NIGHTLIFE AND CRIME

NIGHTLIFE AND CRIME

SOCIAL ORDER AND GOVERNANCE IN INTERNATIONAL PERSPECTIVE

EDITED BY

PHIL HADFIELD

OXFORD
UNIVERSITY PRESS

OXFORD

UNIVERSITY PRESS

Great Clarendon Street, Oxford OX2 6DP

Oxford University Press is a department of the University of Oxford.
It furthers the University's objective of excellence in research, scholarship,
and education by publishing worldwide in

Oxford New York

Auckland Cape Town Dar es Salaam Hong Kong Karachi
Kuala Lumpur Madrid Melbourne Mexico City Nairobi
New Delhi Shanghai Taipei Toronto

With offices in

Argentina Austria Brazil Chile Czech Republic France Greece
Guatemala Hungary Italy Japan Poland Portugal Singapore
South Korea Switzerland Thailand Turkey Ukraine Vietnam

Oxford is a registered trade mark of Oxford University Press
in the UK and in certain other countries

Published in the United States
by Oxford University Press Inc., New York

British Library Cataloguing in Publication Data

Data available

Library of Congress Cataloging-in-Publication Data
Nightlife and crime : social order and governance in international perspective/
edited by Phil Hadfield.
 p. cm.
Includes bibliographical references and index.
ISBN 978–0–19–955974–9 (hardback : alk. paper) 1. Crime. 2. Nightlife.
3. Sociology, Urban. 4. Criminal justice, Administration of. I. Hadfield, Phil.
 HV6025.N544 2009
 364.2—dc22

                                        2008050355

Typeset by Laserwords Private Limited, Chennai, India
Printed by the MPG Books Group in the UK

ISBN 978–0–19–955974–9

1 3 5 7 9 10 8 6 4 2

FOREWORD

When I partnered with Stephen Tomsen in Sydney 20 years ago to begin a scientific exploration of the world of pubs and clubs, I wanted to understand what made some licensed premises violent year after year, while other apparently similar establishments seemed to be able to manage their affairs more peaceably. The research literature on this topic was pretty limited in those days, by far the most illuminating study being the pioneering work by Dr Kathryn Graham in bars in Vancouver a decade earlier. We used the Vancouver findings as the starting point for our investigations, but opted quite deliberately for a fully qualitative, even to some extent ethnographic, methodology. We did this so that we would have the best chance of uncovering those features of Australian drinking environments and regulatory arrangements that were distinctive, not wanting to assume that Sydney was exactly the same as Vancouver.

Our approach was in fact precisely in line with the guiding principles of this excellent book. In the words of Dr Hadfield in the final chapter of this book, 'empirically grounded comparative research on nightlife and crime can only flourish if researchers think locally and work from the bottom up, as well as thinking globally and from the top down in a process of hypothesis testing'. The remarkable achievement of this book is to bring together in one volume so many fine scholars from so many countries, writing not only from diverse disciplinary perspectives but also from a deep knowledge of local history and culture. On this foundation it will be possible, perhaps for the first time, to do some genuine global analyses and hypothesis testing, informed by the rich descriptions of nightlife and crime patterns that are the hallmark of this book.

Especially valuable is the fact that some countries in this volume have only a limited tradition of social scientific investigation and almost no systematic research on alcohol, drugs, drinking establishments, and crime. So in addition to the new analyses and research findings that are reported for those countries where social research traditions are strong (which includes most of the English-speaking and northern European nations), we have illuminating accounts of the dimensions of nightlife and crime in a developing country (South Africa), one Asian city (Hong Kong), a number of southern European countries (Italy, Greece, Spain), and one former member of the Soviet bloc (Hungary). Interestingly, in most of these countries alcohol is not the sole or main focus, in contrast to the preoccupations of many of the other authors in this book.

South Africa has a very high crime rate by international standards, but, as the authors note, it is the 'ferocious violence that often accompanies it' that really distinguishes the country from other parts of Africa. Where does this violence come from? Some have suggested that the enjoyment of violence is a particular feature of southern African culture. Or perhaps it is the history of state-sponsored violence and the violent resistance to such oppression that has been the crucible for South Africa's tortured post-Apartheid crime experience. Actually, the authors propose that while these explanations may have value, the real issue may be 'an insidious culture of daredevil masculinity' wherein young males attempt to appropriate the night. They draw here from the work of a range of scholars, especially Australian sociologist Raewyn Connell's concept of 'hegemonic masculinity', illustrating that although the size of the problem may be unique to South Africa, the shaping influences may be quite universal.

In Hungary, Greece, and Hong Kong, the mix of illicit drugs, prostitution, and organized crime is viewed as being at the heart of nightlife crime patterns, although spending on alcohol may also be high. In Greece, for example, the meaning of nightlife spaces is 'constructed around a controlled loss of control' that may involve staff participating in, or turning a blind eye to, 'hidden' forms of crime such as human trafficking, extortion of legitimate leisure entrepreneurs, or the operation of drug markets. The problems of nightlife in these countries are not so much the kinds of social disorder and incivilities observed in the UK, but, rather, organized illegalities taking place behind the scenes, or in geographical hotspots where drug and sex markets are concentrated. By contrast, in Italy and Spain, nightlife crime and disorder are now firmly linked in the public imagination with young people's leisure activities and their 'takeover of the night', in combination with patterns of alcohol consumption that increasingly resemble 'binge-drinking' practices in northern Europe. These trends are recent, with young people traditionally not being viewed with suspicion as a 'problem' in these countries. The new 'problem' is exacerbated by the shift by young people from private to public places, exemplified by the Spanish *botellón*, regular mass gatherings by young people on weekend nights in public places.

This book is notable not only for the light it shines on under-researched countries but for the new light it sheds on what is going on in countries such as the USA, Australia, and various parts of the UK, where quite a lot is known about alcohol and licensed premises, crime, and illicit drugs, although not necessarily in a form that facilitates understanding of specific nightlife and crime issues. It came as a surprise to me, for example, to learn that there is such sharp differentiation between England and Wales on the one hand and Scotland on the other in terms of 'protecting and improving public health'. This makes Scotland, in a policy sense, much more similar to Canada, New Zealand, Australia, and the Scandinavian countries than to England and Wales, and perhaps helps to explain some of the peculiar features of English law and policy that are well documented in this book and elsewhere.

The Editor's review in Chapter 2 of what has been learned so far about the effects of the UK Licensing Act 2003, a law that is fundamentally deregulatory in purpose and in practice, is particularly important at a time when 'free market' models and British drinking patterns are being successfully exported. The experience in countries such as Australia and Canada with a longer tradition of independent research on alcohol but also with a history of British-style drinking patterns becomes especially valuable in the light of these trends. This is exemplified by very recent Australian work, reported in Chapter 18, that demonstrates the 'non-linear' effects on violence of increases in the geographical density of licensed premises in entertainment areas. It is not just the proliferation of licenses that matters, but how many premises are 'bunched together'; once a density threshold is reached, problems increase exponentially, not in a steady linear (or cumulative) fashion. While this finding is intuitively appealing, to my knowledge it has not previously been demonstrated in a rigorous quantitative fashion. The policy implications are profound in an era of rampant, British-style deregulation.

While an obvious strength of this book lies in the nuanced descriptions of nightlife and its control in a wide range of countries, the book also demonstrates that amidst diversity there is considerable convergence in terms of themes and recurring problems. The convergence of drinking patterns—or the export of British or northern European drinking styles—has already been noted. I was surprised in addition at how ubiquitous conflicts around 'youth culture' appear to be, and at how widespread the technologies of control have become—although 'sonic governance' UK-style, whereby techniques like 'music profiling' are employed as ways of targeting 'risky' groups or channelling crowds, does not yet seem to be the international norm. A theme noted by many authors is the inadequacy of regulatory systems in the face of powerful commercial forces, and the paucity of evidence on what works to reduce crime and violence is noted in more than one chapter. There is a strong and increasing tendency in most countries to locate blame for disorder and violence at the level of the individual reveller or consumer of the nightlife experience, with a corresponding 'light-touch' approach to nightlife operators. Such commonalities invite shared thinking about effective policy responses, thinking that draws on a deep understanding of one's own context while engaging with new ways of seeing suggested by experiences in other cultures.

The dialectic of light and darkness, pleasure and restraint, work and play is the unifying theme of this volume. Such tensions or debates are never permanently resolved, today's solution emerging as tomorrow's problem. Nevertheless the dark side of nightlife, so skilfully depicted from so many perspectives in these pages, does demand a societal response. When 'the froth on life's cappuccino' (below, p 3) conceals or is used to justify the systematic exploitation of sex workers or the callous disregard for human rights by bouncers or police officers, bigger things are at stake. Dr Hadfield reveals something of his personal journey as a scholar *and* human being in the closing sentences of this book, highlighting the policy and personal dilemmas we all face, regardless of nation or race, as we seek to negotiate the shadows cast by the bright lights.

Ross Homel, Officer in the Order of Australia
School of Criminology and Criminal Justice, Griffith University

ACKNOWLEDGEMENTS

Firstly, I would like to thank Karen Hughes, Ross Homel, Tim Stockwell, and Kate O'Brien for assisting me in locating authors from around the world. My colleagues at the Centre for Criminal Justice Studies, School of Law, University of Leeds, provided supportive comments and were always willing to share their insights and their books. Adam Crawford, Anthea Hucklesby, and my research project colleagues Stuart Lister and Peter Traynor deserve a special mention. Also thanks to Robin Jones. Fiona Measham and Teela Sanders were rock steady in their encouragement and enthusiasm for the project and I'll immoderately raise my glass to them.

Thanks must go to the chapter authors for all their hard work and gracious acceptance of my comments and suggestions. Similarly, I am grateful to Lindsey Davis, my editor at OUP, and to Jeremy Langworthy for their assistance in navigating the publication process.

Financial assistance was provided by my Academic Research Fellowship at the University of Leeds and by an award from the Alcohol and Education Research Council (R 03/2006) for the project 'The Orientation and Integration of Local and National Alcohol Policy'. I remain grateful to both organizations for their support.

I owe a great debt to Sarah and my parents, Sam and Una, for their unswerving support in seeing this project to completion.

SUMMARY CONTENTS

PART III CONCLUSIONS

CONTENTS

PART III CONCLUSIONS

CONTRIBUTORS

Noelani Bailey Research Consultant specializing in the study of alcohol, tobacco, and other drug use in urban nightlife settings. She studied dance at the University of New Mexico, earning her Bachelors degree in 2002 and went on to complete a Masters degree in social research methods at Goldsmiths College, University of London in 2004. Under the direction of Helen Thomas, her dissertation explored Israeli club culture in London, focusing on notions of identity, space/place, movement, and nightclub terrorism in new urban contexts. Working alongside Geoffrey Hunt and colleagues, she has subsequently applied her unique perspective to several nightlife studies in the San Francisco Bay Area.

Anabel Rodríguez Basanta Research Officer at the Asociación Centro de Estudios de Seguridad (Centre for Security Studies), Barcelona. Her main research interests focus on constructions of, and institutional responses to, social problems, especially those relating to youth. She has also conducted investigations of policing, drug use, and drug trafficking. In 2007, Anabel and colleague Mila Barruti completed a study of youth violence in the nightspots of Catalonia, as part of the European Union's Daphne II comparative research programme.

Sharon Bernards Research Project Coordinator at the Centre for Addiction and Mental Health (CAMH), London, Ontario. Her current research concerns the area of alcohol and aggression, including research using multi-level models to identify risk factors for bar-room aggression. She is also engaged in cross-national research on gender and alcohol and is co-editor of a book, *Unhappy Hours*, on alcohol and intimate-partner violence in ten countries in the Americas, to be published by the Pan-American Health Organization in 2008.

David Brotherton Professor and Chair of Sociology at John Jay College of Criminal Justice, The City University of New York (CUNY), and a member of the PhD faculties in Criminal Justice, Sociology and Urban Education at The Graduate Center, CUNY. David has been researching the street-life activities of New Yorkers for over a decade and is currently the Principal Investigator of a night-time economy research project at John Jay College. His most recent books are: *Globalizing the Streets: Cross-cultural perspectives on youth, marginalization and empowerment* (co-edited with Michael Flynn, Columbia University Press, 2008), *Keeping Out the Other: Critical analysis of immigration control today* (co-edited with Phil Kretsedemas, Columbia University Press, 2008), and *The Encyclopedia of Gangs* (co-edited with Louis Kontos, Greenwood Press, 2007).

Tanya Chikritzhs Epidemiologist and Senior Research Fellow at the National Drug Research Institute, Perth, Western Australia where she leads the alcohol policy research team. She has published more than 80 scientific articles, book chapters, and reports on the impacts of alcohol policy changes and the epidemiology of alcohol, injury, and disease. Tanya leads a highly regarded national project which tracks trends in alcohol consumption and related harms across Australia. She has first-authored a number of articles on the effects of trading hours for licensed premises on violence and road injury. She has recently been engaged in the development of an Australian model aimed at assisting authorities to determine appropriate liquor-outlet densities for minimizing alcohol-related harms.

Zsolt Demetrovics Head of the Addiction Research Unit at the Institute of Psychology, Eötvös Loránd University, Budapest, where he works as a Clinical Psychologist and Cultural Anthropologist. Zsolt received his PhD in Health Psychology. His primary research focuses on the characteristics of legal and illegal drug use in recreational settings. He also studies aspects of psychoactive substance use and behavioural addictions relating to family life and personality traits.

Martin Elvins Lecturer in Politics at the University of Dundee. His primary research focuses on illegal drugs, and he is the author of *Anti-Drugs Policies of the European Union* (Palgrave Macmillan, 2003). His interest in nightlife dates from 2001–2, when he worked for the University of Durham on a Home-Office-funded study into the measurement of alcohol-related crime in England. He has also conducted research on behalf of the City of Westminster, examining the night-time economy of London's West End, and has appeared as an expert witness in licensing cases. He has a broad research interest in policing and through the auspices of the Scottish Institute for Policing Research is currently co-supervising a project on policing the night-time economy in Scotland.

Galit Erez Sociologist who obtained her Bachelors degree at the University of Colorado, Boulder. She currently works as a Research Associate and Project Manager for the Institute for Scientific Analysis, Alameda, California. Her recent research has focused on the nightlife of San Francisco's Bay Area, with particular reference to dance/party scenes and associated drug use, Asian American youth, and gangs. Galit plans to further her studies in urban sociology and community development at the University of California, Davis.

Kathryn Graham Senior Scientist and Head of Social and Community Prevention Research at the Centre for Addiction and Mental Health (CAMH), London, Ontario, Adjunct Research Professor in the Department of Psychology, University of Western Ontario, and Professor (Adjunct), National Drug Research Institute, Curtin University of Technology, Perth, Western Australia. Her current research focuses on the role of alcohol in aggressive behaviour both in licensed premises and between intimate partners, the social context of aggression, and gender differences in the relationship between alcohol and aggression. Her work in the community has included development and evaluation of the 'Safer Bars' programme to reduce aggression in licensed premises. In 2002, Kathryn received the Queen's Golden Jubilee Medal for her contributions to applying research knowledge to community interventions. *Raising the Bar*, her latest book (with Ross Homel) on preventing bar violence, was published by Willan in 2008.

Paul J Gruenewald Scientific Director and Senior Research Scientist at the Prevention Research Center, Berkeley, California, which is a division of the Pacific

Institute for Research and Evaluation. The Center's work focuses on research and prevention science directed at understanding the social and environmental determinants of alcohol and drug problems. Paul has been involved in empirical and theoretical work relating alcohol availability to alcohol use and associated problems for the past 20 years. His current interests lie in the development of theoretical models for understanding the impacts of over-densities of alcohol outlets upon social structure and social problems in community settings.

Phil Hadfield Senior Research Fellow in the Centre for Criminal Justice Studies, School of Law, University of Leeds. His research interests focus on criminological and regulatory aspects of nightlife. He has worked in this field for over ten years and his publications include *Bar Wars: Contesting the Night in Contemporary British Cities* (Oxford University Press, 2006) and (as co-author) *Bouncers: Violence and Governance in the Night-time Economy* (Oxford University Press, 2003). He has conducted research for the UK Home Office, Economic and Social Research Council, and Alcohol Education and Research Council. Phil has also conducted independent research on nightlife and crime for a number of prominent public and private organizations, including the Metropolitan Police Service, the City of Westminster, and the City of London.

Marja Holmila Research Professor at the National Research and Development Centre for Welfare and Health, Helsinki. Her research has primarily focused on alcohol-related social harms and their prevention. She is editor and main author of the book *Community Prevention of Alcohol Problems* (Macmillan Press Ltd, 1997). Violence related to night-time drinking in licensed premises has been a central theme of much of her work, which has included scientific papers and evaluation projects.

Geoffrey Hunt Social and cultural anthropologist, who has had nearly 30 years' experience in planning, conducting, and managing research in the field of youth studies, and drug and alcohol research. Currently, he is a Senior Research Scientist at the Institute for Scientific Analysis, Alameda, California, and the Principal Investigator on three National Institutes of Health projects. Two of these projects are on youth gangs in the San Francisco Bay Area and the third is on Asian American youth, club drugs and the dance scene in San Francisco. In addition, he has been involved in two large-scale comparative international projects. The first project focused on the study of alcohol treatment systems in 16 countries and led to the publication of the book *Cure, Care or Control: Alcoholism treatment in sixteen countries* (SUNY Press, 1992). A companion volume, *Drugs, Demons and Delinquents: Drug treatment systems in an international perspective* (Sage, 1998), examined drug treatment in 20 different countries. Geoffrey has published widely in the field of substance use studies in many of the leading sociology, anthropology, and criminology journals in the United States and the UK.

Fiona Hutton Lecturer in Criminology at Victoria University of Wellington. Her primary research focuses on gendered experiences of drug use, pleasure, and risk. She is the author of *Risky Pleasures? Club cultures and feminine identities*

(Ashgate, 2006). Fiona's interest in this area stems from her experiences as a volunteer on an English street-based project for sex workers and drug users in the mid-1990s. Since then her research has centred on clubbers' alcohol and illegal drug use, together with broader aspects of youth culture(s), disorder, and social control. She is currently working on an evaluation of harm-minimization information about binge drinking, aimed at students in Wellington, funded by the Alcohol Advisory Council of New Zealand (ALAC).

Vibeke Johannessen Head of the Bergen Clinics Foundation, Drug and Alcohol Competence Centre. Nightlife and crime has become a key policy focus in Norway and Vibeke has played a leading role in supporting the development of local alcohol and drug strategies, nationally. Her work has included projects for the Norwegian Ministry of Health concerning local strategy development, together with preventive and early intervention initiatives for people with substance use problems. Vibeke also assisted in the implementation of a national 'Responsible Server Training' programme for bar staff in Norwegian licensed premises.

Karen Joe Laidler Professor of Sociology and Head of the Department of Sociology at the University of Hong Kong. Much of her research has been conducted in the United States where she has studied the drug-use patterns and violence associated with youth gangs in California, the relationships between alcohol and drug use and violence among female gang members, and alcohol and drug cessation during adolescent pregnancy. She is also working on a number of drug-related studies in Hong Kong, including work on the recent rise of psychotropic drugs, the drug market, the relationship between violence and drug use, and Buddhist interventions with heroin users.

Karen McElrath Reader in Sociology at Queen's University, Belfast. Her current research interests focus on injecting drug use, risk behaviours associated with blood-borne viruses, and methodological issues relating to hard-to-reach or hidden populations. Karen is co-editor of *The American Drug Scene* (with James Inciardi, 5th edn, Oxford, 2008), editor of *HIV and AIDS: A global view* (Greenwood, 2002), and author of *Unsafe Haven: The United States, the IRA and political prisoners* (Pluto, 2000).

Paula Mayock Lecturer in Youth Research at the School of Social Work and Social Policy and Children's Research Centre, Trinity College, Dublin. Her research focuses primarily on the lives and experiences of marginalized youth, covering areas such as drug use and drug problems, homelessness, risk behaviour, and mental health. She is a NIDA (National Institute on Drug Abuse) INVEST Post-Doctoral Fellow and her research on heroin initiation, linked to this Fellowship, is currently ongoing. She is the author of numerous articles, chapters, and research reports, and has recently co-authored a book entitled *Lives in Crisis: Homeless young people in Dublin* (Liffey Press, 2007).

Fiona Measham Internationally renowned researcher with over 20 years' experience in the field of drug and alcohol use, gender, licensed leisure, and cultural criminology. She is co-author of *Illegal Leisure* (1998) and *Dancing on*

Drugs (2001), co-editor of *Swimming with Crocodiles: The culture of extreme drinking* and also of a special issue of the journal *Addiction, Research and Theory* focusing on ketamine use (both, 2008). Her theoretical interests span cultural criminology, gender studies, and the sociology of intoxication, with a particular interest in the boundaries of transgression, the criminalization of leisure, and the problematic–recreational interface in leisure-time consumption.

Molly Moloney Research Associate of the Institute of Scientific Analysis, Alameda, California. Trained in sociology, cultural and media studies, her research primarily focuses on youth, gender, drug users, and dance-music cultures. Molly has recently worked on projects concerning: gang fathers and desistance from crime, ethnicity, identity, drug use among young Asian Americans, and the roles of epidemiology and cultural studies in scholarship on club drugs.

Jane Mounteney Consultant at Bergen Clinics Foundation and a Research Fellow of the Faculty of Medicine, University of Bergen. Jane's previous positions include Senior Researcher and Assistant Director at the Institute for the Study of Drug Dependence, UK (1993–2000). During the 1990s, her work included a historical case study of reported ecstasy use linked to a pan-European project on new drug trends. She was also involved in the development of a London-based 'Safer Dancing' initiative. In 2002, she established the city-level Bergen Earlier Warning System (BEWS) for identifying and monitoring emerging drug trends. Other research interests include community epidemiology, rapid assessment methodologies, drug use among vulnerable groups, and drug and alcohol policy implementation.

Gian Guido Nobili Head of the Department for Local Policing and Safety Policies Research Unit of the Emilia-Romagna Region, based in Bologna. He is also Assistant Lecturer in Criminology at the University of Macerata. Gian Guido is mainly involved in the implementation and evaluation of regional crime-prevention and policing programmes. At a local level, he coordinates research on violence and antisocial behaviour in the public spaces of Bologna. He also collaborates on the region's international projects which have included a comparative study entitled 'Violence among Young People in Leisure Time' funded by the European Union and participation in national and international conferences on the impact, efficiency, and effectiveness of crime reduction programmes.

Richard E Ocejo PhD Student in Sociology at the Graduate Center of the City University of New York (CUNY). His research interests include urban sociology, community studies, urban culture, and public space. Richard is currently completing his thesis, an ethnographic study of the transformation of an urban downtown in a post-industrial city, through the analytical lens of bars, nightlife, and nightlife scenes. In September 2007, Richard began working with his co-author, David Brotherton, and team at John Jay College of Criminal Justice on a project exploring the culture of bouncers within the night-time economy, funded by New York City Council. Richard and David's chapter reports findings from this study, and from Richard's thesis.

Kopano Ratele Professor in the Institute of Social and Health Sciences (ISHS) at the University of South Africa, Lenasia. Kopano has a range of scholarly interests spanning the areas of violence and fatal injury, critical psychology, and men and masculinities. Prior to his post at the ISHS, he was Professor in the Department of Psychology and in Women's and Gender Studies at the University of Western Cape. Kopano has edited or co-edited the following books: *From Boys to Men: Social construction of masculinities in contemporary society* and *Inter-group relations: South African perspectives.* He is chief editor of *African Safety Promotion: A journal of injury and violence prevention* and books' editor at the *South African Journal of Psychology.*

Lillian G Remer MA, GISP Associate Research Scientist at the Prevention Research Center, Berkeley, California, a division of the Pacific Institute for Research and Evaluation. Her primary responsibilities involve database design and development, geographic information systems (GIS), spatial analysis, and computer modelling as applied to substance abuse interventions and problem prevention.

Mohamed Seedat Director of the Institute for Social and Health Sciences, University of South Africa (UNISA), Lenasia, a WHO collaborating centre for violence and injury prevention research and training. He also heads the National Presidential Lead Programme on Crime, Violence and Injury in South Africa, a joint collaboration between the Medical Research Council and the UNISA. In 1989–90 he was a Mid-Career Fellow at Yale University, and in 1990–1 he worked as the Director of the Living after Murder Programme at Roxbury Comprehensive Community Health Care Centre in Boston, United States. In July 2002–May 2003 he was a Visiting Professor at the Indian Institute for Technology, New Delhi, India. He has published widely in the areas of community psychology and development, racism and psychohistory and is chief editor of the book *Theory, Practice and Methods in Community Psychology: South African and other perspectives.*

Rosella Selmini Professor of Criminology at the University of Macerata and Director of the Department for Local Policing and Safety Policies for the Emilia-Romagna Region. Her main work in academia and institutional practice relates to public policies and the local governance of crime, crime prevention, juvenile delinquency, and gender studies in crime and criminal justice. She is the author or co-author of several books in Italian and articles in international journals and edited collections. Rosella recently completed a comparative study entitled 'Violence among Young People in Leisure Time' funded by the European Union. This was one of the first research projects of its kind to be conducted in an Italian context.

Mairéad Seymour Senior Lecturer at the School of Social Sciences and Law, Dublin Institute of Technology (DIT). Prior to her current position, she worked at the Centre for Social and Educational Research, DIT and the Institute of Criminology and Justice, Queen's University Belfast. Her research interests and publications are in the areas of youth offending, comparative youth justice, social order, and reintegration. Her interest in nightlife and crime stems from her previous research studies on persistent young offenders and her involvement with the international self-report delinquency study. Her current research examines the experiences and community context of young people remanded on bail in Ireland.

Arvid Skutle　Research Director at the Bergen Clinics Foundation, one of Norway's main treatment centres for alcohol and other substance abuse. Arvid previously worked as Associate Professor in Clinical and Community Psychology at the University of Bergen. He has conducted clinical and epidemiological studies, particularly among adolescents, and has evaluated a number of prevention programmes. He is currently a member of the Ministry of Justice and Police national accreditation panel for substance user treatment programmes across the Norwegian criminal justice system.

Lu-Anne Swart　Community Intervention Researcher at the University of South Africa's Institute for Social and Health Sciences in Lenasia. She has studied the dynamics of community mobilization and volunteerism in under-served communities. Lu-Anne has expertise in quantitative research methodologies and injury surveillance. Her current research interests include home-based injury, adolescent development, and sexuality and violence in teenage dating relationships.

Andrew J Treno PhD　Senior Research Scientist at the Prevention Research Center (PRC), Berkeley, California, a division of the Pacific Institute for Research and Evaluation. Over the past 16 years, Andrew has specialized in the implementation and evaluation of community-level alcohol-problem prevention programmes. He has published in the areas of community mobilization, alcohol involvement in injury, and evaluation of environmental approaches to the prevention of alcohol-related problems. He is also the instructor of record for courses offered by the University of California, School of Public Health, including the post-doctoral training programme at the PRC.

Patrick Van Calster　Associate Professor in the Department of Criminal Law and Criminology, University of Leiden. He teaches a course entitled 'Safety, Security and Justice', in which he presents a multi-focal perspective on issues of risk and security in constitutional democracies. His research interests include organizational dynamics, policing, narrativity, ethics, and cultural studies. His current research focuses on vigilantism in the risk society.

Joanne van der Leun　Professor of Criminology in the Department of Criminal Law and Criminology, University of Leiden. She teaches a course entitled 'Urban Criminology', which focuses on crime and disorder in public spaces and societal developments which impact on European cities. Her research interests and publications encompass issues of crime and migration in urban contexts and associated policy responses. She recently wrote a report (with Anna Hulsebosch and Heike Goudriaan) for the Municipality of Leiden examining local policy responses to nightlife-related violence.

Ninette van Hasselt　Programme Manager for 'Youth in Recreational Settings' at the Alcohol and Drugs Unit, Trimbos Institute (Netherlands Institute of Mental Health and Addictions). Ninette has 15 years' experience as a public-health professional. She has a particular interest in the development of substance-misuse prevention campaigns in nightlife settings. She coordinates the Trimbos Clubs and Drugs Project and the European Union 'Healthy Nightlife Toolbox' Project. Both schemes aim to spread knowledge of evidence-based interventions among regional professionals. In 2007, Ninette coordinated a national conference on nightlife, aimed at integrating scientific and practitioner approaches to substance use risk management.

Sophie Vidali Assistant Professor in Criminology and Crime Policy at the Department of Social Administration, Democritus University of Thrace. Her recent research includes a qualitative study of the drug economy in Athens and a study of the implementation of rehabilitation services for ex-drug addicts, both for the Ministry of Health and Social Solidarity. Sophie is the author of several recent books and journal articles in Greek, on crime, policing, and criminology.

Katariina Warpenius Senior Researcher at the National Research and Development Centre for Welfare and Health, Helsinki. Her research interests surround the prevention of alcohol-related harms, with particular reference to licensed premises, the development of local prevention initiatives, and the history of the Finnish temperance movement.

PART I

INTRODUCTION

1

NIGHTLIFE AND CRIME IN INTERNATIONAL PERSPECTIVE

Phil Hadfield

It's a balmy summer night and I'm on my way home from the pub as I catch a snippet of hope and lament, 'forget about him, you can do better'. Just ahead of me, two girls in their early twenties are stumbling arm-in-arm along the pavement. As the distance between us shortens, the legs of one of the pair buckle and she falls momentarily to the ground only to regain stance and momentum with the help of her friend; but she's lost one of her shoes. She goes on her way bare foot, now clutching both shoes to her chest. 'Put your shoes on!' her companion demands. 'No, I like it, it's liberating', she replies.

(Town Street, Horsforth, Leeds, UK)

... mice were allowed to self-administer ethanol (10% v/v) vs H_2O in the home cage for 28 days. Alcohol was then removed for 1 or 14 days, and mice were tested in the forced swim test[1] to measure depression-like behavior. After 14 days (but not 1 day), of abstinence from alcohol drinking, mice showed a significant increase in depression-like behavior.

(Stevenson et al, 2008: unpaginated abstract, advance access)

Nightlife. What sort of life is it?—a life-affirming field of dreams, or a cathartic field of sorrows? The chapters in this collection allow us to see that it can be either, and more importantly both, in the space of one single night. Yet, the problem with naming a book 'Nightlife and Crime' is that things immediately get dark, when in fact, nightlife is mostly full of light, with darkness only inhabiting its periphery. Nightlife is often associated with celebration, festival, and community gatherings, so let's not get too serious just yet; nightlife isn't. What nightlife *is* for most who *partake of it*, is a minor, ostensibly frivolous, punctuation of daily routines—a release of pressure; the froth on life's cappuccino. This is not to deny that nightlife is important to many, especially young adults; it plays a role in personal growth and social development, especially in the West and is a sphere of life laden with meaning, notions of

---

[1] The research team employed the 'Porsolt swim test', wherein mice were left to swim in a beaker for six minutes. The more apathetically the mice swam, the more depressed they were assumed to be.

acceptance, conformity, and rebellion (Room, 2005). 'Exploring the nightlife of the city can bring young people closer to a level of maturity and cultural awareness commensurate with the post-adolescent life' (Grazian, 2008: 223). It is a creative outlet for people talented in music, the arts, and entertainment and allows for the development of its own communities of interest, as the many sociological accounts of club culture attest (Jackson, 2004; Malbon, 1999; Thornton, 1995; Wilson, 2007). Such attachment to peer groups and cliques can render participation in nightlife obligatory, as to abstain would be tantamount to 'social suicide' (Winlow and Hall, 2006). Peer and broader societal influences further frame nightlife as a setting in which the inevitable risk-taking and experimentation of youth takes place (Room, 2007). As the authors of the pan-European *Safer Nightlife Projects* report conclude: 'these are not spaces of marginality but spaces of integration where nightlife "consumers" escape from their routine, meet new people, try new experiences and also assume new risks, such as drug taking' (Democracy, Cities and Drugs Project, 2008: 5).

However, the romantic cultural potentialities of nightlife can be overstated, as it is most often bounded by a commercial infrastructure geared toward exploitation of a 'youth leisure market', in which profit is the main driver. To the extent that nightlife spaces are spaces of consumption—a point to which I shall return—they are also, spaces of exclusion. In some countries, nightlife is a significant contributor to the national economy, attracting foreign investment and boosting tourism; in recent years this transnational element has been accentuated by budget air travel and the internet. Such trends are further underlined by the emergence of global nightlife brands such as *Pacha* and *Hed Kandi*,[2] which become embedded within a transnational nightlife culture through clothing, sponsorship, and events-marketing activities. Throughout the world, legal and illegal drug use has been a consistent feature of nightlife and a complex issue to attend. Profit from selling drugs is part of a worldwide legal and illegal industry worth billions and the legislative and enforcement activities of individual states struggle to contain the fluidity of new markets, trends, and psychoactive products, of which partygoers and youth are eager consumers. In addition, important social and cultural changes are taking place in many Western societies, involving changing life transitions, gender relations, technologies, urbanization, and reconfigurations of work and leisure time (Kreitzman, 1999).

In relation to the nightlife and crime situation in England, my colleagues and I have used some pretty gloomy (if, justified) rhetoric: 'the night-time economy poses the greatest threat to public order in Britain today'(Hadfield, 2006: 1), featuring, as it does, 'levels of violence that are unparalleled outside of military and penal institutions' (Hobbs et al, 2003: 147). As implied above, thinking solely in such terms it is easy to allow the 'bad news' to cloud our thinking. Much is lost analytically if we concentrate only on the more negative aspects of the phenomena: blood on streets, shattered glass, hellish Accident and Emergency Departments—the dark sides of the night—cannot and should not be abstracted from the light. The interdisciplinary nature of the research topic makes these concerns especially pertinent. Just as criminologists and public-health researchers may find focusing on the fun, light-hearted, and frivolous

---

[2] See <http://www.pacha.com> and <http://beta.hedkansi.com/Events/Pages/GlobalEvents.aspx>.

aspects of nightlife challenging, so social scientists in other disciplines may find it difficult to accept that nightlife is one important sphere of contemporary social life in which there is an affinity between cultural and leisure activities and crime. Rojek, for example, notes the intellectual challenge faced by 'leisure studies' scholars, for whom:

> the concept of leisure is bound up with capitalist ideology which presents free time as a reward for work. Leisure is overwhelmingly associated with positive characteristics, most commonly, freedom, choice and self-determination. This is one reason why it is so difficult to discuss leisure time and space as the root of negative personal experience or social alienation. (2000: 176)

These interdisciplinary aspects become increasingly apparent the more one explores the *context* of people's behaviours and actions. Attention to context often requires researchers, who are understandably focused on particularities, to move outside their topic-based and disciplinary comfort zones. A key aim of this book is to provide readers with a 'flavour' of nightlife in the 17 countries in question, with chapter authors challenged to provide this contextual element, alongside the reporting of their specific research interests. It will come as little surprise to many readers that the genesis of the book derived from particular aspects of the British condition. Amongst a significant proportion of young Britons, drinking with the intention of getting drunk is an accepted end in itself and the competitive drinking of large quantities of alcohol may be deemed amusing and heroic (Engineer et al, 2003). In the UK, public, media, and professional concern about 'binge drinking' has created a highly sensitized frame of political action (see Chapters 2 and 3). Yet, public drunkenness is still tolerated far more in Britain than in many other societies. This means that the social regulation of drunken comportment through informal controls is comparatively weak (Jarvinen and Room, 2007) allowing increased opportunities for hedonistic aggression. This is particularly observable on Britain's 'night-time high streets'—social environments dominated by the attitudes, expectations and norms of young adult revellers (Hadfield, 2006).

Critical comparisons are often drawn, both in Britain and abroad, between our own approach to nightlife and that of other countries, especially the nations of Southern Europe (Jayne et al, 2008). This is graphically illustrated by media reports of alcohol-related violence involving young Britons on holiday, most recently focusing on the Cretan resort of Malia (Jones, 2008; Lyall, 2008). *British Behaviour Abroad*, a recent report published by the central government Foreign and Commonwealth Office (FCO, 2008) revealed the number of Britons arrested at 15 selected foreign holiday resorts to be increasing by an annual rate of over 16 per cent. The Czech Republic, for example, 'features as one of the countries where most consular assistance is required with a disproportionate number of lost passports, arrests and hospitalisations. This is likely to be due to the massive influx of hen and stag parties to Prague' (p 1), the report concludes. Flows of people, drugs, business enterprise, and cultural influences around the world then, ensure that countries both import and export the symbols and substance of their nightlife and many of its associated problems.

Before outlining the substantive content of each chapter, some explication of the conceptual framework which underpins the book is required.

NIGHTLIFE, SOCIAL ORDER, AND GOVERNANCE

In *Regulating the Night* (Ashgate, 2007), Deborah Talbot links the term 'night-time economy' (NTE) with an entrepreneurial place marketing discourse in which gentrified bars and clubs are framed as integral to the 'regeneration' of urban neighbourhoods; 'regeneration' in this instance implying the transformation of predominately bohemian or working-class districts and industrial quarters into 'playgrounds' for affluent incoming consumers. In her case study of an inner city London borough, Talbot provides strong empirical evidence for such conceptualizations, with the attachment of these meanings being ubiquitous in UK urban practitioner and policy circles from the mid-1990s onwards and still retaining currency today. Thankfully, in academic and literary discourse the NTE concept appears, for the most part, to have retained a somewhat broader definition, referring not only to those facets of night-time activity most visible within a capitalist consumer society—the pub and club scene—but also to other aspects of commercial transaction: the criminal and informal economy, various forms of nightwork, theatre, cinema, bingo, and night-classes etc (Krietzman, 1999; Moore-Ede, 1993; Sandu, 2006). It is clear therefore that the economy of the night involves much more than 'big business' leisure players and urban boosterism. One need think only of London's West End, with its unlicensed flower sellers, hot-dog stalls and pedi-cabs, or of the more hidden activities of organized criminals involved in protection rackets and the localized control of drug markets (Hobbs et al, 2003; Winlow, 2001).

In its defence, one can see that talk of a 'NTE' has had significant utility as a readily identifiable 'rendezvous concept' or analytical lens, through which to explore a range of salient contemporary issues, including: an apparent rise in citizen concern regarding violence, incivilities and so-called 'quality of life' issues in the public realm; reconfigurations in the organization and delivery of policing and crime control; and the relationship between these themes and broader political and economic transformations. Research on the NTE has permitted us to understand 'crime in context' (Taylor, 1999), providing a rich stream of empirically derived, theoretically informed, and policy relevant reflections on the constitution of gender relations, consumption, identity, life-stage transitions and the micro-politics of public space, within contemporary urban milieux. Implicit to Talbot's critique, however, is a more fundamental challenge to unconsidered use of the term—not all night-time activity, and specifically leisure activity, involves monetary exchange. This is, of course, true, as numerous examples from the organized free party and rave scene, to more impromptu home or neighbourhood-based events attest.

For the purposes of this book, nightlife is understood as something broader than the NTE, yet narrower than the entire 'life of night'—the all-encompassing nocturnal social world that includes privatized home-based pursuits, sleeping practices etc, as described by cultural historians and sociologists such as Ekirch (2005) and Melbin (1987). A useful working definition for scholarship in this field, then, might perhaps be: *the night-time pursuit of leisure or work activities outside of the home and the hosting of leisure events in the home.* With this in mind, one sees that the authors in this volume tend to use the terms 'nightlife' and 'NTE' interchangeably, but not inaccurately, as when alluding to the latter they are in accord with common academic discourse in describing that part of nightlife in which economic activity occurs.

Having considered the parameters of what nightlife might be in this context, it is now necessary to consider a second conceptual issue, the sociological question of how such lives may be lived and ordered. As explored in detail elsewhere (Hadfield, 2006; Talbot, 2007), nightlife involves the contestation, not only of ownership over physical spaces and social settings, but also of competing ideologies surrounding questions of lifestyle and values (hedonism v restraint) and citizenship (rights v responsibilities). To the extent that stable social orders, ie patterns of social expectations, interactions and customs surrounding nightlife are constructed and maintained, these must be viewed as subject to myriad adjustments in accordance with the outcome of ongoing cultural, ideological and governmental power plays (Dennis and Martin, 2005; Jasanoff, 2004).

Yet, the conditions essential to the existence of nightlife forms must remain relatively stable over time. In the case of a consumption-oriented NTE these conditions include property, exchange, and power relations, but also cultural forms, communicative systems, and structures of ideological support (Merton, 1959; Ritzer, 2001; Wrong, 1995). Here the opportunities for comparative analyses are, of course, striking; for example, whilst many forms of nightlife might exist in a Muslim country governed by Sharia law, or within a communist control economy, these would be of a very different 'order' from those of Western consumer capitalism. Furthermore, the relative stability required to support such NTEs also presupposes a degree of 'security'—which, following Zedner (2000: 155), may be conceptualized as the 'objective condition' of 'being without threat' and 'being protected from' and the 'subjective condition' of 'feeling safe' and free from anxiety. That a vibrant NTE, tourist industry, or even extensive nightlife, tends not to emerge in societies divided by civil strife is testament to this, whilst the legacy of such security deficits may linger in post-conflict societies for some time (see Karen McElrath's account of Northern Ireland in Chapter 4).

This brings us to the question of how such an order might intentionally be shaped; that is to questions of 'governance' (Parker and Braithwaite, 2003). In the context of nightlife, governance may be conceived broadly to encompass informal street-level strategies and spatial elements of social organization, through to approaches that are embodied in policy guidelines, formal professional criteria, and legislation (Crawford, 2006). However, the chapters in this book are mostly concerned with one subset of governmental activities, namely those which involve policing and regulation. These concerns may be termed those of 'security governance'. Security governance has proved a fertile field of study for criminologists, many of whom have drawn upon the theoretical vocabularies of Michel Foucault and Bruno Latour in attending to the ways in which the state and its agents (primarily the public police) do not monopolize security provision (Dupont et al, 2003). As Wood and Shearing (2007: 9) note, 'The power to shape events is produced not by owning it but by enrolling others to perform actions required to realise one's objectives.' Citing Latour (1987: 273), they note that power, and hence governance, is produced through 'action at a distance', being 'the consequence of an intense activity of enrolling, convincing and enlisting'. This 'nodal' perspective has become influential in contemporary criminological analyses of the ways in which various non-state agents, including private-sector businesses, have become variously enlisted in projects of security governance. These security 'partnerships' may incorporate public, private, and voluntary sector actors, but tend to remain state-directed (Crawford, 2006). The chapters in this book provide many empirical examples of such governmental forms and processes.

OUTLINE OF THE BOOK

Although 'drinking cultures' have formed the focus of earlier scholarly collections (Douglas, 1987; Heath, 1995; Jarvinen and Room, 2007; Wilson, 2005), nightlife, as a whole, and as a context for the consumption of alcohol and other drugs, has received very little research attention from a comparative perspective. Moreover, even less attention has been paid to issues of comparison, convergence, and divergence in relation to night-time contexts for crime and disorder and the policing and regulatory responses to them (although, see Central Cities Institute, (2002) and the collection of papers in Recasens (2007), as isolated, pan-European examples). In response to such lacunae the following chapters provide data and critique from experienced researchers—in some cases, world-renowned experts—and outstanding early-career scholars, tasked with the explication of salient themes and particularities within the countries from which their research is drawn. The book thus represents an initial attempt to help develop an understanding of trends and concerns in academic work on nightlife from around the world. Whilst literatures and debates within the epidemiology of alcohol and drug use are relatively well developed internationally, there is a dearth of research on the *social contexts* in which licit and illicit psychoactive substances are consumed. Context is taken here to denote the social, physical, and temporal constituents of particular *social settings* for such consumption and also for related crime and disorder. Moreover, attention to context involves exploration of matters which go far beyond observable consumer behaviours, to encompass broader, sometimes obscure, processes of governance. Formal and informal agents, from state legislators and municipalities, to criminal networks and others involved in the commission or control of crime or the operation and regulation of legal and illegal markets, all shape and influence such settings.

The social settings of concern to this book have, of course, a distinctly temporal dimension, being found in the evening, night-time and early morning; the period, let us say, between 6.00 pm and 6.00 am. Spatially, nightlife settings are almost exclusively associated in existing academic literatures with privately owned and commercially operated entertainment premises, to which nominally only 'consumers' are granted access, or with the public spaces of urban centres, inner city areas, and suburbs. Whilst the exploration of such settings is necessary, it is not sufficient, as nightlife, particularly of a non-commercial—and what will be described in Chapter 19 as 'organic'—kind occurs across a range of settings from private homes, social housing, or squats (Talbot,

2007), to beaches, national parks, and privately owned rural landscapes, as apparent in various free-party scenes (Collin, 1997; Riley et al, 2008). Some of the authors in this collection touch upon these issues, revealing the potential for future exploration of the ways in which regulatory actors and youthful innovators become embroiled in intricate games of cat and mouse.

Readers should appreciate that across the countries covered there are different approaches, concerns, and degrees of development in relation to the study of nightlife and crime. Furthermore, chapter authors come from a range of disciplines—mostly, criminology, sociology, social psychology, public health, and epidemiology—and thus adopt various methodologies and approaches to their subject matter. In focusing upon their countries of origin, the contributors do not, for the most part, present research that is itself comparative. However, in providing a sample of some of the most exciting work carried out across the world, it is hoped that these summary and review exercises will create an intellectual space in which the seeds of truly comparative and collaborative research agendas may be sown. That nightlife and crime is an issue of such international interest and concern is, as in other areas of the social sciences, 'testimony to the value of, and demand for the exchange of ideas, dissemination of work and development of common understandings' (Ruggiero et al, 1998: 11). Taken as a whole then, the intention of this collection is to encourage the development of outward-looking, internationalist perspectives which stimulate both debate and action.

The book is organized as follows: in Chapter 2, Fiona Measham and I consider the situation in England and Wales, wherein the governance of alcohol, and by extension nightlife, has become nothing less than a national obsession. The chapter highlights changing patterns of alcohol and drug use before exploring three of the most salient themes to have emerged within a recent period of rapid change, including: (1) transformations of the policy and legislative context; (2) the changing role of women as nightlife consumers, offenders, and workers; and (3) the role of the state, the police, and Licensing Authorities in the local governance of nightlife and associated criminalization of youth, across the nightlife spectrum.

Then, in Chapter 3, Martin Elvins reports from post-devolution Scotland in which he identifies an emergent crime-and-health policy discourse which increasingly departs from that of Westminster in highlighting the costs to public expenditure arising from alcohol misuse. With particular reference to policing, he notes how the NTE has various impacts beyond the physical and temporal boundaries that are routinely used to define it, generating political debate as to resource allocation and prioritization, and consequent demands for the adoption of a 'polluter pays' approach, with additional funding for crime control levied from the operators of licensed venues. More broadly, he notes how, in equally emphasizing the criminogenic and public-health aspects of alcohol use and the interconnections between them, the Scottish approach recognizes that nightlife and crime are societal issues which cannot be addressed in piecemeal fashion.

Karen McElrath (Chapter 4) turns our attention to Northern Ireland, many of whose citizens—urban working-class communities, especially—remain riven by legacies of political conflict and sectarian violence. Her account of the routine preplanning and risk management required when traversing the territories of the 'other', or when occupying and returning home from so-called 'neutral' spaces serves as a reminder of the many taken-for-granted assumptions of personal security and political stability that are prerequisite to the development of a vibrant consumerist NTE. She shows how the repression of nightlife was also underpinned by the courts, who until recently imposed very stringent controls over the number of pubs and clubs and their operating hours. On a positive note, McElrath indicates that times are changing—the peace process producing opportunities for a new leisure-and-tourism-based urban renaissance and the removal of conflict-era controls.

In Chapter 5, Mairéad Seymour and Paula Mayock take us south of the border in the island of Ireland. A predominantly Catholic country, Ireland does not have what can be described as a 'temperance culture' and perceived threats to the institution of the pub, related to more stringent drink-driving laws etc, are often seen as an attack on community life and 'tradition'. Nightlife is big business in urban areas, having grown alongside the increasing economic prosperity of recent decades; the totems of its conviviality now exported worldwide in the form of the Irish theme-pub. Prevailing cultural attitudes view drunkenness in a relaxed, non-judgemental, or even positive light, and this, combined with the political influence of the drinks industry, has tended to limit governmental intervention in the spheres of crime control and public health—although the licensing framework applied to venues has a number of stringent features, shared only with Northern Ireland.

Chapter 6, by Patrick Van Calster and colleagues, focuses on The Netherlands and principally Amsterdam, a city regarded around the globe as an emblem of liberalism and freedom of expression. The authors argue that whilst foreigners tend to think of nightlife in The Netherlands in terms of deregulated drug and sex markets, the Dutch themselves are more concerned with other issues, principally alcohol-related violence and street robbery. The authors go on to identify rapidly emerging cracks in the edifice of Dutch liberalism, with the governance of soft-drug use and commercial sex, primarily understood for so long as inhabiting a public health, rather than criminal-justice policy agenda, being drawn into a new security-fixated politics of fear and precautionary restriction.

Skutle and colleagues' account of the Norwegian context (Chapter 7) offers an interesting counterpoint to the Dutch situation, wherein (in tandem with Northern Ireland), the balance of power in nightlife security governance has tipped from a position of long-standing formal and informal restriction, toward processes of increased liberalization. Judged as harm-prevention measures, the controls that are now being dismantled may be understood to have proved particularly effective. Norwegian policymakers are thus in the unenviable position of introducing new deregulatory measures that most experts agree will have a range of harmful and perverse effects (see also, discussion of the genesis of the Licensing Act 2003 in England and Wales, Chapter 2, in this regard). Skutle et al demonstrate the difficulties of weighing crime and public-health concerns against opposing political demands and economic pressures for change and of maintaining a distinctive national approach in the context of inward and out-flowing streams of leisure consumers with increasing demands and expectations.

In Chapter 8, Marja Holmila and Katariina Warpenius examine changing rates of violence in Finnish restaurants, bars, pubs, and nightclubs over a ten-year period. The period in question was characterized by rapid rises in the number of licensed premises and increased consumption of alcohol. However, data shows that the number of violent assaults in licensed premises did not increase during this period, although rises were recorded in public places and private homes. The authors discuss the possible explanations for this in relation to the proportion of alcohol sales derived from on- and off-licensed venues and in terms of the potential efficacy of various harm reduction, situational crime prevention, and law-enforcement initiatives.

The risks associated with concentrating policing and regulatory efforts on creating 'safe' and controlled leisure venues, whilst doing little to address the displacement of alcohol-related violence from licensed premises to public spaces is a theme that is revisited by Rosella Selmini and Gian Guido Nobili (Italy, Chapter 9). Given the warm climate and tradition of spontaneous communal gatherings, open-air drug and alcohol consumption are matters of relatively major concern to the Italian authorities, as the case study of Bologna presented here demonstrates. Despite a history of politically inspired conflict between students and the police, the 'condition of youth' has not normally been associated with danger, risk, or violence; the image of young people being embedded in a culture of paternalism and de-responsibilization, particularly in the case of girls. This stance, they note, is now being replaced by inter-generational conflict and a harsher criminalizing rhetoric, as manifested in recent public and institutional reactions to nightlife and crime.

Anabel Rodríguez Basanta makes similar observations concerning notions of 'unstructured leisure time' as a threat to public order in Spain (Chapter 10). Here, as in Italy, spontaneous outdoor gatherings of intoxicated youth, known as the *botellón*, are seen to undermine harmonious relations between different generations and social groups, and to threaten the interests of towns and cities: their reputations, traditions, and civic laws. Correspondingly, however, the chapter shows how nightlife has become central to the political economy of many Spanish regions, particularly coastal areas, where *sun and party* experiences are the focal concern of young foreign tourists. Other issues concerning the activities of foreigners arise in the province of Catalonia, where French rave organizers cross the border to hold their events in order to circumvent the prohibitive laws adopted in their own country.

Continuing the theme of electronic dance music (EDM), Zsolt Demetrovics provides an authoritative account of drug use across the Hungarian club scene (Chapter 11). He shows how different musical genres may be associated with the use of different illegal substances, and with consumption practices conforming to a social-recreational pattern: that is, (1) frequency of use being predominantly low (usually no more than one occasion per week); (2) with the exception of cannabis, drugs being consumed almost exclusively within the dance event setting; and (3) drug use being associated with social occasions, being rarely practised by individuals in conditions of solitude. Demetrovics goes on to describe how recreational drug use in Hungary has a tendency to follow trends first established in Western Europe. He identifies an apparent disjuncture between the liberal 'harm minimization' approach of the Hungarian National Drug Strategy and current law enforcement which adopts a contradictory hard-line abolitionist stance. The eagerness to prosecute venue operators, he argues, has been counterproductive to the aims of the Drug Strategy, fostering a culture of secrecy and denial with respect to drug-use issues.

In Chapter 12, Sophie Vidali argues that the most evident forms of crime occurring in a Greek nightlife context are not those associated with a general environment of social disorder and incivility, but rather with organized illegalities taking place 'behind the scenes', or in relation to street-level drug and sex markets concentrated in specific geographical 'hotspots'. The latter are spaces of danger, most prominently, for the socially excluded groups who inhabit them. These groups include prostitutes and drugs addicts who are repeatedly victimized, both by criminals and by the police, from whom they receive little protection but a considerable degree of repressive and unwarranted attention. In contrast to the conventional and visible crimes of the street population, forms of criminality linked to the operation of entertainment enterprises often inhabit a 'grey area' in which ostensibly legitimate business practices are used as a 'cover' for organized illegalities. Vidali shows how new opportunities for such crimes have grown in line with urban restructuring and the increasing economic importance of the leisure and tourism sectors.

Paul Gruenewald and colleagues present the first of three reports from the United States of America (Chapter 13.1). Their chapter reviews the four most prominent social ecological theories devised by scholars to explain statistical relationships between the number or density of alcohol outlets and rates of crime and other alcohol-related problems: (1) Availability Theory, (2) Social Disorganization Theory, (3) Drinking Contexts Theory, and (4) Niche Theory. The authors weigh the strengths and limitations of each model, identifying Niche Theory—which stresses the interaction of commercial alcohol markets and social systems—as the most productive conceptual framework for future research. This approach, they note, runs contrary to the prevailing predisposition in the United States to attribute drinking problems solely to drinkers themselves, rather than to the contextual circumstances of their drinking. These assumptions tend to obscure the fact that much crime and disorder related to drinking arises at rather low levels of consumption. Ecological theories provide explanations for this, whilst also proving essential to the development of effective community-based crime prevention and public-health initiatives, they argue.

The formal regulation of nightlife in New York, 'the city that never sleeps', is the focus for Richard Ocejo and David Brotherton (Chapter 13.2). They describe how liquor licensing and enforcement activities, once the sole preserve of the State Liquor Authority and New York Police Department (NYPD) respectively, now incorporate a wider range of actors, including local residents and private security agencies. A case study of Manhattan's Lower East Side is presented which demonstrates the power of the local state in facilitating and shaping the development of nightlife scenes, whilst attempting to confront the 'quality of life' issues that arise for residential communities living in their midst. Yet, noisy, crowded streets, populated by intoxicated consumers signify a healthy nightlife scene and economic regeneration for the area—a new prosperity that the NYPD has no wish to threaten, increasingly relinquishing its role to the bouncers employed by night-time enterprises. Thus, tensions remain unresolved regarding nuisance and street crime, raising questions as to the area's sustainability as a mixed-use commercial, residential, and leisure zone.

Moving from East to West Coast, Moloney and colleagues (Chapter 13.3) also discover narratives of gentrification and displacement in San Francisco, albeit of a quite distinct and local flavour. They describe a process of struggle between different stake-holders over the policing and regulation of nightlife, culminating in 2003 with the creation of a unique multi-agency Entertainment Commission. Although this body now exercises licensing powers formerly held by the police, it is arguable that the latter still retain significant influence over both the form and content of the city's nightlife. This appears to be the case, most controversially, with regard to implicitly racist dis-courses concerning the 'musical profile'—and by extension racial composition—of particular types of club night and their attendant crime risks. However, the authors suggest that nightclub owners and promoters may themselves have internalized the music-profiling message, associating it with 'good management', and strongly avoid-ing musical programming that attracts the 'wrong' crowd. The chapter thus provides empirical evidence as to the degree of scrutiny to which nightlife patrons are now sub-jected, with certain populations identified as unwelcome and targeted for exclusion.

In Chapter 14, Kathryn Graham and Sharon Bernards take us north of the border. They describe the history of nightlife and its regulation in Canada, from the country's early colonial days, through periods of prohibition in the early twentieth century, to today's post-industrial economy. They describe how, throughout this history, secur-ity concerns surrounding public drinking have retained a powerful currency. Whilst the role of the police in responding to such concerns varies between communities and over time, many of the same tensions and ambiguities concerning police activity (and inactivity) arise repeatedly. Canadians were pioneers in the development and evaluation of measures to improve operating standards within licensed premises, yet cultural sensitivities remain concerning the use of closed-circuit television and other surveillance technologies. Today one sees a move toward increasing awareness of nightlife's cultural and economic benefits, together with broader community 'own-ership' of its associated problems.

Hong Kong is the focus for Karen Joe Laidler in Chapter 15 as she traces the shift-ing terrain of government policy toward drug and sex markets. Cross-border flows of sex workers and pleasure seekers exert a powerful influence here, along with the entrenched interests of triad networks in controlling illegal markets. As identified in Italy and Hungary in earlier chapters, drug-use patterns display a shift from the hid-den and socially isolated use of opiates, to public and collective use of 'dance drugs'. In echoes of Irvine Welsh's *Trainspotting*, the author describes a growing awareness amongst heroin users that the social spaces of drug use are changing around them. The gender politics of contemporary nightlife form a further theme; Hong Kong's club scene remaining highly sexualized and sexist, despite women's vastly increased presence as nightlife consumers.

Readers content to muse on nightlife's positive aspects and romantic potentials should avoid Chapter 16. Kopano Ratele and colleagues inject a dose of grim realism in reminding us of the potential for nightlife disputes to descend into ferocious, some-times fatal, violence. Using data from the South African National Injury Mortality Surveillance System they identify marked correlations between evening leisure time and an increased risk of violent death, across four of South Africa's major cities. In their analyses, homicidal violence is mainly a weekend, night-time, seasonal (spring and summer), and youthful phenomenon. It is also predominately male-on-male, a finding they explain in terms of the violent accomplishment of gendered hierarchy, linked to affect: in particular, the destructive anxieties and identity needs of masculinity which draw some young men into contests of 'honour'.

In Chapter 17 we join Fiona Hutton in New Zealand. Tracing nightlife throughout the country's history, she describes how concerns about drunkenness and disorder were rooted in early European settlers' preoccupation with the type of society they were building and their hopes of transforming frontier towns into settled and civilized communities. In addition to 'rough' working-class frontiersmen, Maori populations were seen as another group whose alcohol consumption needed to be controlled to prevent the unleashing of 'savagery'. The history of this indigenous people's difficult relationship with alcohol is revealed as one of the more shameful aspects of colonial history, as prior to contact with Europeans, alcohol played no part in Pacific society. Toward the end of her chapter, Hutton's attentions turn to contemporary towns and cities, the anomalies which surround how crime and disorder is perceived, and the consequent introduction of novel and exclusionary regulatory and policing strategies.

Australia forms the book's final destination, with an authoritative national profile from Tanya Chikritzhs (Chapter 18). It has been said of Australians that 'they work hard at their leisure', with the pub or 'hotel' being an important feature of the leisure landscape. Amongst policymakers, regulators, and enforcers, deregulation and self-regulation have become the common catchphrases of recent decades, a trend prompted by the dictates of central government competition laws. Evidence can be found, however, of growing public concern over the management of the NTE, particularly in relation to violence. The impact of trading hours for licensed venues on crime and disorder has long held public interest whilst debate on the burgeoning numbers of licensed premises is a fresh preoccupation. Australian scholars are at the forefront of research on the criminogenic impacts of extended trading hours and venue densities and Chikritzhs reviews both literatures—one recent study, for example, pointing to a 'critical threshold', above which the bunching of premises substantially increases the risk of violence in immediate and surrounding areas.

In the concluding chapter, Chapter 19, I draw together some of the main themes from the book and make tentative comments as to its omissions and future trajectories for nightlife research.

The potential scope and value of comparative research in the nightlife arena are truly immense and it is my hope that the chapters which follow will provide readers with a taste for adventures to come.

REFERENCES

CENTRAL CITIES INSTITUTE (2002) *Licensing Reform: A cross-cultural comparison of rights, responsibilities and regulation,* London: University of Westminster.

COLLIN, M, with contributions by GODFREY, J (1997) *Altered State: The story of ecstasy culture and acid house,* London: Serpent's Tail.

CRAWFORD, A (2006) 'Networked governance and the post-regulatory state? Steering, rowing and anchoring the provision of policing and security', *Theoretical Criminology,* 10/4, 449–79.

DEMOCRACY, CITIES AND DRUGS PROJECT (2008) *Safer Nightlife Projects*, Brussels: European Commission.

DENNIS, A and MARTIN, P (2005) 'Symbolic interactionism and the concept of power', *British Journal of Sociology*, 191–213.

DOUGLAS, M (1987) *Constructive Drinking: Perspectives on drink from anthropology*, Cambridge: Cambridge University Press.

DUPONT, B, GRABOSKY, P and SHEARING, C (2003) 'The governance of security in weak and failing states', *Criminal Justice*, 3/4, 331–49.

EKIRCH, AR (2005) *At Day's Close: A history of night-time*, London: Weidenfeld & Nicolson.

ENGINEER, R, PHILLIPS, A, THOMPSON, J and NICHOLLS, J (2003) *Drunk and Disorderly: A qualitative study of binge drinking among 18–24 year olds*, Home Office Research Study 262, London: Home Office.

FCO (Foreign and Commonwealth Office) (2008) *British Behaviour Abroad*, London: FCO.

GRAZIAN, D (2008) *On the Make: The hustle of urban nightlife*, Chicago: University of Chicago Press.

HADFIELD, P (2006) *Bar Wars: Contesting the Night in Contemporary British Cities*, Oxford: Oxford University Press.

HEATH, DB (ed) (1995) *International Handbook on Alcohol and Culture*, Westport, Conn: Greenwood Press.

HOBBS, D, HADFIELD, P, LISTER, S, and WINLOW, S (2003) *Bouncers: Violence and Governance in the Night-time economy*, Oxford: Oxford University Press.

JACKSON, P (2004) *Inside Clubbing: Sensual experiments in the art of being human*. Oxford: Berg.

JARVINEN, M and ROOM, R (2007) 'Youth drinking cultures: European experiences', in M Jarvinen and R Room (eds), *Youth Drinking Cultures: European experiences*, Aldershot: Ashgate, 1–15.

JASANOFF, S (2004) 'The idiom of co-production', in S Jasanoff (ed), *States of Knowledge: The co-production of science and social order*, London: Routledge.

JAYNE, M, VALENTINE, G and HOLLOWAY, SL (2008) 'Fluid boundaries—British binge drinking and European civility: Alcohol and the production and consumption of public space', *Space and Polity*, 12/1, 81–100.

JONES, S (2008) 'Antics on Crete would delight Dionysus but the local police are not laughing', *The Guardian*, 16 August, 17.

KREITZMAN, L (1999) *The 24-Hour Society*, London: Profile.

LATOUR, B (1987) *Science in Action*, Cambridge Mass: Harvard University Press.

LYALL, S (2008) 'Some Britons too unruly for resorts in Europe', *New York Times*, 23 August, <http://www.nytimes.com/2008/08/24/world/europe/24crete.html?_r=2&oref=slogin& oref=slogin>, accessed on 5 October 2008.

MALBON, B (1999) *Clubbing: Dancing, ecstasy and vitality*, London: Routledge.

MELBIN, M (1987) *Night as Frontier: Colonizing the world after dark*, London: The Free Press.

MERTON, RK (1959) (Revised and enlarged edition) *Social Theory and Social Structure: Toward the codification of theory and research*, Glencoe, Ill: The Free Press.

MOORE-EDE, M (1993) *The 24-Hour Society: The risks, costs and challenges of a world that never stops*, London: Piatkus.

PARKER, C and BRAITHWAITE, J (2003) 'Regulation' in P Cane and M Tushnet (eds), *Oxford Handbook of Legal Studies*, Oxford: Oxford University Press.

RECASENS, A (ed) (2007) *Violence between Young People in Night-Time Leisure Zones: A European comparative study*, Brussels: Vubpress.

RILEY, S, MOREY, Y and GRIFFIN, C (2008) 'Ketamine: The divisive dissociative. A discourse analysis of the constructions of ketamine by participants of a free party (rave) scene', *Addiction Research and Theory*, 16/3, 217–30.

Ritzer, G (2001) *Explorations in the Sociology of Consumption*, London: Sage.

Rojek, C (2000) *Leisure and Culture*, London: Macmillan.

Room, R (2005) 'Multicultural contexts and alcohol and drug use as symbolic behaviour', *Addiction Research and Theory*, 13/4, 321–31.

—— (2007) 'Understanding cultural differences in young people's drinking', in M Jarvinen and R Room (eds), *Youth Drinking Cultures: European experiences*, Aldershot: Ashgate, 17–40.

Ruggiero, V, South, N and Taylor, I (1998) *The New European Criminology*, London: Routledge.

Sandu, S (2006) *Night Haunts: A journey through the London night*, London: Verso.

Stevenson, JF, Schroeder, JP, Nixon, K, Besheer, J, Crews, FT and Hodge, CW (2008) 'Abstinence following alcohol drinking produces depression-like behavior and reduced hippocampal neurogenesis in mice', *Neuropsychopharmacology*, advance online publication 18 June 2008 (pre-publication ref: doi: 10.1038/npp.2008.90).

Talbot, D (2007) *Regulating the Night: Race, culture and exclusion in the making of the night-time economy*, Aldershot: Ashgate.

Taylor, I (1999) *Crime in Context*, Cambridge: Polity.

Thornton, S (1995) *Club Cultures: Music, media and subcultural capital*, Cambridge: Polity.

Welsh, I (1993) *Trainspotting*, London: Vintage.

Wilson, A (2007) *Northern Soul: Music, drugs and subcultural identity*, Cullompton: Willan.

Wilson, TM (ed) (2005) *Drinking Cultures: Alcohol and identity*, Oxford: Berg.

Winlow, S (2001) *Badfellas: Crime, tradition and new masculinities*, Oxford: Berg.

—— and Hall, S (2006) *Violent Night: Urban leisure and contemporary culture*, Oxford: Berg.

Wood, J and Shearing, C (2007) *Imagining Security*, Cullompton: Willan.

Wrong, DH (1995) *The Problem of Order: What unites and divides society*, Cambridge, Mass: Harvard University Press.

Zedner, L (2003) 'The concept of security', *Legal Studies*, 23/1, 153–76.

PART II

REPORTS FROM AROUND
THE WORLD

2

ENGLAND AND WALES

Phil Hadfield and Fiona Measham

INTRODUCTION

'They scream, they sing, they fall down, they take their clothes off, they cross-dress, they vomit', Malia's Mayor, Konstantinos Lagoudakis, said in an interview. 'It is only the British people—not the Germans or the French.'

(report by Sarah Lyall, New York Times, 2008)

In England and Wales, certain forms of violent crime, criminal damage, and antisocial behaviour have long been concentrated in and around nightlife areas. This may be regarded as a by-product of the intensity of leisure activity in these particular times and spaces, as well as the youthful socio-demographic composition of the nightlife population. It is also a corollary of the forms of commercial leisure one finds there, with much of this leisure activity dominated by the sale and consumption of alcohol. In recent years, there have been two key concerns regarding alcohol consumption in England and Wales: first the exacerbation of long-standing traditions of heavy sessional drinking (Measham, 1996; McKeganey, 1998; McKeganey et al, 1996) and, secondly, an increasingly favourable attitude towards drunkenness amongst British youth, in comparison with young people in most other European countries (Hibell et al, 2004; Jarvinen and Room, 2007). These shifts have been facilitated by the statutory deregulation of licensing laws and entrepreneurial agendas of local economic regeneration (Chatterton and Hollands, 2003; Hadfield, 2006), alongside rapid developments surrounding the sale and consumption of alcohol (Measham and Brain, 2005). The British government has pursued a neo-liberal agenda in its deregulation of potentially addictive legal substances and behaviours (such as alcohol and gambling) (Hadfield, 2007a; Measham and Moore, 2008; Room, 2004), whilst pursuing a new wave of criminalization in relation to alcohol (Hadfield, 2008a) and illicit drug 'misusers' (Moore and Measham, 2008).[1]

The alcohol-driven leisure market is a key component of local economic regeneration in post-industrial Britain and has come to dominate towns and cities after dark. With supply-side controls reduced and access to alcohol increased there has been a renewed emphasis on the self-governance of individual consumers and suppliers (Hadfield, 2006). As Measham (2006) argues, this approach fails to acknowledge the wider social and economic environment within which consumption choices (and competition for sales) take place. Young adults aged 16–35 years represent core consumers of commercial urban leisure and it is toward them that the contemporary branding and marketing practices of the drinks and leisure industries have been most obviously directed (Brain and Parker, 1997; Forsyth, 2001). The potential for violence, public disorder and low-level antisocial behaviour amongst young people has been an important conduit of this process of expansion in the night-time economy (NTE). Against this background, this chapter will focus on three of the most salient themes to have emerged within a period of rapid change in the governance of nightlife: (1) recent transformations in the policy and legislative context; (2) the changing role of women; and (3) the extensive criminalization of youth across the nightlife spectrum. Before exploring these themes, it is necessary to say a little about changing patterns of alcohol and drug use.

CHANGING PATTERNS OF ALCOHOL AND DRUG USE

Young Britons are now socialized into a culture that exhibits a considerable degree of ambivalence toward alcohol. On the one hand, drinking to intoxication is widespread[2] and often regarded as socially acceptable, even expected (Measham, 2004).

---

[1] Whilst illicit drug use has, by definition, involved the criminalization of the possession of controlled drugs under the Misuse of Drugs Act 1971, Measham and Moore (2008) argue that the UK is experiencing a new wave of criminalization of 'recreational' drug users through: (a) the extension of legislation to outlaw emergent drugs increasingly favoured in weekend polydrug repertoires such as ketamine, GHB, and fresh psychedelic mushrooms; (b) a renewed government commitment to a prohibitionist agenda of supply and demand in 2008 with reduced harm reduction services for 'recreational' users (HM Government, 2008a; Hunt and Stevens, 2004); and (c) local policing initiatives which target and harass low-level 'recreational' drug users through the use of sniffer dogs, drug testing, and intimate searches of customers queuing to enter licensed leisure venues within the NTE.

[2] In recent years there has been considerable debate about 'immoderate' drinking and 'binge drinking'. Immoderate drinking is defined as drinking more than the daily benchmark of recommended sensible or 'moderate' consumption. In the UK, the most widely used threshold is four units of alcohol for men and three units for women, with one standard unit of alcohol containing ten millilitres or eight grams of pure alcohol/ethanol (Department of Health, 1995). 'Binge drinking' is also often defined using unit-based measures, most usually the consumption of more than double the daily 'sensible' consumption levels on a single drinking occasion, as recommended by the Department of Health (1995): that is eight units of alcohol for men and six units for women, the equivalent of 64 g and 48 g of alcohol respectively. It has been noted, however, that the calculation of standard units of alcohol consumed is an approximation and not 'very accurate' and therefore it is more useful for assessing changing trends, rather than absolute quantities (The Information Centre, 2007: 5). Historically (Berridge et al, in press) and cross-culturally (ICAP, 1997) there are considerable variations in the definitions and measurement of binge drinking. In Britain, one more

On the other hand, young people may be mindful of the risks associated with heavy sessional drinking and seek to regulate their drinking in order to minimize possible harmful consequences (Measham and Brain, 2005; Szmigin et al, 2008). Important changes have occurred over the past 10–15 years which point to the emergence of a 'new culture of intoxication' amongst a significant minority of young Britons (Measham and Brain, 2005). These changes involve shifts in the societal/cultural framing of alcohol and illegal drug use and involve a willingness to engage in increasingly complex repertoires of weekend polydrug use (the combining of various psychoactive substances in one session) (Moore and Measham, 2008, Williams and Parker, 2001).[3]

Concurrent transformations have occurred in the social environments in which psycho-active consumption takes place and the types of substance/product consumed (Hadfield, 2006; Measham and Brain, 2005; Plant and Plant, 2006). Drinking practices in the NTE are associated with the emergence of new forms of alcoholic beverage, such as 'shooters' and 'ready-to-drinks' (RTDs). Shooters or shots—flavoured, brightly coloured mixtures of spirits and liqueurs served in a small glass and usually drunk in one gulp—have become increasingly popular in British bars within the last decade.[4] RTDs are bottled and branded mixes of spirits, spirit mixers, fruit juice, or flavourings, and sometimes include herbal stimulants such as taurine or guarana. Formerly known as 'alcopops', RTDs were originally introduced into the UK in 1995 in the form of alcoholic lemonades as the spearhead of a re-commodification of alcoholic beverages in the wake of falling sales and a trend in the early 1990s toward bottled water and soft drinks being consumed alongside dance drugs at 'raves' and dance

recently sees a shift in the focus of official policy, away from sessional consumption (such as binge drinking) and toward weekly or regular consumption. Thus, we see 'hazardous drinking' defined as drinking practices which regularly exceed recommended sensible levels (over 4/3 units per day for men/women respectively and more particularly, over 28/21 units per week respectively) and 'harmful drinking', defined in terms of regular heavy intake of over 8/6 units per day, respectively; leading to the consumption of over 50/35 units per week, respectively (HM Government, 2007a).

[3] Much of the focus of criminological research on the British NTE has been on alcohol-oriented leisure, whilst research on 'recreational' drug use has tended to be within public health, cultural studies and club studies (the latter include: Anderson and Kavanaugh, 2007; Malbon, 1999; Redhead, 1993; Sanders, 2006; Thornton, 1995). Yet, there is a strong relationship between the use of controlled drugs and attendance at pubs and clubs. Increased use of drugs such as ecstasy, amphetamines, and LSD was much in evidence in the late 1980s British acid-house and rave scenes (Ashton, 1992; Critcher, 2000; Shapiro, 1999), developing into a broader repertoire of 'club drugs' taken across the course of a clubbing 'lost weekend' (Measham et al, 2001; Riley and Hayward, 2004). The British Crime Survey, the best national self-report data on adult drug use in the UK, shows that frequency of pub/club attendance is statistically significantly associated with the use of illicit drugs. Self-reported prevalence of cocaine use (lifetime, past year, and past month), for example, is highest amongst the 20–29-year-old age group, those who visit pubs and clubs more frequently, residents living in areas of 'urban prosperity', and particularly in London, the north-east and north-west of England (Roe and Man, 2006). However, rather than a blanket growth in Class A drug use across the NTE, emergent research suggests that distinct patterns and repertoires of weekend polydrug-use develop linked to specific stylistic, musical, and geographical 'scenes' both within and between sections of the NTE (Measham and Moore, submitted; see also Anderson, 2009; Demetrovics, Chapter 11, this volume; Moore, 2004). The British Crime Survey, for example, shows that cocaine users under 29 are more likely to be frequent pub-goers than clubbers, whereas cocaine users over 30 are more likely to be clubbers than frequent pub-goers (Roe and Man, 2006: 33).

[4] The *Revolution* chain of Young Person's Venues currently offers a drinks menu containing 25 different flavours of shooter for sale in its bars, with discounts on multiple purchases.

clubs (Collin and Godfrey, 1997; Measham, 2008a ; Measham et al, 2001).[5] In British bars and clubs, these high-strength drinks have been associated with the growth of 'vertical drinking', wherein the consumer remains standing, glass or bottle in hand, in venues with limited seating capacity and music played at high volume. This results in fewer opportunities for conversation and consequently quicker drinking. The popularization of high-strength, often sweet-tasting, alcoholic beverages has encouraged consumers to increase both the speed and quantity of their alcohol intake in each session, with shooters tending to be drunk alongside—rather than instead of—their usual beverage of choice. These practices not only add to the overall quantity of units consumed per session, they also encourage a mixing of different alcoholic drinks (Measham and Brain, 2005).

The advertising of RTDs has focused on youth media in an attempt to create particular brand associations within niche markets. Within a context of conspicuous consumption and competitive individualism (Winlow and Hall, 2006) which sits uneasily alongside the quest for acceptance through conformity to group norms, the image of particular alcoholic products plays its part in the constitution and performance of identity, resulting in both calculated brand choice and brand avoidance by consumers (Lee et al, 2008; Piacentini and Banister, 2008). Alongside the 'right' attitude, body shape, clothes and hairstyle, the bottle-in-hand is imbued with meaning and used as a fashionable adjunct to the presentation of self: a signifier of affluence, virility, and discernment, as recognized by other members of particular urban scenes, cultural or consumer elites (Measham and Hadfield, 2009).[6]

---

[5] Despite criticism that 'alcopops' were enticing young people to drink alcohol at an earlier age by disguising the alcoholic content in flavoured soft drinks (Forsyth, 2001), RTDs proved popular with young adults and particularly female drinkers aged 18–35. By 2002, the market analysts *Mintel* estimated their total market value to be worth £1.6bn, with *Datamonitor* reporting that sales had risen to £5m per day by 2003. More recently, this market share has begun to fall, with drinkers turning to more 'sophisticated' premium and 'heritage' products such as hand-poured cocktails and new premium bottled ciders.

[6] These observations relate mostly to young adults and the night-time leisure market, but should be understood against the backdrop of broader long-term trends in British drinking habits. Over 90 per cent of British adults consistently report drinking alcohol (Office for National Statistics, 2006). The Academy of Medical Sciences (2004) note a 50 per cent growth in per-capita alcohol consumption since 1970 in the UK, with particular rises amongst teenagers and younger women. These trends have been facilitated by an increase in the availability of alcohol through proliferation of off- and on-licensed sales outlets, a fall in the real price of alcohol since the 1970s, and extended trading hours since the 1980s.

As noted in Measham (2008b: 209), alcohol consumption by British adults has declined slightly from a peak around 2001 (Goddard, 2006, 2008). Amongst 16–24-year-olds, the four key indicators of weekly drinking, frequent drinking, immoderate drinking, and binge drinking have all fallen for women and men since 1998. Of note, given the publicity surrounding binge drinking by youth and young adults is that the proportion of young women drinking more than 14 units of alcohol a week fell from 33 per cent in 2000 to 24 per cent in 2005, and the proportion of young men drinking more than 21 units of alcohol a week fell from 41 per cent to 27 per cent respectively (Goddard, 2006: 54). Amongst young people, the ongoing ESPAD surveys confirm the findings from British secondary school surveys (eg, The Information Centre, 2007) that whilst British youth's self-reported experiences of frequent drinking, drunkenness, and binge drinking remain amongst the highest in Europe, there is growing evidence of a downward turn (Hibell et al, 2004). However, despite media coverage to the contrary, recent figures suggest growing polarization within the British youth and young adult population, with increasing numbers of abstainers, as well as increasing numbers who are drinking more heavily (Measham, 2008b).

Hughes et al's (2007) study of drinkers in the Liverpool NTE identified an (unexpected) association between drinkers who report 'pre-loading'[7] and a greater likelihood of heavier drinking and alcohol-related disorder when 'out on the town' later that evening. Such practices are intimately connected to broader-based community norms and socio-economic disparities which influence patterns of consumption and exposure to risk evident in, for example, the regional variations in drinking patterns and alcohol-related harms (APHO, 2007; NWPHO, 2008). Whilst such statistical information provides important aggregate data to inform local, regional, and national initiatives on alcohol, particularly in relation to crime-reduction and public-health policies (HM Government, 2007), it also raises many unanswered questions as to the qualitative dimensions of particular drinking cultures and nightlife contexts (Jayne et al, 2006). Geography, gender, ethnicity, and socio-economic class all become important variables. Trends in women's involvement in nightlife appear to represent one of the most important points of departure in comparison with other countries.

WOMEN AND THE NIGHT-TIME ECONOMY

Women's relationship with alcohol in England and Wales appears to have changed significantly since the early 1990s, with sessional consumption increasing throughout that decade and reaching a peak around the turn of the century,[8] alongside an apparent reduction in the taboos surrounding female public drunkenness (Measham, 2008b). Furthermore, amongst teenagers, there are indications that young women in Britain are currently some of the heaviest female drinkers in Europe (Hibell et al, 2004). The trend toward increased drinking and drunkenness by young women has been attributed to two factors. First, there are lifestyle changes, such as some young women enjoying higher levels of disposable income than women of previous generations and increasing numbers of women delaying marriage, motherhood, and mortgage commitments. These factors have allowed women's drinking patterns, alongside other aspects of their lives, to increasingly emulate men's (the 'convergence' theory, see Bloomfield et al, 2001).[9] Secondly, the 'revolution' in the NTE and the transformation

---

[7] 'Pre-loading' or 'front-loading' appears to be a growing practice in the UK wherein people gather at home to prepare for their night out and drink alcohol purchased from off-trade outlets. These gatherings occur both for social reasons and in order to save money by reducing the group's spending on higher priced on-trade drinks later that same evening. A further money-saving practice is the smuggling of off-trade purchased bottles of spirits into pubs and clubs whereupon the smuggler tops up the drinks they purchase at the bar with extra shots.

[8] A survey of English adults aged 16 and over found that whilst the proportion of men drinking more than the then recommended weekly benchmark of 21 units had remained largely unchanged at 27 per cent in 2002, in comparison with 1992, the proportion of women drinking more than their then recommended weekly benchmark of 14 units had increased from 12 per cent, in 1992, to 17 per cent in 2002 (ONS, 2004). Similarly, between 1992 and 2002, average weekly alcohol consumption by adult women increased from 5.5 units to 7.6 units (ONS, 2004).

[9] There is evidence to link women's growing economic independence with increased alcohol consumption, for example, the highest frequency and quantity of consumption is reported amongst women in managerial and professional occupations (Lader and Goddard, 2004).

of licensed leisure venues from the 'spit and sawdust' backstreet pubs of pre-1980s Britain, to the 'chrome and cocktails' café bar culture of the twenty-first century, have proved appealing to the growing numbers of young women consuming night-time entertainment and leisure spaces (Chatterton and Hollands, 2003; Gofton, 1990; Hadfield, 2006; Measham and Brain, 2005). The expansion of the NTE has also corresponded with the rise of gay and lesbian leisure scenes and an increasing number of 'gay and gay-friendly' venues in English towns and cities (Hindle, 1994; Hobbs et al, 2003; Skeggs, 1999). National statistics (ONS, 2006), public-health data (NWPHO, 2008), and academic research (Jayne et al, 2006) increasingly highlights the importance of regional and ethnic diversity in the drinking patterns of British women.[10]

Despite the more recent falls in overall consumption figures, anxieties about the drinking habits of British women—and especially those under 25—have intensified in recent years. It is young women, rather than young men, who have now come to symbolize the high-profile 'binge drinker' in British public debate (Jackson and Tinkler, 2007; Marsh, 2004) and implicit in these representations is a perception that violence and aggression amongst young females is increasing (O'Brien et al, 2008). A recent survey by *Channel 4 News Online* (2008) asked all 52 police forces in the UK for details of the number of women that had been arrested for drunk and disorderly (D and D) offences in the previous five years. Although 38 forces replied to the survey, only 21 were able to provide like-for-like figures over the five-year period: overall it showed a 53 per cent increase in arrests, from 3,847 in 2003/4, to 5,891 in 2007/8. Fifteen forces, by comparison, found the figures static or lower. The largest rises were in England and Wales. In England, 17 forces reported an increase and nine a fall. In Wales, two forces showed a rise. In Scotland, two forces showed a rise and five a fall, or no change. Police forces in Northern Ireland reported a fall. The biggest increases were in the West Midlands, Gwent, and Leicestershire, with rises of 1,138 per cent, 578 per cent, and 450 per cent, respectively.

Clearly, research is needed as to the bases of such figures. For example, over and above any increases in actually occurring incidents, is there perhaps a growing

[10] For example, since 2000 there have been significant increases in drinking amongst women residing in northern regions, especially the North West, the North East and Yorkshire, recorded at a health authority level.

England and Wales are culturally and ethnically diverse countries and caution is needed in generalizing about the uniformity of the changes identified above, whilst understanding the multi-faceted nature of attitudes and behaviours toward alcohol and drugs. Longitudinal studies of young people show the complexities of how ethnicity, religion, and cultural background, as well as age and generational characteristics, interact to influence young people's drinking-related attitudes and behaviours and why risk-factor analysis cannot fully predict protective or probable high-risk groups. For certain minority ethnic groups, cultural and religious factors will interact with socio-economic status, education, employment, age, and housing conditions. Whilst, for example, British Asian Muslims appear to engage in very little drinking and drunkenness compared with their peers in their earlier teens, there is evidence that by their late teens, some second- and third-generation Asian Muslims who move away from their families and communities become more involved in a social life which includes alcohol (Parker et al, 1998). Amongst minority ethnic adults, apart from Irish respondents, both men and women continue to be less likely than the general population to have had a drink in the week prior to interview, or to have drunk above the daily recommendations. For example, only 1 per cent of Bangladeshi women consumed three or more units on their heaviest drinking day in the previous week, compared with 36 per cent of Irish women, and 30 per cent of the female population in general (ONS, 2006).

willingness on the part of police officers to use powers of arrest, rather than other means of disposal such as 'cautions', in their dealings with female violence and alcohol-related disorder (see Chesney-Lind and Eliason, 2006). In addition and more broadly, such media messages tend to obscure the nuances of women's drinking practices and cultures. Skeggs (1997), for example, has usefully alerted us to the significance of socio-economic class to women's drinking behaviours in her work on 'working-class femininities', whilst Westwood's ethnography explored the complex interaction between class, age, ethnicity, and religion in the drinking practices of a group of female factory workers (Westwood, 1984). Although a small number of studies from the 1980s address the importance of gender to pubs as workplace (Measham, 1988) and leisure space (Hey, 1986; Hunt and Satterlee, 1981), in-depth examinations of the role of gender in contemporary cultures of intoxication are sparse. The relationships between women's drinking practices, the broader socio-economic and cultural changes in their lives, and the gendering of their consumption patterns, have yet to be fully explored (Ettore, 2007; Measham, 2002; Østergaard, 2007).

RECENT DEVELOPMENTS IN POLICY AND PRACTICE

Other countries—principally Australia and New Zealand—have led the way in evaluating the effects of changes in licensing arrangements using such indices as patterns of drink-driving and alcohol-related traffic accidents, rates of alcohol-attributable mortality and violent assault, police work-tasks, and hospital admissions data. With the exception of the latter,[11] comparable studies in England and Wales have been notably absent: a result, in part, of the paucity of public funding beyond the Home Office's own in-house activities, together with a lack of comprehensive, systematic, and comparable regional data. Given the weight of new legislative developments to have emerged since the millennium which impact upon the nightlife field, it is now more important than ever that gaps in knowledge be filled by robust and independent research. Implemented in November 2005, the Licensing Act 2003 (LA2003) and accompanying Guidance (DCMS, 2007), replaced legislation dating back to 1964 and have proved to be the most important statutory developments in alcohol policy for many years. As we shall describe, the Act must be considered alongside the *Alcohol Harm Reduction Strategy for England*, issued in March 2004 (Strategy Unit, 2004) and subsequently developed in *Safe. Sensible. Social. The next steps in the national alcohol strategy* (HM Government, 2007a). Other important policy developments include the introduction of Local Area Agreements (LAAs) requiring public bodies to develop local strategies for preventing alcohol-related crime, and the *Youth Alcohol Action Plan* (DCSF, 2008) which takes forward the government's renewed emphasis on under-age drinking and the consumption of alcohol by young people in public space.

The recently updated British Drugs Strategy for 2008–18 continues a well-established prohibitionist course with its renewed prioritization of the relationship between drug

---

[11] Most prominently in the work of Shepherd and colleagues (eg, Warburton and Shepherd, 2004).

use, crime, and disorder, focusing on drug prevention and enforcement within communities, combined with coercive treatment for 'problem drug users'. Problem drug use is especially associated with opiates and crack, whose users 'account for 99 per cent of the costs to society of Class A drug misuse' (HM Government, 2008a: 50).[12] Meanwhile non-problematic or 'recreational' drug use has remained stable throughout this century with 5.9 per cent of over-16s—nearly two million adults—using controlled drugs *each month* in the UK (HM Government, 2008a: 48; Murphy and Roe, 2007). In terms of 'recreational' Class A drug use, whilst ecstasy use has remained stable or fallen slightly (Measham, 2004), cocaine powder use has increased from 1.3 per cent of 16–24-year-olds reporting past-year use in 1995 to 6 per cent by 2006/7 (Nicholas et al, 2007: 44). The consequent implications of this sustained Class A 'recreational' drug use for policing the NTE include the continued enforcement of drug possession and supply legislation for a growing number of controlled drugs, alongside supply-related violence and disorder (Bennett and Holloway, 2004; Best et al, 2001; Winlow and Hall, 2006), contrasted with reduced harm-minimization service provision for 'recreational' drug users due to the increasing flow of resources to coercive treatment within and attached to the criminal justice system (Hunt and Stevens, 2004; McSweeney et al, 2007; Measham and Moore, 2008).

Returning to the governance of alcohol, the following paragraphs begin by reviewing initial evaluations of the LA2003, before going on to discuss the potential importance of other wide-reaching legislative developments in the alcohol field insofar as they impact upon issues of nightlife, crime, and crime policy.

Before implementation of the LA2003, problems associated with 'fixed' closing times—mostly, 11.00 pm for pubs and 2.00 am for clubs—had been considered a source of concern for many years. The approach of a rigid and, for some drinkers, 'artificially early' time for 'last orders' was thought to encourage people who wished to continue drinking to drink more rapidly and stockpile drinks before closure of the bar. Moreover, standardized trading hours often resulted in the disgorging of customers from venues in various states of intoxication onto the streets, placing pressure on public transport and policing (Hadfield, 2004). Such concerns had been growing since the 1980s when increased consumption of continental lagers by young men combined with associated alcohol-related disorder, led to high-profile media coverage of so-called 'lager louts'. Behind the headlines, however, was a recognition that where transport networks, fast-food outlets, and licensed leisure venues converged and the infrastructure was unable to cope with the pressures of the post-pub 11.00 pm–midnight peak in demand, tensions, frustrations, and high jinks amongst drinkers fuelled the development of disorder hotspots or 'flashpoints' (Hope, 1985; Tuck, 1989).

The LA2003 sought to address these long-standing problems by introducing a system wherein the operators of licensed premises could apply for whatever hours

---

[12] The Misuse of Drugs Act 1971 and subsequent amendments divides illegal drugs into three different categories, or classes. These classes (A, B, and C) carry different levels of penalty for possession and supply according to perceptions of their associated levels of harm (although see Nutt et al, 2007, and their critique of the evidential bases of current rankings). Class A drugs carry the highest penalties and Class C the lowest.

they saw fit, subject to these proposals not being contested by 'responsible authorities' such as the local police and fire services, or 'interested parties' such as local residents. Were no such representations received, the licensing authority was to be duty bound to grant the licence and it was this restriction in the autonomy of local decision-makers, combined with the active political will to increase consumer 'choice' (through increased access to alcohol) that made the Act fundamentally deregulatory in tone. The government's political manoeuvrings in pushing through the legislation included explicit dismissal of an international research literature (Hadfield, 2006: chs 1 and 3) which pointed, almost unanimously, to the various negative public-health and crimi-nogenic effects of recent licensing deregulation in countries such as Ireland (Butler, 2003), Australia (Chikritzhs and Stockwell, 2002; Stockwell and Crosbie, 2001), and Iceland (Ragnarsdóttir et al, 2002). This approach drew criticism from a wide range of scholars, practitioners, and urban stakeholders (Council of HM Circuit Judges, 2005; Hadfield, 2006; LGA, 2002; Measham, 2006; Metropolitan Police, 2004; Plant and Plant, 2005, 2006). The pre-eminence of the British drinks industry and its politi-cal lobby combined with inter-departmental tensions within central government over the divided responsibility for alcohol issues between the Home Office, Department of Health, and the Department for Culture, Media and Sport (DCMS), led one emi-nent alcohol researcher to claim that 'in few (or no) other countries has the alcohol industry more political power than in the UK ... what happens routinely in the UK would be seen as shameful elsewhere' (Room, 2004: 872; see also Burkitt, 2005). Indeed there was even an underlying tone of gratitude to the industry in the National Alcohol Strategy, with its reminder that the NTE employs over one million people and that 'the alcohol leisure industry has supported a revival of city centres across England and Wales' (HM Government, 2007a: 30).

Moreover, of key concern here is the way in which the LA2003 underlined gov-ernment thinking in placing alcohol policy, as with drug policy, predominantly in the realms of crime control. From November 2005 onwards, licensed businesses were required to demonstrate that their operations would not undermine any of the fol-lowing statutory objectives:

- the prevention of crime and disorder
- public safety
- the prevention of public nuisance
- the protection of children from harm.

Another potential statutory objective—included, for instance, in recently reformed licensing legislation for Scotland (Licensing (Scotland) Act 2005)—was omitted from the Act: public health. This omission was notable, given the rises in long-term public ill-health associated with alcohol that have alarmed sections of the British medical com-munity (Academy of Medical Sciences, 2004; BMA, 2008). Legislative drafting appeared to have been driven chiefly by the Department for Culture, Media and Sport (DCMS) in its attempts to combine leisure industry facilitation with certain checks and balances to appease police, local government, Department of Health, and Home Office opinion.

Given its strong emphasis on crime and disorder, it was to the NTE and its associated 'problems' that the objectives of the Act were most clearly addressed.

Subsequent evaluation of its impacts within nightlife areas have presented something of a challenge as many urban entertainment districts inherited extended licensing hours obtained under the old licensing regime (see Hadfield, 2006: Ch 3; 2007b). In evaluating the evaluations it is important to know how and why particular locations were chosen, as qualitative research reveals important local variations (Herring et al, 2008). Some areas have experienced little increase in drinking hours. The established late-night culture of our urban high streets, local market conditions, and the position of individual business interests within them, would appear to exert major influence over decisions to (a) apply for extended licenses and (b) use the full duration of one's licensing hours on any given occasion (Hough et al, 2008). Shifts in consumer behaviour, which may be related to the general economic downturn, are apparent in some areas, with patrons deciding to drink for longer at home, beginning and ending their nights out at a later hour (Hough et al, 2008; Hughes et al, 2007), or choosing to remain in community public houses and visiting centralized nightlife areas less frequently (DCMS, 2008). Moreover, although relevant evaluations have yet to emerge, there are early indications that suburban areas may have experienced the most dramatic changes since 2005, as the extension of licensing hours combined with the expansion of café bars into affluent suburbs diverts customers from city centres and into social drinking locations closer to home.[13]

There remains a considerable degree of policy divergence amongst licensing authorities and magistrates, with some continuing to exercise a restrictive caution in licensing matters, whilst others embrace liberalization or swing from one stance to the other (Hadfield, 2006). In order to produce meaningful results, evaluation studies must account for such differences, focusing on areas in which a quantifiable change in alcohol's availability (through hours of trading and/or number of outlets) can be demonstrated. There are likely to be further intervening variables such as local cultural differentiations in drinking practices, differing degrees of policing and enforcement activity, and uneven access to late-night transportation and other supporting infrastructure. Nonetheless, largely undifferentiated auditing of crime patterns across nightlife's urban heartlands has remained the central focus of Home Office statistical studies (Babb, 2007; DCMS, 2008; Pike et al, 2008; Walker et al, 2006), whilst independent commentators employing a mixed or qualitative methodology (Foster et al, 2007; Hough et al, 2008; LGA, 2008; Newton et al, 2007; Roberts and Eldridge, 2007) have tended to present a more nuanced view. We will begin by reviewing key findings from the former.

---

[13] Chorlton, for example, is an affluent suburb about two miles south of Manchester (situated in the north-west of England, the third largest city in the UK) containing the highest density of bars per square metre to be found outside of Manchester city centre (*South Manchester Reporter*, 2007). Starting with the opening of The Bar in 1993, 20 new bars and pubs opened in the 14-year period 1993–2007, taking the total number of bars and pubs in and around Chorlton to 30 by 2008. Whether or not Chorlton has become a 'drinkers' paradise' or a 'resident's nightmare' is open to dispute; however, the high density of bars with late opening hours (usually extended from 11.00 pm to midnight at weekends) have certainly made the suburb a drinking destination, attracting young adults from outside the area. It has also spearheaded a transformation of the local economy from daytime services toward an expanded local night-time economy, with bars and takeaway food outlets replacing stores, hardware shops, and even a post office.

HOME OFFICE EVALUATIONS

The first quantitative evidence to emerge was the Home Office report *Crime in England and Wales 2005/06* (Walker et al, 2006), which examined the proportion of violent offences and criminal damage occurring over the period October 2004–March 2006. The authors concluded that levels had remained static: 'The data shows no indication of a rise in the overall level of offences, or a shift in the timing of offences as a result of the change in the opening hours of licensed premises' (p 77). However, due to a number of important methodological shortcomings—not least, the failure to record any offences occurring after 2.00 am!—such statements remained moot (Hadfield, 2007b).

The following year saw publication of Babb's (2007) report *Violent Crime, Disorder and Criminal Damage since the Introduction of the Licensing Act 2003*, for the Home Office. This was an important and long-awaited document, being the first systematic analysis, from a government source, of the Act's crime-related impacts. Crime statistics were collected from 30 of the 43 police forces in England and Wales for 'five groups of offences that can occur as a result of alcohol misuse and night-time disorder' (p 1) (criminal damage, harassment, assault with no injury, less serious wounding, and serious violent crime) recorded between October 2004 and September 2006. Eighteen of the sampled forces also provided data for offences recorded as occurring at specified locations such as city centres and in or near licensed premises.

Babb indicates that a 'steep rise appears to occur in the number of offences happening between 3.00 am and 6.00 am in the December 2005–February 2006 period immediately following the introduction of the Licensing Act, with a rise of 22 per cent compared with September–November 2005' (para 3, p 3). More serious violent crimes, whilst falling in number before midnight, increased by 25 per cent between 3.00 am and 6.00 am in the year following introduction of the Act (para 3.2, p 4). Whilst the patterns for each offence category varied, with some offences falling in number before midnight, *all* types of offences were found to rise between the hours of 3.00 am and 6.00 am.

The report concludes that 'the rise from 3.00 am is likely to partly reflect the change to opening hours of licensed premises and the increased numbers of people in a public place at these times, including the police, with greater resources being placed on the streets to deal with disorder' (Summary: i). The report offers no explanation for the fall in some offences before midnight.

The latter point above relates to the truism that the more crime you look for, the more you will find. Whilst it is true to say that the period in question partly coincided with high-profile national police enforcement campaigns (discussed below), it is well established that offences occurring in a nightlife context are likely to be significantly under-reported and under-recorded (Lister et al, 2000; Tierney and Hobbs, 2003). Whilst crimes within the 3.00 am to 6.00 am period represent around 4 per cent of the total recorded crimes in the study, 12 of the participating police forces provided data for the whole 24-hour period. This cannot therefore be taken to imply that only 4 per cent of recorded crimes occurring in city centres at night are occurring between 3.00 am and 6.00 am, as the methodology of the study cannot but produce an underestimate in this respect. In order to obtain more accurate percentage estimates, it would have been necessary to know what the proportion of offences occurring between 3.00 am and 4.00 am was across the 18 forces that provided specific data on city centres and nightlife areas.

In March 2008, Hough and colleagues reported the results of their multi-stranded evaluation of existing sources for the Home Office, focusing largely on the Act's impacts on crime and disorder. The various elements included the statistical review of recorded crime, as reported by Babb; a national Home Office telephone survey of police licensing officers; findings from the British Crime Survey (BCS) Night-Time Economy module covering periods before and after implementation; and detailed case studies of the experience of five towns and cities. Hough and colleagues drew together key findings from these various strands and previously published material on the Act, notably DCMS statistics, HM Revenue and Customs statistics as published by the British Beer and Pub Association (BBPA), independent evaluations of local health authority (particularly hospital accident and emergency departments) data, and interview studies with Local Authority and health staff.

The study found the impact of the LA2003 to have varied from region to region, but that overall the new legislative provisions had made little difference to rates of alcohol-related crime and disorder, despite the increased resources made available to the police. Only a very small minority of licensed premises had applied for 24-hour licences. A fifth had chosen to retain the 11.00 pm closing time, with a half applying for an hour's extension to midnight. The remaining 30 per cent had opted for 1.00 pm closing. The average extension of closing times across all types of on-licensed establishment was 21 minutes (CGA Strategy Ltd, cited in DCMS, 2008: 13). Of those that did apply for 24-hour opening, 65 per cent were hotels, many of which had bars open to residents only. The second largest group was supermarkets and other off-trade stores. The potential for such outlets to contribute to any 'problems' associated with public access to cheap alcohol throughout the night has yet to be explored; however the DCMS (2008: 12) report that some stores are choosing not to open their alcohol aisles for the full 24 hours, 'often following discussions with the police about local issues'.[14] Of the premises that do hold 24-hour licences, many choose not to use them. This is particularly true of the 470 pubs, bars, and nightclubs to have obtained 24-hour licences (ibid).

Across the five towns and cities used as case studies (Birmingham, Blackpool, Croydon, Guildford, and Nottingham), violent crime was found to have fallen by 3 per cent overall in the first 12 months after the change. There were variations between sites: with increases in three locations (Guilford, Birmingham, and Nottingham) and decreases in the remaining two. In accordance with the Babb report, there was evidence of temporal displacement: in four out of five sites there was a fall in levels of violent crime between 11.00 pm and midnight, whilst the small proportion of violent crimes occurring between 3.00 am and 5.00 am rose in all but one of the areas. The authors concluded that these shifts were probably attributable to the changes in licensing hours. The previous concentrations of incidents around closing time were

---

[14] Some supermarkets such as the Asda (Wal-Mart) store in Hulme, Manchester, which had introduced round-the-clock sales, have since decided to terminate their 24-hour alcohol trading.

found to be 'flattening out' in Blackpool and Birmingham, remained unchanged in Croydon and Nottingham, and to have 'moved forward in time into the small hours' in Guildford (Hough et al, 2008: 14).

Further evaluations were conducted by Home Office Regional Government Office researchers in the East of England and Yorkshire and the Humber regions (Pike et al, 2008). Both studies drew on quantitative and qualitative sources and assessed the early experiences of the Act in terms of levels of crime and disorder six months post implementation. Both studies concluded that the new regime did not result in increases in alcohol-related violence, and suggested that the reasons for this lay in the minor changes in opening hours that were actually implemented. Consistent with the Home Office 30-force survey and the case-study sites, evidence of temporal displacement was found, with incidents more likely to occur around the new closing times, and there was some evidence that violent incidents had become less concentrated in time.

INDEPENDENT EVALUATION STUDIES

In one of the first evaluations to appear, Roberts and Eldridge (2007) of the University of Westminster examined the impacts of the Act on dispersal from nightlife areas, drinking cultures, and democratic involvement in the licensing process. The research sought the views of leading late-night operators and representatives from the police and licensed industry. Local case studies were conducted in four areas—the eastern fringe of London, Chelmsford, Newmarket, and Norwich—over a four-month period, including in-depth interviews with residents, licensing officers, senior councilors, and the police.

Many operators were of the view that the longer hours now allowed their customers to leave when they were ready, reducing the rush for late-night transport; others disputed this and felt the busiest period had merely shifted to one or two hours later. The authors see this clash of opinion as a reflection of the many differences in local circumstance. Areas with effective policing and transport strategies, for example, reported more success in ensuring the peaceful dispersal of drinkers, whilst areas with narrow streets, or venues close to residential homes, still experienced problems.

Drinkers in nightlife areas displayed no signs of moving away from heavy sessional-drinking styles (but see Measham, 2008b) and there was little evidence of diversification in the type of nightlife activities to be found on Britain's high streets. However, the report points to improved community relations within its case-study areas, with residents and councilors feeling they had gained a more active role in the local governance of nightlife, through the process of granting and challenging licensing decisions. Operators, it was felt, were now more accountable to their neighbours due to the introduction of an ongoing licensing review process under the Act. 'Under the old licensing regime, licences were renewed every three years. There was limited scope to intervene in the years in between. At renewal it was possible for the licensing magistrates to revoke the licence. This was the only option open to them—it was not possible to add conditions to a licence' (DCMS, 2008: 14). Review procedures—or the threat of them—now provide the police, council environmental-health teams, and residents with an increased capacity to exert pressure on operators to address issues such as noise pollution and 'irresponsible' drinks promotions. This is achieved through a graduated scale of penalties and the ability of licensing authorities to impose legally binding conditions. Review hearings tend to be regarded as a measure of last resort, with the police and operators in many areas drawing up informal 'memoranda of agreements' concerning how premises are to be run. Typically, only those considered to have flouted these agreements, thus failing the 'attitude test', find themselves brought before the licensing authority for formal review proceedings.

The increased influence of local stakeholders is also stressed by Foster et al (2007) of Middlesex University in their survey of local authority areas in England. A telephone/ email survey was conducted aiming to capture the views of key informants—chairs of Licensing Committees and heads of local licensing teams. Respondents were asked for their 'estimates and perceptions' of the first year of implementation of the Act. Two hundred and twenty-five (63 per cent) of the 356 authorities responded. Sixty per cent of respondents who expressed an opinion felt that the changes in licensing and extension of licensed hours in particular would not result in a transformation of British drinking habits and the emergence of a 'café culture' (pp 32–5). In accord with Roberts and Eldridge they found a perceived increase in the capacity of local stakeholders to shape the licensing landscape. The police emerged as the group judged to have the greatest involvement and influence in making representations to the Licensing Authority. The influence of residents was also rated to be high; however, the authors add a cautionary note that 'this might be perception of the *possibility* of influence rather than the actual exercise of influence' (p 38). Only 16 per cent of respondents judged health professionals to be highly involved. This was perhaps due, in part, to the framing of the Act, in which the promotion of public health had not been cited as a statutory licensing objective (although the authors make no comment to this effect). In terms of the Act's impacts at street level, 68 per cent of respondents thought that alcohol-related crime had remained unchanged, 19 per cent thought it had fallen, and 13 per cent thought it had risen; 59 per cent thought that noise levels had remained constant, 32 per cent thought there had been an increase, and 9 per cent a fall. There were few perceived changes in drink-driving. Police activity was seen to have increased, both on the streets and in local decision-making. A sustained commitment from the police was regarded as essential to the control of crime within a licensing framework—licensing authorities could not operate alone in this respect. Licensing authority powers to adopt a 'cumulative impact policy', thereby restricting the number of new licences or extensions to licensing hours in the interests of crime prevention, had been adopted by only 17 per cent of, mostly urban, local authority areas.

In July 2008, the Local Government Association published further research concerning the impacts of the Act (LGA, 2008). In this survey, 51 local authorities (councils), 49 primary care trusts (PCTs),[15] and 20 police authorities were questioned by means of telephone interviews. In answer to the question 'What overall effect do you

---

[15] Primary care trusts (PCTs) are local health organizations responsible for managing local health services. PCTs work with local authorities and other agencies that provide health and social care locally to make sure the community needs are met.

think the Licensing Act 2003 has had on the level of alcohol-related incidents in your area?', seven out of ten respondents reported an increase or no change. PCTs were more likely to say that incidents had increased rather than decreased (29 per cent), compared with 10 per cent of police authorities and 4 per cent of councils. Police and councils were more likely to say that incidents had decreased rather than increased (10 per cent as against 25 per cent, and 4 per cent as against 16 per cent, respectively). However, the majority reported no change at all (57 per cent overall, in addition to 10 per cent who said that they did not know).

Half the police authorities reported that the Act had led to alcohol-related disorder occurring later at night (see also Home Office/KPMG 2008). PCT and police respondents who reported an increase in alcohol-related incidents were also asked what effect this had had on their resources. Eighty-six per cent of the PCT sample reported increased pressure on resources, mainly through a rise in accident and emergency admissions. There were too few police respondents to give meaningful results for this question. Local authorities were also asked this question, with 94 per cent reporting increased resourcing pressures. On a positive note, the new laws were judged to have been effective in streamlining licensing procedures and encouraging closer partnership working between the various public sector agencies.

A survey of 33 accident and emergency departments (AEDs) across England and Wales by the Violence and Society Research Group at Cardiff University found a 2 per cent fall in attendances in 2006 compared with 2005, this fall being concentrated amongst women (Sivarajasingam et al, 2007). Falls were also recorded in a study of AEDs in the Wirral by Bellis et al, (2006). However, countervailing trends were recorded by research teams in London. Newton et al (2007) compared data for the number of people over the age of 16 attending St Thomas' Hospital AED, Central London, between 9.00 pm and 9.00 am during two months—March 2005 and March 2006; one month in the period before, and one month in the period after, introduction of the LA2003. Overnight attendances in March were found to have increased three-fold across the following categories: alcohol-related assaults, alcohol-related injuries, and alcohol-related hospital admissions. The London Ambulance Service (2007) also reported a 2 per cent increase in alcohol-related call-outs in the first ten months following the changes—in accordance with a pre-existing upward trend—and a further 10 per cent increase in the same ten-month period from 24 November 2006.

In March 2008, the DCMS published their own report, *Evaluation of the Impact of the Licensing Act 2003*. This report summarized findings from both the Home Office and independent evaluations. It pronounced the transfer of licensing responsibilities from magistrates to licensing authorities to have been a success, improving democratic accountability and the involvement of residents and other stakeholders in the regulation process. Somewhat refreshingly for an official alcohol policy document it acknowledged that not everything had gone to plan. There was, for example, little indication of diversification within the NTE away from a concentration of drinking venues and current drinking cultures. However, drawing upon their own enforcement statistics, any apportionment of blame was rapidly deflected from the centre to the periphery of state authority. Pointing to a general failure to address problematic premises, licensing authorities and police were told they could do more to apply the 'considerable powers granted by the Act' (p 7). For example: 'the number of licence reviews seems dispro-portionately low compared with the number of test purchase failures' (p 10). In taking forward their review's policing and enforcement priorities, the DCMS point to new legislation to be brought forward by the Home Office (see below).

THE RISE OF LAP-DANCING VENUES

Other concerns surround the way in which the LA2003 permits the incorporation of lap-dancing venues within the standard Premises Licence arrangements which apply to all venues providing alcohol, food, music, and drinking. This legal loophole means that if an establishment already has a licence for a bar and restaurant, it is able to offer lap-dancing without an additional 'Sexual Encounter Establishment Licence' of the type required by cinemas dedicated to pornographic films, strip clubs, and sex shops. This has resulted in a doubling in the number of lap-dancing clubs in Britain from approximately 150 to over 300 in the four years from 2004 to 2008. The proliferation of pole-dancing and lap-dancing in England has occurred within the broader context of a 'normalisation of the sex industry' (Chatterton and Hollands, 2003: 160) involving specialist chains running dedicated clubs, such as the internationally operated *Spear-mint Rhino* brand, to the simple addition of poles and podiums to mainstream pubs and clubs. In the latter, such fixtures may be used not only by professional dancers, but also by female customers performing impromptu dances, as noted in a recent national alcohol industry review (Home Office/KPMG, 2008). In 2008, the Fawcett Society, together with the Object women's organization, launched a campaign entitled 'Strip-ping the Illusion: The Re-Licence Lap-Dancing Campaign', which sought to obtain amendments to the LA2003 so as to close the legal loophole. Whilst the Fawcett Soci-ety's campaign focused on female City workers pressurized into attending lap-danc-ing clubs for corporate entertainment with their firm's clients (*The Guardian*, 2008), Object focused on lap-dancing venues' potential impacts upon their local community and possible relationships between the customers of lap-dancing venues and inci-dents of sexual assault on dancers and residents in the surrounding neighbourhood (Eden, 2007; see also Chatterton and Hollands, 2003). In response, the Lap Dancing Association (LDA) which represents venue operators has been keen to position its members as vendors of entertainment rather than part of the sex industry. However, Stripping the Illusion undoubtedly reflects broader ongoing concerns about the rou-tine sexual harassment of women working in diverse occupational spheres from the NTE (bar staff, waitresses) to finance (City traders), as well as the contested nature of women's presence in licensed premises, both as staff and as customers. The rise of a commercial lap-dancing sector can thus be understood as perhaps the most visible manifestation of an increasingly entrenched 'sexualization' of employment expecta-tions and entertainment in the twenty-first century NTE (Home Office/KPMG, 2008; Measham, submitted). A further issue, articulated by Dan Rogerson MP,[16] concerns

---

[16] Dan Rogerson, Liberal Democrat MP for North Cornwall, has five recently opened lap- dancing ven-ues in his constituency. As he comments: 'The burgeoning number of sex clubs has caused considerable and understandable concern among residents in my constituency. Extraordinarily, it seems what were perfectly

a blurring of the lines between bar and sex club. To this end, a Private Members' Bill, co-sponsored by Dr Blackman-Woods MP and Lynda Waltho MP, was put before the House of Commons in June 2008. Stakeholder consultation on the Bill is currently ongoing.

THE NEW POLICY MIX

Clearly, government aspirations to usher in a new age of 'Continental-style café culture'—as expressed in the White Paper *Time for Reform* (Home Office, 2000) have not been realized. Taken together, the various reviews gave no indication that the Act has so far either delivered significant reductions in alcohol-related crime and disorder or introduced greater diversity into the NTE. The reduction in young-adult drinking discussed earlier in this chapter was evident before the introduction of the Licensing Act and cannot be ascribed to any simple policy change (Measham, 2008b). Although there have been some positive impacts, violent crime and public nuisance during the early hours of the morning appear to have increased and public sector organizations report an *increased* pressure on local services. Moreover, 'a true picture of the impacts may not emerge for a number of years, and in terms of health consequences for many years' (Foster et al, 2007: 42). In addition, there are now a number of policy initiatives aimed at reducing alcohol-related crime and promoting 'sensible drinking', many of which are aimed specifically at the nightlife context. Evaluation of the Act in isolation from these other interventions has, and will continue to, prove difficult. As the DCMS (2008: 17) acknowledge: 'The main conclusion to be drawn … is that licensing regimes may be one factor in effecting change to the country's drinking culture—and its impact on crime—but they do not appear to be the critical factor. The key issue is how they interact with other factors.'

In *Safe. Sensible. Social. The Next Steps in the National Alcohol Strategy* (HM Government, 2007a), focus is placed on a 'root and branch' approach to alcohol-related harm. The National Alcohol Strategy sets out three key objectives:

1. to ensure laws and licensing powers are being used widely and effectively to crack down on crime and disorder, irresponsible management of licensed premises, and to protect young people
2. to 'sharpen the focus' on the minority of drinkers who cause the most harm to themselves and their communities, such as under 18s, 18–24-year-old 'binge drinkers' (drinking more than 8/6 units per session), and 'harmful drinkers' (regularly drinking more than 50/35 units per week)
3. to actively promote 'sensible drinking' drawing on policing, prison, and probation staff, along with local authorities, the NHS, voluntary organizations, the media, the alcohol industry, the wider business community, and local communities.

(Paraphrased from HM Government, 2007a: 6)

ordinary bars can slip into what is effectively a part of the sex industry without any further licensing requirements or consultation with local residents, as though our communities are glorified theme parks for adults' (Morris, 2008: unpaginated).

British alcohol policy currently strives to balance the widely recognized 'pleasures' and benefits of drinking alcohol in the booming British NTE with the necessity to reduce alcohol-related harms to drinkers and wider society and the National Alcohol Strategy (NAS) reflects that precarious balance. The NAS states that drinking brings pleasure to the 'vast majority' of drinkers (HM Government 2007a: 30) and that 'alcohol can play an important and positive role in British culture. It is part of our social and family life, and can enhance meal times, special occasions and time spent with friends' (HM Government 2007a: 5). Indeed, 'alcohol-related harm should not be viewed in isolation, as alcohol consumption can also have positive effects. Drinking at a responsible level can be a source of enjoyment for the vast majority of those who participate' (2007a: 30). However, alongside this government commitment to 'ensuring that people are able to enjoy alcohol safely and responsibly' (2007a:6), the NAS also advocates a 'paradigm shift' in promoting a sensible drinking culture and 'making drunkenness unacceptable' (2007a: 10).

Significantly, there is no official recognition that drinkers might find drunkenness, in itself, pleasurable. The challenge then, for the government, public health, law enforcement, voluntary sector, and alcohol industries in their promotion of sensible drinking, is the thorny problem that there is evidence that some drinkers do find drunkenness in itself a pleasurable state to be actively pursued. Variously described as 'determined drunkenness' (Measham, 2006), 'intense intoxication' (Hayward and Hobbs, 2007), and 'extreme drinking' (Martinic and Measham, 2008), a range of studies, including government-funded research (eg, Engineer et al, 2003; Richardson and Budd, 2003), conclude that drunkenness, for some youth and young adult drinkers in England and Wales, is considered both a motivation for consumption and a positive outcome (Martinic and Measham, 2008). However, this important consumer perspective concerning the pleasures of immoderate consumption remains absent and unrecognized in official alcohol policy documents.

In the NAS, official sanctioning of the social pleasures of moderate alcohol consumption nestles alongside the targeting of what are described as a minority of immoderate drinkers—such as those who participate in harmful or binge drinking. This growing official censure, policing, and criminalization of immoderate consumption fits a broader governmental agenda not only to change the traditional British drinking culture of weekday restraint/weekend excess, but to criminalize the pharmacological pleasures of intoxication per se (Measham, 2008b; Measham and Moore, 2008; see also below). To this end, the NAS includes the aim of challenging 'the attitudes and practices that underlie cultural attitudes towards alcohol' (HM Government, 2007a: 58) and even hints at an underlying abstentionism in its aim to 'create a culture in which young people feel that they can have fun without needing to drink' (2007a: 61). In practical terms, this has meant a focus not only on the 18–24-year-old 'binge drinkers' already the subject of frenzied public and political debate since the late 1990s (Berridge et al, 2007: 32), but also on older home drinkers, whose regular immoderate consumption may also lead to health and social problems, if not the highly visible alcohol-related disorder more usually associated with the NTE.

January 2008 saw the introduction of a 'toolkit' on how to implement the aims and objectives of the NAS at a local level (HM Government, 2008b). This document was designed as a resource to help Alcohol Leads and others within local authorities, PCTs, children's services, and delivery partnerships, such as Crime and Disorder Reduction Partnerships (CDRPs) and Drug and Alcohol Action Teams (DAATs)—the agencies most likely to be responsible for developing and delivering local strategies—to address alcohol-related crime, ill-health, and other harms. The document highlighted a range of activities to achieve the government's aims across three key strategic areas of health, community safety, and children and young people:

1. to reduce the levels of alcohol-related violent crime, disorder, and anti-social behaviour
2. to reduce the percentage of the public who perceive drunk and rowdy behaviour to be a problem in their area
3. to reduce chronic and acute ill-health caused by alcohol, resulting in fewer alcohol-related accidents and hospital admissions.

(HM Government 2008b: 6)

A further strategic milestone was passed in the 2007 Comprehensive Spending Review which set out the government's key policy priorities and outcomes for the 2008–11 funding period. The Review represented a significant step in the development of alcohol policy nationally as it introduced targets and associated funding streams to drive action on alcohol (Ranzetta, 2007: 1). As part of the Review, the government has, for the first time, expressed its priorities on alcohol in the form of a Public Service Agreement (PSA). PSA 25 (HM Government, 2007b) aims to reduce the harm caused by alcohol (and drugs) to: (1) the community as a result of associated crime, disorder, and antisocial behaviour; (2) the health and well-being of those who use (drugs or) drink harmfully; and (3) the development and well-being of young people and families (ibid: 3). The most important local delivery mechanism for PSA 25 is the Local Area Agreement (LAA). LAAs comprise a three-year contract between local and central government, outlining how local priorities on alcohol will be met by delivering local solutions. From summer 2008, LAAs became the central 'delivery contract' between central government and local government and its partners, including the police, PCTs, the voluntary sector, and local businesses, on alcohol strategy implementation.

Further requirements of local partnerships are made under the Crime and Disorder (Formulation and Implementation of Strategy) Regulations 2007 (Home Office, 2007). These regulations implement s 19 of the Police and Justice Act 2006 which required all CDRPs to have conducted a 'strategic assessment' of local priorities and have a strategy in place for tackling crime, disorder, antisocial behaviour, and substance misuse, including alcohol, by April 2008. The most important developments in relation to crime control, however, concern the rapid and unprecedented expansion of police powers.

'THE PARTY'S OVER'? EXTENSIONS OF POLICE POWER

> We are coming down hard on people who cause trouble. These people, often worse the wear for drink or drugs, behave as if they have the right to do whatever they like on our streets. Well they don't. The party's over for people who

make any street in any town or city a no-go area for decent, law-abiding people.
I promised we would get tough and we are doing just that.

(Michael Craik, Chief Constable, Northumbria Police and Association of
Chief Police Officers lead on AMEC, BBC News, 2005)

Branded as *The Party's Over*, a Northumbria Police campaign of summer 2005 foretold the new mood of government and its increasing willingness to partake in 'get tough' rhetoric. The Alcohol Misuse Enforcement Campaign (AMEC) of the summer of 2004 transpired to be the first of five national Home Office campaigns. Supported through the Tackling Violent Crime Programme (TVCP),[17] the exercise was repeated over the Christmas period in 2004, from mid-November to the end of December 2005, and in the summer of 2006. Whilst the exact aims of each campaign varied slightly in emphasis, the most common objectives were the targeting of under-age drinking and alcohol-related violence in areas of high-volume violent crime, at times when violence was known to increase (festive and holiday periods). Police forces in target areas were provided with additional funding to increase high-visibility patrols, enforcement, and awareness-raising activity during campaign periods. The fourth and fifth exercises, the Tackling Underage Sales of Alcohol Campaign (TUSAC) of summer 2007 and the Responsible Alcohol Sales Campaign (RASC) of December 2007 placed particular emphasis on licensed premises themselves and enforcement of the law around serving alcohol to under-18s and customers who were already drunk.[18]

The Home Office campaigns were assisted by an unprecedented acceleration in the number and scope of police, local authority, and court powers in relation to the control of crime, disorder, and public nuisance associated with nightlife. These interventions have tended to take one of three forms, either targeting identified persons and venues, or focusing on designated places. Adapting categories developed by Crawford (2008b: 13–14) for designating antisocial behaviour legislation, these include:

Person-Specific Restrictions

Penalty Notices for Disorder (PNDs) Section 1 of the Criminal Justice and Police Act 2001 gave police officers the power to issue 'on the spot' Penalty Notices for Disorder (PNDs). Similar to a parking fine, a penalty notice provides the opportunity to discharge any liability to conviction for an offence on payment of a fixed fine.

---

[17] The TVCP focused on alcohol-related and domestic violence and was targeted at those 56 of the 373 Crime and Disorder Reduction Partnership (CDRP) areas in England and Wales judged to have the highest volume of recorded violent crimes.

[18] In support of the RASC campaign the Home Office provided guidance notes to police officers on how to identify a person who is drunk, through aspects of their comportment and appearance, including: 'rambling conversation', 'an unkempt appearance', 'being careless with money', 'spilling drinks', 'fumbling for cigarettes', and 'bumping into furniture'. Police were told that the purpose of this 'check-list' was to assist them in gathering evidence to support actions against licensed premises serving alcohol to already intoxicated persons, so as to paint 'such a compelling picture of the level of intoxication of the purchaser that any attempt by the seller to claim a lack of knowledge would be doomed to fail' (Slade, 2007: 5). See also Perham et al, (2007).

Directions to Leave a Locality Section 27 of the Violent Crime Reduction Act 2006 allows the police to require any individual aged 16 or over, to leave a particular locality for up to 48 hours if that person is judged likely to cause, or contribute to, alcohol-related crime and disorder in that locality.

Drinking Banning Order (DBO) This is a civil order introduced by the Violent Crime Reduction Act 2006 (ss 1–14). The order prohibitions persons judged by the courts to pose a risk of committing criminal or disorderly acts whilst under the influence of alcohol from entering licensed premises within a defined geographical area. DBOs may only be issued to over-16s and must have a specified duration of two months to two years. DBOs replaced the previous provisions of the Licensed Premises (Exclusion of Certain Persons) Act 1980 which similarly allowed for exclusion of named individuals from licensed premises.

Venue-Specific Restrictions

Licensing Conditions The LA2003 allows licensing authorities to place additional 'conditions' on a licence which specify how the premises will be operated. Typical conditions may concern the use of door supervisors (bouncers), CCTV, search policies, customer proof-of-age schemes, the prominent display of signage at exits requesting patrons to leave quietly, and involvement in local CDRP initiatives. Following a ban on smoking in indoor public places in 2007, licensed premises are now having to provide outdoor 'smoking areas' and the management of such areas in terms of noise escape and crowd control has become a particular focus for the imposition of conditions.

Licensing Law Enforcement Powers

i. *Sales to Under-Age Drinkers: Test Purchasing.* Part 7 of the LA2003 restates the law concerning the offence of selling/supplying alcohol to persons under the age of 18. A person commits an offence under s 146 if he or she sells alcohol to an under-18-year-old; an offence under s 147 is committed if a person knowingly allows such a sale; s 31 of the Criminal Justice and Police Act 2001 allows that police officers or Trading Standards personnel may check compliance by conducting test-purchases. Juvenile volunteers may be recruited to assist with these operations.
ii. *Sales to Persons who are Drunk: Covert Operations.* In the RASC campaign of December 2007, the Home Office turned their attention to the use of powers contained within the LA2003 to deal with the 'irresponsible' sale of alcohol. The specific aims of the RASC were to encourage and promote the use by police of ss 140 (allowing disorderly conduct on licensed premises), 141 (sale of alcohol to a person who is drunk), 142 (obtaining alcohol for a person who is drunk), and 143 (failure to leave licensed premises), through targeted enforcement activity during the pre- Christmas period.

Noise Abatement Noise-related nuisance is controlled by the imposition of licensing conditions under the LA2003 and also through enforcement by local authority Environmental Protection Teams (EPTs) using powers under the Environmental Protection Act 1990, ss 79–82 of the Noise Act 1996, and the Clean Neighbourhoods and Environment Act 2005, Pts 1–7, and ss 40 and 41 of the Anti-Social Behaviour Act 2003.

Closure Powers Under the LA2003 police have the power to close individual licensed premises, or all licensed premises in a geographical area if there is actual or anticipated disorder on or near those premises. The closure order can last for up to 24 hours. Under s 160, the closure order is obtained through the magistrates' court in advance, and ss 161–70 allow for immediate closure without a court application.

Licence Review The LA2003 provides that at any stage, following the grant of a premises licence, a 'responsible authority' (the police and other statutory bodies, such as EPTs and fire authorities) or an 'interested party' (a person living or working in the vicinity of licensed premises, or a body representing those persons) may ask the licensing authority to review the licence. Licence reviews can only be called in connection with a matter arising at the premises in connection with one or more of the four objectives of the Act. In addition, reviews will normally follow any action by the police to close down the premises for up to 24 hours on grounds of disorder or noise nuisance.

Place-Based Restrictions

Dispersal Powers Part 4, s 30 of the Anti-Social Behaviour Act 2003 gives police and Police Community Support Officers (PCSOs)[19] powers to disperse groups of two or more persons from a designated area, without evidence that they are causing antisocial behaviour. The legislation also provides police with powers to escort home under-16s after 9.00 pm.

Designated Public Places Orders (DPPOs) Section 13 of the Criminal Justice and Police Act 2001 gave local authorities the power to designate public areas in which it is an offence to drink alcohol after being required by a police officer not to do so. The police have the power to require individuals to surrender the alcohol and any opened or sealed containers. Failure to comply without reasonable excuse is an offence. The powers replaced existing local authority 'drinking by-laws' that applied similar place-based restrictions.

Cumulative Impact Policies are not mentioned specifically in the LA2003, but are referred to in the accompanying Guidance (DCMS, 2007: 13.24–13.39). The term refers to the potential impact of a significant number of licensed premises concentrated in one area. Where there is evidence that the cumulative impact of all these premises, taken together, is undermining the licensing objectives relating to the prevention of crime and disorder, and the prevention of public nuisance, licensed authorities may adopt cumulative impact policies (CIPs) in their local Statements of Licensing Policy. Where the local authority adopts a CIP, their Statement of Licensing Policy must clearly show the geographical areas in which the policies apply and the evidence that necessitated them. CIPs typically create a refutable presumption against the granting

---

[19] The Police Reform Act 2002 created the possibility for police support staff, endowed with limited powers, to undertake a variety of uniformed patrolling tasks. These staff are known as Police Community Support Officers (PCSOs) and now play a major role in 'reassurance policing' across England and Wales.

of new premises licences or variations to licences so as to extend opening hours within their designated areas. Importantly, although CIPs are formulated by local authorities, the police still play a key role both in providing much of the evidence base for their establishment and in bringing the necessary representations as an 'interested party' to the application process, thus allowing CIP powers to become operational.[20]

Alcohol-Disorder Zones (ADZs) The Violent Crime Reduction Act 2006, ss 15–20, creates powers for local authorities to designate, with the consent of the police, a locality as an ADZ where there is an ongoing problem with alcohol-related nuisance and disorder. Within the ADZ, local authorities have the power to impose charges on holders of premises licences for the costs of police-initiated crime-control measures. Although now operational in law, no area has so far (as of September 2008) seen fit to impose an ADZ. This may be due, in part, to the accompanying guidance (Home Office, 2008) which frames the creation of an ADZ as an action of 'last resort' to be used only in designated areas where alcohol-related disorder presents serious and chronic challenges that other remedies have failed to address. It may also have to do with the fear of legal challenge from powerful national bar chains (Doward, 2005).

Business Improvement Districts (BIDs) These are a North American model which seeks investment in the local trading environment through the provision of added-value services funded by local businesses. Businesses identify the area and the issues and put together a proposal which includes performance indicators and a management structure. Businesses must vote in favour of a BID in order for it to be established. In accordance with the Local Government Act 2003 and the Business Improvement Districts (England) Regulations 2004, BIDs operate as a partnership initiative between local public- and private-sector organizations, financed by the commercial sector, through a levy approved by a ballot. In November 2007, Nottingham city centre became the first area in the UK to create a Business Improvement District (BID) scheme committed solely to the needs and priorities of the NTE.

Venue-directed powers (both place-based and venue-specific) represent clear attempts to 'responsibilize' licence holders for the control of crime and disorder in, and increasingly around, their premises (Hadfield, 2008b). In practice, the powers are usually used as bargaining tools in negotiated settlements concerning a 'package' of security measures that are struck between police and venue operators; the 'gloves coming off' (as one licensing barrister representing police in a review hearing, put it) only in the case of serious recurrent problems, recalcitrance, or defiance of police authority. Crawford (2008a: 780) reminds us of the similar 'attitude test' applied in the classic street-policing encounter, whereupon the outcome of police decision-making in choosing whether or not to apply their person and/or area-based powers is determined in large degree by the extent to which youth are seen to defer to police authority. In both scenarios, the current level of public, media, and political concern

---

[20] In the absence of representations from an 'interested party', licensing authorities are required by the LA2003 to grant the licence, regardless of the existence of a CIP—licensing authorities cannot act alone in this regard.

about alcohol creates a highly sensitized frame of governmental action in which the symbolism of policies which appear to support a 'get tough' stance appears more important than their substance or efficacy (Crawford, 2008a, 2008b; Jones and Newburn, 2007). This is clearly underlined by the concerns of practitioners, including senior police officers (Doward, 2005) and local government officials (LGA and LACORS, 2005), regarding the viability of ADZs and in relation to the Home Office's failure to pilot or evaluate the effects of many of the recent place-based and person-specific antisocial behaviour powers.

CONCLUSIONS

Against the backdrop of changing patterns of alcohol and drug use, this chapter has considered ways in which the potential for violence, public disorder and low-level antisocial behaviour amongst young people has become an important conduit of the expansion of the NTE in England and Wales. Public, media, and political interest in these issues is exceptionally high and has been reflected in rapid changes within nightlife's formal governmental framework, including transformations in the broader policy and legislative context and specifically targeted extensions of police power. Whilst the reach of the criminal justice system in providing solutions to the problem of intoxication has been extended, official discourse continues to deny the lure of pleasurable substance-enhanced experiences and therefore fails to acknowledge or constructively engage with important facets of contemporary youth cultures, including, perhaps most prominently, the leisure lives and consumption choices of many young women and young men. Alcohol policy continues to be framed most dominantly within a crime, disorder, and enforcement discourse operating within a broader neo-liberal agenda. In practice, this involves the differential application of punitive actions according to official constructions of the 'responsible' and 'irresponsible' supplier and consumer. Whilst the needs and interests of the former category are increasingly well served by a light-touch pro-business regulatory agenda, the activities of those judged by the police, licensing authorities, and the courts to constitute a 'problem' are increasingly criminalized. To a large extent, this constitutes a focus on what Rod Morgan, the former Chair of the Youth Justice Board for England and Wales,[21] has called the 'low hanging fruit' (cited in Crawford, 2008a: 780). In introducing a more diverse and graduated range of powers through which to govern licensed premises, the LA2003 appears to have strengthened the hand of local regulatory stakeholders. This is much more the case, however, in relation to situational and managerial controls which are thought to enhance—or at least not restrict—business opportunities arising within the 'legitimate' arena of moderate drinking and carefully

---

[21] The Youth Justice Board for England and Wales (YJB) is an executive non-departmental public body, whose board members are appointed by the Secretary of State for Justice. The YJB oversees the youth justice system and works to prevent reoffending by children and young people under the age of 18 years.

delineated and pacified pleasures, as supplied by 'responsible' (often large corporate) operators. The difficulties of applying more fundamental supply-side checks on the availability of alcohol and illicit drugs—and on consumers' continued thirst for more than a 'moderate' degree of hedonism—remain largely unresolved.

REFERENCES

All internet sources were accessible 20 August 2008

ACADEMY OF MEDICAL SCIENCES (2004) *Calling Time: The nation's drinking as a major health issue*, London: Academy of Medical Sciences, <http://www.acmedsci.ac.uk/index. php?pid=99and puid=20>.

ANDERSON, T (2009) *Rave Culture: The alteration and decline of a music scene*, Philadelphia: Temple University Press.

—— and KAVANAUGH, P (2007) 'A rave review, conceptual interests and analytical shifts in research on rave culture', *Sociology Compass*, 1/2, 499–519.

APHO (Association of Public Health Observatories) (2007) *Alcohol: Indications of public health in the English regions*, London: APHO.

ASHTON, M (ed) (1992) *The Ecstasy Papers: A collection of ISDD's publications on the dance drugs phenomenon*, London: ISDD.

BABB, P (2007) *Violent Crime, Disorder and Criminal Damage since the Introduction of the Licensing Act* 2003, 2nd edn, Home Office Online Report, 16/07, <http://www.homeoffice. gov.uk/rds/pdfs07/rdsolr1607.pdf>.

BBC NEWS (2005) 'Drunken images released by police', 7 June, <http://news.bbc.co.uk/1/hi/ england/4070630.stm>.

BELLIS, MA, ANDERSON, Z, and HUGHES, K (2006) *Effects of the Alcohol Misuse Enforcement Campaigns and the Licensing Act* 2003 *on Violence: A preliminary assessment of accident and emergency attendances in Wirral*, Liverpool: Centre for Public Health, <http://www.cph. org.uk/showPublication.aspx?pubid=275>.

BENNETT, T and HOLLOWAY, K (2004) 'Possession of illegal guns among offenders in England and Wales', *Howard Journal*, 33/3, 237-52.

BERRIDGE, V, HERRING, R and THOM, B (in press) 'Binge drinking: A confused concept and its contemporary history', *Social History of Medicine*.

—— THOM, B and HERRING, R (2007) *The Normalisation of Binge Drinking? An historical and cross cultural investigation with implications for action*. London: Alcohol Education and Research Council, <http://www.aerc.org.uk/documents/pdfs/finalReports/AERC_ FinalReport_0037.pdf>.

BEST, D, SIDWELL, C, GOSSOP, M, HARRIS, J and STRANG, J (2001) 'Crime and expenditure amongst polydrug misusers seeking treatment: The connection between prescribed methadone and crack use, and criminal involvement', *British Journal of Criminology*, 41, 119–26.

BLOOMFIELD, K, GMEL, G, NEVE, R and MUSTONEN, H (2001) 'Investigating gender convergence in alcohol consumption in Finland, Germany, The Netherlands and Switzerland: A repeated survey analysis', *Substance Abuse*, 22, 39-53.

BMA (British Medical Association) (2008) *Alcohol Misuse: Tackling the UK epidemic*, London: BMA Board of Science.

BRAIN, K and PARKER, H (1997) *Drinking With Design: Alcopops, designer drinks and youth culture*, London: Portman.

BURKITT, H (2005) 'Are alcohol advertisers drinking in the last chance saloon?' in M Grant and E O'Connor (eds), *Corporate Social Responsibility and Alcohol: The need and potential for partnership*, New York: Routledge.

BUTLER, S (2003) 'Paying the price for extended opening hours: A comment from Ireland', *Drugs: Education, Prevention and Policy*, 10/4, 293–6.

Channel 4 News Online (2008) 'Female drink offences soar', Law and Order News, 1 May, <http://www.channel4.com/news/articles/society/law_order/femalepercent20drinkpercent20offencespercent20soar/2115947>.

CHATTERTON, P and HOLLANDS, R (2003) *Urban Nightscapes: Youth cultures, pleasure spaces and corporate power*, London: Routledge.

CHESNEY-LIND, M and ELIASON, M (2006) 'From invisible to incorrigible: The demonisation of marginalised women and girls', *Crime Media Culture*, 2/1, 29–47.

CHIKRITZHS, T and STOCKWELL, T (2002) 'The impact of later trading hours for Australian public houses (hotels) on levels of violence', *Journal of Studies on Alcohol*, 63/5, 591–9.

COLLIN, M and GODFREY, J (1997) *Altered State: The story of ecstasy culture and acid house*, London: Serpent's Tail.

Council OF Her Majesty's Circuit Judges (2005) *Observations of the Criminal Sub-Committee of HM Council of Circuit Judges on 'Drinking Responsibly': The government's proposals*, 13 June, reprinted at: <http://www.ias.org.uk/resources/publications/alcoholalert/alert200502/al200502_p2.html>.

CRAWFORD, A (2008a) 'Dispersal powers and the symbolic role of anti-social behaviour legislation', *Modern Law Review*, 71/5, 753–84.

—— (2008b) 'From the Shopping Mall to the Street Corner: Dynamics of exclusion in the governance of public space', paper presented to the Worldwide Universities Network Colloquium 'International Comparative Criminal Justice and Urban Governance', University of Leeds, 26–28 June.

CRITCHER, C (2000) '"Still raving": Social reaction to ecstasy', *Leisure Studies*, 19, 145–62.

DCSF (Department for Children, Schools and Families) (2008) *Youth Alcohol Action Plan*, London: DCSF, Home Office, Department of Health, <http://www.dcsf.gov.uk/publications/youthalcohol/pdfs/7658-DCSF-Youthpercent20Alcoholpercent20Actionpercent20Plan.pdf>.

DOH (Department of Health) (1995) *Sensible Drinking: The report of an Inter-Departmental Working Group*, Department of Health: London, <http://www.dh.gov.uk/assetRoot/04/08/47/02/04084702.pdf>.

DCMS (Department for Culture Media and Sport) (2007) *Revised Guidance Issued under Section 182 of the Licensing Act 2003*, London: DCMS, <http://www.culture.gov.uk/NR/rdonlyres/597B72E2-61BC-44AD-98D2 6BC7208FD740/0/RevisedGuidance-June2007.pdf>.

—— (2008) *Evaluation of the Impact of the Licensing Act 2003*, London: DCMS.

DOWARD, J (2005) 'Police fear chaos over pub hours', *The Observer*, 20 March, <http://www.guardian.co.uk/society/2005/mar/20/drugsandalcohol.politics>.

EDEN, I (2007) *Inappropriate Behaviour: Adult venues and licensing in London*. London: The Lilith Project, Eaves Housing for Women.

ENGINEER, R, PHILLIPS, A, THOMPSON, J and NICHOLLS, J (2003) *Drunk and Disorderly: A qualitative study of binge drinking among 18–24 year olds*, Home Office Research Study 262, London: Home Office.

ETTORRE, E (2007) *Revisioning Women and Drug Use: Gender, power and the body*, Basingstoke: Palgrave Macmillan.

FORSYTH, A (2001) 'A design for strife: Alcopops, licit drug—familiar scare story', *International Journal of Drug Policy*, 12/1, 59–80.

FOSTER, J, HERRING, R, WALLER, S and THOM, B (2007) *Implementation of the Licensing Act 2003: A national survey*, London: Alcohol Education and Research Council.

The Guardian (2008) 'Lap dance ethos at heart of city sexism, say campaigners', 31 March, 25.

GODDARD, E (2006) *General Household Survey 2005: Smoking and drinking among adults*, London: Office for National Statistics, <http://www.statistics.gov.uk/StatBase/Product.asp?vlnk=5756>.

—— (2008) *General Household Survey 2006: Smoking and drinking among adults*, London: Office for National Statistics, <http://www.statistics.gov.uk/downloads/theme_compendia/GHS06/Smokinganddrinkingamongadults2006.pdf>.

GOFTON, L (1990) 'On the town: Drink and the "new lawlessness"', *Youth and Society*, 29, April, 33–9.

HADFIELD, P (2004) 'The operation of licensed premises', in P Kolvin (ed), *Licensed Premises: Law and practice*, London: Tottel.

—— (2006) *Bar Wars: Contesting the Night in Contemporary British Cities*, Oxford: Oxford University Press.

—— (2007a) 'Party invitations: New Labour and the (de)-regulation of pleasure', in D Downes (ed), *Criminal Justice Matters: 10 years of New Labour*, 67/Spring, 18–19, 47.

—— (2007b) 'A hard act to follow: Assessing the consequences of licensing reform in England and Wales', *Addiction*, 102/February, 177–80.

—— (2008a) 'Policing and regulating the night-time economy in England and Wales: Recent developments in law and practice', paper presented at the European Society of Criminology Conference, September 2008, Edinburgh.

—— (2008b) 'From threat to promise: Nightclub 'security', governance and consumer elites', *British Journal of Criminology*, 48, 429–47.

HARPER, D (1998) 'An argument for visual sociology', in J Prosser (ed), *Image-Based Research: A sourcebook for qualitative researchers*, London: Routledge/Falmer.

HAYWARD, K and HOBBS, D (2007) 'Beyond the binge in 'Booze Britain': Market-led liminalization and the spectacle of binge drinking', *British Journal of Sociology*, 58/3, 437–56.

HERRING, R, THOM, B, FOSTER, J, FRANEY, C and SALAZAR, C (2008) 'Local responses to the Alcohol Licensing Act 2003: The case of Greater London', *Drugs: Education, Prevention and Policy*, 15/3, 251–65.

HEY, V (1986) *Patriarchy and Pub Culture*, London: Tavistock.

HIBELL, B, ANDERSSON, B, BJARNASON, T, AHLSTRÖM, S, BALAKIREVA, O, KOKKEVI, A and MORGAN, M (2004) *The ESPAD Report 2003: Alcohol and other drug use among students in 35 European countries*, Stockholm: The Swedish Council for Information on Alcohol and Other Drugs.

HINDLE, P (1994) 'Gay communities and gay space in the city', in S Whittle (ed), *The Margins of the City: Gay men's urban lives*, Aldershot: Ashgate.

HM GOVERNMENT (2007a) *Safe. Sensible. Social: The next steps in the national alcohol strategy*, London: The Stationery Office.

—— (2007b) *PSA Delivery Agreement 25: Reduce the harm caused by alcohol and drugs*, HM Treasury London: HMSO, <http://www.hm-treasury.gov.uk/media/B/1/pbr_csr07_psa25.pdf>.

—— (2008a) *Drugs: Protecting families and communities: The 2008 Drug Strategy*, London: Home Office, <http://drugs.homeoffice.gov.uk/publication-search/drug-strategy/drug-strategy-2008-2018? view=Binary>.

HM GOVERNMENT (2008b) *Safe. Sensible. Social: Alcohol strategy local implementation toolkit*, London: Home Office, Department of Health, Department for Children, Schools and Families.

HOBBS, D, HADFIELD, P, LISTER, S and WINLOW, S (2003) *Bouncers: Violence and Governance in the Night-time Economy*, Oxford: Oxford University Press.

HOME OFFICE (2000) *Time for Reform: Proposals for the modernisation of our licensing laws*, London: HMSO.

—— (2007) *Crime and Disorder (Formulation and Implementation of Strategy) Regulations 2007*, Statutory Instrument 2007/1830.

—— (2008) *Alcohol Disorder Zones, Sections 15–20 of the Violent Crime Reduction Act 2006, Draft Guidance*, London: Home Office.

——/KPMG LLP (2008) *Review of the Social Responsibility Standards for the Production and Sale of Alcoholic Drinks*, Birmingham: KPMG LLP.

HOPE, T (1985) 'Drinking and disorder in the city centre: A policy analysis', in *Implementing Crime Prevention Measures*, Home Office Research Study No 86, London: HMSO.

HOUGH, M, HUNTER, G, JACOBSON, J and COSSALTER, S (2008) *The Impact of the Licensing Act 2003 on Levels of Crime and Disorder: An evaluation*, Research Report 04, London: Home Office.

HUGHES, K, ANDERSON, Z, MORLEO, M and BELLIS, M (2007) 'Alcohol, nightlife and violence: The relative contributions of drinking before and during nights out to negative health and criminal justice outcomes', *Addiction*, 103, 60–5.

HUNT, G and SATTERLEE, S (1987) 'Darts, drink and the pub: The culture of female drinking', *Sociological Review*, 35/3, 575–601.

HUNT, N and STEVENS, A (2004) 'Whose harm? Harm reduction and the shift to coercion in UK drug policy', *Social Policy and Society*, 3/4, 333–42.

THE INFORMATION CENTRE (2007) *Smoking, Drinking and Drug Use among Young People in England in 2006: Headline figures*, Leeds: The Information Centre for Health and Social Care, <www.ic.nhs.uk/pubs/drugsmokedrinkyoungeng2005>.

INTERNATIONAL CENTRE FOR ALCOHOL POLICIES (1997) *The Limits of Binge Drinking*, ICAP Report No 2, Washington DC: ICAP (also available online).

JACKSON C and TINKLER P (2007) '"Ladettes" and "modern girls": "Troublesome" young femininities', *The Sociological Review*, 55/2, 251–72.

JARVINEN, M and ROOM, R (eds) (2007) *Youth Drinking Cultures: European experiences*, Aldershot: Ashgate.

JAYNE, M, HOLLOWAY, S and VALENTINE, G (2006) 'Drunk and disorderly: Alcohol, urban life and public space', *Progress in Human Geography*, 30/4, 451–68.

JONES, T and NEWBURN, T (2007) *Policy Transfer and Criminal Justice: Exploring US influence over British crime control policy*, Maidenhead: Open University Press.

LADER, D and GODDARD, E (2004) *Drinking: Adults' behaviour and knowledge in 2004*, London: Office for National Statistics.

LEE, M, MOTION, J and CONROY, D (2008) 'Anti-consumption and brand avoidance', *Journal of Business Research, Special Issue on Anti-Consumption*, in press (pre-publication ref: doi:10.1016/j.jbusres.2008.01.024).

LGA (Local Government Association) (2002) *All Day and All of the Night? An LGA discussion paper*, London: LGA.

—— (2008) *Licensing Act 2003 and the Effects of Alcohol*, London: LGA.

—— and LACORS (LOCAL AUTHORITIES COORDINATORS OF REGULATORY SERVICES) (2005) *Local Government Association and LACORS Response to Drinking Responsibly: The government's proposals*, February, London: LGA and LACORS, <http://www.lga.gov.uk/Documents/Briefing/Drinkingpercent20ResponseFeb2005.pdf>.

LISTER, S, HOBBS, D, HALL, S and WINLOW, S (2000) 'Violence in the night-time economy: Bouncers—the reporting, recording and prosecution of assaults', *Policing and Society*, 10, 383-402.

LONDON AMBULANCE SERVICE (2007) *Alcohol-Related Ambulance Calls Rise by 12 per cent in London*, London Ambulance Service, <http://www.londonambulance.nhs.uk/news/latest/latest.html>.

LYALL, S (2008) 'Some Britons too unruly for resorts in Europe', *New York Times*, 23 August, <http://www.nytimes.com/2008/08/24/world/europe/24crete.html?_r=2&oref=slogin&oref=slogin>.

McKEGANEY, N (1998) 'Alcopops and young people: A suitable cause for concern', *Addiction*, 93, 471-3.

——FORSYTH, A, BARNARD, M and HAY, G (1996) 'Designer drinks and drunkenness amongst a sample of Scottish schoolchildren', *British Medical Journal*, 313, (17 August), 401.

McSWEENEY, T, STEVENS, A, HUNT, N and TURNBULL, PJ (2007) 'Twisting arms or a helping hand?: Assessing the impact of "coerced" and comparable "voluntary" drug treatment options', *British Journal of Criminology*, 47, 470-90.

MALBON, B (1999) *Clubbing: Dancing, ecstasy and vitality*, London: Routledge.

MARSH, B (2004) 'The ladette takeover', *Daily Mail*, 19 January, 3-4.

MARTINIC, M and MEASHAM, F, (2008) 'Extreme drinking', in M Martinic and F Measham (eds), *Swimming With Crocodiles: The culture of extreme drinking*, London: Routledge, 1-12.

MEASHAM, F (1988) 'Men buy the beer and the leer: sexual harassment at work in the leisure industry', unpublished MA thesis, University of Warwick.

—— (1996) 'The "Big Bang" approach to sessional drinking: Changing patterns of alcohol consumption amongst young people in north-west England', *Addiction Research*, 4/3, 283-99.

—— (2002) '"Doing Gender"—"Doing Drugs": Conceptualising the gendering of drugs cultures', *Contemporary Drug Problems*, 29/2, Summer, 335-73.

—— (2004) 'The decline of ecstasy, the rise of "binge" drinking and the persistence of pleasure', *Probation Journal, Special Edition: Rethinking Drugs and Crime*, 51/4, 309-26.

—— (2006) 'The new policy mix: Alcohol, harm minimisation and determined drunkenness in contemporary society', *International Journal of Drug Policy, Special Edition: Harm Reduction and Alcohol Policy*, 17/4, 258-68.

—— (2008a) 'A history of intoxication: Changing attitudes to drunkenness and excess in the United Kingdom', in M Martinic and F Measham (eds), *Swimming With Crocodiles: The culture of extreme drinking*, New York and Abingdon: Routledge, 13-36.

—— (2008b) 'The turning tides of intoxication: Young people's drinking in Britain in the 2000s', *Health Education, Special Edition: Drugs in the 21st Century*, 108/ 3, 207-22.

—— (submitted) 'The "barmaid question": Attempts to criminalize female employment in English public houses'.

——ALDRIDGE, J and PARKER, H (2001) *Dancing On Drugs: Risk, health and hedonism in the British club scene*, London: Free Association Books.

—— and BRAIN, K (2005) '"Binge Drinking", British alcohol policy and the new culture of intoxication', *Crime, Media, Culture: An International Journal*, 1/3, 263-84.

—— and HADFIELD, P (2009, forthcoming) '"Your name's not down": Fragmentation, gentrification and criminalization in English clubland', *Addiciones, Special Issue: Selected Papers from the Club Health Conference 2008*.

MEASHAM, F and MOORE, K (2008) 'The criminalization of intoxication', in P Squires (ed), *ASBO Nation: The criminalization of nuisance*, Bristol: Policy, 273–88.

—— (submitted) 'Drugs in the night-time economy: Exploring the relationship between patterns of illicit drug use and leisure type by customers in licensed leisure venues in an English city'.

METROPOLITAN POLICE (2004) *Preliminary Assessment of the Impact of the Licensing Act 2003 on the Metropolitan Police Service*, London: Metropolitan Police Clubs and Vice Operational Command Unit.

MOORE, D (2004) 'Beyond "subculture" in the ethnography of illicit drug use', *Contemporary Drug Problems*, 31/Summer, 181–212.

MOORE, K and MEASHAM, F (2008) '"It's the Most Fun You Can Have for Twenty Quid": Motivations, consequences and meanings of British ketamine use', *Addiction Research and Theory, Special Edition: Ketamine*, 231–44.

MORRIS, N (2008) 'Sex and the citizen: Lap-dancing—a licence to thrill?', *The Independent*, 18 June, <http://www.independent.co.uk/news/uk/home-news/sex-and-the-citizen-lapdancing--a-licence-to-thrill-849233.html>.

MURPHY, R and ROE, S (2007) *Drug Misuse Declared: Findings from the 2006/07 British Crime Survey England and Wales*, Home Office Statistical Bulletin 18/07, London: Home Office.

NEWTON, A, SARKER SJ, PAHAL, GS, VAN DEN BERGH E and YOUNG, C (2007) 'Impact of the new UK licensing law on emergency hospital attendances: A cohort study', *Emergency Medical Journal*, 24, 532–4.

NICHOLAS, S, KERSHAW, C and WALKER, A (eds) (2007) *Crime in England and Wales 2006/07*, Home Office Statistical Bulletin 11/07, London: Home Office, <http://www.homeoffice.gov.uk/rds/pdfs07/hosb1107.pdf>.

NUTT, D, KING, L, SAUSBURY, W and BLAKEMORE, C (2007) 'Development of a rational scale to assess the harm of drugs of potential misuse', *The Lancet*, 369, 1047–53.

NWPHO (North West Public Health Observatory) (2008) *Local Alcohol Profiles for England 2007*, <http://www.nwph.net/alcohol/lape/regions.htm>.

O'BRIEN, K, HOBBS, D and WESTMARLAND, L (2008) 'Negotiating violence and gender: Security and the night-time economy in the UK', in S Gendrot and P Spierenburg (eds), *Violence in Europe: Historical and contemporary perspectives*, New York: Springer.

ONS (Office for National Statistics) (2004) *Living in Britain: Results from the 2002 General Household Survey*, London: The Stationery Office, <http://www.statistics.gov.uk/pdfdir/lib0304.pdf>.

—— (2006) *General Household Survey 2005*, London: ONS, <http://www.statistics.gov.uk/StatBase/Product.asp?vlnk=5756>.

ØSTERGAARD, J (2007) 'Mind the gender gap? When boys and girls get drunk at a party', *Nordic Studies on Alcohol and Drugs*, 24/2, 127–48.

PARKER, H, ALDRIDGE, J and MEASHAM, F (1998) *Illegal Leisure: The normalisation of adolescent recreational drug use*. London: Routledge.

PERHAM, N, MOORE, SC, SHEPHERD, J and CUSENS, B (2007) 'Identifying drunkenness in the night-time economy', *Addiction*, 102, 377–80.

PIACENTINI, M and BANISTER, E (2008) 'Managing anti-consumption in an excessive drinking culture', *Journal of Business Research,* in press. doi:10.1016/j.jbusres.2008.01.035.

PIKE, S, O'SHEA, J and LOVBAKKE, J (2008) *Early Experiences of the Licensing Act 2003 in the East of England and Yorkshire and Humber Regions*, Research Report 05, London: Home Office.

PLANT, E and PLANT, M (2005) 'A "Leap in the Dark?" Lessons for the United Kingdom from Past Extensions of Bar Opening Hours', *International Journal of Drug Policy*, 16, 363–8.

PLANT, M and PLANT, M (2006) *Binge Britain: Alcohol and the national response*, Oxford: Oxford University Press.

RAGNARSDÓTTIR, T, KJARTANSDÓTTIR, A and DAVIDSDÓTTIR, S (2002) 'Effect of extended alcohol serving hours in Reykjavik', in R Room (ed), *The Effects of Nordic Alcohol Policies: What happens to drinking and harm when control systems change?* Publication no 42, Helsinki: Nordic Council for Alcohol and Drug Research, 145–54.

RANZETTA (2007) *Local Action on Alcohol: A new era*, Ranzetta Consulting.

REDHEAD, S (ed) (1993) *Rave Off: Politics and deviance in contemporary youth culture*, Aldershot: Avebury.

RICHARDSON, A and BUDD, T, (2003) *Alcohol, Crime and Disorder: A study of young adults*, Home Office Research Study 263, London: Home Office.

RILEY, S and HAYWARD, E (2004) 'Patterns, trends, and meanings of drug use by dance-drug users in Edinburgh, Scotland', *Drugs: Education, Prevention and Policy*, 11/3, 243–62.

ROBERTS, M and ELDRIDGE, A (2007) *Expecting 'Great Things'? The impact of the Licensing Act 2003 on democratic involvement, dispersal and drinking cultures*, London: Central Cities Institute for the Institute of Alcohol Studies.

ROE, S and MAN, L (2006) *Drug Misuse Declared: Findings from the 2005/06 British Crime Survey*, Home Office Statistical Bulletin 15/06, London: Home Office, <http://www.home-office.gov.uk/rds/pdfs06/hosb1506.pdf>.

ROOM, R (2004) 'Disabling the public interest: Alcohol strategies and policies for England', *Addiction*, 99, 1083–9.

SANDERS, B (ed) (2006) *Drugs, Clubs and Young People: Sociological and public health perspectives*, Aldershot: Ashgate.

SHAPIRO, H (1999) 'Dances with drugs: Pop music, drugs and youth culture', in N South (ed), *Drugs: Cultures, controls and everyday life*, London: Sage, 17–35.

SIVARAJASINGAM, V, MOORE, S and SHEPHERD, JP (2007) *Violence in England and Wales 2006: An accident and emergency perspective*, <http://www.cf.ac.uk/dentl/resources/Trents_violence_England_Walves_2006.pdf>.

SKEGGS, B (1997) *Formations of Class and Gender: Becoming respectable*, London: Sage.

—— (1999) 'Matter out of place: Visibility and sexualities in leisure spaces', *Leisure Studies*, 18/3, 213–32.

SLADE, D (2007) *Sales to Drunks Enforcement and Responsible Alcohol Sales Campaign: Additional information for participating BCUs*, London: Home Office, Police and Partnership Standards Unit.

South Manchester Reporter (2007) '"Drinkers" haven or plain bar-my?', 29 March, 14.

STOCKWELL, T and CROSBIE, D (2001) 'Supply and demand for alcohol in Australia: Relationships between industry structures, regulation and the marketplace, *International Journal of Drug Policy*, 12, 139–52.

STRATEGY UNIT (2004) *Alcohol Harm Reduction Strategy for England*, London: Cabinet Office, Prime Minister's Strategy Unit.

SZMIGIN I, GRIFFIN C, MISTRAL W, BENGRY-HOWELL, A, WEALE L and HACKLEY C (2007) 'Re-framing "binge drinking" as calculated hedonism: Empirical evidence from the UK', *International Journal of Drug Policy*, in press (pre-publication ref: doi:10.1016/j.drugpo.2007.08.009).

THORNTON, S (1995) *Club Cultures: Media, music and subcultural capital*, Cambridge: Polity Press.

TIERNEY, J and HOBBS, D (2003) *Alcohol-Related Crime and Disorder Data: Guidance for local partnerships*, London: Home Office.

Tuck, M (1989) *Drinking and Disorder: A study of non-metropolitan violence*, HORPU Research Report 108, London: HMSO.

Walker, A, Kershaw, C and Nicholas, S (2006) *Crime in England and Wales 2005/06*, Home Office Statistical Bulletin, London: Home Office.

Warburton, A and Shepherd, J (2004) *An Evaluation of the Effectiveness of New Policies Designed to Prevent and Manage Violence through an Interagency Approach (A Final Report for WORD)*, Cardiff: Cardiff Violence Research Group.

Westwood, S (1984) *All Day Every Day*, London: Pluto.

Williams, L and Parker, H (2001) 'Alcohol, cannabis, ecstasy and cocaine: Drugs of reasoned choice amongst young adult recreational drug users in England', *International Journal of Drug Policy*, 12, 397–413.

Winlow, S and Hall, S (2006) *Violent Night: Urban Leisure and Contemporary Culture*, Oxford: Berg.

3

SCOTLAND

Martin Elvins

Alcohol is the problem of our time. This is the major criminal justice, health
and social issue in Scotland . . . we have to take action. Scotland has a cultural
problem. We 'dine out' on the hard-drinking Scottish image and we have to
change that culture. We just allowed our high streets to be taken over.

(Kenny MacAskill, Scottish Government Cabinet Secretary for Justice)

INTRODUCTION

The quote above from Kenny MacAskill is taken from an interview published in
The Guardian newspaper, 14 May 2008. His forceful words encapsulate a number of
important points about the contemporary debate regarding alcohol in Scotland. First
and foremost, it contains the implication that a strong cultural dimension shapes
attitudes and perceptions regarding alcohol within Scottish society. Second, by referring to 'our high streets' the minister locates the debate firmly in relation to ownership of public space and negative associations concerning alcohol use in public.
O'Donnell has pointed to a long-established culture of heavy drinking in Scotland,
further emphasizing that during the past five to ten years 'a marked increase in heavy
drinking and alcohol-related harm' has occurred (2006: 367). Political recognition of
this trend came with the launch of the Scottish Plan for Action on Alcohol Problems
in 2002, marking the first coordinated attempt to challenge the cultural legacy at a
national level (Scottish Executive, 2002).[1] A recent official estimate of the overall costs
of alcohol use and misuse in Scotland—based on 2006/7 data (Scottish Government,
2008a)—led to newspaper headlines highlighting that the estimated cost had doubled
as compared with the previous estimate based on 2002/3 data.[2] The role of alcohol
in relation to nightlife and crime is an oft-discussed aspect of the wider debate but,
partly as a consequence of the very breadth of that debate, it is often very difficult
to isolate the specific factors that shape the scale and form of this phenomenon in

---

[1] An updated version of this plan was published in 2007 (Scottish Executive, 2007a).
[2] See 'Scotland's alcohol shame: Drink abuse costs nation £2.25bn a year', *The Scotsman*, 13 May 2008.

Scotland. This chapter is an attempt to explore that terrain. At this point it may be helpful to explain the contemporary Scottish political and regulatory context within which decisions about alcohol and its socio-cultural and socio-economic dimensions take place.

CULTURAL AND REGULATORY CONTEXT

Few doubt that Scotland has a distinctive and culturally specific relationship with alcohol, although there is no definitive account of why this should be the case. To suggest that the Scottish relationship with alcohol differs significantly as compared with the rest of the UK is borne out by the fact that in 2006 alcohol-related death rates per head of population were more than double in Scotland as compared with the UK as a whole: there were 13.4 deaths per 100,000 people across the UK as a whole, whilst the equivalent rate in Scotland was 27.3 deaths (*The Scotsman*, 26 January 2008). Scotland has a population of a little over 5 million people and since devolution in 1999 has had its own government responsible for the majority of day-to-day Scottish issues, including public health, and the law and home affairs (including most aspects of criminal and civil law; the prosecution system and the courts).[3] Under the devolution settlement, the Westminster Parliament retained legislative responsibility on a UK-wide basis for what are termed reserved matters, such as fiscal policy and trade and industry, including competition and customer protection. The matter of alcohol duty and taxation is, for example, a matter reserved to Westminster.

In Scotland, the regulation of liquor (alcohol) licensing falls under the responsibility of 32 licensing boards made up of a statutorily prescribed number of local councillors, who operate independently of their respective local authority and exercise a quasi judicial function (Cummins, 2005: 840). Licensing boards were introduced by the Licensing (Scotland) Act 1976, which established a system of permitted licensing and trading hours and created two new types of licence, one of which (the Entertainment Licence) has been especially pertinent to the subsequent development of the night-time economy (NTE).[4] Cummins describes how what had been intended as exceptional under the 1976 legislation gradually became normal, and hours became routinely extended based on location and type of licence (with larger, city-centre premises generally getting later hours). The nature of entertainment premises, defined as those premises which are the subject of an entertainment licence authorizing the sale of alcohol as an ancillary to the entertainment provided, had also changed in nature significantly from what had been envisaged under the 1970s legislation:

dance halls gave way to discotheques, discotheques became clubs, and banks became super-pubs, while the proliferation of licences stimulated unprecedented levels of competition and deep-price discounting. (Cummins, 2005: 843)

---

[3] For more detail on the Scottish system of government see McGarvey and Cairney (2008).

[4] A more comprehensive discussion of the historical development of alcohol (liquor) licensing in Scotland can be found in Scottish Executive (2003b: 25–8). See also Cummins (2005) and Scottish Executive (2007b: 6–7).

By 2001 the Scottish government concluded that various social changes meant that major legislative reform was required; a process which culminated in the granting of Royal Assent to the Licensing (Scotland) Act 2005 on 21 December 2005.[5] Reform of licensing laws in Scotland occurred broadly in parallel with reform of equivalent laws applying in England and Wales. The Labour Party held a majority administration in both Westminster and Edinburgh at this time hence it was inevitable that there would be a degree of common ground in relation to the main ideas and principles underlying the reform process. However, with the election of a government led by the Scottish National Party (SNP) in May 2007 the basis for the two administrations to share impetus and political preference for a broadly similar approach was removed (Labour remained in power in Westminster at this time). It will be argued in this chapter that the present Scottish government—of which Mr MacAskill (quoted above) is a senior member—is in fact now showing a degree of divergence from the Westminster approach to alcohol policy and, by extension, to the issue of nightlife and crime.

Returning to the legislation, one sees that the Licensing Act (Scotland) 2005 established five licensing objectives:

(a) preventing crime and disorder
(b) securing public safety
(c) preventing public nuisance
(d) protecting and improving public health
(e) protecting children from harm. (Scottish Executive, 2005: 2)

The equivalent legislation applicable in England and Wales (the Licensing Act 2003, implemented November 2005) contained only four of these five licensing objectives. The objective present in the Scottish legislation but not in its English and Welsh equivalent is objective (d): 'protecting and improving public health'. The inclusion of public health suggests, nominally at least, that the Scottish legislature has embraced a more holistic view of how different aspects of the potentially negative consequences of alcohol use are interrelated. That this has been done via licensing law at first seems surprising, and almost certainly reflects a political environment with more executive flexibility, and without the powerful departmental demarcations—and vetoes—that characterize Westminster-based government. By linking public order and health to alcohol in this way, Scotland has seemingly undergone a shift in its political willingness to recognize alcohol as a societal issue that cannot be addressed in piecemeal fashion. However, the inclusion of health in the remit of the 2005 Act was envisaged prior to the drafting of the legislation, and its final adoption points us to the role played by the Nicholson Committee.

PROBLEM PERCEPTION: THE ROLE OF THE NICHOLSON COMMITTEE

The appointment of the Nicholson Committee was announced on 28 June 2001 by Mr Jim Wallace, then Justice Minister in the Scottish Executive, with the following terms

---

[5] The legislation is being introduced in stages and will enter full force on 1 September 2009.

of reference: 'To review all aspects of liquor licensing law and practice in Scotland, with particular reference to the implications for health and public order; to recommend changes in the public interest; and to report accordingly' (Scottish Executive, 2003b: 1).

The Nicholson Committee report was published on 19 August 2003 and provided some pertinent reflections as to the intersection of emerging health and public order concerns underlying its appointment and underscoring its remit:

there has been growing concern in recent years about the health implications of, for example, binge drinking on the part of the young of both sexes and about the growth of alcohol-related illnesses, affecting all ages. Additionally, those with a concern for public order have become increasingly alarmed at the links between over-consumption of alcohol and the commission of crimes, in particular crimes of violence. (Scottish Executive, 2003b: 28)

Alcohol, nightlife, and crime were thus tacitly accepted by the Committee as having a causal relationship, albeit without providing further exposition or analysis of its nature. The Committee specified what it deemed to be the four most important background facts when forming its recommendations, noting first the emergence of the so-called 'super-pub' 'which generates a much greater density of drinkers' even though the number of public-house licences had remained constant for some time (Scottish Executive, 2003b: 35). Second, a large increase in the number of off-sale licences (allowing alcohol to be bought and taken away) was also noted. Two further—related—developments with direct relevance to the NTE were also noted: third, that since 1976 a very large number of entertainment licences had been granted; and, fourth, that 'the widespread grant of regular extensions to permitted hours . . . has resulted in large numbers of licensed premises, particularly in town and city centres, being open until very late at night' (ibid: 35). The report observed that by 2001 around 90 per cent of all on-licensed premises had extensions beyond the 'normal' closing hour of 11.00 pm that had become standardized in the late-1970s; furthermore, that 'many of those extensions run not just until midnight but often extend until 3 or 4 am or even later. This has given rise to many problems which have been brought to our notice by local residents' and amenity groups' (ibid: 28).[6]

The importance of the Nicholson Committee lies in the fact that it both advocated and validated a broader role for licensing legislation in addressing problems associated with alcohol in the Scottish context, emphasizing the significance of the NTE in the process. However, the report of the Committee made clear that neither its members nor those it consulted considered that changes to licensing law could 'of themselves remove the undesirable consequences of over-indulgence in alcohol. Many of the problems associated with that are deeply engrained in the Scottish psyche, and reform of the law will not of itself bring about changes' (Scottish Executive, 2003b: 1–2).

---

[6] Cummins (2005: 843) notes that at the time he was writing the policy of Glasgow Licensing Board was to allow entertainment premises in Glasgow city centre to routinely remain open until 3.00 am each day of the week. This regime broadly matched that which then applied in London, but was later than the 2.00 am upper limit which applied in the rest of England and Wales at the time.

RESEARCH EVIDENCE

With the honourable exception of three studies of Glasgow (Forsyth et al, 2005; Forsyth, 2006, 2008) research-based knowledge of nightlife and crime in Scotland is relatively limited. Just under 40 per cent of the population of Scotland live in one of only four cities in the country with a population that exceeds 100,000 people: Glasgow, by far the largest city, has a population of around 1.1 million, followed by Edinburgh (the Scottish capital) with 457,000, and Aberdeen and Dundee with 188,000 and 151,000 respectively. The most extensive and spatially concentrated night-time economies in Scotland are to be found in these four cities. In April 2003, there were 295 pubs and nightclubs within a half-mile square area of Glasgow city centre, then estimated to draw 70,000 people to its NTE on the busiest days of the week (Forsyth et al, 2005: 4).

Forsyth et al (2005) and Forsyth (2006) form companion studies, examining Glasgow city-centre pubs and nightclubs respectively. Both studies used consistent observational methods to measure disorder risks arising from licensed premises and provide a rich source of data on the Scottish cultural setting. In the 2005 study, researchers focused on eight pubs, for which all observations were conducted from 9.00 pm to 1.00 am on Friday and Saturday nights to the following mornings; hence, if taken alone, the findings referred only to part of the NTE period. However, the 2006 study examined eight nightclubs, with observation occurring in the period from 11.30 pm to 3.00 am, thus providing a basis for comparison between the two studies.

One of the most significant comparative findings was that the frequency and severity of aggressive incidents witnessed inside nightclubs was much greater (more than double) than in the earlier study of pubs. The research also found that 'drunkenness was the norm' inside the observed nightclubs but concluded that the higher level of disorder was linked to dancing behaviours inherent to nightclubs rather than greater levels of intoxication (see Forsyth, 2006: 102, 117–18). City-centre streets were observed to be less disorderly after nightclub closing time (3.00 am) in comparison with pub closing (12 midnight) as observed in the 2005 study, and it was concluded that a high and visible police presence on the streets and the presence of other night workers (such as 'taxi marshals') at the later, but not earlier, hours combined to make the streets less disorderly (ibid: 108). The report offered a positive view on the use of taxi-rank-marshalling schemes in the city centre in terms of reducing the potential for confrontation and argument amongst those queuing for taxis.

The use of taxi marshals in Glasgow arose from an initiative known as 'Nite Zone' first implemented by Glasgow City Council for a 12-week period starting in December 2005, with cooperation from the local Strathclyde Police and the largest local bus provider (First Group).[7] The scheme also included upgraded lighting, relocation of bus stops and prominent marketing of existing late-night bus services, enhanced CCTV coverage and public 'Help Points', aimed at reducing violent crime, disorder, and anti-social behaviour within the city centre at night. Elements of the Glasgow scheme have

---

[7] See Mistral et al (2007: 51) for a more detailed description of the measures involved. The same report provides data showing that a significant reduction in recorded violent crime and substantial increases in arrests occurred during the 12-week Nite Zone project (ibid: 68).

been retained: taxi marshals are now funded in part by private funding from taxi companies at a cost of £40,000 per year ('Taxi marshal move is a hit with cabbies', *[Glasgow] Evening Times*, 24 April 2008). The Scottish government has recently shown commitment to the broader application of such schemes across Scotland. In September 2007 it announced funding of £1 million for the Christmas and New Year period to be made available for community safety initiatives, including late-night taxi marshal schemes, extra enforcement at known problem spots, and high-visibility policing.[8]

The previous comments point to a diverse range of NTE-related crime reduction initiatives in recent years. The most recent published study by Forsyth (2008) focuses on the specific topic of disorder-related harm arising from the use of glassware in licensed premises in Glasgow. In February 2006, Glasgow City Council imposed—via a local by-law—a restriction on the use of glass drinking vessels in all venues holding an entertainment licence (mostly nightclubs). The by-law required the use of toughened or plastic vessels in an attempt to reduce the incidence of violent 'glassing' attacks in licensed premises. After an initial pilot scheme, a ban on the use of glassware now applies to all pubs and nightclubs open after midnight under regular extension of hours. The Board's justification for its policy can be found in its published Statement of Licensing Policy (as required under the 2005 Act):

From statistical information made available to the Licensing Board, it was clear that the incidence of 'glassing attacks' was considerably greater in 'late opening premises', such as nightclubs which attract an almost exclusively younger clientele, as opposed to other licensed premises which do not operate into the early hours of the morning. Indeed, from the statistical information available, the likelihood of a glassing attack in late opening premises was twice that of other licensed premises. (Glasgow City Licensing Board, 2007: 81)

Plans to introduce a ban applying to all pubs by January 2007 were withdrawn after an application to subject them to judicial review was made by the licensed trade, led by the Scottish Beer and Pub Association ('U-turn on Glasgow pub glass ban', *BBC News Online*, 19 June 2006). Forsyth (2008) found that patrons felt safer in venues adopting the policy and concluded that the policy had the potential to reduce the severity of alcohol-related violence in the NTE.

In Edinburgh, under the auspices of the Edinburgh Community Safety Partnership (one of 32 nationally), the Edinburgh Violence Reduction Programme (EVRP) 2008–2013 was launched in May 2008. The programme, which marks the first initiative of its type for the capital, identifies three so-called 'work streams': violence against women; alcohol and the NTE; and other street violence. A wide range of organizations are affiliated, including police, ambulance and health agencies, as well as the voluntary sector and the licensed trade (see Edinburgh Community Safety Partnership, 2008: 5). The rationale for including alcohol and the NTE is clearly explained:

While 'alcohol' per se is not recorded as a factor in reported crime, anecdotal evidence suggests clear links. Front line officers from Police, Accident and Emergency Departments,

---

[8] This followed a similar scheme a year earlier whereby funding of between £40,000 and £100,000 was provided to four cities and eight towns. See: <http://www.scotland.gov.uk/News/Releases/2006/12/11094524>.

Council Community Safety Teams, and victim support agencies report that the offender, victim, or often both, are regularly found to be under the influence of alcohol at the time an offence is committed.

Of note, the majority of such violence takes pace during the trading hours of licensed premises. In Edinburgh City Centre, Lothian and Borders Police record on average 350 incidents on licensed premises each month, over 4,000 per year. Hot spot[9] mapping for crimes of violence clearly shows a connection between areas with high availability of alcohol and high incidence of violence. (ibid, 2008: 10)

The recent initiatives in Glasgow and Edinburgh described above are certainly the most extensive and high-profile, but even in 2003 an audit of the alcohol harm-reduction initiatives at that time indicated a diverse range of approaches, including a number aimed specifically at night-time issues (Scottish Executive, 2003a). Whilst Scottish police forces have been involved in many NTE-oriented schemes across Scotland there has been no equivalent of the police-led Alcohol Misuse Enforcement Campaigns (AMECs) implemented in recent years across England and Wales with the support of the Home Office (see Chapter 2).

POLICING, SECURITY, AND CRIME CONTROL

Forsyth et al (2005) drew some interesting findings in relation to policing, security, and crime control. Their study concurred with that of Hobbs et al (2002) in that they found Glasgow's NTE to be 'policed' by far greater numbers of door staff in licensed premises than by public police officers. This situation bears direct comparison with the English city of Manchester which has a NTE of broadly comparable size. Hobbs et al found that the preponderance of private policing solutions in Manchester licensed premises made it inevitable that the level of violence that became known to the police as associated with such premises would be grossly underestimated. The authors also suggested that the controlling presence of stewards within licensed premises appeared 'to force up the amount of disorder occurring outside on the streets for police to deal with' (Forsyth et al, 2005: 175). However, neither this, nor the 2006 study by Forsyth, sought to examine the specific challenges of policing the NTE, highlighting a primary area for future research in Scotland.[10]

The Licensing (Scotland) Act 2005 will introduce new powers allowing courts to impose exclusion orders on individuals convicted of violent offences in or close to licensed premises, along with powers for closure of licensed premises by senior police officers under circumstances where serious threats to public order are observed or

---

[9] Author's note: 'hot spot' is a term generally used to define a location at which crimes are clustered based on data held in police recording systems.

[10] Hadfield (2006, Ch 5) provides a model to guide such an approach.

envisaged (Scottish Executive, 2005, Section 7).[11] Research is needed to examine the use and impact of these powers.

The relationship between policing the NTE and overall policing and crime control in Scotland has recently been revealed to have wider and previously unacknowledged consequences. Giving oral evidence before the Justice Committee of the Scottish Parliament on 6 November 2007, Malcolm Dickson, representing Her Majesty's Inspectorate of Constabulary (HMIC) raised a series of points about the NTE and its demands on policing. In response to a question from a Committee member asking whether the requirement for public order policing in urban centres late on Friday, Saturday and Sunday nights meant that fewer resources were available during 'waking hours', he responded as follows:

Local authorities and their Licensing Boards, in particular, must accept that an infrastructure is needed to deal with a town or city centre becoming a venue. It is not sufficient just to rely on the police to sweep up the mess afterwards. It is a fact that the young people who take over city centres at night are drawing more and more officers into policing the night-time economy in the urban centres of a small part of Scotland, and that has an effect for the rest of the week, because there will be fewer officers available at other times.

... On any graph of hot spots of demand for police forces in Scotland, the biggest peaks will be on Friday and Saturday nights in town and city centres. If that is what you want police to do most of, that is fine, but if you also want them to be out where they are visible to the vast majority of the rest of the resident and working population of Scotland, you will need to think about that. (Justice Committee, 2007, cols 269–70)

This exchange identifies a significant emergent discourse about the NTE in Scotland that emphasizes the extent of costs to public expenditure arising from alcohol misuse. It also makes the important point (with specific reference to policing) that the NTE has an impact beyond the physical and temporal spaces that are routinely used to define it, creating a consequent demand for political choices about resource allocation and prioritization. Since taking office in April 2007 the present government, robustly led by the Justice Secretary, has argued in favour of a broad 'polluter pays' approach to this issue. In a quote taken from the same interview cited at the beginning of this chapter, Mr MacAskill explained the core philosophy behind the approach:

When you are given a liquor licence, you are given the right to make a profit, and therefore those who make a profit must meet some of the social and economic costs. ('There is not a God-given right to dispense alcohol', *The Guardian*, 14 May 2008)

Responding to a previous suggestion by the Justice Secretary that a fee on late-licensed premises to help pay for additional policing should be considered, Colin Wilkinson, secretary of the Scottish Licensed Traders Association, made clear that businesses felt that they were 'already paying' for the cost of policing through alcohol duty and

---

[11] It was reported in the *Edinburgh Evening News* on 24 January 2008 that a man convicted of a violent attack became the first person to be banned for *life* from Edinburgh nightclubs, not by the courts, but under a scheme known as UNIGHT involving 21 nightclubs launched in October 2007. The local police force, Lothian and Borders Police, has expressed full support for the scheme ('Police support city nightclubs, Edinburgh', *Lothian and Borders Police Press Release*, 26 October 2007).

commercial rates ('Late night bars face police costs', *BBC News Online*, 29 August 2007). The first tangible manifestation of what is emerging as a battle of wills between the government and the licensed trade has been fought out in relation to the costs of premises licences under the 2005 Act. Following the principle established by the Nicholson Committee that liquor licensing should be a self-financing system, and after a period of statutory consultation between June and September 2007, the government proposed a proportional-fee system, levying higher fees on larger premises. Despite strong opposition from the licensed trade—led by the Scottish Beer and Pub Association—and a difficult passage through the Justice Committee (see Justice Committee, 2008), the measure was passed early in 2008.

On 17 June 2008 the Scottish government launched a consultation document setting out a new strategic approach to tackling alcohol misuse (Scottish Government, 2008b), inviting interested parties to submit their views by 9 September 2008. The document proposes a very broad range of measures, with a proposal to raise the minimum purchase age to 21 for off-sales of alcohol (up from the present 18) garnering most headlines at the time of its launch. Critics immediately argued that this specific measure was contradictory on the grounds that the government was also proposing that the minimum age for alcohol purchase in pubs and nightclubs should remain at 18, whilst it would become 21 for purchases from off-licences or supermarkets. An opposition party (the Conservatives) forced a debate on the measure in the Scottish Parliament on 2 October 2008, which resulted in a defeat for the government as a motion to reject the proposal was carried by a significant majority (72 votes to 47). However, in spite of this defeat, at the time of going to press media reports suggested that the government was still planning to include the measure in a forthcoming Justice and Licensing Bill. This Bill will potentially incorporate the full range of measures included in the consultation document, once the government has reflected on the submissions received via the consultation process.

One measure outlined in the consultation document specifically includes the NTE: the proposal to levy a so-called 'social-responsibility fee' on some alcohol retailers, marking a tangible manifestation of the arguments (led by the Justice Secretary) that have been described above. The consultation invited views on the criteria that should be used to determine the types of premises that should be subject to a fee. The document makes clear that whilst initial government thinking had led to the suggestion 'that the fee should be applied to late-opening city centre premises to contribute to the additional policing costs which are necessarily incurred to deal with the adverse effects of alcohol misuse and subsequent disorder' the proposal now also embraces off-sales premises and the costs of other (unspecified) services (ibid: 31). Some local initiatives, such as schemes to fund taxi marshals, have already found broad support from a number of local authorities and—in the Glasgow example—private businesses too, but the concept of a statutory levy to directly fund extra policing appears to present a far greater challenge. An earlier attempt by the Licensing Board in a small Scottish city (Perth) to fund more city-centre police officers by contributions from pub and nightclub owners was abandoned as unworkable ('Perth plan for pubs to fund police is scrapped', *Aberdeen Press and Journal*, 24 April 2006). In

England and Wales, legislation giving local authorities the power to levy costs on businesses in areas designated as Alcohol Disorder Zones (ADZs) was introduced in June 2008.[12] However, the designation of an ADZ is seen as 'a measure of last resort' (Home Office, 2008: 23) and the practical challenges involved in implementation of charges (and, indeed, ADZs in general) are, at the time of writing, untested and the source of some contention (see House of Lords, 2008).[13]

The outcome of the 2008 consultation process will shape the extent to which the Scottish government is prepared (and indeed able) to legislate for its social responsibility fee in a way that is different from the route chosen in England and Wales (that is, ADZs). Based on the comments attributed to the Justice Secretary it seems reasonable to assume that the Scottish government is seeking a system that is closer to first, rather than last, resort. Other measures put forward for consultation would, if implemented, further differentiate the Scottish approach from that in England and Wales. Proposals to restrict promotional and loss-leading pricing of alcoholic drinks and for minimum retail pricing for alcohol are also under consideration. These measures are intended to encompass concerns regarding the off-sales element, highlighting more general social attitudes to alcohol and its availability, but often directly linked to nightlife through the phenomenon of 'pre- (or) front-loading'.[14] 'Pre-loading' refers to the consumption of alcohol purchased at low prices from supermarkets and other off-trade outlets, with the aim or effect of feeling intoxicated *before* going out to pubs and clubs (which often charge much higher prices for drinks). Exemplifying the intersection of these issues for policymakers, Forsyth found the pre-loading phenomenon to have become a behavioural norm in the Scottish context (2006: 104).

CONCLUSIONS

The consequences of alcohol use have become an increasingly prominent political issue in Scotland in recent years, first as Scottish alcohol licensing law was reformed and particularly so since May 2007, with the SNP-led government elected at that time displaying clear political will to consider and introduce new and in some respects radical policies. Whilst the overall tenor of the debate has been essentially the same as that which has taken place in England and Wales since the early part of the present

[12] For more details on Alcohol Disorder Zones, see Chapter 2, this volume, and Home Office, 2008.

[13] A range of so-called 'irresponsible promotions' will not be permitted in licensed premises once the Licensing (Scotland) Act enters force in full in 2009 (for details see Scottish Government, 2008b: 64). A previous attempt in 2004 by an individual licensing board (Aberdeen) to introduce minimum prices for alcohol under the 1976 legislation was ruled to be *ultra vires* (see 'Time called on booze curb bid', *BBC News Online*, 5 November 2004). From September 2009, licensing boards will also be required to assess the number of licensed premises within their area and develop a policy on 'overprovision' (Scottish Government, 2008b: 29).

[14] See 'Beer cheaper than water drives surge in supermarket drinks sales', *The Scotsman*, 12 February 2008. In 2004, the Daniels Committee had previously identified a significant shift in Scotland towards alcohol purchasing from off-sales, that is from licensed retail rather than entertainment premises (Daniels, 2004, see esp section 1.10).

decade, the most recent period shows that Scotland is entering a phase when more distinctive differences in approach are beginning to emerge as compared with Westminster. Nightlife and crime has figured prominently in the overall discourse in Scotland, with a clear consensus on the need for action to reduce the problems that occur in late-night city and town centres, whilst accepting that this forms only part of a deep-seated set of cultural attitudes towards alcohol. A relatively limited amount of direct government funding has been directed towards NTE-specific interventions and in the main it has been local partnership activities—most notably in Glasgow and Edinburgh—that have characterized attempts to manage issues of crime and violence occurring in the NTE in Scotland.

The findings of the government-appointed Nicholson Committee, published in 2003, have provided the main evidential basis for the first major reform of Scottish alcohol licensing laws since the 1970s. The Committee found that a significant liberalization of the hours of operation and scale and character of the NTE in Scotland had occurred since 1980 and accepted this to be linked directly to a growth in late-night problems around public order and crime in Scottish towns and cities. Scotland had in fact gone further in the liberalization of hours than the majority of the UK, allowing hours that were broadly in line with those which otherwise applied only in London. However, it was the Committee's advocacy of a need to make public health an objective of licensing law that marked a pivotal moment; one at which Scotland began to show a divergence from England and Wales. The subsequent adoption of this recommendation in the Licensing (Scotland) Act 2005 has provided a coherent, galvanizing principle for a more holistic approach to alcohol policy. Why then did Scotland incorporate health when England and Wales had chosen not to during its own licensing-law reforms? The answer almost certainly lies in more prosaic reasons concerned with bureaucratic politics; under the Scottish system ministries have much less power to demarcate issues and veto moves that affect their portfolio. However, the apparent freedom for manoeuvre afforded to the SNP government on this issue exposes another dimension of Scottish politics that has allowed a more strident stance to be taken towards commercial interests with a stake in alcohol. The ability to argue so strongly for a 'polluter pays' approach is born of the post-devolution freedom arising from the fact that whilst Scottish governments are free to legislate on health and crime issues they have a much more indirect relationship with the political pressures that stem from the lobbying power of the drinks industry linked to its fiscal contribution.[15] It is not yet clear the extent to which the present government will be able to implement its preferences—notably the so-called social-responsibility fee—but the prominent highlighting of the cost to public expenditure of the NTE in Scotland is unlikely to go away without action of some form.

On the basis of relatively limited research-based knowledge, but supported by voluminous anecdotal evidence and professional opinion, the essential nature of nightlife and crime in Scotland appears to exhibit many features in common with England and Wales and indeed other parts of the world. Based on their study of Glasgow pubs,

[15] For a recent illustration of the political tensions in England and Wales see 'Drinks industry "flouting voluntary code on sales"', *The Guardian*, 24 July 2008.

Forsyth et al (2005) concurred with the existing academic literature, citing in particular the Canadian study by Graham and Wells (2003) which suggests that alcohol is not the cause of bar-room violence but that consuming it, especially in heavy amounts, allows incidents to escalate and become more serious. However, current tools—most notably the official attempt to cost alcohol use and misuse (Scottish Government, 2008a)—are crude and of very limited value for understanding and extracting data on factors that link crime with nightlife. For example, the section detailing costs attributable to the criminal justice system currently relies heavily on assumptions that the proportion of crimes influenced by alcohol in Scotland match those of England and Wales. Similarly, the same report estimates that 25 per cent of all attendances at hospital accident and emergency departments (AEDs) are alcohol-related, without offering any analyses of the temporal distribution of these admissions or their potential link with crime.[16] There is thus a clear need to conduct research that builds a more robust evidential base for decision-making in Scotland. Alcohol policy in Scotland is entering a very interesting phase and it is essential that research emerges to monitor and inform the debate and policy outcomes in Scotland, particularly in relation to nightlife and crime.

REFERENCES

All internet sources were accessible 20 August 2008

CUMMINS, J (2005) 'The Scottish experience', in P Kolvin (ed), *Licensed Premises: Law and practice*, Haywards Heath: Tottel Publishing.

DANIELS, P (2004) *Off-Sales in the Community: The report of the Working Group on Off-Sales in the Community*, Edinburgh: Scottish Executive, <http://www.scotland.gov.uk/ Publications/2004/02/18764/31741>.

EDINBURGH COMMUNITY SAFETY PARTNERSHIP (2008) *Edinburgh Violence Reduction Programme* 2008–2013, <http://www.edinburg.gov.uk/internet/city_living/community_ safety/crime_and_law_enforcement/crime_prevention/cec_violence_reduction_ programme_2008_-_2013>.

FORSYTH, AJM (2006) *Assessing the Relationships between Late-Night Drinks Marketing and Alcohol-Related Disorder in Public Space*, London: Alcohol Education Research Council.

—— (2008) 'Banning glassware from nightclubs in Glasgow (Scotland): Observed impacts, compliance and patron's views', *Alcohol and Alcoholism*, 43/1: 111–17.

—— CLOONAN, M and BARR, J (2005) *Factors Associated with Alcohol-Related Problems within Licensed Premises*, Glasgow: Greater Glasgow NHS Board, <http://library.nhsggc.org.uk/ mediaAssets/library/nhsgg_pilp_main_report_2005-02.pdf>.

GLASGOW CITY LICENSING BOARD (2007) *Licensing Policy Statement*, <http://www. glasgow.gov.uk/NR/rdonlyres/891F7CC1-62CE-40FC-ABDA-BB9507D0A429/0/ LicensingPolicyStatement.pdf>.

---

[16] A recent statistic serves to emphasize the significance of temporal factors in a Scottish context: in 2007 the Scottish Ambulance Service attended an average of 73 incidents between 1.00 and 2.00 am on Sunday mornings compared with a normal hourly average of 38 incidents (Scottish Government, 2008b: 32).

GRAHAM, K and WELLS, S (2003) "'Somebody's gonna get their head kicked in tonight!' Aggression among young males in bars—a question of values?', *British Journal of Criminology*, 43/3, 546–66.

HADFIELD, P (2006) *Bar Wars: Contesting the Night in Contemporary British Cities*, Oxford: Oxford University Press.

HOBBS, D, HADFIELD, P, LISTER, S and WINLOW, S (2002) '"Door Lore": The art and economics of intimidation', *British Journal of Criminology*, 42/2, 352–70.

HOME OFFICE (2008) *Alcohol Disorder Zones: Sections 15–20 of the Violent Crime Reduction Act 2006. Draft Guidance*, 31 March 2008, London: Home Office, <http://police.homeoffice.gov.uk/publications/operational-policing/alcohol-disorder-zone-guidance>.

HOUSE OF LORDS MERITS OF STATUTORY INSTRUMENTS COMMITTEE (2008) *18th Report of Session 2007–08*, HL Paper 100, 2 May 2008 (London: The Stationery Office Limited), <http://www.publications.parliament.uk/pa/ld/ldmerit.htm>.

JUSTICE COMMITTEE, SCOTTISH PARLIAMENT (2007) *Official Report 6 November 2007*, <http://www.scotlandParliament.cc/s3/committiees/justice/or-07/ju07-0802.htm#Col214>.

—— (2008) *Official Report 22 January 2008*, <http://www.scottish.Parliament.uk/s3/committees/justice/or-08/ju08-0202.htm#Col486>.

McGARVEY, N and CAIRNEY, P (2008) *Scottish Politics: An introduction*, Basingstoke: Palgrave Macmillan.

MISTRAL, W, VELLEMAN, R, MASTACHE, C and TEMPLETON, R (2007) 'UKCAPP: An evaluation of 3 UK Community Alcohol Prevention Programs', *Final Report for the Alcohol Education and Research Council*, University of Bath and Avon and Wiltshire Mental Health Partnership NHS Trust, <http://www.aerc.org.uk/documents/pdfs/finalReport/AERC_FinalReport_0039.pdf>

O'DONNELL, BA (2006) 'Reducing harm and changing culture: Scotland's National Plan for Action on Alcohol Problems', *International Journal of Drug Policy*, 17/4, 367–72.

SCOTTISH EXECUTIVE (2002) *Plan for Action on Alcohol Problems*, Edinburgh: Scottish Executive, <http://www.scotland.gov.uk/Publications/2002/01/10551/File-1>.

—— (2003a) *Liquor Licensing and Public Disorder: Review of literature on the impact of licensing and other controls/audit of local initiatives*, Edinburgh: Reid Howie Associates for Scottish Executive Social Research.

—— (2003b) *The Nicholson Committee: Review of liquor licensing law in Scotland*, Edinburgh: Scottish Executive.

—— (2005) *Licensing (Scotland) Act 2005 (asp 16)*, Edinburgh: Scottish Executive, <http://www.opsi.gov.uk/legislation/scotland/acts2005/pdf/asp_20050016_en.pdf>.

—— (2007a) *Plan for Action on Alcohol Problems: Update*, Edinburgh: Scottish Executive, <http://www.scotland.gov.uk/Publications/2007/02/19150222/0>.

—— (2007b) *Scottish Liquor Licensing Statistics 2006*, Edinburgh: Scottish Executive, <http://www.scotland.gov.uk/Publications/2007/08/21145701/24>.

SCOTTISH GOVERNMENT (2008a) *Costs of Alcohol Use and Misuse in Scotland*, Edinburgh: Scottish Government, <http://www.scotland.gov.uk/Publications/2008/05/06091510/0>.

—— (2008b) *Changing Scotland's Relationship with Alcohol: A discussion paper on our strategic approach*, Edinburgh: Scottish Government, <http://www.scotland.gov.uk/Publications/2008/06/16084348/0>.

4

NORTHERN IRELAND

Karen McElrath

INTRODUCTION

Northern Ireland comprises six counties in north-east Ireland with a population of approximately 1.7 million residents in 2001 (Northern Ireland Statistics and Research Agency, 2002). The region has been characterized as a space of contestation since its creation in 1921, when the British government partitioned Ireland. The contemporary political conflict in Northern Ireland commenced in 1969 and, since then, the British government as well as mainstream British media has portrayed the conflict as one of warring tensions between two factions, ie Protestants and Catholics. This portrayal is limited in two ways. First, it ignores the role of the British state as an active protagonist in the conflict. Second, it suggests that the conflict is 'tribal', and one based on religious grounds only. More accurately, the contemporary political conflict in Northern Ireland has had considerably less to do with religious differences, and more to do with how religious and political identities shape interpretations of historical and current events (Metress, 1995; Parker, 1994; Weitzer, 1995). Religious background and political identity are closely linked. For example, Irish Nationalists support the re-unification of Ireland (north and south) and individuals who identify with Nationalism often come from Catholic backgrounds. Irish republicans also support a united Ireland, and for over two centuries have used political violence in pursuit of independence from Britain for the entire island of Ireland. Unionists argue that Northern Ireland should remain part of the United Kingdom and most Unionists come from Protestant backgrounds. Loyalists are Unionists who believe that violence is justified in order to defend the link with Britain or to oppose those individuals whom they identify with Irish nationalism or republicanism.

Crime and disorder, as well as other social problems, must be understood in the context of Northern Ireland's history and of the political conflict that has resulted (McEvoy and Ellison, 2003). Prior to the 1990s, crime in Northern Ireland was viewed primarily as crime against the state (ie, 'terrorism') but described as politically motivated behaviour by those who engaged in these activities. Behaviours in violation of the criminal law but without political motivation were described as 'ordinary crimes', allowing the state to emphasize the severity of 'terrorism'. Indeed, prisoner data presented by the Northern Ireland Prison Service in the 1990s were officially categorized into two sections: crimes against the state, and 'ordinary' crimes. Offenders who committed the latter were known by the authorities as 'ordinary decent criminals', or simply ODCs, even when they had been convicted of murder or rape, as long as those offences were committed without political motivation.

CULTURAL CONTEXT

Since the 1920s, several villages, towns, and cities in Northern Ireland have comprised areas that have been segregated according to religious background and political identity. These divisions became more pronounced beginning in the early 1970s when large numbers of the population (primarily Catholics) were displaced through extreme sectarian violence. Despite several years of officially acknowledged peace, data collected from a representative survey of people aged 18 and older and residing in Northern Ireland revealed that 68 per cent of respondents reported that most or all of their neighbours shared their religious background (ARK, 2006). This figure increased to 78 per cent among city residents.

Neighbourhoods in Belfast, the largest city in Northern Ireland, are demarcated along boundaries that incorporate religious background, political identity, and class. The city includes areas (ie, East and West Belfast) that extend several square miles with the majority of residents sharing the same religious background and/or political identity. In contrast, the north of the city includes several small neighbourhoods that are locally described as 'Protestant' or 'Catholic' and many of these communities lie adjacent to the community of 'the other'. The university area lies within South Belfast, and is surrounded by middle-class and several working-class neighbourhoods—the latter being defined by the religion and political identity of residents. In some areas of the city, 'peace walls' have been constructed to separate and protect residents who live in close proximity to neighbourhoods of 'the other'. These boundaries serve to create (and reinforce) 'social, political and cultural distance between communities' (Shirlow and Murtagh, 2006: 57). Some walls exceed 25 feet in height and, since the Good Friday Agreement in 1998, additional walls and gates have been erected. 'Mixed' communities are those areas comprising roughly equal numbers of Protestants and Catholics. In their review of census data, Shirlow and Murtagh (2006) observed that only 10.7 per cent of Catholics and 7 per cent of Protestants resided in mixed communities in Belfast in 2001. Further, 58 per cent of Catholics and 44.6 per cent of Protestants resided in areas comprising almost entirely (ie, 91 per cent and higher) residents who shared their religious background. Although some towns and villages can be described as mixed communities, integrated neighbourhoods in Belfast nearly always comprise residents from middle- or upper-income backgrounds.

For many people, the segregated physical geography of Northern Ireland extends to lifestyle. Words, flags, colours, favoured football teams, language (eg, the pronunciation of the letter 'h') are important symbols that often serve to differentiate the communities. The majority of schools are highly segregated and friendships with 'the other' are limited. Representative survey data collected in 2005 (ARK, 2006) revealed that 65 per cent of respondents reported that most or all of their friends were of the same religious background and 87 per cent stated that most or all of their relatives and relatives through marriage shared their religious background. The everyday routines of people, particularly those who reside in segregated working-class areas, have been influenced greatly by the legacy of political conflict. Using qualitative data collected from residents of selected working-class areas in Belfast, Lysaght and Basten (2003) documented how everyday routines were mediated by residents' perceptions of sectarian threat. At times, residents had to move within the other community and the interview data revealed how respondents attempted to mask their identities in order to avoid threat and confrontation.

RESEARCH EVIDENCE: FORMS OF CRIME AND DISORDER

In the preface to his book, Whyte (1991: viii) suggests: 'It is quite possible that, in proportion to its size, Northern Ireland is the most heavily researched area on earth.' However, the vast majority of this research has focused on the extent, nature, or implications of the Irish political conflict. Indeed, scholarly studies of several other social problems in Northern Ireland did not emerge until the 1980s and 90s. Research into crime has for the most part followed the same pattern.

CRIME AND DRUGS, PRE-1990S

Data on non-political crime and disorder prior to the 1990s are very limited. Information on non-political crime reported to police suggests that by comparison with many other parts of Europe, levels were low in Northern Ireland in the period up to the late 1980s (Morison and Geary, 1989). However, the police lacked legitimacy in several communities and it has been suggested that large segments of the population did not report incidents to the police (Garrett, 1999). Ethnographic accounts of non-political crime in Northern Ireland prior to the 1990s could not be located by this author. Regional surveys of crime victims did not commence until the mid-1990s with sponsorship (and authorship) by the Northern Ireland Office.[1] Northern Ireland was one of several countries included in the 1989 International Crime Survey and was reported to have one of the lowest levels of overall prevalence of victimization during the previous year (Van Dijk and Mayhew, 1992). The survey data also revealed that the rate of reporting crime to police in Northern Ireland was comparable to that in several

---

[1] Surprisingly, there has been a lack of critical commentary with regards to the validity of surveys that are sponsored by a state that lacks legitimacy among several subgroups of the population it aims to study.

other countries. However, the survey methodology revealed little information about the background and residence of Northern Ireland respondents who participated in the international study. For example, other research has shown that class, place of residence (urban/rural), and religious identity of the residential area contribute to the reporting of crime to the police in Northern Ireland (O'Mahony et al, 2000). Further, unlike several other countries in the international survey, the response rate for Northern Ireland was not provided because a quota sample was used.

Despite extensive social deprivation, high unemployment, and some of the worst housing conditions in Europe, a review of the available indicators suggests that drug use in Northern Ireland was quite low prior to the 1990s (McElrath, 2004). The high numbers of police and British army, and their extensive use of checkpoints and sophisticated surveillance equipment would have encountered some evidence of large-scale drug markets had such existed. Prior to the 1990s, the annual number of drug seizures tended to be reported in single digits. Data collected and reported from general practitioners and drug treatment staff showed very low numbers of opiates and other drugs during this era. Retrospective accounts from people who have used heroin for many years suggest the presence of very small and close-knit pockets of heroin users residing in or around South Belfast during the 1970s and 80s (McElrath, 2001). With the exception of alcohol and high levels of prescribed benzodiazepines that were exchanged informally among neighbours, friends and relatives, the effects of war in Northern Ireland appeared to shield its residents from the extensive drug use that characterized other areas in close proximity to the region (eg, Dublin, Glasgow, and parts of England).

From the early 1970s to the ceasefires of the mid-1990s, people rarely travelled outside their communities of residence in the pursuit of night-time (or indeed daytime) leisure. This restriction was largely due to personal safety concerns and was most evident in working-class areas. During that period, night-time leisure in Belfast city centre was very limited. The area was not perceived as safe and visits to the city centre at night placed people at risk of assault and other forms of violence. Although several pubs were located in Belfast city centre, these establishments tended to close early. The university area in Belfast also offered fairly limited nightlife during this time. That area, however, was and is still perceived to be 'neutral'. Despite this perception, pubs located in the university area did not escape the bombing campaign.

THE PEACE PROCESS AND ITS IMPLICATIONS FOR CRIME AND NIGHTLIFE

The Irish Republican Army called its ceasefire in 1994. This act was followed by a similar announcement by the Combined Loyalist Military Command, although various loyalist groups persisted in sectarian violence during the years that followed. Nevertheless, with these changes came the *perception* of peace, and in turn more involvement in nightlife activity, eg drinking and socializing excursions outside one's area of residence. Developments in the peace process have not led to an increase in the number of pubs in Northern Ireland. In fact, the number of pubs in the region declined from 2,196 in 1966 (three years prior to the beginning of the most recent era of political conflict) to 1,526 in 2005 (Department of Social Development (DSD),

2005: 30).[2] However, night-time access to pubs has changed considerably with developments in the peace process. For example, pubs located in Belfast city centre now operate with extended opening hours (midnight or later)[3] whereas city-centre pubs tended to close by 7.00 pm during the 1969–94 period of conflict. The pursuit of nightlife and other leisure outside the community of residence has been, and continues to be, mediated by class, space, the degree of sectarian violence, and to a lesser extent gender and ethnicity. Research conducted since the ceasefires has shown that participation in leisure outside one's area of residence is considerably more common among youth from middle-class backgrounds, ethnic minorities, and females (McGrellis, 2004). Further, for people residing in 'interface' areas, movement outside the place of residence has tended to fluctuate with rising sectarian violence (Lysaght and Basten, 2003; Shirlow and Murtagh, 2006).

The perception of peace gave way to the hope for normality. Reflecting similar patterns elsewhere in Europe, the dance and club scene emerged in Northern Ireland in the mid-1990s, coinciding with wider political change and freedom of movement. Data for the first qualitative study into illicit drug use in Northern Ireland were collected in 1997–8 and focused on MDMA/ecstasy (McElrath and McEvoy, 1999). Data for that study were collected through in-depth interviews with 98 respondents, aged 17 to 45 years (mean = 25 years). The majority (92 per cent) had used ecstasy in the six-month period prior to the interview and approximately 44 per cent had used ecstasy on at least 100 different occasions since initiation. In comparison to studies conducted elsewhere in the 1990s (Beck and Rosenbaum, 1994; Solowij et al, 1992), a disproportionate number of respondents in the Northern Ireland study were described as 'heavy' users of the drug.

Respondents in the ecstasy study were asked about relations between Protestants and Catholics in clubs where ecstasy was consumed. A number of respondents reported that ecstasy 'bridged the gap' between Protestants and Catholics:

You would have Catholics and Protestants [in the same club] but you would [also] have loyalists and republicans and to have them in the same place was amazing like, you know? And they couldn't have done that unless they were *off their faces*.[4] (Female, age 22.)

---

[2] A 'surrender' policy operates in Northern Ireland with regard to the grant of new public house or off-sales licences. A new licence cannot be granted unless an old licence is surrendered (for an explanation of the origins of this policy, see DSD, 2005). This has created a lucrative market in the trading of existing licences, often for huge profit. The surrender policy is unique to the island of Ireland and is one of several issues being debated as part of the DSD Social Policy Unit's proposals for reform of current liquor licensing legislation (Licensing (Northern Ireland) Order 1996 and the Registration of Clubs (Northern Ireland) Order 1996). A consultation document, *Liquor Licensing—The Way Forward*, was published in November 2005, with implementation anticipated in 2009. In relation to 'surrender' it notes: 'Since a new pub or off-licence does not have to be in the same area as the premises from which the surrendered licence was acquired, a pub closing in rural Fermanagh could lead to one opening in Belfast city centre. Surrender could, therefore, lead to some rural areas being left without a pub' (DSD, 2005: 30). Any market pressures for expansion of the night-time economy in Belfast and other towns and cities would seem to make this risk to rural life especially pertinent.

[3] Licence applications are administered by the county and magistrates' courts, judges and magistrates receiving advice from the police and other specified parties. In the proposals for reform it is anticipated that district councils will assume jurisdiction for licensing matters, with the option to extend opening hours to 2.00 am Monday–Saturday and to midnight on Sundays.

[4] 'Off their faces' refers to the effects of or intoxication from ecstasy.

Living where I do, which would be perceived as a Protestant, loyalist area, I haven't had much dealings with Catholics, you know. I have made a couple of good friendships [with Catholics] through ecstasy and it doesn't matter to me now . . . Now I don't bother putting my flag out.[5] (male, age 30)

Although several respondents suggested that the pharmaceutical effects of the drug helped foster better relations between Protestants and Catholics, others suggested that these relations were for the most part confined to club settings. Although respondents' descriptions and our observations within nightclubs did not uncover sectarian violence within these settings, a number of respondents reported that anxiety and sometimes fear accompanied their journey home. For people living their nightlives in a divided community, choices about the 'right' taxi company[6] and other lifestyle precautions had become 'second nature'. Travelling on foot or via taxi to the university area was deemed safer in that one's religious background could not be ascertained by destination alone. Stress associated with 'identity management' (McGrellis, 2004: 16) was lessened in these situations. This fear of sectarian attack varied across and within communities. For example, in their study of 1,621 residents from five types of communities in Northern Ireland, O'Mahony et al (2000) found that residents from urban, working-class Catholic areas were more than twice as likely (17.7 per cent) to report being worried about physical sectarian attack compared to residents of other communities (range 0.7 to 6.0 per cent).

The number of sectarian incidents increased from the mid-1990s (Jarman, 2004) and a total of 23 Catholics and two Protestants were murdered by loyalists between July 1996 and March 1999 (for a brief description of these incidents, see McElrath, 2000: 144–5). This figure included three children and a human-rights solicitor. Although the increase in sectarian incidents during this time might have been influenced by changes in the reporting and recording of incidents, many respondents in the ecstasy study would have been well aware of the violence from media coverage at the time. On the journey home, one's 'geography of residence' serves as an identifier of one's perceived religious and political background leading to fear of victimization. Some participants reported that they often had to negotiate a longer route for safety reasons; that is, in order to avoid verbal and physical assault (or the fear of) by members of 'the other' community.

Data from the ecstasy study also found that the extent of 'mixing' in club venues varied across communities. Clubs located in 'neutral' areas tended to be more integrated whereas clubs located in other areas were frequented almost exclusively

---

[5] The 'flag' mentioned here refers to the Union Jack or other symbolic British flag. The Union Jack is often displayed by Loyalist residents during the month of July, in celebration of William of Orange who defeated the last Catholic king of England.

[6] People who travel to segregated areas often attempt to choose a taxi company or taxi driver of the same religious background in order to avoid the possibility of sectarian attack. Customers' identities can be masked during destinations to 'neutral' areas. Additionally, several taxi drivers in Northern Ireland have been assaulted or killed through sectarian violence. In nationalist West Belfast, a large painted mural has been dedicated to taxi drivers who have been killed during the political conflict. For an interesting comparison, Gambetta and Hamill (2005) examine risk avoidance and management amongst taxi drivers in Belfast and New York.

by members of one religious background only. When asked about the link between ecstasy use and relations between Catholics and Protestants, a 23-year-old female reported that she did not know any Protestants at all. Nevertheless, reports by several ecstasy users indicated that mixing with the 'other' in club settings was a relatively new experience for them. Shirlow and Murtagh (2006: 82) observed that following the 1994 ceasefires, some people began to 'cross ethno-sectarian boundaries in the pursuit of consumption and leisure' (Shirlow and Murtagh, 2006: 82). Clubs and other nightlife venues opened in the city centre where some people 'mixed' for the first time socially with members of the 'other' community. Observations among some respondents in the ecstasy study who attributed improved relations between the two communities to the pharmaceutical effects of the drug may have instead reflected political and social changes at a broader level.

Since 1994 and particularly in recent years, economic rejuvenation has transformed the physical appearance of several areas in Northern Ireland. Dozens of hotels, restaurants, clubs, major shopping centres, and up-scale apartments now grace the city landscape of Belfast. Tourism began to increase shortly after the 1994 ceasefires (Lennon and Titterington, 1996) and nightlife activity in Belfast is now fairly extensive, comparable to many other European cities of its size. Economic investment, the progress towards peace, and visible signs of materialism have changed the social fabric of life; yet, these changes have coincided with the perception that (non-political) crime and the threat of crime have increased in Northern Ireland. Police data show that recorded crime increased from 76,644 offences in 1998/9 to 121,144 offences in 2006/7 (Royal Ulster Constabulary, 1999; Police Service of Northern Ireland, 2007). Recorded violent crime also increased from 9,496 (1998/9) to 35,223 (2006/7). One study found that the increase in recorded crime between 2004 and 2006 was most likely due to a greater willingness to report crime by people residing in predominately Catholic areas (Ipsos MORI, 2007). The authors of that study suggested that changes in reporting practices among Catholics might have been influenced by a statement from the republican leadership calling for Nationalists to support the police. However, the available data cannot determine whether this suggestion is valid.

Data from the Northern Ireland Crime Survey 2006/7 reveal that 73 per cent of respondents believed that crime had increased in Northern Ireland in the previous two years, and 44 per cent reported increases in their local area (French and Freel, 2008). The authors noted these figures to be higher than those described in the British Crime Survey of the same year. Respondents' beliefs that crime is increasing are dismissed by the authors who note that there is a 'tendency of most people to believe crime is increasing, even when it is not' (French and Freel, 2008: i). Analyses did not compare people's *perceptions about crime* in their local areas with *recorded crime* in those areas. Nor were people questioned about their perceptions about the types of crime that were increasing. The importance of locale as well as class in relation to crime and reporting has been demonstrated in other research (O'Mahony et al, 2000). The limitations of police and crime victimization data are well documented but are exacerbated in Northern Ireland.

Although sectarian attacks have continued throughout the peace process and threaten night-time leisure in some communities,[7] many offenders in recent years share the same community and religious background as their victims. These attacks have stunned community residents, many of whom survived years of violent political conflict. In September 2007, a well-known resident and owner of a small local business in predominantly Catholic West Belfast left his local pub in the evening hours and walked the short distance to his home. He observed a group of young people near his home, attempting to steal his van. He confronted the youths and was fatally attacked with a screwdriver. The offenders were also from Catholic backgrounds. In March 2008, another Catholic male was murdered after he confronted youths who had repeatedly used the area just outside his home to socialize and drink alcohol. The offender was Catholic and the victim was a well-known Irish republican. Communities whose residents were to a great extent protected from non-political crime by the mechanisms of informal social control (see below), at least anecdotally appear to be changing in terms of the risk of victimization by offenders from the same community. The pursuit of normality in other areas of life may be accompanied by 'normal' patterns of crime and victimization.

POLICING, SECURITY, AND CRIME CONTROL

From the early 1970s until the mid-1990s, various factors contributed to the management of and response to non-political crime. Individual-level factors included personal beliefs with regard to the wider political conflict and how these beliefs shaped offending and crime reporting. For example, Irish republicans and many nationalists regarded the police as the arm of the British state that lacked legitimacy. The effect of political beliefs therefore profoundly influenced people's propensity to report crimes to the police and was mediated by the nature of the community in which individuals resided. In working-class neighbourhoods, victims and witnesses of non-political crime often avoided contact with the police. This avoidance was fuelled by the perception that police failed to respond or were slow to respond to crime in some communities and the fear that contact with the police created the opportunity for police to recruit residents as informers (Weitzer, 1995).

The management of and response to crime in these areas relied greatly on mechanisms of informal social control which were 'sociologically embedded' within these communities (Brewer et al, 1998: 576). Working-class neighbourhoods were often characterized by close-knit and extended family networks, close relations with neighbours, and strong identity with the community in which one resided (McLaughlin, 1993). The wider political conflict in some ways reinforced and may

---

[7] In April 2008, a visitor from the south of Ireland was attending a rugby match in Belfast and was staying with friends in a new hotel, located on the fringe of the city centre and adjacent to a Loyalist area. He ventured out of the hotel alone in search of a late-night restaurant and was brutally attacked in the Loyalist area. Several have speculated that his accent identified him as a Catholic 'outsider' from the Republic of Ireland.

have indeed created community cohesiveness by creating a common enemy. Weitzer (1995: 143–4) observes that 'the mistreatment of individuals appears to have larger neighbourhood effects; that is, harassment [by police] of some residents is defined as repression of the whole community'. Further, the closeness of the community produced a watchful gaze by locals over would-be offenders. Residents interviewed for a qualitative study in Belfast in the 1990s reported that they often or indeed always left the doors to their homes unlocked, despite living in an urban area characterized by extreme political violence (Brewer et al, 1998).

Non-political crimes were often addressed by members of the community, who relied on the power of the neighbourhood 'grapevine' to identify offenders and used this source to confront the actors involved (Brewer et al, 1998). Moreover, victims and witnesses of non-political crime had the option of reporting incidents to the paramilitaries who maintained responsibility for responding to crime (Mika and McEvoy, 2001). This practice continued after the ceasefires in 1994. O'Mahony et al (2000), collecting interview data in 1996, found that urban working class residents were much more likely (35.8 per cent in Catholic areas; 25.8 per cent in Protestant areas) to report crime to paramilitaries than were urban residents of middle-class backgrounds (4.3 per cent) and respondents residing in small towns (less than 3 per cent). The role of the paramilitaries represented another form of social control. They intervened on behalf of the victim and carried out punishments, eg public shaming rituals, beatings, exclusion. Support for these punishments varied although many residents preferred that interventions on behalf of the community be carried out by local paramilitaries rather than the police (Weitzer, 1995). One alternative explanation for the rise in reported crime in Catholic areas is that it has followed and corresponded with calls from the republican leadership for cessation of 'informal policing' by the Irish Republican Army.

Within a context of increased freedom of movement and expanding nightlife, bouncers now serve as the main gatekeepers and security providers in entertainment venues. However, legacies of the conflict remain as some door staff are rumoured to have variously loose or direct connections with paramilitary organizations.[8] These connections may well extend the power of community-based controls to encompass nightlife, helping maintain order within licensed venues. In some areas, fluctuations in sectarian violence pose a risk for door staff whose religious backgrounds are perceived through knowledge of the owner and the background of patrons. Two Catholic doormen were murdered by the Loyalist Volunteer Force in 1998 and 1999. These events prompted several bar owners to introduce CCTV systems and better security at entrances, eg steel gates, buzzers. In the month following the second murder in 1999, one pub owner reportedly sat in his car, armed with a heavy baton each night until closing time. The extent to which this period of sectarian violence deterred would-be patrons is unknown. A third doorman (and alleged drug dealer) was killed in 2007. A republican paramilitary group claimed the murder, citing the victim's previous engagement with criminal activity.

---

[8] A conviction for a political offence can be used legally to exclude people from various occupations. Door work and taxi driving are two occupations that have not typically denied access to former political prisoners.

The British government has long voiced its concern regarding the alleged links between paramilitaries and the private security industry and new regulations are to be implemented in 2010. These regulations are designed to introduce tighter controls over the licences granted to private security firms and to restrict the profile of employees who can be hired. Individuals with prior convictions, including convictions for political offences, will no longer be permitted to work as door staff.

CONCLUSIONS

The sustainability of Northern Ireland's current economic rejuvenation and expanded nightlife depends greatly on a continuation of the region's political stability. Peace is in its infancy and the future influence of political dissenters is unknown. Investors in nightlife and other business ventures therefore have a great deal at stake. If the transition towards peace remains, will 'ordinary crime' become normalized as in other societies? If political stability dissipates, how will people adjust to a return to political violence after they have experienced freedom of movement within their own culture?

Crime in Northern Ireland today must be understood in the context of this legacy of political conflict. Although low levels of 'ordinary crime'—including nightlife-related crime—appear to have characterized much of the 1969–94 period, data from this era are limited (Morison and Geary, 1989) and confounded by the implications of conflict. Police were (and remain) the gatekeepers of recorded-crime statistics and the extent to which sectarian violence was recorded as crime is unknown. A growing body of scholarly research is providing evidence of collusion between the police and Loyalists, in particular (Ní Aoláin, 2000), but the effects of such collusion on data recording are not known.

Crime occurring in a nightlife context continues to be affected by fluctuations in sectarian violence, particularly where residents of working-class and interface areas travel outside their neighbourhoods. There is also speculation that the socio-demographic profile of victim–offender relationships may be changing, with increasing violence within, as well as between, communities. Thus the desire for normalization appears to have implications for both nightlife and crime as part of a continuing process of social and economic change. More research is needed to explore these phenomena in greater detail. Several areas of Northern Ireland were once characterized by strong yet informal social controls. The responsibility of crime management and control may be shifting to the police, who must also adjust to political change. This transition requires close monitoring and accountability. In particular, to what extent are the police willing or able to provide the types of security services that are prerequisite to the development of a vibrant and inclusive night-time economy?

In comparison to many countries, Northern Ireland remains something of an anomaly with regard to the nightlife and crime nexus. However, other countries have also undergone major social and political change in recent years. In-depth cross-cultural studies would greatly assist our understanding of how political change affects nightlife and crime in the context of divided societies.

REFERENCES

All internet sources were accessible 20 August 2008

ARK (Access Research Knowledge) (2006) *Northern Ireland Life and Times Survey, 2005*. ARK Northern Ireland, Economic and Social Research Council, <http://www.ark.ac.uk/nilt/datasets>.

BECK, J and M ROSENBAUM (1994) *Pursuit of Ecstasy: The MDMA experience*, Albany: SUNY.

BREWER, JD, LOCKHART, B and RODGERS, P (1998) 'Informal social control and crime management in Belfast', *British Journal of Sociology*, 49/4, 570–85.

DSD (Department of Social Development) (2005) *Liquor Licensing—The Way Forward: Government proposals to reform liquor licensing law in Northern Ireland*, <http://www.dsdni.gov.uk/lrt_liquor_licensing_consultation_document.pdf>.

FRENCH, B and FREEL, R (2008) *Perceptions of Crime: Findings from the 2006/07 Northern Ireland Crime Survey*, Belfast: Northern Ireland Office.

GAMBETTA, D and HAMILL, H (2005) *Streetwise: How taxi drivers establish customers' trustworthiness*, New York: Russell Sage Foundation.

GARRETT, PM (1999) 'The pretence of normality: Intra-family violence and the response of state agencies in Northern Ireland', *Critical Social Policy*, 58, 31–55.

IPSOS MORI (2007) *Research into Recent Crime Trends in Northern Ireland*, Belfast: Ipsos.

JARMAN, N (2004) 'From war to peace? Changing patterns of violence in Northern Ireland, 1990 to 2003', *Terrorism and Political Violence*, 16/3, 420–38.

LENNON, R and TITTERINGTON, AJ (1996) 'The prospects for tourism in Northern Ireland', *International Journal of Contemporary Hospitality Management*, 8/3, 11–17.

LYSAGHT, K and BASTEN, A (2003) 'Violence, fear and "the everyday": Negotiating spatial practice in the city of Belfast', in EA Stanko (ed), *The Meanings of Violence*, London: Routledge, 224–42.

McELRATH, K (2000) *Unsafe Haven: The United States, the IRA and political prisoners*, London: Pluto.

—— (2001) 'Risk behaviors among injecting drug users in Northern Ireland', *Substance Use and Misuse*, 36, 2137–57.

—— (2004) 'Drug use and drug markets in the context of political conflict: The case of Northern Ireland,' *Addiction Research and Theory* 12, 577–90.

—— and ELLISON, G (2003) 'Criminological discourses in Northern Ireland: Conflict and conflict resolution', in K McEvoy and T Newburn (eds), *Criminology, Conflict Resolution and Restorative Justice*, Basingstoke: Palgrave Macmillan, 45–82.

—— and McEVOY, K (1999) *Ecstasy Use in Northern Ireland*, London: The Stationery Office.

—— —— (2001) 'Fact, fiction and function: Mythmaking and the social construction of ecstasy use', *Substance Use and Misuse*, 36, 1–22.

McGRELLIS, S (2004) *Pushing the Boundaries in Northern Ireland: Young people, violence and sectarianism*, Families and Social Capital ESRC Research Group, Working Paper, London: London South Bank University.

McLAUGHLIN, E (1993) 'Women and family in Northern Ireland: A review', *Women's Studies International Forum*, 16/6, 553–68.

METRESS, S (1995) *Outlines in Irish History: Eight hundred years of struggle*, Detroit: Connolly Books.

MIKA, H and McEVOY K (2001) 'Restorative justice in conflict: Paramilitarism, community, and the construction of legitimacy in Northern Ireland', *Contemporary Justice Review*, 4/3–4, 291–319.

Morison, J and Geary R (1989) 'Crime, conflict and counting: Another commentary on Northern Ireland crime statistics', *Howard Journal of Criminal Justice*, 28/1, 9–26.

Ní Aoláin, F (2000) *The Politics of Force: Conflict management and state violence in Northern Ireland*, Belfast: Blackstaff.

Northern Ireland Statistics and Research Agency (2002) *Northern Ireland Census: 2001 population report and mid-year estimates*, Belfast: Northern Ireland Statistics and Research Agency.

O'Mahony, D (2002) 'Juvenile crime and justice in Northern Ireland', in N Bala et al (eds), *Juvenile Justice Systems: An international comparison of problems and solutions*, Toronto: Thompson, 135–51.

—— Geary, R, McEvoy, K and Morison, J (2000) *Crime, Community and Locale: The Northern Ireland communities crime survey*, Aldershot: Ashgate.

Parker, T (1994) *May the Lord in His Mercy Be Kind to Belfast*, New York: Henry Holt.

Police Service of Northern Ireland (2007) *Chief Constable's Annual Report, 2006–2007*, Belfast: PSNI.

Royal Ulster Constabulary (1999) *Report of the Chief Constable, 1998–1999*, Belfast: RUC.

Shirlow, P and Murtagh, B (2006) *Belfast: Segregation, violence and the city*, London: Pluto.

Solowij, N, Hall, W and Lee, N (1992) 'Recreational MDMA use in Sydney: A profile of "ecstasy" users and their experiences with the drug', *British Journal of Addiction*, 87, 1161–72.

Van Dijk, JJM and Mayhew, P (1992) *Criminal Victimisation in the Industrialised World: Key findings of the 1989 and 1992 International Crime Surveys*, Report presented to the conference: Understanding Crime: Experience of Crime and Crime Control, November, Rome.

Weitzer, R (1995) *Policing Under Fire: Ethnic conflict and police-community relations in Northern Ireland*, Albany: SUNY Press.

Whyte, J (1991) *Interpreting Northern Ireland*, Oxford: Clarendon.

5

IRELAND

Mairéad Seymour and Paula Mayock[1]

INTRODUCTION

In the past twenty years, Irish society has been transformed in ways that few might have anticipated. Depicted by *The Economist* as 'easily the poorest country in rich north-west Europe' in 1988, by the turn of the century, Ireland had managed to establish itself as 'a post-industrial enclave within global capitalism' (Peillon, 2002: 1). What has become known, both colloquially and internationally, as the 'Celtic Tiger' period of economic growth began in the mid-1990s, peaked around 2003, and has precipitated rapid social change.[2] This period has also coincided with increasing rates of public disorder and violence. Levels of crime against the person doubled between 1999 and 2003 (Central Statistics Office (CSO), 2004), the level of minor and serious assault peaked in 2002, and the homicide rate continues to rise (An Garda Síochána, 1996–2005; CSO, 2008; O'Donnell, 2005).

Significant shifts have also taken place in drinking practices over the past two decades. Between 1986 and 2006, alcohol consumption per capita increased by 48 per cent, with the most dramatic rise evidenced between the mid-1990s and 2001 (Hope, 2007). The negative health consequences associated with this rise in consumption are well rehearsed and include increases in hospital discharges related to alcohol (Mongan et al, 2007), a high percentage of alcohol-related injury attendances (28 per cent) in accident and emergency departments (Hope et al, 2005a), and an upward trend in alcohol-related mortality for cirrhosis of the liver and alcohol-related chronic conditions from the 1990s onward (Hope, 2008). The social harms linked to alcohol consumption are also well documented, with alcohol deemed to be involved in half the cases of unwanted sexual experiences in a national study of sexual violence

[1] We would like to thank Dr Shane Butler, Senior Lecturer, School of Social Work and Social Policy, Trinity College Dublin, Dr Eoin O'Sullivan, Senior Lecturer, School of Social Work and Social Policy, Trinity College Dublin, and Professor Ian O'Donnell, Institute of Criminology, University College Dublin, for their helpful comments on earlier drafts of this paper.

[2] Whilst the economic boom of the 'Celtic Tiger' greatly enhanced the economic positioning of a large number of Irish people, it corresponded with a broadening of the margins between rich and poor, contributing to a rise in the level of relative poverty among adults (CSO, 2008; Whelan et al, 2003) and to one of the highest levels of child poverty in the EU (Combat Poverty Agency, 2004).

(McGee et al, 2002). Recent research on domestic violence in Ireland identified alcohol as being directly implicated in over one-quarter of the cases investigated (27 per cent) (Watson and Parsons, 2005).

The manifestations of excessive alcohol consumption are possibly most visible in the scenes played out by intoxicated persons emerging from pubs and clubs in towns and cities across the country. Although media coverage has been charged with fuelling moral panic about crime and disorder in Ireland (McCullagh, 1996; O'Connell, 1999), the available empirical evidence supports the link between alcohol and public disorder during night-time hours (National Crime Council (NCC), 2003). Nightlife in Ireland revolves around the weekend nights of Friday and Saturday (although it extends to weekday nights in the bigger cities, particularly Dublin) and is characterized by the congregation of large groups of predominantly young adults in pubs and clubs until the early hours of the morning. As we discuss in more detail below, the dominant substance ingested is alcohol, which is often consumed in excessive quantities and in mixed combinations including beer, spirits, 'alcopops' and 'shooters',[3] and also with illicit drugs (Mayock, 2004). It is perhaps important to state at this juncture that the 'night-time economy' (NTE), per se, has not been the subject of specific research attention in an Irish context. While the epidemiology of alcohol and drug use is relatively well developed, there is a dearth of research on the *social context* of both licit and illicit substance consumption, whether in clubs, pubs, street-based settings, or the disadvantaged zones of large cities. This is particularly apparent in relation to alcohol, possibly reflecting the cultural ambivalence that surrounds drinking in Ireland.

A NATION CONSUMED BY ALCOHOL?

Stereotypes of the Irish have always included drinking and drunkenness (Stivers, 2000), and alcohol, associated with many aspects of social life, has been a 'recurring motif in the collective representation of Ireland and Irishness' (Kuhling and Keohane, 2007: 129). While stereotypes are usually a mix of myth and truth, recent statistics appear to verify the image of the drunken Irish. Drinking remains intrinsic to many aspects of Irish social and cultural life and is deeply woven into the national identity.[4]

For most of the twentieth century, Ireland had comparatively low levels of alcohol consumption. Reporting on consumption trends in the early 1990s, Coniffe and McCoy (1993: xii) concluded that, although drinking rates had increased between 1960 and 1991, 'it should not be assumed that Ireland has especially high alcohol consumption by international standards'. The authors went on, however, to predict

---

[3] Chapter 2 describes the corresponding rise of 'alcopops' and 'shooters' in England and Wales.

[4] As a predominantly Catholic country, Ireland does not have what has been described as a 'temperance culture' (Levine, 1992). Founded in 1898, the Pioneer Total Abstinence Association is the mainstream Catholic temperance movement in Ireland. However, it is a moderate movement which advocates voluntary abstinence for religious motives and does not see itself primarily as a Catholic lobby for more restrictive alcohol policies (Ferriter, 1999).

an increase in consumption levels in line with what they termed 'income elasticity' (Coniffe and McCoy, 1993: 93). Available evidence now points to the accuracy of their prediction, with a dramatic increase in the total consumption per adult (that is, individuals over 15 years of age) apparent from 1995, coinciding directly with Ireland's economic boom. The period of most rapid growth in consumption was from the mid-1990s to 2001 (Hope, 2007) and, by 2002, Ireland was reported to have the highest alcohol consumption levels among the countries studied in the European Comparative Alcohol Study (Ramstedt and Hope, 2005). While consumption rates declined from their peak of 14.3 litres per adult in 2001 to 13.4 in 2006, the Irish continue to be among the highest consumers in Europe. By 2006, Ireland ranked second after Luxembourg in terms of overall consumption among 15 EU countries (Hope, 2007). This latter study also found Ireland to have the highest proportion of abstainers among the countries surveyed (at 23 per cent of 18–64-year-olds), suggesting that increasing consumption rates cannot be explained by a decline in abstention. This finding also appears to confirm that, in relation to alcohol, Ireland is a 'nation of extremes' (Ferriter, 1999).

Alongside these dramatic increases in alcohol consumption, 20 years of statistical data now points to significant shifts in drinking patterns. Most notable is the rise in 'binge' or heavy episodic drinking, a trend which has been noted in relation to teenagers (Hibell et al, 1997; 2000; 2004) but also among men and women of all ages (Hope, 2007; 2008 ; Hope et al, 2005b; Mongan et al, 2007; Ramstedt and Hope, 2005; SLAN, 2003; Strategic Task Force on Alcohol, 2002; 2004). In relation to school-aged children and young people, specifically, national studies reveal high levels of drinking, irrespective of gender, and there is practically no class effect in the numbers of young people reporting lifetime or more recent drinking (Friel et al, 1999; Kelleher et al, 2003; Nic Gabhainn et al, 2007). Heavy drinking patterns and 'binge' drinking are also recorded among college students (Hope et al, 2005b). Another striking change in consumption patterns relates to gender. Traditionally, drinking in Ireland was considered a male privilege and, until the 1960s, it was not socially acceptable for women to drink in public places (Cassidy, 1997; Curtin and Ryan, 1989). However, pubs are now among the most widespread leisure spaces used by women (Coakley, 2002) and increasing numbers of women of all ages are regular consumers of alcohol. Ramstedt and Hope (2005) found that 31 per cent of 18–29-year-old women exceeded weekly 'low-risk' limits (14 standard drinks), with heavy and risky alcohol consumption far more concentrated in the younger age groups, compared to men. A final significant trend in Ireland since the mid-1990s is the mixing of alcohol with other psychoactive substances, including cannabis, ecstasy, and cocaine (Mayock, 2001; 2004; National Advisory Committee on Drugs, 2003; 2005). Within a variety of social settings, 'going out' increasingly holds the possibility of using illegal drugs. Drug consumption among Irish youth has risen steadily throughout the 1990s and Ireland is ranked as one of the most drug experienced youth populations in the EU (EMCDDA, 2003). Three consecutive 'European School Survey Project on Alcohol and Other Drugs' (ESPAD) studies (Hibell et al, 1997; 2000; 2004) have uncovered close similarities in drug use prevalence rates among 16-year-olds in Ireland and the UK, as noted by Parker (2001: 3):

It is interesting that Ireland comes closer to the UK drugs profile than any other European country but there is no authoritative literature which attempts to explain this extraordinary status.

Irish attitudes to drinking, drunkenness and alcohol-related harm are said to be characterized by cultural ambivalence (Cassidy, 1998, 2003; Morgan and Grube, 1994). Distinctive features include favourable attitudes to the consumption of large amounts (Inglis, 2002) and public tolerance of drunkenness (Moane, 2002). Conversely, Ireland has traditionally had a significant number of total abstainers from alcohol, both in the general population (Cassidy, 1997; Ferriter, 1999) and among young people (Grube and Morgan, 1990; O'Connor, 1978) and, as noted earlier, the percentage of teetotallers remains high. According to Cassidy (2003: 56):

The ability of Irish people (considered as a whole) to admit and accommodate contradictory attitudes towards this most socially defining of ideas [drinking] is evidence of Ireland's wider success as an ambivalent nation of abstainers and swallowers.

The release and publication of evidence pointing to the negative health consequences and social harms associated with drinking have tended to generate sporadic, if sometimes intense, spells of public debate, particularly in the aftermath of highly publicized media reports of alcohol-induced disorder. The tendency, in other words, has been towards an outburst of public and political commentary followed by silence and ultimate inaction. Since the early 2000s, a more sustained public focus on the negative health and social consequences of heavy consumption, supported by clear empirical evidence of widespread social and personal harms, might be expected to have challenged public and political ambivalence about the extent of alcohol-related harm in society. The period between mid-2002 and mid-summer 2003 was one of unprecedented public attention, coupled with persistent and, at times, hostile debate, on the issue of drinking in Ireland (Butler, 2003). During this period, the print and broadcast media devoted sustained attention to alcohol consumption and, in particular, to 'binge' or heavy sessional drinking. Recent survey research on Irish attitudes to drinking in fact suggests quite negative attitudes to drinking and drunkenness but simultaneously demonstrates the persistence of cultural ambivalence towards alcohol. This research, published by Alcohol Action Ireland (2006), found that 82 per cent of people believed current levels of consumption to be problematic; 85 per cent felt that cultural attitudes to alcohol needed to change; and 51 per cent believed that the government was not doing enough to address alcohol problems. However, only 26 per cent of respondents supported the imposition of increased excise duty/tax on alcohol as a measure to curb consumption. The persistence of this deep-seated and complex cultural perspective is expressed succinctly by Butler (2002a: 211):

it [alcohol] is a familiar drug which has always been part of our everyday environment, so that epidemiological and public health arguments that it is a dangerous drug and that consumption levels and drinking patterns should be changed or regulated appear moralistic and out of touch with popular sentiment.

Moreover, propositions aimed at curbing consumption which simultaneously denote expressions of paternalism are clearly at odds with a broadly neo-liberal policy culture in Ireland, where 'the liberalisation of internal markets is matched by the celebration of individual rights and liberties' (Kirby et al, 2002: 7). Later discussion of Irish government policy on alcohol further underscores this tension as expressed between the policy sectors in Ireland which argue, on the one hand, for greater use of alcohol control policies (namely, public health advocates), and, on the other, for the promotion of competition and consumption (the drinks industry).

ALCOHOL CONSUMPTION IN CONTEXT

The pub in Ireland, as a locus of assembly, conversation and expression, is a social institution in its own right and is the drinking context most closely associated with night-time leisure. The essence of pub culture is closely connected in the public consciousness with having the 'craic', a term generally taken to refer to a particularly 'Irish' way of having a 'good time'.[5] Irish pubs are also a major tourist attraction and the drinking of Guinness, in particular, is a well-established element of the experience of visitors to Ireland. Equally, exporting the ambiance of the Irish bar has become a major industry (Brown and Patterson, 2000; Kelley, 2006). There are currently several hundred Irish theme bars in Britain (McGovern, 2002) and Irish branding is now a global licensed-trade phenomenon with over 1,600 new Irish bars opening across Europe, the USA, and the Far East during the 1990s (Irish Pub Company, 1997).

PUBS, CLUBS, AND THE NIGHT-TIME ECONOMY

As the public house is the quintessential location of Irish sociability it is perhaps surprising that this social setting has been the subject of relatively little sociological investigation (Inglis, 2002; Share et al, 2007). It is nonetheless clear that, historically, pubs in Ireland have been closely related to everyday community life (Curtin and Ryan, 1989; Peace, 1992). Until the 1960s, pubs were used routinely for the conduct of business, economic exchange, political and community action, as well as constituting a core social setting (Molloy, 2002). However, over recent decades, the secondary functions associated with trade and politics have moved to other locations and pubs are now associated with the broader leisure and tourism industries (Share et al, 2007). Indeed, a distinctive feature of contemporary drinking in Ireland is its public nature (Conniffe and McCoy, 1993; Morgan and Grube, 1994). At the turn of the century, Ireland had the largest population of 'out of home' drinkers in Europe (Babor et al, 2003), with three-quarters of all alcohol consumed taking place within the confines of a public house. Although recent years have seen an increase in home-based drinking, pubs retain their place as sites of extensive social interaction and might therefore be said to truly represent a 'third place', or home from home (Oldenburg, 1999). Furthermore,

---

[5] The term 'craic' is the subject of some debate among etymologists of the Gaelic language. However, as an everyday term in an Irish context, it usually denotes fun, enjoyment, banter, and generally relaxing, often in association with alcohol and music. There is no English language equivalent and the term has been incorporated into English language usage in Ireland.

perceived threats to the institution of the pub, related to proposed changes in licensing or drink-driving laws, are often seen as an attack on community life and 'tradition' (Share et al, 2007).

As demonstrated, there have been significant changes in both the extent and style of alcohol consumption in Ireland. Correspondingly, pubs are claimed to have undergone an 'accelerated and thoroughgoing transformation' (Kuhling and Keohane, 2007: 129). A whole new range of bars, theme pubs, and club–bar hybrids have been developed and many traditional pubs, particularly in urban areas, have been replaced by pseudo-nightclub settings that facilitate large numbers of people. These establishments often maintain the configuration of a standard pub until the evening time and then transform into 'nightclubs' at 11.30 pm. The development of these larger premises can be partly explained by shifts in licensing legislation. With no new pub licences being issued,[6] pub owners have extended their premises—creating, in some cases, three or four floors of drinking space—to cater for a growing population of young drinkers. According to Kuhling and Keohane (2007: 130), recent years in Ireland have seen

transformations in the social role of the public house from a public institution, a locus of community, conviviality and sociability where behaviour was regulated formally and informally by set opening hours and the normalising gaze of both the publican and the other clientele, to a super-pub, a business corporation whose goal is the maximisation of profits and therefore alcohol consumption at the expense of sociability.

Although the relationship between specific types of venues and antisocial behaviour has not been the subject of rigorous investigation, 'super-pubs' have been implicated in the instigation of public-order problems, particularly in Dublin City, where large groups of intoxicated individuals spill onto the streets from these venues at closing time. It could certainly be argued that the physical design and 'ambience' of these premises—with large areas of standing room, restricted seating facilities and high-volume piped music—is geared towards maximizing consumer drinking space and, ultimately, promoting excess.

Nonetheless, despite claims that traditional pubs have been substantially transformed (Kuhling and Keohane, 2007), 'super-pubs' cannot be said to have eradicated the traditional public house and are, in fact, a predominately urban, indeed Dublin-based, phenomenon. Public houses in Dublin are significantly larger than pubs in other towns and cities throughout the country, with over half in excess of 2,000 square feet, compared to less than one-fifth of those elsewhere. More than one in three Dublin pubs have sales turnovers in excess of €1.25 million per annum, compared to

---

[6] The 1902 Licensing Act and subsequent Licensing Acts restricted the granting of new licences except where an existing licence or two licences could be 'surrendered' in exchange. Licences could only be exchanged within the boundaries of a particular village, town, or county. This system was amended under the Intoxicating Liquor Act 2000, which allowed new licences to be issued in substitution for one existing anywhere in the country (a similar 'surrender' policy applies in Northern Ireland, see Chapter 4, this volume). Although this was a significant departure from the general restrictions in force since the early twentieth century, it remains the case that licences are a finite commodity; no additional ones being granted over and above the number currently in circulation.

just 1.3 per cent of pubs outside Dublin (Foley, 2004).[7] It is important, therefore, not to exaggerate the extent to which pub life has in fact been transformed, particularly in towns and cities outside Dublin. Perhaps the most notable modification to Irish pub scenes in recent years occurred on 29 March 2004 when the government introduced the world's first comprehensive national ban on workplace smoking, which included bars and restaurants. Interestingly, the smoking ban appears not to have significantly altered pub life and has a high level of acceptance in general, and among smokers (Fong et al, 2005). Despite the insistence of the drinks and hospitality industries that the smoking ban would result in job losses, this prediction appears not to be supported by the available evidence (McCaffrey et al, 2006).

ENTERTAINMENT DISTRICTS AND THE NIGHT-TIME ECONOMY

Whilst the expansion of the night-time entertainment industry is a countrywide phenomenon associated with economic growth, Dublin has by far the largest number of late-night venues and the heaviest concentration of these establishments is in the city centre. The Temple Bar district of the city is probably one of the better known of the city's night-time leisure/pleasure zones. To those not familiar with the area, it is useful to comment briefly on how this district has been transformed. Built in the 17th and 18th centuries, until the early 1990s Temple Bar was home to artists and recording studios, book and record stores, and second-hand clothes shops, with many of its buildings in a state of dereliction. Since the development and implementation of an urban regeneration project—The Temple Bar Initiative—in the late 1980s, the district has been transformed both physically and symbolically. Today the area, which retains its cobbled streets, is host to restaurants, hotels, cafés, boutiques, novelty stores, galleries, pubs, and clubs. Driven primarily by 'a "bums on seats" (or punters in the streets) economic logic', it is oriented towards young, single, high-earning consumers, be they local residents or visitors (Corcoran, 1998: 10).

By the mid-1990s, the Temple Bar area had developed a reputation as the 'stag night' capital of Europe (Montgomery, 2004a, b) and concern was expressed that the original cultural objectives of the district's redevelopment had been overshadowed by the proliferation of licensed premises (Harrison, 1996), with their emphasis firmly on 'individualised rather than socialised consumption' (Corcoran, 1998: 13). Around this time, local residents protested the nuisance arising from the expansion of such properties (Maxwell, 1996). According to Montgomery (2004b: 8), public-order issues arising from stag and hen parties, comprising 'groups of young women and men from England' were addressed by 'a coordinated management response by landlords and hoteliers in the area, essentially by refusing accommodation to same-sex groups'. Noteworthy here is the manner in which blame for public disorder is largely

---

[7] Only 5.2 per cent of pubs are part of a chain, although the proportion is higher for Dublin (13.2 per cent) than the rest of the country (4.2 per cent). In another indicator of the key differences, it is reported that almost 79.7 per cent employ a manager compared to non- Dublin pubs (21.9 per cent).

apportioned to tourists. Whilst the problems associated with the arrival of 'stag' and 'hen' night punters into city-centre pub and clubbing locations have attracted significant attention, the participants in these groups of weekend drinkers are not limited to 'outsiders' by any means. Furthermore, despite Montgomery's (2004b) claims that nuisance arising from the large number of young drinkers has been strategically and effectively managed, controversy remains over what the *new look* Temple Bar has become.[8] Media reports and televised screenings of the behaviour of the district's nightlife punters have generated considerable public discussion. Much of the debate about Temple Bar and other areas associated with a concentration of nightlife venues centres on levels of drinking, drunkenness, and public order problems perceived to characterize the social fabric of these districts after dark.

CRIME AND DISORDER

In setting the context for discussion of crime and disorder, it is important to remind readers of the dearth of empirically grounded criminological literature in Ireland (Kilcommins et al, 2004). To date, only one study, commissioned by the National Crime Council (NCC) and conducted by the Institute of Criminology at University College Dublin, has focused exclusively on public order offences in Ireland (see NCC, 2003). The absence of subsequent empirical study forces a reliance on official crime statistics, international comparative research, and media reportage.[9]

While data sources are limited, some key features of public order within nighttime leisure zones can be ascertained from the available data. The only published study on public order in Ireland reports that just over 70 per cent of all public order offences[10] occurred between 10.00 pm and 4.00 am, with the peak times and days being the early hours of Saturday and Sunday morning (NCC, 2003). This research also found that the vast majority of these offences (over 90 per cent) took place 'on the street' or 'on the road' and that a small number of streets accounted for the location of the majority of incidents (NCC, 2003: 15). More recently, official crime-data sources suggest that those areas with the largest urban concentrations have the highest rates of 'disorderly conduct' per 1,000 of population.[11] In 2006, the rates were highest in

---

[8] John Montgomery was commissioned by Temple Bar 91, a group of young businesspeople and entrepreneurs, to advise them in the preparation of a bid for European Union funding for a renewal scheme for Temple Bar which aimed to promote cultural and business interests within the district. It may be reasonable to suggest, therefore, that he had a vested interest in playing down the public disorder or nuisance associated with the area's entertainment venues.

[9] A new system of crime classification, the Irish Crime Classification System (ICCS), was introduced by the Central Statistics Office (CSO) in April 2008 alongside a detailed report of recorded crime from 2003 to 2006 (CSO, 2008). The ICCS replaces the previous system of crime categorization published up to 2005 (An Garda Síochána, 1996–2005). Crimes are categorized differently under each system and datasets are therefore not comparable.

[10] Public order offences were defined as those under the Criminal Justice (Public Order) Act, 1994 (CJPOA) (NCC, 2003).

[11] The category of 'Disorderly Conduct' was introduced as part of the ICCS and includes 'affray/riot/violent disorder, public order, drunkenness offences and air rage'.

the southern (28.09) and eastern (18.61) regions of the Dublin Metropolitan area, followed by Cork (16.58), Ireland's second largest city (CSO, 2008). Overall, from 2003 to 2006, the rate of disorderly conduct in these areas equated to approximately two and a half times the national average in Dublin and more than one and a half times in Cork. In line with the experience in other jurisdictions (Hobbs et al, 2005; Matthews and Richardson, 2005), public order offending in Ireland typically involves young males.[12] Almost half (48 per cent) of those convicted of 'disorderly conduct' in 2006 were aged between 18 and 24 years and 91 per cent were male (CSO, 2008). The most common proceedings taken under the public order legislation (Criminal Justice (Public Order) Act 1994) relate to 'intoxication in a public place' and 'threatening/abusive behaviour', which together account for approximately three-quarters of the total (An Garda Síochána, 1996–2005). It is well acknowledged, however, that public order incidents in the night-time zones of town and cities often lead to more serious and violent consequences (NCC, 2003; O'Donnell, 2005).

No analysis of crime and disorder in Ireland would be complete without reference to the documented increase in alcohol consumption over the past 20 years and, specifically, to the prevalence of heavy episodic drinking. Internationally, 'binge drinking' is increasingly associated with violence among adults and adolescents (Boyle et al, 2007; Bye, 2008; Felson et al, 2008; Hughes et al, 2007; Treno et al, 2007) and its prevalence in Ireland is of particular relevance to criminological analyses of social order within the country's night-time zones. Whilst acknowledging that inconsistencies across available data sources pose serious challenges (Kilcommins et al, 2004; O'Donnell and O'Sullivan, 2001), making the identification of any direct causal link between alcohol and crime 'very much a matter of speculation and conjecture' (Vaughan, 2003: 205), the weight of contextual evidence is substantial. In approximately half of the cases examined in a study of homicide in Ireland (1992–6), the victim, perpetrator or both were intoxicated (Dooley, 2001). Expert commentary on the European Union Survey of Crime and Safety (EU ICS) suggests that rates of violent crime are 'associated with the levels of consumption of alcohol per population' (van Dijk et al, 2005: 2) and identifies Ireland as one of the countries with the highest risk of assault. More specifically, Rossow's (2001) findings demonstrate a positive and significant association between alcohol consumption (in terms of alcohol sales) and homicide rates in five of 14 European countries studied, including Ireland. In explaining the phenomenon, he surmises that differences in the relative impact of alcohol sales on homicides could be attributed to the divergences in drinking cultures across the countries studied, specifically between those with 'explosive' drinking practices leading to intoxication and those where intoxication was seen as socially unacceptable. Ireland could reasonably be said to belong to the former category, certainly in terms of its current drinking culture.

The social and economic changes in Irish society over the last ten years merit specific attention in explaining public disorder and violence. A proliferation of gangland violence, involving 'turf wars' in the drug-market constituencies of the major cities, partly explains increases in violent crime, particularly homicide. Whilst not directly

---

[12] Although an apparent rise in female offences is recorded in England and Wales, see Chapter 2.

related to the NTE there are claims that middle-class drug consumption creates a demand that ultimately fuels criminal networks (O'Donnell, 2007a, b). It has also been suggested that the tension created between those who benefited from the economic output of the Celtic Tiger and those who did not, may have resulted in increased violence in society (Inglis, 2006; McCullagh, 2004). Following a sustained period of high unemployment and mass emigration (Share et al, 2007), the spending power of the young has been greatly enhanced due primarily to increased opportunities for labour-market participation. Indeed, the increase in offences against the person from the mid-1990s has been attributed to 'the tendency for people with greater disposable incomes to spend more time in pubs and clubs, settings where interpersonal confrontations may occur' (O'Donnell, 2007b: 246). Increased affluence, coupled with a culture of ambivalence towards excessive alcohol use, has undoubtedly contributed to rising alcohol consumption (Strategic Task Force on Alcohol, 2002) and also to the proliferation of environments that have the potential to foster public disorder. Whilst street violence in Ireland, as elsewhere, has traditionally been associated with working-class males, a tragic incident in 2000 involving 'respectable' young men catapulted the issue of alcohol and disorder to the forefront of public and media discussion, challenging many taken-for-granted ideas about violence and simultaneously questioning whether Ireland's economic success has been an entirely fortuitous turnabout.

In August 2000, an 18-year-old student, Brian Murphy, was kicked to death outside a well-known nightspot, *Club Annabel*, located in a salubrious area of south Dublin. After emerging from the club, Murphy encountered a group of young men and an altercation ensued involving minor pushing and shoving. This quickly escalated into a violent attack with fatal consequences. The victim and the four youths charged in connection with the incident were all from wealthy middle-class backgrounds. The events surrounding Brian Murphy's death were not dissimilar to those of other incidents in which lives have been lost; what differentiated this case from most others, however, was that it brought violent crime to the doorstep of 'respectable' society (Inglis, 2006). Analysis of causation could not lay the blame on poverty, disadvantage, or inequality in the Murphy case and the sudden manner in which the toxic mixture of alcohol and violence laid tragic consequences at the door of 'respectable' society challenged the national consciousness, generating questions about what had become of Irish society. Cromer (2004: 398) claims that moral panic is usually generated by the perception that crime has increased dramatically, but argues that it may also arise 'from the belief that crime and delinquency have permeated sections of the population hitherto considered to be unlikely or even unable to break the law'. Nowhere was this more discernible than in the Murphy case. Traditional understandings of public disorder as a phenomenon related to 'the drinking practices of the unruly working class' (Jayne et al, 2008: 83) had been challenged. Public disorder was no longer the preserve of the poor, but rather a phenomenon which could transcend all sections of society.

RESPONDING TO PUBLIC DISORDER: POLICING AND OTHER MEASURES

In an attempt to examine the exigencies of policing crime and disorder in nightlife areas, the following discussion examines general trends in public order and liquor licensing proceedings over a ten-year period. This data provides baseline information for analysing the particularities of the Irish context.

Proceedings for public-order offences increased more than three-fold between 1996 and 2005 (An Garda Síochána, 1996–2005; NCC, 2003). Figure 5.1 shows the steady rise from 1996 to 2002, followed by a decline in 2003 and 2004 and further rises in 2005. Whilst this upward trend can be partly attributed to changes in offence recording practices since 2000, it must also be located within the broader criminal justice framework. In particular, the increased emphasis on policing minor infractions following the introduction of 'zero tolerance' policing in 1997 (O'Donnell and O'Sullivan, 2001, 2003) saw proceedings for 'public' offences, including begging, prostitution, and public order, increase across all domains. More recently, the introduction of behaviour orders, aimed at tackling antisocial behaviour among adults and young people, provides further indication of a shift in emphasis towards the policing of particular forms of public conduct (Brown, 2007; Hamilton and Seymour, 2006).

In stark contrast to the rise in proceedings for public-order offences, there has been a steady decline in the number of proceedings per 100,000 of population taken under the liquor licensing legislation since 1997. This is largely explained by a fall-off in the number of proceedings taken against licensees and consumers for breaches of the pub-closing regulations. One possible explanation relates to the extension of opening hours initiated by the Intoxicating Liquor Act 2000,[13] which essentially served to legalize late-night trading. However, the downward trend in proceedings for liquor licensing offences started prior to the introduction of this legislation,

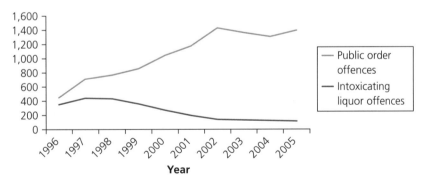

Fig 5.1 Proceedings per 100,000 population 1996–2005

[13] This legislation is discussed in greater detail below.

thus discounting, at least in part, the role of extended opening hours. In light of the increasing police attention to incivility offences, a more persuasive argument is that the emphasis may have shifted away from a concern about offending within the quasi-private domain of licensed premises towards the more public arena of the streets. This is certainly borne out in official statistics, where anomalies exist between the high numbers of proceedings taken against persons for order-related offences in public places compared to the low numbers documented to occur within licensed venues (An Garda Síochána 1996–2005; Courts Service, 2006; CSO, 2008).

Police powers to respond to NTE-related infractions are executed under the Intoxicating Liquor Acts and the Criminal Justice (Public Order) Act 1994, as well as the Criminal Justice (Public Order) Act 2003 and the Criminal Justice Act 2006. Despite the increased emphasis on public order policing, the available research suggests that police discretion is commonly exercised in responding to public order incidents and, in over half of cases, matters are dealt with informally (NCC, 2003). Equally, the use of arrest appears to be as much about apprehending offending individuals as a mechanism to diffuse tension (ibid). Within the policing rubric there is also evidence that officers exercise their discretion more favourably towards those entering city-centre entertainment zones than towards other groups. It could therefore be argued that night-time consumers are viewed as respectable partygoers and treated as such. In contrast, the police response to young people 'hanging about' in their locality has been described as confrontational (NCC, 2003), supporting the notion that 'the location of young people's drinking, as much as the consumption of alcohol itself [has] the potential to be perceived as problematic and disorderly' (Hamilton and Seymour, 2006: 64).

CRIMINAL JUSTICE RESPONSES

The vast majority of offenders under the age of 18 years are diverted to a caution-based Garda Juvenile Diversion Programme (GJDP) for alcohol-related offences. This form of discharge consistently accounts for appoximately one-fifth of all referrals on an annual basis (An Garda Síochána, 1996–2005; CSO, 2008). Adults may also be able to avoid prosecution due to the introduction of a caution scheme and fixed-penalty fines. The adult caution scheme is aimed almost entirely at public order-related offences, including drunkenness, criminal damage (excluding arson), and minor assault. Notwithstanding concerns about net-widening, these new diversionary measures offer the Gardaí (Irish police) an alternative to court proceedings. This is perhaps significant given previous findings that decisions by the Gardaí to proceed with public order charges are sometimes influenced by the perception that the courts do not take public order offences seriously (NCC, 2003).

As Table 5.1 indicates, in some areas of the country a large proportion of cases are 'struck out'. In the Dublin District Courts over a quarter of public-order/assault cases are dismissed. Noteworthy also are the disparities across geographical regions in the outcomes for public-order/assault offences (Courts Service, 2006). Anomalies in sentencing practice across Ireland are well documented (Bacik, 2002; O'Malley, 2000) and are by no means confined to the category of offence in question here. Although information about the sentences imposed for liquor licensing offences is not publicly available, a report of the Government Alcohol Advisory Group (GAAG) in 2008 drew

Table 5.1 Court outcome for public order/assault convictions 2006

	% Struck out	% Imprisoned	% Fined
Dublin (East)	27	8	14
Cork City (South)	16	23	18
Limerick (South-west)	21	14	18
Galway (West)	9	16	33
Donegal (North-west)	7	4	54
Kilkenny (South-east)	12	31	33

Source: Courts Service, 2006

attention to the small number of serious penalties imposed on licensees for breach of the licensing regulations. While legislative provision is available (under the Intoxicating Liquor Acts 2000 and 2003) to impose a temporary closure order against licensed premises for breaches of licensing law, only eight orders of this kind were imposed for the supply of alcohol to intoxicated persons between 2005 and 2007 (GAAG, 2008). Available figures therefore strongly suggest that the enthusiasm with which individuals and consumers are pursued and punished for public order offences is not matched by an equal level of surveillance over their 'suppliers of crime opportunities' (Garland, 2001:127): that is, publicans. Furthermore, it appears that the consequences of the law are experienced most heavily by those on the margins of society. The only national reconviction study in Ireland found that in the offence category of public order, 53.5 prisoners per 10,000 population came from the most deprived areas of Ireland compared to 1.7 from the least deprived (O'Donnell et al, 2007). It seems clear, therefore, that while entertainment districts may be the domain of those with disposable income to engage in hedonistic behaviour, the burden of imprisonment and re-imprisonment (see O'Donnell et al, 2007) for public order offences falls most heavily on individuals and communities with the highest levels of material deprivation.

LOCAL REGULATORY RESPONSES

Local authorities do not play an active role in efforts to address public order issues, despite legal mechanisms for such involvement. Under the Intoxicating Liquor Act 2003 local authorities and the Gardaí must be consulted before a late licence (Special Exemption Order) is granted to a nightclub owner or other licensee to serve alcohol until 2.30 am.[14] Whilst the District Court retains ultimate jurisdiction in granting

---

[14] All licensees are required to apply to the District Court for a Special Exemption Order if they wish to serve alcohol until 2.30 am. Prior to the introduction of the Intoxicating Liquor Act in July 2008, an anomaly in outdated legislation allowed a small number of premises to remain open and serve alcohol beyond 2.30 am. Under the Public Health Acts Amendment Act 1890, holders of public music and singing licences could apply directly to the Revenue Commissioners for a theatre licence without application to the District Court. Theatre licences were granted if it could be proved that a live performance would be held in the venue. There was no specified mandatory closing time and the sale of alcohol was permitted for half an hour after the termination of a performance. In practice, alcohol could be served up to 3.30 am thus giving such licensees an unfair advantage over those granted special exemption orders in the District Court. The aforementioned Act removed this anomaly in the legislation.

these orders, a recent report suggests that none of the local authorities have executed their powers under the Intoxicating Liquor Act 2003 (GAAG, 2008). In contrast, the Gardaí in provincial towns, in particular, have been proactive in seeking reductions in the length of licence extensions on the basis of public order concerns. In these cases, the Gardaí have made representations in court, drawing on CCTV footage of public disorder in some cases, to support their request. The onus on local authorities to work with the Gardaí on public order matters is likely to increase in the near future, following the introduction of Joint Policing Committees under the Garda Síochána Act 2005. Overall, however, the effectiveness of these preventative initiatives, of themselves, is likely to be limited without increased enforcement of the liquor licensing laws and more consistent and severe deterrents imposed against licence holders by the courts. Without such measures, responsibility for preventing and responding to public disorder in night-time leisure areas will continue to fall heavily on the national police force (An Garda Síochána).[15] The limited effectiveness of this approach to controlling alcohol-related public disorder is explained by Hobbs et al (2005: 173) who argue that 'high-profile "law and order crackdowns" may relieve the short-term symptoms but they do nothing to address the political–economic context that feeds the problem'. It is within this context that our final section examines broader public-policy responses to the place of alcohol in Irish society.

NATIONAL RESPONSES TO THE ALCOHOL 'PROBLEM'

Ireland's first national alcohol policy was published in 1996. *National Alcohol Policy— Ireland* was a hard-hitting document based on health-promotional principles which set out a range of strategies aimed at reducing alcohol consumption. The chief issues it considered included access to and availability of alcohol, which it suggested should be regulated through the licensing code; the road-traffic legislation governing drink-driving; the advertising of alcohol; and the taxation and pricing of alcohol. Five years after its publication, the policy was judged to 'have made virtually no impact on public consciousness, on policy or the actual drinking habits here in Ireland' (Butler, 2001: 6). Furthermore and as demonstrated earlier, by the turn of the century, alcohol consumption had reached an all-time high. Today, the recommendations of Ireland's national alcohol policy have yet to be implemented, a situation which has been attributed to the influence of the drinks industry (Hope, 2006). Critics have argued that the industry set out to limit government intervention through the power of persuasion, particularly

---

[15] Door security at night-time entertainment venues has increased substantially in recent years. However, despite 20 years of lobbying, regulation of the wider private security industry did not occur until the Private Security Authority (PSA) was established in 2005 under the Private Security Services Act 2004 (Select Committee on Crime, Lawlessness and Vandalism, 1984; Consultative Group on the Private Security Industry, 1997; PSA, 2008). Furthermore, the absence of research in this area in Ireland means that little is known about the interplay between door security and crime and disorder on the streets.

through the insistence that they had appropriate mechanisms in place to reduce harm and self-regulate. According to Hope (2006: 478–9):

the alcohol industry has to date managed to persuade the government that their proposed strategies to reduce alcohol-related harm are more appropriate and that taxes and marketing regulations should not be part of it.

The Intoxicating Liquor Act 2000 liberalized the licensing laws and extended the opening hours of licensed premises to 12.30 am on Friday, Saturday, and Sunday mornings, with a half-hour 'drinking-up time'. In November 2000, the Commission on Liquor Licensing (CLL) was established by the minister for justice with a remit to review the liquor licensing system (Commission on Liquor Licensing, 2002). Rather than addressing the alcohol problem in its entirety, the Commission focused almost exclusively on issues such as binge drinking and public disorder and the need for individuals to take personal responsibility for their drinking habits. It did, however, recommend the establishment of a Strategic Task Force on Alcohol within the Department of Health and Children 'to bring forward recommendations on specific, evidence-based measures to prevent and reduce alcohol-related harm' (Hope, 2006: 472). The Strategic Task Force on Alcohol (2002) focused heavily on public disorder and, in keeping with the recommendations made in *National Alcohol Policy—Ireland*, called for greater regulation of the industry through limitations on availability, higher taxes, and restrictions on the marketing of alcohol, particularly to young people. Its recommendations aimed to imbue *collective* responsibility for the effects of Ireland's drink habit. This was to be achieved through the implementation of broad strategies, rather than targeting particular populations or groups perceived to be problematic. As Butler (2003) points out, the establishment of the Strategic Task Force on Alcohol in 2002 effectively meant that there were two parallel alcohol policy processes in place, one based in the Department of Justice, Equality and Law Reform and, the second, based at the Department of Health and Children. Whilst the former is dominated by interest groups (including the drinks industry) committed primarily to consumerism, the latter represents a public-health perspective on alcohol. Consequently, there is no integrated or 'joined-up' approach to alcohol and no single government department with overall responsibility for the implementation of a national alcohol policy (Butler, 2002).

The Intoxicating Liquor Act 2003 was presented, following the period of intense media reportage on alcohol-related public disorder referred to earlier, as a tough response to excessive alcohol consumption, binge drinking, under-age consumption, and crime. In reality, however, much of its substance replaced outdated legislation and many of the 'new' provisions introduced were minor, such as reverting closing time on Thursday nights to 11.30 pm and outlawing entertainment during the final thirty minutes of opening time. The ban on 'happy hours' was, at best, one of the more substantive signs of a so-called 'get tough' rhetoric on binge drinking.

In April 2008, the government announced new legislative measures arising from recommendations of the Government Alcohol Advisory Group (GAAG) report published earlier that year. The GAAG had emphasized the need to restrict the availability of alcohol through off-sales and to encourage greater enforcement of the law and harsher sanctions for offences of drunkenness, disorderly behaviour, the provision of alcohol to minors, and for permitting drunkenness and disorderly behaviour on licensed premises. Many of these recommendations were included in the Intoxicating Liquor Act 2008. Under the Act, Gardaí were given the power to seize alcohol from minors and from others seen to present a threat to public order, a fixed penalty scheme was introduced, and District Court fines were increased for public order and liquor licensing offences. Previous GAAG proposals to deploy plain-clothes police officers to detect breaches of the liquor licensing laws were, however, excluded from the legislation. Furthermore, whilst the trading hours of off-licence premises were reduced and restrictions placed on acquiring an off-sales licence, provisions requiring supermarkets and convenience stores to structurally separate the display and sale of alcohol were postponed in favour of a voluntary code of conduct for the responsible sale of alcohol. It remains to be seen if the more general recommendations of the GAAG, including their call for the development of a new national strategy on alcohol, are ever taken forward.

CONCLUSIONS

Levels of alcohol consumption and the number of proceedings taken for public order offences have increased dramatically over the last decade. While legislative change and changes in crime-recording practice partly explain the rise in public order offences, increased economic prosperity, coupled with more stringent policing of public order offences are important contributory factors. Noteworthy is the introduction of a range of criminal justice responses to public disorder at a time when enforcement of the liquor licensing laws has declined steadily. The response to public disorder in the Irish context has therefore been executed via the lens of front-end governance, through 'tackling' alcohol-related crime and disorder on the street without a corresponding emphasis on the need for a broader societal response to the problem of alcohol and the health, social, and economic consequences arising from its misuse. Much of the evidence presented here resonates with Hobbs et al's (2005: 173) suggestion that 'as the state continues to devise authoritarian strategies aimed at managing the poor (Lea, 2002: 163), it also refrains from utilising the full range of preventive measures and police powers for the licensing, regulation and management of the night-time economy'.

As discussed, responsibility for the various aspects of alcohol policy is spread across a number of government departments and there are no mechanisms in place to join up these various sectors (Butler, 2002). This disjointed approach has provided 'fertile ground for the drinks industry to lobby' (Hope, 2006: 469) and to strongly influence the governance of alcohol consumption. There are other factors, however. The paternalistic ideas at the heart of the public-health policy approach to alcohol appear severely at odds with an economy and culture characterized as never before by neo-liberal values. Popular support for a public-health approach is equivocal at best, a situation which provides a 'democratic basis' for 'the refusal of the state to introduce alcohol control policies' (Butler, 2009). Arguably, the ambivalence towards excessive alcohol consumption in Ireland is characterized by a detached political and public attitude and response to alcohol-related harm. In this context, the notion of processing 'disorderly' drinkers through the criminal justice system, whilst at the same time ignoring the larger social ills associated with excessive alcohol consumption, may be appealing to consumers who are, in the main, law-abiding.

REFERENCES

All internet sources were accessible 20 August 2008

ALCOHOL ACTION IRELAND (2006) *Alcohol in Ireland: A survey of Irish attitudes*, Dublin: Alcohol Action Ireland.

AN GARDA SÍOCHÁNA (1996–2005) *Annual Report of An Garda Commissioner 1996–2005*, Dublin: The Stationery Office.

BABOR, T, CAETANO, R, CASSWELL, S, EDWARDS, G, GIESBRECHT, N, Graham, K. GRUBE, J, GRUENEWALD, P, HILL, L, HOLDER, H, HOMEL, R, OSTERBERG, E, REHM, J, ROOM, R, and ROSSOW, I (2003) *Alcohol: No Ordinary Commodity*, Oxford: Oxford University Press.

BACIK, I (2002) 'The practice of sentencing in the Irish courts,' in P O'Mahony (ed), *Criminal Justice in Ireland*, Dublin: Institute of Public Administration.

BOYLE, S, MORTENSEN, L, GRØNBÆK, M and BAREFOOT, J (2007) 'Hostility, drinking pattern and mortality', *Addiction*, 103, 54–9.

BROWN, K (2007) 'Examining the introduction of legislation in Ireland to tackle juvenile antisocial behaviour', *Probation Journal*, 54/3, 239–50.

BROWN, S and PATTERSON, A (2000) 'Knick-knack, paddy-whack, give a pub a theme', *Journal of Marketing Management*, 16, 647–62.

BUTLER, S (2001) 'The national alcohol policy and the rhetoric of health promotion', *Irish Social Worker*, 19/1, 4–7.

—— (2002) *Alcohol, Drugs and Health Promotion in Modern Ireland*, Dublin: Institute of Public Administration.

—— (2003) 'Paying the price for extended opening hours: A comment from Ireland', *Drugs: Education, Prevention and Policy*, 10/4, 293–6.

—— (2009) 'Obstacles to the implementation of an integrated national alcohol policy in Ireland: Nannies, neo-liberals and joined-up government', *Journal of Social Policy* (forthcoming).

BYE, EK (2008) 'Alcohol and homicide in Eastern Europe: A time series analysis of six countries', *Homicide Studies*, 12/1, 7–27.

CASSIDY, T (1997) 'Sober for the sake of the children: the Church, the State and alcohol use amongst women in Ireland', in A Byrne and M Leonard (eds), *Women and Irish Society: A sociological reader*, Belfast: Beyond the Pale Publications, 447–64.

—— (1998) 'Just two will do', in M Peillon and E Slater (eds), *Encounters with Modern Ireland: A sociological chronicle, 1995–1996*, Dublin: Institute of Public Administration, 165–73.

—— (2003) 'Society and alcohol', in S Kilcommins and I O'Donnell (eds), *Alcohol, Society and Law*, Chichester: Barry Rose Law Publishers, 33–59.

CSO (Central Statistics Office) (2004) *Quarterly National Household Survey: Crime and victimisation, Quarter 4 2003*, Dublin: The Stationery Office.

CSO (Central Statistics Office) (2008) *Garda Recorded Crime Statistics 2003–2006*, Dublin: The Stationery Office.

COAKLEY, L (2002) '"All over the place, in town, the pub, everywhere": A social geography of women's friendships in Cork', *Irish Geography*, 35/1, 40–50.

COMBAT POVERTY AGENCY (2004) *Against All Odds: Growing up in poverty*, Dublin: Combat Poverty Agency.

COMMISSION ON LIQUOR LICENSING (2002) *Commission on Liquor Licensing Final Report*, Dublin: Department of Justice, Equality and Law Reform.

CONIFFE, D and MCCOY, D (1993) *Alcohol Use in Ireland: Some economic and social implications*, General Research Series Paper No 160, Dublin: The Economic and Social Research Institute.

CONSULTATIVE GROUP ON THE PRIVATE SECURITY INDUSTRY (1997) *Report of the Consultative Group on the Private Security Industry December 1997*, Dublin: The Stationery Office.

CORCORAN, M (1998) 'The re-enchantment of Temple Bar', in M Peillon and E Slater (eds), *Encounters with Modern Ireland: A sociological chronicle, 1995–1996*, Dublin: Institute of Public Administration, 9–24.

COURTS SERVICE (2006) *Courts Service Annual Report*, Dublin: The Courts Service.

CROMER, G (2004) 'Children from good homes: Moral panics about middle-class delinquency', *British Journal of Criminology*, 44/3, 391–400.

CURTIN, C and RYAN, C (1989) 'Clubs, pubs and private houses in a Clare Town', in T Wilson (ed), *Ireland from Below: Social change and local communities*, Galway: Galway University Press, 128–43.

DOOLEY, E (2001) *Homicide in Ireland 1992–1996*, Dublin: The Stationery Office.

EMCDDA (European Monitoring Centre for Drugs and Drug Addiction) (2003) *Annual Report on the State of the Drugs Problem in the European Union and Norway*, Lisbon: EMCDDA.

FELSON, RB, TEASDALE, B and BURCHFIELD KB (2008) 'The influence of being under the influence: Alcohol effects on adolescent violence', *Journal of Research in Crime and Delinquency*, 45/2, 119–41.

FERRITER, D (1999) *A Nation of Extremes: The pioneers in twentieth-century Ireland*, Dublin: Irish Academic Press.

FOLEY, A (2004) *Survey of Licensed Premises in Ireland 2004, A Report Commissioned by the Drinks Industry Group of Ireland*, Dublin: Drinks Industry Group of Ireland.

FONG, GT, HYLAND, A, BORLAND, R, HAMMOND, D, HASTINGS, G, MCNEILL, A, ANDERSON, S et al (2006) 'Reductions in tobacco smoke pollution and increases in support for smoke-free public places following the implementation of comprehensive smoke-free workplace legislation in the Republic of Ireland: Findings from the ITC Ireland/UK Survey', *Tobacco Control*, 15, Suppl III, iii51–iii58.

FRIEL, S, NIC GABHAINN, S and KELLEHER, C (1999) *The National Health & Lifestyle Surveys: Dublin and Galway*, Health Promotion Unit, Department of Health and Children, Dublin and Centre for Health Promotion Studies, NUI, Galway.

GAAG (Government Alcohol Advisory Group) (2008) *Report of the Government Alcohol Advisory Group*, Dublin: Department of Justice, Equality and Law Reform.

GARLAND, D (2001) *The Culture of Control: Crime and social order in contemporary society*, Oxford: Oxford University Press.

GRUBE, J and MORGAN, M (1990) *The Development and Maintenance of Smoking, Drinking and Other Drug Use Among Dublin Post-Primary Pupils*, Dublin: The Economic and Social Research Institute, General Research Series, Paper 148.

HAMILTON, C and SEYMOUR, M (2006) 'ASBOs and behaviour orders: Institutionalised intolerance of youth?', *Youth Studies Ireland*, 1/1, 61–76.

Harrison, B (1996) 'A tale of two Temple Bars', *Irish Times*, 18 October, 13.

Hibell, B, Andersson, B, Ahlstrom, S, Balakireva, O, Bjarnasson, T., Kokkevi, A and Morgan, M (2000) *The 1999 ESPAD Report: Alcohol and other drug use among students in 30 European countries*, Stockholm: Council of Europe, Pompidou Group.

———— Bjarnason, T, Kokkevie, A, Morgan, M and Narusk, A (1997) *The 1995 ESPAD Report: Alcohol and other drug use among students in 26 European countries*, Stockholm: Council of Europe, Pompidou Group.

—————— Shlstrom, S, Balakireva, O, Kokkevi, A and Morgan, M (2004) *The ESPAD Report 2003: Alcohol and other drug use among students in 35 countries*, Stockholm: Council of Europe, Pompidou Group.

Hobbs, D, Winlow, S, Hadfield, P and Lister, S (2005) 'Violent hypocrisy governance and the night-time economy', *European Journal of Criminology*, 2/2, 161–83.

Hope, A (2006) 'The influence of the alcohol industry on alcohol policy in Ireland', *Nordic Studies on Alcohol and Drugs*, 23, 467–81.

—— (2007) *Alcohol Consumption in Ireland, 1986–2006*, Dublin: Health Service Executive, Alcohol Implementation Group.

—— (2008) *Alcohol-Related Harm in Ireland*, Dublin: Health Service Executive, Alcohol Implementation Group.

—— Dring, J and Dring, C (2005b) 'College lifestyle and attitudinal (CLAN) survey', in *The Health of Irish Students*, Dublin: Health Promotion Unit, Department of Health and Children.

—— Gill, A, Costello, G, Sheehan, J, Brazil, E and Reid, V (2005a) *Alcohol and Injuries in the Accident and Emergency Department: A national perspective*, Dublin: Health Promotion Unit, Department of Health and Children.

Hughes, K, Anderson, Z, Morleo, M and Bellis, M (2007) 'Alcohol, nightlife and violence: The relative contributions of drinking before and during nights out to negative health and criminal justice outcomes', *Addiction*, 103, 60–5.

Inglis, T (2002) 'Pleasure pursuits', in M Corcoran and M Pellion (eds), *Ireland Unbound: A turn of the century chronicle*, Dublin: Institute of Public Administration, 25–35.

—— (2006) 'Club Anabel', in M Corcoran and M Peillon (eds), *Uncertain Ireland: A sociological chronicle 2003–2004*, Dublin: Institute of Public Administration.

Irish Pub Company (1997) *The Irish Pub: A remarkable business opportunity*, Dublin: Irish Pub Company Promotional Literature.

Jayne, M, Valentine, G and Holloway, S (2008) 'Fluid boundaries—British binge drinking and European civility: Alcohol and the production and consumption of public space', *Space and Polity*, 12/1, 81–100.

Kelleher, C, NicGabhainn, S, Friel, S, Corrigan, H, Nolan, G, Sixsmith, J, Walsh, O and Cooke, M (2003) *The National Health and Lifestyle Surveys*, Health Promotion Unit, Department of Health and Children, Dublin and Centre for Health Promotion Studies, NUI, Galway.

Kelley, A (2006) 'Ireland's "crack" habit: Explaining the faux Irish pub revolution', *Slate*, 16 March, <http://www.slate.com>.

Kilcommins, S, O'Donnell, I, O'Sullivan, E and Vaughan, B (2004) *Crime, Punishment and the Search for Order in Ireland*, Dublin: Institute of Public Administration.

Kirby, P, Gibbons, L and Cronin, M (2002) *Reinventing Ireland: Culture, society and the global economy*, London: Pluto Press.

Kuhling, C and Keohane, K (2007) *Cosmopolitan Ireland: Globalisation and quality of life*, London: Pluto Press.

Lea, J (2002) *Crime and Modernity*, London: Sage Publications.

LEVINE, H (1992) 'Temperance cultures: Concerns about alcohol problems in Nordic and English-speaking countries', in M Lader, G Edwards, and D Drummond (eds), *The Nature of Alcohol and Drug Related Problems*, New York: Oxford University Press, 16–36.

MATTHEWS, S and RICHARDSON, A (2005) *Findings from the 2003 Offending, Crime and Justice Survey: Alcohol-related crime and disorder No 261*, London: Home Office.

MAXWELL, R (1996) 'The city takes shape', in P Quinn (ed), *Temple Bar: The power of an idea*, Dublin: Temple Bar Properties Limited, 81–5.

MAYOCK, P (2001) 'Cocaine use in Ireland: An exploratory study', in R Moran, L Dillon, M O'Brien, P Mayock and E Farrell (eds), *A Collection of Papers on Drug Issues in Ireland*, Dublin: Health Research Board, 80–152.

—— (2004) 'Binge drinking and the consumption of pleasure', in M McLachlan and C Smith (eds), *Binge Drinking and Youth Culture: Alternative perspectives*, Dublin: Liffey Press, 113–41.

McCAFFREY, M, GOODMAN, PG, KELLEHER, K and CLANCY, L (2006) 'Smoking, occupancy and staffing levels in a selection of Dublin pubs pre and post a national smoking ban, lessons for all', *Irish Journal of Medical Science*, 175/2, 37–40.

McCULLAGH, C (1996) *Crime in Ireland: A sociological introduction*, Cork: Cork University Press.

—— (2004) 'Random attacks?' in M Peillon and M Corcoran (eds), *Place and Non-Place: The reconfiguration of Ireland*, Dublin: Institute of Public Administration.

McGEE, H, GARAVAN, R, de BARRA, M, BYRNE, J and CONROY, R (2002) *The SAVI Report: Sexual abuse and violence in Ireland*, Dublin, Liffey Press in association with the Dublin Rape Crisis Centre.

McGOVERN, M (2002) 'The 'craic' market': Irish theme bars and the commodification of Irishness in contemporary Britain', *Irish Journal of Sociology*, 11/2, 77–98.

MOANE, G (2002) 'Colonialism and the Celtic Tiger: Legacies of history and the quest for vision', in P Kirby, L Gibbons and M Cronin (eds), *Reinventing Ireland: Culture, society and global economy*, London: Pluto Press, 109–23.

MOLLOY, C (2002) *The Story of the Irish Pub*, Dublin: Liffey Press.

MONGAN, D, REYNOLDS, S, FANAGAN, S and LONG, J (2007) *Health-Related Consequences of Problem Alcohol Use*, Overview 6, Dublin: Health Research Board.

MONTGOMERY, J (2004a) 'The story of Temple Bar: Creating Dublin's cultural quarter', *Planning Practice and Research*, 10/2, 135–72.

—— (2004b) 'Cultural quarters as mechanisms for urban regeneration. Part 2: A review of four cultural quarters in the UK, Ireland and Australia', *Planning, Practice & Research*, 19/1, 3–31.

MORGAN, M and GRUBE, J (1994) 'The Irish and alcohol: A classic case of ambivalence', *Irish Journal of Psychology*, 15/2, 390–403.

NATIONAL ADVISORY COMMITTEE ON DRUGS (2003) *An Overview of Cocaine Use in Ireland*, Dublin: The Stationery Office

—— and ALCOHOL INFORMATION AND RESEARCH UNIT (2005) *Drug Use in Ireland and Northern Ireland, Bulletin 1*, Dublin: National Advisory Committee on Drugs.

National Alcohol Policy—Ireland (1996), Dublin: The Stationery Office.

NCC (National Crime Council) (2003) *Public Order Offences in Ireland: A report by the Institute of Criminology*, Faculty of Law, University College Dublin for the National Crime Council, Dublin: NCC.

NIC GABHAINN, S, KELLY, C and MOLCHO, M (2007) *The Irish Health Behaviour in School-aged Children (HBSC) Study* 2006, Dublin: Department of Health and Children.

O'CONNELL, M (1999) 'Is Irish public opinion towards crime distorted by media bias?', *European Journal of Communication*, 14/2, 191–212.

O'CONNOR, J (1978) *The Young Drinkers: A cross-national study of social and cultural influences*, London: Tavistock Publications.

O'DONNELL, I (2005) 'Violence and social change in the Republic of Ireland', *International Journal of the Sociology of Law*, 33, 101–17.

—— (2007a) 'A society on a knife edge', *Sunday Business Post*, 1 July 2007.

—— (2007b) 'Crime and its consequences', in T Fahey, H Russell and C Whelan (eds), *Best of Times? The social impact of the Celtic Tiger*, Dublin: Institute of Public Administration.

—— and O'SULLIVAN, E (2001) *Crime Control in Ireland*, Cork: Cork University Press.

—— —— (2003) 'The politics of intolerance, Irish style', *British Journal of Criminology*, 43/1, 41–62.

—— TELJEUR, C, HUGHES, N, BAUMER, E and KELLY, A (2007) 'When prisoners go home: Punishment, social deprivation and the geography of reintegration', *Irish Criminal Law Journal*, 17/4, 3–9.

O'MALLEY, T (2000) *Sentencing Law and Practice*, Dublin: Round Hall.

OLDENBURG, R (1999) *The Great Good Place: Cafes, coffee shops, bookstores, bars, hair salons, and other hangouts at the heart of the community*, New York: Marlowe.

PARKER, H. (2001) '"Unbelievable"? The UK's drug present', in H Parker, J Aldridge and R Egginton (eds), *UK Drugs Unlimited: New research and policy lessons on illicit drug use*, New York: Palgrave, 1–13.

PEACE, A (1992) 'No fishing without drinking: The construction of social identity in rural Ireland', in D Gefou-Madianou (ed), *Alcohol, Gender and Culture*, London: Routledge, 167–80.

PEILLON, M (2002) 'Boundaries and the metamorphosis of Ireland', in MP Corcoran and M Peillon (eds), *Ireland Unbound: A turn of the century chronicle*, Dublin: Institute of Public Administration, 1–12.

PSA (Private Security Authority) (2008) *Private Security Authority Progress Report*, Tipperary: PSA.

RAMSTEDT, M and HOPE, A (2005) 'The Irish drinking habits of 2002: Drinking and drinking-related harm in a European comparative perspective', *Journal of Substance Use*, 10/5, 274–83.

ROSSOW, I (2001) 'Alcohol and homicide: A cross-cultural comparison of the relationship in 14 European countries', *Addiction*, 96/1, 77–92.

SELECT COMMITTEE ON CRIME, LAWLESSNESS AND VANDALISM (1984) *Fourth Report of the Select Committee on Crime, Lawlessness and Vandalism*, Dublin, The Stationery Office.

SHARE, P, TOVEY, H and CORCORAN, MP (2007) *A Sociology of Ireland*, 3rd edn, Dublin: Gill & Macmillan.

SLAN (Survey of Lifestyle, Attitude and Nutrition) (2003) *The National Health and Lifestyles Surveys*, Galway: Centre for Health Promotion Studies, National University of Ireland, Galway and Department of Health and Children.

STIVERS, R (2000) *Hair of the Dog: Irish drinking and its American stereotype*, New York: Continuum.

STRATEGIC TASK FORCE ON ALCOHOL (2002) *Interim Report*, Dublin: Department of Health and Children.

—— (2004) *Second Report*, Dublin: Department of Health and Children.

Treno, A, Gruenewald, P, Remer, L, Johnson, F and LaScala, E (2007) 'Examining multi-level relationships between bars, hostility and aggression: Social selection and social influence', *Addiction*, 103, 66–77.

van Dijk, J, Manchin, R, van Kesteren, J, Nevala, S and Hideg, G (2005) *The Burden of Crime in the EU. Research Report: A comparative analysis of the European Crime and Safety Survey (EU ICS) 2005*, EU.

Vaughan, B (2003) 'Alcohol and the criminal justice system in the Republic of Ireland', in S Kilcommins and I O'Donnell (eds), *Alcohol, Society and Law*, Chichester: Barry Rose Law Publishers.

Watson, D and Parsons, S (2005) *Domestic Abuse of Women and Men in Ireland Report on the National Study of Domestic Abuse*, National Crime Council in Association with the Economic and Social Research Institute, Dublin: The Stationery Office.

Whelan, C, Layte, R, Maître, B, Gannon, B, Nolan, B, Watson, D and Williams, J (2003) *Monitoring Poverty Trends in Ireland: Results from the 2001 Living in Ireland survey*, Dublin: Economic and Social Research Institute.

6

THE NETHERLANDS

Patrick Van Calster, Joanne van der Leun, and Ninette van Hasselt[1]

INDRODUCTION

Recent attempts to transform Amsterdam's red-light district into a more 'respectable' area were dubbed 'Amsterdam's war on sex' in *Newsweek*.[2] The question was raised: 'Amsterdam without the red-light district? Wouldn't that be like Paris without the Eiffel Tower!?' A similar question can be raised about cannabis coffee shops. Over the past decade the number of coffee shops has decreased considerably and regulation of those that remain has become more stringent. Without doubt, Amsterdam's nightlife is changing. Most inhabitants of Amsterdam do not consider coffee shops and the red-light district as typical nightlife settings. Tourists, however, do.

Amsterdam's red-light district is a major tourist attraction, drawing millions of visitors from abroad every year. It is therefore not surprising that the recent clampdown on a wide range of problems ranging from sleaziness and disorder to organized crime in the city centre has attracted media attention from all over the world. Amsterdam's mayor, Job Cohen, and his aldermen[3] are very aware of the nostalgia for the red-light district—the world's most famous home of prostitution since the 15th century—which appears to be internationally shared. He is also mindful of the area's economic value. However, many Dutch people believe that the district has become tacky and sleazy and seems to be attracting the 'wrong' public. Thus the aim of the municipality is to transform the red-light district into a more upscale area with trendy restaurants, bars, galleries, and boutiques.

Of course, the red-light district with its high concentration of brothels, bars, and coffee shops does not represent Amsterdam nightlife as a whole, much less that of the Netherlands. Yet, it is relevant to analyse the changes it is undergoing, as it represents the liberal element of Dutch society that is well-known abroad, but now stands under pressure. This may come as a surprise to outsiders, given the image of Amsterdam as

---

[1] All authors contributed equally.
[2] <http://www.newsweek.com/id/109373?gt1=10856>, accessed 8 February 2008.
[3] 'Alderman' is the name given to executive members within Dutch municipal government.

a laid-back place where anything goes. Yet, the lenient Dutch approach is not only subject to profound changes, but also often misunderstood. The aim of this chapter will be to explain the way in which nightlife is conceived, celebrated, and controlled in the Netherlands through the lens of a case-study approach focusing on its most prominent exemplar, central Amsterdam.

In the Netherlands, brothels and designated prostitution zones have been officially 'tolerated' by the authorities for a long time, although owning a brothel was still illegal. In 2000, however, the laws controlling brothels were relaxed bringing prostitution involving consenting-adult sex workers into the mainstream regularized economy. Pimping and the exploitation of prostitutes remain illegal. A recent evaluation of the lifting of the ban on brothels by the Ministry of Justice (Daalder, 2007) shows that decriminalization has gone hand-in-hand with stricter enforcement of existing rules and regulations. This apparent shift from pragmatic 'tolerance' to 'intolerance' is closely connected to broader trends in the Netherlands, involving a more repressive approach to social problems, and the growth of policy 'integration' across various domains (Buruma, 2007). The effects of these socio-political shifts impact directly upon nightlife. Fighting crime and disorder has become much more of a priority than it used to be and the police are no longer seen as the only relevant actors. As noted by Garland (2001) in relation to the UK and US experience, this involves strategies of 'responsibilization' through which the state increasingly seeks to respond to crime not only through its own agencies, but also by co-opting the assistance of non-state organizations and citizens. At the same time, the power and jurisdiction of the police have expanded and public expectations regarding crime reduction have mounted. The public at large supports a toughening of crime policy, expressing the opinion that violent crime, in particular, should be punished more harshly (SCP, 2004).[4] However, trust and reliance on the government and its policy decisions has weakened.

The SCP public-opinion survey mentioned above shows that although stricter approaches towards prostitution and coffee shops may attract attention in the international media, the Dutch public are much more concerned about other nightlife issues, especially violence. This issue touches upon the dilemma of how to balance economic interests against city management. After all, nightlife is very important to the local economy, yet it also produces specific crime problems. As is well known in the field of criminology, the spatio-temporal organization of everyday life and its 'routine activities' allows for greater exposure to crime opportunities and victimization risks in some settings than in others and this is very much linked to people's lifestyles (Felson, 1997). Cities, and certain areas within them, tend to attract criminals, commonly leading to relatively high levels of crime (Glaeser and Sacerdote, 2004). Amsterdam's red-light district, but more so the famous Leidseplein and Rembrandtplein, with their high concentration of bars and clubs, attract many young people who in the process of 'going out' also expose themselves to the risk of being robbed or becoming engaged in a fight. Here economic interests and city management come into conflict. On the one hand, night-time activities in and around Leidseplein and Rembrandtplein are

---

4 The Netherlands Institute for Social Research/SCP is a government agency which conducts research into the social aspects of all areas of government policy.

of major concern to the police, with many fights and drunken people; demonstrating the close relationship between the consumption of alcohol and violence in nightlife settings. On the other hand, restaurants, bars, and clubs in these areas make a major contribution to the city's economic prosperity.

Against this background, our chapter addresses three nightlife issues in Amsterdam: interpersonal violence, 'soft drug' consumption in coffee shops, and prostitution. We begin by discussing the broader cultural context of nightlife and go on to explain the ramifications of this context for crime, disorder, and city governance. We then conclude by summarizing our findings and their wider implications.

THE CULTURAL CONTEXT OF DUTCH NIGHTLIFE

Because Amsterdam is regarded worldwide as an emblem of liberalism and freedom of expression, the political and cultural context in which the city develops is of great importance. In order to understand the Dutch approach to controversial nightlife issues such as prostitution and drugs, it is important to discuss the country's political system and its organizational approach to policy formation. In the Netherlands, governments always consist of a coalition of parties. The need to reach a consensus before action can be taken prevents policy debates from becoming strongly polarized and compromise is traditionally a crucial element. Compromises are achieved by pursuing pragmatic and above all tolerant policies (de Kort and Cramer, 1999). Tolerance is seen as a way of dealing pragmatically with social problems and trying to minimize their negative consequences (Buruma, 2007). Yet, since the mid-1990s, the famous Dutch custom of *gedogen* ('condoning') appears to be losing its positive connotations (Engbersen et al, 2007). In the broad field of public policy, the lenient stance towards welfare-benefit recipients has already been eroded and gradually replaced by a tougher standpoint. Citizens are increasingly regarded as rational actors who are largely the authors of, and therefore responsible for, their own fate. The legitimacy of claims for financial support from the state are now judged in this light (Visser and Hemerijck, 1997). Since the terrorist attacks in the USA and Europe and the Pim Fortuyn crisis (Fortuyn was a popular far-right anti-establishment politician in the Netherlands who was murdered in 2002) the Dutch electorate appears to have become increasingly critical of perceived political indifference and leniency in issues of 'security' (Buruma, 2007).

The shift from condoning to controlling is clearly demonstrated in the Dutch debate on drugs, in which, since the 1970s, a sociologically informed, welfarist, and structural perspective has been central (Boekhout van Solinge, 1999). Drug policy has long focused on the attempt to prevent cannabis users from becoming involved in more harmful drug scenes (de Kort, 1995). In 1976 this led to a formal policy of separating the drug market into 'soft' and 'hard' drugs (Boekhout van Solinge, 1990) and on reducing associated health risks. Coffee shops selling small quantities of cannabis were tolerated and became symbols of this drug policy. Tolerance weakened in the 1990s, when the high concentration of coffee shops began to give rise to complaints from the public (O+S, 2004;[5] Van Laar, 2007). Additionally, increasing cooperation with other EU countries made it more difficult for the Dutch government to maintain its distinct and comparatively liberal approach (Boekhout van Solinge, 1999). New findings about the possible impact of cannabis use on the onset of schizophrenia (Smit, Bolier, and Cuijpers, 2003), especially given increasing THC levels in Dutch cannabis (Van Laar, 2007), have also fuelled a shift in the way the drug is perceived. Since 1995, coffee shops have had to abide by strict rules, and permits for new shops are often refused. Both factors have led to a sharp decline in the number of coffee-shop establishments.

Corresponding shifts have occurred in relation to the governance of brothels. Although the criminal code was amended in 2000 to lift the ban on brothels, what has received less attention is the increase in enforcement activity applied to those forms of prostitution that remain punishable. Government bodies now monitor sex venues more frequently and thoroughly, and owners risk losing their permits if they employ undocumented migrants or minors. In some ways, therefore, prostitution has become *more* criminalized than it was when all forms of prostitution were prohibited (Daalder, 2007: 95).

Although the red-light district attracts a wide range of age groups, Amsterdam nights are dominated by youth and nightlife is an important element of youth culture. From the early 1960s onwards, new rites, music, and codes of conduct among the young led to a rapid growth in the number of bars and clubs (ter Bogt and Hibbel, 2000; Deben, 2007). At the heart of this cultural and economic renaissance was the increase in social-security provisions, set off in 1963 by claims from the labour movement for substantially higher wages. Young workers shared in this increased prosperity, enabling them to spend more time and money on their own pleasure. The stage of life in which this pleasure-seeking was most pronounced (between puberty and becoming parents) also became increasingly long; Dutch youth were in no hurry to 'settle down' (Council of Europe, 2005).

From the 1960s onwards, Dutch society became influenced by a counterculture that positioned itself as a reaction to moral conservatism and the 'pillarized' segregation of different socio-political groups.[6] Young people were the main disciples of this counterculture, and Amsterdam became its Dutch epicentre and site of pilgrimage, attracting many free spirits (de Kort 1995; Stichting Adviesbureau Drugs, 1997). Drug-taking became a symbol of the struggle against traditional culture, first among a bohemian hippie crowd and later spreading to encompass broader groups of teenagers and young adults (de Kort, 1995).

AMSTERDAM AND ITS NIGHTLIFE: SOME FACTS

Amsterdam has a population of just under 750,000 inhabitants (O+S, 2007). The city is located within the urban conurbation of the Randstad, the western part of

---

[5] O+S are the municipal Department for Research and Statistics in Amsterdam.

[6] The term 'pillarization' refers to the vertical separation of Dutch society into well-organized 'pillars' (*zuilen*) of religion and ideology. Within each pillar, ordinary Dutch citizens lived, in some ways, separate lives from those inhabiting other parts of society. However, the leaders of each pillar worked well together, enabling public life to run smoothly.

the Netherlands (Dijkstra, 2002). Despite its relatively small size, it is undoubtedly an international city. Half of Amsterdam's population were born in the Netherlands to parents also born in the Netherlands. Those born to 'non-western' migrant families represent 35 per cent of the city's citizens (O+S, 2007). The population is relatively young and more than half of households comprise one-person living alone. Amsterdam is home to many artists and a variety of people with an alternative lifestyle. Its major attractions for natives and tourists alike include bars, clubs, and cinemas, as well as the brothels and cannabis coffee shops (Boekhout van Solinge, 1999). It is one of three Dutch cities, along with Rotterdam and Utrecht, where influential social trends often begin (Nabben, Koet, and Korf, 2007). Amsterdam's most important industries are banking and financial services, business support services, and ICT. Tourism is also a major source of income, with 8 per cent of the workforce employed in this sector. After a slight drop in 2003, tourism is now growing again (O+S, 2006). The millions of tourists visiting Amsterdam each year[7] are fascinated by the Van Gogh museum and the picturesque canals, but also by the nightlife. Most tourists venture no further than the compact (8 km sq) city centre.

The number of bars and restaurants in Amsterdam has risen by more than 40 per cent over the last 25 years (Deben 2007). Every weekend, young people from across the country and abroad go partying in Amsterdam and visit at least one of the city's 36 discotheques, 1,215 bars, 234 coffee shops, or several dance events.[8] Each night they spend, on average, €24 to €40 in bars, clubs, and discotheques (Van Spronsen and Partners, 2008; Nabben, Benschop, and Korf, 2006). The total number of discotheque visitors in Amsterdam has decreased slightly in the last decade, as has the number of discotheques, whereas the number of people visiting large dance events has increased. In 2006, dance events—130 of which were held in the city's central squares—attracted more than two million visitors. Parties in trendy clubs are also becoming more popular and, given Amsterdam's contemporary profile as a multicultural city, it is not surprising that around one-quarter of discotheque visitors are migrants (Van Spronsen and Partners, 2008). This figure is expected to rise as non-white musical styles and Islamic-oriented events become increasingly prominent.

Drugs, of course, continue to play their part in Amsterdam's nightlife (Van Laar, 2007; O+S, 2008). The first coffee shops (selling cannabis) were founded in the 1970s (O+S, 2003) and, despite recent restrictions, Amsterdam still has more than any other city in the Netherlands (Van Laar, 2007). Highly concentrated in the city centre, either in, or close to, the red-light district, coffee shops hold major attractions for young tourists. The red-light district (located close to the central rail station) has its origins in the 15th century when Amsterdam was frequently visited by sailors. The district is now packed with sex shops, brothels, gay bars, cinemas, hotels, and around 250–400 'red-light windows' announcing prostitutes and other sex-related products and services. It also has several museums which attract visitors during the day, but are closed at night. As a result of globalization and in particular the growth of low-cost

---

[7] In 2006, 4.7 million people stayed in a hotel in Amsterdam and the number of nights city hotel rooms were occupied totalled a record, 8.7 million, <http://amsterdam.nl/nieuws/overzichten/actueel?ActItmIdt=72759>.

[8] O+S Tourism Factsheet: <http://www.amsterdamtourist.nl/nl/home/over+amsterdam/feiten+_xan_+cijfers/default.aspx>, accessed 1 April 2008.

airlines, young people from all over the world visit Amsterdam to party. Spending weekends abroad to party has become a common phenomenon. According to local statistics, a quarter of all tourists who visit Amsterdam attend a coffee shop, and the number of tourists continues to increase (O+S, 2003). The urban sociologist Leon Deben (2007) suggests that central Amsterdam has been 'colonized', or dominated, by visitors. Domination of public space by partygoers inevitably leads to crime-related tensions.

NIGHTLIFE AND CRIME

Although crime is now a major public and political issue in the Netherlands and the lenient stance of the past is frowned upon, Amsterdam's inhabitants continue to feel relatively safe. International comparisons show that this is more so the case than residents of, for instance, Barcelona, Paris, and Leipzig (O+S, 2004). These findings sit uneasily against the high levels of recorded crime: Amsterdam finds itself in the 'top 3' of Dutch cities with the highest number of registered crimes per 1000 residents. This is partly explained by location-specific crimes such as the 9000-plus bicycle thefts reported to the police each year (7 per cent of the total number in the Netherlands as a whole) and the vulnerability of tourists as potential victims. Of course, willingness to report such crimes may be high (O+S, 2004). Nonetheless, high crime statistics cannot be fully set aside when trying to understand city life. Over the past 15 years violent attacks on youngsters in nightlife settings have received nationwide attention. In 2007, a period in which almost all forms of recorded crime fell, public violence increased by 7.2 per cent (Politie Amsterdam Amstelland, 2007).[9] In the following paragraphs we focus forms of nightlife-related crime associated with alcohol, prostitution, and drugs.

ALCOHOL AND NIGHTLIFE VIOLENCE

The general public has little understanding or awareness of drugs, particularly 'hard' drugs, and alcohol is still seen by many as a highly innocent consumer product. Dutch parents, for example, are very relaxed about their children drinking at a young age (de Graaf, Smit, and Verdurmen, 2007). Although alcohol consumption in the Netherlands does not deviate from the European average, Dutch youngsters drink more frequently and start drinking at an earlier age than most of their European peers (Verdurmen et al, 2005). Tolerance is undoubtedly displayed, both in terms of parental attitudes and also in the way that entrepreneurs go largely unpunished for selling alcohol to minors despite this being prohibited by law. Increases in alcohol consumption among youngsters, and new insights into the effects of alcohol on the maturing brain, have led to unprecedented political and societal attention. This is now beginning to

---

[9] General trends in registered crime in the Netherlands show a strong increase between 1960 and 2000, partially due to changes in recording practice and shifting police activity. In recent years, figures for property offences have fallen. Violent crime has risen since 1975. Victimization data confirm this rise, but also demonstrates that the 'dark figure' of violent offences is declining as a result of improved data collection by the police (Wittebrood and Junger, 2002).

have an impact on local and national policies and is, in turn, transforming the regulation of nightlife settings.

In the Netherlands, as in most European countries, alcohol is nightlife's drug of choice. Its use is very common in nearly all youth cultures. At a population level, alcohol consumption increased from the 1960s and peaked in the 1980s. It then decreased a little to the current level of 8.45 quarts (8 litres) of pure alcohol per inhabitant per year;[10] however, among young people, consumption has continued to rise (Verdurmen et al, 2005). Economic growth, strong marketing impulses from the alcohol industry, and the prolonged opening hours of clubs and pubs have all been important factors which may explain these trends. Some claim that alcohol's increasing popularity among the young is related to the rise of an informal lifestyle in which feelings and physical sensations are valued above rationality and fixed moral codes (van den Brink, 2001).

The increases in youth violence and young people's alcohol consumption have both taken place in the last decade. Many socio-economic factors have impacted upon both problems, and it seems likely that the increases are not only parallel, but also related. Dutch research among the instigators and victims of violent crime suggest that: (1) excessive drinking (and drug-taking) is relatively more common among these groups than among the general population (Bieleman et al, 1998); and (2) being drunk increases one's chances of victimization; however, young people expect that others will protect them if they behave foolishly (Van der Linden et al, 2004a, b). Many violent incidents are regarded by the media as 'senseless' to the extent that bystanders see no apparent need or reason for the aggression. Yet, the term is highly problematic as the factors precipitating this kind of violence are often complex and multifaceted (de Haan, 2000). Alcohol appears to play its part in at least two ways. First, it reduces the drinker's ability to decipher and negotiate instances of provocation (Brouwers, 2007). Second, some people seem to associate drinking with the search for a 'Saturday night fight', especially when this involves fighting among rival groups (Terlouw et al, 1999). In this way, alcohol is intentionally used to achieve relaxation and is a source of identification with one's peers (Van der Linden et al, 2004a, b), helping achieve what the Anglo-Saxon world calls 'Dutch Courage'!: the willingness to rise to a challenge.

DRUGS AND NIGHTLIFE

Patterns of drug use in the Netherlands are similar to those in other Western European countries, with cannabis being the most popular controlled substance. 'Party drugs' such as ecstasy and cocaine are rarely used by the general population, but regular participants in nightlife consume them five times as often as those who like to stay at home (Trimbos Instituut, 2007). Despite the relatively high level of drug use in nightlife settings, drug-related crime problems are limited. Heroin users are the only problematic category in this respect. Heroin became popular among some specific groups during the second half of the 1970s (de Kort, 1995). Heroin addicts financed their habits through theft and (street) prostitution (Grapendaal et al, 1991). They did

---

[10] <http://www.rivm.nl/vtv/object_document/o1191n19086.html>, accessed 2 April 2008. RIVM is the National Institute for Public Health and the Environment, an advisory body to the Dutch government.

not participate in nightlife as such, but their 'working area' was the red-light district, where many tourists were confronted with the Dutch heroin scene. Although their visibility led many tourists to think that the Dutch heroin problem was huge, this was never the case. Amsterdam currently has around 4–5,000, mostly male, heroin users. They are an aging population (average ages now exceed 40 years of age) and about half of them receive treatment for their addiction.[11]

Using stimulants (such as cocaine and amphetamines) can play a role in the onset of aggressive and sometimes excessive and unpredictably violent behaviour, in particular, in combination with alcohol (Duijvestijn, 2004). This is of growing concern, as this combination is becoming more popular among clubbers in Amsterdam (Nabben et al, 2007). When offenders engage in violence after having used hard drugs, they tend to feel less responsible for their deeds (Van der Linden et al, 2004a).

Due to its calming effects, the use of cannabis causes very little problems in nightlife. However, in the early 1990s, the high concentration of coffee shops in the centre of Amsterdam did cause much public irritation. In 1995 it was decided that the number of coffee shops would be dramatically reduced by closing all those engaged in illegal activities such as money laundering and the trade in illegal drugs. The remainder were then licensed by the council and the issuing of new licences was frozen. Coffee shops that close are not replaced, so their overall numbers continue to diminish. These policy changes are primarily aimed at fighting organized crime rather than combating drug use.

PROSTITUTION AND CRIME

In a similar way, the relations between prostitution and crime are largely hidden. Now that prostitution is officially permitted, the attention of the authorities has turned towards underlying problems such as human trafficking, exploitation and the extent to which organized crime operates within the city centre's real-estate sector. These problems, however, impact very little on the experience of nightlife for visitors. Tourists are more affected by the pickpockets and thieves who target crowded city-centre venues and outdoor spaces. In 2004, over 8,000 of Amsterdam's foreign visitors reported an offence to the police (8 per cent of all reported crimes). Almost half of these cases pertained to pickpocketing or theft from a car. The offences often took place in the city centre and/or on public transport. Every year, the special NGO Amsterdam Tourist Assistance Service (ATAS) offers support to hundreds of tourists who have become victims of theft or robbery (O+S, 2006). Other problems surround the fear of crime in public spaces, which led in the 1970s and 80s to the decision to close certain alleys.[12] Nowadays this appears to be less of an issue. Local politicians, leisure entrepreneurs, and inhabitants in favour of reclaiming public space have tried to have the alleys re-opened; such plans remain contested.

---

[11] <http://www.iamsterdam.com/introducing/government_politics/policies/drugs>, accessed 29 July 2008.

[12] In the 1970s and 80s the level of (drug-related) crime and incivilities was high (specific areas such as de Zeedijk were even regarded as no-go areas). As a result, the municipality decided to fence off many small public alleyways.

POLICY RESPONSES

So far in this chapter we have argued that nightlife-related crime and public violence in particular, appears to be strongly influenced by the use of alcohol, more so than by prostitution or illicit drugs. One of the difficulties in tackling problems associated with alcohol is the widespread acceptability of its use. People from all walks of life drink alcohol, and above all it is a major source of income for the leisure and tourist economy in Amsterdam. However, the relationship between crime and disorder on the one hand and alcohol on the other is becoming a matter of public concern and of concern to the authorities.

THE TRIANGLE COMMITEE

Amsterdam's mayor (as the head of municipal government) is responsible for maintaining public order in the city and works closely with the chief of police on matters of administrative policing (*bestuurlijke politie*). In relation to judicial and sentencing matters, local police activity is managed by the Public Prosecution Department. All three parties come together in the so-called 'Triangle Committee'. Local crime policies are developed by this committee and measures are fine-tuned to the local context. The Triangle dictates priorities, which, for the city centre, include dealing with 'persistent offenders'—often drug-addicted youngsters—and prostitution.[13]

More specifically, the Triangle Committee provides an overarching framework for the work of the 14 city district subcommittees. Each subcommittee includes a representative of the mayor, a representative of the Public Prosecution Department, and a representative of the chief of police. Through this policy framework and procedure all of the city's officials play an important role in developing crime-prevention strategies for their area. The mayor also coordinates the Amsterdam Safety Policy which strives for an integrated approach with input from various public and private partners. The Policy has a social safety component and a physical safety component. The first aims to establish safety by focusing on the persistent offenders who are responsible for a high proportion of the city's crime. The second component, physical safety, focuses on fire, disaster, and accident prevention, prioritizing work around large public events.

In terms of policy development and implementation, both arms are steeped in a partnership approach. Local public authorities such as the police and the administration of justice are engaged in partnerships with hospitals, department stores, the tax office, bars and restaurants, among others. The operators of bars, clubs, discotheques, and coffee shops, together with private security companies, the organizers of dance events, and brothel owners, work with the public authorities in tackling problems of crime and disorder. This line of communication allows intelligence-led security policies to be moulded. Moreover, in engaging with partners, the state's monopoly on crime control is broken. Amsterdam's authorities aim, where possible, to develop alternatives to the criminal justice system, custom-made to fit the specificity of local security issues. To this end, the City has created the post of 'Neighbourhood

---

[13] <http://www.eenveiligamsterdam.nl/themas/stadsdelen/centrum>, accessed 27 July 2008.

Coordinator' (*Buurtregisseur*). The Coordinators, who are typically (but not exclusively) police officers, act as 'champions' for their local area, collecting data, bringing parties together, and attempting to enrol and empower people, institutions, and enterprises in the fight against crime. There are 220 Neighbourhood Coordinators across Amsterdam as a whole. Remaining at an area-specific level, the following paragraphs focus on nightlife and its governance in two of Amsterdam's major party zones.

POLICING THE LEIDSEPLEIN AND THE REMBRANDTPLEIN

Each week the Leidseplein and the Rembrandtplein areas of the city attract tens of thousands of visitors. The charm of both squares lies in their restaurants, bars, theatres, and cinemas. During the evening and for much of the night, this mixture spells amusement, but also disorder: pickpocketing, violence, and alcohol abuse. Annually, 1,500 cases of violence are recorded in these Amsterdam squares alone.[14] Most violence takes place when the nightclubs and discotheques close and the squares fill with people. Since 1998, many new measures have been taken to try to address these problems.

One such measure is the introduction of a so-called 'cool-down' hour. Discotheques are allowed to stay open after their official closing time, on the condition that bartenders stop selling alcohol to the clients. In this way, the authorities hope to accomplish a more gradual departure of people from the squares. Moreover, by introducing alternative routes for taxi drivers, noise pollution decreases; whilst public transport providers ease the busyness of the squares by providing bus services between 2.00 and 4.00 am. In addition, bars and cafés are subject to very strict rules and regulations. These regulations are intended to secure, among others things, the health and safety of venue staff, their clients, and the general public. These measures are contained in the Alcohol Licensing and Catering Act (7 October 1964 and amendments) which, among other things, forbids the sale of alcohol to children and to drunks. The Act also controls the training of bar managers and stipulates house rules for bars and cafés. Bouncers, for example, have to qualify for the profession, which means they are trained in social skills and specific sections of the penal code. Body-searching by bouncers has become a normal procedure in Amsterdam. Most cafés and bars have even installed metal detectors. When confronted with the illegal possession of firearms or drugs, bouncers must place the items in specially made deposit boxes, emptied every Monday morning by the police. Police and bouncers meet two or three times a year to discuss both problems and solutions. There have been other specific initiatives in the squares, such as 'Project Streetwise'. This police campaign, informed by 'Broken Windows Theory' (Wilson and Kelling, 1982) focused on public urination, aggressive behaviour, and vandalism. The police are now very strict in relation to these matters and do not condone any disorderly behaviour. In addition, cameras and other electronic surveillance measures have moved to the fore.

Drug use in the Netherlands is controlled by the Opium Act (4 October 1919 and amendments). The Act draws a distinction between drugs with particularly high health

---

14 <http://www.eenveiligamsterdam.nl>, accessed 29 July 2008.

risks ('hard' drugs such as heroin and cocaine) and cannabis products (hashish and marijuana). This enables the criminal justice system to focus on the trafficking and dealing of hard drugs (Boekhout van Solinge, 1999). The sale of cannabis is tolerated and even regulated, yet not fully decriminalized. Although in principle people can be prosecuted for drug possession, in practice, this tends not to occur. This is because the Dutch Ministry of Justice applies the *gedoogbeleid* (tolerance policy) with regard to 'soft' drugs: an official set of guidelines telling public prosecutors under which conditions not to prosecute an activity that is officially forbidden. *Gedoogbeleid* is in fact the institutionalized version of a practice commonly found in other countries, namely that law enforcement officers have to make priorities on which offences are important enough to spend limited resources on. Coffee-shop owners have to comply with many rules which stipulate that they are forbidden from advertising, must not allow the sale and use of hard drugs on their premises, must not sell to minors, must prevent public disturbances, and must not exceed a quantity threshold of five grams of cannabis per customer. Five grams has long been the officially tolerated amount for personal use. Cannabis was only policed where persons were found to possess larger amounts which led to the suspicion that they were dealers, or where drug use was implicated in public disturbances. However, Van Bakkum (2008) has highlighted the increasingly hard line adopted by police in pursuing 'fixers', those people who do not consider themselves to be dealers, but who adopt the role of obtaining drugs in bulk for a group of their friends. Van Bakkum regards this shift in police practice as symptomatic of wider moves from liberal tolerance to repression in Dutch drugs and criminal justice policy. Drug researchers at Amsterdam's Trimbos Institute have recently argued in favour of an evaluation of the Dutch National Drugs Policy. According to these experts, the distinctions drawn between the effects of hard and soft drugs were never fully evaluated. In March 2008, the Dutch government agreed to their demands and ordered an evaluation of 30 years of Dutch drug policy.

Police drug enforcement operations receive assistance from the so-called *Horeca-Interventieteam* (HIT).[15] The HIT is a body with overarching authority for labour inspection, taxation, food and goods standards, and the investigation of social security fraud, among other duties. It consequently has the authority to close bars and discotheques where there is evidence of hard-drug use and other safety irregularities during dance events. The HIT scans businesses for tax evasion and illegal labour. It also checks if bars, pubs, and restaurants comply with licensing and hygiene instructions. Its main goal is to encourage bona fide businesses by tackling dishonest competition. It is also concerned with the prevention of human trafficking.

In comparison with the policy responses to disorderly behaviour, responses to prostitution have taken a somewhat different path. As noted, up until 2000, prostitution was legally forbidden, yet officially 'tolerated'. Following the legalization of brothels in 2000, a further law was introduced on 1 October 2002 penalizing all forms of exploitation in the prostitution sector, including the employment of under-18-year-olds (s 250(a) of the Dutch Criminal Code was tightened, extended, and renumbered, resulting in a new set of laws under s 273(f)). Administrative responsibility in this field lies with

---

[15] <http://www.politie-amsterdam-amstelland.nl/frameset/get.cfm?id=85>, accessed 29 July 2008.

local authorities (Daalder, 2007) and the city of Amsterdam promotes an integrated policy on prostitution, focusing on three issues. First, brothels are only allowed in areas approved by the municipal zoning plan and up to a specified maximum number. Second, it imposes ordinances prescribing instructions for hygiene and security. Third, brothel operators are banned from employing illegal immigrants and minors.

Finally, new legal instruments and measures are being introduced in an attempt to tackle infiltration of the brothel, coffee shop, and other licensed sectors by organized crime. Under the Public Administration Probity Screening Act (20 June 2002), commonly termed the 'BIBOB Act', administrative bodies have the power to refuse to issue, or to withdraw, licences if there are serious risks that they are, or may be, used to facilitate crime or obtain financial benefits from illegal activities. In 2006, the Amsterdam authorities began to use criminal record 'integrity tests' to evaluate those wishing to operate a brothel (Daalder, 2007) and recently revoked the licences of two well-known sex venues.

WHO OWNS THE NIGHT? SOME FINAL REMARKS

According to Ulrich Beck (1992), political debates and discourses about crime and insecurity are in some ways hypocritical, since a number of important problems seem to result from regulatory failure. For each solution, additional problems arise. Moreover, measures often result in unintended outcomes (Van Calster, 2007; Van Calster and Verfaillie, 2007). From this critical angle one could go as far as arguing that policymakers increasingly find themselves incapable of exercising influence and can do little more than seek refuge in symbolic action and rhetoric. Several years ago, the political scientist Van der Wouden (1995: 50) warned that policymaking in the Netherlands had descended into 'administrative fuss' and 'symbolic policy'. For him, too many measures were being applied at the same time, leading to aimless malaise. As a result, political decision-making and implementation falls back into old routines under new labels. Public authorities are primarily concerned with reassuring the public and upholding the idea that crime and insecurity can be controlled. In combination with the fact that feelings of insecurity are very hard to influence at a local level, and the complication that powerful economic interests must also be reconciled, crime and disorder goals appear even more difficult to meet.

Is this also the case for the city of Amsterdam? In 2005, Amsterdam's local audit concluded that both reported crime and the fear of crime had reduced. Victimization surveys confirmed that the improvements were more pronounced than elsewhere in the country (Rekenkamer, 2005). According to the audit, however, it is not clear to what extent these changes may be directly related to local policy initiatives. Policy goals had been formulated only vaguely and in most cases overlapped with earlier policy goals. In sum, the audit was highly critical of the municipality, remarking on its lack of vision and coordination (Rekenkamer, 2005: 122). Understandably, the City chose to focus on the positive outcomes of the report and claimed success.

In this chapter we have tried to show that nightlife problems do not arise in a social vacuum. They are the result of far-reaching social changes and are not necessarily driven by public policy. Second, when a precise analysis of the problems and intended outcomes is lacking, measures may misfire and evaluation is nigh impossible. Whilst the tolerance and leniency of the past are now blamed for many tenacious crime problems, the new concerted repressive and preventative approach may raise its own specific problems and backlashes.

Will the new 'tougher' measures lead to a safer nightlife? With the work of Beck (1992) in mind, one could also ask what their unintended effects might be. Will the red-light district really be transformed into an upscale area where laws and regulations are obeyed and which attracts a 'better' segment of the tourist market? Will it lose its heart and soul, as some fear? Or will the city centre retain its old character, despite all efforts to change it? Whatever the outcomes may be, we have tried to make clear that contrary to what outsiders may think, nightlife problems appear to be less related to prostitution and drugs than to the use of alcohol. Public violence, for example, goes hand-in-hand with the misuse of alcohol, sometimes combined with drugs. Dutch youngsters drink more than many of their European counterparts and this, combined with society's tolerant attitude towards alcohol, means that the problem will not disappear any time soon.

Over the past few years much knowledge has been gained concerning the most effective means of preventing alcohol-related harms (Anderson and Baumberg, 2006). These measures should be an integral part of the crime prevention package, but do not always find favour with the operators of pubs and clubs since they often involve a reduction in alcohol's availability and hence its sales. Due to the economic importance of their industry, the position of café and bar owners is strong and one wonders how likely it is that the partnership approach will be fully embraced when economic interests are threatened. In addition, there is little cooperation between health promotion workers and the police despite strong evidence that the success of alcohol interventions in nightlife settings depends on strong multi-agency partnerships between health, criminal justice, and private businesses in implementing a combination of interventions (Bellis and Hughes, 2008).

Helped by its free-bird image, Amsterdam still attracts millions of tourists each year. These visitors contribute to the cosmopolitan atmosphere of the city's nightlife and to its economy. Yet, as we have tried to show, the Netherlands is currently witnessing a strong turnaround in all public policy domains and this has directly impacted upon Amsterdam's nightlife. Crime is redefined in more diffuse terms such as 'insecurity' and 'disorder' which policymakers try to combat with new plans and regulations within the framework of a partnership approach. From a dialectic perspective, the current breakdown in tolerance with respect to prostitution and drugs can even be understood as a new countermovement. Repression and prevention are visible in all domains and tolerance of disorder and organized crime has eroded.

The changes in Amsterdam are still too new for us to speculate as to what intended or unintended outcomes will prevail. Yet, it is clear that crime is fully interwoven with the night-time economy. In the 1980s, the New York Police Department deployed the slogan: "We own the night" to underline that the police ruled the city. In 2007, the same sentence found expression in the movie *We Own the Night* (dir. J. Gray) in which a New York nightclub owner had to choose between submitting to extortion from the Russian mafia and obeying American law. In Amsterdam we might conclude that the night can never be owned by one single party. Many problems of crime and disorder are directly related to mainstream 'routine activities'. Laws, regulations, professionals and partnerships can only control urban nightlife to a limited extent. Amsterdam without its nightlife would certainly be like Paris without the Eiffel Tower.

REFERENCES

All internet sources were accessible 20 August 2008

ANDERSON, P and BAUMBERG, B (2006) *Alcohol in Europe*, London: Institute of Alcohol Studies.

BECK, U (1992) *Risk Society: Towards a new modernity*, London, Sage.

BELLIS, MA and HUGHES K (2008) 'Comprehensive strategies to prevent alcohol-related violence', *IPC Review*, 2, 137–68.

BIELEMAN, B, MAARSINGH, H and MEIJER, G (1998) *Aangeschoten Wild: Onderzoek naar Jongeren, Alcohol, Drugs en Agressie Tijdens het Uitgaan*, Groningen: Stichting Intraval.

BOEKHOUT VAN SOLINGE, T (1999) 'Dutch drug policy in a European context', *Journal of Drugs Issues*, 29/3, 511–28.

BOGT, T TER and HIBBEL, B (2000) *Wilde Jaren: Een eeuw Jeugdcultuur*, Utrecht: Uitgeverij Lemma.

BROUWERS, R (2007) *Impulsief Gewelddadig Gedrag*, Nijmegen: WLP.

BURUMA, Y (2007) 'Dutch tolerance on drugs, prostitution and euthanasia', in MH Tonry and CCJH Bijleveld (eds), *Crime and Justice in the Netherlands*, Crime and Justice, 35, Chicago, Ill: University of Chicago Press, 73–113.

Council of Europe (2005) *Recent Demographic Developments in Europe*, Strasbourg: Council of Europe Publishing.

DAALDER, AL (2007) *Onderzoek en Beleid: Prostitutie in Nederland na Opheffing van het Bordeelverbod*, The Hague: Wetenschappelijk Onderzoek- en Documentatiecentrum van het Ministerie van Justitie/Boom Juridische Uitgevers.

DEBEN, L (2007) *De Amsterdamse Binnenstad en de Openbare Ruimte: Gebruik, Beheer en Beleving*, Amsterdam: University of Amsterdam.

DIJKSTRA, LW (2002) 'Amsterdam, Netherlands', in M Ember and C Ember (eds), *Encyclopedia of Urban Cultures*, Danbury, Conn: Grolier Publishers.

DUIJVESTEIN, HH (2004) *Uitgaansgeweld: Oorzaken en Preventie*, The Hague: Stichting Maatschappij en Onderneming.

FELSON, R (1997) 'Routine activities and involvement in violence as actor, witness, or target', *Violence and Victims*, 12/3, 209–21.

GARLAND, D (2001) *The Culture of Control: Crime and social order in contemporary society*, Oxford: Oxford University Press.

GLAESER, EL and SACERDOTE, B (1999) 'Why is there more crime in cities?', *The Journal of Political Economy*, 107/6, 225–58.

GRAAF, I DE, SMIT, E and VERDURMEN, J (2007) *Uitstellen van Alcoholgebruik Door Jongeren: Hoe stel je Regels in de Opvoeding?* Utrecht: Trimbos Instituut.

GRAPENDAAL, M, LEUW, E and NELEN, H (1991) *De Economie van het Drugbestaan: Criminaliteit als Expressie van Levensstijl en Loopbaan*, Arnhem: Gouda Quint.

HAAN, W DE (2000) *Geweld: Gemeld en Geteld*, The Hague: WODC.

KORT, M DE (1995) *Tussen Patient en Delinquent: Geschiedenis van het Nederlandse Drugsbeleid*, Hilversum: Uitgeverij Verloren.

—— and CRAMER, T (1999) 'Pragmatism versus Ideology: Dutch drugs policy continued', *Journal of Drugs Issues*, 29/3, 473–92.

NABBEN, T, BENSCHOP, A and KORF, DJ (2006) *Antenne 2005: Trends in Alcohol, Tabak en Drugs bij Jonge Amsterdammers*, Amsterdam: Rozenberg Publishers.

—— KOET, S and KORF, DJ (2007) *Nl.Trendwatch: Gebruikersmarkt Uitgaasdrugsin Nederland 2006–2007*, Amsterdam: Rozenberg Publishers.

O+S (Department for Research and Statistics, Amsterdam) (2003) *Amsterdamse Coffeeshops: Gereguleerde Attractie*, <http://www.os.amsterdam.nl/pdf/2003_factsheets_5>.

—— (2004) *Urban Audit: Amsterdam in Europees Perspectief*, Factsheet, Amsterdam: Bureau Onderzoek en Statistiek.

—— (2006) *Factsheet Toerisme*, <http://www.os.amsterdam.nl/pdf/2006_factsheets_1.pdf>.

—— (2007) *Kerncijfers Bevolking*, <http://www.os.amsterdam.nl/tabel/7206/>.

—— (2008) *Less Coffee Shops in Amsterdam, 22–05–2007*, <http://www.os.amsterdam.nl/nieuws/10316>.

POLITIE AMSTERDAM AMSTELLAND (2007) *Jaaroverzicht 2007*, Amsterdam; Politie Amsterdam Amstelland.

REKENKAMER AMSTERDAM (2005) *Van Beleid naar Uitvoering, Deelstudie Centrale Stad*, Amsterdam: Rekenkamer Amsterdam.

SCP (Sociaal Cultureel Planbureau) (2004) *In het Zicht van de Toekomst: Sociaal en Cultureel Rapport 2004*, Den Haag: SCP.

SMIT, F, BOLIER, L and CUIJPERS, P (2003) 'Cannabisgebruik Waarschijnlijk Oorzakelijke Factor bij het Ontstaan van Latere Schizofrenie', *Nederlands Tijdschrift voor Geneeskunde*, 147/44, 2178–83.

STICHTING ADVIESBURO DRUGS (1997) *Disco and Drugs: Een Analyse van de Relatie Tussen Uitgaan en Drugs*, Amsterdam: Stichting Adviesburo Drugs.

TERLOUW, GJ, HAAN, WJM DE and BEKE, BWMA (1999) *Geweld, Gemeld en Geteld*, Arnhem: Advies en Onderzoeksgroep Beke.

TRIMBOS INSTITUUT (2007) *Factsheet: Alcohol- en Drugspreventie in het Uitgaanscircuit*, Utrecht: Trimbos Instituut.

VAN BAKKUM, F (2008) 'Zero (in)tolerance: Counteracting the sliding scale of Dutch drug policy to repression', paper presented at Club Health 2008, Santa Eularia, Ibiza, June.

VAN CALSTER, P (2007) 'Politietechnieken en Methoden: Balans of Regelrechte Contradictie', in P Van Calster, S De Kimpe, A Dormaels and E Hendrickx (eds), *Wie is de baas van de Lokale Politie? Balans tussen Community Policing en het Gebruik van Ingrijpende Politietechnieken*, Brussels: Politeia, 133–46.

—— and VERFAILLIE, K (2007) 'Het Strafrechtsysteem als Narratief Proces. Over de Illusie van Maakbaarheid en Controle', in P Van Calster, E Christiaens, A Enhus, S Nuytiens and S Snacken (eds), *Liber Amicorum Christiaen Eliaerts*, Brussels: University Press Brussels, 319–32.

VAN DEN BRINK, G (2001) *Geweld als Uitdaging: De Betekenis van Agressief Geweld bij Jongeren*, Utrecht: NIZW Uitgeverij.

VAN DER LINDEN, J, KNIBBE, RA, VERDURMEN, JEE and VAN DIJK, AP (2004a) *Geweld bij Uitgaan op Straat: Algemeen Bevolkingsonderzoek naar de Invloed van Alcohol- en Drugsgebruik*, Maastricht: Universiteit Maastricht.

VAN DER LINDEN, KNIBBE, RA and JOOSTEN, J (2004b) *Daders en Slachtoffers aan het Woord: Een Exploratief Onderzoek naar Uitgaansgeweld*, Maastricht: Universiteit Maastricht.

VAN DER WOUDEN, R (1995) 'Integraal Veiligheidsbeleid tussen Symboliek en Bestuurlijke Drukte', *Justitiële Verkenningen*, 5, 49–61.

VAN LAAR, M (2007) *Nationale Drugs Monitor, Jaarbericht 2006*, Utrecht: Trimbos Institute.

VAN SPRONSEN AND PARTNERS (2008) *De Discotheek 2008, Profiel van de Discothekenbranche*, Leiderdorp: van Spronsen and Partners.

VERDURMEN, J, ABRAHAM, M, PLANIJE, M, MONSHOUWER, K, DORSELAAR, S van, SCHULTEN, I, BEVERS, J and VOLLENBERGH, W (2005) *Alcoholgebruik en Jongeren Onder de 16 Jaar. Schadelijke Effecten en Effectiviteit van Alcoholinterventies*, Utrecht: Trimbos Instituut.

VISSER, J and HEMERIJCK, A (1997) *A Dutch Miracle: Job growth, welfare reform and corporatism in the Netherlands*, Amsterdam: Amsterdam University Press.

WILSON, JQ and KELLING, GL (1982) 'Broken windows: The police and neighborhood safety', *The Atlantic Monthly*, March, 29–38.

WITTEBROOD, K and JUNGER, M (2002) 'Trends in violent crime: A comparison between police statistics and victimisation surveys', *Social Indicators Research*, 59/ 2, 153–73.

SELECTED WEBSITES FOR FURTHER INFORMATION

<http://www.amsterdam.nl/>.
<http://www.eenveiligamsterdam.nl/>.
<http://www.rivm.nl/vtv>.
<http://www.newsweek.com>.
<http://www.iamsterdam.com>.

7

NORWAY

Arvid Skutle, Jane Mounteney, and Vibeke Johannessen

INTRODUCTION

Norway is a sparsely settled country with a population of approximately 4.5 million. Most urban areas are concentrated along the southern coasts and valleys, where the cities of Oslo, Bergen, Stavanger, Kristiansand, and Drammen are located. Further north along the coast is Trondheim and in the extreme north are Narvik, Tromsø, and Hammerfest. The standard of living is relatively high and crime and illegal drug consumption rates are low in comparison with most other European countries (Politidirektoratet, 2007). Norway is renowned for its restrictive alcohol and drugs policies. For much of the 20th century, alcohol was both limited in availability and high in price, with the sales of wine, liquor, and strong beer being controlled by the government-owned Norwegian Wine and Spirits Monopoly. The Norwegian temperance movement has a long and active history. Regulatory policies and strategies have been prioritized, including the use of alcohol monopolies, restrictions on sales and serving times, prohibitions on advertising, strict age limits, and high taxation. Such approaches have played an important role in ensuring that Norway has unusually low levels of alcohol consumption and alcohol-related harms in a European context (NOU, 2007). However, despite the apparent success of Norwegian alcohol policies, it is now possible to identify important liberalizing and countervailing trends. Whilst some municipalities still prohibit alcohol sales outside of the state-controlled outlets, the numbers adopting this approach are dwindling. The sale of beer and cider in supermarkets is now permitted in most areas and the traditional government wine monopolies have had a facelift, shifting from counter service to self-service, supermarket-style trading formats.

Pressure to deregulate has arisen as a result of political campaigning by liberal reformers and as an adjunct to the growing economic importance of the entertainment industry. Norwegian policymakers now face a major challenge in finding ways to accommodate the increasing number of restaurants, nightclubs, and pubs, whilst retaining measures that will limit alcohol-related harm and preserve public safety. Over the last decade there has been a significant increase in the number of licensed premises and this, alongside an extension in opening hours, has contributed to a rise in crime and disorder in nightlife settings. Recent years have also witnessed a steady rise in national levels of alcohol consumption. The typical Nordic drinking culture, characterized by infrequent but intense sessions, has become more widespread, especially among young adults. However, increasing numbers of Norwegians are also adopting 'Continental European' drinking habits involving more frequent, but moderate, consumption. The nature of socializing and of leisure time is also changing, particularly in cities, where designer bars, pavement cafés, and themed pubs are increasingly popular as a new type of meeting place.

This chapter begins by outlining the unusual history of alcohol regulation in Norway. It goes on to describe some particular aspects of the nation's drinking culture and their associations with nightlife and crime. The chapter then moves to a consideration of wider recreational drug use in Norway's second largest city, Bergen. Informed by the previous work of one of the authors (Mounteney and Leirvåg, 2004), this discussion focuses on an innovative approach to the monitoring of substance use trends. In the penultimate paragraphs, the chapter locates various policy responses to alcohol- and drug-related harm within the shifting context of Norway's new 'nighttime economy'. The chapter concludes by sketching out the political and economic dimensions of such problems and the challenges that lie ahead for public health and criminal justice agencies.

ALCOHOL LEGISLATION

Historically, alcohol has not been readily available in many areas of Norway. The Ministry of Health and Social Care has primary responsibility for national alcohol policy and for 'Alkoholloven', the law introduced in 1989 to regulate sales of alcoholic beverages in order to limit social and individual harm. This legislation forbids the sale of alcohol to anyone under the age of 18, and drinks of over 22 per cent proof cannot be sold to anyone under 20. The law also prohibits licensed premises from selling alcohol to persons who are 'obviously under the influence of alcohol or drugs'. Under this law, local authorities are responsible for issuing and enforcing liquor licences in their area, on the basis of local-level assessments. Licences have a four-year duration period and are granted on the basis of criteria such as the number of existing venues in an area and other environmental factors: the venue's target audience, traffic and transport issues, and local business and community impact. Some authorities maintain a restrictive approach and there are still towns where beer can only be bought in the local beer monopoly. Authorities also use the licensing system to control the opening and closing times of venues.

Local authorities are required by law to conduct at least three enforcement visits ('controls') per year to check compliance at the establishments they licence. They can recruit their own group of part-time inspectors or alternatively hand the job over to a private security company. Either way, the local authority remains responsible for training the inspectors. Venues which contravene the licensing laws face having their licence revoked for a period decided by the local authority. One of the idiosyncrasies of the Norwegian system is that such sanctions can differ considerably from one local authority to another. In 2006, almost half of Norwegian local authorities withdrew licences from one or more premises in their area.

Despite this enforcement activity, the availability of alcohol has increased markedly in almost all of the country's 431 municipalities. Since the mid-1990s, there has been a doubling in the number of licensed premises in urban areas and 60 per cent of local authorities have now extended opening hours beyond midnight (Lauritzen, 2008). Moreover, although taxes levied on alcohol in Norway are among the highest in Europe, an increase in average income levels has made drinking more affordable.

NORWEGIAN DRINKING CULTURE

Norway has a strong temperance tradition and levels of alcohol consumption among the general population remain among the lowest in Europe. As indicated, however, there are signs of change. In 1995, annual registered sales were estimated at 4.8 litres of pure alcohol per inhabitant aged 15 years or more; by 2006 this had risen to 6.4 litres (Bryhni, 2007). Homemade beer and spirits have historically been the main alcoholic beverages and around one-third of all alcohol consumed is obtained unofficially (and untaxed) through smuggling, private winemaking, and home distilling.

The high price of drinks in official outlets has fuelled a cultural phenomenon known as the *vorspiel* or pre-party. *Vorspiel* involves meeting and drinking at someone's home in the evening, before later going out to a bar or club at around midnight. After a few hours 'on the town', it is not uncommon to end up at a *nachspiel*—an after-hours party—also in a private home, where people continue drinking into the early hours. Norway has a tradition of 'binge drinking', with consumption of large quantities in one session often leading to inebriation. The historical roots of such practices may be traced to Viking times when drinking to intoxication was an end in itself. This is still evident in the weekend drinking culture, especially common among younger groups.

Each year, Norwegian students celebrate the end of their 13-year school career with a public party known as *russefeiring*—a highly visible, but little researched, Norwegian phenomenon. Almost all students completing sixth-form education adopt the traditional uniform of red dungarees and hat and participate in public partying, games, and drunkenness for 17 days between the 1 May and the Norwegian National Day on the 17 May. To wash one's uniform during this period appears to be against the protocol! Sande (2000) describes the *russefeiring* as a modern-day rite of passage from childhood to adulthood, where alcohol plays a key role. The roots of the tradition lie in a 19th-century initiation ritual for wealthy students joining Oslo University. Students elect their own council each year, which decides on a programme and set of rules (*knuteregler*) for conducting the list of wild and boundary-breaking tasks the '*russ*' must perform in public to win a symbol (*knute*) for their hat. These tasks include various challenges: for example, drinking 24 bottles of beer in 24 hours, or running naked through the town centre. Such rules and pranks change from year to year. Sande describes *russefeiring* as a kind of alcohol-related sport, where the goal is to get as drunk as possible and get as many symbols as you can during the period. It is also common for '*russ*' participants to team up in small groups and buy a vehicle, usually an old van (always painted red and decorated for the period). These notoriously unreliable vans become a home-away-from-home and means of travel from party to party. Unsurprisingly, these hedonistic celebrations are a cause for concern for many parents, police, and health promotion agencies, whilst providing a supply of extravagant stories for the media.

Wine consumption and high-frequency low-dosage drinking has also become more widespread, especially among affluent young Norwegians. Modern designer cafés have become very popular as a meeting place for these groups. A typical example is when four friends in their early 20s meet at a down-town café in the afternoon, are served by trendy waiters, and order one glass of wine, one café latte, one bottle of water, and one beer (Aasmundstad, 2003). They relax, talk with friends, or just read a newspaper. The setting encourages drinking, but not to excess.

NIGHTLIFE AND CRIME

ALCOHOL-RELATED VIOLENCE

Norway has enjoyed a relatively stable general crime rate, with figures for 2006 being the lowest for twelve years. However, a study of violent crime over the 1983 to 1994 period revealed significant increases in 1993–4, coinciding with the period in which the recent liberalization of liquor licensing first began (Olaussen, 1996). More recently a national study found that where consumption increased by one litre of pure alcohol the associated rate of violence increased by 8 per cent, when controlling for a number of social and economic factors (Bye, 2007). Whilst alcohol consumption in Norway has increased over the last decade by an average of 30 per cent among the general population and 60 per cent among adolescents, recent analyses of annual trends data indicate that alcohol-related violence has not increased to the same degree. This suggests that alcohol consumption levels alone do not determine rates of violence (Bye and Ingeborg, 2008). Olaussen (1995) describes how typical drinking settings in Norway have changed significantly since the 1970s. Increases in violence, especially on weekend evenings, may be associated, he argues, with a number of factors: higher incomes and more affordable alcohol and drugs, more alcohol outlets, more time to party due to extended hours, more people on the streets at night, and less informal social control due to the main social setting being outside of the home and family or community occasions.

Police in a number of cities now report a concentration of violence on Saturday nights/Sunday mornings, with incidents peaking between 3.00 and 4.00 am, as the patrons of pubs and clubs disperse. Although much anecdotal evidence is emerging at the local level, estimations of the scale of alcohol-related violence across Norwegian nightlife areas nationally are hampered by a lack of robust data. Existing datasets largely pertain not to street-level disorder, but rather to licensed premises and the enforcement of licensing laws concerning the serving of alcohol, smoking in a public place, the sale and consumption of illegal drugs, and drink-driving.

NIGHTLIFE AND DRUGS: THE CASE OF BERGEN

Monitoring drug-use trends in nightlife environments constitutes a real challenge as the situation is both complex and fluid. Recreational users are generally socially integrated and not in touch with drug services, and in-situ surveys are often too expensive to repeat at regular intervals. In 2002, the Bergen Earlier Warning System (BEWS) was established with the aim of monitoring consumption trends in Norway's second city (Mounteney and Leirvåg, 2004) and facilitating early intervention by policymakers and practitioners.

The BEWS draws information on patterns and trends in drug consumption in the city every six months, using 50 data sources. Both quantitative and qualitative data are utilized, including a schools survey, secondary data such as police arrests, seizures, treatment demand data, and alcohol sales, as well as a media-monitoring element which follows local newspapers, publications for youth and drugs-related professionals, and drug-user websites. A central component of the BEWS is its key-informant panel. Prior to the establishment of this panel, the BEWS team undertook a 'cultural mapping' of the city's drug scene. This included an exploration of the city's music scenes, focusing on the recreational drug-use patterns linked to specific music genres, subcultures, and venues. Following this mapping, ten 'key informants' from the city's nightlife and avant-garde scenes were recruited as panel members. These nightlife informants comprised personnel working in pubs and clubs such as doormen, serving staff, and disc jockeys and also nightlife patrons. Each informant was linked to a different musical or subcultural milieu—the aim being to provide breadth of coverage rather than a representative sample. Informants completed a semi-structured questionnaire on their observation of drug-use trends in their milieu in the previous six months, a small number were interviewed in-depth on an annual or biannual basis. Panel attrition was handled by recruiting a new informant from the same milieu.

DRUG-USE TRENDS IN BERGEN

The key-informant panel has provided unique insight into drug-use trends within the city. Results indicate a limited repertoire of substance use which largely reflects patterns in other European cities. Alcohol, cannabis, cocaine, and amphetamine were the most commonly reported substances in 2002–7. Key informants were asked every six months whether any new drugs had appeared in their particular social group and the results showed that no completely new substances had been observed during the five-year period. However, both cocaine and anabolic steroids were reported on several occasions as being substances that had gained in popularity among key groups, expanding from minority choices to wider acceptance. In-depth interviews provided useful insights into cocaine and anabolic steroid users' motivations and patterns of consumption. Two steroid-using cultures were reported in the nightlife scene—the first associated with bouncers and security staff, the second involving young men out pubbing and clubbing who were using steroids to enhance their physical appearance. Key informants highlighted the seasonal nature of use, with winter bodybuilding regimes followed by a rest in the summer. According to informants, the majority of steroids were purchased directly from the internet, although local drug dealers were also named as suppliers. In 2002, cocaine use was limited to a small clique of wealthy partygoers, but from 2004 onwards it was found to spread more broadly across the nightlife scene. Cocaine users were reportedly 'getting younger', although the 'typical user' was described as 25–35, male, and in employment. Polydrug use, involving the combining of alcohol and illegal substances, was reported repeatedly. The mixing of alcohol with cannabis or cocaine proved the most popular choice. Some informants described drinking alongside cocaine use, followed by the smoking of cannabis or the ingestion of benzodiazepines to relax and 'chill out' after a weekend's partying.

In terms of popularity among users, cocaine moved into 'third place' ahead of amphetamine from 2004 onwards. Other drugs consistently present in the nightlife scene at lower levels included ecstasy, magic mushrooms, Valium, and anabolic steroids. In 2002, Rohypnol appeared as one of the three most popular drugs in the city's pubs and clubs, only to entirely vanish from the scene by 2005. Nightlife patrons could be clearly differentiated from other types of drug user by the absence of opiates and medicines from their repertoire. The three most commonly reported substances— alcohol, cannabis, and cocaine—all displayed rising trajectories of use across the five-year period. The same was true for anabolic steroids. Ecstasy, amphetamine, and Rohypnol use fell in nightlife environments, whilst use of Valium remained stable. The price of cannabis, cocaine, and ecstasy remained stable over the BEWS reporting period, whilst amphetamine became cheaper (around half the price of cocaine per gram by the end of 2007).

Key informants also reported on the health and social implications of drug consumption. Alcohol was consistently identified as the root of most problems in nightlife environments, primarily linked to aggression, violence, and accidents. Problems linked to cannabis use increased significantly over the five years, to the extent that, by the end of 2006, it almost equalled alcohol in its reported associations with depression, anxiety, and lethargy. Cocaine was linked to relatively few problems. When Rohypnol use peaked in 2002, very high levels of harm—principally, aggressive behaviour, loss of control, and memory loss—were reported, particularly where the drug was used in combination with alcohol.

Though a relatively small city, Bergen (circa 250,000 inhabitants) has a dynamic and fast-changing nightlife scene. Drug-use trends are interlinked with music and youth culture. The declining House music scene is mirrored by reduced interest in ecstasy, whilst the rising popularity of Hip Hop has coincided with increasing use of cannabis. The city-level profile corresponds with nationally reported prevalence rates for 21 to 30 years olds (Ødegård, Skretting, and Lund, 2007) and with wider European trends, both of which indicate rises in cocaine use and the falling popularity of ecstasy (EMCDDA, 2007).

As a multi-source and multi-method approach, the BEWS has proved to be a particularly effective tool for monitoring a nightlife environment characterized by uncertainty and change. The use of key informants represents an efficient method for following changes and new developments whilst maintaining a level of anonymity as to the specific establishments and clubs involved. Moreover, the twice-yearly reporting to policymakers and practitioners has provided opportunities for relatively rapid response to new and emerging trends. A number of prevention, harm-reduction, and control measures have been put in place during the years that BEWS has been in operation and it is assumed that the system's public reporting has played a role in this. One example has been a focus on anabolic steroids, where the city outreach team included this as a theme in a rapid assessment in the city, resulting in the establishment of a project working with young steroid users. A second issue relates to Rohypnol which was reclassified from a B- to an A-rated (more stringently controlled) medicine and finally removed from sale in Norwegian pharmacies in 2004. In addition, the Bergen Violence Reduction Initiative was established to monitor increasing levels of alcohol consumption and the connections between alcohol, nightlife, and violence in the city.

POLICING, SECURITY, AND CRIME-CONTROL RESPONSES

Recent years have seen an increased focus on violence linked to nightlife settings, which has led to debate around the use of more visible policing strategies and changes in licensing hours. In their national plan for fighting drug-related crime, the Norwegian police have identified a range of approaches relating to the control of youth entertainment venues (clubs, concert venues, dance events). Strategies include a focus on improving standards in the entertainment industry concerning matters such as 'temperature, drinks, sound levels, chill out zones, in addition to strategies related to age limits, opening times, serving of alcohol and security and inspection arrangements' (Politidirektoratet, 2003: 2). In 2007, the Norwegian Police Authority recommended increasing the number of high-visibility police patrols in crime hotspots (particular places where crime is concentrated) at peak times. Violent and sexual crimes were prioritized on the basis that reported incidents had doubled since 1993. Local police forces were required to develop specially tailored action plans to tackle violent crime based on a local analysis of needs.

The City of Bergen has drawn up a multi-agency plan aimed at reducing street violence. The City's partners include police, youth outreach and drug prevention workers. Key hotspots and problem areas, primarily associated with nightlife and weekends, have been identified. A range of concrete activities have been proposed, including:

- provision of non-alcoholic drinks for those waiting in taxi queues
- review of the location of bus and taxi stops
- cleaning of the city centre at night
- improved street lighting in certain risk areas
- use of CCTV in the city centre
- implementation of the 'Responsible Hosts' programme (see below)
- reduction in venue opening hours.

In some Norwegian cities 'protected' zones have been established in residential areas, where alcohol is not available after 1.00 am.

Further responses have been made by the voluntary sector. The 'Night Ravens' scheme aims to ensure that responsible and sober adults are always a visible presence on the streets during weekend evenings. Volunteers, who wear a clearly recognizable uniform, patrol nightlife areas, not as vigilantes or police spies, but rather to provide assistance and support for young people.

THE 'RESPONSIBLE HOST' PROGRAMME

In several Norwegian cities, a 'Responsible Hosts' programme has been implemented in response to alcohol-related violence, over-serving, and the serving of alcohol to minors. The programme was devised in response to evidence which indicated over-serving (ie, the serving of alcohol to persons who are already drunk) to be common-place, especially during the later trading hours, at crowded venues, when the music was loud, and where other customers were drinking to excess. These practices, it was found, were contributing to an escalation in alcohol-related violence within licensed premises and their surroundings. Under the programme, bar staff receive training on how to avoid over-serving and regular inspections are conducted to check compliance.

In Bergen more than 1,200 serving staff have attended the training course since 2000. In addition to alcohol-sales issues, the training also covers issues such as conflict management and the prevention of drink-related violence. In 2003 the programme became compulsory for bar staff in the city. Only eight violations have been detected in Bergen in the course of seven years and over 7,000 inspections. This surprisingly low figure prompted an evaluation project in 2006 in which test purchases, performed by actors playing the role of inebriated customers, were conducted in a number of pubs and restaurants (Lauritzen and Baklien, 2007). The low number of recorded violations was found to result from the poor operation of the programme rather than the high operating standards of licensed premises. The project revealed an urgent need for improvements to the training programme, especially regarding the employment of practical steps to enforce the law. The project also revealed evidence of inadequacies in the system's ability to apply legal sanctions, particularly withdrawal of a venue's alcohol licence.

NATIONAL POLICY GUIDANCE

Following the lead of the World Health Organization, Norway's Social and Health Directorate (SHD) has developed a national multi-sector strategy for the prevention of drug-related harms, to be implemented by local authorities. The SHD has issued guidance to all Norwegian local authorities on strengthening drug and alcohol harm-prevention work. The Guidance provides advice on topics such regulating the availability and marketing of alcohol through pricing and taxation, changing the context of drinking, and influencing social norms concerning drink-driving. Each authority is responsible for developing a local Alcohol Action Plan, under which the prevention of crime in nightlife environments may be addressed under the stated policy aim of creating 'Safe Communities'.

One of the most effective preventive measures is to reduce the availabilty of alcohol by limiting the number of licensed premises and restricting their opening hours (Babor et al, 2003). By preventing the sale of alcohol early in the evening, the *vorspiel* or pre-party drinks period can be shortened and people are encouraged to both go out and return home earlier. However, such wide-ranging restrictions are unpopular among Norway's liberal political wing. Other measures discussed, and sometimes implemented, include: reducing the number of patrons allowed entry to a venue, denial of admission to intoxicated persons, and having strict and clear drinks ordering procedures to prevent arguments and fights.

THE NEW NORWEGIAN NIGHT-TIME ECONOMY

The birth of mass tourism to Mediterranean countries during the 1960s and 70s allowed many Norwegians their first taste of inexpensive and readily available alcohol. Holidaymakers returning from destinations such as Benidorm, Palma, and Ibiza began to demand that alcohol become more available in their own cities. At the same time, Norway itself became a very popular tourist destination, and the leisure and tourism sector began to feature heavily in the deliberations of local authorities when deciding whether new licences should be granted. During the summer, Norway's main cities are now filled with tourists, and the number of licensed premises has grown significantly. Bergen, for example, has become the most popular harbour for cruise ships in northern Europe and this is reflected in the vibrancy of its city-centre restaurants and pubs. Some premises have been granted extended opening times to 3.00 am and are frequented more by local people than by tourists. This new lifestyle, with more venues for socializing and meeting friends outside the home, and a more lively nightlife, has been welcomed by most. But the question remains as to whether the price, in terms of alcohol- and drug-related harm and the financial burden on society, is too high. This tension is perhaps most graphically illustrated in the scenes one witnesses in the city's hospital accident and emergency department (AED) on Friday and Saturday nights (Steen and Hunskaar, 2004).

The political and economic aspects of this dilemma clearly involve a struggle between free-market liberalism with its focus on meeting consumer demand and providing lifestyle 'choices' and the social democrat agenda of state regulation. However, as in other countries, city centres offer the greatest challenge regarding alcohol-related disturbances and violence. Empirical evidence points to problems associated with the unrestricted 'bunching' of licensed premises (see Chapter 18 of this volume), leading to a crowded nightlife, many people leaving pubs and clubs at the same time, and fighting for the few available taxis. In accordance with traditional Nordic drinking patterns, licensed premises remain highly dependent on the weekend custom of young adults.

In an attempt to address problems associated with the new 'night-time economy', Norwegian authorities have adopted a number of individually targeted and community-level strategies. Targeted approaches tend to emphasize the need for solutions such as more police on the streets, training bar staff to avoid over-serving, encouraging patrons to drink more moderately, punishing offenders, and generally stressing the responsibility of individuals to control their own actions. Community-based approaches aim to prevent night-time public spaces from becoming an extension of the nightclub, ensuring that alcohol policies do not in any way facilitate the kinds of problem they were intended to address. Evidence indicates that the majority of crime, disorder, and nuisance incidents occur after midnight. In response to this, some city authorities have chosen to restrict the opening hours of city-centre premises, whilst introducing more effective public transport to get people home.

CONCLUSIONS

During the 1990s, harm-reduction funding, policies, and initiatives linked to nightlife were concerned primarily with the use of ecstasy and synthetic drugs on the Electronic Dance Music (EDM) scene. These issues have now been superseded. In accordance with European trends, cocaine has become more popular on the nightlife scene, cannabis remains popular, but ecstasy use has waned. It is perhaps telling that the Futures Project, run by Oslo and Bergen outreach agencies in clubland dance environments, no longer exists. Alcohol use among youth, and alcohol-related violence most specifically, has moved up the policy agenda.

There is evidence to suggest that some affluent Norwegians are drinking moderately as part of a new urban café culture, switching from beer and spirits to wine, which is taken frequently in low-dosage, often as part of a meal, 'Mediterranean' style. These, however, are minority practices. From a pan-European perspective, Norway and the other Nordic countries are witnessing significant rises in alcohol consumption, especially among younger age groups. It would appear that our binge drinking heritage—exacerbated by the increasing availability of alcohol—remains hard to challenge. Norwegian cities, for a long time regarded as relatively safe places to visit by European standards, now contain areas that many citizens consider it unwise to enter during the late evening. The perpetrators and victims of alcohol-related street violence are most often intoxicated young men. Most altercations occur between strangers, often over matters which, to the sober person, in the light of day, appear trivial. Enforcement measures, such as the withdrawal of alcohol-serving licences, have not been adequately applied.

Norwegian licensing authorities are sovereign in their decisions as long as they stay within the legal limits of the Alcohol Law. They do, however, face pressure to deregulate from the rising political and economic influence of an 'alcohol lobby' comprising alcohol manufacturers, nightlife operators, liberal right-wing politicians, and the service and tourism sector. These actors are pitted against a similar coalition of health and judicial authorities and Christian Democrat and socialist politicians. In a comprehensive review of international literature on the prevention of alcohol-related harm, the restrictive measures for which Norway is renowned were shown to be especially effective when compared to individualized competence-enhancement measures, such as public health education campaigns, often favoured by the 'alcohol lobby' (Babor et al, 2003). Norwegian authorities now find themselves in the paradoxical situation of being encouraged to promote forms of deregulation which are almost guaranteed to undermine their previous policies' successes.

A comprehensive approach to harm reduction encompassing both restrictive and competence-enhancing elements would appear to be the best way forward for Norwegian health and criminal justice agencies. Changing trends in nightlife and crime demand robust approaches to data collection and monitoring. The main challenge will be to develop an evidence base to identify clear and concrete objectives. The BEWS has proved to be one effective way of obtaining well-documented sources of information and the Bergen model has been adopted by other cities in Norway and beyond. One interesting possibility may be to develop this city-level key-informant-panel methodology internationally, perhaps by means of a pan-European network from which comparative data could be drawn.

REFERENCES

All internet sources were accessible 20 August 2008

AASMUNDSTAD, L (2003) 'Café con Trivseselsvakt', *Rus og Avhengighet*, 3, 7–9.

BABOR, T, CAETANO, R, CASSWELL, S, EDWARDS, G, GIESBRECHT, N, GRAHAM, K, GRUBE, J, GRUENWALD, P, HILL, L, HOLDER, H, HOMEL, R, OSTERBERG, E, REHM, J, ROOM, R, and ROSSOW, I (2003) *Alcohol: No Ordinary Commodity*, Oxford: Oxford University Press.

BRYHNI, A (2007) 'Alcohol and drugs in Norway', *The Norwegian Institute for Alcohol and Drug Research*, Oslo, SIRUS rapport, ISBN 82–7171–311–9.

BYE, EK (2007) 'Alcohol and violence: Use of possible confounders in a time-series analysis', *Addiction*, 102/3, 369–76.

—— and INGEBORG, R (2008) 'Is the impact of alcohol consumption on violence relative to the level of consumption?', *Journal of Scandinavian Studies in Criminology and Crime Prevention*, 9/1, 31–46.

EMCDDA (The European Monitoring Centre for Drugs and Drug Addiction) (2007) *The Drug Situation in Europe: 2006 Annual Report*, Lisbon: EMCDDA.

LAURITZEN, HC (2008) *Kommunenes Forvaltning av Alkoholloven 2007*, Oslo: SIRUS rapport.

—— and BAKLIEN, B (2007) *Oppfølging av Evalueringen av 'Ansvarlig Vertskap' i Bergen*, Oslo: SIRUS rapport nr. 5/2007, ISSN, 1502–8178.

MOUNTENEY, J and LEIRVÅG, S-E (2004) 'Providing an earlier warning of emerging drug trends: The Føre Var system', *Drugs: Education, Prevention and Policy*, 11/6, 449–71.

NOU (Norwegian Public Reports) (2007) 'En Vurdering av Særavgiftene', *Utredning fra et Utvalg Oppnevnt av Finansdepartementet* 1, Oslo: NOU.

OLAUSSEN, LP (1995) *Beruselse, Utelivsdeltakelse og Utsatthet for Vold*, Rapport 3:1995, Oslo: Politihøgskolen, ISBN 82–7808–004–6.

—— (1996) *Alkoholpolitikk og Vold-Finnes det en Sammenheng?* Rapport 1:1996, Oslo: Avholdsfolkets Landsråd.

POLITIDIREKTORATET (2003) *Politiets Narkotikabekjempelse 2003–2008*, Oslo: Politidirektoratet.

—— (2007) *Tendenser i Kriminaliteten—Utfordringer i Norge i 2007–2009*, POD publikasjon 2007/01, Oslo: Politidirektoratet, Seksjon for analyse og forebygging.

SANDE, A (2000) 'Den Norske Russefeiringen', *Nordisk Alkohol og Narkotikatidskrift*, 17/5–6, 340–53.

STEEN, K and HUNSKAAR, S (2004) 'Violence in an urban community from the perspective of an accident and emergency department: A two-year prospective study', *Med Sci Monit*, 10/2, 75–9.

ØDEGÅRD, MK, SKRETTING, A and LUND, KE (2007) *Rusmiddelbruk Blant Unge Voksne, 21–30 år. Resultater fra Spørreskjemaundersøkelser 1998, 2002 og 2006*, Oslo: SIRUS rapport nr 8/2007.

8

FINLAND

Marja Holmila and Katariina Warpenius

INTRODUCTION

On the basis of statistics and official records this chapter examines changing rates of violence in Finnish restaurants, bars, pubs, and nightclubs over a ten-year period. The period in question was characterized by rapid rises in the number of licensed premises and increased use of alcohol. However, data shows that the number of violent assaults in licensed premises did not increase during this period, although rises were recorded in public places and private homes. We argue that one likely reason for this is that, whilst the country's total consumption of alcohol reached new peaks, the proportion of alcohol sales from on-licensed venues remained static. Another explanation could be that the harm-reduction initiatives targeting on-licensed premises, including campaigns of licensing-law enforcement, proved successful. In the concluding section we discuss the potential for using situational crime-prevention measures as part of an overall strategy for reducing alcohol-related harm.

BACKGROUND

The Finnish population's alcohol consumption has increased almost every year for the past 20 years. The greatest annual increase occurred in 2004, when alcohol prices were reduced due to cuts in tax duties, and consumption of alcoholic drinks grew by 10 per cent (Mäkelä and Österberg, 2006: 322–3). This growth was reflected in a rise in alcohol-related harms, including assaults and homicides (National Research Institute of Legal Policy, 2007: 444–5). Drinking culture in Finland is similar to that of the other Nordic countries: alcohol is mostly consumed in 'time-out' contexts, and not necessarily with meals. Intoxication is common and semi-acceptable even in public. Beer and hard liquor are the favourite types of beverage, although consumption of wine has increased in recent years.

During the last 10–15 years, efforts to reduce violence in and around licensed premises have incorporated elements of situational crime prevention in addition to more traditional Finnish approaches such as the targeting of welfare and treatment services towards a reduction in the number of heavy alcohol users (Kivivuori, 2008: 378).

Licensed premises are expected to comply with regulations and to serve alcohol responsibly in order to reduce harms. In this chapter we will describe these preventive efforts, together with trends in nightlife-related violence. Statistics derived from police records provide insight into the locations in which violence takes place. Crime locations where alcohol is served for consumption on the premises are coded as 'licensed premises'. Premises which serve alcohol for consumption off the premises are not included. It is not possible to obtain more detailed data broken down into specific types of on-licensed venue as police statistics do not record this. Thus, in what follows, the term 'licensed premises' is used to encompass a range of different venue types (restaurants, bars, pubs, and nightclubs).

ALCOHOL AND VIOLENCE IN FINLAND

Rossow's (2001) pan-European study points to correlations between the growth in alcohol consumption and rising rates of violence in Scandinavian countries. In a Finnish time-series study covering 1950–2000, Sirén (2002) estimated that for every annual increase in consumption of one litre of 100 per cent alcohol per capita, there had been a corresponding 3–6 per cent increase in incidents of assault. In Finland the annual rate of assaults has roughly paralleled trends in alcohol consumption and the population's rising affluence (National Research Institute of Legal Policy, 2007: 445). Crimes, especially robberies, carried out under the influence of other drugs also grew during the 1990s. This growth stopped in the 2000s, and alcohol remains the main intoxicant in criminal offences.

The perpetrators of violent crime are predominately young and this is particularly true in relation to fights between males on the streets and within licensed premises. Assault rates are highest among 15–24-year-olds, reducing with age (Kivivuori, 2008: 29). Most assault victims also fall within this age range. In one survey (Lehti, Sirén, and Hinkkanen, 2007: 49–73), every eighth young male and every tenth young woman, reported that they had been a victim of physical violence during the last year, whilst the corresponding number across all age groups was 5 per cent. According to police records from 2002 to 2006, 79 per cent of homicide offenders committed their offence whilst under the influence of alcohol. In assault offences, the corresponding figure was 67 per cent. Similarly, in robberies, 43 per cent of offenders were under the influence of alcohol (Lehti, Sirén, and Hinkkanen, ibid).

Finland's heavy and intoxication-oriented drinking culture has led researchers to see alcohol's presence in the commission of so many crimes as one of the reasons for its relatively high levels of fatal violence in comparison with other Scandinavian countries. For example, in 2006, the number of the homicides in Finland was 2.6 per 100,000 inhabitants, whilst the corresponding figures for Sweden and Denmark were 1.1 and 1.2, respectively (Lehti and Kivivuori, 2007: 72). There also appears to be a prima facie socio-economic explanation given that the highest rates of lethal violence were found among unemployed, marginalized, and alcoholic Finnish men for whom welfare policies have not succeeded in providing adequate support (Kivivuori and Lehti, 2006: 75–8).

THE GROWTH OF URBAN NIGHTLIFE

Major urbanization in Finland began as late as the 1960s and has been especially rapid when one considers that the majority of its people now live in towns and cities. Unsurprisingly, corresponding changes have occurred in the location of violent crime. Public life has become more commercialized, people have more money to spend, the number of licensed premises has grown, and women have taken their place in nightlife. Spending time in licensed premises has generally become more important in the lives of young adults. Young adults also drink a considerable amount at home before entering the pubs and nightclubs and this drinking is often intoxication-oriented (Törrönen and Maunu, 2007). The increasing function of pubs and nightclubs as the settings for young people's partying has perhaps increased the opportunities for formal surveillance and harm-reduction efforts attached to the management of drunkenness, yet it has also introduced new challenges. For instance, when venues close, large groups of drunken people leave the premises and start to queue for snacks or transport home in the otherwise empty city.

Numbers of licensed premises have more than doubled in the last two decades (STAKES, 2007: 117), whilst the physical capacity of venues, measured in terms of 'customer places', increased by 200 per cent from 1997 to 2006 (see Fig 8.1). Although increased prosperity has fuelled this expanding leisure market, growth was also been encouraged by changes to the alcohol legislation enacted in 1995 (Finnish Alcohol Law 1143/1994) and by the High Court's subsequent interpretation of these laws in 1997 (Alavaikko, 2001: 166; Korkeimman Hallinto-oikeuden Päätös, 19.6, 1997). Formerly, when considering an application for a new liquor licence, the authorities were obliged to assess whether the proposed location already contained large numbers of licensed premises and whether there was any consequent 'need' for more services of a similar kind. Any potential impact of increasing the density of outlets was thus—at least in theory—assessed in terms of its effects on public health and civil order. Following the High Court ruling in 1997, the authorities no longer applied this test and

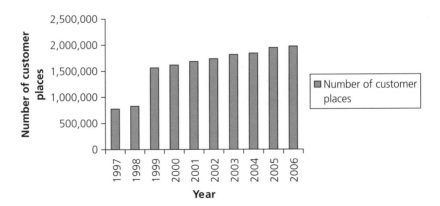

Fig 8.1 **Capacity figures for all licensed premises in Finland, 1997–2006**

Source: *Yearbook of Alcohol and Drug Statistics 2007*

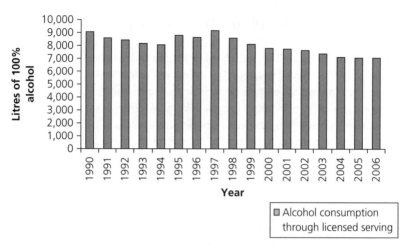

Fig 8.2 Total consumption of alcoholic beverages in licensed premises (litres of 100 per cent alcohol), 1990–2006

Source: *Yearbook of Alcohol and Drug Statistics 2007*

sought to evaluate only the 'respectability' and professional skills of the applicant. The underlying emphasis of regulation therefore changed from public protection to non-intervention in that the freedom of the business community was now curtailed as little as possible, thus promoting economic growth.

A further effect of the new licensing laws has been to extend the opening hours of licensed premises. Venues are now generally permitted to remain open until 1.30 am and with 'special permission' may operate to 2.30 or 3.30 am. People have begun to visit licensed premises later at night: in 1992 only 18 per cent of all drinking occasions in restaurants, pubs, bars, and nightclubs continued past 2.00 am; by 2000 this figure had risen to 27 per cent. Similarly in 2000, even though Finns reported often drinking to intoxication at home, in the early hours of the morning the greatest numbers of intoxicated persons were to be found in city-centre licensed premises (Holmila, Metso, and Österberg, 2003). Yet, in spite of a considerable growth in total alcohol consumption at a population level, sales of alcohol in on-licensed premises have not grown since the end of the 1990s (see Fig 8.2). This suggests that many people prefer to buy their drinks from shops, possibly as a result of price differentials; prices in retail outlets often being considerably lower.

TRENDS IN VIOLENT CRIME

In analysing violence at licensed premises the patterning of police-recorded assaults is a commonly used indicator (Wallin, 2004), these statistics being a more valid measure than the comparatively rare cases of homicide. However, the recording of non-fatal

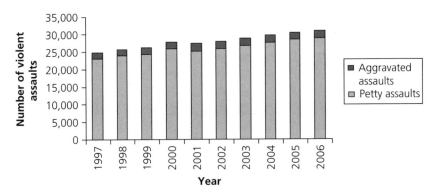

Fig 8.3 Assaults (petty and aggravated) in Finland, 1997–2006

Source: Lehti, Sirén, and Hinkkanen, 2007 (Statistics Finland)

assaults is often influenced by police activity, requiring that some caution be exercised when examining trends. Also, during the 1990s, changes were made to the way in which statistics were collated and for that reason we limit our examination to the 1997–2006 period for which data is comparable. Official police-derived crime statistics have been complemented by victimization surveys since 1980, these studies revealing that the majority of violent crimes go unreported. The 2006 survey found that only a fifth of the violent incidents reported by victims had been recorded by the police. People's willingness to report crimes of violence has grown, however, and is now four times higher than in 1980 (Lehti, Sirén, and Hinkkanen, 2007: 70). Figure 8.3 displays the steady increase in the total number of violent assaults recorded in police registers from 1997 to 2006. As noted, alcohol prices were radically reduced in 2004 and this factor, together with the reform of the licensing laws, indicates a correlation between alcohol policy liberalization and rises in violent crime. Rates of assault were highest in the country's most densely populated regions.

Despite this general rise there was no recorded increase in the number of assaults occurring on licensed premises. The biggest increases were recorded on the streets and other public places and especially in private homes. Indeed, expressed as a proportion, the number of assaults on licensed premises slightly decreased during the period (Fig 8.4). Of course, it is possible that some of the violence was simply displaced from licensed venues to other locations, especially in the early hours of the morning as drunken customers entered the streets. However, only a part of the increase in violence is likely to be even indirectly related to on-licensed venues. It is possible, for example, that there is now an increased willingness to report incidents of domestic violence thus increasing the relative proportion of assaults recorded for private residential locations. Domestic violence is itself often linked to the use of alcohol. Furthermore, it has always been common for young people and heavy drinkers to gather in streets, parks, near festival grounds and other public places, especially in the summertime, and reductions in the price of drink are likely to have had a disproportionate influence upon alcohol's availability to these groups through off-licensed sales.

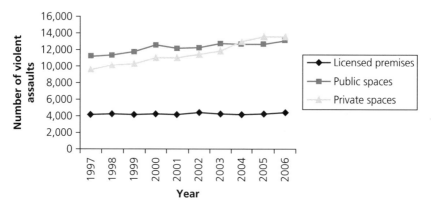

Fig 8.4 Assaults in private and public spaces and in licensed premises, 1997–2006

Source: Lehti, Sirén, and Hinkkanen, 2007 (Statistics Finland)

SITUATIONAL CRIME PREVENTION AS A METHOD OF HARM REDUCTION

One reason for the relatively low level of violence in licensed premises in comparison with other locations is likely to be the fact that although total consumption of alcohol has reached new peaks, the proportion of alcohol consumed in licensed premises has remained largely static (see Fig 8.2). Another explanation could be that the harm-reduction strategies applied in licensed premises have proved to be effective.

Previous studies indicate that social atmosphere, staff behaviour and other specific environmental factors, such as noise levels and overcrowding, can influence levels of risk for violence in licensed premises (Graham et al, 2006; Quigley et al, 2003). Reviews of the evaluation literature indicate that multi-component interventions combining bar-staff training, written house policies, and stricter enforcement of the licensing laws increase the possibilities of reducing alcohol problems within the venue (Graham, 2000; Homel et al, 2001). Improving the environment and operating standards within licensed premises can thus reduce the risks of acute alcohol-related harm. These principles clearly chime with the idea of situational crime prevention (Clarke, 1992) as underlined by regulations from the Finnish liquor licensing authorities. Since the late 1990s, these authorities, together with licensed-trade associations and trade unions have developed guidelines and protocols for Responsible Beverage Service (RBS). Legislation implemented in 2003 (Laki Alkoholilain Muuttamisesta 764/30.8.2002) requires that at least one member of staff, who has attended a special educational course and passed a test in RBS, must be present at all times that premises are open to the public.

Surveillance of licensed premises by the liquor licensing authorities was decentralized in 2004. These tasks are now the responsibility of district-level authorities rather than central government, which has meant greater levels of enforcement activity, as can be seen from Fig 8.5. In 1996, only five licensed premises were sanctioned by

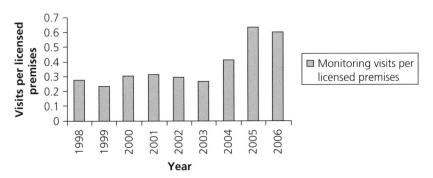

Fig 8.5 Number of liquor licensing enforcement visits per premises, 1998–2006

Source: National Product Control Agency for Welfare and Health

permanent closure. In 2004, by comparison, more than 60 premises lost their licence as a result of prosecution for unlawful business practices.

Increasing the efficiency of surveillance has led to positive developments. Previous studies on preventive interventions have shown that RBS training exerts only a limited influence over server practices and violence unless supported by increased liquor licensing enforcement (Stockwell, 2000; Wallin, 2004; Wallin et al, 2003; Warburton and Shepherd, 2006). In addition to the requisite knowledge and skills, bar personnel have to have a strong motivation to take on the demanding task of regulating patrons' intoxication levels and associated behaviour. Awareness of the possibility of surveillance and consequent sanctions increases this motivation and is thus an important factor in shaping the attitudes of owners and managers in promoting a professional working culture within their venues.

The Ministry of Justice and the Ministry of the Interior have established working groups to coordinate and develop the prevention efforts of various authorities, NGOs, business associations, and trade unions. On the basis of recommendations from these working groups, the government has formulated a national programme for reducing violence. It is recommended that the police intervene, in systematic fashion, to disrupt all public drinking sessions that could disturb other citizens' and their use of public amenities, or pose a risk to public safety. The police have suggested that municipalities should increase their use of private security agents and cameras to control drinking activities in public areas. Within licensed premises it is recommended that attention be paid to RBS and other situational control measures (Ministry of Justice Publications, 2005; Sisäisen Turvallisuuden Ohjelman Toimeenpano ja Tulokset, 2004–2007).

There are some evaluated experiences of local efforts to implement these kinds of preventive methods in Finland. The community-based Lahti-project of 1994-5 included RBS training (Holmila and Haavisto, 1997). Another project developed the licensees' own voluntary actions to carry out routine surveillance of staff practices ('self-surveillance') and cooperation between licensed premises and the local police was enhanced (Haavisto et al, 2002). In Tampere, the local police, liquor licensing authorities, and social workers conducted a combined 'crackdown' operation on licensed premises in 1999–2000 (Korander and Soine-Rajanummi, 2002). Elsewhere, close cooperation between venue operators and the police has developed on a voluntary basis (Hyttinen, 2005).

The demonstration project Local Alcohol Policy (PAKKA) in 2004–2007 systematically combined law enforcement, RBS training, media advocacy, and broad cooperation between local authorities and leisure entrepreneurs (Holmila and Warpenius, 2007). The licensed premises component aimed at limiting the service of alcohol to intoxicated and/or under-age customers, and further reducing alcohol-related harms. Liquor licensing authorities increased their monitoring visits to restaurants, pubs, bars, and nightclubs in order to enforce the licensing laws. An RBS training programme was incorporated, consisting of a half-day drama-education course. The training provided information on alcohol law and advised servers on how to improve their working methods. The enforcement and training was then combined with opinion-building campaigns and community-wide media advocacy, creating public discussion on safety and drinking norms in licensed premises.

The project was evaluated by means of test-purchasing operations which measured the frequency of alcohol service to intoxicated clients on licensed premises in the intervention areas and in other comparison sites. These comparisons revealed that the interventions were having a significant impact, with the over-serving of alcohol being much less apparent in the town where the RBS training, increased law enforcement, and sanctions had been applied (Warpenius et al, 2009). Findings from the PAKKA project thus support the belief that local multi-component prevention efforts can have an impact on server behaviour in licensed premises. Further analyses are required to establish what, if any, impacts, these harm-reduction efforts have had on rates of violence in public places.

CONCLUSIONS

COMBINING ALCOHOL CONTROL, WELFARE POLICIES, AND SITUATIONAL CRIME PREVENTION

The relatively late growth of the urban night-time economy in Finland has changed the country's crime profile, adding new elements to long-established problems associated with heavy sessional drinking and alcoholism. In a response to changing times, preventive work to reduce violence has increasingly focused on situational crime prevention (Kivivuori, 2008: 378) whilst retaining targeted welfare policies where crime is understood to be a by-product of poverty and marginalization. Attempts to reduce intoxication in licensed premises represent one important element of situational prevention. Here the active intervention of bar staff is crucial as the responsibility for preventing excessive intoxication belongs not only to the drinker, but also to the server. Recent legislative changes, decentralized liquor licensing jurisdictions, and local demonstration projects seem to have had a positive impact by encouraging social responsibility within the night-time economy. However, it is important to remember that these promising developments are only one side of the coin. There is a risk that if overall crime prevention is forgotten and harm-reduction policies concentrate all their efforts on creating 'safe' and controlled premises where customers can drink, alcohol-related violence may still be displaced from licensed premises onto the streets and parks. There is compelling evidence to suggest that an individual's criminality often goes hand in hand with their heavy use of alcohol whilst, at a population level, the total growth of alcohol consumption has corresponded with rising overall rates of violent crime in recent years. In the long term, a sustainable night-time economy must find other sources of income and provide alternative leisure options in addition to the excessive use of alcohol. Until then the risks of alcohol-related harm need to be managed through balanced strategies which acknowledge that the different areas of preventive, enforcement, and welfare work are all important and reinforce each other. In addressing the issue of violence, situational crime prevention is a promising addition to the overall package of control methods.

REFERENCES

All internet sources were accessible 20 August 2008

ALAVAIKKO, M (2001) 'Alkoholi- ja Huumekenttien Muutos Paikallisesta Näkökulmasta', *Yhteiskuntapolitiikka*, 66/2, 159–68.

CLARKE, R (1992) *Situational Crime Prevention: Successful case studies*, New York: Harrow and Heston.

GRAHAM, K (2000) 'Prevention interventions for on-premise drinking: A promising but under-researched area of prevention', *Contemporary Drug Problems*, 27, 593–668.

—— BERNARDS S, OSGOOD DW and WELLS S (2006) 'Bad nights or bad bars? Multi-level analysis of environmental predictors of aggression in late-night large-capacity bars and clubs', *Addiction*, 101, 1569–80.

HAAVISTO, K, HOLMILA, M, AHTOLA, R and WARSELL, L (2002) 'Alcohol and drug problems: The views of bar staff and their patrons', in M Holmila (ed), *Alcohol and Drug Problems in Residential Areas: An evaluation of community-based prevention in Tikkurila and Myllypuro*, Study 122, Helsinki: National Research and Development Centre for Welfare and Health (STAKES), 102–19.

HOLMILA, M and HAAVISTO, K (1997) 'Responsible service and drinking environments', in M Holmila (ed), *Community Prevention of Alcohol Problems*, Basingstoke: Macmillan Press Ltd, 123–35.

—— METSO, L and ÖSTERBERG, E (2003) 'Longer opening hours lead to increased intoxication', *Dialogi*, 8, 16–19.

—— and WARPENIUS, K (2007) 'A study of the effectiveness of local alcohol policy: Challenges and solutions from the PAKKA project', *Drugs: Education, Prevention and Policy*, 14/5, 1–13.

HOMEL, R, MCILWAIN G and CARVOLTH, R (2001) 'Creating safer drinking environments', in N Heather, TJ Peters and T Stockwell (eds), *Handbook of Alcohol Dependence and Alcohol-Related Problems*, New York: JOHN WILEY and SONS, 721–40.

HYTTINEN, N (2005) *Pieni Askel Yhdelle Ravintolalle, Suuri Kaupungille. Järvenpään Ravintola-Projektin Toteutus- ja Vaikuttavuusarviointi.* Järvenpää: DIAK publication series D 35.

KIVIVUORI, J (2008) *Rikollisuuden Syyt* (The Causes of Crime), Jyväskylä: Gummerus.

—— and LEHTI, M (2006) 'The social composition of homicide in Finland, 1960–2000', *Acta Sociologica*, 49/1, 67–82.

KORANDER, T and SOINE-RAJANUMMI, S (2002) *Kahdeksalta Koskarille—Saman Tien Sakot. Tampereeen Nollatoleranssikokelu, 1999–2000: Historiallinen Konteksti, Vastaanotto ja Vaikuttavuus.* Helsinki: Studies of the Police Polytechnic 13.

KORKEIMMAN HALLINTO-OIKEUDEN PÄÄTÖS (Decision of the Finnish High Court), 19.2.1997/626.

LAKI ALKOHOLILAIN MUUTTAMISESTA (Changes to the Alcohol Legislation) 764/30.8.2002.

LEHTI, M and KIVIVUORI, J (2007) 'Kuolemaan Johtanut Väkivalta' (Fatal Violence), in *Oikeuspoliiittisen Tutkimuslaitoksen Julkaisuja* (Crime and Criminal Justice in Finland), 229, Helsinki: Publications of the National Research Institute of Legal Policy, 15–47.

—— SIRÉN, R and HINKKANEN, V (2007) 'Muut Väkivaltarikokset' (Other Violent Acts), in *Oikeuspoliiittisen Tutkimuslaitoksen Julkaisuja* (Crime and Criminal Justice in Finland), 229. Helsinki: Publications of the National Research Institute of Legal Policy, 49–65.

MÄKELÄ, P and ÖSTERBERG, E (2006) 'Alkoholin Kulutus Kasvaa—Lisääntyykö Hyvinvointi? (The Consumption of Alcohol is Growing—Does Welfare Increase?), in M Kautto (ed), *Suomalaisten Hyvinvointi* (Finnish Welfare), Helsinki: STAKES, 306–28.

MINISTRY OF JUSTICE (2005) *Kansallinen Ohjelma Väkivallan Vähentämiseksi* (National Programme for Violence Reduction 2), Helsinki: Edita Prima Oy.

NATIONAL RESEARCH INSTITUTE OF LEGAL POLICY (2007) 'Crime trends in Finland, summary', in *Crime and Criminal Justice in Finland*, Helsinki: National Research Institute of Legal Policy, 444–65.

QUIGLEY, BM, LEONARD, KE and COLLINS, RL (2003) 'Characteristics of violent bars and bar patrons', *Journal of Studies on Alcohol*, 64, 765–72.

ROSSOW, I (2001) 'Alcohol and homicide: A cross-cultural comparison of the relationship in 14 European countries', *Addiction*, 96 (Supplement 1), 77–92.

SIRÉN, R (2002) 'Trends in assault: On the relationship between the assault rate and selected social indicators in post-war Finland', *Journal of Scandinavian Studies in Criminology and Crime Prevention*, 3, 22–49.

SISÄASIAIN MINISTERIÖ (Ministry of the Internal Affairs) (2007) *Sisäisen Turvallisuuden Ohjelman Toimeenpano ja Tulokset 2004–2007* (Implementation and results of the Internal Security Programme 2004–2007), Helsinki: Sisäasiain Ministeriö.

STAKES (National Research and Development Centre for Welfare and Health) (2007) *Yearbook of Alcohol and Drug Statistics 2007*, Helsinki: STAKES.

STOCKWELL, T (2000) 'Responsible beverage service: Lessons from server training and policy initiatives around the world', in K Elmeland (ed), *Lokalt Alkohol Och Drogförebyggande Arbete i Norden* (Local Alcohol and Drug Prevention in the Nordic Countries), NAD publication nr 38, Helsinki: Hakapaino Oy, 113–25.

TÖRRÖNEN, J and MAUNU, A (2007) 'Whilst it's red wine with beef, it's booze with a cruise! Genres and gendered regulation of drinking situations in diaries', *Nordic Studies on Alcohol and Drugs*, 24/2, 177–99.

WALLIN, E (2004) *Responsible Beverage Service: Effects of a community action project*, Stockholm: Karolinska Institutet.

—— NORSTRÖM, T and ANDRÉASSON, S (2003) 'Alcohol prevention targeting licensed premises: A study of effects on violence', *Journal of Studies on Alcohol*, 64, 270–7.

WARBURTON, AL and SHEPHERD, JP (2006) 'Tackling alcohol-related violence in city centres: The effects of emergency medicine and police intervention', *Emergency Medicine Journal*, 23/1, 12–17.

WARPENIUS K, HOLMILA M and MUSTONEN, H (2009) *Effects of a Community Intervention on Over-Serving at Licensed Premises*, Helsinki: STAKES.

9

ITALY

Rosella Selmini and Gian Guido Nobili

INTRODUCTION

In contemporary Italian society, 'nightlife' is a concept whose importance has increased enormously in many different contexts: as a key element in understanding the changing nature of young people's lifestyles, a central aspect of urban governance, including crime control and place marketing, and as an issue of public debate. In Italy, as elsewhere, nightlife is also an important issue in two different and conflicting ways: on the one hand, improving access to leisure helps drive and sustain economic development and cultural vibrancy. On the other, nightlife is still associated with feelings of public anxiety and insecurity and with some established and chronic forms of crime and disorder. These different ways of interpreting and attaching meaning to nightlife lie at the core of conflict among different social groups concerning the ways in which nightlife should be regulated.

Despite the increasing importance of nightlife as a criminological issue in Italy, academic and policy-oriented research has not emerged to the same degree as in other European countries (Recasens, 2007). Although a handful of remarkable studies relating to nightlife have been conducted in disciplines such as urban sociology (Dal Lago, 1995), youth research (Canevacci, 1999), and cultural planning (Bianchini, 1995), Italian criminologists have had little to say on such matters. This lacunae is all the more surprising when one considers that the main issues raised in Italian public debate about nightlife concern themes of violence and disorder. In tentatively initiating a filling of this 'knowledge gap', this chapter will begin by outlining some general features of the relationship between youth nightlife and crime in an Italian context. It will then go on to report the findings of a qualitative research project conducted by the authors in the northern city of Bologna.[1] This case study, it is suggested, offers

[1] Daphne European Commission project: JAI/DAP/2004-1/133/Y – 'Violence Amongst Juveniles in Leisure Places: A Status Report and Measures Adopted by Institutional Stakeholders', June 2005– May 2007.

important insights into the way in which the governance of nightlife plays out in specific urban contexts.

NIGHTLIFE AND YOUNG PEOPLE

In Italy, the lack of research attention to nightlife may be partly explained by a more general failure to prioritize or, more accurately, 'problematize' the behaviour of young people. Viewed from an outside perspective, this may be understood as a peculiar feature of Italian culture and society. The 'condition of youth' has never been associated—at least until recently, and with a few exceptions—with the categories of danger, risk, or violence. Historically, the image of young people[2] has been firmly embedded in a culture of protection and de-responsibilization. This tradition continues to inform many aspects of the social welfare and criminal justice systems, from policy to practice.

The first true public awareness of the 'dangerousness' of nightlife emerged in the 1980s and concerned the issue of road-traffic safety (the so-called 'Saturday night slaughters'[3]). It is in this regard that we find the first signs of social and institutional concern about nightlife and young people's behaviours. We also see the emergence of new ways of conceptualizing the relationship between leisure time, alcohol and illicit drug use, and social hazards. Public alarm concerning these issues resulted in important changes to the regulation of time and space for leisure activities. Access to nightclubs, in particular, became more restrictive and expensive, with greater attention paid to their hours of trading. This process fostered the beginnings of a shift in young people's night-time leisure, from privately owned and controlled indoor spaces, to public, open-air environments. In the last decade, attention has increasingly turned to young people's night-time of such spaces. More generally, one sees the beginnings of a paradigm shift in social policy. Paternalistic and welfarist understandings of the young as vulnerable subjects, requiring protection and having little formal accountability for their actions, are being replaced by a more harsh view of youth as a condition of danger, both to young people themselves and to the rest of society. Despite the powerful continuing legacy of welfarism, young Italians are now increasingly criminalized[4] and their actions related to issues of community safety, fear of crime, and incivilities. It is within this new context that we explore public and institutional reactions to young people's night-time leisure.

---

[2] In referring to 'young people' we will follow the term's application in common discourse which encompasses individuals below the age of 30. This extended definition of youth is widespread in Italian sociological literature and in the labour laws.

[3] This term is usually applied to the death of people in car crashes, which has been found to peak on Saturday nights as intoxicated drivers make their way home from nightclubs.

[4] A tendency illustrated by attempts to lower the age at which young people are deemed to assume criminal responsibility for their actions (currently set at 18 years of age), in order to make penalties more severe and to limit many of the alternatives to imprisonment once provided for young offenders.

ALCOHOL AND DRUG CONSUMPTION

ALCOHOL

Important changes have also occurred in relation to young people's alcohol and drug consumption. Drinking practices among the young are different from those of older generations. Alcohol consumption is both increasing in quantity and becoming more akin to northern European models in terms of the ways in which it is consumed. Nonetheless, consumption rates remain lower than those of most northern European countries and it is not surprising that a recent study by ISTAT (the Italian National Institute of Statistics, 2008) begins at page 1 by reminding us that: 'In Italy, consumption of alcohol is traditionally moderate and it is represented mostly by the consumption of wine during meals.' The same research points out, however, that between 1998 and 2007, the largest increase in alcohol consumption has been among young women (7 per cent) and 11- to 15-year-olds (20 per cent).[5] Moreover, young Italians are forsaking the traditional glass of wine with dinner for a focus on drinking in its own right at other times of day (15.2 per cent to 22.7 per cent) (see Fig 9.1). The ISTAT study reveals a distinct, if not dramatic, shift toward consumption of alcohol beyond mealtimes, increasing sessional consumption (binge drinking), and the mixing of different beverage types. Eighteen- to thirty-four-year-olds, especially males in Northern regions, are considered to be the most 'at risk'. As we shall describe, this increased drinking is strongly related to new forms of leisure activity, wherein young people stay out late at night in public spaces. This tendency has been fuelled, in part, by recent laws prohibiting smoking inside bars, pubs, and restaurants (L n° 3, 16 January, 2003).

DRUGS

Trends in illegal drug markets and drug consumption in Italy are similar to those found in other European countries over the past 20 years. Two central and connected issues are of note:

1. The social profile of drug users: drug consumption is no longer identified primarily with heroin addiction among the poorest, most marginalized inner-city youth.
2. The wide variety of drugs available: there has been a widespread diffusion of 'soft' drugs (eg, marijuana), synthetic drugs (eg, amphetamines, LSD, ecstasy), and cocaine. At the same time, heroin use has strongly decreased.

Locating reliable sources of data concerning patterns of drug use is not easy. However, some information is available.[6] In its annual report on drug crime, the Ministry of the

---

[5] This was despite Art 689 of the Italian Penal Code which strictly forbids the sale of alcohol to under 16-year-olds.

[6] We refer here to the Ministry of the Interior annual reports on drug crime using incidents recorded by the police and reported to the Prefecture, together with Drug Addiction Social Services data and our own qualitative research in Italian towns.

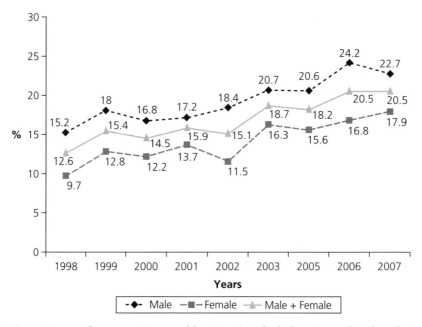

Fig 9.1 Persons from 14 to 17 years old consuming alcohol at times other than during meals. Distinction by gender (in percentage)
Source: ISTAT, 2008

Interior (2007) reports increases in police-recorded marijuana offences from 42 per cent of all drug-related offences among 14–65-year-olds in 1991 to 74 per cent in 2006, whilst cocaine offences among the same group rose from 5 per cent in 1991 to 14 per cent in 2006. By comparison, the proportion of drug offences relating to heroin diminished from 50 per cent in 1991 to 8 per cent in 2006.[7] Although Italian research on drug consumption patterns and drug-taking careers is not extensive, some researchers identify a tendency toward 'normalization' (Frontini, 2007: 346; Paoli, 2003: 87). Over the past decade, as a result of globalization, cultural transmission, and cross-border travel, young people have increasingly begun to see recreactional drug use (mainly involving cannabis, amphetamines, cocaine, and ecstasy) as an acceptable lifestyle choice.

THE CHANGING CHARACTERISTICS OF ITALIAN NIGHTLIFE

The distinctive features of young people's contemporary lifestyles and values, transformations in the labour market, and the changing political and economic fortunes of Italian towns and cities, are manifested no more so than in the content of young

[7] Barbagli, Colombo, and Savona (2003: 85) provide more detailed remarks and analyses concerning drug assumption in Italy and its changes over the years. Other comparative data, available in the European schools survey, ESPAD Report (although not updated), shows that consumption of drugs among 15–16-year-old Italian students is high in comparison with many other countries (Hibell et al, 2000), this is particularly the case for heroin consumption (Paoli, 2003: 93).

people's leisure activity and its visibility in time and space. Cavalli, De Lillo, and Buzzi (2002) found that 60 per cent of young Italians aged 18–24 years old went out at night more than twice a week. Participation in nightlife was greater for boys, with girls often remaining subject to different parental rules and expectations. Girls came out above all on Fridays and Saturdays and were usually obliged to return home earlier than boys. These differences were especially evident in the southern regions of the country where traditional patriarchal and paternalistic values remain strong. Whilst clubs remained an important facet of night culture, with 70 per cent of respondents saying that they regularly attended such venues, the second most important activity was to 'hang around with my friends' (62 per cent)—as encompassed by the British concept of 'loitering'—followed by going to pubs and bars (50.2 per cent) and inviting friends round to their home, or meeting up at a friend's home (41.4 per cent).

The most important change in young Italians' 'leisure worlds' has involved a move *from the inside to the outside*. From the 1990s onwards, the nightclub, as the traditional 'container' of youth leisure activities, started to lose its pre-eminence and appeal (Chiarello, 2000; Torti, 1997, 1998). Through the diffusion of DIY rave culture and of new forms of youthful congregation and appropriation, a new model of leisure emerged based around the spatial fragmentation of different youth tribes and an extension of 'party time', further into the night. Nightlife became open to different possibilities and constituencies. In addition to pubs, bars, and restaurants, locations for youth nightlife might include abandoned industrial buildings, beaches, caves and opens spaces in the country. More visibly, the public streets and squares of towns and cities became increasingly important sites for youthful leisure, especially at night. This later phenomenon is more evident in the university cities of Bologna, Florence, and Milan in northern and central Italy. However, the establishment of several university centres in smaller provincial towns such as Ferrara, Forlì, Cremona, Rimini, and Ancona has encouraged the spread of similar phenomena across many areas, nationally.

Public space offers a section of youth—particularly those who cannot afford to attend nightlife venues, or who lack the capacity and resources to travel to commercial entertainment hubs—an accessible opportunity to socialize. This is understandable when one considers that a single bottle of beer costs 7 or 8 euros and they would need to spend 50 euros or more just to enter a nightclub and enjoy a few drinks. This search for a more affordable leisure experience has also favoured small ethnically owned convenience stores which are able to sell cans and bottles of beers and wine at reduced prices because their customers do not need, or expect, table service from waiters and they do not need to wash glasses, cutlery, or tableware. Young people simply consume their drinks in public space, directly from the bottle or can. Such venues also save money because the cost of liquor licences and planning permits is calculated according to a venue's size and facilities.

As discussed below, the regulation of night-time leisure is not well organized, being fragmented across different institutional actors. Nightclub closing times are determined by regional laws and fixed by municipal government, usually cohering around 4.00 am. It is forbidden to sell alcohol in the last hour before closing time and music volume must also be reduced at this time. The general framework of municipal regulation applied to bars and pubs allows for much local discretion, with different rules applied in different regions of the country and sometimes in different areas of the same city.

NIGHTLIFE IN BOLOGNA: A CASE STUDY

In most Italian towns, especially university towns, nightlife is now segmented into three different leisure scenes: the 'mega-discos', bars, pubs, and restaurants, attended by the most affluent groups of young people; the 'alternative venues'—such as social centres—for smaller, more politicized groups seeking alternatives to egalitarian lei-sure; and finally, public space for the mass gatherings of those who cannot afford to attend licensed nightclubs and only occasionally visit the second tier of the leisure market—the more affordable bars, pubs, and clubs. The first two scenes are based around music, dancing, and other formally organized leisure experiences as the main attractions which bring people together. Public space, of course, offers a more informal context for leisure in which young people must find their own amusement. Conflicts and tensions related to crime and disorder are qualitatively similar across the three scenes, differences lying in their level of intensity and the varying capacity of actors to exercise control. Control measures are much stronger in the venues, and especially nightclubs, than they are in public space. What all three scenes share is a focus on the consumption of alcohol and drugs as a normal and expected way for the young to spend time together (although scenes differ in relation to participants' drugs of choice and their specific consumption practices). The three scenes are not completely segmented and many young people retain the ability to choose which they wish to par-ticipate in. This is particularly the case for users of public and alternative spaces who may intersperse their activities between each within the course of the same evening. It is much less true of the nightclub scene which has become increasingly exclusive and geared toward the demands of a specific affluent audience (see Hadfield, 2008).

Bologna, with its university district and central square, the Piazza Verdi, is an inter-esting area in which to explore these changes in nightlife, youth lifestyles, crime and disorder, and related governmental responses.[8] Until a decade ago, the square, and the university area in general, was surrounded by nightclubs, social centres, and theatres. Within the space of a few years these businesses and facilities either closed down or moved to outlying neighbourhoods. At the same time, the university area was deeply affected by other changes. Most of the original bookshops and small grocers were replaced by bars. Pubs opened, or were enlarged. Above all, a concentration of small, ethnically owned grocery shops selling cheap alcohol emerged. These businesses chose to remain open late at night despite a series of administrative orders to the contrary. At the same time, Bologna's university area became known as having one of the largest street-level drug markets in northern Italy. However, this image of disorder

---

[8] Our research strategy consisted of 20 semi-structured interviews with civil servants of the Bologna Municipality's Social Services Department, local police officers, bouncers, shopkeepers, members of citizens' committees, students, and members of a youth subculture known as the *punka bestia*. Participant observa-tion was also conducted three times a week on the streets and in two of Bologna's nightclubs, between November 2006 and January 2007. See also, Pavarini (2006).

and decline went hand in hand with the retention of more positive perceptions of a tolerant and lively neighbourhood. The University of Bologna remains one of the top academic centres in Italy and for students the attractiveness of this institution and the city in which it is located, remains as strong as ever.

Our fieldwork found that young people met in the square and then spent the night drinking and talking, sometimes moving from one bar to another one, but always within a very limited area. Sometimes there were concerts in the square organized by the owners of one of the largest bars, by the municipality, or by youth associations. In these circumstances, leisure activity was more structured and music became the main attraction and focus. These cultural events were, however, unusual and for most of the time venues in the area offered a standardized 'bar-room' experience. Nonetheless, drinks prices were high and for this reason many young people arrived with their own home-brewed beverages, or bought alcohol in the convenience stores at significantly lower prices than to be found in the area's bars and pubs. Unsurprisingly, young people's differing economic capacities tended to channel them into separate leisure scenes. The high cost of cultural attractions such as cinema, theatre, and live music acted as a deterrent to many who spent their night in the square. At the same time, public transport in Bologna was very limited after 9.00 pm and they could not easily reach other spaces, such as the social centres, located far from the centre of town. Neither could they afford the more expensive out-of-town nightclubs.

Many buildings in Bologna's historic university quarter contain residential accommodation rented to students. Students in the area often hold large parties, attracting numerous people: both invitees and gatecrashers. These leisure activities are not explored in this study other than to note the view of many interviewees concerning their effects on surrounding public spaces. We were told that during and after the parties, people go in and out from the buildings and their presence increases the number of people present in the square. Moreover, arguments over admission to student parties could provoke conflict among young people. However, the most important conflicts arose in relation to problems of noise for other residents.

Young people who used the square at night tended to share a propensity to view leisure time as unstructured time spent loitering with a glass of beer, talking to each other, smoking (usually marijuana), using amphetamines and, less frequently, heroin. In this way, they seemed to keep alive the old collective traditions of using the urban square as a civic meeting place. The numbers involved, however, are without precedent; average occupancy at any one time being 50–60, but rising to several hundred during the summertime and at weekends. The crowds usually gather in late afternoon and stay in the square until 3.00 am, or beyond. The phenomenon is the same—albeit with reduced numbers—in smaller university towns across central and northern Italy. Even those revellers who purchase their drinks in the bars often choose to take their drinks outside. Many of the venues are small and, especially following the ban on smoking in enclosed spaces,[9] people usually stay inside for a short while only to join the throng outside in the street or under Bologna's famous arcades which provide a

[9] Law no 3, 16 January, 2003 strictly forbids smoking inside bars, shops, pubs, etc. This has further increased the number of young people populating the streets and squares.

canopy over the pavement. These seem to be the favoured socializing spots for students and visitors from out of town alike.

The objectives of revellers, as expressed in our interviews, were simply those of staying 'out and about', drinking, seeing, and being seen. This seems to confirm that the leisure values preferred by young people in this context are related to the importance of social relationships and social identity (they like to stay in the square because it is the place to meet friends and acquaintances, week in, week out). They also enjoyed the opportunity to meet in a space that was considered 'free'—both in financial terms, and to the extent that their actions in such space were ungoverned and, to some extent, ungovernable; the street being a space where they felt they could do whatever they wanted. Above all, they could break the rules and transgress. It was not clear to what degree the wish to define communal leisure in such terms was spontaneous or provoked by the conditions of the leisure market and the economic constraints young people faced. It seems likely, however, that such considerations mutually inform one another. By contrast, police, local government, and residents tended to view unstructured leisure time as a threat to public order. Integration into the commercial nightlife scene was seen as a protective factor which reduced the risk of violence and antisocial behaviour through the application of formal control by venue management.

YOUTH GROUPS IN THE UNIVERSITY AREA

It was possible to distinguish four different groupings of young people who frequented the nightlife of Bologna. Their norms, values, and lifestyles were found to influence the ways in which each group approached and used public spaces:

1. The so-called *punka bestia* are a group of young urban travellers who live on the streets with their dogs (Cardinali, 2001). The label may be attached to a small group of marginal young men and women (about 50 persons), who have been the target of many, generally ineffective, social interventions. *Punka bestia* are characterized by their multiple social problems: most of them are drug or alcohol addicted (or both), some are mentally or physically ill (pneumonia, HIV). Their lifestyle involves loitering during the day and for much of the night. They are also involved in begging, street-level drug dealing, vandalism, petty crime, and various minor incivilities. As a result, the police, local government, and residents view them as the most problematic group and many efforts have been made to provide support services (in 2001, for example, a shelter was created to host people and their dogs in an area outside the city centre. Unfortunately, this facility has now closed[10]). The phenomenon of the young urban traveller seems to be widespread across many different European countries, providing further confirmation of the 'globalization' in young people's attitudes, lifestyles, and emerging subcultures.[11]

2. The so-called 'normal students' are young men and women who migrate to the city, usually from other regions of Italy, in order to study. They face a daily struggle to

---

[10] According to a statement by the Municipality, the centre closed due to its high running costs and because it had failed to deter the *punka bestia* from loitering in Bologna's historic city centre.

[11] See Pattegay (2001) regarding the traveller phenomenon in France.

meet the high costs of university tuition fees, housing, and other costs of living on a low income. They favour the old attractive features of the town and appreciate the lively street life, both for its own qualities and because more expensive leisure options are beyond their reach. Many are attracted to the seemingly carefree and rebellious lifestyle of the *punka bestia,* adopting similar fashions and loitering habits, whilst generally avoiding the more serious forms of substance misuse, ill health, and criminality. These stylistic emulators are sometimes called the *punka fiction.* Yet, social workers report an increasing number of borderline situations in which youthful rebellion translates into students unable to complete their courses, developing gradually higher levels of drug and alcohol addiction, and being at risk of long-term marginalization and criminal careers.

3. North African drug dealers form the third notable group. Some are as young as 10 years old, many are teenagers, whilst a few are older, up to the age of 40. This group is, of course, considered problematic due to the nature of their criminal activity, but also because they are present in the square for much of the day and night. They are perceived to be violent and aggressive and many carry knives. A high proportion of the violent incidents—including assaults and brawls—that occur in outdoor leisure contexts are related to their presence. Much of this violence is induced by quarrels between the different drug suppliers, or between dealers and their clients. Other tensions surround attempts by this group to incorporate themselves into the leisure activities of the students and *punka bestia.*

4. Fourthly, there are the 'visitors'. These are tourists and young people coming into the city centre for the night. The presence of visitors is most noticeable on Fridays and Saturdays. As noted, Bologna, despite its problems, is still considered a lively town, rich in opportunities. Many young people from other towns and regions travel to Bologna for their entertainment. Visitors are much less likely than the other groups to use the square as the focus for their leisure activities. More often, they cross the square and its surroundings, looking for a place (pub or bar) to spend the night. It is during these movements that they sometimes find themselves in conflict with members of the other groups.

With the exception of most of the 'visitors' group, what these different tribes of adolescents and young adults share is a conception of public space as anomic space—a space where anything can happen, everything is allowed, and where rules, even if represented by a strong police presence, cannot be enforced. At the same time, they express dissatisfaction with their economic status and the often mundane nature of their leisure activities, regretting that they cannot afford more interesting activities, or blaming the municipal government for its poor leisure and cultural facilities.

CONFLICT AND VIOLENCE IN THE SQUARE

In the square and surrounding streets, it is not so much crime, but a general climate of intolerance, fear, and hostility which haunts young people's opportunities for leisure. In our interviews, this atmosphere was perceived by young participants and regulators alike. It sat uneasily alongside more utopian conceptions of a communal liminal zone, free from the strictures of the old, the dour, the authoritarian, and the greedy. Certainly, the square could be a dangerous place, but the term 'conflict' was used much more often than 'violence' or 'crime'. Conflict, from young people's perspectives, meant the propensity for verbal jousts to be provoked for what—when removed from the social context of an encounter—often seemed trivial reasons: a look, a comment about a girl, a misread gesture. Informants did not define these honour contests as 'violent' but, rather, perceived their leisure time as embedded in an egoistic social setting in which people were competitive and intolerant of others around them. Most conflicts were not collective, but arose between two people. These incidents could then escalate to involve others in the square (usually friends of the initial interlocutors).[12] In a worst-case scenario, arguments would degenerate into physical violence. In the opinion of many interviewees, drug and alcohol consumption lay behind the squabbling. Conflict increased late at night, usually after 11.00 pm when states of intoxication reached their peak.

Use of the square did sometimes involve contestation between different groups. In the case of the *punka bestia*, conflicts often related to the difficult conditions of street life, to drugs, and to involvement in petty larceny.[13] *Punka bestia* were without doubt the most quarrelsome and challenging group, squabbling between themselves, challenging police authority, clashing with the other young people in the square. Incidents involving North African dealers were less frequent, but often more serious due to the severity of physical injury sustained in knife attacks. Violence of this kind usually began with a quarrel over a drug deal (the price, or the quality of drugs, etc), especially when the client was a *punka bestia*.

There were interesting gender-related aspects to the conflicts in the square. Interviewees often noted that young women could be equally as aggressive as men. However, the research also highlighted the extent of physically abusive relationships between couples. This was particularly apparent among the *punka bestia*, where girls were sometimes battered by their partners, or forced to prostitute themselves to pay the North African drug dealers. Moreover, a number of rapes had occurred in the area, not all of which had been reported to the police. This remained something of a hidden problem as only the most notorious cases had received coverage in the press. The North African dealers were regarded as the main sources of harassment and violence against women, further underlining the danger derived from their presence in the university area.

In relation to many types of conflict in the square it was difficult to distinguish 'victim' from 'aggressor': in a socially disorganized setting, these roles would overlap throughout the course of an evening. There was an expectation of low-level conflict and the less serious incidents appeared to have no lasting consequence for the relationships between the people involved: the night after, both parties would be drinking together once again, last night's passions seemingly forgotten. The only group to which the label 'typical victim' might less problematically be attached were the visitors. This

---

[12] Interviewees associated fear and stress with the presence of aggressive dogs. This was because dogs were often involved in the quarrels and brawls involving *punka bestia*.

[13] But, as a social worker reminded us, when someone steals your jacket, and it is cold and you are living on the street, the loss experienced may be far from 'petty'.

group might become embroiled in conflicts while crossing the square or drinking outside the bars and pubs. Local press reports tended to emphasize this view of the urban 'riff raff' preying upon 'nice young people' from out of town who found themselves involved in dangerous situations they could not avoid or control. Conflicts also arose between users of the square and other actors, principally, residents, police, and shopkeepers. It was in this context that we found cases of collective reaction to control situations in which the fragmented groups within the square seemed to find a sort of temporary solidarity.

In the collective memory of the city, this solidarity echoes the political agitation of the late 1960s and 70s. During this era the university area and the Piazza Verdi were the scenes of fighting between the radical leftist Movimento degli Studenti and the police, including infamous incidents in which students lost their lives. Although both the context and the issues at stake are now very different, the local 'sense of place' in these areas nonetheless retains its associations with protest, rebellion, and conflict, especially between young people and the police.

Some local politicians, social workers, and students believed that one should look beyond the everyday situational precursors to conflict and violence, to deeper structural problems. These included the city authorities' hostility toward young people, the difficult conditions of many students' lives, and their lack of opportunity to pursue others forms of leisure. Such explanations conformed to the welfarist perspective discussed earlier. Other interviewees, such as residents and private security guards, took a different view. For them, the roots of conflict in the square were to be found in a clash of values, and a lack of respect for others, an ethic to which the young people involved did not seem to adhere. The complaints of residents mostly surrounded issues of social and physical disorder related to the presence of young people in the square and surrounding streets. Such views were communicated strongly to those police and municipal government officials involved in local community safety. In this respect, the main conflicts were not between the young themselves, but between young people and the city, its rules, established order, and traditional way of life.

POLICING, SECURITY, AND CRIME CONTROL

Italy has five types of police organization, each with its own peculiar structure and functions:

1. the *Polizia di Stato*: the nationwide civilian police force
2. the *Carabinieri*: armed services permanently employed as police for the preservation of public security
3. the Financial Police: have a customs and excise role
4. the Forest Rangers (forestry police)
5. Penitentiary Police (prison guards).

In addition, some provinces have their own provincial police and all city councils have a municipal police force. These municipal forces are charged with traffic control and enforcement of city ordinances and regional laws. In addition to their specific duties, all police organizations are expected to assist one another in preserving public security and order. In accordance with a community-policing ethos, city governments depend upon their provincial and municipal police to address petty crime and incivilities. Contact and dialogue with citizens is promoted by these local police teams, acting in a proactive manner to reassure the public, act as mediators, and resolve conflicts. At the same time, these officers may be called upon to act immediately and authoritatively to suppress low-level crime and antisocial behaviour. Local police teams are tasked with enforcing local government by-laws prohibiting certain behaviours. Many by-laws apply to activities commonly associated with night-time leisure in Italy, for example, drinking alcohol in certain areas at certain times of night, and setting up unlicensed campsites in public areas. Regulators tend to regard ordinances and by-laws as the most appropriate preventive measures against low-level incivility. However, at night, police numbers are not sufficient to enforce them city-wide (Pavarini, 2006) and, even when there are prosecutions, penalties are quite lenient and do not deter repeat offenders.

Municipal governments have invested in situational crime prevention measures such as CCTV and improved street lighting for their city streets and squares. Recent years have also seen the introduction of street-warden schemes in several Italian cities, specifically to address crime and disorder in leisure time. These volunteers act as a link between council services and other agencies, especially the police. Close working relationships between municipal district councils and area-based municipal policing teams have increased the effectiveness of surveillance in specific locations, such as concert halls and theatres. One of the most important causes of disturbance to residents is the noisy gatherings of people who congregate in front of nightclubs, pubs, and other leisure venues. Police Commissioners have the power to suspend the licence of a venue where serious incidents of disorder have occurred, or where the location presents a danger to public order or the safety of citizens. If the events that have caused the suspension are repeated, Law no 773 Royal Decree June 18 1931 Art 100 (TULPS) allows for the licence to be permanently revoked. There are also national laws that allow municipalities to enact administrative rules in order to control the number of bars and nightclubs and the times they close. These regulations usually involve 'zoning' wherein different rules apply to different areas of a city.

In December 1999, central government and the SILB (a trade organization representing the Italian nightclub industry) signed a Protocol of Agreement[14] concerning the professional training of nightclub personnel, especially bouncers. The content of this training was specified to include knowledge of youth lifestyles, drug identification, drug cultures and the law, mediation, crowd control, and emergency and first-aid procedures concerning alcohol and drug misuse. Nightclub operators were also enrolled in public programmes to promote drug and alcohol awareness through youth education campaigns, the promotion of non-alcoholic drinks, and a reduction in noise levels inside nightclubs. On 28 February 2001 the Ministry of the Interior

---

[14] A Protocol of Agreement is not a contract in the technical sense but a voluntary undertaking which is codified in an administrative document. As a voluntary code of practice its enforcement is left to the discretion of the institutions involved.

and the SILB signed a further Protocol of Agreement called 'ClubSafe'. This protocol stressed the importance of cooperation between bouncers, nightclub managers, and the police and sought to incorporate this within the leisure industry's professional training courses. In 2000 the Municipality of Bologna, in cooperation with the SILB and national police headquarters, developed Italy's first training course for bouncers. Seventy hours of training is now available to bouncers and nightclub managers and the course is also taken by police officers from the national and local forces in order to foster greater cooperation. Unfortunately, the effectiveness of these preventive initiatives has not been evaluated and there seems little chance that public monies will be made available to fund appropriate research.

CONCLUSIONS

To conclude, our research suggests that, in Italy, issues of conflict and violence in the context of nightlife are of increasing public and institutional concern. The attention now paid to criminogenic features of young people's leisure activity represents a further step in changing cultural perceptions of youth. In a country where young people had long been considered not fully responsible for their actions—more in need of counsel and protection than repression and punishment—this is a profound step. There is a growing perception of the dangerousness of youth and of social hazards related to juvenile behaviours. Yet, despite these increasing concerns, there remains a paucity of research on youth crime in general, and crime and disorder related to nightlife specifically.

Changing political, economic, and social conditions undoubtedly exert important pressures on contemporary youth. The commercial entertainment market has become increasingly segmented, presenting differing opportunities (and forms of exclusion) to different groups of young people. The greatest gap is in the dichotomy between leisure activity in public space and leisure in the nightclubs. The former is largely informal, uncontrolled, and partly founded on the attractions of deviance inherent in the infringement of civic rules; the latter is increasingly standardized, regimented, accountable to regulators, and embedded in broader official control mechanisms— some would say, sanitized. In both contexts, however, conflict and violence are closely associated with the sale and consumption of alcohol and drugs. The incidents occurring in public space are qualitatively similar to those in nightclubs, as both relate to the darker, egoistic, and competitive face of nightlife. Yet, the conflicts in public space have their own, especially poignant resonance. Students and other young people feel abandoned by civic institutions and under-protected against the presence of groups such as the *punka bestia* and drug dealers, with whom they must share leisure space. Whilst much of the crime and disorder that occurs in nightclubs and commercial venues goes unnoticed, the leisure life of our public spaces is widely condemned as a menace. Such public gatherings are seen to undermine harmonious relations between different generations and social groups, and to threaten the interests of towns and cities: their reputations, traditions, and civic laws.

Politicians, local governments, and police have failed to develop consistent strategies for controlling nightlife. In particular, there has been a lack of coordinated action between the different governmental actors. Attempts to intervene in the public spaces of the university areas and historical centres of Italian towns and cities have failed to produce sustainable resolutions to the conflicts which surround their appropriation by youth. This has only fuelled public concern regarding the insecurity of nightlife and the dangerousness of youth.

REFERENCES

All internet sources were accessible 20 August 2008

BARBAGLI M, COLOMBO, AD and SAVONA, EU (2003) 'Le Sostanze Legali e Illegali', in M Barbagli, AD Colombo and EU Savona (eds), *Sociologia Della Devianza*, Bologna: Il Mulino, 73–105.

BIANCHINI, F (1995) 'Night cultures, night economies', *Planning, Practice and Research*, 10/2, 112–26.

CANOVACCI, M (1999) *Culture Extreme*, Rome: Meltemi.

CARDINALI, M (2001) 'I Nomadi della Nuova Era: Uno Studio di Sociologia della Devianza', *Dei Delitti e Delle Pene*, 1/3, 265–301.

CAVALLI, A, DE LILLO, A and BUZZI, C (eds) (2002) *Giovani del Nuovo Secolo: Quinta Indagine IARD Sulla Condizione Giovanile in Italia*, Bologna: Il Mulino.

CHIARELLO, F (2000) 'Le Derive della Notte, I Giovani e le Discoteche', *Minori e Giustizia*, 2, 68–82.

DAL LAGO, A (1995) *I Nostri riti Quotidiani. Prospettive Nell'analisi della Cultura*, Genoa: Costa and Nolan.

FRONTINI, M (2007) 'L'Addiction: Propensione Individuale e Influenza del Contesto', in C Buzzi, A Cavalli and A de Lillo (eds), *Rapporto Giovani. Sesta Indagine dell'Istituto IARD sulla Condizione Giovanile in Italia*, Bologna, Il Mulino, 341–52.

HADFIELD, P (2008) 'From threat to promise: Nightclub "security", governance and consumer elites', *British Journal of Criminology*, 48, 429–47.

HIBELL, B, ANDERSSON, B, AHLSTROM, S, BALAKIREVA, O, BJARNASSON, T, KOKKEVI, A and MORGAN, M (2000) *The 1999 ESPAD Report: Alcohol and other drug use among students in 30 European countries*, Stockholm: Council of Europe, Pompidou Group.

ISTAT (National Institute of Statistics) (2008), 'L'Uso e l'Abuso di Alcol in Italia', *Statistiche in Breve*, Rome: ISTAT.

MINISTRY OF THE INTERIOR (2007) *Drug Offences in Italy: Central Drug Unit Annual Report 2006*, Rome: Ministry of the Interior.

PAOLI, L (2003) 'Il Mercato delle Droghe', in M Barbagli (ed), *Rapporto sulla Criminalità in Italia*, Bologna: Il Mulino, 81–108.

PATTEGAY, P (2001) 'L'Actuelle Construction, en France, du Problème des Jeunes en Errance. Analyse Critique d'une Catégorie d'Action Publique', *Déviance et Société*, 25/3, 257–77.

PAVARINI, M (2006) 'La Costruzione Sociale della Sicurezza a Bologna', *Metronomie*, 32-33 June–December, 37–65.

RECASENS, A (ed) (2007) *Violence Between Young People in Night-Time Leisure Zones*, Brussels: Brussels University Press.

TORTI, MT (1997) *Abitare la Notte*, Genoa: Costa and Nolan.

—— (1998) 'La Seduzione della Notte', *Animazione Sociale*, May, 10–14.

10

SPAIN

Anabel Rodríguez Basanta

INTRODUCTION

In recent decades, Spain has undergone the transition from a dictatorship which placed great restrictions on the private and public life of its citizens to a European consumer society. Youth nightlife has mirrored the path of this transition. From the 1970s onwards, young people began to frequent nightlife venues in large numbers with their peer groups, commencing the process of separating the young from the community-focused leisure spaces and times they had shared with older adults, and marking the emergence of an important economic sector in this field. The process reached its peak from the mid-1990s onwards: leisure options multiplied and diversified, the users of commercial nightlife increased in number, and the young consolidated their takeover of the night.

This chapter will describe how changing patterns of alcohol consumption have been a major aspect of this transition and the bedrock of a new leisure economy. Spanish drinking practices have come closer to the models more typically seen among the cultures of northern Europe, the aim being to obtain the desired state of festive euphoria through rapid intoxication. The considerable increase in nightlife options has been similarly accompanied by a popularization of the recreational consumption of narcotic substances. Over recent years, 'partying' holidays in the sun have become the focus for young foreign visitors to an unprecedented degree, thanks to the emergence of low-cost airlines and package tourism.

Spanish research in the field of youth leisure has primarily focused on analyses of individual and group values in relation to time use and risk-taking behaviours, such as recreational drug use, sexual practices, driving risks, etc (Aguinaga and Comas, 1997; Comas, 2003; Elzo, 1999; González et al, 1997; Megías, 2001). However, there has been little research into the problems of public security generated by the nightlife economy, or any assessment of institutional strategies in this field. This chapter will examine how growth of the leisure economy has taken place without a clear model of public management. The reactions of official institutions have not been consistent across Spain's three tiers of government (state, autonomous regions, and individual towns). In many cases, governmental initiatives have simply responded to occasional bouts of social alarm by instigating repressive enforcement measues against the most visible manifestations of the problem: leisure venues themselves. There has been a distinct failure to integrate nightlife concerns into the pre-planning of routine policing and other public services, such as transport. Moreover, regulatory action has proved ineffectual in tackling countervailing pressures towards excess from powerful economic agents, such as the alcohol industry. The chapter will go on to describe the increasing importance of informal leisure practices among young people in public spaces, in particular, the so-called *botellón* phenomenon, involving mass gatherings of young people drinking alcohol in the street. It will be argued that the rise of the *botellón* highlights the effects of an increasingly exclusive commercial leisure scene.

FROM POPULAR LEISURE TO THE LEISURE ECONOMY

In their review of the evolution of Spanish nightlife spaces from the post-Civil War period onwards, Pallarés and Feixa (2000)[1] describe how, with the country undergoing social and economic reconstruction, and with limited free time, leisure was confined to communal spaces (parks, boulevards). These spaces were characterized by strong informal community-based controls over the activities of youth. Dance halls, which had benefited from certain relaxations during the pre-war period, were widely demonized in public discourse as 'immoral' locations, frequented only by the lowest classes.

From the mid-1960s onwards, new forms of youth leisure began to emerge which broke with parental control and marked a clear distinction between the leisure spaces of young and old. These venues were known as *guateques* and *boîtes*, the latter with their origins in tourist areas, in particular the Balearic Islands, and the Mediterranean coast. Bars and pubs associated with the cultural and political mood of the transitional period began to appear in the mid-1970s. In particular, a middle-class political movement known as the *movida* set the scene for a break with the ethical and moral values of the dictatorship. The period marked the beginning of a shift in the hours of nightlife towards later times.[2]

---

[1] Analyses of the recent evolution of formal and informal youth leisure, together with changing trends in young people's drug consumption can be found in Pallarés et al (2006).

[2] The previous regulations dating back to 1935 imposed a general closing time of 1.30 am with only 'cabarets' permitted to open until 5 am. Royal Decree 2816 of 27 August 1982 introducing a new set of 'General Police Regulations for Public Performances and Recreational Activities' adapted to the new leisure practices that had emerged since 1960s, including the opportunity for later closing times to be negotiated with the authorities.

Nightclubs proliferated in the 1980s and began to specialize (in terms of musical styles and aesthetics) in order to attract different types of patron and become more 'sophisticated'. On the outskirts of cities, more egalitarian 'mega-clubs' also began to appear. The 1990s witnessed the rise of a 'party-oriented' hedonistic approach to nightlife: between 1996 and 2003 the number of teenagers and young people going to nightclubs doubled (Comas, 2003). The weekend became consolidated as the time for leisure, and for the establishment of social boundaries between adults and young people. The diversification of leisure options intensified towards the end of this period (with a clearer distinction, for example, between winter and summer nightlife). Over the course of the decade, clubbing sessions became longer and longer, and in response to the demand from a sector of users, after-hours venues began to emerge.[3] In the last decade, a number of independent club promoters from northern Europe have begun to arrive, seeking to operate their 'brands' in the resorts, principally in Ibiza. These foreign leisure businesses have been assimilated by the local commercial sector through the use of nightclub venues. Over recent years, the success of summer music festivals has led to further diversification of leisure options. Leisure is now central to the political economy of many Spanish towns and cities, particularly in coastal areas where 'sun and party' tourism has become very popular among young foreign visitors. Finally, the emergence of a large immigrant community has also increased the heterogeneity of Spain's leisure map. Some groups of immigrants, in particular those from Latin America, have organized their own leisure scene.[4]

PROBLEMS ASSOCIATED WITH LEISURE PRACTICES

ALCOHOL-RELATED TRAFFIC ACCIDENTS

In Spain, more than 50 per cent of young people going out on the town travel in a private car, either as a driver or passenger (RACC, 2006). Car use has, meanwhile, become a very important element of identity for young people. In a country where the cost of housing often prevents young people from 'flying the nest' until the age of 30, buying a vehicle means establishing a private space and has become a badge of social distinction.

Figures for accident and fatality rates in traffic accidents show the greatest risks emanate from 18- to 30-year-olds at night during weekends. Around 40 per cent

---

[3] For most young people, the final stage of nightclub partying takes place between 3.00 and 6.00 am at which point some will go on to an after-hours establishment. After-hours venues are unregulated and generally operate illegally under a licence for some other type of activity.

[4] Economic migration into Spain is, in comparison with other European countries, a fairly recent phenomenon. Beginning in earnest in the 1980s, it reached a new peak during the period of strong growth in the Spanish economy from 2000 onwards. Barcelona's immigrant population, for example, increased from a level of 5 per cent in 2001 to 15.5 per cent in 2007, and more than 40 per cent in some districts. Seventy per cent of this immigration is from developing countries (Ajuntament de Barcelona, 2007). This rapid increase in immigration has had a major impact on the social and demographic profile of many areas.

of those killed in traffic accidents test positive for alcohol (Instituto Nacional de Toxicología, 2002) and the popularization of recreational-drug use at leisure events has increased traffic risks. A lack of equipment to perform roadside drugs tests has focused the efforts of authorities on controlling the possession and consumption of drugs in public places.[5] Alcohol and drug checkpoints target this age group, with the police often performing operations close to nightlife areas. General prevention campaigns have also promoted the practice of using a 'designated driver' who abstains from drinking alcohol or taking drugs.

Some studies question the effectiveness of such measures as around 30 per cent of young drivers exiting nightclubs are still found to be over the permitted blood alcohol limit (RACC, 2005). More recent studies, however, indicate a slight reduction in such problems (RACC, 2006) although it is not possible to say if this is due to the campaigns. As noted below, in many areas, the main obstacle to effectively reducing this type of risk surrounds the lack of public transport services at night, such services offering the most accessible alternative to the use of private vehicles.

ILLEGAL DRUGS

The *movida* movement of the 1970s was associated with the rise of experimental drug use, involving substances such as cannabis, LSD, and heroin. In terms of crime, this new Spanish drug culture was associated with working-class youths and the consequences of their heroin addiction on the rates of property offences. Drug use during this period had little connection with leisure environments.[6] By the 1990s, the numbers of property crimes perpetrated by drug users began to fall.[7] Concern shifted from the prevention and treatment of private and street-level heroin addiction[8] towards nightlife environments. 'Techno' venues, in particular, became associated with the increasing popularity of synthetic drugs such as ecstasy.

The Spanish association between nightlife and synthetic drugs began in the 1970s on the Balearic Islands, but gained a massive resurgence with the arrival of the 'Acid House' scene of the late 1980s (Gruppo Abele, 2004). This new drug scene was introduced by tourists from northern Europe and at first remained limited to small, elite groups. The early 1990s saw these leisure and consumption practices gradually transfer to the mainland via tourist destinations such as the Levante coast. This form of nightlife then became further popularized with the setting up of mega-clubs and clubbing routes (the most famous being the *bakalao route* between Madrid and Valencia) allowing young people to spend the whole weekend travelling non-stop from one club to another.

---

[5] The Protection of Public Safety Act 1992 is an administrative law under which fines are levied for the possession and consumption of controlled drugs. In the case of drug dealing and trafficking, penal laws apply and the typical tariff is imprisonment.

[6] Recasens (2001) provides an analysis of the main security problems in Spain in the 1980s and 90s.

[7] This was the result of a combination of various factors: HIV infection; deaths by overdose; damage limitation and substitution programmes (methadone); education, social and employment integration programmes; and broader economic recovery and employment opportunities.

[8] A general overview of legal, social, and public-health responses to the drugs issue in Spain from the beginning of the democratic era can be found in Arana et al (2000).

Surveys of self-reported drug use also reveal increases in the use of cocaine from the mid-1990s onwards.[9] Cocaine use is associated with older clubbers who have greater purchasing power than the teenagers consuming ecstasy and other designer drugs. In the second half of the 90s, a number of tragic episodes involving young people dying as a result of polydrug use at raves (typically the combination of synthetic drugs and alcohol) served to generate a state of public alarm, forcing the authorities to react. Public funding became available for drug agencies engaged in risk-reduction programmes at nightlife venues (information about the risks, pill testing, etc). This network of agencies has now consolidated, becoming an essential point of reference for leisure entrepreneurs and public bodies concerned with the promotion of 'safe clubbing' environments. Voluntary organizations have even become interlocutors between businesses and regulators, groups who are often at odds as a result of the interventionist approach of the authorities in regulating and controlling nightlife operations.[10]

Nonetheless, governmental action in this field has more often been repressive. Both criminal and administrative law allow for penalties to be imposed based on involvement in, or simply tolerance of, the sale and consumption of illegal drugs at venues. However, the authorities often have difficulty obtaining the necessary evidence to prove this participation.[11] They therefore adopt a two-fold indirect strategy to control both the operation of the venue and its patrons. First, they intensify inspection and monitoring of the regulatory conditions for the venue to operate (licence, health and emergency regulations, monitoring of opening hours and capacity, qualifications of private security staff, etc). Secondly, police controls are stepped up at the exits, checking patrons for the possession of drugs and breath testing those about to drive.[12] Venues bear the brunt of this official scrutiny in terms of fines and loss of custom, leading many operators to increase security at their establishments to prevent the sale of narcotic substances and more obvious acts of consumption.

THE PROTECTION OF CHILDREN

State legislation[13] prohibits all persons under the age of 16 from entering nightclubs and dance halls and places the responsibility for legal compliance on the owners of

[9] Drug use among 15–64-years-olds in Spain is measured every two years, see Ministerio de Sanidad y Consumo (Ministry of Health and Consumption) (2007).

[10] One result of this cooperation is the *Guía Preventiva y de Seguridad para Espacios de Música y Baile* (Security and Prevention Guide for Music and Dance Spaces) (Energy Control, 2006), produced jointly by a number of NGOs, venue managers, and public representatives and featuring recommendations on how to reduce the social and health risks associated with drug consumption.

[11] For example, it is hard to prove that staff are tolerating the consumption of drugs given the nature of consumption (pill-taking can be very inconspicuous), the location where drugs are consumed (queues, toilets), and the range of precautions which may have been taken.

[12] For example, on 28 June 2002 the Catalan parliament presented a motion on drug policy to the regional government, calling for increased preventive policing at major nightlife venues. This led to the instigation of 'peaceful Saturday' campaigns, with police units being deployed in nightlife areas to conduct mass alcohol and drug testing.

[13] Royal Decree 2816 of 27 August 1982 introduced the General Police Regulations for Public Performances and Recreational Activities.

the venues. Until recently, 16 was also the minimum age at which a person could buy alcohol. However, from 2002 onwards, some of Spain's autonomous regions chose to raise the age limit for alcohol purchases to 18 for all licensed premises, including night-life venues, bars, and shops. Inspections have focused mainly on ensuring compliance with the ban at nightlife venues. As explained below, this policy has led to a reduction in the number venues focusing on the 16- and 17-year-old market, without having effectively reduced this group's access to alcohol.

VIOLENCE

In the early 1990s the figure of the 'violent youth' began to replace the stereotype of the delinquent heroin addict as Spain's most prominent folk devil.[14] This was fuelled by the visibility of various 'urban tribes' (Feixa et al, 2006) and violent episodes involv-ing groups of young skinheads, sometimes involved in football hooliganism (Barruti, 1993). In the second half of the decade, this violent image spread through the presence of groups adopting a skinhead aesthetic in nightlife venues. These were youths from inner-city areas imitating the image and behaviour of hardcore skinhead groups and frequenting venues playing the most unrelenting electronic music (known as *mákina*, *bakala*). This led to various labels being attached to such groups, including the *mak-ineros, bakalas, pastilleros, quillos*, and *nacional-bakalaeros* (Viñas, 2004). A number of tragic episodes on the club scene were blamed on youths adopting these negatively perceived styles, leading, in the manner of a classic 'deviancy amplification spiral', to further increases in the perceived seriousness of the situation.

From this point on, those venues and young people associated with violence were placed under considerable pressure by the public authorities. Some regions even approved the adoption of specific regulations restricting access to venues by individu-als displaying violent attitudes, or wearing clothing or symbols inciting violence.[15] There was a parallel increase in police surveillance of the public spaces surrounding such venues.

Other incidents resulting from the actions of bouncers served to reinforce the per-ception of nightclub violence and led some Spanish regions to implement measures to improve the qualifications of security staff. According to state regulations, sur-veillance and security duties inside nightlife establishments can only be performed by private security guards, and not by door staff. These regulations are nonetheless subject to certain difficulties which have limited their application in practice.[16] As a result, venue owners generally form security teams using bouncers who end up taking on wide-ranging policing and security duties both on the door and inside the venues.

---

[14] Crime surveys consistently show juvenile violence to be one of the greatest issues of public concern (Sabaté et al, 2000).

[15] In Catalonia, for example, Generalitat Decree 200 of 27 July 1999 regulates the right of entry to public establishments hosting performances and recreational activities.

[16] Private security companies are generally reluctant to accept this type of work as their staff can find themselves involved in complaints of assault and because contracts are generally for only around eight hours per week, meaning that the company has to make up the security guard's salary with other jobs, complicat-ing staff administration.

Catalonia has acknowledged this situation and introduced regulations governing staff qualifications allowing, under certain circumstances, the role of security guard to be substituted by a doorman. In order to be receive approval, a bouncer must not have a criminal record and must have successfully completed a training course.[17]

INTEGRATING LEISURE WITH URBAN GOVERNANCE

In Spain, the granting of licences for leisure establishments—and hence the planning of what facilities are available—is the responsibility of local councils. This occurs within a framework of general regulations established by the state and the regions concerning opening hours, rights of admission, emergencies, use of private security staff, etc. Inspections and the administration of penalty proceedings are usually the responsibility of the local bodies. Local councils differ according to the political and economic significance they attach to the administrative governance of leisure. Some, for example, base much of their tourism on nightlife, whilst others may impose restrictions in order to win local votes. Councils enjoy the discretion to be more or less permissive or restrictive in terms of imposing closing times and the maximum capacity for venues, etc.[18] This geographical divergence can have a negative impact, since when nightclubs close in a restrictive borough their patrons sometimes move on to continue partying in towns with more permissive opening hours, with a consequent increase in the risk of traffic accidents.

   This heterogeneous approach also applies to the spacing and placing of leisure, with some leisure areas in heavily residential city centres and some on the outskirts of town—some concentrated, some scattered. There has been virtually no political or scientific debate as to the impact of spatial policies on the risks associated with leisure, including crime, public order, and road safety. One study in Catalonia analysed conflicts and official mechanisms for conflict resolution in three leisure areas across two boroughs bordering metropolitan Barcelona (Barruti and Rodríguez, 2007). The study serves to illustrate some current approaches to the integration of leisure space:

- In one of the boroughs, leisure facilities were integrated within the mostly residential central district. These comprised mostly bars and pubs frequented during the earlier part of the night (from midnight to 3.00 am).
- A 'clubbing' scene could be found on the outskirts of both boroughs in an area formerly occupied by industrial units. This scene covered the second part of the night (3.00 am to 5–6.00 am), venues were very large, and attracted patrons from surrounding towns.

---

[17] Door staff are regulated by two Catalan government decrees: the aforementioned Decree 200/1999 on the right of admission, and Decree 348, of 20 July 2004 governing the qualifications and roles of door staff for certain establishments and recreational activities.

[18] Over recent years, however, these discretionary powers have been questioned by the courts. A number of judgments (Provincial High Court of Seville, Section 5, of 24 September 2004; Supreme Court of Justice of Valencia, Administrative Litigation Division, of 7 April 2006) have criticized municipal authorities for failing to control the noise pollution generated by leisure establishments.

- One of the towns featured an emerging leisure area of bars and clubs organized in accordance with the needs of a recently arrived immigrant community from South America.

In the first area, the position of the local council had traditionally been to grant very few licences for this type of activity. This had resulted in a leisure scene characterized by limited capacity venues and low spatial concentration. The owners, workers, and patrons of the venues generally lived within the town itself. Informal regulation and self-regulation were considerable, with few interpersonal or public order disturbances. Local residents (very often parents or relatives of the young patrons) did not perceive either the clientele or the venues to be problematic.

The second area, characterized by 'mega-clubs', was controlled by established business owners with considerable experience in the sector. Nonetheless, the venues had a history of disputes with the authorities, exemplified by the two-fold strategy of public authority pressure referred to above. Prior to their current location, some of these operators had traded in residential areas. During the 1990s, as a result of the popularity of one particular club, a number of lower-quality 'satellite' venues had begun to appear. These attracted troublesome patrons who were involved in fights and attacks. Moreover, the large capacity of the venues (attracting around 6,000 people) had created some disturbance for local residents. In the light of residents' complaints, the local council began to exert regulatory pressure on the establishments themselves and to call for intense policing of surrounding public areas. They also began to close venues down and only the most financially secure owners survived. The council subsequently introduced new regulations outlining stringent conditions for the granting of new licences, whilst encouraging the more professional owners to move their operations to the outlying industrial area.

Within the 'clubbing' area, factors such as spatial agglomeration, greater consumption of alcohol and other drugs, and an aura of hedonism, were particularly present to observers and served to increase the risk of interpersonal conflict. However, venue operators had also implemented enhanced security measures. They operated a strict door policy, intended to deny entry to young people seen as troublemakers and those not corresponding to the style and image sought by the venue. Large security teams had also been established to deal with any incidents inside. Yet, conflict still occurred outside the venues, particularly involving those refused entry and patrons entering the street at closing time when the evening's high spirits were at a peak.

In the third area, one sees a new profile of patrons and owners whose leisure practices enter into conflict with indigenous Spanish society. As other studies have confirmed (Feixa et al, 2006), in Spain, Latin American youth are stereotypically associated with violence and the concerns of residents in this area revolved around the use of public spaces (streets and squares) for which they now had to compete with Latino juveniles. In relation to the new Latin venues, residents' complaints had more to do with noise pollution. In many cases the establishments were operating as 'disco bars' without having the necessary licence, or appropriate soundproofing. This created an emergent problem to which the authorities were required to react. On this occasion the position adopted by the town council was one of mediation and progressive adaptation of the venues to required standards, through voluntary compliance and minor penalties. In some cases there was a lack of resources to bring penalty proceedings to a successful conclusion, or else legal limitations prevented such penalties from being enforced. However, the council's stance may also have been informed by the need to integrate an immigrant population's demands for leisure facilities and therefore avoid alienating a section of society who would soon be entitled to vote in municipal elections.

CHALLENGES FOR AN ADMINISTRATIVE GOVERNANCE OF LEISURE

The Mass Influx of Tourist Revellers

As noted, leisure is the economic powerhouse of many Spanish towns. The arrival of low-cost flights and package tourism has brought Spain ever closer to the rest of Europe. Among younger age groups, one significant tourist sector is that attracted by the warm climate and the nightlife on offer. Spain is a key destination for stag and hen weekends and 'beach and party' package tourism from northern Europe, for which the consumption of alcohol is a defining feature. In the last decade, some coastal towns with intense tourist traffic and a great concentration of nightlife options, have begun to experience chronic security problems, especially fights, public disorder, and sexual assaults. In cities such as Barcelona, for example, public order disturbances involving young tourists have led to an increase in complaints from residents. The official response has involved a tightening of formal control over public spaces through an increased police presence. Many local councils have also approved public order regulations penalizing typical revellers' excesses such as property damage and urination in the street, with fast-track payment systems that can be easily applied to foreign visitors and other non-locals.[19]

The Non-integration of Policy Responses

As noted, from the 1990s onwards, the authorities began to exert greater control over leisure venues through various policing and licensing enforcement measures. Pressure was applied on venue operators to drive drugs out of their establishments and inspection visits were conducted to ensure compliance with the regulations on age restrictions for admissions, under-age alcohol sales, drink-driving, the exclusion of violent patrons, and the professional credentials of security staff. These measures appear to have contributed to a pacification of licensed premises (Pallarés, 2006), a decline in the consumption of alcohol among young drivers, and an easing of public anxieties concerning leisure venues.[20] Nonetheless, the conflicts and risks associated with night-time leisure have not disappeared, but rather have been dispersed to

---

[19] For example, Barcelona's 'Regulations to Promote and Guarantee Communal Use of Public Spaces', approved in December 2005. This measure was accompanied by a suspension in the granting of new licences for nightlife venues.

[20] The repeat survey of *Enquesta Joventut i Seguretat* (Departament d'Interior–Departament d'Ensenyament, 2002; Departament d'Interior, Relacions Institucional i Participació–Departament d'Educació, 2006) reveals a drop in the percentage of secondary-school students who associate pubs and clubs with the risk of violent assault.

other spaces. For example, although recorded drug offences in and around venues have reduced there has been no clear decline in the overall incidence of dealing and consumption. These activities simply occur in less visible spaces.

Interpersonal disputes and public disorder in the vicinity of establishments remain a major concern for the authorities, particularly in areas which attract large concentrations of revellers. Many of these incidents are occurring in the early hours when comparatively few formal and informal control mechanisms exist to curb the hedonistic excess and public transport services are insufficient to provide egress (Barruti and Rodríguez, 2007; Calafat et al, 2000). Some localized schemes have sought to increase public transport services at night, or adapt the closing time of venues to match such services, but this has been sporadic.[21] The main measures to address crime and disorder in public space have focused on strengthening the police presence.

In regions where the minimum permitted age for purchasing alcohol has been raised from 16 to 18, venue operators are now reluctant to provide entertainment for 16- and 17-year-olds, whom they regard as both more problematic and less profitable than older customers (Barruti and Rodríguez, 2007; Calafat et al, 2005; Megías, 2007). Although local councils organize various leisure facilities for this age group they do not fill the gap left by such establishments in meeting demand from young people keen to enter the partygoing nightlife scene as soon as possible. These younger groups—together with others, excluded from formal leisure establishments because they do not correspond to the increasingly sophisticated image required—are generating their own alternative leisure practices.

THE BOTELLÓN PHENOMENON

In Spain, the name *botellón* is used to refer to the regular mass gatherings of young people that occur on weekend nights in public spaces, especially the main squares of villages, towns, and cities (Baigorri and Chaves, 2006; Baigorri and Fernández, 2003). Those attending the *botellón* tend to be aged from 14 to 23. For the youngest, the *botellón* represents an alternative to the formally regulated commercial leisure scene from which they are increasingly excluded; for older participants it is simply the start of a partygoing route, which will later proceed to nightlife venues. The main activities of the *botellón* are socializing, drinking alcohol, and listening to music (Elzo et al, 2003). Before meeting up with their peers, young people often club together to buy their alcohol from supermarkets or grocery stores. Narcotics are also used during *botellón*, especially cannabis. Navarrete and colleagues (2003) estimate that, depending on the city in question, somewhere between 10 and 30 per cent of juveniles use cannabis at most or every *botellón*.

---

[21] In Catalonia the opening hours of venues have been extended in order to alleviate problems associated with the mismatch between the time when venues close (5.00 am) and the time when public transport begins (around 6.00 am). The aim has been to avoid the concentration of young people in public spaces awaiting the first metro or train. The underground rail service in Barcelona has been running all night on Saturday–Sunday mornings since April 2006. The main challenge, however, involves the provision of night-time public transport systems in smaller towns which lack such developed infrastructure.

Official debate has classified this phenomenon as a public-health problem, due to its association with teenage alcohol consumption. Moreover, in residential areas, the mass concentrations of young people on the streets until late into the night have often given rise to intergenerational and community conflicts concerning noise, litter, and damage to urban fixtures, etc. It now seems that the young, who had achieved their emancipation (at least symbolically) through the rise of age-specific nightlife venues, are now occupying public spaces during the time of rest for adults. Rodríguez and Megías (2001) have shown how some adults perceive juvenile leisure practices involving the youthful appropriation of space and time in terms of social confrontation. Unsuprisingly, the police and municipal governments have responded to this occupation of space by applying stringent controls to ensure public order.[22] Under the aegis of their responsibilities for safeguarding public health, some regions have approved legislation completely banning the consumption of alcohol in public (except at café terraces, tables, and during local fiestas).[23] The state has also created legal mechanisms such as the Noise Act 2003 to allow local councils to impose penalties on individuals and businesses in the event of antisocial behaviour. The civic conduct regulations mentioned above should be understood within this context.

In an attempt to reconcile the rights and interests of all social groups, some regions, such as Andalusia and Extremadura have chosen not to repress the *botellón*, but to restrict it to specific, non-residential areas of the town, whilst continuing to uphold the prohibitions on under-age drinking. Whilst in some regions it is still possible to buy alcohol from the age of 16, even in areas which have raised the minimum age to 18, the authorities have not applied the same degree of pressure to off-licensed supermarkets and smaller convenience stores as they have to bars and clubs. This has meant that young people still have ready access to alcohol as demonstrated by the results of a school-administered survey (PNSD, 2006) which found that 90 per cent of teenagers expressed the view that alcohol was easy or very easy to obtain.

Until recently, juvenile alcohol consumption was not considered a genuine public-health problem in Spain. Parents and other adults were more concerned about the consumption of narcotics (Rodríguez and Megías, 2001). Similarly, Spanish culture tended to attribute the excesses of young adults to a lack of experience, simply a phase in the process of learning 'how to take one's drink'. However, drinking practices among Spanish teenagers are increasingly diverging from the traditional patterns of Mediterranean countries (consuming alcohol slowly, together with food) (Cortés et al, 2005). Although total alcohol consumption among Spanish youth appears to have reduced in recent years, the ways in which alcohol is consumed have become increasingly akin to those previously more typical of Nordic countries (imbibing large quantities of alcohol in a short time to *hit the spot*, if not get completely drunk).

[22] Leisure events in public spaces involving radical youth groups have sometimes led to major confrontations with the police (eg, the Fiestas de Gracia in Barcelona in August 2005, the frustrated *macrobotellón* in Barcelona and Girona in March 2006, and the event marking 2 May in Madrid in 2007). They have even served as justification for the intervention of more militarized Special Operations Group police units.

[23] The first region to bring in such legislation was Madrid, which passed its law in 2002. The same pattern has been followed by Catalonia, Cantabria, Castile-Leon, Valencia, and the Canary Islands.

Data from the *Encuesta Estatal sobre Uso de Drogas de Enseñanzas Secundarias* of the Plan Nacional Sobre Drogas (National Drugs Strategy) (PNSD, 2006), a major drug-use survey among Spanish secondary school students aged 14–18, reveals that between 1994 and 2006:

- 80 per cent of secondary school students had consumed alcohol at least once in their lifetime. This rate of prevalence remained roughly consistent between 1994 and 2006.
- Over the same period, the average age for beginning weekly consumption of alcohol was 15.
- Prevalence rates for the consumption of alcohol on a school day during the previous 30 days had fallen from almost 30 per cent of students to 14 per cent . This indicates the consolidation of juvenile consumption around weekend leisure times.
- Prevalence of recent consumption at a weekend fell from 65 to 55 per cent.
- However, there was a clear increase in the number of students who said they had 'got drunk' on at least one occasion during the month prior to the survey (from 20 per cent to over 40 per cent).

These changing patterns of consumption suggest that whilst a growing number of young people abstain from alcohol use, those who do drink are drinking more heavily. However, as the schools-survey data illustrates the situation among the adolescent population throughout Spain, it should be considered independent of the *botellón* since in some regions the phenomemon has not caught on. In these areas, young people adopt different approaches, occupying the street in smaller groups or gathering in private homes, etc.[24]

A further fundamental challenge to the implementation of public-health policies arises from the economic interests of alcohol producers and distributors. One example of this has been the recent failure of a White Paper presented by the Ministry of Health which intended to introduce a blanket ban on the sale of alcohol to under-18s. The Bill was dropped three months before the regional and municipal elections in May 2006 in the face of determined opposition from the wine trade.[25]

RAVE PARTIES

As noted, foreign leisure entrepreneurs have played a prominent role in integrating rave events within Spain's formal licensed leisure economy by entering into partnership with indigenous nightclub operators. In Catalonia, the illegal-rave phenomenon has nonetheless enjoyed a long lease of life. In 2001, the French government introduced

[24] The consumption of alcohol in the street is no novelty in Spain: there is a long tradition of drinking on café terraces, at the doors of bars, etc. It is however true that from the 1980s onwards, other drinking practices emerged in public spaces, organized by young people themselves. The typical practice at the time was to share *litronas* (litre bottles of beer). According to recent research (Megías et al, 2007) the *botellón* is a practice indulged in by less than half of Spanish teenagers: 45 per cent drink in bars and a further 25 per cent at home or on private premises.

[25] In Spain, young people are major consumers of wine, in particular of *calimocho*, a mixture of wine and coca-cola.

a law regulating this type of gathering which required rave organizers to apply for official authorization of their events (Pourtau, 2005). Since then, groups of partygoers have been crossing the border to organize raves in Catalonia.

Informal rave events often raise a number of risks connected to the consumption of drugs and a failure to adhere to basic public-safety standards. During fieldwork for two recent research projects (Barruti and Rodríguez, 2007; Gruppo Abele, 2004) the author had the opportunity to learn how the authorities had sought to address such issues. The official response was found to be quite limited. Such gatherings are organized at short notice taking advantage of new technologies (email, social-networking websites, and mobile phones) meaning that the authorities find it difficult to learn of their locations. Even when this information can be found, other problems arise. Many events are held on isolated private property, requiring the police to receive a complaint from the property owner before they are able to intervene. Administrative proceedings remain similarly ineffective as there are no legal mechanisms for precautionary action (such as the seizure of sound equipment). Once the event has commenced, enforced interruption or termination involves a serious risk of confrontation between revellers and the police. The tactic consequently adopted is to organize police surveillance teams. As a result of two rave parties held during several days on industrial estates very close to residential areas, there has been an increase in media and public pressure for the authorities to adopt a more repressive stance. A law is currently passing through the Catalan parliament which will empower the police to adopt precautionary measures to halt the organization of such parties. These measures include the seizure of property.

CONCLUSIONS

In Spain, the emergence of the night-time leisure practices now typical of global consumer economies has occurred at a rapid pace and without an appropriate process of official reflection and planning. Public institutions have been reactive in their approach to the governance of nightlife, responding disproportionately to those issues which are publicized, and almost always exaggerated, by the media. Responses have thus focused mainly on the regulation and control of licensed leisure establishments. A certain *pacification* of such establishments has been achieved, although at the cost of effectively discriminating against large groups of young people (under 18s and all youth who do not fit the aspirational image and style required by leisure businesses). Such groups have sought out alternative leisure options in public spaces. The conflicts which play out in such spaces then take the form of public-order issues and inter-generational and intra-community tensions. Nonetheless, economic factors remain salient as the consumption of alcohol is a key element of all forms of nightlife. The alcohol industry has a major interest in retaining its youngest customers regardless of the spaces they choose to occupy when consuming its products. The *botellón*, one of the most problematic leisure practices in terms of youth drinking and social conflict, has served to stimulate further lines of research. Other important issues for future research include exploration of the alcohol industry's role in shaping national public-health and security agendas. Most importantly, there remains a general paucity of knowledge concerning the development and effectiveness of strategies for governing night-time leisure in all its formal and informal manifestations.

REFERENCES

All internet sources were accessible 20 August 2008

AGUINAGA J and COMAS D (1997) *Cambios de Hábitos en el uso del Tiempo: Trayectorias Temporales de los Jóvenes Españoles*, Madrid: Instituto de la Juventud.

AJUNTAMENT DE BARCELONA (2007) *Informes Estadístics: La Població Estrangera a Barcelona. Gener 2007*, <http://www.bcn.cat/estadistica/catala/dades/inf/pobest/pobest07/pobest07.pdf>.

ARANA, X, MARKEZ, I and VEGA, A (2000) *Drogas: Cambios Sociales y Legales ante el Tercer Milenio*, Instituto Internacional de Sociología Jurídica de Oñati, Madrid: Dykinson.

BAIGORRI, A and CHAVES, M (2006) 'Botellón: Más que Ruido Alcohol y Drogas (la Sociología en su Papel)', *Anduli: Revista Andaluza de Ciencias Sociales*, 6, 159–73.

BAIGORRI, A and FERNÁNDEZ, R (2003) *Botellón: Un Conflicto Postmoderno*, Barcelona: Icaria.

Barcelona, Generalitat de Catalunya, Diputació de Barcelona, Agencia de Salut Pública de Barcelona.

BARRUTI, M (1993) *El Món dels Joves a Barcelona: Imatges I Estils Juvenils*, Barcelona: Ajuntament de Barcelona, Àmbit de Benestar Social.

—— and RODRIGUEZ, A (2007) 'Violence in Nightspots: A case study in Catalonia', in A Recasens (ed), *Violence between Young People in Night-time Leisure Zones. A European comparative study*, Brussels: Vubpress, 141–72.

CALAFAT, A, JUAN, M, BECOÑA, E, CASTILLO, A, FERNANDEZ, C, M, PEREIRO, C and ROS, M (2005) 'El Consumo de Alcohol en la Lógica del Botellón', *Adicciones*, 17/3, 193-202, <http://www.irefrea.org/archivos/sa/logica_botellon.pdf> .

—— —— —— FERNÁNDEZ, C (2000) *Salir de Marcha y Consumo de Drogas*, IREFREA–Ministerio del Interior.

COMAS, D (2003) *Jóvenes y Estilos de Vida: Valores Riesgos en los Jóvenes Urbanos*, Madrid: Injuve–FAD.

CORTÉS, MT, GIMENEZ, JA, MESTRE, MV, NACHOS, MJ, SAMPER, P and TUR, A (2005) *Los Padres Ante las Nuevas Formas de Consumo de Alcohol de sus Hijos*, Ponencia Presentada al II Congreso Hispano Portugués de Psicología, II Congreso Hispano-Portugués de Psicología, <http://www.fedap.es/IberPsicologia/iberpsi10/congreso_lisboa/cortes/cortes.htm>.

DEPARTAMENT D'INTERIOR–DEPARTAMENT D'ENSENYAMENT (2002) *Enquesta Joventut i Seguretat*, <http://www.gencat.net/interior/docs/text_integre.pdf>.

DEPARTAMENT D'INTERIOR, RELACIONS INSTITUCIONALS i PARTICIPACIÓ–DEPARTAMENT D'EDUCACIÓ, (2006) *Enquesta de Convivència Escolar i Seguretat a Catalunya: Curs 2005–2006*, <http://www.gencat.net/interior/departament/publicacions/estudis/ecesc.htm>.

ELZO, J (1999) 'Jóvenes en Erisis. Aspectos de Jóvenes Violentos: Violencia y Drogas', in D Rechea (ed), *La Criminología Aplicada II*, Cuadernos de Derecho Judicial, Madrid: Consejo General del Poder Judicial.

—— Laespada, MT and Pallarés, J (2003) *Más allá del Botellón: Análisis Socioantropológico del Consumo de Alcohol en Los Adolescentes y Jóvenes*, Madrid: Agencia Antidroga de la Comunidad de Madrid.

Energy Control (2006) *Guía Preventiva y de Seguridad Para Espacios de Música y Baile*, <http://www.energycontrol.org/flash/attachs/guiaseguridad.pdf>.

Feixa, C, Porzio, L and Recio, C (eds) (2006) *Jóvenes Latinos en Barcelona: Espacio Público y Cultura Urbana*, Barcelona: Anthropos.

González, MA, Martínez García, JM, López Martínez, JS, Martín López, MJ and Martín Carrasco, JM (1997) *Comportamientos de Riesgo: Violencia, Prácticas Sexuales de Riesgo y Consumo de Drogas Iilegales en la Juventud*, Madrid: Entinema.

Gruppo Abele (ed) (2004) 'Synthetic Drugs Trafficking in Three European Cities: Major trends and the involvement of organised crime', Final report by Gruppo Abele, Institute de Estudios Sobre Conflictos y Accion Humanitaria and Transnational Institute, *Trends in Organized Crime*, 8/1, September, 1084–4791.

Instituto Nacional de Toxicología (2002) *Memoria. Análisis Toxicológico. Muertes en Accidentes de Tráfico*, <http://www.mju.es/toxicologia/documentos/documentos.htm>.

Megías, E (ed) (2001) *Valores Sociales y Drogas*, Madrid: FAD.

—— (ed) (2007) *Adolescentes ante el Alcohol: La Mirada de Padres y Madres*, Colección Estudios Sociales, 22, Obra Social-Fundación 'La Caixa', <http://media.lacaixa.es/descarga/obrasocial/pdf/Llibre22_es.pdf>.

Ministerio de Sanidad y Consumo (Ministry of Health and Consumption) (2007) *Encuesta Domiciliaria Sobre Alcohol y Drogas* (Household Survey of Alcohol and Drug Use), Madrid: Delegación del Gobierno para el Plan Nacional sobre Drogas. Calle Recoletos, <http://www.pnsd.msc.es/Categoria2/observa/estudios/home.htm>.

Navarrete, L et al (2003) *El Fenómeno del Botellón. Estudio Comparado en Madrid, Galicia y Jaén (2002–2003)*, <http://www.pnsd.msc.es/Categoria2/publica/pdf/JuventudDrogo dependencias4.pdf>.

Pallarés, J, Díaz, A., Barruti, M, Espluga, J and Canales, G (2006) *Observatori de Nous Consums de Drogues en l'àmbit Juvenil: Metodología i Informe Evolutiu 1999–2005*, Barcelona: Generalitat de Catalunya.

—— and Feixa, C (2000) 'Espacios e Itinerarios para el Ocio Juvenil Nocturno', *Revista de Estudios de Juventud*, 50, 23–41.

PNSD (Plan Nacional Sobre Drogas) (2006) *Encuesta Estatal Sobre uso de Drogas en Estudiantes de Enseñanzas Secundarias (Estudes)*, <http://www.pnsd.msc.es/Categoria2/observa/estudios/home.htm>.

Pourtau, L (2005) 'Les Interactions entre *Raves* et Législations Censées les Contrôler', *Déviance et Société*, 29/2, 127–39.

RACC (Automóvil Club) (2005) 'Press Report', *El Mundo*, 17 January, <http://www.elmundo.es/2002/01/17/catalunya/1093967.html>.

—— (2006) *X Encuesta RACC de Movilidad y Seguridad Vial*, press report, <http://www.racc.es/index.racc/mod._GLOBAL/mem.descargar/f._zjw_pub_zjw_ficheros_zjw_prensa_zjw_notaprensa_dp_x_encuesta_jovenesmadrid_jzq_7b07d6b1.pdf/chk.cee7076 19c855bccc48faa90cf8af893.html>.

Recasens, A (2001) 'Politiques de Sécurité et de Prévention dans l'Espagne des Années 1990', *Déviance et Société. Les Politiques de Sécurité et de Prévention en Europe*, 25/4, 479–97.

Rodríguez, E and Megías, I (2001) 'Estructura y Funcionalidad de las Formas de Diversión Nocturna: Límites y Conflictos', *Revista de Estudios Juventud*, 54, 9–34.

Sabaté, J, Aragay, JM and Torrelles, E (2000) '1999: *La Delinqüència a l'Àrea Metropolitana de Barcelona. 11 Anys d'enquestes de Victimització*', Barcelona: Institut d'Estudis Metropolitans de Barcelona.

Viñas, C (2004) *Skinheads a Catalunya*, Barcelona: Columna.

11

HUNGARY

Zsolt Demetrovics

INTRODUCTION

Information concerning nightlife-related crime in Hungary remains limited. Police data is recorded and analysed in relation to acts prohibited by the criminal law, but these are not categorized according to the settings in which they occur. Moreover, neither the police, nor criminologists, have identified nightlife as a particular environment in which criminal acts should be explained or analysed. Academic literature in the field is therefore very limited and the domain has yet to be systematically explored. The only related issues to have generated official interest in recent years are recreational alcohol and drug use at nightclubs and other dance events (Demetrovics and Rácz, 2008). There is no available data concerning other issues such as violence and vandalism in a nightlife context. Even the drug markets that operate in this arena remain unexplored, drug *consumption* remaining the only developed scientific field. Yet, although Hungarian society strongly associates drug use with entertainment venues, dancing facilities, and the world of parties, the actual extent of this scene's importance to psychoactive drug consumption nationally, is not known. Some epidemiological data indicates that—at least in the case of certain psycho-stimulants[1]—the relation is significant.

The use (or possession) of illegal substances is punishable by up to two years of imprisonment in 'basic' cases (personal use, small amount of drugs). However, where large quantities of drugs are seized or special circumstances give rise to the offences being judged more seriously (for example, adults supplying drugs to schoolchildren or others below 18 years of age) then penalties can rise to 5–8 years of imprisonment. In Hungarian law there is no classification system based on the different risks of illicit

---

[1] Psycho-stimulants or CNS (central nervous system) stimulants are drugs (psychoactive substances) that can increase alertness and intensify moods. The most frequently used illegal drugs which belong to this group are cocaine, amphetamine, and ecstasy (MDMA).

drugs such, as the ABC system in the UK or Schedule I–IV in the USA. However, Hungary, like many other countries, has introduced a system of 'diversion into treatment' which requires those arrested for the simple acquisition or possession of illicit drugs in small quantities to be referred to a six month educational, treatment or other programme as an alternative to incarceration.

This chapter will begin by reviewing the available literature on recreational-drug use in nightlife settings. It will then go on to discuss various drug policies, initiatives, and interventions aimed at reducing drug-related harms in the Hungarian context.

HISTORICAL BACKGROUND AND CULTURAL CONTEXT

Most of Hungary's nightlife is concentrated in the capital, Budapest. This was demonstrated in research conducted in 2005 in which 365 dance-music venues were identified in ten large cities and their surroundings. Sixty-two per cent of the venues were located in the capital, with the remainder fairly evenly distributed across the other nine cities (Demetrovics et al, 2008). Furthermore, whilst most of the entertainment venues in Budapest were open almost every night, in provincial areas venues tended to open on Friday and Saturday nights only. This limited focus on weekend trading is characteristic of traditional nightclubs. In the 1980s and early 90s these clubs were the only entertainment venues playing popular music and providing facilities for youngsters to dance. In this period, illegal drug use was not a feature of the scene, alcohol being the drug of choice for music and dancing occasions. Drink-driving and alcohol-related violence were the main issues of criminological interest in this field, although no systematic studies were conducted.

In Hungary, the rise of electronic dance music (EDM) and related nightlife occurred some years later than in Western European countries. Fejér (2000) dates the first underground events (known as 'acid parties') in Hungary to 1993. In that year, he identified only one subcultural group in the capital, whose origins lay in the metropolitan underground movement of the late 1980s.[2] Wider adoption of a Techno-Acid style dance scene in Budapest clubs began the following year (Fejér, ibid). Fejér (1998) provides the only data available concerning this early period. He used participant observation and other fieldwork methods, allowing insight into the underground and subcultural characteristics of the phenomenon. In Hungary, as elsewhere, the EDM scene has fragmented into subcultures, or even sub-subcultures. The original Acid scene that emerged in 1993 repeatedly splintered and mutated from its original

---

[2] The metropolitan underground movement was a group of young people (mostly, university students) who followed an alternative music scene based around a number of popular bands. These bands wrote songs that criticized elements of life under socialism and discussed many of the most controversial issues in Hungarian society. Since the lyrics of the songs were not explicit in their criticism of the socialist government, the music could not be banned and their presence was more or less tolerated.

form (Fejér, 1995). From the mid-1990s onwards, Techno and House sounds began to permeate the traditional disco scene. This created a division between underground and overground (mainstream) party cultures which continues to this day (Rácz and Geresdi, 2001). Further differentiation of the scene occurred and there are currently six important EDM styles: House, Techno, Trance, Goa, Drum and Bass, and Breakbeat, and several less prominent ones: experimental Electronica, Noise, and Nu Skool (Csák et al, 2008; Demetrovics, 2005). The capacity of different EDM scenes to assume the characteristics of a distinct subculture varies. Underground scenes tend to have more markedly subcultural characteristics, whilst overground trends are comparatively diluted and permeable. At the same time, a popularization and commercialization of certain styles has occurred, implying a degree of fluidity and movement, with aspects of previously esoteric underground cultural forms infiltrating the overground (mainstream). A recent study by Csák et al (2008) identified three main Hungarian EDM scenes: Drum and Bass/Breakbeat; Goa; and Techno. The first two were classified as underground scenes, although elements of popularization could be observed even there.

One of the most important trends to occur since 1994 has been for 'disco' type settings to increasingly turn over to EDM (Demetrovics and Rácz, 2008). This has occurred in two ways: first, pop/dance and electronic music styles are represented in different rooms, within the same venue, at the same time; secondly, separate 'nights' are organized, in which the whole venue is turned over to a particular musical genre. In both cases, the most popular genres—Techno, House, and Trance—prevail, whilst Breakbeat, Drum and Bass, and Goan Trance have a more irregular presence. By the end of the 1990s, a further three-way division of recreational *settings* was identifiable involving: discos (open at weekends, fixed location, pop/dance music, with some electronic trends); parties (occasional events, linked to particular promoters not locations, strongly EDM- and disc-jockey-oriented); and thirdly, clubs (fixed locations, open all week, setting conditions allow for conversation and other entertainment besides dancing) (Demetrovics, 1998).

Alongside the broadening and fragmentation of dance culture and its settings one finds an extension of the times in which such recreation is available. Such activity is no longer predominately restricted to weekends. Different types of EDM event can be found almost every night of the week. Moreover, events organized during the week tend to promote diversification as they are more likely to focus on smaller subcultural scenes (Csák et al, 2008). This extension in the times and spaces available to EDM is most apparent in the capital (Demetrovics et al, 2008). In Budapest, the various scenes are 'bounded to location' by their association with particular entertainment venues which focus exclusively on electronic music trends, either in terms of particular genres, or broader selections on different days of the week. Beyond the capital, EDM parties have tended to remain discrete events featuring only the most popular and overground trends. Of the 365 dance-music entertainment venues identified by Demetrovics et al (2008) across Budapest and nine other large Hungarian cities, 18 were classified as dance-scene-oriented 'party' venues (see above). Of these, 13 were located in the capital. Five cities had no venues of this kind whatsoever.

DRUG USE IN THE HUNGARIAN DANCE SCENE

SURVEY RESEARCH

Three large-scale surveys and two smaller qualitative studies have been conducted on recreational-drug use in Hungary. The first quantitative survey was conducted in Budapest in autumn 1997 (Demetrovics, 1998). Anonymous questionnaires were used to survey 373 young people during 17 data-collection exercises across seven different locations, including EDM party venues, clubs, and discos.[3] Respondents had an average age of 20.6 and 61 per cent were male. The majority (89.3 per cent) were aged between 17- and 26-years-old. Among this sample as a whole, lifetime prevalence of drug use was 68.6 per cent and 55.2 per cent indicated having used illicit drugs and/or inhalants in the past month. However, significant divergences in drug use were found across the different recreational settings. At EDM party events, lifetime prevalence was 95.2 per cent and last month prevalence was 87.5 per cent. In clubs, the figures were 81.7 per cent and 64.3 per cent respectively. In discos the values measured were roughly half of those found in these more dance-scene oriented venues: 40.9 per cent and 26.6 per cent.

The next drug-use survey, conducted two years later in autumn 1999, adopted a nationwide approach (Demetrovics, 2001b). Data was collected on 60 occasions across 27 sites. These included four regional centres/capitals (Szombathely, Miskolc, Debrecen, and Pécs) representing all the large regions of Hungary, together with Budapest. Among the 1,507 respondents (51.4 per cent male, average age 21.2 years), lifetime prevalence of drug use was 52.6 per cent (62.3 per cent for men and 42.1 per cent for women), with last month prevalence rates of 29.5 per cent (39.1 per cent for men and 18.7 per cent for women). In Budapest, lifetime prevalence was 72.5 per cent, whilst last month use was 41.2 per cent. Patterns of drug use across the various types of recreational setting were similar to those found in the previous study. Lifetime prevalence of drug use was 82.5 per cent in parties (last month prevalence 56.8 per cent), 63.3 per cent in clubs (33.9 per cent for last month), and 33 per cent in discos (16.8 per cent).

Between September and December 2003 a third survey was conducted which focused on the Budapest party scene (Demetrovics, Nádas, and Kun, 2008). In contrast to the earlier projects, only youth attending electronic music parties were questioned; disco and club goers were not included in the sample. Moreover, whilst the previous studies had used only face-to-face in situ interviews as data-collection techniques, research methods for the 2003 study also involved the distribution of questionnaires (and stamped addressed envelopes) to young people during and after dance events. Data was collected at 33 parties. On 19 occasions both interviews and questionnaire distribution was employed, whilst on the remaining 14 occasions only questionnaires

---

[3] Methodological note: Although it was not possible to obtain a representative sample of venues across the locations, we tried to obtain full coverage of the club scene in Budapest. Two EDM party locations were visited (on four occasions), two discos (five occasions), and three clubs (eight occasions). The four party events were all organized in the period of the survey. Discos and clubs were selected as being the most popular places in Budapest. Some other venues were also selected, but the owners did not grant access for the research. Subjects were not selected systematically. Peer interviewers were present at the locations and they asked patrons of the venues to fill out the questionnaires in situ.

were used. Sixty per cent of the 1,051 respondents were male, with the mean age of the sample being 23 years. Across the sample as a whole, the extent of drug use was similar to that found in the previous studies. However, the findings also indicated that there might be significant differences in the characteristics of drug use among young people involved in different EDM scenes. For example, participants at Goa parties reported the highest prevalence rates for cannabis, amphetamine, cocaine, LSD, and herbal drugs, and the second highest for ecstasy. Techno events featured the highest lifetime prevalence of ecstasy use and also very similar results to the Goa parties for amphetamine use. Of the Techno party attendees, almost two-thirds had tried amphetamine and three-quarters had tried ecstasy at some point in their lives. Nonetheless, lifetime prevalence of amphetamine and ecstasy use was also high among those attending House and Trance parties.[4] Techno devotees also reported outstanding levels of ketamine and PCP use. The different trends are summarized in Table 11.1.

Read in combination, the three surveys provide a comprehensive picture of the extent and characteristics of illegal drug use across various recreational settings. Close interrelationships between party culture and recreational-drug use—primarily that of psycho-stimulants and hallucinogens—have been repeatedly confirmed. Although cannabis is the most widespread drug in Hungarian society, in recreational settings psycho-stimulants tend to be the drug of choice. Respondents almost exclusively associated the use of such drugs with dance-music entertainment settings. Cannabis, though markedly present in these environments, was associated with a wider range of settings. It is useful to compare data from the 2003 survey with the findings of more general studies of drug use among the 18–34-year-old population such as Paksi (2007). This comparison indicates that lifetime prevalence of cannabis use among those attending party events is 2.6 times higher than that of the general youth population. Comparable ratios for other drugs are 4–6 times higher. Thus, one finds prevalence rates for amphetamine use of × 4.6, ecstasy use of × 4.2, cocaine use of × 6.4, and LSD use of × 5.2, the drug use prevalence rates of the Hungarian youth population in general (see Fig 11.1).

Despite the high lifetime prevalence rates for drug use among dance-event attendees, consumption habits tended to conform to a social-recreational pattern, that is: (1) frequency of drug use was predominantly low (usually no more than one occasion per week); (2) with the exception of cannabis, drugs were consumed almost exclusively within a dance-event setting; and (3) drug use was associated with social occasions, being rarely practised by individuals in conditions of solitude (Demetrovics, 2001a; Demetrovics and Rácz, 2008). Moreover, the only deviance identified in this population was illicit drug use itself. Socio-demographic indicators relating to work and study, as well as the psychological profile of the recreational drug user population, revealed no otherwise unusual features (Demetrovics, 2001a). Indeed, the income and education levels of those surveyed in recreational settings were found to be generally higher among drug users than among those who had never taken illicit drugs.

---

[4] However, results should be considered tentative due to the limited sample of respondents from House and Trance parties.

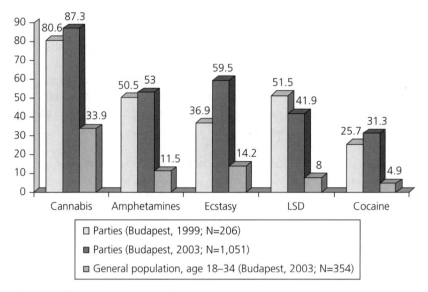

Fig 11.1 Lifetime prevalence of drug use among Budapest partygoers (1999 and 2003) and in the general youth population (2003)

QUALITATIVE STUDIES

As noted, in addition to the quantitative surveys, two qualitative studies have been conducted in similar recreational settings. Csák et al's (2008) research employed in-depth interview and focus-group methods to explore the views of key actors associated within the electronic music scene and its control in Budapest. Informants included partygoers, party event organizers, doctors, criminal-justice personnel, and prevention and harm-reduction professionals. The study explored two main topics: the characteristics of drug use on the scene, and informants' experiences of prevention and harm-reduction activities related to such use. The patterns of drug use reported corresponded closely to those found in previous research. However, Csák et al's most important results involved the identification of a four-phase trajectory in personal recreational-drug use careers: trying, experimenting, active drug use, and normalization. Informants described how use-levels typically increased toward the beginning of a drug-use career, only to peak and then decrease in later stages (see Table 11.2).

Csák et al (2008) also point to different patterns of drug use across the various party scenes. They found Techno events to be dominated by amphetamine and ecstasy. Cocaine and nitrogenous-oxide were also particularly prevalent within this sub-scene. Conversely, cannabis appeared to play a less prominent role than in other scenes. Stimulants (amphetamine, ecstasy) were similarly popular at Drum-and-Bass and Breakbeat events, although this sub-scene was more strongly associated with cannabis use. Further differences were noted within this scene. Drum-and-Bass parties were especially popular with the younger, 14–17-year-old age range, whilst Breakbeat events were preferred by older groups. Alcohol use—sometimes in large quantities,

Table 11.1 Lifetime prevalence in the use of different drugs across various EDM scenes

	N	Cannabis	Amphetamine	Ecstasy	Cocaine	LSD/magic mushroom	Herbal drugs	Ketamine	PCP	GHB
Drum and Bass	201	91.5	48.8	56.7	32.8	51.7	36.5	16.4	11.9	8.5
Breakbeat	221	85.1	39.6	45.2	23.9	48.0	27.0	11.9	4.6	2.7
Goa	203	93.6	66.5	73.8	42.5	62.6	50.3	29.3	9.5	8.9
Techno	159	79.9	66.0	74.1	28.3	39.6	15.7	41.5	15.1	10.1
House	35	80.0	57.1	65.7	40.0	48.6	25.7	28.6	2.9	11.4
Trance	39	79.5	59.5	63.2	24.3	23.1	8.1	21.6	8.1	2.6

Table 11.2 Phases and patterns of personal drug use

Phase	Typical drugs	Intensity of drug use	Attitudes, motivations
Trying	Tobacco Alcohol Cannabis	Occasional	Curiosity—Peer group influence—Breaking of norms
Experimenting	Whole spectrum of available drugs	Intensive	Curiosity—Experiencing different states of consciousness—Acquisition of experiences
Active drug use	Tobacco Alcohol Cannabis Ecstasy Speed Hallucinogens	Regular drug use (fortnightly and monthly use of stimulants and hallucinogens, sometimes daily use of cannabis)	Altered consciousness sought—The drug use experience—'Partying' as a lifestyle focus
Normalization	Tobacco Alcohol Cannabis	Occasional drug use built into a 'normal' lifestyle	'Relaxation'

From Csák et al 2008: 235

inducing drunkenness—was a characteristic of the latter and appears to be a new phenomenon on the party scene. Goa parties were strongly identified with stimulants and hallucinogens and had higher general levels of drug use than any of the other EDM sub-scenes.

Similar findings were demonstrated in a national-level qualitative study conducted in spring 2005 (Demetrovics et al, 2008). In this research, 99 structured interviews with experts working in or around the night-time leisure scene were conducted, across 10 cities. Informants included professionals working on harm-reduction programmes and at drug outpatient facilities, doctors working in crisis intervention centres, police officers, and the owners and employees of entertainment venues. The interviews aimed to explore the characteristics of nightlife-related drug use and the views of informants concerning the effectiveness of current and possible future interventions. The results indicate that drug use in the party scene continues to grow, albeit more slowly than in recent years. Such findings correspond with those of general population studies (Elekes and Paksi, 2000; Paksi, 2007); however, due to methodological difficulties, such as the absence of a common and systematic sampling frame, it is not possible to compare data and calculate trends with any degree of precision. Certainly, there appears to have been a shift toward the earlier onset of drug-taking careers, young people beginning to use entertainment venues from an earlier age, particularly in relation to certain types of venue. How might we explain these trends?

As noted, many leisure venues have transformed the musical entertainment on offer, shifting away from pop-dance music and toward EDM. This broadening and differentiation of EDM trends has meant that the number of young people exposed to 'dance culture' has increased and the constitution of dance crowds, in terms of age and social background, has widened. Reductions in the age of participation did not occur within any of the established EDM scenes, but rather was symptomatic of this popularization and commodification of related styles. As electronic-music venues are more strongly associated with drug use than traditional discos (Demetrovics, 1998, 2001b), it seems likely that rises in the proportion of young people who take drugs may be related to their age group's increasing exposure to social environments in which illicit drug consumption is the norm. In view of these factors one should not be surprised to find that decreases in the age at which people begin to attend EDM events should correspond with the earlier onset of recreational-drug consumption.

In relation to gender, the three quantitative studies indicate higher prevalence of illicit drug consumption among males (Demetrovics, 2001b). Male consumption patterns were characterized by greater intensity of use, experimentation with a wider range of substances, and more frequent sessions of polydrug use (Demetrovics, 2004). Qualitative data support the finding that amphetamine and cannabis use—especially of a regular and intensive nature—is less characteristic of females. By contrast, ecstasy appears to be more popular among young women than young men (Demetrovics et al, 2008). In interview, treatment experts and other harm-reduction professionals expressed the opinion that female users were often less willing to talk openly about their drug use. They were therefore also less likely than males to seek help in addressing their drug problems, despite, according to Milani et al (2004), reporting a higher proportion of psychological symptoms.[5]

In comparing data on the extent and structure of recreational drug use it can be concluded that there are few significant differences between Budapest and most other major European cities (Demetrovics, 2001b; Tossmann, Boldt, and Tensil, 2001). The most marked difference between Hungary and Western European countries has been in the lower incidence of cocaine use. The most likely explanation for this disparity has been economic; cocaine's generally high street-value having coincided with comparatively lower levels of disposable income among Hungarian youth. Price sensitivities are notable in relation to other substances, with relatively cheap drugs such as amphetamine having greater popularity in Budapest in comparison to Berlin, Prague or Zurich[6] (see Table 11.3).

---

[5] Anecdotal evidence suggests that young men are more likely to display 'pride' in their drug use, or at least to consider it a symbol of independence. These attitudes are less characteristic of women, who often try to deny or downplay their drug use. Further research is needed to unpick these interesting gendered dimensions.

[6] In the case of hallucinogens, LSD use in Hungary is high in comparison to Western European countries, whilst prevalence of more expensive natural hallucinogens, such as peyote and magic mushrooms, is substantially lower. The most recent data, however, suggests a decrease in LSD use and a parallel increase in magic mushroom and herbal-drug use in Budapest.

Table 11.3 Lifetime use of different drugs in European cities (per cent)

	A'dam[a]	Berlin[a]	Prague[a]	Zurich[a]	B'pest[b]
Cannabis	91.7	78.6	88.2	85.8	80.6
Amphetamine	61.3	46.1	46.1	38.6	50.5
Ecstasy	83.4	44.6	38.2	51.8	36.9
Hallucinogens	66.8	41.6	48.7	54.4	54.4
Cocaine	59.6	33.2	21.3	37.8	25.7

[a]Tossmann, Boldt and Tensil, 2001
[b]Demetrovics, 2001a

Cocaine is now becoming more widespread and its increased use in entertainment venues is a significant development (Demetrovics and Rácz, 2008). In Hungary, cocaine has long been associated with older and more affluent drug users who are not core participants in dance culture (Demetrovics et al, 2008), yet although its price has not significantly reduced it has become more widely available, gaining popularity with a broader range of (younger and poorer) people. In this respect, Hungarian trends continue to reflect those of Western Europe, albeit incrementally and subject to a degree of time-lag.

POLICING AND HARM-REDUCTION ACTIVITIES

The 'National Strategy to Combat the Drug Problem' adopted by the Hungarian Parliament in December 2000 (Ministry of Youth and Sport, 2000) contains specific aims concerning drug use in dance-music entertainment venues. In a chapter addressing the theme of 'community and cooperation', long-, medium- and short-term aims are outlined. Long-term proposals include 'increasing the number of safe entertainment venues'; medium-term measures involve 'supporting the establishment of drug-free programmes and scenes' and 'decreasing the number of disco accidents'; whilst 'analysis and necessary modification of the legislative environment', 'establishment of local prevention services', and 'establishment and control of local forms of regulation' are short-term goals. In a further chapter on 'treatment' the Strategy refers to a reinforcing of outreach activities in recreational settings, whilst reducing the supply of drugs is also mentioned as a clear aim. Without describing these aims in detail, it is sufficient to note that the Hungarian government has sought to strengthen its position in this field. To this end, the Ministry of Youth and Sport has recognized the main problems relating to recreational drug use in entertainment settings and has outlined them in a coherent strategy document. There is now a clear set of official aims and objectives concerning the public and private management of substance use, based mainly around the initiation of measures to prevent and reduce harm.

THE SAFE ENTERTAINMENT VENUES PROGRAMME

The Hungarian government's increasing commitment to recreational-drug policy was further illustrated by development of the 'Safe Entertainment Venues Programme'. The origins of the Programme date back to 1999 with the drafting of plans to implement the National Drug Strategy through partnership working between various agencies and stakeholders involved in nightlife, its regulation, and the provision of support services (Demetrovics and Pelle, 2000). In May 2000, the Ministry of Youth and Sport (ISM), in collaboration with the National Crime Prevention Council, began to coordinate fortnightly discussions among 24 prominent entertainment-venue operators and representatives of other relevant organizations such as the police, ambulance services, municipal governments, and the Ministry of Economics (who are responsible for the regulation of venues through national licensing law).

The aim of these meetings was to draw up a partnership agreement and develop a code of practice which would serve as a model for the safe operation of dance venues. Under the outline programme design of July 2000, the model venue would be drug-free and operated in such a way as to eliminate or minimize public-health hazards and other social harms. The Association of Safe Entertainment Venues (ASEV), established to implement the programme, was founded at the end of that same year (Demetrovics and Pelle, 2000).

Following establishment of the SEV Programme the state refocused its efforts toward the dissemination of knowledge on the topic and the provision of financial support for drug welfare agencies. To this end, the ISM organized three national conferences to raise awareness of the SEV Programme and announced a grant scheme titled 'Safe Entertainment Venues' as part of the PHARE funding programme. This initiative was of limited success, as in its first phase only 20 per cent of available funds were distributed due to the limited number of active organizations in the field and the poor quality of funding applications received.

OTHER PREVENTION AND HARM-REDUCTION ACTIVITIES

In Hungary, harm-reduction activity in clubland settings began in earnest in January 1999 with the launch of the Blue Point Drug Counselling and Outpatient Centre's so-called 'Party Service' (Rácz, Urbán, and Lencse, 2000). This service—working in the underground party scene, primarily in and around Budapest—has operated continuously ever since. Qualitative studies indicate that the owners and operators of entertainment venues often adopt an ambivalent attitude toward such service providers, sometimes refusing them access to their venues. This is particularly true of more mainstream party scenes (Csák et al, 2008; Demetrovics et al, 2008) as building harm-reduction services into the operation of one's venue implies acknowledgement that one's customers are drug users. Such considerations appear to inform the reticent or obstructive position of many venue owners, whose primary concern is to avoid any related stigmatization of the setting, possibly involving increased police activity. Many operators adopt this unhelpful strategy of denying or, at best, seeking to underplay the extent of young people's drug use at their events. The stance is maintained regardless of the views and interests of their customers, many of whom clearly view these types of intervention as useful. Nonetheless, several in-situ drug-service initiatives have been adopted throughout the country in recent years, some, typically in smaller cities, linked to specific entertainment venues, and others which have a presence in several different locations.

CONCLUSIONS

Research shows the extent of recreational-drug use in Hungarian clubland to have increased in recent years, albeit at a lower pace than in the 1990s. Due to the decreasing age of youngsters attending electronic dance music (EDM) events, recreational-drug use has also begun to start at an earlier age. Differences have been found in relation to the substances and patterns of drug use associated with different EDM styles. These variations relate to the repertories of drugs that are chosen and the intensity at which they are consumed. Whilst one sees a decrease in the popularity of certain substances, such as LSD, it is also possible to identify the spread of new 'highs' (eg, magic mushrooms, herbal drugs, ketamine and GHB) that were not previously seen on the Hungarian party scene (or else present, but of relatively little significance). Recreational-drug use in Hungary has a tendency to follow trends first established in Western Europe, as has occurred in relation to significant growth in the cocaine market.

Harm-reduction and treatment services have been established across Hungary in an attempt to reduce the attendant health risks of recreational drug use. Although drug support agencies receive adequate state funding, their success has been only partial. Leisure industry operators have been notably reluctant to embrace such initiatives fearing negative repercussions arising from any acknowledgement that their venues might have an associated 'drug problem'. This ambivalence is understandable when one considers the conflicted stance of the Hungarian government. Whilst the National Drug Strategy counts focused action on harm reduction among its fundamental aims, and the state has taken a number of practical steps toward achieving such goals, present approaches to drugs law enforcement adopt a contradictory hard-line abolitionist stance. Prevailing criminal law threatens with closure any entertainment venue in which drug use is found. Given the wish to avoid stigmatization, criminalization, and a possible loss of livelihood, cultural entrepreneurs who embrace the harm-reduction agenda play for high stakes. It is understandable that many may wish to deny or downplay the extent of drug use among their patrons and other young people on the dance scene.

REFERENCES

All internet sources were accessible 20 August 2008

CSÁK, R, FORSTNER, M, MÁRVÁNYKÖVI, F and RÁCZ, J (2008) 'Kvalitatív Panelvizsgálat a Budapesti Elektronikus Zenei Partiélet Szereplői, Valamint a Drogpolitika Megvalósítói

Körében (Qualitative panel study among the stakeholders of the Budapest party scene and drug-policy decision-makers)', in Z Demetrovics and J Rácz (eds), *Partik, Drogok, Ártalomcsökkentés. Kvalitatív Kutatások a Partiszcénában.* Budapest: L'Harmattan, 225–91.

DEMETROVICS, Z (1998) *Drugs and Discos in Budapest: Smoking, alcohol consumption and drug-using behaviour amongst youth in clubbing subcultures,* Budapest: Regional Resource Centre.

—— (2001a) 'Cultural changes and the changing face of youth subculture and drug use: Some comparisons between Western and Eastern Europe', in M Nechifor and P Boisteanu (eds), *Pharmacodependences: Mechanisms, clinical aspects, treatment,* Iasi: Editura Glissando, 109–17.

—— (2001b) *Droghasználat Magyarország Táncos Szórakozóhelyein (Drug Use in the Hungarian Party Scene),* Budapest: L'Harmattan.

—— (2004) 'Nemi Különbségek a Rekreációs Droghasználatban (Gender differences in recreational drug use)', *Addictologia Hungarica,* 3/4, 533–42.

—— (2005) 'A Rekreációs Környezetben Megjelenő Droghasználat Alakulása Magyarországon (Recreational drug use in Hungary)', in É. Borsi and P Portörő (eds), *Jelentés a Magyarországi Kábítószerhelyzetről,* Budapest: Ministry of Youth, Family, Social Affairs and Equal Opportunities, 81–98.

—— KUN, B, NÁDAS, E and VADÁSZ, P (2008) 'A Magyarországi Táncos-Zenés Rekreációs Színtéren Megjelenő Droghasználat Jellemzői (Characteristics of drug use in the Hungarian recreational party scene)', in Z Demetrovics and J Rácz (eds), *Partik, Drogok, Ártalomcsökkentés. Kvalitatív Kutatások a Partiszcénában,* Budapest: L'Harmattan, 25–223.

—— NÁDAS, E and KUN, B. (2008) 'Rekreációs Droghasználat Magyarországon: Előzmények (Recreational drug use in Hungary: An historical overview)', in Z Demetrovics and J Rácz (eds), *Partik, Drogok, Ártalomcsökkentés. Kvalitatív Kutatások a Partiszcénában.* Budapest: L'Harmattan, 13–24.

—— and PELLE, A (2000) '"Biztonságos Szórakozóhely Program". Ajánlás Valamint Elméleti és Jogi Háttéranyag a Táncos Szórakozóhelyek Biztonságos Üzemeltetéséhez ("Safe Entertainment Venues Programme": Recommendations, theoretical and legal background to the safer operation of clubs)', *Addictologia Hungarica,* 8/6, 433–41.

—— and RÁCZ, J (eds)(2008) *Partik, Drogok, Ártalomcsökkentés. Kvalitatív Kutatások a Partiszcénában (Parties, Drugs, and Harm Reduction: Qualitative studies in the party scene),* Budapest: L'Harmattan.

ELEKES, Z and PAKSI, B (2000) *Drogok és Fiatalok (Drugs and Youth),* Budapest: Ministry of Youth and Sport.

FEJÉR, B (1995) 'Acid Történet (Acid Story)', *Törökfürdő,* 1, 22–6.

—— (1998) *Az LSD Kultusza. Egy Budapesti Kulturális Színpad Krónikája (The Cult of LSD: The chronicle of a cultural scene in Budapest),* Budapest: MTA PTI.

—— (2000) 'A Parti. Antropológiai Sűrű Leírás (The party: An anthropological description)', *Törökfürdő,* 1, 22–6.

MILANI, RM, PARROTT, AC, TURNER, JJ and FOX, HC (2004) 'Gender differences in self-reported anxiety, depression, and somatisation among ecstasy/MDMA polydrug users, alcohol/tobacco users, and nondrug users', *Addict Behavior,* 29/5, 965–71.

MINISTRY of YOUTH and SPORT (2000) *National Strategy to Combat the Drug Problem: Conceptual framework of the Hungarian government's anti-drug strategy,* Budapest: Ministry of Youth and Sport.

PAKSI, B (2007) 'A Magyar Társadalom Drogérintettsége (Drug use in Hungary)', in Z Demetrovics (ed), *Az Addiktológia Alapjai I,* Budapest: ELTE Eötvös, 255–94.

Rácz, J and Geresdi, Z (2001) 'Az Underground Partikultúra Értékvilága Magyarországon (The culture of the underground party scene in Hungary)', *Educatio*, 10/3, 530–42.

—— Urbán, B and Lencse, M (2000) '"Biztonságosabb Táncolás"—Party Service ("Safer dancing"—Party Service)', in Z Demetrovics (ed), *A Szintetikus Drogok Világa. Diszkódrogok, Drogfogyasztók, Szubkltúrák*, Budapest: Animula, 241–63.

Tossmann, P, Boldt, S and Tensil, MD (2001) 'The use of drugs within the techno party scene in European metropolitan cities', *European Addiction Research*, 7/1, 2–23.

12

GREECE

Sophie Vidali

INTRODUCTION

Stereotypical representations of nightlife in Greece frame this social realm within the discourses of entertainment and leisure and it is rare to encounter discussions of associated criminality, incivilities, or the fear of crime. Up until the late 1970s, the social history of Greek nightlife was, however, littered with accounts of deviance and petty criminality. Since then, the influence of criminal organizations in shaping social and economic relations within a free-market night-time economy (NTE) has been of primary importance. Despite these links, nightlife and entertainment do not represent core components of crime policy for the Greek authorities. This apparent contradiction may be explained in the following ways:

1. The major topics of public concern ensure that the priorities of the police and other crime prevention and security agencies are mainly targeted at the activities of illegal immigrants, street-level drug dealers, and prostitutes, together with the control of conflict between young people (mostly students) and the police.
2. Lawbreaking by the owners and operators of nightlife enterprises is governed primarily by the civil rather than criminal code, ensuring that their criminal activities remain comparatively obscure and marginal to mainstream crime and disorder policy.
3. The activities of nightlife's criminal organizations are not recorded as a separate category in crime statistics.
4. Opportunities for survey research and ethnography in this field are limited and studies have yet to emerge.
5. Crime-control agencies have a tendency to evaluate criminal episodes independently of their structural contexts, as symptoms of personal choice. Thus, when nightlife's criminal lynchpins are brought to justice their actions are evaluated as isolated law infringements in the context of a healthily functioning system, like 'a bad apple in a barrel of good apples' (Sutherland and Cressey, 1978: 12).

Identification of these 'knowledge gaps' leads to the conclusion that the study of nightlife's relationship with crime and disorder in Greece should be extended to include the crimes of those individuals and groups who organize and govern nightlife enterprises.

Given the absence of empirical research in a Greek context, the aims of this chapter are modest and exploratory. What follows will draw together findings from research (Lazos, 2002; Vidali et al, 2008) and official publications (EKTEPN, 2006, 2007) in associated fields, together with knowledge from media sources, including newspapers and the web pages of political parties. This tentative exploration of nightlife and crime in Greece is conducted through the lens of urban governance wherein social and economic relations are shaped by legal and illegal forces operating within a free-market economy.

NIGHTLIFE AND SOCIAL CHANGE

The place of commercial night-time leisure in Greece can only be understood within the context of broader economic developments within the country—particularly the entrenchment of a free-market model from the mid-1980s onwards. Slightly later, one sees the imposition of concrete measures to control an expanding NTE. In 1994, licensing hours for night-time entertainment enterprises were extended to 3.00 am.[1] This allowed greater access to nightlife and has provided employment for some of the many young adults who leave education with poor qualifications and must therefore seek informal or part-time employment. In a post-industrial context of 'flexible' labour markets the borders between legal and the illegal activities in the workplace become blurred. For example, the security policies adopted by nightlife enterprises are frequently beyond and in conflict with the law (Hobbs et al, 2003) and new informal codes acquire peculiar significance (see below). The creation and maintenance of alternative social orders governed by illicit forces facilitates the formation of protective bubbles in which more serious forms of criminal activity—over and above the mostly petty crimes of patrons— may be pursued.

In Greece, the development of illicit social orders has been intrinsic to the historical evolution of cultural traditions and social relations, forming a constituent of the country's transition to modernity. Moreover, since the inter-war years (1919–39), a strong artistic tradition and folklore has emerged surrounding famous groups of 'rebetes'.[2] Thus, nightlife and entertainment have long been part of everyday life for

---

[1] Min Dicr, 1169/1994, FEK (GOG), B', 96/1994, Art 14, L 2194/1994, FEK A', 43/1994.

[2] *Rebetes* were groups of musicians who played traditional musical instruments (the bouzouki, outi, gouras) and wrote passionate songs ('*rebetika*'). The original *rebetes* were socially excluded people, mainly refugees from Asia Minor, who resisted the Europeanization of their way of life. Their urban folk songs are often compared to genres such as the American blues, The lyrics narrated the misfortune of poor people's lives, their relations with politicians, the state and its laws (police, prison, drugs), their cultural values (especially concerning money, prosperity, and leisure) and love stories; dances such as the '*hasapikos*' and '*zeimbekikos*' are associated with their songs. *Rebetes* were persecuted due to their drug use, and their story is strongly connected with the history of the 'drug problem'; its social construction and law enforcement. They were often involved in petty criminality and were regarded by the state and the bourgeoisie of the time as 'public enemies'. During the Metaxas dictatorship (1936–40) their music was forbidden, *rebetes* were arrested and their musical instruments destroyed. During the 1950s, these songs and traditions were revisited by the great Greek composers M Chatizdakis and M Theodorakis. The musical style of the '*rebetika*' has since became the root of much contemporary Greek music, as represented in famous films such as *Stella*,

the Greek people, even though different meanings have been attached to such activities throughout the years. The commercial side of nightlife and entertainment is also a far from new phenomenon, being influenced by trends in the arts, entertainment, and music, particularly since the 1950s. The marketing and expansion of nightlife has had important cultural effects, contributing to the wide-scale transformation of everyday entertainment habits. However, the notion that peculiarly Greek forms of entertainment play a role in keeping aspects of traditional culture alive is still present in today's free-market NTE, if only in new and transformed forms.

NIGHTLIFE AND URBAN RESTRUCTURING

The story of contemporary nightlife in Greece begins in earnest in the late 1980s (Vidali, 2007) with the establishment of large-scale entertainment enterprises. As in other post-industrial economies, the deregulation of traditional controls such as liquor licensing and the rise of free-market forces transformed leisure into a key sector of the economy (Hobbs et al, 2005; Taylor, 1999). At the same time, the sector's associations with crime became increasingly marked by the rise of protection rackets and infiltration of the leisure industry by criminal organizations (Vidali, 2007). Affluence and leisure consumption, rather than poverty and exclusion from such consumption, became the precursors of criminal opportunity (Ruggiero, 1996). This led to erosion in the traditional culture of tolerance toward acts of deviance in entertainment time. Concurrently, in the Greek live-music halls and Western European and American-influenced venues alike, artistic and musical appreciation was being replaced by a new entertainment culture of hyperbole and kitsch.

In the Athens region today, nightlife is concentrated within de-industrialized areas of the city centre and around the coast. Local municipal authorities have encouraged such concentration through policies of land-use planning, the licensing of entertainment venues, and through marketing of the coasts and beaches as tourist and leisure destinations (*Eleftherotypia*, 7 June 2003b; Maloutas, 2000; Municipal Authority of Athens, 2008; Vidali, 2007). Similar processes have taken place in other areas, including Patras, Piraeus, and Thessaloniki.

FORMS OF CRIME AND DISORDER

Development of the NTE as a liminal space (Hobbs et al, 2003) has created much ambiguity concerning associated forms of crime and disorder, particularly in relation to the links between nightlife enterprises and criminal business. Organized crime takes the form of economic crimes such as fraud, money laundering, and extortion,

Never on Sunday, and *Zorbas*. In the 50s, shortly after the Greek Civil War (1943–50), a new generation of *rebetes* emerged. These musicians were, for the most part, socially accepted and the *rebetiko* became central to Greek folklore, music, and notions of national unity. The commercialization of *rebetes'* dances, leisure-entertainment patterns, and musical style has more recently contributed to the development of nightlife-entertainment and tourism (Chatizdakis, 1949; Damianakos, 2001; Petropoulos, 2000).

together with human-rights violations such as the maltreatment of immigrants and/or sex workers. Here one finds a grey area in which it is sometimes difficult to decipher where an extended informal (legal) economy merges with criminal enterprises (Ruggiero, 1996). Nightlife and crime in Greece may be understood as inherent in three main realms of economic activity. First, it is related to the operation of indoor entertainment enterprises; secondly to street-level illegal and semi-legal markets; and thirdly, to night-time services which complement the main entertainment activities such as illegal taxi and parking enterprises. The following paragraphs will outline criminogenic aspects of the first and second categories. The third category will not be discussed here as its contours remain largely unexplored and data is both limited and anecdotal.

A multitude of local and national, public and private, legal and illegal interests influence the development of nightlife and thus shape the methods by which criminal enterprises exploit opportunities, infiltrate, and retain a presence within the market. In Athens, protection rackets and the extortion of nightlife entrepreneurs by criminal organizations have been a long-standing problem. Furthermore, opportunities for fraud and corruption surround the administration of licence permits for entertainment premises.[3] The bureaucratic complexities of law in this area provide a fertile breeding ground for legal violations and deviant solutions. Such problems are so widespread as to make engagement with bribery and corruption a virtual precondition of the securing of a licence and thus entry into the leisure market (see also Hadfield, 2006: 173).[4]

The dual pressures of extortion and official corruption thus embed criminal action within both the initiation and maintenance of nightlife enterprises. The majority of venues operate in the absence of any licence, or, where a licence is held, it may permit very different types of services to the public from the ones that the operators actually offer.[5] Conflicts over the land-use plans of private developers which compromise the public interest[6] constitute further opportunities for corruption among local 'growth coalitions' comprising private entrepreneurs and state, police, or municipal authorities (*Eleftherotypia*, 7 June 2003a and 3 May 2008). Such corruption results from the pressures generated by legitimate and illegitimate businesses alike in their drive to achieve designated goals. This aspect of the NTE is especially remarkable as it reveals something of the little understood continuum along which sharp practices melt into criminality.

When attempting to manipulate the system, powerful individuals and groups variously apply techniques of introduction, adaptation, and maintenance to achieve or defend their position in the market. In this arena, legal and criminal demands or motivations may respectively give rise to criminal or legal solutions. The application of

---

[3] The Presidential Decree 410 (PD 410/1995, FEK {GOG} A, 231) transferred responsibility for the licensing of entertainment premises from the police to municipal authorities.

[4] Anoihti Poli (2007), *Eleftherotypia*, 5 February 2007.

[5] *Eleftherotypia*, 7 June 2003a, Prefecture of Athens, Press Releases, 7 July 2007 and 26 July 2007.

[6] This issue has recently been at the centre of intensive public disputes and even violent conflicts between entrepreneurs and their personnel on the one side and local municipal authorities, residents, and politicians on the other (*Eleftherotypia*, 3 May 2008).

these solutions then influences the forms of private order which emerge in nightlife, all of which are related to criminal actors' attitudes toward the law, as outlined in the following typology:

1. Law attachment: Businesses display formal attachment to the law in all of their 'front stage' dealings with the authorities. This approach may be used as a technique to deflect attention away from the 'back regions' inhabited by serious forms of criminality upon which the enterprise is founded. For example, venues may simply operate as a vehicle for the laundering of drugs money or for the provision of private sitting rooms in which specific clients obtain unlicensed and/or illegal prostitution services (Vidali et al, 2008).

2. Tolerance to criminality: This attitude implies a willingness to bend the rules so as to increase one's profits to a level which exceeds that which could be obtained by legitimate means alone. For example, nightlife enterprises, even if they have been legally funded, choose to tolerate drug use and dealing in order to increase the popularity of their venue and gain competitive advantage over their rivals (Vidali et al, 2008).

3. Direct involvement in 'hidden' crimes: A further technique to increase profits. Here otherwise legal nightlife entertainment enterprises break the law by placing their clients at risk (ignoring health and safety regulations, illegally serving alcohol to under-17-year-olds) or by employing illegal immigrants, or other forms of off-the-books labour.

The majority of these crimes are 'hidden' to the extent that they are not recorded in official crime statistics. One of the most common crimes in Greek live-music halls is alcohol recycling wherein, at the end of the night, bar staff refill bottles with the contents of partially-consumed drinks. The recycled vessels and contents are cleaned and sealed for resale together with previously sold flowers collected from the floor where customers have dropped them which are then made into fresh bunches. The adulteration of alcohol (to form super-strength 'bomb' drinks) is a further 'sharp practice' stimulated by tax evasion, but which can have dramatic and harmful effects upon the drinker (*To Vima*, 8 February 1998, 17 November 2002).

In bars and clubs mostly frequented by the young and especially in Techno/Trance music venues the use and trading of illegal drugs are commonplace (EKTEPN, 2007; *Kathimerini*, 14 October 2003, 10 December 2004, 28 January 2005; Vidali et al, 2008). Venue staff often use drugs themselves and the safety of drug-using patrons is sometimes seriously compromised when, for example, the reactions of staff to instances of overdose are conditioned by the interests of the enterprise in concealing such occurrences (Vidali et al, 2008). In the Greek live-music halls very little drug use or trading occurs; nonetheless, the artists (mostly singers and musicians) employed in such venues often become drug users/addicts in order to keep themselves active and in 'high spirits' or to cope with the stresses of nightwork (*To Vima*, 9 December 2007; Vidali et al, 2008).

Strip shows are associated with further very specific aspects of nightlife and crime. Here the role of the dancers (who are not exclusively women) includes prostitution (*Ta Nea*, 28 January 2003). The criminality of these arrangements inheres in the status of the artists who are prostituted. Most are young (adolescent) females from Eastern European and African countries residing in Greece without official authority. They are often the victims of trafficking and are controlled and extorted by criminal networks (*Eleftherotypia*. 23 November 2002; *Ta Nea*, 25 September 2004; *To Vima*, 13 November 2005). This phenomenon constitutes a sizable problem. In 2003, approximately 80 nightlife enterprises of this kind, employing around 2,000 young women, were uncovered in the Attica region alone (*Ta Nea*, 28 January 2003).

THE ACHIEVEMENT OF ORDER

In nightlife venues social order is not spontaneous and unstructured but actively accomplished and shaped by processes of security production and reproduction. The main objective of this purposive action is to create an environment conducive to the enhancement of profits for the entrepreneur and enjoyment for the patron. As noted above, this environment may not necessarily be 'safe' in that it may incorporate opportunities for transgression and crime. Clients' attitudes are crucial here. The participation of adolescents and young adults within 'consumerist cultures of transgression' with high spending on alcohol (Hobbs et al, 2005: 168) allows for the meaning of nightlife spaces to be constructed around a controlled loss of control.

Order is achieved through concrete security measures such as access control (door supervision) and also by the willingness of staff to work in furtherance of the economic interests of the enterprise, which, as described, may be realized by tolerating, or even participating in, 'hidden' forms of crime. Thus crime may become a regular part of the 'job'. As in other countries, door supervision has been linked to criminal gangs and networks (*To Vima*, 4 November 2007) and anecdotally to the extortion of legitimate leisure entrepreneurs. Work on the doors is usually offered to young adults, whose muscular body is the main qualification and tool for their trade. As a result, those employed in door supervision have the capacity to apply physical force and intimidation. The order imposed by door teams is sometimes threatened by antagonistic groups who seek to wrestle control of particular nightlife enterprises in pursuit of their own ambitions for extortion or the control of lucrative drug markets. Such groups effectively govern nightlife in Athens by their own informal means (Hellenic Police Headquarters, 2005: 19m; *Ta Nea*, 12 February 2000 and 3 February 2005).

THE PLACE OF ALCOHOL IN NIGHTLIFE

In Greece, alcohol consumption is not usually associated with drunkenness (WHO, 2004: 32, table 10, 33) and is low at a population level, in comparison with almost all West European countries (WHO, 2004: table 3, 12). One recent national survey suggests that alcohol consumption has sharply decreased during the past 20 years (EKTEPN, 2006: 97). Such surveys are not entirely comprehensive, however, as a considerable quantity of wine is produced and consumed at home and therefore does not form part of the official 'alcohol industry' (see also WHO, 2004: 15). More specifically, the years 1999–2003 saw a drop in the proportion of alcohol consumed in licensed premises and increased drinking in the home (EKTEPN, 2006: 99). In 2006, home drinking accounted for 41 per cent of whisky sales and 25 per cent of the sales of ouzo, the take-home market comprising a total of 57,600 litres of alcohol (*To Vima*, 27 July 2008: B8–B9). Levels of alcohol consumption are higher in rural and semi-rural regions than in Attiki, the region which includes the Greek capital (EKTEPN, 2006).

During 2006, 61.9 per cent of consumers surveyed reported having consumed alcohol in entertainment venues (EKTEPN, 2007: graph 43,100). Age was found to be a very significant variable, with more than 40 per cent of respondents in each of the age categories (12–17, 18–24, 25–35) reporting that they regularly consumed alcohol in bars, clubs, and discos. The highest percentage for participation in entertainment venue drinking was recorded among 18–24-year-olds (65.6 per cent) and the data provides evidence to suggest that illegal sales of alcohol to under-17s is rife. In the previous year (2005) approximately 70 per cent of 12–17-year-olds reported having consumed alcohol in indoor entertainment spaces (EKTEPN, 2006: 101), with hangovers the next day recorded as the most common negative consequences (57.6 per cent) (EKTEPN, 2006: 96). Overall, the two surveys confirm that alcohol consumption outside the home is predominately popular among young people, and 18–24-year-old adults especially (EKTEPN, 2007: graph 44, 101).

Perhaps the most negative effects of alcohol consumption relate to drink-driving and road traffic accidents. Road traffic police (RTP) conduct systematic stop-and-breathe-test operations at night-time and severe penalties are imposed on drivers found to have exceeded the legally permitted limit for blood-alcohol concentration. In Athens, the recent extension of Metro light rail services to 2.00 am has contributed to a decrease in the number of alcohol-related road accidents. During 2007 and the first half of 2008, only 3.1 per cent and 3.0 per cent respectively of those stopped by the RTP were found to be intoxicated (Ministry of the Interior, 2007a). Additionally, among a total of 6,263 road traffic accidents involving injury in the first half of 2008, only 157 were linked to drink-driving (Ministry of the Interior, 2007b). The number of accidents involving drivers who have consumed illegal drugs is not recorded.

STREET CRIMES

In the municipality of Athens and much of the rest of Greece, street-based nightlife is mainly concentrated in certain squares, with associated crime being related to drugs and prostitution.

STREET-LEVEL DRUG MARKETS: THE OMONIA AREA

The Omonia area at the heart of Athens city centre is the only area in Greece where the trading of drugs is tolerated. This 'tolerance zone' was created in the 1990s to accommodate the expulsion of drug addicts from other parts of the city. Since then, police raids, city-centre restructuring, and the increasing involvement of immigrants has led to the spread of drug-related activities into neighbouring streets. The square is now a symbolic location for crime, and its inhabitants have been blamed for street crimes and creating a zone of fear for local citizens. Drugs are traded and distributed between Greeks and immigrants in the square 24-hours a day (Vidali et al, 2008).

PROSTITUTION

The drugs market has close affinities with the sale of sexual services. As noted above, Greek law regulates the status of persons who may engage in prostitution (Lazos, 2002: 74) and most prostitution is conducted in brothels. The social composition of the sex trade has been completely transformed during the last ten years due to a massive influx of immigrant sex workers. Whilst some of the foreign sex workers are victims of trafficking, others are drug addicts whose habit is supplied by their pimp for whom they must now work to fund their drug consumption (Vidali et al, 2008).

In Athens, street prostitution is mainly found in five of the city's squares[7] all of which are sited near entrances/exits to the city's entertainment and/or tourist zones. Thus the spatial distribution of street prostitution appears to follow that of other nightlife activities in the city. At street level these markets are governed by pimps, but the relationship, if any, between the organization of illegal street markets and legal brothel-based sex work is not known. Apart from the sex workers themselves, whole networks of people, including criminal gangs, earn money from the sale of sex in brothels and on the streets (Lazos, 2002). There are said to be around 2,000 women working within the legal sex industry in Athens and a further 9,000 working illegally (*Ta Nea*, 16 July 2008). These figures do not account for the further market in male prostitution, mainly supplied by young immigrants and drug addicts and purchased by older gay men. Further hidden aspects of illegal sex work include crimes of violence against prostituted persons, both by their 'controllers' and by clients.

POLICING, SECURITY, AND CRIME CONTROL

Pimps, drug dealers, and others involved in the illegal street markets impose their own forms of order which serve to regulate street life (Vidali et al, 2008). However, whilst nightlife is 'policed' in a number of ways by various formal and informal agencies, the Hellenic Police Force (HP) remains the most dominant actor in maintaining public order on the streets. For various reasons related to Greek police history and culture and the failure of reformist efforts, the HP continues to adopt a militarized mode of policing (Vidali, 2007). Although a problem-oriented policing strategy was nominally adopted in 2004, in practice, this has produced little more than randomly targeted repressive police operations aimed at prostitutes, immigrants, and drug addicts in the nightlife street markets. The selection of 'targets' appears to be influenced by political

---

[7] These are: (1) Solonos/Kolonaki Square, (2) Sugrou Avenue, (3) Votanikos/St Polykarpos/Iera Odos, (4) Kavalas Street, and (5) Eyripidou Street/ Threatrou Square (Omonia area). It is notable that the city of Athens does not have areas that are purely residential. Land uses in the city are mixed and commercial activities are found in all but a few small neighbourhoods.

factors surrounding public anxieties and the various moral panics which periodically erupt in relation to different groups of urban 'others' (Robinson, 2003).

In policing nightlife venues themselves, the activities of the HP are strictly restrained by laws which require specific evidence that a crime has been committed and therefore limit discretionary powers of access to conduct routine inspections. On the other hand, public agencies tasked with the governance of public health, commerce, and economic crime have a clear remit to inspect nightlife entertainment enterprises and their standards of operation. The state's role in enforcement activity, as in the administration of licensing, is conditioned by extra-legal factors such as stereotypical assumptions and unfair discrimination in the exercise of discretion which may be influenced by various forms of malpractice, including corruption (*Ta Nea*, 25 September 2004). Despite the quasi-public character of entertainment venues, the maintenance of order and security within them remains largely a function of private governance as imposed by operators and their door teams, as described above. State control over these liminal spaces is conditioned, among other things, by the recognition that these are not spaces of marginality and that strong-arm tactics and undue interventions into law-abiding people's leisure time are likely to prove politically unpopular and subject to challenge.

CONCLUSIONS

In Greece, the most evident forms of crime occurring in a nightlife context are not those associated with a general environment of social disorder and incivility, but rather organized illegalities taking place 'behind the scenes' or in relation to street-level drug and sex markets concentrated in specific geographical hotspots. The latter are spaces of danger, most prominently, for the socially excluded groups who inhabit them. These groups include prostitutes and drugs addicts who are repeatedly victimized, both by criminals and by the police, from whom they receive little protection but a considerable degree of repressive and often unwarranted attention. The markets which fuel this misery remain largely tolerated, with those most directly affected left to the robust self-regulatory efforts of the criminal networks who govern them. In every transition from one type of economy to another there are always winners and losers (Melossi, 2002: 48). The primary losers are those identified as 'pathological' or 'problematic' populations to be eliminated, abandoned to elimination by others, treated, excluded, or 're-socialized'. These are the people who inhabit the illegal street markets of Athens.

In contrast to the conventional and visible crimes of the street population, forms of criminality linked to the operation of entertainment enterprises inhabit a 'grey area' in which ostensibly legitimate business practices are used as a 'cover' for organized illegalities. New opportunities for such crimes have grown in line with urban restructuring and the increasing economic importance of the leisure and tourism sectors. Powerful social actors form coalitions to exploit the ineptitude of state agencies in their attempts to control a society in transition. These forms of resistance and corruption are a historical component of the struggle by powerful groups in Greek society to maintain the status quo and avoid the democratization of power relations (Charalabis, 1985 and 1989; Vidali, 2007). At the same time, nightlife exists as a social arena which is not and cannot be controlled by traditional police methods. In Greece, nightlife's liminal markets and spaces constitute social ghettos in which governance is ceded to what are often criminally inclined and conflicting private interests.

Western societies appear to be on the cusp of a new era in which the regulatory technologies of the industrial era are beginning to wane and attempts to control the business of pleasure exist as archaic mechanisms of marginal utility to the engine of neo-liberalism. However, the history of capitalist development in Greece has taken very specific forms which have favoured the maintenance of pre-industrial institutions such as the extended family network and their traditional social roles. The contemporary informal economy, political corruption, and organized crime all have their roots in such relations, with important consequences for the borderline between legality and illegality, the promotion of private (extra-institutional) legal and illegal interests, and for the nation's crime control policies.[8] The Greek situation and that of other countries which retain strong cultural legacies which influence the regulation of a supposedly 'free' market economy constitute important cases for reflection on the power structures which infuse urban governance, nightlife, and crime.

REFERENCES

All internet sources were accessible 20 August 2008

References marked * are published in Greek

ANOIHTI POLI (2007) 'What's going on with nightlife entertainment enterprises?', Press release, 1 February 2007, <http://www.anoihtipoli.gr>.*

CHATZIDAKIS, M (1949) 'Interpretation and standing of the modern folk song', in M CHATZIDAKIS, official website, ergography link: <http://www.hadjidakis.gr>.

CHARALAMBIS, D (1985) *The Army and Political Power: The structure of power in post-Civil War Greece*, Athens: Exantas.*

—— (1989) *Clienteles and Populism: Extra-institutional consensus in the Greek political system*, Athens: Exantas.*

DAMIANAKOS, S (2001) *A Sociology of the Rebetiko*, Athens: Plethron.*

EKTEPN (National Documentation and Information Centre for Drugs) (2006) *Annual Report on the Drugs and Alcohol Situation in Greece, 2005*, Athens: EKTEPN.*

—— (2007) *Annual Report on the Drugs and Alcohol Situation in Greece, 2006*, Athens: EKTEPN.*

HADFIELD, P (2006) *Bar Wars: Contesting the Night in Contemporary British Cities*, Oxford: OUP.

HELLENIC POLICE HEADQUARTERS (2005) *Annual Report on Organized Crime in Greece 2004*, Athens: Hellenic Police Headquarters.*

HOBBS, D, HADFIELD, P, LISTER, S and WINLOW, S (2003) *Bouncers: Violence and Governance in the Night-time Economy*, Oxford: OUP.

---

[8] For further exploration of these important cultural and political themes and their history, see: Charalabis, 1985; Sotiropoulos, 2001; Vergopoulos, 1984; Vidali, 2007; Voulgaris, 2001).

—— WINLOW, S, HADFIELD, P and LISTER, S (2005) 'Violent hypocrisy: Governance and the night-time economy', *European Journal of Criminology*, 2/2: 154–76.

LAZOS, G (2002) *Prostitution and Trafficking in Contemporary Greece*, Athens: Kastaniotis.*

MALOUTAS, T (ed) (2000) *The Cities: Social and economic atlas of Greece*, Athens: Volos, EKKE, University Edition of Thessalia.*

MELOSSI, D (2002) *Stato, Controllo Sociale, Devianza*, Milan: Bruno Mondadori.

MINISTRY OF THE INTERIOR (2007a) 'Road Police Statistical Data', <http//.www.astynomia. gr/images/ stories/NEW/methi.pdf>.

—— (2007b) 'Road Police Statistical Data Update', <http://www.astynomia.gr/images/ stories/NEW/66.pdf>.*

MUNICIPAL AUTHORITY OF ATHENS (2008) *Project on the Development of the Municipality of Athens*, <http://www.cityofathens.gr>.*

PETROPOULOS, E (2000) *Songs of the Greek Underworld: The Rebetika tradition*, London: Saqui Books.

ROBINSON, BM (2003) 'The mouse who would rule the world! How American criminal justice reflects the themes of Disneyification', *Journal of Criminal Justice and Popular Culture*, 10/1: 69–86.

RUGGIERO V (1996) *Economie Sporche: L' Impresa Criminale in Europa*, Turin : Bollati Boringhieri.

SOTIROPOULOS, S (2001) *Greece during the Restoration of Democracy: Political and social developments, 1974–1988*, Athens: Livanis.*

SUTHERLAND, EH and CRESSEY, DR (1996) [1978] *Criminologia*, Milan: Giuffré.

TAYLOR, I (1999) *Crime in Context: A critical criminology of market societies*, Cambridge: Polity.

VERGOPOULOS, K (1984) 'The creation of the new bourgeois class', in AAVV, *Greece 1940–1950: A nation in crisis*, Athens: Themelio.*

VIDALI, S (2007) *Crime Control and State Police: Ruptures and continuities in crime policy*, vol II, Athens: Ant N Sakkoulas.*

—— PAPATHEODOROU, C, KOULOURIS, N, GASPARINATOU, M, STAMOULI, S, CHAINAS, E, KAMPANAKIS, J and BOGDANOU, G (2009) *The Drug Economy: Factors which influence the effectiveness of prevention policies: Qualitative research in the city of Athens*, Final Report, Project Equal, Entaxi-OKANA (Greek National Organization against Drugs). Athens: Daradanos.*

VOULGARIS J (2001) *Greece after the Restoration of Democracy, 1974–1990*, Athens: Themelio.*

WHO (World Health Organization) (2004) *Global Status Report on Alcohol*, Department of Mental Health and Substance Abuse, Geneva : WHO.

NEWSPAPERS

Eleftherotypia, <http://www.enet.gr>

23 November 2002, 'Everyday Slavery', <http://www.iospress.gr>.

7 June 2003a, KYRIAKOPOULOS, K and CHATZIGEORGIOU, A, 'Piraeus: "Raining" lawsuits but waterproof enterprises'.

7 June 2003b, KYRIAKOPOULOS, K and CHATIZGEORGIOU, A, 'Seaside stories of madness'.

5 February 2007, 'Nightlife places: In front patrons—behind bureaucracy'.

3 May 2008, CHATIZGEORGIOU, A, 'Embarrassment'.

Ta Nea, <http://ta-nea.dolnet.gr>

12 February 2000, NESFYGE, L and BAILIS, P, 'Exchanging gunshots and millions'.
28 January 2003, KAGIOS, P, 'Here society throws off its clothes'.
25 September 2004, ATHANSIOU, A, 'They expel us, and the procurers remain unpunished'.
3 February 2005, NESFYGE, L, 'Blackmailers' broom'.
16 July 2008, KANELLOPOULOU, D, 'Criminality will increase if brothels close'.

To Vima, <http://tovima.dolnet.gr>

8 February 1998, 'Night belongs to . . . "Bombs"', Art Code, B12467A591, ID: 64110.
17 November 2002, 'The consequences of a "bomb" explosion'.
13 November 2005, LAMBROPOULOS, VG, 'Dossier: Dolls'.
4 November 2007, LAMBROPOULOS, VG, 'The "bad" apples of the Hellenic Police'.
9 December 2007 LAMBROPOULOS, VG, 'The artistry of cocaine's hot-spots'.
27 July 2008, TSAKIRI, T, 'Clashes and re-classifications in the alcohol market'.

Kathimerini, <http://www.kathimerini.gr>

14 October 2003, 'Penal prosecutions against 14 youngsters'.
10 December 2004, 'Raid in bar: 90 brought by force to police stations'.
28 January 2005, 'Raid in bar: 13 arrests for drugs'.

13

UNITED STATES OF AMERICA

REPORT 1 ALCOHOL OUTLETS, CRIME, AND DISORDER IN THE UNITED STATES OF AMERICA

Paul J Gruenewald, Lillian G Remer, and Andrew J Treno[1]

INTRODUCTION

In this chapter we suggest that statistical relationships between numbers and densities of alcohol outlets and rates of crime and related problems are well established in the research literature. However, theoretical explanations for these relationships have not been adequately formulated or tested. The chapter discusses how five theories have been introduced to explain these relationships: (1) Availability Theory, (2) Social Disorganization Theory, (3) Routine Activities Theory, (4) Drinking Contexts Theory, and (5) Niche Theory. The chapter then remarks upon the benefits and limitations of these theoretical models in light of the social responsibilities of commercial sellers and individual consumers of alcohol. It is suggested that Niche Theory provides a conceptual framework in which effective public health approaches to the prevention of crime and disorder related to alcohol outlets may be developed. In the final paragraphs of the chapter it will be argued that the observed effectiveness of community-based preventive interventions in the United States (US) in reducing crime and disorder associated with alcohol outlets demonstrates that social ecological approaches have much to offer with regard to the improvement of health and safety in our communities.

Drinking is commonplace in commercial establishments where night-time entertainment is offered such as bars and restaurants, cafés and nightclubs, concert halls, and other public spaces. These establishments provide entertainment for many, employment for some, and income for owners and operators of these alcohol outlets (Kolvin, 2004). Unfortunately, these benefits are accompanied by societal costs related to the health and social problems that arise from drinking in these places. While the full extent of these problems is not known, it is known that several forms of crime and

[1] Research and preparation of this manuscript were supported by Research Center Grant Number P60-AA06282 and Merit Award R37-AA 012917 from the National Institute on Alcohol Abuse and Alcoholism, National Institutes of Health, USA.

disorder are associated with drinking at these venues. What is now being discovered are the social mechanisms by which alcohol outlets maintain and sometimes aggravate these problems.

The number of problems associated with drinking at alcohol outlets is many and most of these problems may not be directly preventable by the owners and operators of drinking establishments. The research supporting this view has been developed over the past half century by researchers in many countries (especially Australia, New Zealand, Great Britain, Sweden, Norway, Finland, and the United States: Babor, et al, 2003; Roman, et al, 2008; Stockwell, et al, 2005). Best documented among these problems are violent assaults related to on-premise drinking places such as bars and taverns. This association has been observed across community areas, over time, independent of other causes of violence (eg, the illegal drug trade), and at many levels of analysis (from neighbourhoods to cities). Less well documented, but certainly true, are relationships of alcohol outlets to drunken driving and alcohol-related motor-vehicle crashes. Here, too, similar associations have been observed. Less understood, but more troubling, are the roles that alcohol outlets may play in under-age drinking (Treno et al, 2008b), pedestrian injury collisions (LaScala et al, 2004), child abuse and neglect (Freisthler et al, 2007), and intimate partner violence (Quigley and Collins, 2003; Quigley and Leonard, 2000). Statistical associations of outlets with these problems have been observed, but the specific roles of outlets in these problems are not well understood.

THE UNITED STATES CONTEXT

In the US today, none of the states universally prohibit alcohol sales. However, a few states actively restrict sales of specific beverages (ie, spirits), others permit local prohibitions on sales (eg, the state of Kentucky), and a minority of so-called monopoly states still monopolize some aspects of either the wholesale or retail distribution of alcohol (usually again focused on spirits). All states maintain control over alcohol sales through restrictions on production, wholesale and retail licensing (numbers and types), licence densities (ie, numbers per population) and through sales taxes and markups on alcoholic beverages. Most often, local jurisdictions are responsible for licensing, although states may set general limitations and intervene actively in this process (eg, by enabling the privatization of sales through many different outlets). Importantly, despite continued pressure to raise alcohol taxes, the price of alcohol adjusted for inflation has declined continuously over the past decades, continues to decline today, and the lowest prices for alcohol are sometimes less than the price of equivalent volumes of soft drink (Treno et al, 1993). Alcohol is both widely available and very affordable in the US. While alcohol purchases and drinking take place more often among the wealthy, problems related to alcohol are more evident among ethnic minorities living in low-income areas (a phenomenon called the 'minority paradox':

Galvan and Caetano, 2003). Not surprisingly, these are the same areas where alcohol outlets (especially off-licensed shops and liquor stores) typically concentrate in urban and suburban communities (LaVeist and Wallace, 2000), leading researchers to suggest that at least some part of the minority paradox may be explained by the over-concentration of outlets in these areas (Gruenewald et al, 2006).

As this outline suggests, the commercial market for alcoholic beverages is well established in the United States, reflecting the broad acceptability of drinking in association with many night-time activities throughout the country. Perhaps more unique to the United States is the predisposition to attribute drinking problems to drinkers themselves rather than the social ecological circumstances of their drinking. This view is particularly noticeable whenever the US beverage industry encourages users to 'drink responsibly', focusing the onus of responsibility for drinking problems upon the individual. However, this attitude is also reflected in programmes to detect, treat, and/or jail problem drinkers through targeted case-finding and enforcement efforts (Peele, 1993) and in research that focuses upon personal characteristics that promote problem drinking (eg, Lapham et al, 2001, 2006). The presumption is that problem drinkers cause drinking problems and, with enough resources, these drinkers can be found, incarcerated, treated, or otherwise removed from the population (Peele, 1985).

The US focus on the 'problem drinker' stands in stark contrast to alternative criminological and public-health perspectives which view the social ecological circumstances of drinking as intimately tied to the incidence and prevalence of alcohol problems among all who drink, not just the problem drinker (Treno et al, 2008a). This point of view does not deny that some individuals are disproportionately responsible for the alcohol problems that occur; some persons suffer very significant problems from drinking (eg, the repeat drunken driver). However, this point of view does suggest that much crime and disorder related to drinking arises at rather low drinking levels among large populations of users. Impairments in judgement (Vuchinich and Heather, 2003), motor performance (Moskowitz and Fiorentino, 2000), and elevated risk-taking and aggression (Burian et al, 2002) occur at low levels of use. Alcohol-related motor-vehicle crashes, for example, arise at very low drinking levels (ie, at blood-alcohol concentrations as low as 0.04 per cent by volume: National Highway Traffic Safety Administration, 2005). Since most individuals drink at these relatively low levels most of the time, these otherwise low-risk drinkers account for a large proportion of drinking problems.

Viewed from this public-health and criminological perspective, retail alcohol outlets are part of the social ecology of drinking that provides places where individuals are encouraged to drink and are at risk for some alcohol-related problems. In these circumstances, drinking habits (good and bad) can be learned and reinforced, and problem-drinking maintained in our communities (Sanchez et al, 2007). Of course, there are many contexts in which people drink, but alcohol outlets are unique since they form part of a commercial market that profits from alcohol sales and have an interest in encouraging and maintaining alcohol use.

HOW ARE OUTLETS RELATED TO PROBLEMS?

There are five general theories that have been developed to explain how problems are related to alcohol outlets: greater numbers of outlets may lead to more drinking and problems (Availability Theory), they may affect neighbourhood conditions that lead to problems (Social Disorganization Theory), they may affect the social use of public spaces (Routine Activities Theory), they may provide places where problems can occur (Drinking Contexts Theory), or they may differentially attract problem drinkers (Niche Theory).

AVAILABILITY THEORY

Availability Theory—greater numbers of outlets make it easier to find and purchase alcohol in different places, increasing alcohol use and related problems. The idea here is that there is an additional cost to the consumer when it is difficult to find alcohol, and this inconvenience lowers use and, consequently, problems. In support of this explanation of outlet effects, large reductions in availability (eg, prohibition and rationing) have been shown to decrease alcohol use (see Babor et al, 2003). However, there is contradictory evidence indicating that changes in numbers of outlets may not affect use in developed markets where alcohol is widely available (Gruenewald et al, 2002; Pollack et al, 2004). The addition or subtraction of a few outlets in markets which fully meet alcohol demand may appear to make little difference to levels of use.

SOCIAL DISORGANIZATION THEORY

Social Disorganization Theory—greater numbers of outlets: (a) reduce normative constraints over crime and violence (eg, norms against aggression), (b) signal places where crime and violence go unpunished (eg, areas with less policing and place management), or (c) affect the collective efficacy of neighbourhoods (eg, reduced social capital with which to respond to crime). The idea here is that some neighbourhoods are troubled by poverty, poor housing, homelessness, high rates of immigration, and residential instability (eg, rapid turnover in residents) and these conditions lead to weakened norms against violence and crime, unwillingness to intervene in criminal activities, and lack of community resources for policing (Morenoff et al, 2001; Sampson et al, 1997). Alcohol outlets are assumed to play a role among these several causes of crime and violence by adding to social disorganization. Certainly, indices of social disorganization, such as poverty and poor housing, are related to greater levels of crime and violence, but the contributions of alcohol outlets are ambiguous, shown to add to problems in some areas, but not others (Gruenewald et al, 2006).

ROUTINE ACTIVITIES THEORY

Routine Activities Theory—greater numbers of alcohol outlets promote night-time recreational activities that expose drinkers to greater risks for problems under conditions of low guardianship. Routine activities theorists focus upon the human ecologies of places to assess the degree to which population movement and the use of local environments are related to the incidence of problems. It is quite clear that the use of bars and other alcohol establishments is related to alcohol problems and that the degree of crowding in these places may be a significant risk to patrons (Haines and Graham, 2005). It is also clear that levels of guardianship around these places can affect crime: for example, the presence of private or public enforcement agents in and around alcohol outlets is an essential ingredient in deterrence (Hadfield, 2004). While to some degree the over-concentrations of alcohol outlets seen in some areas of communities may explain excessive levels of crime (creating crime 'hotspots': Roncek and Maier, 1991), this is not true across all areas of communities. Greater densities of outlets may be related to high rates of crime in one area and low rates elsewhere (Banerjee et al, 2008).

DRINKING CONTEXTS THEORY

Drinking Contexts Theory—the characteristics of drinking places provide contexts in which social interactions may amplify into problems. Advocates of this theoretical approach point out that some characteristics of drinking places (eg, noise levels, crowding, and music) or drinkers in these places (eg, young males) are associated with problems like aggression and violence. These studies suggest aspects of outlets and alcohol service that may be changed to mitigate problems (eg, crowd control, bouncers), but do not explain why greater numbers of outlets should lead some outlets to have these characteristics (Haines and Graham, 2005).

NICHE THEORY

Niche Theory—greater numbers of outlets provide more choices of places to drink, encourage the segregation of drinkers into drinking subgroups, and provide attractive venues for problem drinking. The idea that alcohol outlets are attractive to drinkers should surprise no one. This theory gains force by noting that alcohol outlets compete for drinkers, market to specific subgroups, and maximize profits by selling to specific 'niches' (subgroups of consumers who share common characteristics). The theory argues that greater numbers of outlets increase niche competition, facilitate the segregation of drinkers into different social groups (eg, singles bars), and enable the reinforcement of problem-drinking behaviours among those groups. Thus, the origin of violent bars, so often the focus of studies of drinking contexts, is viewed as a natural consequence of the interaction of commercial alcohol markets and social systems (Gruenewald, 2007; Parker, 1993).

The strength of niche theory is that it motivates explanations of relationships between outlets and problems in terms of the dynamic interaction of markets and drinkers. Alcohol markets efficiently meet the demand for alcohol. Alcohol consumers prefer to drink in places with other drinkers similar to themselves. The interaction of these processes predicts the conditions under which outlets will be related to more problems. For example, in rural markets where the availability of alcohol may not yet meet demand, greater numbers of outlets will encourage drinking outside the home, more contacts among problem drinkers, and greater levels of crime associated with alcohol outlets (Wood and Gruenewald, 2006). In urban markets saturated with alcohol outlets, greater numbers of alcohol outlets may have no effect on problems (Gruenewald et al, 2006). Importantly, independent of population size and drinking levels, the theory predicts greater problems when densities of establishments increase. High-risk drinkers will continue to segregate into different drinking environments leading to accelerated risks. Thus, niche theory identifies how problems seemingly unrelated to outlets may become associated with drinking establishments. For example, Freisthler et al (2007) argue that the incidents of child neglect persistently related to densities of bars in community-level studies may be understood in terms of the ways in which parents selectively drink in these places outside the home. On the other hand, a similarly persistent correlation of off-premise outlets with child abuse is supported by the observation that these parents purchase alcohol for drinking in the home.

WHO IS RESPONSIBLE?

To what extent are owners and operators of alcohol outlets responsible for alcohol-related problems? Are outlets simply responsible for providing an in-demand product and individuals responsible for the consequences of its use? Are consumers the unwilling victims of market activities that encourage greater problems in their lives? Like all false dichotomies, neither of these points of view is correct, but each provides a kernel of truth. It would be easy to rush to judgement and indict the alcohol and hospitality industries for their role in alcohol problems. As noted above, it is in the interests of alcohol outlets to efficiently market alcohol to as many different drinking groups as possible. For this reason it is inevitable that, at some point, these market activities will capitalize upon some facet of drinking subgroups that is related, for example, to violence (eg, marketing to young single males). The fact that outlet owners engage in a social process that leads to violence does not make them solely culpable for the violence that occurs. Individual actors remain responsible for their actions. From a public-health perspective, the assignment of responsibility one way or the other is irrelevant. The most rational response to these issues is to recognize that the alcohol environment can be engineered in different ways so that individual benefits may be maximized while minimizing social costs. How many outlets are associated with how much risk and under what circumstances can, in some instances, be measured (Gruenewald and Remer, 2006), but the ultimate question is how to regulate competition in the alcohol market so as to minimize the shared social risks of alcohol use.

At this juncture, a more comprehensive understanding of the roles of alcohol outlets in communities, better assessments of the numbers of different problems that arise in association with drinking at these outlets, and some determination of the economic and social costs of alcohol-related problems are required. While much of this work is under way (Stockwell et al, 2005) we still cannot determine an optimal number of outlets to maintain access to alcohol while minimizing associated risks. Theoretical work indicates that in any sizable community (of 50,000 or more persons), there will be a rapid phase transition: as numbers of outlets increase from zero, drinkers rapidly utilize those outlets, until the market saturates and outlet use diminishes (a form of diminishing returns in the alcohol market: Gorman et al, 2006). Empirical exploration of these relationships will no doubt deliver avenues for future research. In the meantime, alcohol researchers and criminologists have been exploring policing and environmental prevention efforts that can effectively reduce problems related to alcohol outlets.

WHAT WORKS TO PREVENT PROBLEMS ASSOCIATED WITH OUTLETS?

The good news regarding crime and the disorder that takes place on or near alcohol outlets is that police enforcement can work (Hadfield, 2004). Within some limits, rates of drunken driving and related motor-vehicle crashes can be reduced through greater enforcement of drunken-driving laws and lower blood–alcohol limits (Babor et al, 2003). Greater enforcement has also been shown to reduce under-age youth access to alcohol (Treno et al, 2007), procedures for crowd control can mitigate violence (Haines and Graham, 2005), and, although it is very hard to detect intoxicated patrons at bars and other on-premise establishments, the international literature indicates that police presence can stem some problems related to drunkenness at these drinking places (Treno et al, 2008a).

Beyond policing, community prevention efforts can also work. In the last decades of the 20th century, several important community-based environmental preventive intervention studies were undertaken demonstrating this fact. The 'Saving Lives Project' was conducted in six communities in Massachusetts and was designed to reduce alcohol-impaired driving and related problems such as speeding (Hingson, et al, 1996). Project programmes included media campaigns, business information programmes, speeding and drunk-driving awareness days, speed-watch telephone hotlines, police training, high school peer-led education, 'Students Against Drunk Driving' chapters, and college prevention programmes. Over five years, Saving Lives cities experienced a 25 per cent decline in fatal crashes when compared to the rest of Massachusetts, a 47 per cent reduction in the number of fatally injured drivers who tested positive for alcohol, and an 8 per cent decline in crash injuries among 15–25-year-olds. The 'Communities Mobilizing for Change on Alcohol' (CMCA) project was designed to reduce access to alcohol among youth under the legal drinking age of 21 (Wagenaar and Toomey, 2000; Wagenaar et al, 2000). The project was composed of five core components intended to influence: (1) community policies, (2) community practices, (3) youth alcohol access, (4) youth alcohol consumption, and subsequently (5) youth alcohol problems. Results showed reduced sales to minors (Wagenaar et al, 1996), reduced alcohol use among teens, and reduced propensity to provide alcohol to other teens (Wagenaar et al, 2000). The project also found significant declines in drinking and driving and disorderly conduct arrests among young people (Wagenaar and Toomey, 2000). The Community Trials Project was a five-component, community-level intervention conducted in three experimental communities to reduce alcohol-related harm. The components of the project promoted community organization to support the goals of the project, intervened to encourage responsible beverage service at outlets and reduce sales to under-age youth, encouraged increased enforcement related to drunken driving, and attempted to reduce the availability of alcohol. The project showed a significant 10 per cent reduction in night-time injury crashes, a 6 per cent reduction in crashes in which the driver was found by police to 'have been drinking', concurrent reductions in rates of assault injuries observed in emergency departments (a decline of 43 per cent), and reductions in self-reports of heavy drinking and driving while intoxicated (Holder et al, 2000). Finally, the Sacramento 'Neighborhood Alcohol Prevention Project' reduced youth and young-adult access to alcohol, risky drinking, and associated problems, in low-income ethnically diverse neighbourhoods. The five project interventions were similar to those of Community Trials, but neighbourhood focused and addressing only youth and young-adult drinking and related problems. The project showed significant reductions in assaults and motor vehicle accidents as reported by police and emergency medical systems (fire and ambulance).

CONCLUSIONS

The contribution of alcohol outlets to crime and disorder in cities in the US is one part of the larger puzzle of determining the sources of these problems in our communities. The research evidence currently indicates, rather conclusively, that some problems are related to outlets (eg, drunken driving, motor-vehicle crashes, and violence), but not exclusively so. These crimes also originate from other sources (eg, driving after drinking at friends' homes, violence related to illegal drug markets). The roles that commercial alcohol outlets play in community environments, however, are unique. These outlets serve as dispensaries for an intoxicating substance that can and does affect individual judgement and may accelerate rates of related problems through a variety of mechanisms. Research is only beginning to understand these relationships.

The search for culpable parties responsible for the crime and disorder associated with alcohol outlets is, from a public-health point of view, irrelevant to identifying the community sources of these problems. Current theoretical models recognize that interlocking social mechanisms are responsible for problems related to alcohol outlets and encourage the viewpoint that the dynamic interaction of commercial markets and individual interests determines the patterns of problems observed in communities in the US. From this point of view no one and everyone is responsible for drinking problems, and the social issue of central importance is how to maintain a commercial alcohol market that minimizes harms to drinkers and non-drinkers alike? Remarkably, community-level environmental prevention programmes of the latter 20th century have demonstrated that it is possible to move beyond enforcement programmes alone to create safer alcohol environments and reduce alcohol-related crime and disorder in communities. The challenges for the future are to assess the balance of problems related to alcohol outlets, determine the social mechanisms that maintain these problems, and invent effective social remedies for the reduction of alcohol problems related to these commercial markets.

REFERENCES

All internet sources were accessible 20 August 2008

BABOR, T, CAETANO, R, CASSWELL, S, EDWARDS, G, GIESBRECHT, N, GRAHAM, K, GRUBE, J, GRUENEWALD, P, HILL, L, HOLDER, H, HOMEL, R, OSTERBERG, E, REHM, J, ROOM, R, and ROSSOW, I (2003) *Alcohol: No Ordinary Commodity: Research and Public Policy*, Oxford: Oxford University Press.

BANERJEE, A, LaSCALA, EA, GRUENEWALD, PJ, FREISTHLER, B, TRENO, A and REMER, L (2008) 'Social disorganization, alcohol and other drug markets, and violence: A space-time model of community structure', in I Cheung (ed), *The Geography of Illegal Drug Markets*, National Institute on Drug Abuse and American Association of Geographers (in press).

BURIAN, SE, LIGUORI, A and ROBINSON, JH (2002) 'Effects of alcohol on risk-taking during simulated driving', *Human Psychopharmacology: Clinical and Experimental*, 17, 141–50.

FREISTHLER, B, GRUENEWALD, PJ, REMER, LR, LERY, B and NEEDELL, B (2007) 'Examining child abuse and neglect over space and time: Exploring the spatial dynamics of alcohol outlets and child protective service referrals, substantiations and foster care entries', *Child Maltreatment*, 12, 114–24.

GALVAN, F and CAETANO, R (2003) 'Alcohol use and related problems among ethnic minorities in the United States', *Alcohol Research and Health*, 27, 87–94.

GORMAN, D, MEZIC, I, MEZIC, J and GRUENEWALD, PJ (2006) 'Agent-based modeling of drinking behaviors: A preliminary model and potential applications to theory and practice', *American Journal of Public Health*, 96, 2055–60.

GRUENEWALD, PJ (2007) 'The spatial ecology of alcohol problems: Niche theory and assortative drinking,' *Addiction*, 102, 870–8.

—— FREISTHLER, B, REMER, LG, LaSCALA, EA and TRENO, AJ (2006) 'Ecological models of alcohol outlets and violent assaults: Crime potentials and geospatial analysis,' *Addiction*, 101, 666–77.

—— and REMER, LG (2007) 'Changes in outlet densities affect violence rates', *Alcoholism: Clinical and experimental research*, 30/7, 1184–93.

—— TRENO, AJ and JOHNSON, F (2002) 'Outlets, drinking and driving: A multilevel analysis of availability', *Journal of Studies on Alcohol*, 63, 460–8.

HADFIELD, P (2004) 'The prevention of public disorder', in P Kolvin (ed), *Licensed Premises: Law and practice*, West Sussex, Great Britain: Tottel Publishing.

HAINES, B and GRAHAM, K (2005) 'Violence prevention in licensed premises', in T Stockwell, PJ Gruenewald, J Toumbourou and W Loxley (eds), *Preventing Harmful Substance Use: The evidence base for policy and practice*, New York: John Wiley, 163–76.

HINGSON, R, McGOVERN, T, HOWLAND, J, HEEREN, T, WINTER, M and ZAKOCS, R (1996) 'Reducing alcohol-impaired driving in Massachusetts: The Saving Lives program', *American Journal of Public Health*, 86, 791–7.

HOLDER, HD, GRUENEWALD, PJ, PONICKI, WR, TRENO, AJ, GRUBE, JW, SALTZ, RF, VOAS, RB, REYNOLDS, R, DAVIS, J, SANCHEZ, L, GAUMONT, G and ROEPER, P (2000) 'Effect of community-based interventions on high-risk drinking and alcohol-related injuries,' *Journal of the American Medical Association*, 284, 2341–7.

KOLVIN, P (2004) *Licensed Premises: Law and practice*, West Sussex, Great Britain: Tottel Publishing.

LAPHAM, SC, DE BACA, JC, McMILLAN, GP and LAPIDUS, J (2006) 'Psychiatric disorders in a sample of repeat impaired-driving offenders', *Journal of Studies on Alcohol*, 67, 707–13.

LAPMAM, SC, SMITH, E, C'DE BACA, J, CHANG, I, SKIPPER, BJ, BAUM, G and HUNT, WC (2001) 'Prevalence of psychiatric disorders among persons convicted of driving while impaired', *Archives of General Psychiatry*, 58, 943–9.

LASCALA, EA, JOHNSON, FW and GRUENEWALD, PJ (2004) 'An ecological study of the locations of schools and child pedestrian injury collisions', *Accident Analysis and Prevention*, 36, 569–76.

LAVEIST, TA and WALLACE, JM, Jr (2000) 'Health risk and inequitable distribution of liquor stores in African American neighborhoods', *Social Science and Medicine*, 51, 613–17.

MORENOFF, JD, SAMPSON, RJ and RAUDENBUSH, SW (2001) 'Neighborhood inequality, collective efficacy, and the spatial dynamics of urban violence', *Criminology*, 39, 517–59.

MOSKOWITZ, H and FIORENTINO, D (2000) 'A review of the literature on the effects of low doses of alcohol on driving-related skills', Washington, DC: National Highway Traffic Safety Administration, <http://www.nhtsa.dot.gov/people/injury/research/pub/Hs809028/Title.htm>.

NATIONAL HIGHWAY TRAFFIC SAFETY ADMINISTRATION (2005) 'Crash risk of alcohol-involved driving: A case-control study', DOT NHTSA DTNH22–94–C–05001, <http://www.dunlapandassociatesinc.com/crashriskofalcoholinvolveddriving.pdf>.

PARKER, R (1993) 'Alcohol and theories of homicide', in F Adler and WS Laufer (eds), *New Directions in Criminological Theory: Advances in criminological theory*, vol 4, New Brunswick, NJ: Transaction Publishers, 113–41.

PEELE, S (1985) *The Meaning of Addiction*, San Francisco: Jossey-Bass.

—— (1993) 'The conflict between public health goals and the temperance mentality', *American Journal of Public Health*, 83, 805–10.

POLLACK, CE, CUBBIN, C, AHN, D and WINKLEBY, M (2004) 'Neighbourhood deprivation and alcohol consumption: Does the availability of alcohol play a role?', *International Journal of Epidemiology*, 34, 772–80.

QUIGLEY, BM and COLLINS, L (2003) 'Characteristics of violent bars and bar patrons', *Journal of Studies on Alcohol*, 64 (6), 765–72.

—— and LEONARD, KE (2000) 'Alcohol and the continuation of early marital aggression', *Alcoholism: Clinical and Experimental Research*, 24/7, 1003-10.

ROMAN, CG, REID, SE, BHATI, AS and TERESHCHENKO, B (2008) *Alcohol Outlets as Attractors of Violence and Disorder: A closer look at the neighborhood environment*, Final Report to the National Institute of Justice, Washington, DC: The Urban Institute.

RONCEK, DW and MAIER, PA (1991) 'Bars, blocks, and crimes revisited: Linking the theory of routine activities to the empiricism of "hot spots"', *Criminology*, 29/4: 725–53.

SAMPSON, RJ, RAUDENBUSH, SW and EARLS, F (1997) 'Neighborhoods and violent crime: A multilevel study of collective efficacy', *Science*, 277, 918–24.

SANCHEZ, F, CASTILLO-CHAVEZ, C, GORMAN, D and GRUENEWALD, P (2007) 'Drinking as an epidemic: A simple mathematical model with recovery and relapse', in K Witkiewitz and GA Marlatt (eds), *Therapist's Guide to Evidence-Based Relapse Prevention*, 3 New York: Elsevier.

STOCKWELL, T, GRUENEWALD, PJ, TOUMBOUROU, J and LOXLEY, W (2005) *Preventing Harmful Substance Use: The evidence base for policy and practice*, New York: John Wiley.

TRENO, AJ, GRUENEWALD, PJ, LEE, J, FREISTHLER, B and REMER, LG (2007) 'The Sacramento Neighborhood Alcohol Prevention Project: Outcomes from a community prevention trial', *Journal of Studies on Alcohol and Drugs*, 68, 197–207.

—— NEPHEW, TM and PONICKI, WR (1993) 'Alcohol beverage price spectra: Opportunities for substitution', *Alcoholism: Clinical and experimental research*, 17, 675–80.

—— HOLDER, HD and GRUENEWALD, PJ (2008a) 'Environmental approaches to the prevention of alcohol, drug use and related problems', in AW Graham, TK Schultz, MF Mayo-Smith, RK Ries and BB Wilford (eds), *Principles of Addiction Medicine*, 4th edn, Chevy Chase, MD: American Society of Addiction Medicine (in press).

—— PONICKI, WR, REMER, LG and GRUENEWALD, PJ (2008b) 'Alcohol outlets, youth drinking and self-reported ease of access to alcohol: A constraints and opportunities approach,' *Alcoholism Clinical and Experimental Research* (in press).

VUCHINICH, RE and HEATHER, N (2003) *Choice, Behavioral Economics and Addiction*, New York: Pergamon Press.

WAGENAAR, AC, MURRAY, DM, GEHAN, JP, WOLFSON, M, FORSTER, JL, TOOMEY, TL, OERRY, CL and JONES-WEBB, R (2000) 'Communities mobilizing for change on alcohol: Outcomes for a randomized community trial', *Journal of Studies on Alcohol*, 61: 85–94.

—— and TOOMEY, TL (2000) 'Communities mobilizing for change on alcohol: Effects of a randomized trial on arrests and traffic crashes', *Addiction*, 95/2, 209–17.

—— TOOMEY, TL, MURRAY, DM, SHORT, BJ, WOLFSON, M and JONES-WEBB, R (1996) 'Sources of alcohol for underage drinkers', *Journal of Studies on Alcohol*, 57/3, 325–33.

WOOD, DS and GRUENEWALD, PJ (2006) 'Local alcohol prohibition, police presence, and serious injury in isolated Alaska native villages', *Addiction*, 101, 393–403.

SELECTED READINGS

BABOR, T, CAETANO, R, CASSWELL, S, EDWARDS, G, GIESBRECHT, N, GRAHAM, K, GRUBE, J, GRUENEWALD, P, HILL, L, HOLDER, H, HOMEL, R, OSTERBERG, E, REHM, J, ROOM, R, and ROSSOW, I (2003) *Alcohol: No Ordinary Commodity: Research and Public Policy*, Oxford: Oxford University Press.

FREISTHLER, B, GRUENEWALD, PJ, REMER, LR, LERY, B and NEEDELL, B (2007) 'Examining child abuse and neglect over space and time: Exploring the spatial dynamics of alcohol outlets and child protective service referrals, substantiations and foster care entries', *Child Maltreatment*, 12, 114–24.

GRUENEWALD, PJ (2007) 'The spatial ecology of alcohol problems: Niche Theory and assortative drinking', *Addiction*, 102, 870–8.

—— FREISTHLER, B, REMER, LG, LASCALA, EA and TRENO, AJ (2006) 'Ecological models of alcohol outlets and violent assaults: Crime potentials and geospatial analysis,' *Addiction*, 101, 666–77.

HAINES, B and GRAHAM, K (2005) 'Violence prevention in licensed premises', in T Stockwell, PJ Gruenewald, J Toumbourou and W Loxley (eds), *Preventing Harmful Substance Use: The evidence base for policy and practice*, New York: John Wiley.

MORENOFF, JD, SAMPSON, RJ and RAUDENBUSH, SW (2001) 'Neighborhood inequality, collective efficacy, and the spatial dynamics of urban violence,' *Criminology*, 39, 517–59.

PARKER, R (1993) 'Alcohol and theories of homicide', in F Adler and WS Laufer (eds), *New Directions in Criminological Theory: Advances in criminological theory*, vol 4, New Brunswick, NJ: Transaction Publishers.

SANCHEZ, F, CASTILLO-CHAVEZ, C, GORMAN, D and GRUENEWALD, P (2007) 'Drinking as an epidemic: A simple mathematical model with recovery and relapse,' in K Witkiewitz and GA Marlatt (eds), *Therapist's Guide to Evidence-Based Relapse Prevention*, New York: Elsevier, 354–68.

STOCKWELL, T, GRUENEWALD, PJ, TOUMBOUROU, J and LOXLEY, W (2005) *Preventing Harmful Substance Use: The evidence base for policy and practice*, New York: John Wiley.

TRENO, AJ, HOLDER, HD and GRUENEWALD, PJ (2008) 'Environmental approaches to the prevention of alcohol, drug use and related problems', in AW Graham, TK Schultz, MF Mayo-Smith, RK Ries, and BB Wilford (eds), *Principles of Addiction Medicine*, 4th edn, Chevy Chase, MD: American Society of Addiction Medicine (in press).

REPORT 2 NIGHTLIFE IN NEW YORK CITY—REGULATING THE CITY THAT NEVER SLEEPS

Richard E Ocejo and David Brotherton

INTRODUCTION

This chapter explores how New York City's (NYC's) nightlife is formally regulated. As an example of a post-industrial American city, New York has a substantial leisure economy featuring a wide variety of night-time amusements. The development of nightlife scenes, however, has produced conditions of disorder ranging from violent crime to quality of life issues and has led to many conflicts within the night-time economy (NTE) and changes in nightlife regulation. Historically, the regulation of nightlife has occurred across two arms of the local state—liquor licensing and enforcement, which fall within the jurisdiction of the State Liquor Authorities and City Police Force, respectively. We discuss how, today, a new mode of nightlife regulation has emerged to incorporate a wider range of actors, including local residents and private security agencies, especially bouncers. A case study of the Lower East Side (LES) of Manhattan is presented to demonstrate the power of the local state in facilitating and shaping the development of nightlife scenes, while confronting criminogenic features of these scenes and the demand for new regulatory configurations. While addressing the need to maintain public safety, these regulatory frameworks also act to maintain and improve quality of life aspects of the urban nightscape. Yet, in our case study area, such efforts have contributed to further tensions between venue operators and the police, between bouncers and the police, and between bouncers and the leisure businesses who employ them.

New York City (NYC) is an international nightlife leader, as it is in many cultural and economic categories. Known as the 'city that never sleeps', its nightlife has always been an important aspect of its social and economic history (Caldwell, 2005). Today, the city's nightlife is well integrated into its post-industrial leisure economy of entertainment and cultural activities (Currid, 2007; Lloyd, 2006; Zukin, 1995 and

2004). NYC features several 'urban nightscapes' (Chatterton and Hollands, 2003)—landscapes of nightlife consumption, that have transformed neighbourhoods and generated conditions of public disorder. These disorders have ranged from violent crime (assaults and homicides) to quality-of-life offences (noise, overcrowding, and property defacement). Key conflicts over these issues have developed in dense night-life areas, particularly between the nightlife industry and the police and the nightlife industry and local residents and community groups. Violent incidents, in particular, have formed the catalyst for regulatory reforms. The new nightlife regulation represents a shift in licensing policies and enforcement mechanisms. Long-established regulatory players such as the local state and police have developed new roles and forged new relationships with other actors, such as local community groups, bar owners, and bouncers. Policy implementation within this new regulatory frame has had important effects on local nightlife conditions, while illuminating complex relations between modes of regulation, economic development, and the politics of urban culture and space.

This chapter begins by introducing a number of regulatory issues pertinent to NYC. It begins by setting the governance of the city's nightscape in its local and national context. The empirical focus of the chapter is NYC's Lower East Side (LES), a gentrifying area that features Manhattan's largest and most dense concentration of bars. The chapter discusses the contemporary development of this area as a regionally important nightlife scene. The recent history of nightlife on the LES has been one of liquor-licensing deregulation, public disorder, and the emergence of local conflicts. The chapter goes on to consider how such issues led to a shift in modes of regulation in the area and the formation of new roles and relationships among regulatory actors. The chapter concludes by examining the implications of these emergent roles and relationships for the governance of night-time public space.

FORMAL NIGHTLIFE REGULATION IN NEW YORK CITY

The historical and contemporary regulation of nightlife in American cities varies tre-mendously depending on local conditions, policies, and legal structures. The single most important historical event to affect American nightlife in general was National Prohibition—the banning of alcohol sales and manufacturing. Beginning in 1920 with the ratification of the 18th Amendment to the United States Constitution, Pro-hibition was based on a highly moralistic public policy whose spirit and implementa-tion discriminated against urban groups such as immigrants, African-Americans, and the working classes. Prohibition arose as a result of the increasing national political influence of the decades-old Temperance Movement. The Temperance lobby con-sisted largely of native-born, Protestant, non-urban actors who framed alcohol con-sumption, particularly that which occurred within the urban working-class saloon, as an immoral social problem (Gusfield, 1963 and 1996). Such activities were understood to compromise core 'American' values, such as the Protestant work ethic (Bell, 1976; Peretti, 2007).

Despite their political success in instigating radical legislative change, the Temperance Movement's efforts at social engineering had adverse results. Rather than scaling it back, Prohibition popularized nightlife, emphasizing its mystique as an intriguing, chic, and desirable aspect of urban life. During Prohibition, nightlife culture was consumed in 'speakeasies'—spaces that were intentionally hidden and discrete in order to avoid the attentions of the authorities.[1] The secretive nature of the speakeasies enhanced nightlife's appeal, particularly as they featured unusual levels of gender, racial, ethnic, and social-class mixing, as well as elements of celebrity, criminality, entertainment, and heavy alcohol consumption (Douglas, 1995; Lerner, 2007; Peretti, 2007). The cosmopolitan element of these nightlife spaces helped assimilate aspects of youth deviance and minority culture into the more liberal elements of American society. Aided by media dissemination, the underground nightlife culture of the Prohibition era entered middle-class consciousness, leading to a change in social relations within nightlife spaces and in nightlife's cultural positioning within the United States that was to continue throughout the 20th century (Blumenthal, 2000).

Ratified in 1933, the 21st Amendment to the United States Constitution repealed the 18th, ended Prohibition, and established the modern era of nightlife regulation. The 21st Amendment gave each individual state the right to either continue prohibiting the sale and manufacture of alcohol, or to regulate it themselves. Each state therefore became either a 'Control State', in which alcohol is sold in government-run stores, making the state the wholesaler or retailer,[2] or a 'Licensing State', in which the state grants individuals the ability to sell alcohol through the issuing of a permit. Most states, including New York, became Licensing States. In such states, the law allows a high degree of local regulatory autonomy and discretion, with core categories and policies (ie, closing times, application processes) varying significantly, both between and within each Licensing State. For example, many states allow municipalities and counties to make certain decisions, including whether or not to even permit the sale of alcohol.

All nightlife venues in NYC selling alcohol for consumption on their premises are regulated by the New York State Liquor Authority (SLA). While the SLA has a division of enforcement that conducts investigations on licensed establishments all around New York State, it mostly relies on other government agencies—especially the local police—to enforce licensing conditions. This combination of SLA and New York Police Department (NYPD) activity—as the state's agents of licensing and enforcement, respectively—has shaped NYC nightlife historically. As the following paragraphs will discuss, recent public-disorder issues have underlined the continuing importance of these actors, while re-shaping aspects of their roles, and the configurations of nightlife regulation more generally.

---

[1] They were so-named because a patron had to 'speak easy', or know the right language, code, or password to gain entry.

[2] Alcoholic beverages in the United States are broken down into three categories: beer, wine, and liquor. Some Control States only directly control the sale of liquor, allowing licensed stores to sell wine and beer. Others directly control both their liquor and wine sales, allowing licensed stores to sell only beer. Only one Control State (Utah) directly controls the sale of all three categories.

NIGHTSCAPE DEVELOPMENT ON THE
LOWER EAST SIDE

Nightlife has had a transformative impact upon many areas of NYC. An illustrative case is the Lower East Side (LES) of Manhattan. In the 1970s and 80s, the LES lacked capital investment and featured high crime rates and numerous signs of disorder. Despite its slum-like conditions, local residents—ethnic groups, artists, political radicals—created numerous formal and informal nightlife spaces and cultures (Talbot, 2007). Since the 1980s, however, most areas of the LES have experienced ongoing gentrification—capital investment in residential and commercial real estate, an influx of new, mostly white and well-educated, residents, an overall decline in crime, and a re-imagining of the area from dangerous slum to chic downtown (Abu-Lughod, 1994; Curtis et al, 2002; Mele, 2000; Smith, 1996). Within the context of the city as a whole, the LES has shifted from the margins of the city's economic, social, and cultural life to a position of centrality (O'Connor and Wynne, 1996; Shields, 1991).

Nightlife has been an important aspect of this transition. Since 1985, the number of bars on the LES has increased ten-fold. As of April 2008, there were 692 on-premises licences, including bars, restaurants, and other establishments that sell alcohol for on-premises consumption, within the 1.8 square mile area of the LES.[3] Bars are diffused throughout the district, with dense concentrations on large commercial avenues and smaller residential streets alike. They mostly occupy small commercial spaces in residential tenement apartment buildings. Some of these spaces had previously been empty or abandoned, while others had contained long-established bars, or other types of small business.

Night-time consumption spaces and nightlife activities have replaced local cultures and transformed the area into a 'night-time entertainment district' featuring numerous amusements (Hannigan, 1998). The types of establishment range from bars and restaurants to dance and music clubs. The LES is a popular nightlife destination where residents of the city and metropolitan area and tourists spend all or part of their night out. Individual venues vary, but overall, the nightscape has racially and ethnically diverse clienteles, with the predominant groups being young, white, middle and upper-middle class. Where establishments are located close together, their customers are very evident on the streets and sidewalks at night. The fact that night-time venues are mostly located in residential buildings and on residential streets has caused numerous quality-of-life concerns for many of the area's residents. Drug activity has shifted from rampant dealing and consumption in public spaces to lighter and more discrete use by patrons within night-time establishments, while violent crime overall has declined tremendously (Curtis et al, 2002). Our qualitative case study methodology places distinct limits upon the ability to generalize, however, it seems fair to conclude that the LES is an exemplar of several post-industrial processes, such as gentrification and consumption-driven urban development, which are paralleled in other American cities. Although further research is needed on other areas of NYC, the LES provides a prominent and dynamic context for exploring the development and regulation of central NYC nightscapes.

---

[3] This data was obtained from the New York State Liquor Authority on 14 April 2008.

While gentrification processes have provided a favourable economic context for nightlife development on the LES, the local state has also played a major role in the construction of this new urban nightscape. As we shall describe, the SLA's deregulation of liquor licensing may be understood as an example of 'urban entrepreneurialism', wherein the state adopted policies which directly encouraged private investment and development as a means of urban growth and the gaining of competitive advantage (Harvey, 1989).

In 1993, New York State amended its Alcoholic Beverage Control (ABC) Law by placing restrictions on the spatial concentration of licensed venues. Known as the '500 foot rule', it applies to all cities, towns, or villages, with a population of 20,000 or more people and prohibits the issuance of new on-premises liquor licences in any area which already has three or more such licences within a 500-foot radius of the proposed establishment.[4] This anti-concentration law has three important exceptions. The first two (a 'grandfather clause' and a 'renewal clause') have allowed high concentrations of licensed premises to remain, provided long-standing licences are transferred between owners or renewed, both of which often occur. The third exception has proved the most contentious. It relates to that section of the law permitting dense concentrations of licensed establishments and the construction of nightlife scenes in circumstances where

The Authority may issue a retail license for on-premises consumption for a premise which shall be within five hundred feet of three or more existing premises licensed and operating . . . if, after consultation with the municipality or community board, it determines that granting such license would be in the *public interest*. Before it may issue any such license, the authority shall conduct a hearing, upon notice to the applicant and the municipality or Community Board. (Section 64–a, 7d, New York State Alcohol Beverage Control Law; emphasis added)

In other words, the burden is on the applicants to demonstrate that their establishment will somehow benefit the public. Although the law is unclear on what 'public interest' concerns may entail, it lists several factors that SLA board members may consider in making their decision on a licence. These include the number and characteristics of other licensed premises in the area, and the effect on vehicular traffic, parking, and noise levels that another licensed establishment might have upon the neighbourhood, ie quality-of-life concerns. The law requires local input from the Community Board (discussed below) in such matters, but judgement as to whether another licensed establishment would serve the public interest ultimately rests with the SLA.

Until 2006, the SLA interpreted the latter exception broadly, including such reasons as 'increasing the tax base', 'improving the neighbourhood', and 'providing employment'—all signifiers of economic development—as being in the public interest and therefore permissible in relation to the discounting of any competing concerns regarding increased density levels. Growth centred on night-time entertainment and the cultural production of nightlife became paramount in areas such as the LES, regarded as changing neighbourhoods with favourable conditions for development. The SLA's 1996 Annual Report bluntly stated that one of the agency's goals was to

---

[4] There are many licensing designations under the ABC Law. The 'Full Operating On-Premises Licence' (or OP Licence) permits the sale and on-premises consumption of beer, wine, and distilled spirits. It is the most common retail licence for bars and restaurants.

'Reduce regulatory burdens which hinder economic growth for the industry' (New York State Liquor Authority Annual Report 1996, Introductory Letter). Similarly, an introductory letter from the governor accompanying the same agency's 2000 Annual Report (and copied word for word in each subsequent letter until 2005) states:

This Annual Report clearly portrays the State Liquor Authority as an agency dynamically involved in the resurging private sector economic development. Information, licensing activities, and support services are readily available to the full spectrum of the state's entrepreneurial interests . . . culminating in our vital retail trades. (New York State Liquor Authority Annual Report 2000, Introductory Letter)

This stance and its implementation, allowing unprecedented growth in the number of licensed premises on the LES, demonstrates how a local government agency was able to successfully create (de-)regulatory conditions suitable for profitable economic development by private interests at the same time as the area was gentrifying (Hannigan, 1998; Harvey, 1989). However, our case study reveals how this new nightscape was to produce its own unpredictable conditions, leading to further transformations in the governance of NYC nightlife.

LOCAL CONFLICTS AND POLITICAL ACTION

The most important forums for citizens to engage with the liquor-licensing process in NYC are the Community Boards. Composed of residents, Community Boards offer opportunities for liaison between neighbourhoods, government agencies, and elected officials. They also serve a political function as advisers on city and state policy. According to New York State law, all applicants seeking a liquor licence in NYC must appear before a Community Board before applying to the SLA. Community Boards will either approve the application with stipulations as to how the licensee will operate his or her establishment (closing times, use of spaces such as backyards, etc), or deny the application on the basis of local considerations. In adjudicating each application, the SLA then considers whether or not to incorporate the Community Board's recommendations into the terms of the licence.

The LES's Community Board (CB3) has the most strict and active liquor-licensing committee in the city. During the late 1990s and early 2000s, CB3 continually denied licences. It cited the 500-foot rule, stating that the conditions produced by the saturation of nightlife venues and activities were not in the interests of many areas of the district. Some committee members saw the nightscape as a threat to their quality of life and as intrinsic to the ongoing gentrification of the area. They experienced the new entertainment venues negatively, alongside escalating rents, the displacement of local services, and local businesses' increasing focus on the consumption preferences of a newly incoming metropolitan middle class (Lloyd and Clark, 2001). LES residents regularly attended CB3 meetings and organized themselves into block and tenants' associations to protect the interests of their streets and buildings. These bodies learned the proper procedures for making formal complaints against a licence application, opposing the opening of more bars within their neighbourhood. They also lobbied locally elected officials and the police to gain support for their cause. These efforts helped push quality-of-life offences within the nightlife scene into the media and political spotlight.

However, as explained above, Community Boards only play an advisory role in the local governance of nightlife and their recommendations do not become legally binding on licensed operators unless government officials and agencies take them into account in their decisions. Thus, regardless of the advice of the Community Boards, the SLA was able to continue pursuing its deregulatory agenda, approving liquor licences and loosely interpreting the 500-foot rule. A representative for two consecutive elected members of the NYC Council—the city's local legislative body—on the LES provided a typical synopsis:

Up until 2006, they [the SLA] were still just rubber stamping everything. If you applied for a licence, they approved, it didn't matter if it was contrary to the 500-foot rule, they would always find some way to say that it was in the public interest. And it's pretty clear if you look around here that it's not in the public interest.

LES residents understood their attendance at CB3 meetings to offer a direct recourse under state law for getting their voices heard at the SLA. However, they confronted venue operators and protested liquor-licence applications at these meetings only to see the proposed bars opening up a few months later. The efforts of the block and tenants' associations therefore had little or no effect in improving quality of life in their areas, or on slowing the pace of nightscape development. The views of one active long-time resident express this well:

The bar proliferation thing's been so frustrating because we put our faith in this Community Board process and didn't quite understand that 'advisory' *really* meant advisory. Like, we thought, 'Wow! That's six [applications] before the Board and they rejected these licences and the SLA or somebody must take this in, it must account for something', and it never did.

Along with its failure to control density levels, the SLA also did not regulate the types of establishments that were opening. The LES had many examples of individual owners who agreed to particular modes of operation in their licence applications, only to change these methods later on, often introducing types of activity that had more negative consequences for local quality of life (eg, staying open later, adding live music). This led to significant conflict between residents and the nightlife industry, as well as between residents and the SLA.

It was not until 2006, when several high-profile violent incidents occurred—especially two particular homicides that appeared in the local media—that the state began to take action and re-examine its regulatory policies.[5] There were three unprecedented regulatory developments. First, from September 2006 until the end of that year, the SLA initiated a moratorium on all full, on-premises liquor licences that represented 500-foot cases. Praised by local residents and Community Boards who had seen their own liquor licence moratoria ignored by the SLA for many years, and condemned by the nightlife industry who considered it repressive and unfair to their business interests, this state-wide moratorium gave the SLA time to evaluate its licensing policies. Secondly, the SLA announced the appointment of a Taskforce for the Review of On-Premises Licensure, which brought together representatives from many different

---

[5] One of the authors, David Brotherton, knew the victim of one of these homicides, Imette St. Guillen, who was a student at his college, John Jay College of Criminal Justice, CUNY. The bar from which she was abducted is located in a neighbourhood adjacent to the Lower East Side.

groups—the SLA, the police, Community Boards, locally elected officials, and the nightlife industry—to discuss licensing matters. This group met three times during the fall of 2006, releasing a report of their discussions and a list of ten recommendations at the end of that year. Along with the SLA's own reforms, the Taskforce encouraged greater transparency at the agency and tighter collaboration between the SLA, Community Boards, the police, and other city agencies. Whereas previously the SLA had operated independently—but effectively in the interests of private actors and in opposition to those of local communities—today it highly values local voices in the licensing decision-making process. This is especially so in deciding what qualifies as being in the 'public interest', with the closer links with external actors being drawn upon for the purposes of making such assessments.

The third development dealt more directly with nightlife enforcement and public safety. At the same time as the SLA Taskforce was in operation, New York City Council held a Nightlife Safety Summit, which also brought together disparate nightlife stakeholders and resulted in a report with a list of policy and legislative recommendations. Entitled 'Safer Nights, Safer City', this report focused on strengthening the city and state's ability to regulate leisure establishments through licensing legislation, private-security matters, and through the establishment of closer working relationships between venue operators and the police. This led to the publication of the 'Best Practices for Nightlife Establishments' guidelines in October, 2007. Developed by the city council, in cooperation with the police and the nightlife industry, this document presented a set of recommendations to guide owners and managers in the operation of their establishments. This dissemination of 'best practice' by public authorities, around which the activities of private actors are increasingly expected to cohere (and who are subject to censure if they do not), has become a common strategy in post-industrial urban governance (Belina and Helms, 2003).

In sum, the re-regulation of NYC nightlife developed out of the contradictions that accompany nightscape development, namely quality-of-life issues, social disorder, and violent crime (Hobbs et al, 2003; Talbot, 2003). The result has been the development of a new, 'flexible' mode of nightlife regulation in the form of a decentralized SLA, with stricter licensing policies arising from its inclusion of Community Board input in licensing decisions. As the following paragraphs will explain, it has also involved a ceding of public policing duties to venue-owner-implemented private-security measures and the incorporation of such private-policing solutions within neighbourhood policing strategy.

IMPACTS OF RE-REGULATION: NEW ROLES AND RELATIONSHIPS

As nightlife scenes have expanded, local police have reduced their role in nightly 'on the ground' interaction. Instead, the police, along with local politicians and Community Boards promote private-security mechanisms as fundamental to ensuring not only leisure-time safety, but also quality of life for residents. While it is not unusual for private-security solutions such as bouncers, surveillance cameras, and ID scanners, to be used to prevent and manage violent incidents at larger venues such as dance clubs, such measures are becoming increasingly common at smaller bars and restaurants, such as those on the LES. CB3 often recommend that licencees employ private security and the renewed strength of the residential voice has meant that it is more typical on the LES for bouncers to be hired primarily to control quality-of-life offences, such as noise and littering, as opposed to any more 'serious' criminogenic features of the nightlife environment.

The police have also emphasized the new importance of private security. Developed in the 1990s, the 'Compstat' management information and control system is now used to regulate and direct precinct-level policing in NYC. Compstat maps crime statistics and allows police managers to devise local strategies, often informed by the 'zero tolerance' approaches that originated in NYC in the 1980s and have spread to cities around the world (Kelling and Coles, 1996). Compstat has made local policing highly accountable to police leaders and politicians who place significant pressure on precinct divisions to reduce crime and quality-of-life statistics under their command. For precinct police chiefs, who lack the resources to monitor large nightscapes, bouncers serve the dual function of handling quality-of-life issues, as well as much of the criminal or violent activity that occurs. As employment of bouncers and the operation of surveillance cameras are private rather than public security initiatives, the police welcome cooperation and communication between themselves and venue owners in order to regulate their district.

The LES, then, demonstrates an interesting development in nightlife regulation: 'quality-of-life bouncing'. Our observations at several locations on the LES demonstrate that bouncers are typically used to check the IDs of patrons at the door, which reduces the work of bartenders and protects the establishment from receiving costly fines for violation of the law against serving alcohol to minors. Their other primary roles include attempting to regulate the behaviour of patrons located outside the venue and dispersing crowds from its frontage at closing time. However, the facades and sidewalk spaces of LES bars are relatively small and the large number and dense concentration of licensed establishments means that patrons regularly flood the streets and sidewalks at night, making it impossible for bouncers to exercise control over noisy crowds. Patrons also often ignore or barely acknowledge bouncers when they instruct them to be quiet or move from the front of establishments, effectively turning them into nightlife 'non-persons'—figures within social scenes whose presence and authority go unrecognized (Goffman, 1959: 151). Meanwhile, bouncers, who approach their job at smaller bars with the mindset that a violent incident may occur, are often limited in their ability to handle such situations as a result of the venue and its method of operation, such as when an establishment hires a single bouncer instead of a pair or a team, encourages overcrowding, or utilizes low-visibility spaces such as backyards and basements.

Thus, despite the degree of attention that the new forms of nightlife regulation now pay to relatively minor neighbourhood incivilities, their initiatives have so far proved ineffectual in resolving such issues to the satisfaction of residents. Noisy, crowded streets, populated by intoxicated consumers signify a healthy nightlife scene, as permitted and (formerly) promoted by the state. Although these nightlife spaces are undoubtedly 'disorderly', the police do not impose heavy-handed 'quality of life' tactics and increasingly relinquish their policing role to the private sector. Thus, it appears that the NYPD applies different approaches to different communities and chooses not to apply measures which may threaten the lifeblood of the LES's new leisure economy. This has led to two sets of tensions and conflicts: first, between the nightlife industry and local residents and, secondly, between the nightlife industry and the police. Community Boards and residents have continued their opposition to nightlife development. Since their efforts at combating the conditions that the nightscape has already created have been limited due to the number of existing licensed premises, they continue to have issues with owners. With greater authority and support from the SLA, their recommendations of spatial-use restrictions, earlier closing times, and enhanced private security have made it difficult for owners to freely operate their establishments, forcing them to alter their methods.

Venue operators also find themselves in a new relationship with the police as quasi-partners in crime prevention and the management of quality-of-life offences. The LES nightlife scene consists of small bars, lounges, and restaurants. In many cases, the new measures required by the police and SLA have achieved little more than to introduce a new culture of securitization, of which local licensees have little previous experience. Meanwhile, bouncers are located in between the police, who are interested in public safety and quality-of-life maintenance, and their employers, who are interested in the promotion of their businesses and profit maximization.

CONCLUSIONS

This chapter has examined the transformation of formal nightlife governance in NYC. As the city has developed, the nightlife of the LES has entered the political and economic realm in ways which reflect the growing importance of the leisure industry in contemporary urban policy. Local government and community actors have responded to the conditions of disorder within nightlife scenes by encouraging the growth of private securitization strategies typical of daytime consumption zones (Davis, 1990; Zukin, 1995). While violent crime remains an important factor, what is fascinating about the NYC case is the extent to which these regulatory shifts have focused on quality-of-life issues. Further exploration of these issues may serve as a window to our understanding of many other urban issues, such as the contested uses and meanings of public space, of which nightlife disorder is but a part.

The United States is a large and diverse nation in which liquor-licensing and law-enforcement priorities differ from state to state and city by city. Moreover, historical and contemporary attitudes to nightlife vary by region and any discussion of associated crime-and-disorder patterns and their regulation must take account of such local distinctions. We suspect that many American cities are undergoing similar developments to those in NYC, from the comparably massive nightscapes of Las Vegas, Los Angeles, and other metropolitan centres, to those of smaller cities, which may be relatively modest in scale, but which have major local ramifications for their gentrifying downtown and suburban areas (Grazian, 2003 and 2008). The United States presents enormous potential for sociologists interested in these and many other unexplored nightlife themes.

REFERENCES

All internet sources were accessible 20 August 2008

ABU-LUGHOD, J (ed), (1994) *From Urban Village to East Village: The battle for New York's Lower East Side*, Oxford: Blackwell Publishers.

BELINA, B and HELMS, G (2003) 'Zero tolerance for the industrial past and other threats: Policing and urban entrepreneurialism in Britain and Germany', *Urban Studies*, 40/9, 1845–67.

BELL, D (1976) *The Cultural Contradictions of Capitalism*, NY: BasicBooks.

BLUMENTHAL, R (2000) *Stork Club: America's most famous nightspot and the lost world of café society*, NY: Little, Brown and Company.

CALDWELL, M (2005) *New York Night: The mystique and its history*, NY: Scribner.

CHATTERTON, P and HOLLANDS, R (2003) *Urban Nightscapes: Youth cultures, pleasure spaces, and corporate power*, NY: Routledge.

CURRID, E (2007) *The Warhol Economy: How fashion, art, and music drive New York City*, Princeton, NJ: Princeton University Press.

CURTIS, R, WENDEL, T and SPUNT, B (2002) 'We deliver: The Gentrification of drug markets on Manhattan's Lower East Side', Grant #1999-IJ-CX-0010, Final Report to the National Institute of Justice.

DAVIS, M (1990) *City of Quartz: Excavating the future in Los Angeles*, NY: Vintage.

DOUGLAS, A (1995) *Terrible Honesty: Mongrel Manhattan in the 1920s*, NY: Farrar, Straus and Giroux.

GOFFMAN, E (1959) *The Presentation of Self in Everyday Life*, NY: Doubleday.

GRAZIAN, D (2003) *Blue Chicago: The search for authenticity in urban blues clubs*, Chicago: University of Chicago Press.

—— (2008) *On the Make: The hustle of urban nightlife*, Chicago: University of Chicago Press.

GUSFIELD, J (1963) *Symbolic Crusade: Status politics and the American Temperance Movement*. Urbana: University of Illinois Press.

—— (1996) *Contested Meanings: The construction of alcohol problems*, Madison, WI: University of Wisconsin Press.

HANNIGAN, J (1998) *Fantasy City: Pleasure and profit in the postmodern metropolis*, NY: Routledge.

HARVEY, D. (1989) 'From managerialism to entrepreneurialism: The transformation in urban governance in late capitalism', *Geografiska Annaler, Series B, Human Geography—The Roots of Geographical Change*, 1973 to the Present, 71/1, 3–17.

HOBBS, D, HADFIELD, P, LISTER, S, and WINLOW, S (2003) *Bouncers: Violence and Governance in the Night-time Economy*, Oxford: Oxford University Press.

KELLING, GL and COLES, CM (1996) *Fixing Broken Windows: Restoring order and reducing crime in our communities*, NY: The Free Press.

LERNER, MA (2007) *Dry Manhattan: Prohibition in New York City*, Cambridge, MA: Harvard University Press.

LLOYD, R (2006) *Neo-Bohemia: Art and commerce in the postindustrial city*, NY: Routledge.

——— and CLARK, TN (2001) 'The city as an entertainment machine', *Critical Perspectives on Urban Redevelopment*, 6, 359–80.

MELE, C (2000) *Selling the Lower East Side: Culture, real estate, and resistance in New York City*, Minneapolis, MN: University of Minnesota Press.

New York State Alcoholic Beverage Control Law, Division of Alcoholic Beverage Control, New York State Liquor Authority.

NEW YORK STATE LIQUOR AUTHORITY *Annual Report* 1996, Introductory Letter, Chairman Edward F Kelly.

——— *Annual Report* 2000, Introductory Letter, Chairman Edward F Kelly.

O'CONNOR, J and WYNNE, D (eds) (1996) *From the Margins to the Centre: Cultural production and consumption in the post-industrial city*, Aldershot: Arena.

PERETTI, BW (2007) *Nightclub City: Politics and amusement in Manhattan*, Philadelphia: University of Pennsylvania Press.

SHIELDS, R (1991) *Places on the Margin: Alternative geographies of modernity*, NY: Routledge.

SMITH, N (1996) *The New Urban Frontier: Gentrification and the revanchist city*, NY: Routledge.

TALBOT, D (2003) 'Regulation and racial differentiation in the construction of night-time economies: A London case study', *Urban Studies*, 41/4, 887–901.

——— (2007) *Regulating the Night: Race, culture, and exclusion in the making of the night-time economy*, Aldershot: Ashgate.

ZUKIN, S (1995) *The Cultures of Cities*, Oxford: Blackwell Publishing.

——— (2004) *Point of Purchase: How shopping changed American culture*, NY: Routledge.

REPORT 3 NEW FORMS OF REGULATING THE NIGHT-TIME ECONOMY—THE CASE OF SAN FRANCISCO

Molly Moloney, Geoffrey Hunt, Noelani Bailey, and Galit Erez[1]

INTRODUCTION

Few cities would seem to encapsulate better the model of shifting to an idea-, entertainment-, and service-based economy, away from traditional industrial models, than San Francisco. Close to Silicon Valley and the home of many technology-oriented companies, San Francisco's economy is increasingly dependent on conventions, entertainment, tourism, the arts, and multimedia (Godfrey, 1997). The city has long been associated with night-time entertainment. In the 1940s the club scene in the Fillmore District was referred to as the 'Harlem of the West' (Miller, 2007; Pepin and Watts, 2006). The Avalon Ballroom and the Fillmore Auditorium were famous in the 1960s for dance events, hallucinogenic experiences, electronic sound, and flashing lights (Beck and Rosenbaum, 1994). San Francisco's importance in the night-time club scene has been attributed to a number of elements, including its role in the 1960s acid rock and psychedelic movement, the strength of its gay community and their involvement in the club scene, and more recently its proximity to Silicon Valley and the development of 'cyber/tech' culture (Silcott, 1999).[2]

[1] Corresponding author, Geoffrey Hunt, e-mail: huntgisa@ix.netcom.com. Collection of data for this article was made possible by funding from the National Institute on Drug Abuse (R01-DA014317), administered by Moira O'Brien.

[2] In one measure of nightlife, San Francisco boasts a ratio of restaurants/bars/entertainment venues to population (39 to 10,000) just under that of New York City (40) and twice that of Los Angeles (17) (Mayor's Office of Economic and Workforce Development and IFC International Economic Planning Systems, 2007: 81).

With the dot-com boom and economic expansion of the late 1990s, the night-life industry achieved great success in San Francisco. The city seemed to be filled with young people with unheard of amounts of money, ready to spend it lavishly on entertainment. Clubs were booming with long lines of patrons seeking admission. During this period of economic prosperity, nightclub operators and promoters began to organize to change the regulatory process shaping San Francisco night-life. This shift, decreasing police control of nightlife in favour of a more business-oriented model, is reflective of trends observed elsewhere; UK scholars have observed a 'new nightlife regulatory regime', moving from government control of nightlife to new forms of governance involving stakeholders from business and the community (Chatterton and Hollands, 2003: 46). In San Francisco this has taken the form of the creation of the Entertainment Commission (EC) in 2003 to oversee and issue permits for late-night entertainment venues and nightclubs, removing these powers from those who traditionally had them, the police. In so doing, the Commission radically restructured the permitting process for night-time entertainment venues in the city. In charting these developments, we draw on media reports, primary court/grand jury documents, and 16 key-informant interviews we conducted with police, night-club owners, city officials, and event promoters.

SAN FRANCISCO'S NEW NIGHTLIFE REGULATORY PARADIGM: THE ENTERTAINMENT COMMISSION

In 2003 the San Francisco Board of Supervisors voted to create a new regulatory body, the 'Entertainment Commission' (EC), which shifted to civilian responsibility regulatory duties over nightlife that were previously handled by the police. The EC consolidated a number of related permits (cabaret permit, dance-hall permit, and place of entertainment permit) into one entertainment permit. The licensing process for nightlife nevertheless remains complicated, requiring approval from the state Alcoholic Beverages Commission (ABC) to sell alcohol, as well as fire and health codes to pass and zoning requirements to comply with. While the EC can advise applicants about the whole process, it does not have direct control over any of the other regulators. The seven-member EC comprises representatives from the Police Department, nightclubs, neighbourhood groups, city planning, and public health, appointed by the mayor and the Board of Supervisors. The EC was given ten main tasks in its mandate: 'to have a system of coordinated planning and permitting for cultural, entertainment, and similar events and establishments throughout the City, to promote such establishments and events for the economic and cultural enrichment of San Franciscans and visitors ... and to celebrate the diverse communities within SF.' Its mandate included assisting operators in obtaining permits, promoting responsible conduct in nightlife, promoting the development of the night-time economy, fostering harm-reduction policies, and developing 'good neighbour policies' to help mediate disputes between local residents and nightlife operators (San Francisco Administrative Code, Section 90.1).

The increasing economic strength of the entertainment industry influenced the creation of the Entertainment Commission. One media report from the time noted that the legislation's sponsor, Supervisor Leno, 'said San Francisco's entertainment venues—a key to reviving the city's flagging tourist trade—were stumbling under the weight of a confusing, Prohibition-era system that puts the police in charge of issuing permits. Critics say the restrictions are "a war on the creative class", shooing artists out of town or forcing them to hold events illegally' (Garofoli, 2002). During this period, a number of our respondents report that there were increases in raids on underground parties, and the police, who were in charge of issuing and enforcing night-time entertainment permits, used their powers both to limit the expansion of nightlife and to demand onerous restrictions on licensed night-time venues. One night-time industry lawyer we interviewed referred to this period as a 'nightclub war'. But unlike 'wars' in previous periods, many of those involved in the scene, both as producers/owners and consumers/attendees, were suddenly quite affluent due to dot-com success: 'Some of these guys with money started dumping $50,000 checks' to a late-night oriented political action committee 'and it became very politically powerful at this point', he reports.[3] Nightlife operators argued that the previous permitting process was labyrinthine and capricious, with ambiguous rules. More specifically, there was discomfort over the role of the Police Department in the permitting process. Under the previous regime, the police were in charge of issuing the permits, in addition to their duties to enforce permitting rules and to revoke licenses for venues deemed noncompliant. Critics of the process charged that the police thus had a conflict of interest, that they were both 'judge and executioner' (Sanders, 2002) in late-night matters. One night club owner argued that 'The Police Department has a vested interest in denying permits if they think they'll have to be responding to noise complaints there later . . . They're very strict to the point of being unfair' (Garofoli, 2002). Proprietors of late-night entertainment businesses claimed that police were too punitive with possible violators, too restrictive in issuing new permits. The police were seen as setting public policy (rather than merely enforcing it), such as through a police-imposed de facto moratorium on late-night/after-hours licences.

One representative of the Entertainment Commission argued that police control of the licensing process had been like 'the fox in the chicken coop'. It had been increasingly difficult for night-time venues to get licensed because the police 'don't want to be out late at night cleaning up what they consider your mess; they had the attitude generally that the later you're open the more problems you're going to have, the [more] work they gotta do'. This perception was shared by a club promoter, who argued that 'permits existed but you couldn't get one . . . there were unspoken moratoriums . . .

---

[3] One significant fact here that sometimes gets lost is that it was not only operators/managers who were organizing, but also patrons of nightlife; in the current moment (2008), though, it is more difficult to find evidence of such organizing or activism on the part of night-time entertainment consumers. By 2003, with the EC in operation, the whole context of the economic power of nightclubs was quite different from those early days of organizing—the dot-com boom had bust and the ability to sustain quite so strong a night-time economy was strongly diminished. This did not necessarily diminish advocates' arguments for the importance of the EC, however; they pointed instead to the waning of the night-time economy as proof of the need for policies that encourage growth, not repression.

from the standpoint of the Police Department . . . the less work they had, the more they could devote resources to other things'. Even one police officer we interviewed conceded that in the past 'the Police Department was very heavy-handed and arbitrary in their dealings with these things'. This respondent suggested that perhaps the police were not always the appropriate body to mediate nightlife conflicts: 'When all you have is a hammer, everything looks like a nail. When all you have is policemen, well . . . we did way overkill.'

The creation of the Entertainment Commission was sparked, in part, by a few notorious cases of police crackdowns at night-time events. One key event was the 1995 police raid on an (unlicensed) HIV/AIDS fundraising party, in which the police's heavy-handed tactics garnered copious negative publicity for the city and a successful lawsuit on the part of the party's organizers. Interviews with key informants indicate that this was a galvanizing moment for many who began to organize the nightlife owners and create political action committees. Another controversial case came in 2000, when the San Francisco Police Department reached a settlement with a prominent nightclub, which had been in a dispute with the city and which the police had been threatening to close down. The settlement allowed the club to stay open, but only after it agreed to conditions such as a mandatory search of all patrons entering the premises, security cameras monitoring every inch of public space except for bathrooms, and turning over to the police all people found with any amount of drugs (Nowinski, 2000). This was cited by advocates for the creation of the Entertainment Commission as proof of the overreach of the Police Department. Supervisor Leno argued, 'Many aspects of this settlement are quite disturbing . . . if anything, the situation calls out for an entertainment commission, which I have been proposing' (Nowinski, 2000). Police officials were quoted as saying, 'I would not make this demand on everyone . . . each club is individual', but rather than mollifying critics, such statements seemed to bolster the charge that there were uneven and unpredictable requirements established by the police for different venues. Concerns about the role of police in administering entertainment permits were bolstered by the findings of a 1999–2000 San Francisco Civil Grand Jury report. The grand jury found that club owners were being unfairly held accountable by the police for incidents they had no control over (eg, fights or crime off their premises): 'Such vague and subjective bases for setting permit conditions do not make for just decisions about business permits . . . they do not know what standards they are being measured against or what requirements will next be instituted by a permit officer' (San Francisco Civil Grand Jury, 2000). In the end, they argued that 'Removing the permit process from the police who could focus on enforcement of the laws applicable to clubs, instead of the administration and adjudication of permits, is a sensible solution that recognizes the rights of clubs that operate responsibly and the efforts of the police in protecting citizens and maintaining the peace.'

The EC has been described as 'The first of its kind in California and, perhaps the nation—an organization solely established to oversee permits and promote the development of a vibrant late-night entertainment industry' and 'perhaps the only Commission in the country with such duties and powers that strives to balance the benefits of a vibrant entertainment and late-night entertainment industry with the needs of residents and businesses in the vicinity of entertainment venues' (Harnden, 2006). The Commission's creation was supported not only by night-club operators and groups like the Late Night Coalition (SFLNC) but also (perhaps somewhat surprisingly) by the police themselves. One permit officer is quoted in the media as saying: 'The police would like nothing more than to shed entertainment permit duties . . . We support the establishment of an Entertainment Commission' (Garofoli, 2002). Another officer concurred: 'That's 450 permits we don't have to deal with' (Sanders, 2005).

This transformation of the regulatory regime for the night-time economy in San Francisco is resonant with changes noted elsewhere. In examining the UK night-time economy, Chatterton and Hollands (2003) found a 'shift towards a more pro-active business-led entrepreneurial local state is now a common feature not just of main-stream economic development but also of the cultural and night-time economies' (Chatterton and Hollands, 2003: 61). One part of this is the trend within post-indus-trial service economies for nightlife to be promoted as a significant aspect of a city's economy (Grazian, 2008).

REGULATORY CAPTURE?

With representatives from the nightlife industry serving on the Commission, and with explicit directives in the EC's mandate to 'promote the development of a vibrant entertainment and late-night entertainment industry within the City' (San Francisco Administrative Code, 90.1), San Francisco's EC would seem to be an example of the trend toward cities/governments granting increasing power to the nightlife indus-tries and their agendas and needs, paralleling the 2003 Licensing Act in England and Wales, which sought 'to broadly encourage entertainment activity—or at least prevent licensing authorities from creating conditions that curtail such activities to the detriment of the "cultural diversity" in the community' (Talbot, 2006: 161). Indeed, at first glance, the EC may appear to be a classic example of what econo-mists refer to as 'regulatory capture': the idea that regulators tend to get co-opted by the industries they are regulating (Laffont and Tirole, 1991; see Hadfield, 2006 for an analysis of these processes in the UK context), a point raised by a residents' group representative: 'I'm concerned about who will be the appointees and why there might be industry members on a commission meant to regulate the nightlife industry. The Commission came on too fast, with little neighborhood input' (Sand-ers, 2002). In part, such worries might seem to be borne out by the findings of a 2007 grand jury follow-up report which found that the EC had consistently failed to exercise authority against problem operators, only suspending or revoking licenses in very few instances. Critics charge that the EC 'has no teeth' and the report asks whether 'the pendulum has swung too far in the opposite direction'. The grand jury notes the perception that 'the Commission is too favourable in its determinations toward the entertainment industry to the detriment of residents' (San Francisco

Civil Grand Jury, 2007: 26).[4] However, it is not entirely clear that the reason for the lack of strict enforcement on the EC's part is simply because the chickens are ruling the roost. Instead, insufficient funding, an unclear mission, and poor communication between the EC and other agencies also seem to be major potential culprits. One police officer who works with the EC lays the blame squarely at a lack of resources. He even speculates that it was 'designed to fail . . . either by default or design . . . it's not funded; . . . you got a three-person office to administer the permits for an entire city of three quarters of a million people'.

If the Entertainment Commission were fully captured by the night-time industries, one might expect that the promotion of the night-time economy would be one of its major objectives. But, although one of the EC's explicit duties is to promote development in the night-time entertainment economy, the grand jury follow-up report found this to be one of the least fulfilled aspects of the EC's mandate. 'So far, in its brief history, the Entertainment Commission has engaged in very limited promotion of the development of a vibrant entertainment and late-night entertainment industry in SF' (San Francisco Civil Grand Jury, 2007: 6). The EC has primarily engaged in the issuance of permits, some mediation of disputes, and (to a far lesser extent) enforcement/revocation of permits. One nightclub owner we interviewed pointed to the nightlife-promotional duties of the EC and bemoaned their lack of fulfilment, something he attributed to 'direct political pressure' from groups that oppose nightlife expansion. An underground party organizer complained: 'They can't make anything happen, I mean at best they, you know, have some input into the regulation of clubs, but they've not really been able to substantially change anything in the club scene.'

According to economists, part of the ability of regulatees to 'capture' their regulators has to do with the large resources (both time and money) that regulated industries may be able to invest in the process and with asymmetric information, in which the industry may have greater technical knowledge than the regulators/staff, who come to rely on industry contacts for assistance and guidance. It may be the case, though, that the night-time industry in San Francisco is not nearly so organized that it could apply such leverage. One EC staff member commented on the difficulties of organizing those working in nightlife: 'Night-time economies don't organize very well . . . people who run night-time businesses don't coordinate . . . they're like herding cats around; . . . The folks who run night-time business aren't up during the day . . . they can't demand in an organized way the things that they really need.'

Another factor is the lack of consolidation of nightclub ownership in San Francisco. Unlike in the UK, which is described by many as increasingly dominated by a few chains of branded bars, pubs, and clubs (Chatterton and Hollands, 2002; Talbot, 2007) (and certainly such chains exist in other parts of the US as well), such multiples have not established a foothold in San Francisco. Indeed, San Francisco has specific growth-control ordinances aimed at stopping chain bars (or restaurants or clothing

---

[4] However, very recently, the EC has stepped up its permit suspensions and the number of hearings in respect of violating clubs, so it is possible that this lenient trend is now changing (Goodyear, 2005; Martin, 2006 and 2007a).

stores) from becoming too dominant within the city's landscape.[5] Instead, the vast majority of bars and clubs in the city remain local, independent establishments.[6] These local/independent establishments (or groups of establishments—a few of the more prominent proprietors own multiple clubs in the city), may lack the large-scale resources to truly capture regulators. Moreover, particularly in the current period of economic downturn, the various owners may be too much in competition with one another to unite sufficiently to push their collective interests more effectively than other stakeholders, like the local police or neighbours' groups. Attempting to combat these trends, some prominent nightclub owners are currently seeking to form a night-life association modelled on, or possibly as an adjunct to, the city's restaurant associations, which are seen as having been more effective at mobilizing to get their interests met; whether or not this aspiration will be achieved is not yet clear.

THE ENTERTAINMENT COMMISSION AND THE POLICE

The relationship between the Entertainment Commission and the police, overall, has been mixed. As Chatterton and Hollands (2003) put it (discussing the British context): 'Policing urban nightlife, then, is caught between competing discourses of law and order and the imperatives of growth' (pp 55–6). One Entertainment Commission representative describes one of the unique challenges facing her office: 'To balance essentially the vibrancy of night-time activities with the peace and quiet of neighbourhoods as much as is humanly possible.' While the police officials spoke out in favour of the creation of the Commission in 2002, in the ensuing years relationships between the two seem to have soured considerably. Though the EC's own annual Effectiveness Reports tout the positive and ongoing relationship between the two, police complained to the 2006–7 San Francisco Grand Jury about lack of communication and unresponsiveness on the part of the EC in relation to police complaints or calls to action.[7]

One reason for friction between the two agencies may be a more deeply rooted tension between the goals of expanding the night-time economy versus restricting nightlife-related crime, delinquency, or quality-of-life issues. 'At least two of the Commissioners themselves frequently opine during Commission hearings that the Broadway entertainment trade is now moribund because of the enthusiastic efforts of the Police Department to curb that night-time street scene . . . One Commissioner

---

[5] For an examination of the uneven history of growth and anti-growth activism in San Francisco see Godfrey (1997).

[6] However, according to one of our police interviewees, the adult entertainment venues/strip clubs in the city (which we are not focusing on in this chapter) tend to be owned by one company located out of state.

[7] There may also be financial frictions between the two: 'There is a perception on the part of Commissioners and staff of the Entertainment Commission that too much of the Commission's budget is paid to the SFPD to defray the cost of policing relative to the entertainment industry and that if not for these payments, the EC would be self-sustaining' (San Francisco Civil Grand Jury, 2007: 18).

stated that authorities "had to make sure while clearing the streets they did not kill the businesses"' (San Francisco Civil Grand Jury, 2007: 6). On the other hand, one police official told us he had received little support from the EC and that he had been called (by those in the entertainment industry) a 'new prohibitionist' for his efforts to combat crime in his district. This officer was also of the view that the EC did not sufficiently take the resources or needs of the police into consideration when making its decisions. As Talbot (2007) points out, 'The shifting nature of regulatory strategies, and the colliding interests of cultural regeneration versus social order and fear of the night has continued to haunt debates as to the function and problematic of the night-time economy' (Talbot, 2007: 18).

Shifting the power to grant or revoke entertainment licences to the EC has not removed police from the equation entirely. In addition to their enforcement duties in respect of entertainment permits, the police continue to have a strong role in recommending to the state Alcoholic Beverages Commission (ABC) who should get a liquor licence. A number of the nightlife operators we interviewed complained that the police short-circuited the EC's new role by getting sanctions against the clubs through the ABC. One of the police we interviewed conceded they do this because the EC is an overly 'permissive granting agency', explaining how he leverages his power in making ABC recommendations to achieve the restrictions he deems necessary on clubs' operations. This demonstrates the continued police presence in determining who does and does not get allowed to operate nightclubs in San Francisco, despite initial appearances to the contrary due to the creation of the EC. It also shows the significance of the state government in shaping local nightlife policies. While a great deal of nightlife regulation proceeds through the application of local/municipal rules, there are limits to how much change can be achieved by a city alone. Municipalities must still comply with the broader requirements of state (and federal) law. One illustration of this is in the failed attempts to allow for extended drinking hours in the city.

In 2004, State Assembly Member, Mark Leno (the former SF supervisor who sponsored the EC legislation in the first place), proposed Assembly Bill 2433, which would extend alcohol 'last call' in some cities to 3.30 or 4.00 am. This was supported by owners of bars and clubs in San Francisco. One nightclub owner argued for it on the grounds that 'the initiative would calm crowd noise by creating a "trickle out" effect. Also, he said, because most nightclub patrons don't go out until 11 pm or so, and last call is generally at 1:30 am, the short drinking time creates "an atmosphere of frenzy and binge"' (Martin, 2007b). The legislation also had considerable political support in the city. 'The SFLNC, the Entertainment Commission, 9 out of 11 (city) supervisors, and Mayor Gavin Newsom approved it, and a busload of SF clubbers went to Sacramento to support it' (Martin, 2007b). Despite garnering such support in San Francisco, Leno's proposals were not well received at the State Assembly. 'Police Officers from Oakland, a MADD mother,[8] and members of the Youth Leadership Institute spoke in opposition . . . the proposal didn't make it out of committee' (English, 2004). The fact that it had such overwhelming support in San Francisco, but still was not able

---

[8] Mothers Against Drunk Driving (MADD) is a campaign group which lobbies on alcohol issues in the United States, see <http://www.madd.org/>.

to pass in Sacramento, indicates that while much of nightlife policy is controlled on the local/city level, it is still within the general confines of state legislation to which the cities must accede.

As a result, efforts to have extended closing times in San Francisco now centre on obtaining 'after hours' permits, which allow clubs to stay open past last call, but without the ability to continue serving alcohol. These permits are defended on the grounds that it allows for staggered closing times (rather than all bars and clubs emptying at the statewide 2.00 am closing) and allows for a cool-down period before (inebriated) patrons flood the streets. A perceived moratorium on these permits was one of the galvanizing factors in the creation of the EC, and the number of permits granted for this has grown a great deal since the EC's inception (of the 108 current permits, 25 have been issued since 2004: Sanders, 2005). At the SF Nightlife Safety Summit in 2008, however, some club owners complained that it was still 'impossible' to get extended-hours permits due to the zoning restrictions that applied in their district, which are the purview of a further administrative agency; namely, the Planning Commission.

NEIGHBOURLY DISPUTES

While those in favour of nightlife expansion may clash with the police, even bigger disputes arise between nightlife operators and residents' or neighbour groups. One EC representative opined that 'neighbors and police are always going to align, always, always, always'. Writing in the media, one proponent of San Francisco nightlife has identified such disputes as the biggest thorn in the side of the city's night-time economy: 'One of the biggest obstacles to a healthy nightlife in San Francisco is other San Franciscans. Neighborhood groups hold far more power than local businesses, artists, and musicians. One resident citing noise issues can put a club that serves hundreds of people out of business—because city regulations place a higher value on residents than on nightlife businesses' (English, 2004). This is a very different impression from that which has been noted in the UK: 'In spite of small victories which residents might gain, their perception is that licensing procedures are heavily weighted in favour of the trade, its legal advisors, statutory agencies, and the court, who all use the system regularly' (Chatterton and Hollands, 2003: 65). One difference here may be in the power of 'repeat players' versus 'one-shotters' (Galanter, 1974). As discussed in the sociology of law, 'repeat players' are often able to work the system in a way that benefits them in the long-term and thus have advantages over the less-resourced 'one-shotters' whose priorities are more short-term and thus disadvantaged. While the repeat players are generally thought of as large corporate interests (as in the case of the corporate bars in the UK), within the context of San Francisco, it may actually be the neighbourhood groups and the police who are the repeat players and thus at some advantage.

While these factors point to structural elements of the regulatory field which give rise to certain types of conflict management, we must also look to structural issues in the city's planning that lead to these conflicts in the first place. San Francisco is a geographically small (48 square miles) dense city (among major US cities it is second only to New York in population density) (Godfrey, 1997), which increasingly has 'mixed-use' development—residences and (late-night) businesses are often in very close proximity. The 1990s brought increasing numbers of expensive condominiums, 'live/work' spaces, and loft developments into areas formerly dominated by warehouses, which during the warehouse party era had developed a vibrant nightlife. In these areas the new, often very wealthy, residential population soon came into conflict with night-time entertainment owners. The Entertainment Commission and SF nightlife more broadly, then, should be understood as operating within a context in which 'entertainment venues and residences may be uncomfortably close and that goodwill must be fostered by all sides to keep the city both a wonderful place to live and a wonderful place to play', as the grand jury report put it (San Francisco Civil Grand Jury, 2007: 22). This represents a twist on some classic scenarios of gentrification and nightlife expansion. It is not so much that the clubs, restaurants, and parties are invading previously residential areas, but the reverse.

We can particularly see this in 'SoMa', the area south of Market Street in San Francisco.[9] Once a largely industrial part of the city, over the past decade, neighbourhoods and high-end condominium projects have popped up all over the district, in addition to being a hub of dot-com and other new technology-focused companies and 'multimedia clusters' (Graham and Guy, 2002). Even in this time of real-estate contraction across much of the country (and much of the SF Bay Area), new condo developments are being built and continue to sell in the city.[10] One newspaper account reports that of the new buyers in the area 'about 50 per cent hold at least a graduate degree . . . Almost all earn at least $100,000 and many make between $250,000 and $500,000. Buyers most commonly work in high tech or high finance' (Temple, 2008). According to one estimate, 83 per cent of the SoMa residents have moved in since 1990 (South of Market Health Center, 2007). With (middle-class) families with children increasingly priced out of San Francisco (and/or avoiding the SF public [state] schools), two other groups primarily comprise this market: young well-to-do professionals and 'empty-nesters' whose own children have grown up. Access to San Francisco nightlife seems to be a driving factor for the first group, but a source of conflict for the latter. The SoMa area has long been a scene of nightlife in San Francisco, preceding the entry of these residential developments, with its many warehouses being a prime spot for underground parties and artist studios, and with a number of nightclubs peppered throughout the region

---

[9] This is not the only story of nightlife transformation in the city, however. For example, in the nearby Mission district, traditionally the home of working-class immigrant groups, particularly Latinos, families have been increasingly pushed out due to rising housing costs and increasing evictions, as new, wealthy, and primarily white, residents move in, thus following more familiar gentrification patterns. Expanded nightlife has played a role in this gentrification. Although working-class families and recent immigrants from Latin America still call the Mission home, a recent influx of young, upwardly mobile professionals is transforming the neighbourhood's character. High-end restaurants, night spots, and live/work spaces have displaced low-income households and local-serving businesses (Alejandrino, 2000). We do not wish to imply that low-income residents have not been displaced by gentrification in the SoMa district as well; however, much of this displacement occurred decades ago, prior to the recent nightlife expansions in the district (Graham and Guy, 2002).

[10] So-called 'live/work' spaces have been one of the district's fastest growing segments. These are exempt from the city's requirements that developers set aside a percentage of units for affordable housing, thus further contributing to the low- and middle-income housing squeeze in San Francisco (Alajandrino, 2000: 9).

(Godfrey, 1997).[11] There are at least 50 venues in the district offering dancing and entertainment, and over 100 sites with liquor licenses. But, whereas these nightclubs were once in areas that did not have sleeping residents nearby, condos are being built next to or on top of these venues—and not all of the new condo owners appreciate their nightlife neighbours. One nightlife advocate argues, 'It's easier to understand and accept noise complaints where nightlife venues have moved into residential neighborhoods and pumped up the volume. In most cases, however, the grievances come from new tenants concerning clubs that long preceded them. If you want to shut down a club, just build a live-work loft in the neighborhood and start making phone calls about the noise. And yet would anyone move next door to a church and start complaining that the bells wake them up too early when they're hungover . . . Just as a single loud venue can change the character of a sleepy part of town, a single sleepy yuppie can change the character of a nightlife neighborhood' (English, 2004). The trope of the 'one angry neighbour' came up throughout our interviews—both with representatives of the Entertainment Commission and with nightclub owners and managers. Even the police are frustrated with some of these neighbours, describing in our interviews 'chicken littles' who overwhelm police resources with often trivial complaints. One nightclub promoter lays the blame for these clashes squarely at the feet of the Planning Commission, the agency seen as responsible for allowing residential units to be placed in industrial and nightlife areas of town:

The largest nightclub in San Francisco . . . when it was opened . . . had . . . not one residential unit anywhere near it. It had no soundproofing, it had windows; it had great outdoor Sunday parties and then the Planning Department authorized the conversion of a manufacturing building that was next door to it, to subsidized family housing. . . And so, the Planning Department created a conflict which has gone on for the last 15 years every weekend . . . so it forced the club to encase itself in 10 inches of concrete, block off all the windows; basically turn it into a fortress in an attempt to keep the sound inside and not allow it to escape-and it's still not good enough.

Similarly, a promoter of underground parties reports that while the area was once popular for such events, as the warehouses seemed to be ideal settings, now, due to the increasing power of developers and neighbours' groups, the parties are receiving increased scrutiny and many have been closed down by the police as a result. Underground or unlicensed dance events/parties have an ambiguous place in the regulatory framework of the San Francisco night-time economy. While there have been raids of the parties in the past (most notably in the 1990s) and police-closings do still occur (particularly since the internet makes the parties easier to find not just for patrons but also for police and regulators), for the most part, the parties seem to be tolerated/allowed to continue, except for when receiving sufficient residential complaints. While underground parties were once associated primarily with being

---

[11] Of course, this region was not empty before the bars, nightclubs, restaurants, etc started opening in the 1980s, and it was not always dominated by industry. In the first half of the 20th century working-class families and industry populated the region, though by the 1950s the families had largely been pushed out by 'urban development' and revitalization strategies, such as the building of a convention centre (see Godfrey, 1997 for more on this history).

truly alternative or oppositional, many of the present-day events appear to differ from mainstream nightclubs only to the extent that they are unlicensed (and hence more profitable for organizers), but without a noticeably different ethos. The events may also be less security-focused (both in the positive sense of having less onerous surveillance and in the negative sense of having more dubious safety/fire plans), although bouncers checking identification at the door is not uncommon. Among our interviews with nightclub operators there seemed to be a split in opinion about underground parties. Some resented those who threw underground parties, for not having to go through the regulatory hoops that they themselves had to, and for bringing a bad name to all clubs when problems arose. Others saw the underground events as positive and adding to the overall vibrancy of San Franciscan nightlife.

NIGHTLIFE AND VIOLENCE

While the major source of complaints and actions against clubs are connected to noise issues, the second most pressing social problem connected to nightlife, according to our respondents, was 'undesirable patrons' and violence (as drug researchers, we were struck by how far removed issues related to drug use were in the problems-narratives of our respondents, be they police officers, nightclub owners, or city officials). As one club promoter put it, 'I'd trade the guns for the drugs any day. I'd trade the drugs for the knives . . . I mean a knife or a gun is most likely going to be a serious if not fatal decision. Most of the cases with drug use (in the 1990s), we did not see death.'[12] The city and the police clearly see violence as a major problem facing (and stemming from) night-time entertainment venues. In January 2008, after two shootings outside nightclubs within days of each other, the mayor's office convened a 'Nightlife Safety Summit' bringing together police, security companies, nightclub owners, and promoters. Nightclub owners, and by extension the Entertainment Commission, were chastised for not exerting greater control over nightlife: 'It won't be allowed to continue . . . We're here to help you, but we are going to make some changes', a city official pronounced (Bulwa, 2008). Future increases in police inspections were announced, perhaps indicating a swing back to police control.[13]

---

[12] The original Grand Jury Report advocating the creation of an Entertainment Commission did address some drug issues, and 'harm reduction' is explicitly within the EC's mandate. However there was consensus among our respondents (police, city officials, and owners/operators) that drugs just 'aren't that big of a problem' in nightclubs at the present moment. Some compared the present day to the 1990s, when the rise of club-drugs did lead to some prominent drug overdoses at clubs. It was not entirely clear from the interviews, however, whether they felt that: (a) drugs are now used less, or (b) drugs are still widely used in clubs, but no longer create major problems (use is more discreet/there are fewer health problems), or (c) drugs are a problem, but one which is dwarfed by the problem of violence.

[13] One EC representative complained that while the Commission had been receiving a lot of 'heat' recently, the nightclubs that have been the sites of violence were actually the ones that had been licensed by the police, under the pre-EC regime. As he stated: 'if the police had the ability to proactively, through a magic wand or a piece of paper, make it safer, then how come the violence that we have seen has primarily occurred at venues that the Police Department gave and conditioned those permits?' (interview).

There is an ongoing debate among stakeholders in San Francisco nightlife about the relationship between nightclubs and violence. To what degree is violence engendered by night-time entertainment? Are nightclub operators to blame for violence that happens outside their premises? Those who defend the nightclubs frequently point out that there is violence and shootings in many parts of San Francisco life, not just in the night-time economy. At both the Nightlife Safety Summit, and in our interviews, nightclub owners brought up the example of a recent shooting at the Metreon mall, in which a teenager shot someone, allegedly for moving too slowly on the escalator. They argue that violence is possible anywhere, even somewhere as innocuous as a mall, so it does not seem fair that night-time venues should be seen as particularly problematic. One nightclub owner similarly claimed that responsibility was a societal one, not something specific to the clubs. Closing down clubs was not the solution, he argued. 'The nightclubs don't create the problems, they're created by society and are played out at the nightclub, just like the problems of poverty are played out by shoplifters or other emotional problems, but they're not caused by the stores. The existence of the store does not make someone a thief, just like the existence of a nightclub doesn't make them a homicidal maniac.'

Yet, at the same time, nightclub owners and those working in nightlife security do concede that violence is a problem in their industry in a way that it never was 10 or 20 years ago. Throughout the Nightlife Safety Summit, people referred to a 'sea change' that has happened, with problems with patrons reaching levels never previously experienced in the 1980s or 1990s. Most of the nightclub owners and promoters we spoke with identified the need to defuse potentially violent situations in and around their club, as well as effectively 'weeding out' potentially problematic patrons before they are even admitted to the club, as among the greatest challenges in the night-time economy today. The ability to properly attract or dissuade the right patrons emerged repeatedly in interviews as a defining characteristic of the good/effective/responsible nightlife operator. Talbot (2006) in her London, UK-based case study found that regulators used business competence to define desirable nightlife operators and that they 'tended to associate "good business practice" with the ability to maintain order' (p 164). These discourses were similarly commonplace in our interviews. One police officer said of nightclub owners: 'All I'm asking for is good management', explaining that 'it begins with the people you hire, your dress code . . . before you open at 8.00 or 9.00 pm that night . . . know who your promoter is.' Another officer described with disdain those club owners who were 'in way over their head', and got pushed around by promoters,[14] letting problems spiral out of control. On the other hand, he deemed

---

[14] Independent promoters, contracted by nightclub owners to drum up business for the club, and who typically receive the money from the door-entry costs (whereas the owners receive the money from the bar) are frequently cited by other stakeholders as the source of problems. Police and nightclub owners in our interviews and at the Nightlife Safety Summit described problems with promoters bringing in too large a crowd, filled with the 'wrong sort' of people. One of the hallmarks of a bad manager/owner, according to our interviews, was handing over too much power to promoters whom they knew little about. The problem with promoters, they argued, stemmed from their short-term interests and commitments to the business (versus the long-term interests of club owners), and while owners had to go through extensive vetting during the licensing and permitting process, promoters were typically accountable to no one. One of the key outcomes of the Nightlife Safety Summit in which this topic was discussed, was therefore to increase the scrutiny and surveillance of this group through the development of new regulations requiring the official registration of all those seeking to promote one or more event in the city per year.

those clubs in his district as competent, receiving far less scrutiny from the police: 'I don't even call, except to say "Hi, how are ya?"' Some nightclub owners also appeared to have internalized this normative code, bemoaning the 'irresponsible' conduct of their industry peers: 'People don't wanna treat this like a business—they want to treat it like a personal playground, and a lot of operators are like, "Oh, I have so much fun." Well that's true, but then at the end of the day, you gotta make ends meet too', one nightclub manager told us. As he saw it, it was the common inability to act responsibly that accounted for the high rate of business failures in his industry.

Running throughout the narratives of good versus bad managers and their skills or shortcomings one finds frequent reference to attracting the 'desirable' and dissuading the 'undesirable' patron. Nightclub owners' talk of 'desirable' versus 'undesirable' patrons is generally connected to their perceptions of who will or will not cause confrontations, fights, or other problems for the club: 'Good behavior is people that go out, enjoy themselves, leave and don't cause a ruckus on the way out'; bad behaviour is 'people who take out their inability to problem solve and their aggressions in physical ways—that's bad behavior.'[15] One former nightclub owner described what he saw as a continuum between problematic and non-problematic nightlife. At the non-problematic end he (intriguingly) placed gay leather bars (whose clientele are older and less likely to cause problems), while at the problematic end were clubs which played 'gangsta rap'. The key differences, according to him, were the propensities for violence. Often, this issue of desirable (or acceptable) patrons gets mixed up with issues of musical genre—with some musical content (most notably, hip hop) presented as being more problem-prone than others (although rarely stated outright, assumptions about the 'problems' posed by patrons who follow hip hop, particularly young African American or 'urban' men, formed the subtext to the responses we received from a number of interviewees). In the days before the Entertainment Commission, the police were often explicit in the connections they made between undesirable patrons and undesirable music. The courts subsequently held that police permitting requirements for nightclubs which 'sometimes forbade clubs from playing rap music or loud rock music' (Harnden, 2006) and thus regulated the musical content of the club's entertainment offer, were a First Amendment violation. This issue was one of the many which stimulated calls for the creation of the EC; the police being regarded as having 'gone too far' in attempting to impose restrictions of this nature: 'The foes of hip-hop nightclubs make no bones about their position. "Rap music attracts a certain 'element' that may or may not be desirable"', one neighbor group representative is quoted as saying. According to this account, a police captain argued that 'hip-hop music often draws gang members. And for him, avoiding rival gang confrontations is worth censoring the Mission's music choices' (Miller, 2002).

An EC staff member conceded that 'music profiling' was once a common tool of police practice in governing nightlife through the issuance of permit conditions, but was adamant that such practices no longer occurred: 'that's racist and it's

---

[15] This informant also identified a 'middle group': those who are not starting fights or being blatantly inappropriate, but whose noise, such as loud cell-phone conversations outside the venue, infuriate neighbours and bring unwanted regulatory attention (interview).

unconstitutional, and so we don't regulate content'. However, it is not clear that such profiling is entirely obsolete and some argue that it still occurs, albeit in more subtly ways. For example, one promoter involved in the EC told us that he saw hip-hop as a major source of problems, arguing that he would never play it (or certain variants of it) within his clubs: 'If you play gangsta rap and thug hip-hop, you're gonna have somebody killed outside your venue eventually . . . doesn't matter where it is, it's not the place, it's the programming which attracts the patronage.'[16] Thus, to the degree that promoters and owners have themselves internalized the music-profiling message, associating it with 'good' management, and strongly avoiding programming that attracts the 'wrong' crowd, it seems that it may not even be necessary for regulators to enforce such exclusions, the end result being the same.

One club manager explained that his venue got no 'hassle' or surveillance from the police, because 'it's not the sort in which fights break out'. He contrasted this with problem clubs: 'I'm not saying African American, but I'm saying, if somebody's using ghetto thug music, like people smoking marijuana outside the club, or people hiding Hennessey in the bottle outside drinking and stuff, I'm sure police would keep an eye on it . . . you don't do that kind of party. You have to be smart enough not to deal with that. It's too risky.' Here, as in some of our other interviews, 'ghetto thug music', drugs, inappropriate behaviour, and the mentioned-but-not-mentioned African Americans, are interwoven. All are seen as sources of 'too risky' activity, 'not worth it' for the smart businessperson. A Bay Area disc jockey we spoke to summarized the widespread concerns about hip hop: it attracts people who are 'lower class' or 'ghetto' and therefore 'undesirable', he told us.

The place of musical programming in security management is however a contested arena. Others on the club scene, including, unsurprisingly, those involved in promoting hip-hop events, argue that it is not music in and of itself that leads to violence. For example, at the Nightlife Safety Summit, one promoter argued that, while there had been some melees associated with hip-hop events, this had had more to do with the fact that the events were promoted endlessly on the radio and did not have a cover charge. This had led to crowds that were much too large to control, a factor exacerbated by insufficient staffing levels at the events. These factors were to blame, rather than some innate tendency to violence in hip-hop music and its followers. 'It's not the program, but the execution of the program', he argued.

Yet, even among those who support hip hop, or who oppose profiling based on musical content, certain forms of the hip-hop genre appear to be regarded as more or less acceptable. For example, the EC staff member who opposed the idea that music is the problem and the practice of music profiling in licensing/enforcement, still identified one form of music as troublesome—'hyphy', a local hip-hop variant: 'hyphy promotes go crazy, go wild, crazy ass shit, and although fun in theory, in practice, if you want to go crazy and do the hyphy thing you're going to cause problems'. In

---

[16] One police officer, who was rather disdainful of the EC in general for being too permissive, laughed at the idea that it may be denying permits to hip-hop clubs. In his opinion, the EC would give permits to anyone: 'if you said you were gonna have baby-throwing contests on the weekends, they'd [still] give you the licence' (interview).

this interview, as in others, even in the midst of arguing that no particular type of music (or music fans) are the problem, such opinions manage to sneak in. In the Nightlife Safety Summit, some major hip-hop promoters argued that they would not programme hyphy because of the problems it entails: kids that 'act up'; violent, uncontrolled energy; kids who cannot get into clubs because of money or age restrictions loiter outside the events and cause problems.

These narratives concerning the importance of 'weeding out' those who are not wanted as part of nightlife indicate that while various stakeholders talk about diversity, inclusion, and expanding the night-time entertainment economy, certain forms of exclusion remain fundamentally central. As Chatterton and Hollands (2003: 184) has argued 'spaces of consumption, then, are an important component of social exclusion.'

CONCLUSIONS

As we have indicated in this chapter, the establishment of the Entertainment Commission in San Francisco reflects the changing nature of urban economies and the increasing need today, given financial crises, for cities to enhance their revenues from tourism and from the service sector more generally. However, the night-time has always been a contested and liminal arena, associated rightly or wrongly with crime and deviance, a time which has traditionally been the object of great social control and regulation. The establishment of the EC will not necessarily overcome those more structural rifts. This chapter has attempted to illustrate these issues through a discussion of the Entertainment Commission as a window on the tensions and contests between stakeholders in the night-time economy, including nightlife operators, the police, and neighbours/residents.

In viewing these developments in San Francisco, we must remember the extent to which ways of regulating and controlling the night-time economy in the US vary between different states and even between individual cities within the same state. In fact a striking contrast can be seen between San Francisco and Oakland, California. These two cities are separated by the San Francisco Bay and commuting between the two cities (in both directions) for work and for leisure is common. However, the two cities possess very different structures and attitudes to the issue of regulating nightlife. Whereas San Francisco has been at the forefront of experimenting with alternative models of nightlife regulation, Oakland's licensing and regulation of night-time entertainment remain much more traditionally organized, with the police (in combination with city officials) having a dominant role in licensing decisions. Though in recent years urban regeneration and development has been a major theme in Oakland city politics, these concerns may be dwarfed by the rising numbers of violent crimes in the city, with the latter outweighing the former in policy priorities. Whether these two nightlife regulatory models will continue to coexist side by side, or whether one will become the more dominant model uniformly across the region, only time will tell. While the role of the police in issuing licences and in more general regulation of nightlife in San Francisco may have diminished (although, even this claim is contestable, as we have shown), it is certainly not the case that nightlife in the city is any less 'policed'—indeed, with the growing number of security cameras, rigid security rules, and high numbers of private security guards having a visible presence within nightlife venues in both Oakland and San Francisco, patrons of nightlife may now be under greater scrutiny and surveillance than ever before.

REFERENCES

All internet sources were accessible 20 August 2008

ALEJANDRINO, SV (2000) *Gentrification in San Francisco's Mission District: Indicators and policy recommendations*, Report for the Mission Economic Development Association (MEDA).

BECK, J and ROSENBAUM, M (1994) *Pursuit of Ecstasy: The MDMA experience*, Albany: State University of New York Press.

BULWA, D (2008) 'New violence draws safety warning to S.F. clubs', <http://www.sfgate.com/cgi-bin/article/article?f=/c/a/2008/01/18/BALMUHAP>.

CHATTERTON, P and HOLLANDS, R (2002) 'Theorising urban playscapes: Producing, regulating and consuming youthful nightlife city spaces', *Urban Studies*, 39/1, 95–116.

—— —— (2003) *Urban Nightscapes: Youth cultures, pleasure spaces and corporate power*, London: Routledge.

ENGLISH, C (2004) 'Bad reputation: Or, how to shut down nightlife and why we shouldn't', *San Francisco Bay Guardian*, 16–22 June, 38/38, <http://www.sfbg.com/38/38/cover_nightlife.html>.

GALANTER, M (1974) 'Why the "haves" come out ahead: Speculations on the limits of legal change', *Law and Society Review*, 9/1, 95–160.

GAROFOLI, J (2002) 'A push for the right to party loudly in S.F.', *San Francisco Chronicle*, 1 July, B1.

GODFREY, BJ (1997) 'Urban development and redevelopment in San Francisco', *Geographical Review*, 87/3, 309–33.

GOODYEAR, C (2005) '2 Permits suspended for mission rock club', *San Francisco Chronicle*, 21 April, B4.

GRAHAM, S and GUY, S (2002) 'Digital space meets urban place: sociotechnologies of urban restructuring in downtown San Francisco', *City: Analysis of Urban Trends, Culture, Theory, Policy, Action*, 6/3, 369–82.

GRAZIAN, D (2008) *On the Make: The Hustle of Urban Nightlife*, Chicago, IL: The University of Chicago Press.

HADFIELD, P (2006) *Bar Wars: Contesting the Night in Contemporary British Cities*, Oxford: Oxford University Press.

HARNDEN, A (2006) *San Francisco Entertainment Commission: How this city manages entertainment and events*, Responsible Hospitality Institute, <http://www.rhiclearinghouse.net/RHICH_ShowColumns.aspx?RecID=448>.

LAFFONT, JJ and TIROLE, J (1991) 'The politics of government decision making: A theory of regulatory capture', *Quarterly Journal of Economics*, 106/4, 1089–127.

MARTIN, A (2006) 'Club six not deep-sixed—yet', *San Francisco Examiner*, 7 June, <http://www.examiner.com/a-768098~Club_Six_not_deep_sixed_yet.html>.

——— (2007a) 'City suspends North Beach club's permit', *San Francisco Examiner*, 22 March, <http://www.examiner.com/a-632745~City_suspends_North_Beach_Club_s_permit. html?cid=sfor-article-solar_panels>.

——— (2007b) 'Forum: Close clubs at 4 a.m., offer owners training', *San Francisco Examiner*, 14 April, <http://www.examiner.com/a-673772~Forum__Close_clubs_at_4_a_m___offer_ owners_training.html>.

MAYOR'S OFFICE OF ECONOMIC AND WORKFORCE DEVELOPMENT and ICF INTERNATIONAL ECONOMIC AND PLANNING SYSTEMS (2007) *Sustaining Our Prosperity: The San Francisco economic strategy*, <http://www.sfgov.org/site/uploadedfiles/yw1/SFES090607final.pdf>.

MILLER, C (2002) 'Show's over: Why the hell do the cops get to decide what kind of music plays in SF?', *San Francisco Bay Guardian*, 23 October, <http://www.sfbg.com/37/04/cover_ show_over.html>.

MILLER, LE (2007) 'Racial segregation and the San Francisco Musicians' Union, 1923–1960', *Journal of the Society for American Music*, 1/2, 161–206.

NOWINSKI, A (2000) 'Big brother is watching at Ten 15 Folsom', *San Francisco Bay Guardian*, 14 June, <http://web.archive.org/web/20030823192013/http://www.sfbg.com/News/34/37/ 370gten.html>.

PEPIN, E and WATTS, L (2006) *Harlem of the West: The San Francisco Fillmore Jazz Era*, San Francisco: Chronicle Books.

San Francisco Administrative Code, Chapter 90, Section 90.1, <http://www.ci.sf.ca.us/site/ entertainment_page.asp?id=18156#sec90.1>.

SAN FRANCISCO CIVIL GRAND JURY (2000) 'Club Permits', *1999–2000 San Francisco Civil Grand Jury Report*, <http://www.sfgov.org/site/courts_page.asp?id=3731>.

——— (2007) 'The Entertainment Commission: A work in progress', *2006–2007 San Francisco Civil Grand Jury Report*.

SANDERS, A (2005) 'Late night wakes up in the city', *San Francisco Business Times*, 8 April, <http://www.bizjournals.com/sanfrancisco/stories/2005/04/11/story3.html?page=2>.

SANDERS, J (2002) 'Nightclub supporters get glimmer of hope', *San Francisco Chronicle*, 12 September, p D1.

SILCOTT, M (1999) *Rave America: New school dancescapes*, Toronto: ECW Press.

SOUTH OF MARKET HEALTH CENTER (2007) 'SOMA's Story—The Evolution of a Community', <http://www.smhcsf.org/soma.html>.

TALBOT, D (2006) 'The Licensing Act 2003 and the Problematisation of the Night-Time Economy: Planning, licensing and subcultural closure in the UK', *International Journal of Urban and Regional Research*, 30/1, 159-71.

——— (2007) *Regulating the Night: Race, culture and exclusion in the making of the night-time economy*, Hampshire, England: Ashgate.

TEMPLE, J (2008) 'Shifting demographics hint at SoMa's future', *San Francisco Chronicle*, 9 March, A1.

14

CANADA

Kathryn Graham and Sharon Bernards

One of the earliest enactments of the Manitoba legislature had been a law to regulate and control the liquor traffic . . . During the boom everybody with a ten-or twelve-roomed house rushed to get into the hotel business, and all efforts to regulate the behaviour of the saloons collapsed as the courts split their legal hairs into the finest filaments. Winnipeg, they ruled in 1883, had power only to licence, not to regulate.

When nightly riots developed in the Main Street bistros, police action was limited to arresting the evictees as they were bounced from the bars into the perpetually self-renewing quagmire that was Main Street most of the year. As Chief Murray explained, his force functioned more as a shepherding agency than one concerned with incarcerative action against drunks, even though they jailed more than 2,000 of them in 1882. There had been a problem with the policemen themselves becoming intoxicated, so after several were fired for being drunk on duty they were forbidden to enter the bars except in cases where brawling got completely out of hand . . .

But because of the lenient attitude which constitutional uncertainty forced upon the police, maintaining a semblance of order on the streets became increasingly difficult, not only in Winnipeg but everywhere else. In Portage la Prairie, for example, things got so badly out of hand that the police decided to haul the barkeepers into court under a town by-law. All were convicted and fined. They appealed the conviction, and won acquittal on the grounds the regulations were ultra vires, and the appeal judge ordered judgment for costs against the magistrate who had presided at their trial. To save the magistrate's home from seizure, the Manitoba Temperance Alliance in an emergency convention undertook to raise the required $1,500.

(Gray, 1995: 10–12)

INTRODUCTION

Consistent with its Wikipedia definition,[1] 'nightlife' in Canada is generally understood to be synonymous with going out drinking or, more recently, 'clubbing' and has been strongly associated with crimes of violence (including sexual assault and robbery), vandalism, and disorder. As described in the above quotation, the link between

---

[1] <http://www.en.wikipedia.org/wiki/Nightlife>.

violence and consuming alcohol in licensed drinking establishments began at least a century ago. More recently, surveys of crime victims (Besserer and Trainor, 2000) and research on offenders (Pernanen et al, 2002) indicate that alcohol contributes to a substantial proportion of violent crimes in Canada. Time-series analysis has also shown a positive association between homicide rate and per capita alcohol consumption, over time (Bunge et al, 2005).

The link between crime and nightlife drinking was identified in community-level studies in the late 1970s (Pernanen, 1991) with victimization in bars, especially after midnight, accounting for 24 per cent of male and 5 per cent of female survey respondents who were victims of violence in Thunder Bay, Ontario. In Hamilton, Ontario, at about the same period, police data revealed that alcohol was involved in over 60 per cent of violent crimes committed between midnight and 4.00 am (Gerson and Preston, 1979). This study also found that the rate of violent crime was positively associated with the mean alcohol consumption in licensed premises. More recently, a general population survey of adults aged 18–60 years in the province of Ontario (Graham et al, 2002) found that involvement in physical aggression (as a victim, perpetrator, or both) was more likely to occur in or near licensed premises than in any other location. Among respondents who reported involvement in an incident of physical aggression in the past year, 44 per cent of males aged 18–24 reported that the most recent incident occurred in or near licensed premises. This proportion was 59 per cent for males aged 25–34, 32 per cent for females aged 18–24, and 23 per cent for females aged 25–34.

Although frequency of engaging in any night-time activities (eg, sports, work, classes, a movie, as well as going to a bar) has been found to be linked to increased risk of victimization from a variety of crimes, violent victimization has been linked more strongly with frequency of going to bars than for other evening activities (Kennedy and Forde, 1990). Similarly, bars or restaurants are the most frequent location for sexual assault (20 per cent) and second most frequent for other types of physical assault (11 per cent) when spousal violence is excluded (Gannon and Mihorean, 2005).

Because of the close link between nightlife and violence, this chapter focuses primarily on violent crime relating to licensed drinking establishments. Specifically, we explore the history of this link, including the nature of past problems and past attempts at solutions. We then examine the contemporary relationship between nightlife and crime, including recent approaches to addressing nightlife-related problems.

HISTORICAL PERSPECTIVE

Recent research (Purcell and Graham, 2005) suggests that nightlife in Canada, especially with regard to entertainment areas, looks very much like nightlife elsewhere in the world, with large dance clubs, highly sexualized environments, and a strong presence of security staff. However, historical descriptions of public drinking and its regulation provide a broader cultural context for interpreting the current relationship between nightlife and crime.

In British North America and New France, taverns or public houses were public places where early settlers socialized, very similar in function to taverns in Europe. Alcohol use of all kinds was ubiquitous and alcohol was available at all hours of day or night. For example, in 1830s Toronto, there was one tavern for every 119 inhabitants (Heron, 2003: 27). Prohibitionist thinking began to grow in the latter half of the 19th century, possibly in reaction to increasing levels of serious drunkenness, possibly spreading from sentiments in the US, or possibly because 'in the larger cities more drinking was taking place among workmates and strangers in new commercialised settings, further from the context of home and family' (Heron, 2003: 52). Problems with alcohol were seen to be primarily related to consumption by men in contexts that were not integrated with meals and family. Descriptions of pre-prohibition public drinking (see below) often included 'macho' behaviour and fighting not unlike that found in research on contemporary public drinking behaviour of young men in Canada (Dyck, 1980; Graham and Wells, 2003), the UK (Benson and Archer, 2002; Tuck, 1989), and Australia (Tomsen, 1997):

The men often roamed between hotel bar-rooms on a Saturday night or a public holiday, extending the stage for their loud performances on the street. In their drunkenness, they could brag expansively, insult or offend others, and easily take offence – expressing racist comments about blacks, confronting a strikebreaker, defending the honour of their women-folk or their own reputations. . . . It was not uncommon for their highly theatrical braggadocio to erupt into fights. (Heron, 2005: 427)

Although prohibition of alcohol generally had some supporters, widespread support was only achieved when the prohibition movement focused on problems related to public drinking (Gray, 1995; Heron, 2003) as also occurred in the US (Popham, 1962). And, as the 'Banish-the-Bar' slogan gained in popularity, taverns or 'saloons' became increasingly marginalized with more and more restrictions on entertainment and hours of operation (Heron, 2003: 158). Restrictions on licensing also resulted in the closing of smaller premises, with those remaining squeezed out of residential neighbourhoods and increasingly concentrated in commercial and downtown working-class areas (Heron, 2003), thereby creating de facto 'entertainment districts'. The closure of bars began in 1915–16 with prohibition implemented in most provinces by 1919. Even though prohibition was short-lived in most provinces and never fully implemented (eg, it was not illegal to manufacture alcohol and alcohol could be purchased with a doctor's prescription), its impact on public drinking endured for some time. Home drinking mostly replaced public drinking, and widespread problems with public drinking did not re-occur for some decades (Gray, 1995: 212).

The history leading to prohibition highlights a number of trends that helped shape the current form and function of the drinking establishments that define nightlife in Canada. In particular, during the course of the latter half of the 19th century, drinking establishments were the target of a variety of controls that limited hours of operation, activities of patrons, types of beverages served and various other aspects. Through these controls, establishments became increasingly marginalized from conventional and middle-class society. In the 20th century, these restrictions and limitations were first strengthened when licensed drinking establishments re-emerged following prohibition (Campbell, 2001; Heron, 2003) and then, during the latter half of the 20th century, gradually eliminated or at least greatly reduced. It is useful to examine the nature of these early restrictions because they constitute some of the primary tools used to address nightlife-related crime, especially violence and disorder.

THE POST-PROHIBITION RE-EMERGENCE OF PUBLIC DRINKING

Licensed drinking establishments ('beverage rooms', 'beer parlours', and 'cocktail lounges' as they were called) re-emerged at various times in different provinces and numbers increased very slowly (Marquis, 2000). For example, in 1953, Toronto had 145 taverns with a legal capacity of 32,000 for a population of 711,199 (ie, one tavern to every 4,905 inhabitants compared to one tavern for every 119 inhabitants in the 1830s, as noted above). The concentration of premises into marginalized areas continued, with about half located in poor or industrial areas, 45.5 per cent in lower-income areas, 6.2 per cent in higher-income areas and none at all in the highest-income areas (Popham, 1982: 19).

Licensed drinking in Canada is regulated primarily at the provincial level (eg, permitted drinking ages vary from 18 years in some provinces to 19 in others). Controls are also exercised at the level of the local community in the form of health-and-safety regulations and, sometimes, input into the licensing process. When public drinking was reintroduced following prohibition, most provinces adopted similar restrictions, with the possible exception of Québec, where the largely Francophone population maintained a more European style of drinking and adopted fewer of the Protestant-based restrictions on drinking (Cosper et al, 1987; Heron, 2003). Specifically, patrons in most provinces were required to be seated at a table in order to be served and to remain seated when consuming alcohol. Tables held a maximum of four men, thereby limiting the extent of round-buying and raucous behaviour. There were also tight controls on activities, including little or no entertainment; women were not allowed to be present either as patrons or servers (Heron, 2003; Marquis, 2003). Despite these restrictions, the popularity of licensed premises increased, and following the Second World War, entertainment and other amenities were added through a gradual bending and liberalization of the rules (Campbell, 2001; Heron, 2003).

It is difficult to know whether the tightly controlled post-prohibition drinking environment actually had less violence and other criminal behaviour compared with pre-prohibition drinking establishments. Certainly, the association between public drinking and violence was still evident in legal and media reports of the time (Campbell, 2001). In addition, there was evidence that post-prohibition public drinking establishments still provided the stage where men could play out 'the ritualised performances of outlandish masculine bravado' (Heron, 2005: 435). Consequently, when the next major transition of nightlife occurred in the 1970s, one of its main goals was to address male violence by 'civilizing' and 'gentrifying' the public drinking environment, as described in an article published in a national magazine of the time:

The (Well-Scrubbed) Face on the Barroom Floor. One midnight last fall, Edmonton tavern owner Ernie Wolver ordered a rock band playing in his pub, the Kingsway, to pack it in for the night. The band refused, so he pulled the plug on the power. With that, the, 250 customers remaining in the 600-seat tavern turned ugly. Battles erupted, the crowd spilled into the park-ing lot, and a squad of police reinforcements had to be rushed in to put down the mini-riot. At the time, the brawl was just a typical tavern happening in Alberta. But it may have been an historic last whoop-up: the beer barns that spawn nightly rowdyism and vandalism are being banished. Sprouting up in their place are expensive drinking spas—featuring water-falls, chesterfields, palm trees and dress regulations. 'The same people are drinking in the new taverns,' says Peter Elliott, Chairman of the Alberta Liquor Control Board (ALCB) 'but they look a lot different.' They are also, tavern owners report, behaving a lot better amid the velvet chairs and potted plants. (Zwarun, 1978: 22–3)

This initiative of the Alberta Liquor Control Board was noteworthy in that its goal was to encourage moderate drinking by taking the emphasis *off* drinking (the only activity in the spartan and highly regulated beverage rooms) and placing the empha-sis *on* socializing. And, unlike similar initiatives in other provinces, the policy change included researchers contracted to evaluate its impact on the rate of drinking, with evidence suggesting that patrons drank more slowly, but stayed longer, when engaged in other activities (Ratcliffe and Nutter, 1979; Ratcliffe et al, 1980).

However, the 'civilized', aggression-free nightlife culture envisioned as part of this gentrification did not wholly materialize. From the 1980s onwards, premises became larger (Purcell and Graham, 2005), intoxication was still widespread (Graham, Osgood, et al, 2006), and male-on-male displays of machismo remained very much in evidence in Canadian drinking establishments (Graham and Wells, 2003; McKeen, 2004). More-over, in the presence of women, this machismo was now accompanied by rampant sex-ual harassment and assault (Graham, Tremblay, et al, 2006)—thereby demonstrating that being well dressed and middle class did not necessarily confer immunity to bar vio-lence (Graham, Bernards, et al, 2006). The following section on contemporary night-life reveals how 'the beer barns that spawn nightly rowdyism and vandalism' described by Zwarun (above) may have morphed into equally large nightclubs that continue to 'spawn rowdyism and vandalism', along with the occasional stabbing and shooting.

NIGHTLIFE AND CRIME IN CONTEMPORARY CANADA

To our knowledge, there has been no systematic quantitative analysis of the extent of nightlife-related crime in Canada. Violent crime, in general, declined in the 1990s (Bunge et al, 2005; Ouimet, 2002), levelling off, or increasing slightly, in the first part of the 21st century. At present, the rate of homicide in Canada is considerably less than that of the US, slightly less than Scotland and Sweden, but higher than Japan, England, and Wales (Dauvergne and Li, 2006).

Because no research has focused specifically on nightlife-related crime, the follow-ing discussion uses media and agency reports to describe the nature of the current problem and the types of solutions undertaken. It should be noted that although these sources help to characterize the problems, they do not necessarily provide an objective and reliable assessment of the magnitude of the problem or a systematic review of solutions. We begin by using Alberta as a case example because it has both experienced significant nightlife-related problems and undertaken multiple initiatives to address them.

RECENT NIGHTLIFE-RELATED PROBLEMS IN ALBERTA

Economic prosperity due to a boom in the oil industry has brought a large number of young men to Alberta to work in the oil fields, with a corresponding increase in licensed premises. Similar to the effects of such migration to western Canada a century before (Gray, 1995), the combination of alcohol, young men, and the physical and social atmosphere of drinking establishments in close proximity to one another has been associated with problems such as fighting and brawls. This has been especially notable in the major cities of Calgary and Edmonton.

Calgary

On busy nights in the late 1980s, up to 10,000 people congregated in the 24 bars located in the one and a half block area of 11th Avenue South West, known as 'Electric Avenue' (Calgary Police Service, 1994). Nightlife-related problems, including assaults and homicides, had a substantial impact on the neighbouring residential community as well as on the city generally, with other types of businesses moving out of the area due to noise and crime, and police and other resources increasingly allocated to dealing with nightlife problems.

To address these problems, a Mayor's Task Force was formed including representatives from the police, planning, licensing, fire and law departments, together with the provincial Liquor Licensing Authority and the bar operators on Electric Avenue (Calgary Police Service, 1994). This initiative included:

- over $800,000 to redesign the space using 'Crime Prevention Through Environmental Design' principles
- formulating and endorsing an Area Development Plan
- creation of the 11th Avenue Business Association
- a three-year campaign to increase awareness of the need to address problems in the area
- establishment of a Coordinated Response Team.

Ultimately, re-zoning regulations aimed at limiting the size and number of bars, together with police enforcement activities led to the Electric Avenue entertainment area being closed down in the late 1990s (Phair, 2007). However, problems soon re-emerged in a nearby nightclub strip, including stabbings, beatings, and shootings (White, 2003) such as one incident involving the knifing of a nightclub doorman after he refused admission to a group of men (Wood, 2002). Initiatives to address these problems included a police-led community response involving bar owners (Wood, 2002) and proposals to install closed-circuit television cameras (Walton, 2001) and limit the number of bars with dance floors (Wood, 2002). However, violence on the strip continued (*Edmonton Journal*, 2006). In one incident in January 2007, a brawl involving 50 people got out of hand, with shots fired and one bar employee sent to hospital after being struck by a car which had been used as a weapon (Fernandez, 2007). In the same year, the Calgary Police Service suspended a programme of bars employing off-duty police officers because of a lack of evidence to indicate any positive impact, although at least one bar owner claimed that security staff employed by the bars would be unable to handle the organized crime and gang activity in the bars without police support (Saelhof, 2007). In April 2008, the installation of 24 closed-circuit television cameras was approved by the city council despite local opposition (Mattson, 2008).

Edmonton

Although crime in Edmonton declined during the 1990s, this trend began to reverse in 1999 (Murphy and Clarke, 2005). Nightlife problems were mostly concentrated in two entertainment hubs, the West Edmonton Mall and the Old Strathcona District (Whyte Avenue), although nightlife-related violence also occurred in other city locations (Montgomery, 2006).

West Edmonton Mall

In 1998, the West Edmonton Mall (which bills itself as the world's largest entertainment and shopping centre[2]) had six different drinking establishments. The large number of intoxicated young adults leaving these premises at closing time and the associated noise, vandalism and violence led to multiple complaints from residents in nearby suburban neighbourhoods. For example, one brawl in the parking lot at closing time (3.00 am) involved 30 people fighting with knives, belts, and pieces of wood, while 300 people watched. One police officer was kicked and punched when she tried to help the victim of a stabbing (Ward, 1998). When the adjacent nightclub later went out of business, the owners filed a $15 million lawsuit against the police arguing that police action had forced them out of business by scaring off customers with public warnings about the premises. In their defence, the police argued that the club owners had used the warnings to *promote* the club and that attendance had actually increased after the warnings (Blais, 2000). The Board noted that the police were entitled to warn the public about establishments that were dangerous; however, it found that police officers were guilty of discreditable conduct as they had publicly linked the venue owners to organized crime, without supporting evidence (Cowan, 2001).

In 1998, a 'Barwatch' programme was initiated by the Edmonton police (Bradley, 1998; Laghi, 1998). Six bar owners at the Mall agreed to participate in the voluntary programme which required the bars to:

- purchase and install a security camera at the entrance, and monitor and archive the tapes for 6 months
- attend monthly meetings
- allow police to do background checks on bar staff
- ban patrons from wearing 'gang clothing'

[2] <http://www.westedmall.com/home/default.asp>.

- have security staff trained to eject patrons and break up fights without using excessive force
- install fax machines and pagers so that the identity of patrons who caused problems could be shared with other bars.

Although police praised the programme and one bar manager credited the Barwatch cameras with a decline in incidents and for making it possible to absolve staff of wrongdoing (Bradley, 1998), a Calgary lawyer and member of the Freedom of Information and Privacy Association of Alberta complained that the cameras were an invasion of privacy (Laghi, 1998).

The considerable police resources required at the Mall (O'Donnell, 2003; Sands, 2003) led to a dispute over who should pay for the extra policing (Gerein, 2003; O'Donnell, 2003) which was ultimately resolved by including such costs in the police budget (WEMASIST, 2004). By 2003, the Mall had nine nightclubs, with the four largest (combined capacity of 6,500 persons) in close proximity to one another. Fights and brawls among hundreds of drunken patrons frequently occurred in the parking lot on weekends after closing (Loyie, 2003). Despite media coverage suggesting that extra policing was helping reduce violence (Loyie, 2003), problems continued with two men stabbed during a brawl in 2007 (*Edmonton Sun*, 2007).

Whyte Avenue / Old Strathcona

Whyte Avenue in the historic Strathcona district of Edmonton experienced difficulty balancing its role as a centre for shopping, dining, and the arts, with the expanding focus of the area on nightlife and entertainment (Mah and Gerein, 2004; Responsible Hospitality Institute, 2006). Problems persisted (Gerein, 2005) despite initiatives undertaken in the late 1990s and early 2000s to address violence and other problems— for example, an unsuccessful attempt to implement a Barwatch programme and the use of closed-circuit television cameras (deemed ineffective and discontinued after two years) (Edmonton Police Service, 2006), as well as tougher occupancy limits on licensed premises (Mah and Gerein, 2004). In 2005, the police reported responding to over 3,600 calls from the area and a further 2,400 calls from nearby residential neighbourhoods (Edmonton Police Service, 2006).

In 2006, the Responsible Hospitality Institute, a private company from California, was contracted to hold consultations and recommend a plan for development of the Old Strathcona district. Recommendations, many of which were adopted at a provincial level (see later sections), included:

- create a formal network of city and provincial representatives for managing Old Strathcona and other entertainment areas
- recognize entertainment areas as economic assets
- adopt a coordinated approach to licensing, education, and enforcement
- use the community and policing protocols normally implemented for special events (eg, portable toilets, higher levels of policing) to manage entertainment areas on Friday and Saturday nights (implemented in 2007 –*Edmonton Journal*, 2007)

- conduct a patron responsibility campaign. (Responsible Hospitality Institute, 2006)

Other measures implemented as a result of the Responsible Hospitality Institute report included the allocation of $410,000 from the city budget to address nightlife-related problems (Kent, 2007b) and the formation of a public-safety compliance team, consisting of police, fire, Gaming and Liquor Commission inspectors. This team was tasked with increasing enforcement of the regulations governing the operation of licensed venues through fines, penalties, and other conditions (Kent, 2007a).

COORDINATED EFFORTS TO REDUCE NIGHTLIFE-RELATED CRIME IN ALBERTA

The Alberta Server Intervention Program (ASIP)[3] was launched in 2004. Identity scanners were implemented in drinking establishments in various locations between 2004 and 2007, in order to allow storage of patron identification information (including photographs). Venues have used these systems to track and exclude troublemakers, sharing information among venues by means of computer linked programs. The scanners remain controversial, however, with their use banned at one location by Alberta's Privacy Commission in response to a specific complaint of misuse of information (McIntyre and Landry, 2008). Despite these concerns, some reports attributed significant reductions in violence to installation of the scanners (Cormier, 2008; Kennedy, 2004).

By 2005, awareness of the need for coordination and cooperation at all levels to deal with violence in and around licensed premises led to the establishment of two forums involving the Alberta Gaming and Liquor Commission, government agencies, industry and municipal associations, bar and club owners, police, researchers, and addictions counsellors (Government of Alberta, 2006). Research was also commissioned to identify regulatory and operational best practices (Stockwell, 2008). Subsequent partnership initiatives included the launch of 'Cage your Rage',[4] a public awareness campaign to reduce bar violence, together with the hiring of seven new Liquor Inspectors (*Daily Herald-Tribune*, 2007) and the launch of ProTect,[5] a mandatory training course for security staff based on the 'Safer Bars' programme first developed in Ontario (Graham, Osgood, et al, 2004).

NIGHTLIFE-RELATED CRIME IN OTHER PROVINCES

The following paragraphs summarize some of the main issues relating to nightlife and crime evident from media reports and official publications in three other Canadian cities.

[3] <http://www.aglc.gov.ab.ca/responsibleliquorservice/albertaserverintervention program.asp>.
[4] <http://www.aglc.gov.ab.ca/responsibleliquorservice/cageyourrage.asp>.
[5] <http://www.aglc.gov.ab.ca/responsibleliquorservice/ProTectsecuritystafftraining.asp>.

Toronto, Ontario

According to its official website,[6] Canada's largest city (population five million in the Greater Toronto area) is one of the most multicultural cities in the world and ranked as the safest city in North America. Despite Toronto's relatively low overall crime rate (Bunge et al, 2005; Silver, 2007) media reports of nightlife-related crime and violence are common, especially problems in the city's largest entertainment district (*CBC News*, 2006a; *Globe and Mail*, 2008; Green, 2006; Huffman, 2004; Powell, 2005; Varano, 2006). This area had up to 90 nightclubs and 130 bars and restaurants attracting 30–60,000 nightly patrons on weekends (Burnett, 2007). Noise from venues, violence and illegal activities, rowdyism, littering, graffiti, and vandalism by bar and club patrons, particularly at closing time, have caused problems for residents of the area (Bielski, 2008; Leeder, 2006; Ruryk, 2007).[7,8]

Entertainment districts receive a substantial proportion of media attention, possibly because they serve as 'crime attractors' (Visschedyk, 2008). For example, according to the Toronto Police Chief (Powell, 2007), a third of people charged or victimized in the entertainment district live outside Toronto. However, nightlife-related crime also occurs in other parts of the city (Cairns, 2007) including suburban and industrial areas (Doucette, C, 2006). In one alarming incident at a suburban bar, the owner and manager were charged with various offences after they allegedly put two shooting victims (shot inside the club) outside on the sidewalk, locked the doors and tried to clean up the blood before allowing police access (Lamberti, 2006). Similarly, nightlife-related problems have caused consternation among residents in various areas beyond the entertainment district (Cheney, 2007, Cusenza 1998, Ontario Ministry of Consumer and Commercial Relations, 2000). One study of bar-room aggression found, with other factors controlled, that rates of aggression in suburban bars and clubs were higher than those of comparable city-centre venues (Graham, Bernards, et al, 2006).

Although newspaper reports highlight the most serious and spectacular of nightlife-related crimes, there are no official statistics on the extent of more routine problems. Recent research in large-capacity bars and clubs in Toronto (Graham, Osgood, et al, 2004) suggests that nightlife-related violence may not be as frequent as media reports imply. Observational research in relatively high-risk premises documented moderate (eg, pushing) or severe (eg, punching) aggression in less than one in five visits made late on Friday and Saturday nights in the two-and-a-half hours preceding and following the closure of venues.

Vancouver, British Columbia

The city of Vancouver, British Columbia, has a population of around 600,000 people and more than two million in its region.[9] While the Downtown Eastside is an area known for illicit drugs, prostitution, and crime (Mopas, 2005),[10] nightlife problems

---

[6] <http://www.toronto.ca/toronto_facts/diversity.htm>.
[7] <http://www.toronto.ca/planning/pdf/king_spadina_final_pt1.pdf>.
[8] <http://www.king-spadina.com>.
[9] <http://vancouver.ca/aboutvan.htm>.
[10] <http://en.wikipedia.org/wiki/downtown_Eastside>.

are also associated with bars and clubs in other areas. For example, one newspaper account of a Friday night on Granville Street (one of the main entertainment areas) reported four fights, 'countless' men urinating, heckling of police officers, and people vomiting (Eustace, 2007). Other reported incidents have included a gun battle in a club which left two people dead (*Toronto Sun*, 2003), a fight between two women over a 'bump' on the dance floor in which one slashed the other in the face with broken glass (Lazaruk, 2007), and four women sexually assaulted after their drinks were drugged (Hall, 2007).

Other problems noted in the media include nightclubs owned by gang members (Hall, 2003), gang-related shootings in restaurants and bars (Fong, 2007), illegal drug use by minors at all-night raves (Eustace, 2006), and unlicensed night-spots allegedly operated by organized crime (Bolan, 2007). Issues relating to noise, violence, and other nightclub-related problems have also emerged for Vancouver residents (Bula, 2000) and business owners (Yoo, 2007), although nightclubs are also seen as important sources of employment and revenue (*Vancouver Province*, 2003).

Halifax, Nova Scotia

Halifax is a city of around 400,000 people on the east coast of Canada. Media stories give account of fights, assaults, and deaths related to bars and clubs in the downtown area (Moore, 2008; Patten, 2006). Recent research on nightclub security staff (Rigakos, 2008) provides some indication of the extent of nightlife-associated problems in the city, noting, for example, that on busy nights, 'bouncers' outnumber on-duty police officers by a ratio of ten to one. Security staff who worked in the city's licensed premises were found to be significantly more likely than local police officers to report experiencing physical violence in the past year (Rigakos, 2004). As described in the excerpt below, street violence appears to be closely linked to the club experience, especially among patrons who have been ejected from venues against their will:

> Once banned individuals are outside, doormen are not particularly concerned with what happens to them. They are typically left to their own devices, and bouncers are loath to interfere. They prefer to 'let the police handle it', because drunken revellers on city streets are 'no longer a nightclub issue'—a strange declaration, considering the nightclub produced them, excited them, frustrated them, and then abandoned them. (Rigakos, 2008: 223)

EFFORTS TO ADDRESS NIGHTLIFE-RELATED VIOLENCE IN CANADA

Across the country, provincial licensing authorities, community groups, and police have implemented a variety of solutions to address bar violence, generally similar to many of those undertaken in Alberta (described earlier in this chapter). As described below, these approaches have included controls used historically to manage public-drinking establishments in Canada and elsewhere (Graham, 2005) such as policy and regulatory approaches and enhanced policing, as well as a greater focus on staff training and new approaches targeting specific types of problems.

POLICY AND REGULATORY APPROACHES

In Canada, addressing nightlife-related crime through regulations and restrictions on drinking establishments is a fluid process, generally involving ad hoc responses to critical incidents and public opinion rather than a strategic analysis of the situation. For example, although limiting the number of bars and clubs was a major strategy for controlling nightlife-related problems in the first half of the 20th century (Heron, 2003), this strategy is used less frequently in contemporary Canada. Even though media coverage suggests that a number of communities have proposed such limitations, especially to control areas with very high bar densities,[11] only a handful of communities have implemented even the most temporary of limits or 'freezes' on the number of licences (Mah and Gerein, 2004; *Ottawa Citizen*, 2006). Furthermore, there has been controversy over whether it should be the city or the province that controls the number of venues (Goddard, 2007; Ruryk, 2007; Rusk, 2007 and 2008). These debates echo the jurisdictional wrangling that occurred in Manitoba in the 1880s (described in the quotation from Gray (1995) at the beginning of this chapter).

Traditional methods of control have included restrictions on the hours and days of sale, size and location of establishments, permissible activities, pricing and types of beverage, licence conditions, and legal liability. These types of measures were used in the 20th century, first to marginalize public drinking through strict regulation and later to 'normalize' it through more lenient 'lighter touch' controls. For example, increasingly later closing times have been adopted in the past few decades, with arguments for later closing based on profitability, competitiveness, and tourism, while arguments against focus on increased drunkenness, drunk-driving, and violence (Abbate and Grange 1995; Baglole and Bohn, 2004; Patten, 2006).

Many contemporary policies tend to be 'harm reduction'-oriented, that is, directed toward specific problems, rather than toward the licensing of premises, or alcohol consumption more generally. For example, recent reform of the Ontario Liquor Licence Act included provisions to allow patrons to take drinks into a hallway or washroom in order to protect women from exposure to date rape drugs (Alcohol and Gaming Commission of Ontario, 2007a) and prohibiting sale of Alcohol Without Liquid (AWOL) vaporizers (Alcohol and Gaming Commission of Ontario, 2007b) which are thought to have particular health risks for the consumer.

POLICING AND POLICE-LED INITIATIVES

The need for police resources to control nightlife-related problems has increased in some cities[12] (Bonokoski, 2003; Bula, 2007a; *CBC News*, 2006b; Doucette, K, 2006) and communities often struggle with who should pay for additional policing, as occurred in the case of the West Edmonton Mall. The position adopted by many residents' groups is that the costs should be borne by the drinking establishments rather than the community as a whole (Bielski, 2008; Visschedyk, 2008). As described above, one

---

[11] <http://www.toronto.ca/planning/pdf/king_spadina_final_pt1.pdf>.
[12] <http://ogov.newswire.ca/ontario/GPOE/2007/06/10/c2957.html?lmatch=andlang=_e.html>.

solution in Calgary has been to allow drinking establishments to employ off-duty police officers (McGinn, 2007; Murphy and Clarke, 2005). However, this practice has risks as well as benefits and has been banned in some jurisdictions (Saelhof, 2007; *Winnipeg Free Press*, 2007). In terms of police tactics for preventing nightlife-related crime, the *Toronto Sun*, for example, reports that police review the activity in the entertainment district after every weekend, plan ahead for special occasions (eg, Halloween and New Year's Eve) and increase the number of officers (including vice, parking enforcement, and officers on horseback) on the streets on Friday and Saturday nights at bar closing time (Green, 2006). Police also participate in and often lead community responses and task forces (as described above for Alberta).

Problems relating to police behaviour have also emerged. Just as intoxication among officers who policed the saloons became a problem in 1880s Winnipeg, corruption has been reported within the 21st-century policing of nightlife. For example, the plainclothes unit of the Toronto Police was disbanded and four officers charged after a probe revealed that police had demanded cash from bar owners in Toronto's entertainment district in exchange for advance warning of forthcoming visits from liquor inspectors (*CBC News*, 2004a and 2004b); this led to the establishment of a new team of detectives to police the entertainment district (Huffman, 2004; Powell, 2004). Similarly, complaints about overly aggressive security staff at the West Edmonton Mall led to a police disciplinary hearing concerning the behaviour of the officers who were working alongside the aggressive security staff (Farrell, 2006).

STAFF TRAINING AND PRIVATE POLICING

Training in Responsible Beverage Service (RBS) has been available in Canada for several decades. More recently, provinces have focused on the licensing and training of security staff, such as the mandatory ProTect training in Alberta, mentioned above. Some provinces require criminal-record checks for venue and security managers, and in Manitoba, every new venue licence application must include a security plan.[13] In British Columbia all security staff must be licensed (Cernetig and Hall, 2007).[14]

As in other countries, such as England, private security personnel are now playing an increasing role in the control of nightlife (Hobbs et al, 2005). Private security currently outnumber public police officers in Canada (Swol, 1998) and their role in nightlife policing continues to expand (Mopas, 2005), a result, in part, of decreasing levels of funding for the public police (Murphy and Clarke, 2005). While police in some jurisdictions (eg, Edmonton) appear to have maintained control over most of their nightlife-related functions even when delegated to others, elsewhere control by public police has been considerably weakened (Murphy and Clarke, 2005). The effectiveness of this shift toward private-policing solutions is open to question given that private-security personnel receive considerably less training than public police officers (Murphy and Clarke, 2005; Swol, 1998). Furthermore, questions have been raised regarding whose interests are being protected by private police.

---

[13] <http://www.crfa.ca/news/2008/liquor_changes_on_tap_in_manitoba.asp>.
[14] <http://www.mcscs.jus.gov.on.ca/english/police_serv/PISG/training_testing.html>.

LOCAL ASSOCIATIONS AND BARWATCH PROGRAMMES

Local associations, similar to the 'Alcohol Accords' that operate in Australia and New Zealand (see Chikrizhs, Chapter 18, this volume, and Graham and Homel, 2008) have also emerged as one response to nightlife-related crime. Sometimes these involve bar owners coming together of their own accord (Belanger, 2008; Bula, 2007b; Leeder, 2006), but more often, they form part of a wider police or municipal government-led initiative (Calgary Police Service, 1994; Horwitz, 2008; Ontario Ministry of Consumer and Commercial Relations, 2000), including the promotion of a Barwatch programme (Bradley 1998).[15] Barwatch programmes appear to have originated in the UK where they are known as 'Pubwatch' schemes (MCM Research, 1993). The core function of Barwatch is to establish an agreement among licensees (often working with police) to identify troublemakers, share this information with other licensees, and to deny the identified persons entry to all licensed premises in the area, either for the night on which they have caused problems, or for a longer period of time. Such programmes tend to be popular among bar owners because they focus on individual troublemakers, not on the operating standards of bars (Pursaga, 2007). As described above, however, the police-led Barwatch in Edmonton required much greater commitment from bar owners than a simple agreement to track and inform one another of troublemakers. It resulted in the development of a broader local association tasked with security in and around licensed premises at the West Edmonton Mall.

ENVIRONMENTAL APPROACHES

Closed-circuit television (CCTV) surveillance is not as common in Canada as in other countries, such as the UK, and has often elicited controversy related to privacy and other concerns (Hier et al, 2007; Mopas, 2005). Nonetheless, proposals to install such cameras in nightlife areas have emerged in a number of cities (Bohn, 2006; Hier et al, 2007; Patten, 2006; Verma, 2003) with surveillance systems implemented both by police[16] (Hier et al, 2007; McGinn, 2007) and individual bar owners (Kuxhaus and Santin, 2007; Maughan, 2006).

Most of the focus of transportation options has been on managing taxi services, although at least one community has introduced late-night bus services to transport students back to campus from downtown bars after closing time (Stead, 2004). In Vancouver, police set up a designated taxi stand and insisted that taxi drivers take passengers who wanted to leave the downtown areas between 1.00 and 4.00 am (Bellett, 2007). In a similar initiative in Toronto, 35 taxi drivers were charged in one weekend for various offences from refusing passengers in the entertainment district to demanding payment up-front (*CityNews Staff*, 2008).

Other environmental solutions have also been tried. For example, one establishment in Ottawa, Ontario erected a fence to keep its patrons out of nearby residential areas (Rupert, 1999). Bars in Vancouver agreed not to allow further entries after 2.00 am

---

[15] <http://www.nanaimo.ca/uploadedfiles/Site_Structure/Corporate_Services/Corporate_Administration/Regulation_and_Risk_Management/liq_barwatch.pdf>.
[16] <http://www.torontopolice.on.ca/media/text/20061214-tps_cctv_project.pdf>.

so that queues would disappear before the bars closed (Bellett, 2007),[17] and another Vancouver strategy involved closing some blocks of the main entertainment district to vehicular traffic.[18]

CONCLUSIONS

Although there are no good estimates of actual rates of nightlife-related crime, the recent media and policy literature reviewed here would suggest that many of the nightlife problems first recorded in the 19th century continue to remain salient in the 21st century. Just as the actual relationship between nightlife and crime is difficult to quantify, there is little objective evidence of the effectiveness of various strategies for reducing nightlife-related crime. Although police and media have claimed success for particular measures (Bellett, 2007; Bonokoski, 2003; Calgary Police Service, 1994; Cormier, 2008; *Hamilton Spectator*, 2003; Kennedy, 2004; Loyie, 2003; Stead, 2004; Wood, 2002), these pronouncements have not been backed by strong evidence of effectiveness. Statistics showing reductions in crime are usually unreliable because most preventive initiatives are reactive, being undertaken at times when problems are at their peak, with subsequent reductions often, at least in part, reflecting natural fluctuations.

This is not to say that all responses have proved ineffective, it is merely to point out that a lack of research evidence makes it difficult to confirm the effectiveness of different strategies in order for practitioners to choose between them. To our knowledge, only the Safer Bars programme has been the subject of a formal evaluative study. Safer Bars was shown to be effective in reducing aggressive behaviour in a randomized control trial in large capacity bars and clubs in Toronto (Graham et al, 2005; Graham, Osgood, et al, 2004), however its efficacy in other contexts has not been tested.

One of the primary targets of prevention and often the main impetus for action is the impact of drinking establishments on nearby residents, especially at closing time. The reintroduction of licensed premises following prohibition involved clustering these establishments in poor, marginalized communities (Popham, 1982). This may have minimized complaints for a time, but issues of neighbourhood amenity seem to have become more salient in recent years as wealthier, more powerful people take up residence in the inner-city neighbourhoods where drinking establishments have traditionally been located. Neighbourhood impact has also been apparent in suburban areas where mini-entertainment areas operate, such as the cluster of establishments at the West Edmonton Mall.

In addition to the effects on residents, the growth of drinking establishments, especially large capacity nightclubs in close proximity to one another, results in problems such as conflict associated with movement between bars, in addition to that which

---

17 See the discussion of 'lock outs' in Chapter 18, this volume (Australia).

18 <http://www.mayorsamsullivan.ca/mayor-and-councillor-welcomes-success-of-vpd-project-to-reduce-disorder-in-entertainment-district.html>.

may be associated with individual establishments. This clustering phenomenon can pose significant problems for policing by making it more difficult to link problems to specific establishments in order to apply sanctions, although some have argued that clustering can actually make policing and provision of transportation easier (Livingston et al, 2007). As in 1880s Winnipeg, the police bear a large share of the burden of nightlife-related crime and are usually integral to local preventative efforts. What is clear from the available evidence, however, is that the role of the police varies among communities and over time, and many of the same tensions and ambiguities arise repeatedly. Who should pay for extra policing if it is needed in an entertainment district? Is it good or bad policy to allow bars and nightclubs to employ off-duty police officers? What is the appropriate balance between private and public policing and what should their working relationship be? What are the acceptable boundaries of personal privacy when using new surveillance technologies to monitor the movements of nightlife patrons? What forms of relationship should exist between police and the owners and staff of licensed premises?

Private policing and its increased use is probably the least explored of the recent approaches to preventing nightlife problems. Within a relatively short time period, the role of maintaining order in drinking establishments in Canada has become the almost exclusive domain of security staff, reinforced by provincial decisions to require their presence[19] and to enact training and licensing legislation.[20] Internationally, there is no evidence of positive impacts from this unprecedented growth in the private policing of bars and clubs and at least some evidence that the macho culture of security staff may actually encourage violence (Graham and Homel, 2008; Hobbs et al, 2002, 2003, and 2007; Lister et al, 2000 and 2001; Monaghan, 2002, 2003, and 2004; Wells et al, 1998; Winlow, 2001; Winlow et al, 2001). Moreover, more general concerns have been raised (Rigakos, 2005) regarding the implications for accountability and the social contract of replacing public with private policing.

Along with the greater focus on the role of security staff in drinking establishments, another non-traditional approach adopted in recent years is the increased emphasis on staff training. In much of the early literature on public drinking, the role of staff in preventing (or encouraging) violence and even drunkenness was largely ignored (Graham and Homel, 2008). Canadians were pioneers in the development and evaluation of Responsible Beverage Service training (Gliksman et al, 1993) and such training has become standard, if not mandatory, in most provinces. Recently, bar-staff training has been expanded to include communication and problem-management skills to prevent and better manage violence and other problems (eg, Safer Bars—see Graham, Osgood et al, 2004; ProTect[21]). This increasing focus on staff training may well be a necessary outcome of the deregulation of barroom environments that occurred in the latter half of the 20th century.

Other contemporary approaches to addressing nightlife problems include bar-owners' associations, community coordinating groups (typically including police, bar

---

[19] <http://www.toronto.ca/planning/pdf/king_spadina_final_pt1.pdf>.
[20] <http://www.aglc.gov.ab.ca/responsibleliquorservice/ProTectsecuritystafftraining.asp>.
[21] <http://www.aglc.gov.ab.ca/responsibleliquorservice/ProTectsecuritystafftraining.asp>.

owners, municipal authorities, sometimes representatives of residents' associations, and others) and a greater focus on the environmental features of the area surrounding licensed premises. Although the associations and community groups tend to focus on traditional targets for prevention, namely banning individual troublemakers (Heron, 2003), these associations reflect a change in orientation from historical times where bars were viewed solely as disreputable enterprises. Today one sees a move toward community 'ownership' of nightlife with broad awareness of its cultural and economic benefits, as well as its problems. The greater focus on the environment, including use of CCTV and enhanced transportation options, reflects one of the major issues of contemporary nightlife, namely a large proportion of problems occurring on the streets particularly after the bars close. Street problems appeared to have been less evident during the period of Canadian history when bars were scarce, people were obliged to sit at tables that held no more than four people in order to be served a drink, and music, dancing, and other activities were not permitted.

In sum, the quote at the beginning of this chapter, describing late 19th-century western Canada, has highlighted a number of themes that remain important in Canada and other countries today. First, it makes it clear that the link between drinking in licensed premises and crime and violence has existed for some time. Secondly, it suggests that controls often prove ineffective and sometimes even backfire. Thirdly, although problems relating to drinking establishments often become the responsibility of the police, police may have neither the powers, nor the capability, to handle such problems and may even contribute to them. Finally, the quote illustrates how the sale and consumption of alcohol and its relationship to the governance of nightlife involve many competing interests.

REFERENCES

All internet sources were accessible 20 August 2008

ABBATE, G and GRANGE, M (1995) 'Ontario considers extending hours of licensed bars, current 1 a.m. closing earliest in country, but critics fear increase in drunk driving', *Globe and Mail*. 16 December, <http://www.lexisnexis.com/us/lnacademic/search/homesubmitForm.do>.

ALCOHOL and GAMING COMMISSION OF ONTARIO (2007a) 2006–2007 *Annual Report*, <http://www.agco.on.ca/pdf/Non-Forms/20062007AnnualE.pdf>.

—— (2007b) *Information Bulletin No 013, Liquor Licensing Act Regulatory Amendments*, <http://www.agco.on.ca/pdf/Non-Forms/9013B_e.pdf>.

BAGLOLE, J and BOHN, G (2004) 'Bar owners win the day at council: Vancouver will retain 3 a.m. closing despite complaints', *The Vancouver Sun*, 19 November, B1.

BELANGER, J (2008) 'Bar owners band against violence', *London Free Press*, 17 January, C1.

BELLETT, G (2007) 'Granville Street policing "pays off"', *Vancouver Sun*, 6 June, B1.

BENSON, D and ARCHER, J (2002) 'An ethnographic study of sources of conflict between young men in the context of the night out', *Psychology, Evolution and Gender*, 4, 3–30.

BESSERER, S and TRAINOR, C (2000) *Criminal Victimisation in Canada*, 1999, Statistics Canada (catalogue no 85-002-XIE, vol, 20/10), Ottawa, Canada: Canadian Centre for Justice Statistics, Minister of Industry.

BIELSKI, Z (2008) 'Club district no party for fed-up residents', *National Post*, 26 January, A1.

BLAIS, T (2000) 'Crowds increased after warning, cop tells hearing', *Edmonton Sun*, 2 December, 18.

BOHN, G (2006) 'Crackdown', *Vancouver Sun*, 8 November, B1.

BOLAN, K (2007) 'Drink inc.; How illegal bars are fuelling organised crime in the lower mainland', *Vancouver Sun*, 28 April, A1.

BONOKOSKI, M (2003) 'Club squad's NRG pays off: Halton cops keep tight rein on night spot', *Toronto Sun*, 4 May, 14.

BRADLEY, K (1998) 'Managers praise Barwatch: Nightclub cameras cut violence and lawsuits', *Edmonton Sun*, 13 December, 14.

BULA, F (2000) 'As neighbours fume, noisy club points to city's approval process', *Vancouver Sun*, 17 July, B4.

—— (2007a) 'Police seek extra money for patrolling entertainment district', *Vancouver Sun*, 8 November, B2.

—— (2007b) 'We've a plan to tackle mayhem: Bar owners', *Vancouver Sun*, 26 March, A2.

BUNGE, VP, JOHNSON, H and BALDÉ, TA (2005) *Exploring Crime Patterns in Canada*, Statistics Canada (catalogue no 85-561-MIE, no 005), Ottawa, Canada: Canadian Centre for Justice Statistics, Minister of Industry.

BURNETT, T (2007) 'The city's entertainment district used to make headlines for all the right reasons; Now it's too often merely the scene of the crime', *Toronto Sun*, 10 January, 10.

CAIRNS, A (2007) 'Not so cool; Police: During fight at nightclub, suspect accidentally shot self and pal', *Toronto Sun*, 5 January, 5.

CALGARY POLICE SERVICE (1994) 'Police lead effort to improve safety of popular nightspot: Electric Avenue—"The Place to Go"', *Problem Solving Quarterly*, 7/6–8, Washington, DC: Police Executive Research Forum, <http://www.popcenter.org/library/awards/goldstein/1994/94–03(w).pdf>.

CAMPBELL, RA (2001) *Sit Down and Drink Your Beer: Regulating Vancouver's beer parlours, 1925–1954*, Toronto: University of Toronto Press.

CBC News (2004a) 'Four cops arrested in bribery case', 4 May, <http://www.cbc.ca/canada/Toronto/story/2004/05/04/to_cops20040504.html>.

—— (2004b) 'More charges in kickback scandal', 5 July, <http://www.cbc.ca/canada/Toronto/story/2004/07/05/to_copcharges20040705.html>.

—— (2006a) 'Nightclub shooting victim was intended target: Police', 18 July, <http://www.cbc.ca/canada/toronto/story/2006/07/18/shooting-volume.html>.

—— (2006b) 'Police take aim at Vancouver's entertainment district', 7 November, <http://www.cbc.ca/canada/british-columbia/story/2006/11/07/bc-police-bars.html>.

CERNETIG, M and HALL, N (2007) 'Victoria proposes to license bouncers: Public complaints process to be established', *Vancouver Sun*, 13 March, B1.

CITYNEWS STAFF (2008) 'Cops launch crackdown on cab drivers who refuse to pick up passengers', 14 April, <http://www.citynews.ca/news/news_21695.aspx>.

CHENEY, P (2007) 'It takes a city to kill a bad liquor licence: Getting rid of an unruly bar in Toronto isn't easy', *Globe and Mail*, 10 February, M1.

CORMIER, R (2008) 'Nightclub vows to appeal ruling on id scan—Bar owners argue system helps ban violent customers', *Edmonton Journal*, 22 February, B2.

COSPER, R, OKRAKU, I, and NEUMANN, B (1987) 'Tavern going in Canada: A national survey of regulars at public drinking establishments', *Journal of Studies on Alcohol*, 48, 252–9.

COWAN, P (2001) 'Two cops guilty of discreditable conduct', *Edmonton Sun*, 9 June, 4.

CUSENZA, S (1998) 'Organising to reduce neighborhood alcohol problems: A frontline account', *Contemporary Drug Problems*, 25, 99–111.

Daily Herald-Tribune (2007) 'More liquor inspectors will be patrolling bars to try to curb growing violence', 12 November, 7. <http://cgi.bowesonline.com/pedro.php?id=1&x=story&xid=353424>.

DAUVERGNE, M and LI, G (2006) *Homicide in Canada, 2005*, Statistics Canada (Catalogue no 85-002-XIE, vol, 26/6), Ottawa, Canada: Canadian Centre for Justice Statistics, Minister of Industry.

DOUCETTE, C (2006) 'Gunfire at bar last straw? Bid to have its licence revoked', *Toronto Sun*, 14 April, 5.

DOUCETTE, K (2006) 'Halifax violence summit wins provincial commitment for more police by April', *Canadian Press Newswire*, 9 November, <http://proquest.umi.com/pqdweb?did=1159857241andsid=3andFmt=3andclientId=11263andRQT=309andVName=PQD>.

DYCK, N (1980) 'Booze, barrooms and scrapping: Masculinity and violence in a western Canadian town', *Canadian Journal of Anthropology*, 1, 191–8.

Edmonton Journal (2006) 'Bars should lose their licence if drugs sold there: Solicitor General', 12 August, <http://proquest.umi.com/pqdweb?did=1100574961andsid=2andFmt=3andclientId=11263andRQT=309andVName=PQD>.

—— (2007) 'Late-night open-air urinals working well on Whyte Ave., Official Says', 8 September, B12.

EDMONTON POLICE SERVICE (2006) *Report to the Edmonton Police Commission, June 16, 2006*, <http://www.edmontonpolicecommission.com/pdfs/meetings/june2006-5-3.pdf>.

Edmonton Sun (2007) 'Walk-by stabbing', 11 November, 46.

EUSTACE, C (2006) 'RCMP on drug patrol at today's rave scene', *Vancouver Sun*, 4 November, F1.

—— (2007) 'Granville Street is like a "ticking time bomb"', *Vancouver Sun*, 26 March, A1.

FARRELL, J (2006) 'Hearing to examine police policy', *Edmonton Journal*, 16 September, B6.

FERNANDEZ, P (2007) 'Top cop promotes bar help: Beaton touts working with them to curb violence', *Calgary Sun*, 9 January, 5.

FONG, P (2007) 'Police get new weapon to fight Vancouver street war: Officers to arrest bar patrons linked to gang activities', *South China Morning Post*, 8 October, 12.

GANNON, M and Mihorean, K (2005) *Criminal Victimisation in Canada, 2004*, Statistics Canada (Catalogue no 85-002-XPE, vol, 25/7), Ottawa, Canada: Canadian Centre for Justice Statistics, Minister of Industry.

GEREIN, K (2003) 'On cost of policing, treat us like Whyte, WEM tells city', *Edmonton Journal*, 28 October, B3.

—— (2005) 'Whyte Avenue bar scene no better under new rules', *Edmonton Journal*, 20 September, B3.

GERSON, LW and PRESTON, DA (1979) 'Alcohol consumption and the incidence of violent crime', *Journal of Studies on Alcohol*, 40, 307–12.

GLIKSMAN, L, SINGLE, E, McKENZIE, D, DOUGLAS, R, BRUNET, S and MOFFAT, K (1993) 'The role of alcohol providers in prevention: An evaluation of a server intervention programme', *Addiction*, 88, 1189–97.

Globe and Mail (2008) 'Two men leaving club stabbed with bottle', 21 April, A19.

GODDARD, J (2007) 'Club plan sparks infighting: Lawsuit within Ontario liquor licence, Regulator argues for removal from entertainment district', *Toronto Star*, 22 August, A7.

GOVERNMENT OF ALBERTA (2006) *Alberta Roundtable on Violence In and Around Licensed Premises: Exploring the issues, 22–23 November, 2005 and 31 March, 2006*, <http://www.aglc.ab.ca/pdf/news/ALGCRoundtableReportWeb.pdf>.

GRAHAM, K (2005) 'Public drinking then and now', *Contemporary Drug Problems*, 32, 45–56.

—— BERNARDS, S, OSGOOD, DW and WELLS, S (2006) 'Bad nights or bad bars? Multilevel analysis of environmental predictors of aggression in late-night large-capacity bars and clubs', *Addiction*, 101, 1569–80.

—— and HOMEL, R (2008) *Raising the Bar: Preventing aggression in and around bars, pubs and clubs*, Cullompton: Willan.

—— JELLEY, J, and PURCELL, J (2005) 'Training bar staff in preventing and managing aggression in licensed premises', *Journal of Substance Use*, 10, 48–61.

—— OSGOOD, DW, WELLS, S and STOCKWELL, T (2006) 'To what extent is intoxication associated with aggression in bars? A multilevel analysis', *Journal of Studies on Alcohol*, 67, 382–90.

—— —— ZIBROWSKI, E, PURCELL, J, GLIKSMAN, L, LEONARD, K, PERNANEN, K, SALTZ, RF and TOOMEY, TL (2004) 'The effect of the *Safer Bars* programme on physical aggression in bars: Results of a randomised controlled trial', *Drug and Alcohol Review*, 23, 31–41.

—— TREMBLAY, PF, WELLS, S, PERNANEN, K, PURCELL, J and JELLEY, J (2006) 'Harm and intent and the nature of aggressive behaviour: Measuring naturally-occurring aggression in barroom settings', *Assessment*, 13, 280–96.

—— and WELLS, S (2003) '"Somebody's gonna get their head kicked in tonight!" Aggression among young males in bars – a question of values?', *British Journal of Criminology*, 43, 546–66.

—— WELLS, S and JELLEY, J (2002) 'The social context of physical aggression among adults', *The Journal of Interpersonal Violence*, 17: 64–83.

GRAY, JH (1995) *Booze: When whisky ruled the west*, Calgary, Alberta: Fifth House.

GREEN, S (2006) 'T.O. cops on top of it: Weekend mayhem in entertainment district sends 11 people to hospital', *Toronto Sun*, 14 November, 8.

HALL, N (2003) 'Hells angels member to open nightclub in Gastown', *Vancouver Sun*, 7 November, A1.

—— (2007) 'Police seek more details in date-rape drugging case', *Vancouver Sun*, 20 September, B2.

Hamilton Spectator (2003) 'Police, citizens share awards: NRG project, citizens on patrol, repeat-offender effort all win honours and reduce crime', 26 July, N01.

HERON, C (2003) *Booze: A distilled history*, Toronto, Canada: Between the Lines.

—— (2005) 'The boys and their booze: Masculinities and public drinking in working-class Hamilton, 1890–1946', *The Canadian Historical Review*, 86, 411–52.

HIER, SP, GREENBERG, J, WALBY, K and LETT, D (2007) 'Media, communication and the establishment of public camera surveillance programmes in Canada', *Media, Culture and Society*, 29, 727–51.

HOBBS, D, HADFIELD, P, LISTER, S and WINLOW, S (2002) '"Door Lore": The art and economics of intimidation', *British Journal of Criminology*, 42, 352–70.

—— —— —— —— (2003) *Bouncers: Violence and Governance in the Night-time Economy*, Oxford: Oxford University Press.

—— —— —— —— (2005) 'Violence and control in the night-time economy', *European Journal of Crime, Criminal Law and Criminal Justice*, 13, 89–102.

—— O'BRIEN, K and WESTMARLAND, L (2007) 'Connecting the gendered door: women, violence and doorwork', *The British Journal of Sociology*, 58, 21–38.

HORWITZ, L (2008) 'Clean, safe downtown should be city priority', *Windsor Star*, 7 January, A.7.

HUFFMAN, T (2004) 'Nightclub owners rapped by police', *Toronto Star*, 17 August, B02.

KENNEDY, A (2004) 'ID scanners cutting down on rowdies at corral', *Daily Herald-Tribune*, 18 August, 3.

KENNEDY, LW and FORDE, DR (1990) 'Routine activities and crime: An analysis of victimisation in Canada', *Criminology*, 28, 137–51.

KENT, G (2007a) 'New bartenders shut down private club', *Edmonton Journal*, 7 February, B3.

—— (2007b) 'Council to double fines for Whyte Avenue rowdiness', *Edmonton Journal*, 10 April, B3.

KUXHAUS, D and SANTIN, A (2007) 'Clubs may be required to beef up security', *Winnipeg Free Press*, 24 July, A6.

LAGHI, B (1998) 'Why pubs put patrons in the picture—Will a new take on video surveillance reduce personal privacy as well as rowdiness?', *Globe and Mail*, 26 May, A2.

LAMBERTI, R (2006) 'Adding insult to injury: Danforth Club accused of giving shooting victims the bum's rush', *Toronto Sun*, 13 October, 5.

LAZARUK, S (2007) 'Mutilated victim not enough to convict in nightclub attack', *The Province*, <http://www.canada.com/theprovince/news/story.html?id=ee259b7f-bbfe-4cb2-a75b-62733a6abc92>.

Leeder, J. (2006) 'The music doesn't rule the night. Talks often produce compromise solutions; Residents send bar owners a message. Work with us to reduce noise conflict', *Toronto Star*, 26 July, B.01.

LISTER, S, HADFIELD, P, HOBBS, D and WINLOW, S (2001) 'Accounting for bouncers: Occupational licensing as a mechanism for regulation', *Criminology and Criminal Justice*, 1, 363–84.

—— HOBBS, D, HALL, S and WINLOW, S (2000) 'Violence in the night-time economy. Bouncers: The reporting, recording and prosecution of assaults', *Policing and Society*, 10, 383–402.

LIVINGSTON, M, CHIKRITZHS, T and Room R (2007) 'Changing the density of alcohol outlets to reduce alcohol-related problems', *Drug and Alcohol Review*, 26, 553–62.

LOYIE, F (2003) 'No more brawls at the Mall', *Edmonton Journal*, 8 February, B9.

McGINN, D (2007) 'It's hard out there for a bouncer: Club security has gone from fistfights to brass knuckles and bulletproof vests', *Globe and Mail*, 17 February, M4.

McINTYRE, D and LANDRY, F (2008) '"Chalk one up for the bad guys": Bar owner says ID scanner banned by Privacy Commissioner had improved safety', *Edmonton Sun*, 21 February, 23.

McKEEN, S (2004) 'Testosterone and too much alcohol a dangerous mix', *Edmonton Journal*, 12 January, B.1.

MAH, B and GEREIN, K (2004) 'Bars fear city rules will kill them', *Edmonton Journal*, 30 October, A3.

MARQUIS, G (2000) 'Civilised drinking: Alcohol and society in New Brunswick, 1945–1975', *Journal of the Canadian Historical Association*, 11, 173–203.

—— (2003) '"A reluctant concession to modernity": Alcohol and modernisation in the Maritimes, 1945–1980', *Acadiensis*, 32, 31–59.

MATTSON, A (2008) 'Downtown surveillance cameras a concern to wary Calgary resident', *Calgary Journal*, 2 April, <http://www.calgaryjournal.ca/detail.php?id=925>.

MAUGHAN, C (2006) 'Man gunned down outside bar—Why should we be afraid?', *Toronto Star*, 3 July, B01.

MCM Research (1993) *Keeping the Peace: A guide to the prevention of alcohol-related disorder*, London, England: Portman Group.

MONAGHAN, LF (2002) 'Regulating 'unruly' bodies: Work tasks, conflict and violence in britain's night-time economy', *British Journal of Sociology*, 53, 403–29.

—— (2003) 'Danger on the doors: Bodily risk in a demonised occupation', *Health, Risk and Society*, 5, 11–31.

—— (2004) 'Doorwork and legal risk: Observations from an embodied ethnography', *Social and Legal Studies*, 13, 453–80.

MONTGOMERY, S (2006) '3 shot dead in Edmonton club: Residents used to seeing fights at bar. Recent killings in city linked to gangs', *Toronto Star*, 30 October, A6.

MOORE, O (2008) 'Cheap booze comes with a heavy price', *Globe and Mail*, 11 January, L1.

MOPAS, M (2005) 'Policing in Vancouver's Downtown Eastside: A case study', in D Cooley (ed), *Re-Imagining Policing in Canada*, Toronto: University of Toronto Press, 92–139.

MURPHY, C and CLARKE, C (2005) 'Policing communities and communities of policing: A comparative study of policing and security in two Canadian communities', in D Cooley (ed), *Re-Imagining Policing in Canada*, Toronto: University of Toronto Press, 209–59.

O'DONNELL, S (2003) '$20M tax bill should buy police PROTECTION, WEM says', *Edmonton Journal*, 19 September, B1.

ONTARIO MINISTRY OF CONSUMER AND COMMERCIAL RELATIONS (2000) *Building Safer Communities: Safer communities through co-operative enforcement (discussion paper)*, <http://www.ontla.on.ca/library/repository/mon/ont/Cc/2000/BldgSaferComm.pdf>.

Ottawa Citizen (2006) 'Council freezes opening of new clubs in Market', 24 August, B.5.

OUIMET, M (2002) 'Explaining the American and Canadian crime "drop" in the 1990s', *Canadian Journal of Criminology*, 44, 33–50.

PATTEN, M (2006) 'Halifax stabbing sparks debate on bar closing. U.S. sailor was stabbed to death during weekend fight outside popular nightclub', *Globe and Mail*, 7 November, A6.

PERNANEN, K (1991) *Alcohol in Human Violence*, New York: The Guilford Press.

—— COUSINEAU, MM, BROCHU, S and SUN, F (2002) *Proportions of Crimes Associated with Alcohol and other Drugs in Canada*, Ottawa, Canada: Canadian Centre on Substance Abuse.

PHAIR, M (2007) *Knives and Violence: Report for Community Services Committee*, 26 February, <http://webdocs.edmonton.ca/OcctopusDocs/Public/Complete/Reports/CS/Elected-1995/2007–02–26/2007PDD004%20–%20Knives%20and%20Violence%20(M.%20Phair).doc.>.

POPHAM, RE (1962) 'The urban tavern: Some preliminary remarks', *Addictions*, 9, 16–28.

—— (1982) *Working Papers on the Tavern 3: The contemporary tavern*, Substudy, 1232, Toronto: Addiction Research Foundation.

POWELL, B (2004) 'Clubland's new sheriff', *Toronto Star*, 6 August, B03.

—— (2005) 'Long nights loom for cops on clubland beat. Nightclub district a policing puzzle', *Toronto Star*, 23 April, B1.

—— (2007) 'Merchants pick up the pieces: it's not just club goers and police who deal with the aftermath of a clubland shooting spree', *Toronto Star*, 3 November, A06.

PURCELL, J and GRAHAM, K (2005) 'A Typology of Toronto nightclubs at the turn of the millennium', *Contemporary Drug Problems*, 32, 131–67.

PURSAGA, J (2007) 'City-wide bar ban sought: List of offenders needed says club security boss', *Winnipeg Sun*, 24 October, 8.

RATCLIFFE, WD and NUTTER, RW (1979) *Drinking in Edmonton Taverns and Lounges*, Alberta: Final report to the Alberta Alcoholism and Drug Abuse Commission.

—— —— HEWITT, D, CAVERHILL, KM, FLANDERS, PL and GRUBER, GP (1980) *Amenities and Drinking Behaviors in Beverage Rooms*, Alberta: Report to the Alberta Alcoholism and Drug Abuse Commission.

RESPONSIBLE HOSPITALITY INSTITUTE (2006) *Edmonton-Old Strathcona Leadership Summit: Planning for Development Summary Report, June 5–6, 2006, June 11, 2006*, <http://www.rhiweb.org/edmonton/roundtable/report.pdf>.

RIGAKOS, GS (2004) 'Nightclub security and surveillance', *Canadian Review of Policing Research*, 1, 54–60.

—— (2005) 'Beyond public–private: Towards a new typology of policing', in D Cooley (ed), *Re-Imagining Policing in Canada*, Toronto: University of Toronto Press, 260–319.

—— (2008) *Nightclub: Bouncers, risk, and the spectacle of consumption*, Montreal: McGill-Queen's University Press.

RUPERT, J (1999) '13 arrested after brawl at *Gatineau* nightclub: Two face assault charges after violent melee in parking lot', *Ottawa Citizen*, 17 October, A11.

RURYK, Z (2007) 'Councillor urges lid on nightclub district: Noise levels disturb residents', *Toronto Sun*, 5 May, 19.

RUSK, J (2007) 'Huge nightclub struggles to open: 55,000-square foot *Circa* facing unusual appeal of its liquor licence', *Globe and Mail*, 24 August, 11.

—— (2008) 'Gatien wins ruling on liquor licence', *Globe and Mail*, 28 March, A12.

SAELHOF, T (2007) 'Club cop cuts "big problem"', *Calgary Sun*, 29 March, 4.

SANDS, A (2003) 'WEM bars should pay to combat brawls: Cops; taxpayers foot bill now', *Edmonton Sun*, 2 March, 4.

SILVER, W (2007) *Crime Statistics in Canada*, 2006, Statistics Canada (Catalogue no 85-002-XIE, vol, 27/5), Ottawa, Canada: Canadian Centre for Justice Statistics, Ministry of Industry.

STEAD, H (2004) 'Downtown violence waning, city police statistics suggest', *Guelph Mercury*, 12 March, A3.

STOCKWELL, T (2008) *Operator and Regulatory Best Practices in Preventing and Responding to Violence in and Around Licensed Premises: A review of Australian and Canadian research*, Report commissioned by the Alberta Gaming and Liquor Commission, Edmonton, Alberta.

SWOL, K (1998) *Private Security and Public Policing in Canada*, Statistics Canada (Catalogue no 85-002-XIE, vol 18/13), Ottawa: Canadian Centre for Justice Statistics, Ministry of Industry.

TOMSEN, S (1997) 'A top night out: Social protest, masculinity and the culture of drinking violence', *British Journal of Criminology*, 37, 990–1002.

Toronto Sun (2003) 'Club gunfight leaves 2 dead: Vancouver cops busy grilling 70 witnesses', 17 August, 19.

TUCK, M (1989) *Drinking and Disorder: A study of non-metropolitan violence*, Home Office Research Study, 108: London: HMSO, 11–103.

Vancouver Province, (2003) 'Millions invested on club row', 14 August, A40.

VARANO, L (2006) 'Holiday shooting renews calls for crackdown on nightclubs', *National Post*, 28 December, A14.

VERMA, S (2003) 'Police claim cameras can help fight crime', *Toronto Star*, 7 August, A17.

VISSCHEDYK, N (2008) 'Men arrested in violent entertainment district sex attack', *National Post*, 4 January, <http://network.nationalpost.com/np/blogs/toronto/archive/2008/01/04/men-arrested-in-violent-entertainment-district-attack.aspx>.

WALTON, D (2001) 'Police plan to install street-watch cameras', *Globe and Mail*, 22 June, A6.

WARD, J (1998) 'Cop bashed, 3 stabbed in mall brawl—30 people scrap as 300 more watch,' *Edmonton Sun*, 17 August, 4.

WELLS, S, GRAHAM, K and WEST, P (1998) '"The Good, the Bad and the Ugly": Responses by security staff to aggressive incidents in public drinking settings', *Journal of Drug Issues*, 28, 817–36.

WEMASIST (West Edmonton Mall Area Stakeholders Integrated Service Team) (2004) August update, <http://www.edmonton.ca/CommPeople/wemasist_update_august_19_stakeholders.pdf>.

WHITE, T (2003) 'Bar stabbing "raises red flag": Incident second in six weeks', *Calgary Herald*, 29 September, B1.

WINLOW, S (2001) *Badfellas: Crime, tradition and new masculinities*, Oxford: Berg.

——— HOBBS, D, LISTER, S and HADFIELD, P (2001) 'Get ready to duck: Bouncers and the realities of ethnographic research on violent groups', *British Journal of Criminology*, 41, 536–48.

Winnipeg Free Press (2007) 'Blaming police for nightclub mess makes no sense', 23 October, A3.

WOOD, M (2002) 'City to target bar strips: Licensing motion eyed as way to curb Calgary's nightclub bloodshed', *Calgary Sun,* 14 April, 4.

YOO, C (2007) 'Vancouver violence puts end to 60-year history', *Globe and Mail*, 15 November, A17.

ZWARUN, S (1978) 'The (well-scrubbed) face on the barroom floor', *MacLean's*, 20 March, 22–33.

15

HONG KONG

Karen Joe Laidler

INTRODUCTION

From atop Victoria Peak, busloads of Chinese tourists from the mainland peer down on Hong Kong's hazy sunset and skyline, greyed by the winds of Southern China's industrial pollution. Before them, they bare witness to Deng's call—'to get rich is glorious'—and take in the monumental office skyscrapers, shopping malls, and 60-story luxury apartment complexes. The first location mainland tourists zoom in on is the impressive Central District, the financial and political heart of the city. Here numerous mirror-windowed skyscrapers vie for recognition. The latest addition, the International Finance Center (IFC) 2, at 88 stories, stands as the tallest building in Hong Kong, surpassing the tip of the pyramidal atrium at the 78th floor of Central Plaza. At dusk, office lights dim, and neon lights flicker on, jettisoning and reflecting rainbows of colour onto Hong Kong's waterfront. The neon lights of the Central Plaza glow, changing colour every 15 minutes to keep the public informed of the precise time. The expressway is jammed with commuters in Mercedes Benzs, BMWs, and other luxury sedans, red and green taxis, beige-coloured mini-buses, and multi-coloured double-decker buses, making their way to the Hong Kong Island cross-harbour tunnel and the residential areas of Kowloon and the New Territories. This spectacular view reinforces what many mainland Chinese have imagined from their controlled exposure to the glamorous and financially successful Hong Kong promoted in China's state-censored media.

Since the British handover of Hong Kong to China in 1997, the number of mainland visitors has climbed largely due to government efforts to encourage cross-border economic and cultural exchange. The cross-border exchange has been gradual, first permitting limited and controlled group travel and later, in 2003, introducing the individual visitor's visa. In 2007, over 15.5 million of Hong Kong's 28.2 million visitors travelled from the mainland (Hong Kong Government, 2008). Beyond its status as a major international financial centre, Hong Kong has the added appeal of being regarded as one of the safest cities in the world (UN Habitat, 2007). Police and victimization data are consistent in showing that the city's crime rate is low, even compared to other Asian locales like Singapore and Japan (UN Habitat, 2007). The overall crime rate has been relatively constant over the past decade, and in 2007, the police recorded 1,167 crimes per 100,000 of the population (Hong Kong Police, 2008). The violent crime rate is also low with the police reporting 216 violent crimes per 100,000. Much of this violence is non-lethal. The annual number of recorded murders has remained under 70 for the past decade, and reached a low of 18 in 2007. This is all the more remarkable given that Hong Kong's 6.9 million residents live in highly crowded conditions with a population density of 6,422 people per km, ranking among the highest in the world (UN Population Division, 2006).

Despite its reputation for safety, Hong Kong is not without crime and disorder. The government has been mired in the increasingly visible problem of domestic violence, ignited in 2004, when a Hong Kong husband killed his migrant mainland wife and twin daughters. Since then, a number of family murder/suicides have occurred involving Hong Kong husbands married to migrant women from mainland China (*South China Morning Post* (SCMP), 2007a). Although the government has introduced a number of legal and welfare initiatives, social workers complain of high caseloads (SCMP, 2008a), police indicate a 60 per cent increase in reported domestic violence from 2006 to 2007 (Hong Kong Police, 2008), and the media blame the stress and violence at home on the growing disparity between rich and poor (SCMP, 2007b).[1] Night-drifting among young people has been another outcome of the increasing economic divide. Teenaged night-drifters, faced with everyday boredom and alienated family and school relations, gather in the evening in various public places where there is little chance of informal and formal surveillance (Lee, 2000). Much of their time is spent 'hanging around' which, according to social workers' observations, involves vandalizing public property, chasing and fighting each other, flirting, smoking, swearing, drinking beer, and sometimes being recruited by triad-affiliated gangs (Lee, 2000 and 2005).

Triads have had a long-standing presence in Hong Kong's crime scene; originally organized as secret political societies, triad networks gradually mutated into criminal syndicates in a corrupt and symbiotic relationship with the police. After an aggressive assault on corruption in the late 1970s, the triads transformed into smaller, loosely organized affiliations (Chu, 2005). Today, triad activities are opportunistic and enterprising; they range from involvement in traditional crimes such as vice, drugs distribution, gambling, and protection, to the creation of new legitimate monopolies and markets, including interior decorating, the sale of new residential flats, and investment in the night-time entertainment industry (Chu, 2005). The changing nature of this latter sphere of business forms the central focus of this chapter.

---

[1] Hong Kong's Gini-coefficient, an indicator of income disparity, rose from 0.483 in 1996 to 0.500 in 2006 (Hong Kong Census and Statistics Department, 2007). By comparison, the disparity, as reflected in the Gini-coefficient, is lower in China (47.0 in 2007), the United Kingdom (34.0 in 2005), Australia (32.5 in 2006) and Canada (32.1 in 2005) (CIA, 2008).

CULTURAL CONTEXT

Drugs and prostitution have played a central role in Hong Kong's nightlife, dating back to its early colonial days. Government policy toward these two dimensions of nightlife has swung from legalization and regulated control to criminalization. This is most clear in the case of drugs. If the British had not seized upon the profitable opportunities of the opium trade, Hong Kong would most likely be a very different place today (Booth, 1996). For the British, opium offered the possibility of revenue and the furthering of its empire in Asia. In 1844, the colonial government legislated to gain control over Hong Kong's domestic consumption, selecting one 'opium farm' as the official source of the drugs' manufacture and distribution (Joe Laidler, 2005; Miners, 1983; Traver, 1992). Three years later, having been unable to enforce their monopoly, the same authorities introduced a licensing system for opium sales. By 1858, the colonial government reverted to the monopoly on farms and licensed dens, thereby increasing its revenues and protecting its market from underground smuggling and illegal sales.

These twin objectives—revenue and the protection of markets—were particularly important given the influx of political and economic refugees, many of who were opium users (Booth, 1996; Joe Laidler, Hodson and Traver, 2000; Traver, 1992). Yet opium's attraction was not only among the impoverished; it cut across class boundaries. The Chinese elite considered its purchase and consumption a mark of wealth, status, and a social aphrodisiac (Booth, 1996; Dikotter, Laamann and Xun, 2004). The colonial government's reliance on the revenue generated from opium increased over the next 60 years, peaking in 1918 when it accounted for 46 per cent of its total revenue (Joe Laidler, Hodson, and Traver, 2000; Traver, 1992). Yet, from the late 1800s until the start of the Second World War, the British faced mounting pressures domestically and internationally to prohibit its use. In 1945, after the demise of the Japanese occupation, the British resumed control of the colony and criminalized opium by means of a 'Dangerous Drugs Ordinance' (Miner, 1983).

Heroin entered the scene as a 'cure' for opium addiction in the early part of the 1900s, and to quell the competition, colonial authorities classified it as a dangerous drug in the 1920s (Joe Laidler, Hodson, and Traver, 2000). But it was not until after opium's prohibition that heroin came to dominate the market in Hong Kong. Aside from the transformation of opium's legal status, heroin had a number of advantages, including its lack of odour, compact nature, ease of transport, relatively little paraphernalia and convenient use (Traver, 1992). From the 1960s through to recent years, heroin became the principal drug of choice in Hong Kong. Having lost its prior connections to the wealthy 'opium connoisseur' (Dikotter, Laamann and Xun, 2004), heroin went on to be largely associated with lower- and working-class adult males (Hess, 1965). In the initial stages of their drug career, most users employ a method known as 'firing the ack-ack gun', whereby the drug is inhaled through a cigarette topped with heroin, or by 'chasing the dragon' which entails the placement of heroin on a piece of foil, heating the underside of the foil with a candle and inhaling the fumes through a paper tube. Intravenous injection of the drug normally begins only after a regular habit has been formed. Given their need to purchase on the street and their gaunt stature, users are highly visible but rarely pose a threat to others due to the drug's sedative qualities. Heroin users typically fund their habit through non-violent, property-related crimes. The attraction of heroin to other sections of the community, especially youth, is low. It is a drug that is culturally associated with the 'hardcore addict' who has reached the point of no return.

The last decade has seen significant diversification in Hong Kong's drug scene. Official reports indicate that 'psychoactive drugs' (non-opiates), particularly ecstasy and ketamine, have gained unprecedented popularity among young people and that there are increasing shifts toward polydrug use (Central Registry of Drug Abuse, 2007). These trends have been intimately connected to new and distinctive forms of nightlife. Ecstasy first emerged in Hong Kong in the early 1990s at raves largely organized by, and popular among, British and other Western expatriates; however, the dance-drug scene did not take hold in earnest until the latter part of that decade. From then on, ecstasy, ketamine, and latterly cocaine, became increasingly important constituents of the local drug market. Concurrently, the last ten years have seen a growth in the number of permanent dance clubs, discos, karaoke bars, and lounges. The region now has a burgeoning and highly lucrative night-time entertainment industry, located in Hong Kong's long-standing central entertainment districts, its outlying areas, and across the border with mainland China (Joe Laidler, 2005).

Prostitution has also played a vital role in the development of Hong Kong's night-life. In its early days as a colony, Hong Kong witnessed significant industrial growth, attracting an influx of male migrants from Southern China in search of work and business opportunities. In response to an unmet demand, 'When the Colony of Hong Kong was first established, in 1842, it was forthwith invaded by brothel keepers and prostitutes from the adjoining districts of the mainland of China' (Lethbridge, 1978: 152).[2] As with the drugs trade, sex work was regulated by the colonial authorities in pursuit of their own self-interest. 'Enterprising' businessmen such as Charles May, the superintendent of police, developed a highly lucrative business, establishing brothels that catered to the labouring and the wealthy and the Chinese and European alike (Lethbridge, 1978). Brothel owners found the government licensing fees a small price to pay given the profits to be derived from a thriving business. However, in 1857, the colonial authorities introduced a 'Contagious Diseases Ordinance' due to concern over the spread of venereal disease, especially among its military forces (Howell, 2004). Howell describes this 'regulationism' as a component of colonial discipline, requiring not only the licensing of brothels, but also the registering and compulsory medical examination of prostitutes and the designation of areas where licensed brothels could operate. Although the Ordinance applied ostensibly to all, only Chinese prostitutes catering to European clients were subject to compulsory medical examinations. A decade later, the Ordinance was revised, appointing an Inspector of Brothels to ensure that all prostitutes had a medical examination. As the Inspector was also

---

[2] Lethbridge quotes from the 'Report of the Commission to Enquire into the Working of the Contagious Diseases Ordinance 1867' (Hong Kong: Noronha and Sons, 1879).

empowered to police and pursue unlicensed brothels, this led to much corruption and abuse (Lethbridge, 1978).

Compulsory medical examinations ended in 1887, but the registration of brothels and prostitutes remained until the 1930s. By this time it was estimated that there were over 7,000 licensed prostitutes operating from 200 legal brothels. As a result of international pressures from the League of Nations, the government slowly moved toward prohibition of the sex trade. With the closure of brothels, prostitution took to the streets and residents began to complain to the authorities about soliciting and touting in their neighbourhoods. The Japanese reintroduced a regulatory system in the Wan Chai area, a locale later immortalized in the 1960 film adaptation of Richard Mason's book *The World of Suzie Wong*. To this day, the area remains a site for streetwalkers and 'girlie' bars. However, after the British resumed control of Hong Kong in 1945, the new colonial government effectively removed much of this street-based sex work (Lethbridge, 1978). Their policies combined toleration for prostitution itself, with the criminalization of almost all activities associated with it—soliciting, living from its proceeds, etc. Unsurprisingly, indoor spaces—villas, motels, and guesthouses—then re-emerged as more discreet spaces for prostitution wherein the regulations might be circumvented. The one-woman brothel—where one sex worker services one client at a time—was distinctive as it was the only site in which prostitution was not illegal. All forms involving more than one sex worker were considered illegal organization and implied the prohibited intent to live from its proceeds.

During the 1960s, such 'vice establishments' are known to have operated through police pay-offs (Lethbridge, 1978) and it was not until the corruption crackdowns of the late 1960s and early 1970s that links between triads operating in the sex trade and the police were severed. Nonetheless, new opportunities emerged for enterprising triads in other areas of the sex trade. Many operated go-go bars, nightclubs, escort services, and hostess bars, whilst facilitating the entry of migrant sex workers, particularly Filipinas, Thais, Malay, and Columbians (Whitehead and Vittachi, 1997). For the reasons outlined below, organized crime's attention has more recently turned to the influx of sex workers from mainland China.

DRUGS AND SEX: THE CHANGING FACE OF ILLICIT LEISURE

In discussing contemporary nightlife in Hong Kong it is difficult to escape the importance of drugs and sex. In relation to drugs, two distinctive scenes are especially salient: the heroin scene and the 'dance-drug' scene. First, despite dramatic changes to Hong Kong's society, the world of heroin users appears to have remained remarkably stable. As noted, there appears to be a cultural tolerance to heroin users given that their illegal activities are generally non-threatening to local residents. Though heroin users might commit crimes to fund their habit, these tend to be relatively petty in nature—shop theft, burglaries, and selling small quantities of drugs. The transporting and selling of

pirated and stolen goods is also a major source of finance, typically occurring in the
city's night markets:

Kai is a 34-year-old heroin user who has worked in a variety of legitimate jobs since the age 14,
including truck driving, bar tending, air conditioning repair and as a foreman on a construction site. He began using heroin when he was 16. At the height of his career as a construction
site boss man, his best friend (who introduced him to heroin) framed him in a corruption
scandal. Since then, he reports that his life has been on the decline. He turned to a variety of
illegal jobs to pay for his habit including heroin delivery, pirated videodisc and smuggled
cigarette seller. (Joe Laidler, Hodson, and Traver, 2000: 41)

Like most other long-term heroin users, Kai worries about getting arrested for selling
illegal goods. Whilst feeling especially vulnerable to detection given their distinctive
heroin user 'look'—thin, gaunt cheekbones, pasty grey skin—they feel they have limited choices. Work in the night-time economy (NTE) lessens their visibility. As Lin
describes:

I turned to selling pirated video discs for a while and smuggling cigarettes because I was
unemployed. I wanted to get quick money to buy heroin. Moreover at the time, I was very thin
and looked horrible because I injected too much. I couldn't find any jobs, so I decided to do
illegal jobs. I also transported drugs … (Joe Laidler, Hodson, and Traver, 2000: 47)

Field observations indicate that heroin is easily obtained day or night, in a variety of
settings from public parks, corners of housing estates, 'drug stores', divans, and near
methadone clinics. 'Copping' areas are situated off main thoroughfares, public parks,
stairwells in public estates, and hidden spots under the expressways.

THE NEW DANCE-DRUG SCENE

The world of heroin stands in distinct contrast to the burgeoning dance-drug scene.
Heroin users are well aware that the social spaces of nightlife and drug use are changing. They've seen and heard about ecstasy, 'the head shaking tablet' and ketamine, the
hallucinatory powder used in the growing number of discos, clubs, and lounges scattered throughout the entertainment areas, outlying districts, and across the border
in the neighbouring Chinese city of Schenzen. Older heroin users, like Kai and Lin,
distance themselves from this scene. They've heard that these drugs, unlike heroin,
induce stimulatory and hallucinogenic effects and they feel they simply won't 'fit in'.

The heroin world, although initially a sociable one, becomes, with time, increasingly isolating. At first, users smoke or chase the dragon with a few friends in a small
group in a quiet and discrete area of a public housing estate or public park, but eventually, the convenience, discreteness, and shared experience are perceived as disadvan-
tages. Some refuse to move onto injection use for fear of the full-fledged stigma of
addiction, but also due to the health risks and possibilities of overdosing. To maximize
their use, they begin using at home or, if forced to rely on others, sharing with one or
two others in those discrete but familiar locales of public housing estates and parks.

Mei has been using heroin for the past seven years. 'I have been using heroin for a long time
and my appearance has really changed. I've become very thin and my face is yellowish, I've

got the heroin look. No one wants to employ me…One of my triad brothers introduced me to it in the rubbish room of the public housing estate. At first, I felt strange, wanting to vomit, but after a few more times smoking it with a group of friends, was very happy.' Within six months, she was chasing the dragon once a day and if she had enough money, would do it twice a day at home.

Other heroin users, however, gradually make the shift to injection use, signalling a change in physical and psychological addiction as well as increasing isolation from other users as well as loved ones. Kai recounts his shift to injection use:

After I started injecting, I became very thin. I looked bad because of the needle holes, the skin near my veins was green and swollen and I had a bad rash around the injecting areas. I couldn't find a job… I felt sad for my girlfriend too. I felt so inferior to her, ashamed of myself. I left her because I didn't think I made a good boyfriend. I was very depressed about it… When I have money, I use it alone. But if I don't have money, I share with others.

The new youth-based dance scene has produced a very different social context for drug use, one which is alien and oppositional to heroin users' relations and experiences.

The dance-drug scene emerged in Hong Kong in the late 1990s, much later than in many other parts of the world. As noted, large-scale warehouse parties were the first to appear, but these remained occasional events. The scene became more established through the proliferation of permanent venues for dancing and socializing; discos, clubs, and karaoke bars emerged, tailored to all budgets, and many connected to organized crime (Joe Laidler, Hodson, and Traver, 2000). These new-style venues tended to cater for either small groups of 50 to 100 or larger crowds of 300 people or more. Since 2006, chic, dimly lit lounges with warm, glowing lights have opened in the Central District for a more up-market crowd. Some of these venues have gained popularity from their endorsement by local pop celebrities whose party exploits are photographed by the Chinese press. Although ecstasy was initially the exclusive drug of choice among young dance-goers, this changed rather quickly. Users now show a preference for topping up their ecstasy intake with powered ketamine, a drug described in a popular dance song as the 'poor man's cocaine' (Joe Laidler and Hunt, 2008). This combination allows clubbers to merge their euphoric waving with the hallucinatory experience of flying, as described in the following field observations:

We arrived at the X club at about 1.00 am. Many people were already queuing. The queue was just starting to turn the corner. Everyone was staring at the entrance, waiting to get in, looking very patient. At 1.30 am, there were already 150 people waiting outside, and by 2.00 am, it seemed as if there were about 250 people. The male to female ratio was about 50:50. While we were waiting to get in, I noticed the ages of the crowd; about 80 per cent were between 18 and 25 years old. The remainder of people were something of a mixture, some were 'middle aged' (30s and 40s), some Southeast Asians, others, mainland sex workers.

Most of the young girls wore low waist jeans and tiny sleeveless tops. They were very slim (under 100 pounds). They had put some effort into the evening, their hair neatly brushed and faces coloured with make-up and glitter. Some wore sunglasses. Most of the girls were in mixed groups including some guys. About half of the guys were plainly dressed in jeans and t-shirts or other casual wear. Some of the males wore earrings, skateboard shorts and t's, and had gelled orange or yellow tinted hair. These guys wanted to be noticed, strutting up and down the street, alongside the queue, with the '*gwoo wak jai*' (bad boy) gait.

At 1.50 am, ten police officers stepped out from the disco. They brought their van around from the other side of the street. Eight male and two female suspects were escorted out to the van in front of the disco. The crowd stared at the scene. Just another night of alcohol licensing checks, a routine method in which police stop the music, flip on the lights and check everyone's Identification Card for age—it's also to control the distribution and use of drugs in these venues. No one around us made any comments about the raid and the arrests. The police car departed at 2.05 am and it started raining. No one left the queue. Five minutes later, the ticket booth opened and the staff allowed groups of people to pass. Although most people were in groups, they purchased tickets individually. The girls proceeded to check their bags at the cloakroom. We paid the Saturday night entrance fee of US$32 for males and US$25 for females. The weekday prices were cheaper at US$19 for males and US$10 for females. The ticket included one drink. Monday and Tuesdays are 'ladies night' with no entrance fee for women.

At 2.15 am we were moving into the disco, first through a security check by four guards, then getting a special infrared stamp on our hand. A sign on the wall reminded us, 'People under 18 are not allowed to enter the disco. Please cooperate with the staff. If staff ask you to show your Identity Card, please let them check it.' Once through security we entered the 'cyber tunnel'—a glitzy elevator ascending to the main venue. More than ten security guards were standing on the side of the corridor trying to control the flow, ordering people to move on, and not chat or wait in the middle of the hall. We turned right. There were two to three 'sitting areas' along the corridor towards the dance floor. Each area had about four or five seats and a small table. A sign at one of the tables said, 'Minimum charge—US$128'. No one was seated at any of these tables.

Two security guards were sitting up high on tall-legged chairs on either side of the entrance to the dance room. There were also two rows of tall bar stools and bar tables in front of the dance floor. Some 'older' people sat there alone with their eyes closed, moving their bodies to the rhythm of the music. The dance floor was *really* big, over 8,000 square feet. There were two bars serving drinks on either side of the dance floor. Most people were drinking water, beer or alco-pop. The DJ and the audio-visual system were on an elevated stage in the middle of the dance floor. Local re-mix music blared from the loudspeakers. The dance floor was only half full, with fewer than 300 people. This was unusual as Saturday was normally packed with little room to stand …

At 3.15 am, I went to the toilet, located between the dance floor and the lounge. The queue was long, with about 15 girls and young women in line. The queue at the male toilet was smaller, with only about five guys. The main doors of the toilet were open, and you could clearly see inside. A security guard was sitting in the middle of the two rooms. The girls in front of me were talking, with one of them bragging to the other that she had gotten in free to this club many times, including tonight. Her friend laughed. Later, I discovered that the club advertises: 'Ladies who wear a bra top and short pants can enter free.' So I guess she dressed like that to get in, and changed her clothes when she got in, as she wasn't dressed in that fashion.

I was stuck in the line for over ten minutes. There were six stalls in the toilet. A big sign on the wall facing the main toilet door announced, 'No drugs allowed in the disco. If you find anyone with drugs, please call the staff at XXXXXXXX. You can receive a $ reward if you make a report.' The mobile phone number and the amount of the reward, however, were rubbed out. A bathroom attendant strutted around in the toilet, using a stick to knock on the doors, shouting, 'Be quick! Don't occupy the toilet too long.' No one seemed to hear or care about her pronouncements. When the girls came out from the toilet, they had runny noses. They were wiping their nose clean with tissues. From the blue ketamine wrappers on the floor, it appeared that they had just finished snorting.

While I waited for my friend to check out the male toilets, I was standing nearby and found two guys having difficulties standing. They tried to rest against the wall, and their friend came up to them as said, 'I told you not to "explode" [take] too much …' My friend reported back from the male toilet. It sounded pretty similar to the female one. Most of the boys had opted for the stalls instead of the urinals, stayed in the stall a long time and a male attendant yelled at them to hurry up. When the guys came out of the stalls, they too had runny noses, but simply wiped it with their hand.

By 4.15 am, the dance floor crowds had filled to around 500 people. The crowd seemed to be dancing more freely than before. Three young women were holding on to the bar table and wildly shaking their bodies for several songs. Several ladies and men were in a group, holding the pillars and shaking their heads. Others were sitting on the bar chairs, closing their eyes and waving their bodies. On the dance floor, a lot of the guys and girls were hugging and kissing.

At 5.00 am the toilet was still busy. The girls seemed very hot and sweaty. Their make-up was fading and smearing. Their eyes looked tired. Some of them rested against the wall or sink. They couldn't seem to stand up straight. There were not as many queued up for the stalls, but the ones who came out were sneezing. There were several ketamine wrappers at the top of the garbage bin.

At 5.15 am we walked back to the open bar area of the lounge. It was full of people, mostly older than those on the dance floor. They were drinking wine and beer. One of the small sitting areas along the hall (with the US$128 minimum charge) was occupied by a group of men in their late 20s to mid-30s. They were smoking a lot, drinking beer, talking on their mobile phones, and looking around all the time. Two of them went in and out of the VIP room. They had that 'triad look'—with the muscles, tattoos, big gold chain necklaces, highlighted hair, and attitude.

At 5.30 am, we took the elevator to leave. About eight fellow passengers discussed which disco to go to next. When we left, it was still raining. Maybe that's why it was quieter than usual.

As this field work illustrates, the dance party scene has become an established and highly lucrative industry, of a very different nature from that of the heroin trade and its associated social scenes. Dance-goers have a range of venue choices, including numerous night spots within a short train ride of Hong Kong, across the Chinese border. This mainland scene attracts teenagers and young adults alike, mainly for the variety, but also because of its accessibility and lower prices (Joe Laidler, 2005). Venues on both sides have become sophisticated, designed for a variety of customers ranging from the middle to working classes, from the single to the married, from those in their late teens to those in their late 20s, and for gays and for straights (Joe Laidler, 2005).

THE NEW SEX-WORK SCENE

Although Hong Kong is not a site for sex tourism, it continues to have a thriving sex industry. Available figures estimate the number of female sex workers at 200,000 (Chan, Ho, and Lo, 2002). The Hong Kong and Chinese governments now operate a strategy of 'one country, two systems' to promote cross-border economic and cultural exchange, including leisure and tourism. Since British rule ended, the lucrative opportunities associated with cross-border travel have been both legitimate and illegitimate, with Hong Kong's commercial sex industry a key example. According to Hong Kong Immigration Department statistics, the number of mainland Chinese women arrested for suspected involvement in prostitution grew steadily from 3,002 in 2000 to 9,916 in 2004, whilst decreasing to 6,934 in 2005. Importantly, the women's entry to Hong Kong requires some level of organization and mainland Chinese sex workers operate in many business modes, often under third-party control, sometimes with connections to the Hong Kong or mainland triads. These developments—China's market reforms, economic disparities among its urban and rural populace, the expansion of floating populations, 'one country, two systems' and its changes to immigration policy, emerging legitimate and illegitimate economic opportunities—all of these provide the backdrop to our understanding of mainland Chinese women's experiences in coming to Hong Kong (Joe Laidler, Emerton, and Petersen, 2007).

Young Chinese women hear of the chances of a 'better life' in Hong Kong from colleagues and friends. Most are aware of the nature of 'work' on offer but remain attracted by the ability to earn higher (and faster) wages than their jobs on the mainland allow.

18 year old Ah Lai moved to Shenzhen with her mother from a city in Guangdong Province to look for work. She started out as a waitress in a karaoke club, but was dissatisfied with the RMB$500 monthly wage. She had heard from friends that she could make a lot more money working in Hong Kong and asked them for an introduction to someone who could help with arrangements. She eventually met up with the 'Hong Kong boss' who told her she could make between 6,000 and 7,000 HK$ per week as a sex worker. On her first trip, she earned HK$1,500. She returned to work in Hong Kong the following month as she, in her own words, became 'more ambitious to earn more money than the first visit' and on this second trip she netted HK$3,000. Her most recent trip, for which she was convicted, was also prompted by her desire to increase her earnings.

Whilst local sex workers tend to operate from one-woman brothels, thus attempting— not always successfully—to avoid interaction with the police, migrant women often lack the means to run their 'businesses' independently. Some are deceived as to their potential earnings and the exact nature of the 'hostess' work they are offered. Others pay exorbitant fees to a 'middle-man' to arrange the visa and/or to a 'minder'. Debts often accrue which must be paid off. These may equate to the monies earned from servicing the first 150 or more clients. Moreover, women operating under the auspices of a 'minder' are often forced to remain in their rooms having been warned that their visibility on the streets increases the chances of police detection. As described below, encounters with the criminal justice system tend only to exacerbate their problems.

POLICING, SECURITY, AND CRIME CONTROL

To understand why Hong Kong is considered one of the safest cities in the world and yet is able to sustain such a colourful nightlife, one must consider a number of factors. First and foremost, police presence is comparatively high with 389 officers per 100,000 residents. Approximately 10 per cent of the governments' expenditure goes toward security (UN Habitat, 2007). As observed in the thriving nightclub scene, CCTV abounds and private security personnel are a formidable force at 1,872 per 100,000 persons (UN Habitat, 2007). In the government's attempts to address the rise in psychotropic drug use, the police, since the late 1990s, have conducted routine raids of licensed and unlicensed dance venues. As described above, these raids involve turning on the lights, stopping the music, checking individual identification, and trying to detect drugs. However, they are hampered by the fact that once the lights are switched on, drugs are dumped on the floor and it becomes impossible to determine possession. When the police succeed in terminating a licence, venue operators simply diversify, moving from one locale to another. This leaves the police to face yet another challenge. Most recently, the Police Licensing Office has prevented the licensing of several well-known establishments; as a result, many young people are now crossing the border where the nightlife scene is, from their point of view, less restricted.

Another factor accounting for Hong Kong's reputation for safety is its incarceration rate. Imprisonment of 156 persons per 100,000 (in 2007) makes Hong Kong's stance tough in comparison with that of nearby Japan and Korea (UN Habitat, 2007). Yet, whilst the general level of incarceration is not especially high by international standards, a recent report by the International Centre for Prison Studies on World Prison Populations reveals that Hong Kong has the largest proportion of incarcerated females in the world (22 per cent of its total prison population). The international average ranges from 2 per cent to 9 per cent (Walmsley, 2007). Women from mainland China consistently number 70–88 per cent of the female prison population. The majority are imprisoned for sex-work-related activities such as soliciting, or for breaching the conditions of their visa (Joe Laidler, Emerton, and Petersen, 2007). The imprisonment of these women is costly to the public (approximately US$3,000 for each woman who serves the two month sentence for breaching her conditions of stay), whilst the women themselves are doubly punished. In addition to serving their sentence, they must live with the consequences of their lost earnings on release. These may include mounting debts to their 'middleman' and fines at the border by the Chinese authorities as they attempt to return home (see, Joe Laidler, Emerton, and Petersen, 2007).

CONCLUSIONS

Life for Hong Kong's traditional drug user—the male lower-class heroin addict—remains relatively stable. The wider community tolerates them as long as they remain passive and submit to the well-established medico-legal disciplines of methadone prescription. Relations between heroin users themselves are fragile, but steady; some join together to buy their drugs when money is tight, but most prefer to conduct their drug-taking in isolation. Juxtaposed to these hidden scenes, a younger generation is also seeking temporary escapism by more visible means. Dance-drug enthusiasts distance themselves from heroin users, whom they perceive as having reached a 'terminal point'. Young clubbers—both males and females—see themselves as more connected, but with a distinctive spin, to mainstream society. Their drug use is almost a celebration of contemporary capitalism, rather than an act of resistance to it. Unlike its colonial predecessors, the Hong Kong government of today adopts an anti-drugs stance, with heavy emphasis on enforcement as well as education. Given the region's historical associations with heroin, the government has a comprehensive programme in place for dealing with the problems which attend its use. In its efforts to grapple with ecstasy, and particularly with ketamine, it has recently introduced a health-check initiative to encourage users to seek help. After several years of judicial debate, the sentencing policies for ecstasy and ketamine have been separated and the tariff for both drugs increased.

Sex workers, whether from the mainland or local residents, are increasingly operating out of one-woman brothels to avoid trouble with the police. Appointments are increasingly arranged via online advertisement (Liu and Lau, 2006) although the recent 18-month imprisonment of a website operator for sex-work services may result in other possibilities (SCMP, 2008b). Whilst one-woman brothels afford better privacy and protection compared to street solicitation, they can, paradoxically, heighten the risks and dangers to sex workers as illustrated by the recent robbery and murder of sex workers in their own homes (SCMP, 2008c). Policymakers are confronted with the costs of imprisoning large numbers of migrant women involved in sex work. Although the number of women imprisoned has declined somewhat in the last year, it is not clear whether this is due to the government's punitive approach or whether more lucrative sex markets or legitimate alternatives are emerging within China itself. There has been some limited discussion in legislative council meetings of the possibility of creating a regulated 'Red Light District'. However, such schemes will not resolve the problems faced by migrant sex workers. Under current law, their work is not recognized as a formal occupation, yet they continue to face punishment for violating the conditions of their stay by taking work. More radical proposals, such as legalization and decriminalization, have yet to be confronted.

Despite broader political, economic, and social changes, it remains the case that drugs and prostitution are central facets of Hong Kong's NTE. In comparison to the colonial period, this NTE has experienced unprecedented and highly lucrative expansion, with phenomenal growth in the opportunities for using psychotropic drugs in entertainment and public settings—from raves to discos, lounges, semi-private parties and karaokes—on both sides of the border. Recent years have also seen the creation of 'new' sex work locales, including villas, hotel rooms, and brothels, and new forms of soliciting—from the streets, to the newspapers, to the internet. This expansion has been connected to, but certainly not controlled by, a number of enterprising business-men, many of whom have affiliations with organized crime. Although beyond the scope of this paper, it seems likely that the burgeoning of Hong Kong's NTE, as in the UK, has been linked to the shift from an industrial to a post-industrial age (Hadfield, 2006; O'Brien, Hobbs, and Westmarland, 2008).

What has also changed is the articulation and participation of consumers and workers in Hong Kong's NTE. Although in need of further investigation, it appears that women are increasingly at the forefront of this economy, in part due to the height-ened sexualization of women in marketing and advertising in the entertainment and sex-work industries. Women's sexual commodification in online advertisements for sex work has made it easy for potential customers to scan the photographs, particular characteristics and services of sex workers, as well as obtain feedback from previous customers. In this facet of the NTE, women continue to play to the conventions and violations of femininity for their customers and minders. Unlike the marginal role of women in the heroin world, the contemporary entertainment scene, in targeting young adults, has paid special heed to the demands of their new customers—young women with disposable incomes, without immediate aspirations of marriage and who want to move beyond conventional femininity. Ironically, their consumption needs are being fuelled by highly sexualized advertising and marketing—such as ladies nights with free entry and drinks for women arriving in heels or sexy apparel—all of which may further bind them to highly patriarchal sites of interaction.

REFERENCES

All internet sources were accessible 20 August 2008

BOOTH, M (1996) *Opium: A history*, London: Simon and Schuster.

CIA (Central Intelligence Agency) (2008) *The World Factbook: Distribution of family income*, <https://www.cia.gov/library/publications/the-world-factbook/fields/2172.html>.

CENTRAL REGISTRY of DRUG ABUSE (2007) *56th Report (1997–2006)*, Hong Kong: Hong Kong Narcotics Division.

CHAN, MKT, HO, KM, and LO, KK (2002) 'A behavior sentinel surveillance for female sex workers in the social hygiene service in Hong Kong (1999–2000)', *International Journal of Sexually Transmitted Diseases and AIDS*, 13, 815–20.

CHU, YK (2005) 'Hong Kong triads after 1997', *Trends in Organised Crime*, 8/3, 5–12.

DIKOTTER, F, LAAMANN, L, and XUN, Z (2004) *Narcotic Culture*, Hong Kong: University of Hong Kong Press.

HADFIELD, P (2004) *Bar Wars: Contesting the Night in Contemporary British Cities*, Oxford: Oxford University Press.

HESS, A (1965) *Chasing the Dragon: A report on drug addiction in Hong Kong*, Amsterdam: North Holland Publishing Co.

HONG KONG CENSUS and STATISTICS DEPARTMENT (2007) *Thematic Report: Household income distribution in Hong Kong*, Hong Kong Government: <http://www.censtatd.gov.hk/products_and_services/products/publications/index.jsp>.

HONG KONG GOVERNMENT (2008) *Tourism Fact Sheet*, <http://www.gov.hk/en/about/abouthk/factsheets/docs/tourism.pdf>.

HONG KONG POLICE (2008) *Crime Statistics*, <http://www.police.gov.hk/hkp-home/english/index.htm>.

HOWELL, P (2004) 'Race, space and the regulation of prostitution in colonial Hong Kong', *Urban History*, 31/2, 229–48.

JOE LAIDLER, K (2005) 'Club drugs in Hong Kong', *Substance Use and Misuse*, 40, 1257–78.

—— EMERTON, R and PETERSEN, C (2007) 'Bureaucratic justice: The incarceration of mainland chinese women working in Hong Kong's sex industry', *International Journal of Offender Therapy and Rehabilitation*, 5/1, 68–83.

—— HODSON, D and TRAVER, H (2000) *The Hong Kong Drug Market. A Report for UNICRI on the UNDCP Global Study in Illicit Drug Markets*, Hong Kong: Centre for Criminology.

—— and HUNT, G (2008) 'Sit down to float: The cultural meaning of ketamine use', *Addiction, Theory and Research*, 16/3, 259–71.

LEE, F (2000) 'Teens of the night: The young night drifters in Hong Kong', *Youth and Society*, 31/3, 363–84.

—— (ed) (2005) *Working with Youth at Risk in Hong Kong*, Hong Kong: University of Hong Kong Press.

LETHBRIDGE, H (1978) 'Prostitution in Hong Kong: A legal and moral dilemma', *Hong Kong Law Journal*, 8, 149–73.

LIU, G and LAU, J (2006) 'Sexuality as public spectacle', in PL Law, L Fortunati and S Yang (eds), *New Technologies in Global Societies*, New Jersey: World Scientific, 2259–89.

MASON, R (1957) *The World of Suzie Wong*, London: Collins.

MINERS, M (1983) 'The Hong Kong government opium monopoly', *The Journal of Imperial and Commonwealth History*, 1, 275–99.

O'BRIEN, K, HOBBS, D and WESTMARLAND, L (2008) 'Negotiating violence and gender: Security and the night-time economy in the UK', in S Body-Gendrot and P Spirerenburg (eds), *Violence in Europe*, New York: Springer, 161–73.

SCMP (*South China Morning Post*) (2007a) 'City of sorrow: This week's murder-suicide is the latest chapter in a community's tale of hardship', 20 October, 16

—— (2007b) 'Tin Shui Wai cries out for help and support: Family disputes can have deadly impact as people who have been left out of the economic boom feel the pressure', 22 October, 6.

—— (2008a) 'Concern over caseloads for social workers; Increasing workloads "shameful"', 19 May, 11.

—— (2008b) 'Jail for prostitute website operator', 16 May.

—— (2008c) 'Violence and robberies pose a daily threat to prostitutes trapped by laws that dissuade them from going to the police', 23 March, 9.

TRAVER, H (1992) 'Opium to heroin: Restrictive opium legislation and the rise of heroin consumption in Hong Kong', *Journal of Policy History*, 4(3), 307–24.

UN HABITAT (2007) *Global Report on Human Settlements*, Nairobi, Kenya: United Nations Human Settlements Programme, <http://www.unhabitat.org>.

UN POPULATION DIVISION (2006) *World Population Prospects: The 2006 Revision*, New York: United Nations Population Division, <http://www.un.org/esa/population/unpop.htm>.

WALMSLEY, R (2007) *World Female Imprisonment List*, London: International Centre for Prison Studies, <http://www.kcl.ac.uk/depsta/law/research/icps/downloads/women-prison-list-2006.pdf>

WHITEHEAD, K and VITTACHI, N (1997) *After Suzie: Sex in South China*, Hong Kong: Chameleon.

16

SOUTH AFRICA

Kopano Ratele, Lu-Anne Swart, and Mohamed Seedat

INTRODUCTION

The immensity of South Africa's crime problem is well known. In 2006/7 there were 19,202 reported cases of murder, 20,142 attempted murders, 218,030 incidents of assault with intent to inflict grievous bodily harm, and 52,617 cases of rape (CIAC, 2007). The rates for each of these are respectively 40.5, 42.5, 460.1, and 111.0 per 100,000 of the population. By most accounts these are high levels of crime. The horrific stories of interpersonal violence that appear in the national media on a seemingly daily basis, only serve to further fuel this perception. Some researchers are of the opinion that the country's crime epidemic may be distinguished from that of other African nations not so much by the quantity of its crime as by the ferocious violence that often accompanies it (Altbeker, 2007).

The Crime Information Analysis Centre (CIAC) of the South African Police Service produces regular reports on national, regional, and local crime statistics and trends (ibid). Statistics South Africa has conducted a number of victimization surveys (Central Statistical Service, 1996; Statistics South Africa, 1999) and the Crime and Justice Programme of the Institute for Security Studies produces the *SA Crime Quarterly* and has undertaken a sustained programme of research. The Centre for the Study of Violence and Reconciliation conducts work in the area of violence prevention and the Medical Research Council has a number of programmes running in collaboration with the Institute of Social and Health Sciences at the University of South Africa. There are, therefore, a range of organizations and research expertise within the fields of crime, violence, and related areas. However, due to a number of factors, including, above all, the scale of the crime problem, there remain gaps in the research literature concerning South Africa's violent crime. For example, most studies, if they do remark on the location of offences, fail to consider temporal aspects of the phenomenon, or do so only in passing. This chapter aims to initiate a filling of this gap.

Rather than encompass all forms of recorded violent crime, this chapter will be concerned only with violent deaths. The quantitative data we analyse was obtained from the South African National Injury Mortality Surveillance System (NIMSS) (Prinsloo, 2007). The NIMSS was launched in 1999 to record the extent of deaths from non-natural causes. The goal has been to establish a permanent system that will, among other objectives, help describe the incidence, causes, and consequences of non-natural deaths, prioritize injury and violence prevention actions, identify new injury trends and emerging problems, and monitor longitudinal changes in the profile of non-natural fatalities. An important shortcoming of the NIMSS is that it is currently restricted to victimization data and does not include information concerning the perpetrators of violence, or the social context of fatal injury—that is, whether the deaths occurred, for example, during civil unrest, a bank robbery, vigilantism, or xenophobic attacks.

In the following paragraphs we will analyse the relative significance of a number of key variables regarding victims of fatal violence and external causes of death, specifically time of death and other temporal factors. The chapter begins with a general overview of the violent crime situation in South Africa that is not intended to be read as a systematic review of the field internationally. Our aim is rather to assess some explanations for the particularly high levels of violence and violent deaths in our country. The chapter then turns to studies that have considered time in analysing fatal injury, before reporting the findings of one of our own recent studies. The final section employs theories of masculinity to help explain the observed patterns of fatal injury.

RECREATIONAL VIOLENCE

In his account of the lives of male miners, historian Keith Breckenridge argues that 'violence is endemic in southern Africa because people enjoy it' (1998: 672). He offers support from interviews and work by other scholars. That said, considerably more—as well as different kinds of—evidence would be needed to confirm the hypothesis that southern African men enjoy violence. Nonetheless, Breckenridge is not alone in proposing that there may be a culture of recreational violence among at least some men. His contribution takes things further in stressing the importance of affectivity within this cultural hypothesis. As he states, 'The aesthetics of violence, its lurid power, and the emotional investment that men, in particular, make in it has to be acknowledged if we are to make any sense of its ubiquity and endurance' (1998: 672).

One obstacle to the development of a 'culture of violence thesis' is the reluctance of scholars to open themselves to the charge of racism. Racialized, often racist, politicizations of culture have haunted South Africa for many years and residues of this and other forms of contestation around culture continue to trouble society in the post-apartheid era. For example, proponents of cultural explanations for violence may be suspected of having dubious political motivations, similar to those of the bigoted, repressive, and colonialist 'bantustan' governments of the apartheid era. Bantustan is the term often used to refer to those arid areas, nominally outside of South Africa, to which, in the 1960s to 1980s, the apartheid governments forcibly removed millions of black people because they were said to belong in their own Bantu homelands and not in 'white South Africa'. Homelands such as the Transkei (for the amaXhosa) were economically untenable and dependent on appropriations from the South African government. They were governed by individuals with close ties and sympathies to the apartheid regime and hostile to the so-called terrorist, liberation movements.

For Schönteich and Louw (2001) any predilections to violence in South African society are likely to have been produced and mediated by social, economic, and political conditions: the effects of apartheid, years of political upheaval, and continued exposure to poverty in the home and neighbourhood. This combination of factors, they suggest, nurtures a destructive culture which manifests itself in what has been referred to as 'murderous intolerance'. South Africans, it appears, quickly resort to violence as a means of resolving conflicts—whether in domestic, social, or work environments. Schönteich and Louw generally support this line of explanation, whilst noting the importance of other factors contributing to South Africa's high levels of crime. They explain that part of the strategy of the internal freedom movement of the 1980s and early 1990s was to make the country ungovernable. This, unfortunately, had other, unintended, effects:

In the process of destabilising black local government, leading violent campaigns against black policemen, and urging a people's war which involved the youth in particular, massive violence was unleashed in black communities which bred a culture of violent lawlessness and a distrust of authority. Since 1994, little has been done to reverse these tendencies and to draw young South Africans, in particular, back into a society governed by the rule of law. (unpaginated)

Parker, Dawes and Farr (2004: 22) note that high levels of state violence were a feature of the undemocratic apartheid regime, just as large numbers of young criminal homicide victims are a feature of today's democratic South Africa. Violence, they say, is 'embedded' in the country's history. However, they provide little evidence for the contention that violence is an entrenched feature of South African culture. The second claim they make is that youth, and male youth specifically, account for the majority of victims of violence. This claim, to which we shall return shortly, is not as difficult to substantiate. It is also, we argue, a pointer to more convincing explanations concerning the role and propensity of violence in South African society.

In his book *A Country at War with Itself: South Africa's Crisis of Crime*, Altbeker (2007) expresses a similar claim. 'The institutional architecture' on which the successive apartheid governments and their predecessors in South Africa were predicated, he says, nourished 'a violence-rich male subculture' (p 98). This subculture was embodied in the life of 'mining hostels and the prisons [where] men, torn from the bosoms of their families, lived in a pressure-cooker world where the resort to violence to protect oneself and one's property was common, accepted and necessary' (ibid). Altbeker's book is not a rigorous scientific study of crime or violence, but is rather addressed to the popular reader. For that reason we should not hold him to provide better proof.

As noted, a major aspect of the scholarly hesitation to fully embrace cultural explanations derives from an awareness of the topic's fraught historical legacy. However, we believe it is possible to employ the language of culture without lending support to retrogressive and oppressive discourses. There is something which we can happily refer to as a culture that propagates violence in South Africa. What is meant by a culture of violence here then is a set of beliefs and material practices which groups of people, young men in particular, engage in, support, and even enjoy. These beliefs and practices are related, not to race, but to gender. NIMSS reports for recent years attest to the fact that the majority of those who die from non-natural causes are males (Matzopoulos, 2005; Prinsloo, 2007). This finding is supported by other research indicating males to be the main perpetrators of violence, both against other males and against females (Jewkes et al, 2006). There may, of course, be significant unexplained differences relating to social class and, as we shall see, to age. Concerning social class, the recent report on trends and spatial distribution of crime in South Africa by the CIAC (2007: 24) contends that economic hardship, coupled with rapid urbanization, high degrees of relative deprivation, and lack of supportive social networks, are all major factors which increase the risk of criminal behaviour.

Men's disproportionate involvement in violence is not a uniquely South African phenomenon. Intentional injury accounts for loss of life on a global scale and explanations need to be situated in their global and African regional context. Krug et al's (2002) report for the World Health Organization (WHO) indicates that 506,000 of the lives lost were female, with male victims numbering 1,659 000. The estimated rate of mortality due to intentional injury was 28.8 per 100,000 of the male population and 17.3 per 100,000 of the female population, worldwide. On a regional basis, high-income countries (as defined by the WHO) have, on average, less than half the rates of intentional injury-related male deaths of low- and middle-income countries (a rate of 14.4, compared with 32.1 per 100,000 population) (Krug et al, 2002). Male and female mortality rates in the African region are higher than those of any other part of the world. The rate of male mortality caused by all intentional injury for the low- and middle-income countries of the European region is estimated to be 49.6, whilst the rate for low and middle income countries in Africa is 60.9.

Intentional violence accounts for 26 per cent of injury-related deaths worldwide; in South Africa, the figure can be as high as 50 per cent (Krug et al, 2002; Matzopoulos, 2005). Among male South Africans, violence ranks alongside HIV/AIDS as the primary cause of reduced life expectancy (Bradshaw et al, 2004). Homicide rates for South African males are over 6.6 times higher than those of females, with the 15–44-year-old group disproportionately represented in non-natural mortality figures (Matzopoulos, 2005; Prinsloo, 2007). In the 7th Annual Report of the National Injury Mortality Surveillance System, Prinsloo (2007) indicates that, of cases in which the gender of the victim was known, over 80 per cent of victims were male. Violence was the leading cause of death among males, whilst females were more often killed in road traffic accidents. However, even in relation to these transport-related fatalities, considerably more males than females died. Prinsloo shows the average age of victims to be 33.2. Both males and females between the ages of 15–44 were considerably more likely to die from violence than any other non-natural cause. This contrasted with the age groups 0–14 and 45 and above in which 'transport' was the leading non-natural cause of death. In the age group 45–54 though, whereas violence was the second leading cause of death, the statistical difference between the leading cause of death, transport, and violence was small (Prinsloo, ibid).

Although further data is needed to confirm the gender of the perpetrators of these violent acts (but see, eg, Centre for the Study of Violence and Reconciliation, 1998), available sources of victimization data (Central Statistical Service, 1996; Statistics South Africa, 1999) lead us to the conclusion that the prevalence of deadly force in South Africa may be situated within an insidious culture of daredevil masculinity. This is an observation to which we will return. The following paragraphs outline a number of South African studies that have considered the temporal aspects of violent fatality. Thereafter, we report the findings of our own study on time and fatal injury in four South African cities.

THE TIMING OF FATAL INJURIES

In their study of Tshwane City Municipality, Raquel Mahoque and Joanne Gouveia (2007) show that fatal injuries from firearm discharge rise sharply from approximately 6.00 pm, only to fall again after 5.00 am. Their findings show the most dangerous times to be around 8.00 pm, followed by the 10.00 pm to 11.00 pm, and 1.00 am periods. This pattern of night-time concentration is similar for fatal injury from sharp objects, except that those incidents peak in the early hours of the morning, at around 1.00 am and 4.00 am, with smaller concentrations around 8.00 pm, 9.00 pm and 11.00 pm. Similar patterns are reported by Bowman, MacRitchie, and Gouveia (2006). Taking all violence-related fatal injuries together, they observe the peak periods for violent death to be 1.00 am–5.00 am (23.2 per cent), followed by 8.00 pm–10.00 pm (11.6 per cent) and 11.00 pm–midnight (6.6 per cent). In both studies, the increased risk at night-time is attributed to factors such as alcohol use, a sense of anonymity, and a sense, among young males, of what could be referred to as 'owning the night'.

The pattern of death from gun crime and sharp objects contrasts dramatically with that of fatal injury from burns and strangulation. In the case of burns, the most risky period is between 3.00 am and 6.00 am, after which risk patterns reduce and flatten before dropping to minimal levels between 9.00 am and 1.00 pm. The next most risky period for burn fatalities is between 1.00 pm and 3.00 pm, followed by the time between 5.00 pm and 7.00 pm, 7.00 pm and 9.00 pm, and 9.00 pm and 11.00 pm. The morning pattern coincides with the period when families are waking up and preparing to go work, school, or crèche; afternoon to evening patterns relate to the times at which adults are returning from work, and 1.00 pm to 3.00 pm is indicative of children returning from school (Prinsloo, 2007).

It is instructive to contrast these patterns with those of transport-related fatalities, specifically driver fatalities. The most likely time of the day for a driver to suffer fatal injury is between 6.00 pm and midnight. The increased risk is likely to be attributable to increased traffic, driver fatigue, decreased visibility, and possibly alcohol use. In all cases, it would appear that the likelihood of injury is strongly related to 'human ecology'—that is, to people's daily routines and their occupancy of particular places at particular times.

METHODOLOGY OF THE PRESENT STUDY

LOCATIONS

For the study reported here, data were obtained from the NIMSS for the period 2001–5. All deaths classified as homicide during this period were identified across four major cities in which the NIMSS had full coverage of non-natural fatalities: Cape Town, Durban (eThekwini), Johannesburg, and Pretoria (Tshwane).

DATA INSTRUMENTATION AND COLLECTION PROCEDURES

The NIMSS collates a wide range of secondary data concerning medico-forensic investigative procedures, including post-mortem reports, police investigative records, chemical-pathology laboratory results, and criminal-justice data. The information is combined into a single data form consisting of 21 items. For every non-natural death that enters the forensic medico-legal system in the participating facilities the NIMSS classifies the primary medical cause of death using the International Classification of Diseases version 9 (ICD 9). Demographic information is recorded and the laboratory reports provide details about the presence of alcohol in the deceased. In line with the aims of our research, we were specifically concerned to extract information about the time and location of injury, which the NIMSS also captures.

NIMSS procedures begin with the routine data collection activities of police officers and pathologists. Thereafter, mortuary clerical staff enter the information onto a computerized database and it is sent to the South African Presidential Crime, Violence and Injury Lead Programmes office[1] where all data from mortuaries and forensic chemistry laboratories is combined, cleaned, and analysed.

DATA ANALYSIS

Descriptive statistics of the key variables relating to the homicide victim (age, sex, blood-alcohol concentration (BAC)), external cause of death, and to the environment (month and day of death) were calculated in the form of frequency distributions and percentages. Pearson's chi-square tests were then used to measure any significant night-time and daytime differences.

RESULTS

A total of 33,365 deaths from homicide were registered at the four cities' mortuaries between January 2001 and December 2005. Time of death was recorded for 26,025 (78 per cent) of these deaths. Of the homicide deaths where time was recorded, the

---

[1] The Crime, Violence and Injury Lead Programme is co-directed by the Medical Research Council and the University of South Africa's Institute for Social and Health Sciences.

Table 16.1 Homicide deaths by time of day in four cities, 2001–5

	2001	2002	2003	2004	2005	Total
Cape Town						
Day	969 (41.7)	821 (37.4)	624 (39.0)	573 (38.8)	368 (43.5)	3355 (39.8)
Night	1352 (58.3)	1372 (62.6)	975 (61.0)	903 (61.2)	478 (56.5)	5080 (60.2)
Durban						
Day	732 (37.8)	750 (37.3)	458 (33.7)	599 (34.4)	439 (31.4)	2978 (35.3)
Night	1204 (62.2)	1260 (62.7)	902 (66.3)	1144 (65.6)	957 (68.6)	5467 (64.7)
Johannesburg						
Day	744 (37.7)	700 (35.1)	417 (35.3)	451 (36.9)	457 (37.7)	2769 (36.5)
Night	1232 (62.3)	1295 (64.9)	764 (64.7)	772 (63.1)	754 (62.3)	4817 (63.5)
Pretoria						
Day	36 (52.2)	81 (36.3)	78 (28.9)	120 (39.9)	111 (35.8)	426 (36.3)
Night	33 (47.8)	142 (63.7)	192 (71.1)	181 (60.1)	199 (64.2)	747 (63.7)

majority (16,348, or 62.8 per cent) occurred at night (8.00 pm to 5.00 am) with the remaining 9,677 (37.2 per cent) occurring during the daytime (6.00 am to 7.00 pm) period. This pattern—showing the majority of homicides to occur at night—was consistent across the four cities (see Table 16.1). Overall, there were 1.7 night-time homicide deaths for every daytime homicide death.

CHARACTERISTICS OF HOMICIDE VICTIMS

Gender

Of the 27,378 homicide deaths where the gender of the victim was recorded, 24,118 (88.1 per cent) were male and 3,260 (11.9 per cent) were female. Overall, there were 7.4 male homicide deaths for every female homicide death. The male to female ratio was even higher for night-time homicides (8.4:1) than for daytime homicides (6.5:1). Among male homicide victims, 12,210 (63.4 per cent) of deaths occurred in the evening and there were 1.74 night-time homicides for every homicide occurring during the day. Among female victims, 1,455 (57.4 per cent) of homicide deaths took place at night. The night to daytime ratio was somewhat lower among female victims, with 1.35 female homicide deaths occurring at night for every one occurring during the day.

Age

Most homicide fatalities fell within the 15–44-year-old age group (87.6 per cent). Homicide victimization rises dramatically from the age of 15 years, peaking among the 25–29-year-old age group, and tapering off from the age of 45 upwards. Figure 16.1 illustrates this age-range peak to be considerably more pronounced for homicide deaths occurring at night. For every homicide in the day there were 1.09 deaths at

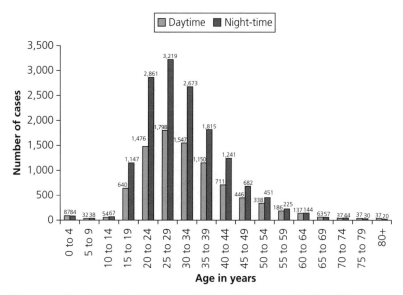

Figure 16.1 Homicide deaths by age and time of day across the four cities, 2001–5

night in the 0–14 age group, 1.85 at night among 15–29-year-olds, 1.68 deaths at night in the 30–44 age group, and 1.3 deaths at night in the 45–years-and-older range. These patterns are further elaborated in Table 16.2, which provides a breakdown of death by homicide for different age groups, by gender and time of day.

External Cause of Death by Time of Day

The majority of deaths due to 'external causes' were related to firearms (18,377: 55.1 per cent), sharp objects (9,744: 29.3 per cent), and blunt objects (3,927: 11.8 per cent)—the remaining 1,157 (3.5 per cent) being the result of strangulation, hanging, burns, and drowning. Figure 16.2 illustrates the higher proportion of homicide deaths due to firearms (9,573: 58.7 per cent) and sharp objects (5,075: 31.1 per cent) occurring at night, in comparison with the daytime (firearms = 4,913: 51.1 per cent; sharp objects = 2,702: 28.1 per cent).

Table 16.2 Homicide deaths by time of day for males and females, by age

	Males				Females		
Age group	6am–7pm n (per cent)	8pm–5am n (per cent)	Total	Age group	6am–7pm n (per cent)	8pm–5am n (per cent)	Total n (per cent)
0–14 yr	85 (47.5)	94 (52.5)	179	0–14 yrs	60 (50.4)	59 (49.6)	119
15–24 yr	1557 (34)	3025 (66.0)	4582	15–24 yrs	208 (41.4)	295 (58.6)	503
25–34 yr	2447 (35.3)	4486 (64.7)	6933	25–34 yrs	308 (41.6)	432 (58.4)	740
35–44 yr	1398 (38.2)	2264 (61.8)	3662	35–44 yrs	199 (39.4)	306 (60.6)	505
45+ yr	876 (44.0)	1117 (56.0)	1993	45+ yrs	204 (46.5)	235 (53.5)	439

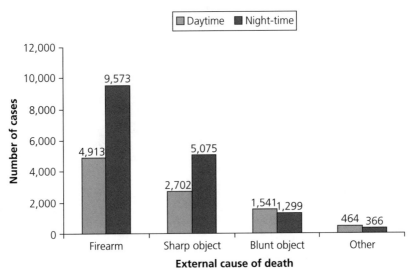

Figure 16.2 Homicide deaths by external cause of death and time of day across the four cities, 2001–5

Scene of Injury

Scenes of injury were recorded for only 17,418 (52.2 per cent) of homicide deaths. Of these, private dwellings (4,868: 27.9 per cent) were the most common scene of injury, followed by roads/highways (4,445: 25.5 per cent), informal settlements (depressed areas with inadequate housing) (3,028: 17.4 per cent), residential institutes (homes for the aged, hotels, and hostels, the latter traditionally being male-only units built by

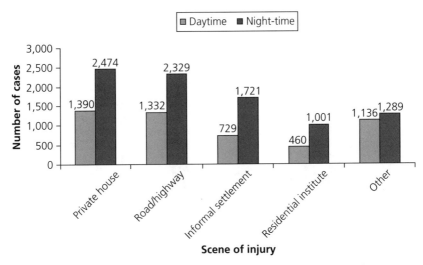

Figure 16.3 Homicide deaths by scene of injury and time of day for the four cities, 2001–5

employers and shared by several men) (1,745: 10 per cent), and other scenes, such as open land, or retail centres (3,332: 19.1 per cent). These trends were similar for both the homicides that occurred at night and those occurring during the day (Fig 16.3).

Homicide Fatalities by Month and Day

Limited information was recorded for the date and time of *injury*, and we therefore report on the date and time of *death*. Whilst death would have occurred at the time of injury for a majority of cases, some victims will have died hours or days after the injury itself and this bias must be kept in mind when reading the relevant tables and charts.

Month of Death

Month of death was recorded for 32,957 cases. Between 7.4 per cent and 8.4 per cent of homicide deaths were recorded for each of the months January to September. Homicide deaths, however, appear to rise towards the end of the year. The peak month for homicides was December (3,525: 10.6 per cent), followed by October (2,908: 8.8 per cent) and November (2,893: 8.8 per cent). This peak in homicides towards the end of the year was apparent among both night and daytime incidents.

Day of Death

Day of death was recorded for 32,957 homicides. Homicide deaths peaked on Saturdays (7,917: 24 per cent) followed by Sundays (6,756: 20.5 per cent), and Fridays (4,482: 13.6 per cent). Figure 16.4 reveals that homicide deaths occur more often in the evening for all the days of the week. However, the ratio of night to day homicide deaths is more notable over the weekend period, where almost twice as many homicides occur during the evening as they do during the day.

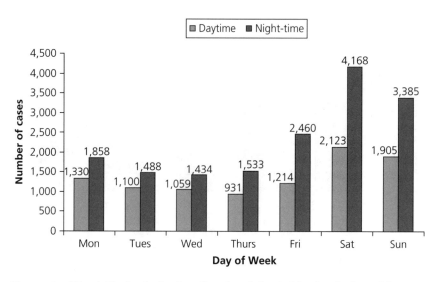

Figure 16.4 Homicide deaths by day of week and time of day for the four cities, 2001–5

Blood-Alcohol Concentration (BAC) Levels

Blood-alcohol analyses were conducted in 20,279 homicide fatalities. Just over half (10,208: 50.3 per cent) of these cases tested positive for alcohol, with a mean concentration of 0.16 g/100 ml (SD = 0.9). In addition, of the victims tested for alcohol, the majority of those whose death had occurred at night (54.8 per cent) were found to test positive, compared to only 42.4 per cent of those who died during the day (Fig 16.5).

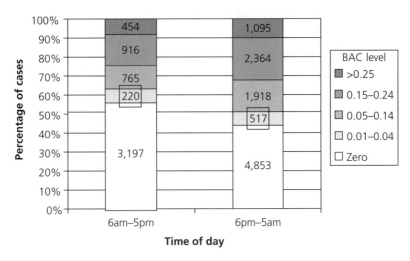

Figure 16.5 Homicide deaths by BAC level and time of day cross the four cities, 2001–5

DISCUSSION

To summarize, although we cannot be certain about the date and time of *injury*, the results show that homicide deaths rise towards the end of the year, with a peak in December, followed closely by November and October. The most likely explanation is that these are holiday months in South Africa when young people go on their long recess from schools and universities, and most working adults receive their income bonuses and take holidays away from their places of employment. There appears to be a clear temporal correlation between leisure time and an increased risk of violence, as further indicated by the time of day and day of the week data.

On all days of the week, violence-related deaths occur more frequently at night. However, more deaths occur on Saturday and Sunday nights than during weekday nights. The weapons most commonly used to inflict fatal injury are firearms, followed by sharp objects. The majority of night-time homicide victims test positive for alcohol consumption and a number of measures point to the importance of evening leisure time as a socio-temporal context for violence. However, this does not necessarily correspond to the use of leisure *spaces*. Private houses are the most likely scenes of fatal injury, followed closely by roads and highways. It is interesting to note that informal settlements, which feature overcrowding, little formal governance, and few infrastructure services, such as electricity, have lower levels of violent mortality than areas with formal housing. Homicide rates rise dramatically from the age of 15 years, peak among 25–29-year-olds, and then decline significantly from the age of 45. Male deaths from violence-related injury outnumber those of females by more than 7:1. This male to female ratio increases still further during the evening. Among males, two out of every three violent deaths occur at night.

Available data lends strong support to the hypothesized relationship between being young, being male, and being at particular risk of fatal violent crime. As Schönteich and Louw (2001, unpaginated) note, 'Young people are disproportionately likely to be victims of crime—especially young urban males . . . Their lifestyles and the fact that they are less risk averse than older people (by, for example, frequenting high crime areas, late at night), place them at higher than average risk of being victimized by criminals, especially in respect of violent crime.'

The gendered nature of such victimization in South Africa is further underlined by the finding that 'females accounted for an average of only 13 per cent of homicide victims from 1999 to 2001' (Matzopoulos, 2004: 12; see also Prinsloo, 2007). This, of course, is not to suggest that females face little risk of interpersonal violence (see Jewkes et al, 2006); it is merely to note that, in comparison with males they are less likely to be *killed* as a result of it.

Qualitative studies from South Africa and elsewhere note how, for some men, authority over women and children is assumed to be a rightful part of social relations and estimations of manhood (Lindsay, 2007; Wood and Jewkes, 2001). Likewise, some men see dominance over other men as being equally important to notions of masculinity (Barker and Ricardo, 2005). In a range of contexts, this authority-play between men often relies upon the use of—or more often, the threat of—force. It has been said that physical violence is a 'central feature of the upbringing of both white and black South African men, [being] integral to the political-economic structure that encompasses both groups' (Breckenridge, 1998: 674). In their discussion of young men, violence, and conflict in sub-Saharan Africa, Barker and Ricardo make the link, not just with the struggle for authority, but specifically with masculinities, noting that:

There are direct links between violence and conflict and the way that manhoods or masculinities are constructed …While some of the armed insurgencies have clear ideological causes, many are directly related to an attempt by young men to acquire power, or to question the power of specific groups of older men, and to live up to a specific version of manhood … At the most basic level, boys involved in these most brutal of armed insurgencies become 'big men' by being in control of a given setting and able to exert violence on those around them. In addition to immediate survival, they achieve and wield power. (2005: 24)

Many scholars in South Africa and elsewhere cohere in the view that violence lies at the core of some men's self-image, in relation to how they both define themselves and categorize and rank other men. The problem of male violence has received increasing attention from researchers interested in exploring the concept and meaning of masculinity/ies (Gibson and Hardan, 2005; Mac an Ghaill, 1996; Lindsay and Miescher, 2003; Morrell, 2001; Ouzgane and Morrell, 2005; Ratele, 2006; Ratele et al, 2007).

An influential theoretical framework often applied in the literature on male violence has been Connell's concept of hegemonic masculinity (Carrigan, Connell, and Lee, 1985; Connell, 1995). Hegemonic masculinity aims to convey the idea that contrary to the notion of sex-roles, which view males as homogeneous in their roles as boys and men, a number of masculinities are operative in any one arena, be it a pub, playground, prison, or political party. More significantly, Connell's framework stresses the recognition that not all masculinities are valued equally by men, women, and society in general. Masculinities are organized hierarchically, with the most valued forms perched at the top, and other subordinate ways-of-being-a-man arranged below. This implies that men are engaged in an ongoing struggle over which characteristics are truly representative of 'manliness', and thus around which *men* most embody this elusive, but most sought, of qualities. According to this nuanced view, moreover, expressions of masculinity are subject to historical change, cultural dynamics, intra-male group rivalry, inter-gender struggles, and psychic ambivalence (Connell and Messerschmidt, 2005).

'OWNING THE NIGHT': THE TEMPORAL DIMENSIONS OF VIOLENT GENDER ACCOMPLISHMENT

Whilst more statistical data is needed to profile the perpetrators and victims of violent crime in relation to gender and socio-economic status, this study indicates that, in South African cities, homicidal violence is a mainly weekend night-time, spring and summer seasons (end of the year), male-on-male, and under-45 years of age phenomenon. It seems that when young men come out to play on a weekend night they tend to play with other young men as much they may do with women. Forms of play occurring between males, and between males and females, appear to have different consequences. One of these differences is that when males play with each other, masculine orders and identities are at stake.

The accomplishment and reproduction of male hierarchy and manhood occurs at both a social and psychological level, established in ongoing activity, of which violence, or violent potential, may be one constituent. It is not that young men go out of their homes with the aim of reproducing their masculinities. The process happens, for the most part, unconsciously or as an aspect of other activities. The unconscious elements are likely related to affectivity, a felt need to prove oneself through the display of character: fearlessness, defence of honour, willingness to meet a challenge.

Interpersonal violence has powerful performative dimensions. Young men recognize this, acting out a 'violent version of manhood, seeking to instill fear and to make their presence known before a terrified audience' (Barker and Ricardo, 2005: 24–5). Yet, as Blackbeard and Lindegger (2007) describe in their study of teenage boys, the discursive positioning of male actors in relation to their masculinity may be multilayered, the boys seeing themselves 'in real and imagined space and in relation to imaginary sets of norms and audiences, such as the male peer group...' (p 42).

The statistical analyses presented here lead us to the opinion that there may be a temporal dimension to these psycho-social struggles. Specifically, we argue that young males in South Africa attempt to appropriate the night as a time for staking their claim as 'big men'. In their nightly sojourns, young men are drawn to act out exaggeratedly potent fantasy versions of masculinity. Yet, the world of fantasy feeds that of the everyday, and day-to-day events are the foundations on which fabrications about masculinity are built. These attempts to accomplish masculinity may be tenuous and performative but they are nonetheless important. They have implications, not just for policing, but also for broader policies of urban governance, economics, social development, education, and employment. Moreover, they have historically led to destructive consequences, both for those who follow such a path and for those around them. If the night-time is the right time for struggles for hegemony to be played out, there are prices to be paid. The dearest price of all is life itself.

REFERENCES

ALTBEKER, A (2007) *A Country at War with Itself: South Africa's crisis of crime*, Johannesburg and Cape Town: Jonathan Ball Publishers.

BARKER, G and RICARDO, C (2005) *Young Men and the Construction of Masculinity in Sub-Saharan Africa: Implications for HIV/AIDS, conflict, and violence*, Paper no 26, Social Development Papers: Conflict Prevention and Reconstruction. Washington, DC: World Bank, Social Development Department.

BLACKBEARD, D and LINDEGGER, G (2007) '"Building a Wall around Themselves": Exploring adolescent masculinity and abjection with photo-biographical research', *South African Journal of Psychology*, 37/1, 25–46.

BOWMAN, B, MacRITCHIE, V and GOUVEIA, J (2006) 'Patterns of fatal violence in Tshwane', presented at the World Cup Cities, World Class Safety Workshop, 16 August 2006, Tshwane, South Africa.

BRADSHAW, D, NANNAN, N, LAUBSCHER, R, GROENEWALD, P, JOUBERT, J, NOJILANA, B, NORMAN, R, PIETERSE, D and SCHNEIDER, M (2004) *South African National Burden of Disease Study 2000: Estimates of provincial mortality*, Cape Town: South African Medical Research Council.

BRECKENRIDGE, K (1998) 'The allure of violence: Men, race and masculinity in the South African goldmines, 1900–1950', *Journal of Southern African Studies*, 24/4, Special Issue on Masculinities in Southern Africa, 669–93.

CARRIGAN, T, CONNELL, RW and LEE, J (1985) 'Toward a new sociology of masculinity', *Theory and Society*, 14/5, 551–604.

CENTRE FOR THE STUDY OF VIOLENCE AND RECONCILIATION (1998) *Into the Heart of Darkness: Journeys of the Amagents in crime, violence and death*, Report for the Council for Scientific and Industrial Research (CSIR), <http://www.csvr.org.za/wits/papers/papcsir.htm>.

CENTRAL STATISTICAL SERVICE (1996) *Living in South Africa: Selected findings of the 1995 October Household Survey*, Pretoria: Central Statistical Service.

CIAC (Crime Information Analysis Centre: South African Police Service) (2007) *Crime Situation in South Africa, April–September 2007: Trends, spatial distribution and interpretation*, Cape Town: CIAC, <http://www.saps.gov.za/statistics/reports/crimestats/2007/_pdf/crime_situation1.pdf>.

CONNELL, RW (1995) *Masculinities*, Cambridge: Polity Press.

—— and Messerschmidt, M (2005) 'Hegemonic masculinity: Rethinking the concept', *Gender Society*, 19, 829–95.

GIBSON, D and HARDAN, A (eds) (2005) *Rethinking Masculinities, Violence and Aids*, Amsterdam: Het Spinhuis.

JEWKES, R, DUNKLE, K, KOSS, MP, LEVIN, JB, NDUNA, M, JAMA, M and SIKWEYIYA, Y (2006) 'Rape perpetration by young, rural South African men: Prevalence, patterns and risk factors', *Social Science and Medicine*, 63, 2949–61.

KRUG, E, DAHLBERG, LL, MERCY, JA, ZWI, AB and LOZANO, R (eds) (2002) *World Report on Violence and Health*, Geneva: World Health Organization.

LINDSAY, LA (2007) 'Working with gender: The emergence of the "male breadwinner" in colonial southwestern Nigeria', in C. M. Cole, T. Manuh and S. F. Miescher (eds) *Africa after Gender?*, Bloomington, IN: Indiana University Press. 241–52.

—— and Miescher, SF (2003) *Men and Masculinities in Modern Africa*. Portsmouth, NH: Heinemann.

MAC AN GHAILL, M (ed) (1996) *Understanding Masculinities: Social relations and cultural arenas*, Buckingham: Open University Press.

MAHOQUE, R and GOUVEIA, J (2007) 'Profile of fatal injuries in Tshwane, 2001–2004', presentation prepared for the Tshwane Mayoral Safety Committee, 22 March, Tshwane.

MATZOPOULOS, R (2004) 'The burden of injury in South Africa: Fatal injury trends and international comparisons', in S Suffla and A van Niekerk (eds), *Crime, Violence and Injury Prevention in South Africa: Developments and challenges*, Lenasia/Tygerberg: Medical Research Council (MRC)/ University of South Africa (UNISA), Crime, Violence and Injury Lead Programme.

—— (ed) (2005) *A Profile of Fatal Injuries in South Africa: 6th Annual Report of the National Injury Mortality Surveillance System 2004*. Lenasia/Tygerberg: MRC/UNISA Crime, Violence and Injury Lead Programme.

MIESCHER, SF, COLE, CM and, MANUH, T (eds), *African After Gender?* Bloomington: Indiana University Press.

MORREL, R (ed) (2001) *Changing Men in Southern Africa*, Durban: University of Natal Press.

OUZGANE, L and MORRELL, R (eds) (2005) *African Masculinities: Men in Africa from the late-nineteenth century to the present*, New York: Palgrave Macmillan.

PARKER, Z, DAWES, A and FARR, V (2004) 'Interpersonal youth violence prevention', in S Suffla and A van Niekerk (eds), *Crime, Violence and Injury Prevention in South Africa: Developments and challenges*, Lenasia/Tygerberg: MRC/UNISA Crime, Violence and Injury Lead Programme.

PRINSLOO, M (ed) (2007) *A Profile of Fatal Injuries in South Africa: 7th Annual Report of the National Injury Mortality Surveillance System, 2005*, Lenasia/Tygerberg: MRC/UNISA Crime, Violence and Injury Lead Programme.

RATELE, K (2006) 'Ruling masculinity and sexualities', *Feminist Africa* 6 (*Subaltern Sexualities*), 48–64.

—— FOUTEN, E, SHEFER, T, STREBEL, A, SHABALALA, N and BUIKEMA, R (2007) '"Moffies, jocks and cool guys": Boys' accounts of masculinity and their resistance in context', in T Shefer, K Ratele, A Strebel, NJ Shabalala and R Buikema (eds), *From Boys to Men: The social construction of masculinity in contemporary society*, Landsdowne: University of Cape Town Press.

SCHÖNTEICH, M and LOUW, A (2001) *Crime in South Africa: A country and cities profile*, Institute for Security Studies, Occasional Paper No 49–2001, <http://www.issafrica.org/Papers/49/Paper49.html>.

STATISTICS SOUTH AFRICA (1999) *Victims of Crime Survey 1998*, Pretoria: Statistics South Africa.

WOOD, K and JEWKES, R (2001) '"Dangerous love": Reflections on violence among Xhosa township youth', in R Morrell (ed), *Changing Men in Southern Africa*, University of Natal Press/Zed Books.

17

NEW ZEALAND

Fiona Hutton

INTRODUCTION

This chapter aims to highlight a number of issues relating to alcohol, crime, and disorder in New Zealand. Alcohol consumption and the perceived rise in disorderly behaviour associated with 'binge drinking'[1] are often linked to crime. The Alcohol Advisory Council of New Zealand (ALAC) (2002) identifies 785,000[2] New Zealand adults as regularly indulging in binge drinking, an activity that is often blamed on young people. Legislation in New Zealand is increasingly concerned with how to control the effects of binge drinking in public places and this chapter will discuss these measures and their effectiveness. In New Zealand, although the negative repercussions of drinking are often frowned upon or viewed with disgust, drinking as a means to bond relationships, to relax, and have a good time is positively encouraged. One of ALAC's objectives is to change these attitudes. This chapter will trace some of the historical and cultural issues related to the development of alcohol consumption and control, highlighting the historical legacy of focusing on specific groups and their public consumption of alcohol. The liberalization of New Zealand's liquor laws and subsequent changes in the availability and accessibility of alcohol have been subject to much research and debate. Changes in the drinking environment resulting from the Sale of Liquor Act 1989 and subsequent amendments[3] will be considered, alongside their effects on alcohol consumption.

---

[1] Binge drinking is a term that has a wide range of definitions. A widely used definition in New Zealand is: consuming six or more drinks on one occasion for men, and consuming four or more drinks on one occasion for women (Bhatta and Casswell, 2001; Dacey and Barnes, 1998). Two widely used definitions in the UK are consuming double the daily recommended/'sensible' amounts of eight units of alcohol for men and six units for women, or consuming more than half the weekly recommended 'sensible' levels of ten and a half units for men and seven units for women in one session (Measham, 2004: 316).

[2] The total population of New Zealand is approximately four million.

[3] Significant amendments to the Sale of Liquor Act 1989 are those enacted in 1999 and 2004. These allowed for the liberalization of alcohol policy: in 1999 supermarkets were permitted to sell beer as well as wine, and pubs and off licences were permitted to trade on Sundays. Most significantly, in 1999 the legal drinking age

The chapter will go on to discuss the introduction of new security measures to address crime and disorder relating to street drinkers and young binge drinkers in specific areas of the city of Wellington. It will be noted that alcohol is not the sole focus of disorder initiatives by local councils and central government in New Zealand. New laws have recently been proposed to address public concerns about graffiti.[4]

CULTURAL CONTEXT

New Zealand has a history of both drinking alcohol and of trying to control the problems and issues associated with excessive alcohol consumption. It is argued that New Zealand's drinking culture developed from specific social, cultural, and historical circumstances (Philips, 1996). Alcohol and its consumption played an important role in early colonial New Zealand. In the 1800s a certain type of man was identified as emigrating to the 'new world'; one that was tough, adventure-seeking, and masculine. This ideal 'frontier man' was also often socially isolated, young, and single and so flocked to the emerging pubs and hotels with their promise of warmth, companionship, and alcohol. As Philips (1996: 34) states, 'There can be no question of the centrality of the pub to frontier male culture', as they were a focus for entertainment and information. In addition, during the 1800s alcohol was seen as a nourishing food and a stimulant at a time when town water supplies were often polluted and undrinkable, and other alternatives were expensive and spread disease. Alcohol was seen as a 'safe' alternative, so much so that hospitals often used alcohol to 'build up' their patients. One patient in Wellington hospital in 1880 was supplied with '581 ounces of sprits, 696 ounces of wine, 88 bottles of port and 16 bottles of claret and champagne in less than six months' (Eldred-Grigg, 1984: 60).

However, despite these popularly held views, alcohol aroused the anxieties of early colonial New Zealand. In early frontier settler societies concerns grew about the alcohol-related disorder associated with male drunkenness. These anxieties were rooted in fears about civilization (or lack of it) in the 'new world' (Philips, 1996: 48). As New Zealand towns developed there was less tolerance of social disorder and drunkenness. On the frontier such behaviour had little effect, but 'in town' such behaviour was more disruptive; women were frightened for themselves and their children, and men were frightened for their land and property; 'cities brought new expectations of order, routine and public decorum' (Philips, 1996: 49). Thus, binge drinking is not a new phenomenon in New Zealand, as male frontier workers frequently came into the

---

was lowered from 20 to 18 years of age. In 2004, vineyards were allowed to sell their own wine on Easter Sunday.

[4] Amendments to the Summary Offences Act 1981 have created a specific offence of graffiti vandalism, tagging, and defacing; limited the sale of spray cans to those 18 years or over; and require that spray cans must be kept securely so that members of the public cannot gain access easily to them. It also gives judges the option of imposing a community sentence that would include the removal of graffiti from vandalism and tagging sites. See <http://www.parliament.nz/en-NZ/SC/SubmCalled/d/3/8/48SCLOtagging200803111 -Summary-Offences-Tagging-and-Graffiti-Vandalism.htm>.

towns and settler societies for drinking sprees which were seen as socially disruptive. The effects of drinking were usually *publicly visible* as men had to get home after their drinking bouts. Drunkenness was seen as a serious social problem throughout the 1800s. For example, from the 1840s to the 1860s New Zealanders drank more than the British and drunk more heavily than subsequent generations; it was not unusual to start drinking mid-morning and continue until late at night (Eldred-Grigg, 1984).

Controls on drinking in early colonial New Zealand were fairly relaxed, with Maori tribes permitting places for alcohol consumption, for which they levied taxes. It was not until after the creation of a colonial state in 1840 that the control and regulation of alcohol began in earnest, with 51 Acts of Parliament brought into force by 1881. The state derived a large income from the tax on alcohol, although the moral question of it profiting from the liquor traffic was not raised. This theme gained greater prominence in 1854 after a government select committee[5] specifically identified 'the vice of drunkenness' as 'the main cause of crime in the colony' (Eldred-Grigg, 1984: 67).

The control of alcohol in New Zealand often centred on specific groups and it was working-class men, in particular, who were targeted by legislators. For example, the licensing Ordinance Act of 1842, and the Vagrant Act of 1866 targeted working-class drunks and also defined a new type of 'habitual drunkard' branded as idle and disorderly (Eldred-Grigg, 1984). Public drunkenness and the harassment of 'respectable' citizens at public gatherings and in towns in the evenings meant that there had become a significant division between 'respectable' and 'rowdy' or 'disreputable' masculinity. In this regard, the popular working-class practice of 'shouting'[6] was made illegal in 1916 under a War Regulation Amendment Act, as it was seen as building bonds between men and encouraging drunkenness. Communities of 'mates' had become 'morally dangerous in the eyes of the respectable' (Philips, 1996: 71). In addition, sexual vice was linked to alcohol consumption and as the 'quickest solution to sexual vice would be the early closing of pubs' (Philips, 1996: 72); the infamous 'six o'clock swill'[7] then developed as a result of a 6.00 pm closing time. Although this piece of legislation was enacted to contain male vice and soldiers' behaviour during the First World War, it was made permanent in 1918. This only served to encourage the speedy consumption of large amounts of alcohol and a cementing of the male drinking culture that it sought to destroy. The 'six o'clock swill' was also credited with the development of an unhealthy binge-drinking culture. The 1967 Sale of Liquor Act extended pub opening hours to 10.00 pm, although it was not until the 1989 Sale of Liquor Act that New Zealand's strict alcohol laws were more dramatically liberalized.

Maori populations were seen as another group that needed to be controlled. Alcohol consumption did not feature in traditional Maori society, but by the 1860s, through contact with settlers, drunkenness among Maori had become commonplace.[8] Fear of

---

[5] Select Committee findings debated, PD, 1854, second session, p 409 (cited in Eldred-Grigg, 1984: 260).

[6] 'Shouting' refers, in this context, to buying rounds of drinks when drinking in groups.

[7] The 'six o'clock swill' refers to the time when working men gathered in pubs after work from about 4.30–5.00 pm in large numbers for the speedy consumption of as much alcohol as they could manage, before the pubs closed at 6.00 pm (see similar discussion in Chapter 18, Chikritzhs, 'Australia').

[8] Sadly there is also evidence that alcohol damaged Maori society and that it was used to deliberately poison or debilitate Maori populations. It was also exchanged for land (Eldred-Grigg, 1984).

disorder meant that by 1847 the sale or supply of spirits to Maoris was banned in some districts. Maori drinking was further criminalized through an amendment to the Licensing Act in 1910 which prohibited the sale of alcohol to 'an intoxicated male Native' or to 'any female Native not being the wife of a person other than a Native' (Philips, 1996: 66). Fear of groups associated with disorder or the unleashing of 'savagery' was behind these types of legislation. Maori drunkenness was also argued to be policed more vigorously to 'maintain the illusion of state control' (Bull, 2004: 505) as settlers would soon lose confidence in the impartiality of the legal system if Maori drunkenness was ignored.

The conflicting cultural expectations and values placed on drinking alcohol differ not only between countries but also within countries. Maori and Pacific people's drinking patterns could be argued to have been shaped by the cultural background and context in which they developed. Pacific peoples, for example, are less likely to be drinkers compared with the general New Zealand population (Huakau et al, 2005). However, those Pacific Islanders who do drink consume larger quantities of alcohol, a larger number of drinks per session, and more often drink to get drunk than the general New Zealand population. While Pacific peoples' drinking patterns appear to be more harmful than those of the general New Zealand population, cultural factors are also likely to have influenced their use of alcohol. Before contact with Europeans there was no alcohol in Pacific society and the acceptability of drinking is low in Pacific cultures (hence the substantially higher figure of abstainers). Alcohol also plays a similar role to food in Pacific cultures and the quantity of alcohol provided at social or group gatherings represents the generosity of the group. Like food, alcohol is consumed until it is finished, which perhaps sometimes underlies Pacific peoples' larger volume of alcohol consumption (Huakau et al, 2005). Maori are often identified as binge drinkers, and disorder related to alcohol consumption has been explained, in part, as a response to disempowerment through colonization (Hill, 2002).

The development of alcohol use and its control in New Zealand is a complex story. However, there are some themes that can be identified and related to contemporary concerns about alcohol use and governance of the night-time economy (NTE). Visible drunkenness and the problems associated with binge drinking are at the forefront of contemporary anxieties about the drinking culture in New Zealand. This means that in contemporary society some groups are the focus for legislation and control, such as young people and street drinkers. Particularly forceful or hidebound forms of 'doing' masculinity are still seen as a threat, as it is largely unruly young men who are at the forefront of concerns about disorderly behaviour. Drinking by young women is also highlighted as problematic in contemporary New Zealand, with rises in consumption and indicators of bingeing by young women (Bhatta and Casswell, 2001). Young women's drinking has raised different concerns in comparison to their male counterparts. Female deviance is often subject to sexualization and anxieties are raised about the moral status of young women (Carrington, 2006). Again, it is only *some* group's *public* drinking that is deemed problematic and these tensions have a long historical legacy.

Cities such as Auckland and Wellington are increasingly marketed as cultured and cosmopolitan places to visit, with varied leisure and consumption opportunities, such as theatre, ballet, opera, dining out, and shopping. Nightlife is socially and economically important as it attracts large numbers of tourists and students, eager to sample the delights of the bars and clubs that New Zealand's cities have to offer. The *Lonely Planet Guide* describes Courtney Place as 'The nightlife centre of Wellington. Blair and Allen Street . . . are fertile hunting grounds for booze and music' (Bain et al, 2006: 421). There is a tension between this entrepreneurial agenda of developing 'cultural life' for students and tourists in order to keep Wellington (and other cities) 'thriving' and the concerns of agencies working to minimize alcohol-related harms.

The development of Wellington as a city with a sophisticated 'café culture' and a thriving nightlife can be traced back to the liberalization of the liquor laws. The Sale of Liquor Act 1989 radically changed New Zealand's alcohol policy, partly in response to the wish to compete in the international tourist market. The 1989 Act introduced a relaxation of the licensing application process, leading to an increase in licensed premises and increased availability of alcohol. With the introduction of such liberalizing measures it is perhaps unsurprising that alcohol consumption has again become the focus for contemporary concerns and that associated health and social problems have not declined (Bhatta and Casswell, 2001). There are now additional concerns about the governance of the night-(and day)-time street, linked to the behaviour of particular groups and associated with their public use of alcohol.

The control and availability of alcohol have always been subjects of tension between those who profit from the trade in alcohol and those who have concerns about its effects and the harms that it causes. From early exchanges between prohibitionists and the liberal government of the late 1800s (Eldred-Grigg, 1984) to contemporary developments in the alcohol liberalization debate, the control of alcohol has been vigorously contested. This tension between public-health groups and commercial interests is evident in industry opposition to policies that are most likely to be effective in reducing alcohol-related harm. These have been identified as: reducing the accessibility of alcohol, strengthening drink-driving laws and restricting the marketing of alcohol (Casswell and Maxwell, 2005: 119). These measures do not appeal to the alcohol industries who want their products to be readily available and affordable to a wide range of people. A source of specific discontent is the excise tax described as a 'burden on the alcoholic beverage industry' (Stewart, 2001 cited in Casswell and Maxwell, 2005: 120). While the abolition of excise tax has not been achieved, the 1989 Liquor Act's liberalized regime allowed that, in cities such as Auckland, 'By 1995, the number of on and off licensed premises and clubs selling alcohol . . . almost doubled' (Bhatta and Casswell, 2001).

From 1990, supermarkets and other main grocery outlets were allowed to sell wine. Alcohol availability, which has been linked to heavier and more frequent drinking, increased. In addition, hours of trading restrictions were lifted meaning some premises could trade twenty-four hours a day (Bhatta and Casswell, 2001). Measures to encourage healthy drinking environments such as requirements for establishments to provide non-alcoholic drinks and food had limited impact as host responsibility training for managers was not mandatory until 1999. However, the effectiveness of monitoring and enforcement of these expectations has been improved with the introduction of liquor licensing liaison teams and last-drink surveys.[9] In addition, in 1999 (under an amendment to the Sale of Liquor Act) promotions, competitions, and pricing structures that encouraged excessive drinking were prohibited, although monitoring of these measures remains under-resourced. In Auckland, in 2005, there were 1,500 licensed premises and only four district licensing inspectors and five liquor licensing police officers (Casswell and Maxwell, 2005: 128).[10]

Increasing the minimum age at which alcohol can be purchased is argued to be one of the most effective measures to reduce alcohol-related harm (Casswell and Maxwell, 2005). However, as noted, under an amendment to the Sale of Liquor Act, New Zealand lowered the age limit in 1999 from 20 to 18 years of age. Industry groups argued that this change 'normalized' drinking in a safe environment and the Liquor Advisory Committee stated that the purchase age was immaterial as young people were accessing alcohol through parents or other adults. With renewed concerns about binge drinking and disorder among young people a Bill was introduced in Parliament in 2006 to increase the legal age at which alcohol could be purchased back up to 20. This Bill was defeated in November 2006.

The Sale of Liquor Act 1989 also changed the way liquor licences were granted. Instead of granting new licences where community 'need' could be shown, as was the case up until 1990, the 1989 Act introduced the criteria that licences be granted provided the applicant was 'suitable' and had a valid planning certificate under the Resource Management Act 1991. Community concerns over the density of liquor outlets—both on- and off-licensed—remain unaddressed, as the legislation contained 'narrowly prescribed grounds for objection' (Casswell and Maxwell, 2005: 126).[11] By the mid-1990s, the number of liquor licences had doubled across the country to 11,280. This upward trend continued with 14,131 liquor licences by 2002 and 15,242 by 2004 (Lash, 2005: 20).

Increases in the availability of alcohol have been linked to increased alcohol consumption by some population groups such as Maori and young people. Rises in the related harms suffered from increased alcohol consumption have also been noted. Maori are over-represented in the figures for binge drinkers and, as noted, they are often cited as drinking larger amounts of alcohol per drinking session (Dacey and Barnes, 1998; Hutt, 2003; Ministry of Health, 2007). Maori women are more likely to suffer from alcohol-related problems. Their morbidity rate from alcohol-related causes was recorded as 2.9 times that of non-Maori females for the 1989–91 period (Pomare and De Boer, 1991, cited in Hutt, 2003: 81). Maori youth are also more likely to have consumed large amounts of alcohol at least once a week compared to young people from non-Maori populations (Ministry of Health, 2007). Legislative developments have made it illegal to refuse to sell alcohol on the basis of race (Sale Of

---

[9] Last-drink surveys, to monitor where those involved in crime or injury purchased their last drink, have been used in some areas of New Zealand since 1994. In 2005, they were incorporated into a national scheme entitled 'Alcolink', <http://www.alcohol.org.nz/CaseStudy.aspx?PostingID=870>. Liquor-licensing teams have been in existence since 1990.

[10] Other liberalizing measures included allowing alcohol brands to advertise in the print media and on television after 8.30 pm, rather than the previous time of 9.00 pm (Bhatta and Casswell, 2001).

[11] Similar problems in challenging liquor licence applications in the UK are discussed in Hadfield (2006).

Liquor Act 1962), and the urbanization of many Maori throughout the 1970s and 1980s was associated with heavier drinking. Therefore increasing the availability of alcohol appears to have been more harmful for some sections of the population, with research pointing to correlations between ease of access to alcohol at 15 and drinking on licensed premises at 18. Drinking on licensed premises at 18 and access to licensed premises were also correlated with more frequent drinking sessions and larger quantities of alcohol consumed (Casswell, Pledger, and Pratap, 2002). It has been argued therefore that a large amount of the alcohol-related harm in New Zealand is the result of heavier drinking with increases in several measures of binge drinking being identified. These measures are cited as: increases in the typical quantities consumed, frequency of drinking to get drunk, and frequency of drinking larger amounts (Bhatta and Casswell, 2001). The increases in these measures were also higher among those in the 14–19 age groups and in men under 30 who were the group who drank the most heavily (ibid). Women of all ages also increased their consumption although on average they reported drinking smaller quantities than men.

As noted above, the drinking environment has changed significantly in New Zealand, with an increase in the number of licensed premises in cities such as Auckland and a broader range of places allowed to sell alcohol, such as supermarkets. It would appear therefore that although policymakers have done all they can to *encourage* drinking, they are now wringing their collective hands about the *problems* associated with increased alcohol consumption. Having highlighted some of the issues relating to the liberalization of New Zealand's licensing laws the discussion will now turn to the debates surrounding alcohol, crime, and disorder.

ALCOHOL, CRIME, AND DISORDER

As noted above, alcohol was linked to crime in New Zealand as early as the 1850s and prohibitionists eagerly leapt on the suggestion that temperance had caused a decline in crime. However, caution was called for, with clergymen and lawyers at the time stating 'always in social phenomena we have to deal with composite and complex causation' (Eldred-Grigg, 1984: 214). As numerous scholars have illustrated, alcohol is associated with several kinds of offending behaviour such as violence and disorder. Parker (1996) points out that alcohol-related crime results from a number of interrelated factors, not just alcohol consumption. Alcohol could be operating alongside factors such as poverty, unemployment, boredom, peer pressure, use of drugs, the pursuit of fun, and mental-health concerns. In addition, alcohol is not always a factor in criminality, as many crimes are committed in the absence of intoxication, highlighting that more complex explanations for criminal activity are required. Researchers have argued that specific crimes are more likely to be influenced or affected by alcohol consumption, such as violent crimes, rather than acquisitive property offences (Pernanen, 1991). A causal link between alcohol and crime cannot be readily identified, although correlations between alcohol and crime are often indicated. Plant, Plant, and Thornton (2002) state that it is likely that alcohol consumption does increase aggression and violence in both men and women but they also point out that most drinking occasions do not end with this kind of behaviour. They reach similar conclusions to those of Parker (1996) asserting that how alcohol affects a drinker is dependent on the setting and the characteristics of the drinker, emphasizing that the link between alcohol, disorder, and violence is by no means clear cut and involves complex interrelating factors (see the leading work of Graham and colleagues in this area, Chapter 14).

Significant controls on alcohol and 'problem' groups such as street drinkers and young people have been proposed or implemented in response to concerns from Central Business District (CBD) retailers about harassment and antisocial behaviour. While it may be the case that concerns are based on unpleasant and abusive behaviour there remains a question mark over whether there has been a real increase in alcohol-related disorder. Police figures do indicate a rise in disorder offences from 1998 to 2007 from 20,395 to 24,609 (Statistics New Zealand, 2007a) but the population has also risen from 3,814,670 in 1998 to 4,228,170 in 2007 (Statistics New Zealand, 2007b). Therefore, a rise in the number of offences would be expected, as demographics are one of the significant factors that affect crime rates (Gurr, 1981). Several researchers have questioned whether there has actually been an increase in offensive or disorderly behaviour, and that if this supposed increase in disorder is based on people's *perceptions* then, there is 'little justification for widening the scope of criminal prohibitions to address the situation' (Husak, 2006: 92). Bottoms (2006) and Husack (2006) both highlight the role that public perceptions play in shaping criminal justice responses to crime and disorder. The concept of 'governing through crime' (Simon, 2007) is pertinent here; the public are seemingly so obsessed with the criminality of particular social groups such as young people, that governments gain political favour by responding to largely misguided public opinion. This has been argued to be a particular phenomenon in New Zealand as a result of 'penal populism'[12] (Pratt and Clarke, 2005). Other commentators have focused on the selective crime reporting of the media as a melting pot for contemporary fears and anxieties about criminal or disorderly groups. One of the results of these kinds of developments is the introduction of measures such as CCTV to soothe public fears about disorder and to regulate deviance.

From early colonial times to the present day, it would seem that this is what the 'public' want: to be reassured that disorderly groups and behaviours are being controlled and that 'respectable' society will not be harmed by such groups and their behaviours. What often remain unacknowledged are the concerns of the groups identified as disorderly. Wooden's (1997) research shows that many young people themselves do not like to encounter the visible signs of violence, alcohol, or drug use as this makes them afraid in public spaces (cited in White, 2008: 233). Young Wellingtonian clubbers also expressed anxieties about traversing the city at night and elaborated on how they stayed safe and the risks that they took in participating in the NTE. Gender is also significant in negotiating the night-time street. A study of female clubbers in Manchester, England showed that they felt they were targets for harassment by men simply by being visible, in public, and out in the city at night (Hutton, 2006). Also

---

[12] This term refers to a reframing of the terms of penal debate around the power and influence of perceived public opinion and pressure groups that campaign on issues of law and order.

unacknowledged by policymakers in New Zealand is the potential for discrimination inherent in the introduction of crime-prevention measures. For example, public-place liquor bans target only those who drink on the streets and CCTV has been used to move on individuals who have not offended, but who are considered suspicious, with young people being particularly vulnerable to this kind of exclusionary practice (Williams and Johnstone, 2000). In addition, clubbers are often a group of young people that are targeted as 'disorderly' and in need of control. A study focusing on young Wellingtonian clubbers and their use of recreational drugs, such as ecstasy, found that they often felt demonized in the press and unfairly targeted by government legislation[13] (Hutton, 2005). So how have perceptions of these 'disorderly' groups impacted upon governance of the night-time street?

POLICING, SECURITY, AND CRIME CONTROL

New Zealand has seen a variety of criminal-justice responses to the crime and disorder associated with increased availability of alcohol and expansion of its NTE. One of the most significant measures introduced to target alcohol-related disorder has been the 'Alcolink' project, implemented in 2005. 'Alcolink' is argued to provide information, enabling a detailed analysis of the role of alcohol in crime. Police record whether alcohol was involved in an incident and, if so, where the offender had their last drink. In conjunction with this, police have carried out targeted operations on certain groups such as Operation Hurricane, which focused on public-place drinking, youth problems, and violence in Wellington city (Sim, Morgan, and Batchelor, 2005). Yet, as Casswell and Maxwell (2005) identify, enforcement of the liquor-licensing law has not been adequately resourced. The Sale of Liquor Act 1989 states that alcohol must not be served to intoxicated persons. Enforcement of this requirement was evaluated in Wellington to see if it had had any effect on crime and disorder (Sim, Morgan and Batchelor, 2005). Overall, this study did show some reduction in alcohol-related harm and offences but it was not clear if this could be attributed solely to increased enforcement, or to other factors such as 'Operation Hurricane' which were influencing the drinking environment at the time.

Local councils in New Zealand have also tried to address problems of governing the central city and public perceptions of rises in disorder through the development of 'Walkwise' programmes. 'Walkwise' provides a visible 'reassurance policing' function, through the conduct of foot patrols in central city areas. In Wellington, these are run by a private security company, Armourguard Security Ltd.[14] Such schemes can be understood as part of the privatization of crime prevention. The patrols are designed to act as a deterrent to crimes such as graffiti and vandalism, and to enhance the 'eyes

---

[13] For example, the use of 'nos' (nitrous oxide) was made illegal in 2005 and in 2008 the use of benzylpiperazine (BZP)-based party pills was banned.

[14] Lower Hutt and Manukau have adopted the same 'Walkwise' model for their city spaces and Dunedin and Porirua have also adopted similar models: <http://www.safecommunities.org.nz>.

and ears of the police'. Part of their role is also stated as 'promoting the public image of the "safe city"' (Safer Communities Foundation, 2008). A Wellington City Council resident satisfaction survey found that respondents' *perceptions* of safety increased substantially after the introduction of 'Walkwise' and other crime-prevention initiatives[15] from 2001 onwards.

A significant measure introduced to try to curb disorderly behaviour associated with alcohol is the liquor ban. In Wellington, for example, there is a permanent liquor ban in force in the city centre which prohibits the consumption and possession of open drinking vessels in public places at particular times (Wellington City Council, 2008). However, there remain concerns about the effectiveness of such a ban, particularly in relation to the displacement of drinking, disorder, and crime to neighbouring locations. Due to alleged increases in alcohol-related disorder and violence, Wellington City Council is now proposing to introduce a 24-hours-a-day, seven-days-a-week ban on street drinking in the central city. This is part of a larger plan to address perceived problems in the Courtney Place area of Wellington,[16] including the introduction of CCTV cameras, improved street lighting, and enhanced traffic management (*Dominion Post*, 8 March 2008). Critics point out that such 'situational measures' do not address the underlying issues associated with alcohol-related disorder, and that they will simply serve to further stigmatize and criminalize already marginalized populations, such as street drinkers, while putting pressure on police to enforce the extended ban. For example, ALAC identify the issues surrounding public drinking as 'ease of access to alcohol, boredom or lack of other alcohol-free activities, parental awareness and responsibility, and the health of young people' and point out that these are issues that cannot be addressed by regulatory measures alone. ALAC also highlight the importance of local government policy that 'targets the wider impact of alcohol misuse on the community and the issues that lead to misuse *in addition* to attempts to regulate public drinking' (ALAC, 2002: 3, emphasis in the original). It is also noteworthy that Wellington City Council's redevelopment of Glover Park in 2004 served to displace the street drinkers that congregated there to Cuba Street, where arguably they became more of a problem.[17] Researchers such as White (2008) have argued that in some public spaces there is an expectation and tolerance of disorder and that the over-sanitization of public spaces stops people from utilizing them, just as antisocial behaviour does. Courtney Place could be argued to be such a place; there is not the expectation that people will act with decorum. White (2008) also points out that the 'public' are not a homogeneous group and the competing demands of different groups who use public space are not easy to meet.

---

[15] In addition, Wellington City Council has introduced a liquor ban, a Homeless Taskforce, and a community-policing base in Cuba Street (Wellington City Council, 2008).

[16] Courtney Place in central Wellington is the heart of bar/club culture and the main entertainment district of the city. It has a large number of bars, clubs, and restaurants and is frequented at the weekends by large numbers of, mainly young, drinkers.

[17] Cuba Mall is an area that has a proliferation of shops and is a busy, well used street; Glover Park is an area slightly off the main thoroughfare. Recent newspaper headlines reading: 'Fed-up Cuba Mall retailers want total booze ban' (*Wellingtonian*, 21 February 2008) illustrate the problems now occurring in this area.

CONCLUSIONS

It is clear that alcohol consumption and associated disorderly behaviours are a source of anxiety and tension in contemporary New Zealand society; although, early controls and debates about alcohol show these behaviours and the anxieties attached to them to be far from new. The issues discussed in this chapter emphasize that one of the challenges surrounding the governance of nightlife, crime, and disorder is sustaining a balance between the competing interests and concerns of the different groups who use the spaces of the city.

The issues raised in this chapter focus on public drinking by specific groups of people and this focus relates to wider debates about anomalies between the perceptions and realities surrounding crime and disorder. Increasingly, policy and legislation have responded to public demands for 'something to be done' which are not always based on accurate information. In addition, New Zealand appears to be adopting situational crime prevention and place-management measures such as liquor bans and CCTV that have not been proven to be effective, may be discriminatory, and foster social exclusion. Also, as the ALAC highlights, these kinds of measures do not tackle the underlying reasons for heavy alcohol consumption, binge drinking, and disorder.

There are, therefore, many areas in which research could usefully inform policy and contribute to the debates about alcohol, crime, and disorder in New Zealand. As noted in a report focusing specifically on Dunedin (Kypri, 2003) there have been no formal evaluations of liquor bans and their effects so this is an area requiring urgent research attention. A suggested focus for research in the short term would be the development of robust tools for evaluating the effectiveness of measures such as 'Alcolink', transport solutions, and CCTV, with a focus on any inherent issues of displacement. Thorough appraisals of this nature may encourage the development of more overarching inter-related strategies for addressing the harms associated with alcohol consumption.

In New Zealand, further reconsideration of the alcohol and crime nexus is required. Alcohol is often unproblematically linked to crime and a simple cause-and-effect relationship assumed. Yet, many criminal offences and acts of an 'antisocial' nature are committed by those who have not consumed alcohol and any links between alcohol and crime are surely complex. As Parker (1996: 296) suggests 'alcohol is an accessory both to crime and a lawful good time. There is perhaps no definitive criminological message in a bottle.'

REFERENCES

All internet sources were accessible 20 August 2008

ALCOHOL ADVISORY COUNCIL OF NEW ZEALAND (2002) *Regulation of the Drinking of Alcohol in Public Places*. Policy Statement 3, Alcohol Advisory Council of New Zealand: Wellington, <www.alac.org.nz/FileLinks/11614_PolicyDrinkingPublicPlaces2002.e76a1785.pdf>.

BAIN, C, DUNFORD, G, MILLER, K, O'BRIEN, S and RAWLINGS-WAY, C (2006) *New Zealand*, London: Lonely Planet Publications Ltd.

BHATTA, K and CASSWELL, S (2001) *A Decade of Drinking: Ten-year trends in drinking patterns in Auckland, New Zealand, 1990–1999*, Alcohol and Public Health Research Unit: Auckland, <http://www.aphru.ac.nz/projects/decade%20TC.htm>.

BOTTOMS, A (2006) 'Incivilities, offence and social order in residential communities', in A von Hirsch and AP Simester (eds), *Incivilities: Regulating offensive behaviour*, Portland: Hart Publishing, 91–113.

BULL, S (2004) 'The land of murder, cannibalism and all kinds of atrocious crimes? Maori and crime in New Zealand, 1853–1919', *British Journal of Criminology*, 44, 496–519.

CARRINGTON, K (2006) 'Does feminism spoil girls? Explanations for official rises in female delinquency', *The Australian and New Zealand Journal of Criminology*, 39, 34–53.

CASSWELL, S and MAXWELL, A (2005) 'What works to reduce alcohol-related harm and why aren't the policies more popular?', *Social Policy Journal of New Zealand*, 25, 118–41.

CASSWELL, S, PLEDGER, M and PRATAP, S (2002) 'Trajectories of drinking from 18–26 years: Identification and prediction', *Addiction*, 97, 1427–37.

DACEY, B and BARNES, MH (1998) *Te Ao Waipiro: Maori and alcohol in 1995*, Auckland: Whariki Maori Health Research Group.

Dominion Post (2008) 'Party zone, radical plan to revamp city centre', Wellington, 8 March, 2.

ELDREG-GRIGG, S (1984) *Pleasures of the Flesh: Sex and drugs in colonial New Zealand 1840–1915*, Wellington: Reed Ltd.

GURR, T (1981) 'Historical trends in violent crime: A critical review of the evidence', *Crime and Justice*, 3, 295–353.

HADFIELD, P (2006) *Bar Wars: Contesting the Night in Contemporary British Cities*, Oxford: Oxford University Press.

HILL, L (2002) *Alcohol and Violence: What's the connection?* Alcohol and Public Health Research Unit: Auckland, <http://www.aphru.ac.nz/hot/violence.htm>.

HUAKAU, J, ASIASIGA, L, FORD, M, PLEDGER, M, CASSWELL, S, SUAALII-SAUNI, T and LIMA, I (2005) 'New Zealand Pacific peoples' drinking style: too much or nothing at all?', *The New Zealand Medical Journal*, <http://www.nzma.org.nz/journal/118–1216/1491/>.

HUSAK, D (2006) 'Disgust: Metaphysical and empirical speculations', in A von Hirsch and AP Simester (eds), *Incivilities: Regulating offensive behaviour*, Portland: Hart Publishing, 239–80.

HUTT, M (2003) *Te Iwi Maorime te Inu Waipiro: He Tuhituhinga Hitori (Maori and Alcohol: A History)*, Wellington: The Printing Press.

HUTTON, F (2005) 'Kiwis, clubs and drugs', Unpublished conference paper at Club Health 2005, Sydney.

—— (2006) *Risky Pleasures? Club Cultures and Feminine Identities*, Aldershot: Ashgate.

KYPRI, K (2003) 'Maori/non-Maori alcohol consumption profiles: Implications for reducing health inequalities', *The New Zealand Medical Journal*, <http://www.nzma.org.nz/journal/116-1184/643/>.

LASH, B (2005) *Young People and Alcohol: Some statistics to 2003 and 2004 on possible effects of lowering the purchase age*, Wellington: Ministry of Justice.

MEASHAM, F (2004) 'The decline of ecstasy, the rise of "binge" drinking and the persistence of pleasure', *Probation Journal*, 51, 309–26.

MINISTRY OF HEALTH (2007) *Alcohol Use in New Zealand: Analysis of the 2004 New Zealand Health Behaviours Survey—Alcohol Use*, Wellington: Ministry of Health.

PARKER, H (1996) 'Young adult offenders, alcohol and criminological cul-de-sacs', *British Journal of Criminology*, 36, 282–98.

PERNANEN, K (1991) *Alcohol in Human Violence*, New York: Guilford Press.

PHILIPS, J (1996) *A Man's Country? The image of the Pakeha male—A history*, Auckland: Penguin.

PLANT, M, PLANT, M and THORNTON, C (2002) 'People and places: Some factors in the alcohol–violence link', *Journal of Substance Use*, 7, 207–13.

PRATT, P and CLARKE, M (2006) 'Penal populism in New Zealand', *Punishment and Society*, 7, 303–22.

SAFER COMMUNITIES FOUNDATION (2008) *Case Study: Walkwise Wellington (ADT Armourguard)*, <http://www.safecommunities.org.nz/resources/cs/ww/download>.

SIM, M, MORGAN, E and BATCHELOR, J (2005) *The Impact of Enforcement on Intoxication and Alcohol-Related Harm*, <http://www.police.govt.nz/resources/2005/wgtn-city-alcohol-enforcement-report/>.

SIMON, J (2007) 'Governing through crime', in M Vogel (ed), *Crime, Inequality and the State*, London: Routledge, 589–95.

STATISTICS NEW ZEALAND (2007a) *National Annual Recorded Offences of the Latest 10 Calendar Years*, <http://wdmzpub01.stats.govt.nz/wds/TableViewer/tableView.aspx?ReportId=2182>.

—— (2007b) *National Population Estimates: December 2007 Quarter*, <http://www.stats.govt.nz/products-and-services/hot-off-the-press/national-population-estimates/national-populations-estimates-dec07qtr-hotp.htm>.

WELLINGTON CITY COUNCIL (2008) *Central City Liquor Ban: 24/7 Liquor Control Bylaw came into effect on 31 July 2008 at 5.00 pm*, <http://www.wellington.govt.nz/services/commsafety/centralliq/centralliq.html>.

Wellingtonian (2008) 'Fed-up Cuba Mall retailers want total booze ban', 21 February, Wellington.

WHITE, R (2008) 'Public Spaces, consumption, and the social regulation of young people', in SA Venkatesh and R Kassimir (eds), *Youth, Globalisation and the Law*, Stanford: Stanford University Press, 223–48.

WILLIAMS, K and JOHNSTONE, C (2000) 'The politics of the selective gaze: Closed circuit television and the policing of public space', *Crime, Law and Social Change*, 34, 183.

18

AUSTRALIA

Tanya Chikritzhs

INTRODUCTION

It has been said of Australians that 'they work hard at their leisure' (Horne, 1971: 18). Since the early days of the male-dominated colonies, the pub or 'hotel' has been an important feature of the leisure landscape. Given this, it is surprising that only fragments of information are available on the perceptions and experiences of Australians in the late-night leisure environment. This chapter argues, however, that evidence can be found for growing public concern over the regulation and management of the night-time economy (NTE). It shows how the impact of trading hours for licensed venues on crime and disorder has long held public interest, while discourse and debate on the burgeoning numbers of licensed premises is a fresh preoccupation.

Current policy relating to the NTE is a mix of potentially mutually exclusive principles. Most state and territory liquor Acts refer to the need to minimize harm arising from the sale and supply of alcohol. At the same time, deregulation, self-regulation and the removal of liquor restrictions which might hamper industry competitiveness have been widely embraced. Policy regimes which bear on the management of the late-night economy are, by all accounts, a great frustration to the police, to whom the practical responsibility of maintaining peace and good order falls. These same systems, it is suggested, appear to offer little comfort to communities seeking relief from violent crime and disorder, declining safety and amenity linked to the late-night economy.

In an Australian context, nightlife, crime, and disorder are tightly knitted to alcohol and licensed premises and it is 'violent' crime which is salient to most. The widely perceived interconnection between pubs and clubs, violent crime and alcohol in the NTE is evident in history, media reports, national and state inquiry directives, public opinion surveys, police policy, community action, and research endeavours. In very recent years, fuelled in large part by extensive media coverage of violent street crime, community awareness and concern over safety in the late-night leisure environment appears to have escalated. Government responses to public outcry have been piecemeal, deflecting the need for social and systematic regulatory change. One-off legislative changes such as the recent Western Australian 'one-punch laws' which focus on violent offenders who kill their victims with a single blow[1] meet the public-relations requirements of the moment and may improve awareness in the short term but do little to foster enduring change.

By world standards, however, Australia is not a 'violent' place (Chappell et al, 1991). National surveys reveal that the large majority of Australians feel safe or very safe in their homes, although females less so. Most people perceive problems with crime in their own neighbourhoods (70 per cent), but few believe that drunkenness (13 per cent) or illegal drugs (10 per cent) are the major causes (ABS, 2005).

Australian national surveys do not routinely or specially enquire about violent crime in and around the NTE but they do occasionally shed a little light on dark places. A 2002 survey indicated that about one in three assaults involving a male victim occurred in a 'place of entertainment or car park' or 'street or open land'. About half of the time, female victims of assault reported their own home as the place of attack, with only about 13 per cent assaulted at a place of entertainment or in the street. In relation to sexual assault, given the nature of the crime, it is striking that well over one-third of women report being assaulted in a public venue—almost as many are sexually assaulted in their own or someone else's home (40 per cent) (ABS, 2002). Recent population surveys have reported that alcohol-related incidents outnumber those related to illicit drugs (all combined) by at least two to one. In 2007, an estimated three-quarters of a million people were physically abused by someone under the influence of alcohol and a further 6.7 million were verbally abused or 'put in fear' (AIHW, 2008).

Community sentiment toward alcohol policy has changed substantially in the last few years. Support for a range of policies—including reductions in numbers of outlets licensed to sell alcohol, reductions in trading hours for pubs and clubs, restrictions on late-night licensed venues, and strict monitoring of late-night licensed premises—all increased significantly from 2004 to 2007. The proportion of respondents who supported these measures ranged from 32 per cent for reducing the number of outlets, to 75 per cent in favour of the strict monitoring of venues. The policy which gained the largest increase in community support over the three years was reduced trading hours for pubs and clubs (22 per cent) (AIHW, 2008).

In the absence of regular and standardized national monitoring, it is difficult to know whether increased media attention and changes in public concern relating to crime and the NTE reflect changes in actual levels of problems. Market research commissioned by the newly formed National Alliance Against Alcohol-Related Violence[2] claimed that about half of all Australians are concerned about alcohol-related violence when visiting entertainment districts after dark and similar numbers of people are more concerned about alcohol-related violence now than they were three years ago (AERF, 2008). One of the few studies to have tracked trends in serious alcohol-related assaults showed that levels were relatively stable in most jurisdictions throughout the 1990s, despite the uptake of a raft of policy and policing measures (Matthews, et al, 2002)—the most notable of which will be discussed here.

---

[1] <http://www.abc.net.au/news/stories/2008/06/20/2280699.htm>.
[2] <http://www.news.com.au/heraldsun/story/0,21985,23540518–2862,00.html>.

CULTURAL CONTEXT

Alcohol has played a central role in the Australian pursuit of leisure, in celebration and commiseration, since the early days of colonization. In the 19th century, a prediction for drinking outdoors or at a 'public house' rather than in the home was firmly established as a way of life and mainstream Australians have demonstrated an enduring interest in 'social' drinking ever since. A session at the local pub is where 'mates' will 'shout' their friends (take it in turns to buy drinks for all), a practice which is more socially acceptable than 'drinking with the flies' (drinking alone). Hosts who serve up an alcoholic beverage which falls short of the drinker's standards may be accused of serving up 'lollywater'. Those who question the central role of alcohol in society or who suggest restraint are, to this day, in dire danger of being labelled that most un-Australian of creatures: the 'wowser'—a person regarded as obnoxiously puritanical.[3]

The dominant working-class 'pub' environment of the mid- to late 1800s was once described as a 'rollicking man's world of booze and two-up'[4] (Horne, 1971: 28) amid austerely furnished drinking barns. Drinking to midnight, unprecedentedly high rates of public drunkenness and violence dominated the nightly scene, while the local pub was a place that women rarely entered. Public drunkenness was a serious problem for authorities, and hotel[5] closing hours, in particular, were a contentious issue (Room, 1988). Toward the end of the 19th century the national focus shifted in favour of industrialization and suburbanization which emphasized 'material security and relied heavily on order, authority and conformism' (Midford, 2005: 891). From here, the traditional man's drinking world succumbed to the pressure of the temperance movement, and the requirement of six o'clock closing[6] for all alcohol sales was adopted during the First World War (Room, 1988: 424).

Contrary to expectations, the most wide-ranging effect of six o'clock closing was to create a single hour of frenzied drinking. Between finishing work at 5.00 pm and hotel closing time at 6.00 pm, herds of drinkers would clamour to the bar with the aim of imbibing as much liquor as was possible in the short amount of time. In the words of a Sydney barmaid in 1924: 'It was a revolting sight . . . the shouting for service, the crash of falling glasses, the grunting and shoving crowd . . .' (Room, 1988: 424).

---

[3] <http://www.thefreedictionary.com/wowser>.

[4] Two-up is a gambling game in which coins are spun in the air and bets placed on a showing of two heads or two tails.

[5] In the context of Australian night-life, the term 'hotel' refers to public houses or 'pubs'. In some states it remains the case that as well as having a licence to sell alcohol for on-premise alcohol consumption, a 'hotel' must provide some level of accommodation. In a more general sense, 'hotel' may also refer to an establishment for which the predominant service is accommodation rather than the sale of alcohol (eg, five-star complexes which attract large numbers of tourists).

[6] Prior to six o'clock closing, most hotels and taverns closed at midnight or 11.00 pm. The temperance movement argued that the then 6.00 pm closing laws for general business establishments (eg, shops) should equally apply to public drinking houses. During a wave of First World War 'patriotic fervor' and 'temperance sentiment', given a choice of 6.00 pm or 11.00 pm closing, South Australian electors voted in absolute majority for the former and set an example soon followed by New South Wales, Victoria, and Tasmania (Room, 1988: 424).

This wretched display was coined the 'six o'clock swill' (Room, 1988) and despite the undesirable consequences, six o'clock closing was maintained in most states until well into the 1950s.

In contemporary Australia, alcohol is freely available for purchase by adults (18 years and older). Alcoholic beverages are widey and openly promoted, over 80 per cent of the population consider themselves to be 'current' drinkers—many times the proportion who identify themselves as current illicit drug users (13 per cent—mostly cannabis) (AIHW, 2008). Women are numerously if not equally represented among hotel patrons, and 24-hour-trading and 'vertical drinking' establishments are growing features of popular late-night entertainment districts (Roche et al, 2007). The spacious, noisy and unfurnished environments of the vertical drinking venues are evocative of the austere, masculinized Australian drinking barns of the 19th century.

The concept of regulating the night-time environment with the intent of reducing undesirable outcomes caused by a few—and potentially curtailing the leisure activities of the many—may seem antithetical to the stereotypical Australian drinking culture. Nonetheless, since the late 1990s, governments in most Australian jurisdictions[7] have incorporated 'harm minimization' principles,[8] as either primary or secondary objectives, into their liquor laws. This was a major achievement as the focus of most past Acts had been to support the liquor, hospitality, and tourism industries (Chikritzhs, 2004).[9]

---

[7] Liquor laws, their administration, and enforcement, are the domain of the states and territory governments (eight in all) and as such there is substantial variation between individual Liquor Acts. In each jurisdiction Acts are administered via a single Liquor Licensing Department or Commission which deals with the day-to-day management of new and existing liquor licences, inspections, alterations, and objections to new licences and so on for the entire jurisdiction. Local councils (many within each state) may indirectly influence liquor licensing decisions via local planning regulations such as zoning for appropriate land use, parking-bay requirements, and local amenity by-laws. The Commonwealth government may also indirectly affect the content and operation of state and territory liquor laws with overriding national policy, as is the case with National Competition Policy. The Commonwealth government is solely responsible for the charging and collection of taxes on alcoholic beverages.

[8] Liquor Acts in New South Wales, Western Australia, Victoria, Queensland, and the Northern Territory specifically refer to the minimization of harm from alcohol, as either a primary or secondary objective. South Australia and the Australian Capital Territory (ACT) refer to the promotion of responsible sales, consumption/consumer attitudes and community amenity, while the Tasmanian Act makes no reference to either harm minimization or responsible sales and supply (Loxley et al, 2007). State/territory Liquor Acts also vary in their definitions of 'harm minimization' and their statements of intent in relation to such objectives. For instance, the NSW Liquor Act 2007 under Objects of Act part (2) is quite specific and states: 'In order to secure the objects of this Act, each person who exercises functions under this Act (including a licensee) is required to have due regard to the following: (a) the need to minimise harm associated with misuse and abuse of liquor (including harm arising from violence and other anti-social behaviour); (b) the need to encourage responsible attitudes and practices towards the promotion, sale, supply, service and consumption of liquor; (c) the need to ensure that the sale, supply and consumption of liquor contributes to, and does not detract from, the amenity of community life.' The Victorian Liquor Control Reform Act 1998 is less specific and couches the primary objective in terms of 'contribution to' harm minimization, as far as 'practicable': 'to contribute to minimising harm arising from the misuse and abuse of alcohol . . . by such means as restrictions on supply and responsible liquor service . . . providing adequate controls . . . as far as practicable'.

[9] In Western Australia, for example, the original Liquor Licensing Act 1988 identified four primary objectives, centred around the development of liquor, hospitality, and tourism. The amended Act (amended in 1998) pointedly identified harm minimization as one of three primary objectives: 'The primary objects of this Act are: (a) to regulate the sale, supply and consumption of liquor; and (b) to minimise harm or ill-health caused to people, or any group of people, due to the use of liquor; and (c) to cater for the requirements of consumers for liquor and related services, with regard to the proper development of the liquor industry, the tourism industry and other hospitality industries in the State.'

The last few decades have also witnessed a proliferation of licensed premises, the trend toward unfettered growth exemplified in the state of Victoria. The current Victorian Liquor Control Act (1987), with its deregulatory approach, was based on the advice of the 'Nieuwenhuysen Report' (1986). Nieuwenhuysen argued that not only were controls on the availability of alcohol clumsy, antiquated, and ineffectual, they also discriminated against the majority of people who consumed alcohol in a harm-free fashion. Later commentary on the new Victorian liquor laws asserted that the previous compulsory trading hours and limits on liquor outlets 'were an economic burden'. With the adoption of a deregulated approach, the number of licensed premises in Victoria has increased faster than anywhere else in the country (Loxley et al, 2007)—club, hotel, restaurant, and off-premise licences more than doubled between 1991 and 2006 (Livingston, 2008b). This rapid growth has lifted Victoria from one of the lowest per-capita rates of licensed premises to the highest.

The failed social experiments of the temperance era are often recalled as evidence in support of deregulation. The 'six o'clock swill' has, for example, been cited by politicians in several states who have supported longer trading hours. During parliamentary debate of the New South Wales Liquor Bill in 1982, it was recommended that extended trading be introduced into licensed premises with the explicit reasoning that doing so would reduce binge drinking and allow drinkers to 'pace themselves'. The state of New South Wales currently has some 70 per cent of the nation's 24-hour-trading premises.

Under the Howard Commonwealth government (1996–2007) the concept of alcohol as an 'ordinary commodity' was, for the first time, embedded in official government policy. National Competition Policy (NCP), the essential aim of which is to weed out anti-competitive government practices in a range of areas, obliges state and territory governments to remove regulation which might 'unjustifiably' reduce liquor trade competition (eg, limitations on numbers of premises, trading hours). The aims of the NCP in relation to the sale and supply of alcohol are potentially at odds with state and territory Liquor Acts for which the minimization of harm is a primary or secondary objective. Commonwealth government funds have been withheld from jurisdictions which have failed to adequately comply (National Competition Council, 2005) but most have introduced the required changes, including the removal of trading hours restrictions for some types of licences and requirements of 'social impact' tests for new licence applications.

Only very recently has evidence of the potential impact of ongoing deregulation on the late-night economy begun to emerge. Active commitment to deregulation of the liquor industry began first and has been most enthusiastic in Victoria. Coincident to rapid growth in the number of licensed premises in that state has been a rapid increase in the population rate of alcohol-attributable hospitalizations in its capital city, Melbourne. In Melbourne, the rate of increase in alcohol-attributable hospitalizations between 1999 and 2004 was at least twice the national average (Loxley et al, 2007). The *Herald Sun* newspaper reported on a police document 'leaked' to the Victorian state opposition which showed 'a record 1.4 per cent increase in violent crime' in 2007/8 while crimes such as handling stolen goods, homicide, and drug trafficking had fallen substantially.[10] The ABC news reported Victoria's Deputy Police Commissioner Kieren

---

[10] <http://www.news.com.au/heraldsun/story/0,21985,24090627–5005961,00.html>.

Walshe as saying that police have been introducing new initiatives to tackle crime but that 'there has been a deterioration in public order and we've seen an increase in assaults in and around licensed premises'.[11] Even so, other states have announced intentions to follow the Victorian liquor-licensing model.[12]

RESEARCH EVIDENCE

SITUATIONAL FACTORS

There is apparent consensus among Australian researchers that not all licensed premises are problematic, but that there are volatile night-time 'hotspots' where violence and disorder are predictable, ongoing, and fuelled by excessive alcohol consumption (Briscoe and Donnelley, 2001 and 2003a; Doherty and Roche, 2003; Homel and Tomsen, 1993; Indermauer, 1999). Within inner-city areas of Sydney, Newcastle, and Wollongong an estimated 8–12 per cent of hotels account for up to 80 per cent of all police reported assaults on such premises (Briscoe and Donnelly, 2001 and 2003a). Perth assaults show a similar distribution of risk (Stockwell, 1997) with the most troublesome nightspots often located in close proximity to one another (Catalano and Stockwell, 2002).

Most Australian jurisdictions distinguish between four functionally distinct liquor licence types depending on their trading hours and requirements to provide food. Most numerous among the on-premise licences, restaurants/cafés, typically include the condition that alcohol may only be served with a substantial meal.[13] For most jurisdictions standard closing time for hotels or 'pubs' is midnight but all allow licensees to apply for a delay in closing, commonly to between 1.00 am and 3.00 am. Nightclub or 'cabaret' licences typically allow trade up to 3.00 am or 6.00 am, with later opening hours than pubs. Liquor store or 'packaged liquor' licences typically restrict sales to off-premise consumption and trading times vary substantially across jurisdictions (Loxley et al, 2007).[14]

The risk of violence occurring in and around licensed premises varies substantially by licence type. Drink-for-drink, pub and nightclub patrons are at higher risk of being involved in violent assaults than patrons of restaurants/cafés (Chikritzhs et al, 2007; Stockwell et al, 1992a and 1992b). This may be due to physical characteristics

---

[11] <http://www.theage.com.au/national/violent-crime-jump-police-leak-20080728–3maz.html? skin=text-only>.

[12] <http://www.theage.com.au/news/national/victoria-best-bar-none-says-keating/2007/09/26/ 1190486400390.html>.

[13] The traditional 'restaurant' licence is currently undergoing change with some states tending toward removing food provision conditions, such that these establishments may now operate more as pseudo 'hotels' than 'restaurants' in the traditional sense.

[14] There are various other liquor licences available, including, social club, canteen, vessel, and special-purpose licences (eg, wineries) which are functionally diverse but which are typically distinguishable by the type of persons or organizations which are able to possess such a licence (eg, in the case of a social-club licence, the licensee must be, or represent, a registered 'club').

and management practices and also to the fact that in almost all restaurants, alcohol sales are only permitted where accompanied by a meal, with the customer seated at a table.[15]

Perhaps the most robust finding to have emerged from police records is that violence in and around late-night entertainment areas peaks between midnight and 3.00 am and is most frequent on Friday, Saturday, and Sunday nights (Briscoe and Donnelly, 2001; Chikritzhs et al, 1997; Devery, 1992; Ireland and Thommeny, 1993; Jochelson, 1997). In inner-Sydney, New South Wales, where many premises trade for 24-hours, Briscoe and Donnelly (2003a) observed that reported levels of violence were higher between 3.00 am and 6.00 am than they were between 9.00 pm and midnight—despite the fact that fewer licensed premises were operating after 3.00 am and that venues were less populated during these early hours of the morning. The authors identify 'increased levels of intoxicated patrons during these peak times and the pooling of intoxicated patrons into premises with later closing times' (p 4) as key explanatory factors.

PHYSICAL CHARACTERISTICS OF LICENSED VENUES

Beyond differences arising from licence types, establishments also differ in more subtle ways which are largely influenced by management style and practice. Although there are laws and regulations which govern basic amenity, safety, and service provision by licensees, there are several factors within the licensed environment that remain unregulated and almost entirely determined by the management practices of individual venues.

Poor physical characteristics of a licensed environment can lead to patron discomfort, frustration, and aggression—especially where patrons are intoxicated. Noise,[16] crowding, poor ventilation, smoky air, inadequate seating, difficult bar and toilet access, general lack of cleanliness, and bad floor planning leading to 'bottlenecks' in crowd flow, have all been demonstrated to be associated with patron aggression (Homel and Clark, 1994; Homel et al, 1992). Yet the associations are not necessarily straightforward. The relation between crowding and aggression, for instance, depends on whether an individual perceives a particular crowded situation as either a positive or negative experience. A crowded dance floor, for example, may be perceived as a non-stressful situation and even preferable to an empty one, but large crowds queuing for access to bars and toilets or restricted traffic flow at exits and entrances may induce feelings of frustration which may in turn lead to aggression (MacIntyre and Homel, 1997). In Australia, as in other countries, there are regulations which set legal limits on the number of persons allowed in such venues,[17] nonetheless, the degree to which these regulations are enforced by local authorities and ignored by licensees is unknown.

---

[15] When food is present in the gut the intoxicant effects of alcohol on the body are slowed.

[16] Noise has been identified as one physical factor associated with aggression. Homel and colleagues (1992) concluded that it was not the level of noise per se but rather the presence of 'bad' bands or poor sound quality which contributed to greater levels of overall aggression and heavier drinking.

[17] A minimum of 1 metre square, per person, in most jurisdictions.

It has also been suggested that actual physical size of a venue (eg, number of bars, number of patrons in view, seating capacity) correlates only weakly with levels of violence and is a less important predictor of problems than crowding and patron discomfort (Homel and Clark, 1994). Along the same lines, Lang and colleagues (1992) found that injured persons were more likely to report that their public-drinking location at the time of injury was either full or mostly full compared to non-injured patrons who reported drinking in licensed premises which were only a quarter full. It is reasonable to expect that certain characteristics of venues may cue patrons to act out perceived expectations about acceptable behaviour: 'attractive, nicely furnished, well-maintained premises give a message to the patron that the managers do not anticipate physical violence and associated damage to furnishings' (Homel et al, 2001: 724).

On the other hand, shabby, run-down premises with broken, uncomfortable, or inadequate furniture (seating, bench tops) may encourage some patrons to perceive a degree of permissiveness for disorderly or aggressive behaviour—'the first clue the patron has as to what kinds of behaviour will be tolerated is the care and maintenance of the bar' (Graham and Homel, 1997: 173).

TRADING HOURS

Situational factors matter when it comes to violence in and around late-night venues, but there is also strong evidence for a direct effect of regulatory policy on levels of violence associated with licensed premises in Australia. Throughout the 1970s and 80s, a great deal of work was done by Dr Ian Smith on the effects of licensed trading hours on road crashes in Australia (eg, see Chikritzhs, 2004); however, it was not until the 1990s that the focus on trading hours expanded to include violent crime and disorder.

The first in a series of studies on licensed premises in Perth demonstrated that hotels which applied for and received an extended trading permit (ETP) to operate past midnight (usually to 1.00 am or 2.00 am) increased alcohol sales by an average of 63 per cent more than matched control venues. The timing of assaults which occurred in and around late-trading venues also shifted to coincide with the new closing hours. As a result, more problems occurred throughout the early hours of the morning when police shifts were likely to be under-resourced and emergency rooms overburdened. Patrons leaving late-trading venues at closing time would also have found it difficult to access public transport, as public buses and trains ceased after midnight, leaving only the bravest of taxi operators[18] to service the throngs of intoxicated patrons (Chikritzhs et al, 1997).

A subsequent time-series analysis was applied to investigate the effect of granting ETPs to some, but not all, pubs in the Perth metropolitan area between 1991 and 1997 (Chikritzhs and Stockwell, 2002). After controlling for the overall trend in reported assaults throughout Perth pubs, assaults occurring in and around hotels with a one- or two-hour extension in closing time rose significantly by an average of 70 per cent.

---

[18] During night-time hours, busy taxi ranks are particularly prone to violence and disorder as concentrations of intoxicated patrons compete for limited transport services (Doherty and Roche, 2003).

Almost 80 per cent of the increase in assaults was explained by simultaneous increases in alcohol sales among the late-trading pubs. The study was unable to determine whether the concurrent increases in alcohol sales and levels of violence were due to increased numbers of patrons (presumably attracted to longer drinking hours) or an increase in the amount of alcohol consumed by individuals, but concluded that it was probably a combination of both. A subsequent study confirmed that young men aged between 18 and 25 years who had had their last drink at hotels after midnight had higher blood alcohol levels than their counterparts who drank at hotels with standard hours. Older males and females did not show increased levels of intoxication regardless of where they drank (Chikritzhs and Stockwell, 2007).[19]

New South Wales, Australia's most populated state, also has more hotels and nightclubs licensed to trade for 24 hours than any other jurisdiction.[20] Results from a study of inner-Sydney late-night-entertainment precincts highlighted the additional burden of violent crime associated with 24-hour trading. Briscoe and Donnelly (2003a) demonstrated that hotels with 24-hour trading had greater numbers of assaults than those with 'normal' extended trading hours (ie, up to 3.00 am closing time). In turn, hotels with 'normal' extended hours had higher levels of recorded assaults than hotels with standard trading hours (ie, no extension of closing time). Of the hotels that were associated with more than ten assaults in a 24-month period, 74 per cent had 24-hour trading and the remaining 26 per cent were attributed to hotels with shorter extended trading hours.

A licensee's decision to apply for a late-night or 24-hour trading permit is made within the context of a highly competitive, profit-driven industry. From a business perspective, the potential gains (eg, greater profits, increased competitiveness) must be weighed against the likely costs (eg, application fee and legal advice, increased wages, power costs, inconvenience, potential legal costs if the licence is opposed).[21] Even before they apply, venues for which late-trading hours are sought are different in several ways from those which continue to trade with normal hours, including: location (more likely to be inner-city); the proportion of high- to low-alcohol-content beverages sold (more of the former compared to other premises); younger clientele; and higher likelihood of association with drink-driver road crashes (Chikritzhs and Stockwell, 2002, 2006 and 2007).

Given this, it is reasonable to postulate that the self-selecting nature of the late-trading process is more appealing to those venues which are predisposed—by virtue

[19] Young females showed lower levels of intoxication at specific times of day.

[20] NSW has about 70 per cent of the some 600 currently in operation throughout the country (personal communication, Director, New South Wales Bureau of Crime Statistics and Research).

[21] It was not possible to identify any specific information regarding the degree to which licensees in possession of a 24-hour permit actually use the full complement of hours available to them. There is evidence, however, which shows that in areas where larger numbers of 24-hour trading permits are granted, assaults occur more frequently into the early hours of the morning (ie, greater proportions of assaults occur between 3.00 am and 6.00 am) pointing to use of the 24-hour permits at least up until 6.00 am (Briscoe and Donnelley, 2001). In the case of shorter extensions of trading hours (eg, one to three hours) there is evidence to suggest they are well-used by most licensees. It was noted in the Western Australia study of extended trading permits (ETPs), that all hotels which gained an ETP later applied for a continuation at their own expense (every 6–12 months) and all were granted. Discussions with key Liquor Licensing Department informants confirmed that the large majority of ETPs were in full use (Chikritzhs and Stockwell, 2006).

of their management practices, location, and the nature of the clientele they purpose-fully attract—to reap the greatest benefits of longer trading hours. However, to a large extent, the 'benefits' enjoyed by licensees are ultimately redistributed as 'costs' to the night-time environment, the communities which they serve, and the police.

OUTLET DENSITY

While the potential impacts of trading hours on the late-night environment have been salient since the early 1900s, consideration of the potential problems arising from the sheer volume or 'outlet density' of licensed premises has only recently become salient for the wider Australian population—and for researchers. This is in large part due to the rapid proliferation of licensed premises under increasingly deregulated policy frameworks.

Unlike the majority of outlet-density studies conducted elsewhere which rely on counts of outlets per se (eg, Gruenewald et al, 1993; Scribner et al, 1995), much Austral-ian work on the effects of outlet density on violence and crime has relied on volumes of alcohol purchases (sales data) made by licensed premises. This is arguably a superior means of measuring the impact of premises on violent crime because it may account for individual variation among premises regarding capacity to sell quantities of alco-hol (Chikritzhs et al, 2007).

Stockwell et al (1998) examined the strength of association between per-capita alcohol sales and police-reported assaults across 130 geographic regions in Western Australia. Assaults during night-time hours (ie, 10.00 pm to 6.00 am) increased as alcohol consumption increased and were highest when alcohol was purchased from either a hotel or liquor store. A more recent, methodologically comparable study supported these early findings and added that the strength of the associa-tion between consumption and violence varied depended on both licence type and where the offence occurred (ie, in the street, in the licensed premises, or on private premises). It was estimated that one additional hotel with an average annual alcohol turnover of some 65,000 litres of full-strength beer would result in an additional ten assaults each year across the state—some four out of five of which would occur on private premises (eg, house, flat) as opposed to a licensed premises (Chikritzhs et al, 2007).

Studies based on New South Wales alcohol-sales data confirm the links between per-capita alcohol consumption and violence in city areas (Stevenson et al, 1999a) and malicious damage to property and offensive behaviour rates across all areas (Stevenson et al, 1999b). Donnelly and colleagues (2006) reported on the links between residents' perceptions of neighbourhood drunkenness, property damage, and assault victimiza-tion in the home and their geographic proximity to licensed premises. People who lived closest to licensed premises (proximity) and people who lived in areas with highest outlet density reported the highest levels of drunkenness and property damage in their neighbourhoods. Evidence of a non-linear relationship between disorder and outlet density was also found, such that at the highest outlet densities the rate of associated neighbourhood problems increased more steeply.

Expanding on the concept of non-linear relationships between outlet density and violence, Livingston (2008a) explored the spatial relationship between alcohol outlet density and night-time violence in Melbourne, Victoria using both linear and non-linear models. The study showed evidence of a 'critical threshold' for hotel and pub licence density, at which point, the bunching of such establishments substantially increased the risk of violence in and around surrounding areas. Specifically, from one to 25 outlets the number of assaults expected per year remained stable at about 12, but as the number of venues increased from 30 to 40 premises, the number of assaults increased more sharply to almost 40 assaults per year. Using longitudinal data Livingston (2008b) also showed that changes in numbers of outlets over time were strongly related to changes in levels of violence in Victoria, but the relationship depended on the socio-demographic characteristics of the affected community. Hotels were particularly problematic in inner-city entertainment precincts, while off-premise outlets were more highly associated with violence in suburban areas.

The theoretical underpinnings of the relationship between alcohol-outlet density, violence and disorder are still developing. Early outlet-density research relied heavily on the classical postulates of 'alcohol availability theory' (Single, 1988) and in doing so, strongly favoured 'supply' as the main mechanism by which outlet density influenced violence. Livingston and colleagues (2007) proposed a theoretical framework whereby the impact of 'proximity' effects (similar to the concept of physical availability) and 'amenity' were considered independently. Within this framework 'proximity' relates to how easily individuals can access alcohol and 'amenity' relates to how licensed premises influence the characteristics of the local community surroundings.

The proximity effect, which relates closely to alcohol availability theory, operates to influence the convenience costs of obtaining alcohol, such as distance to travel and price. As new outlets appear, accessibility and the intensity of competitive pricing practices may be increased thus enhancing access to alcohol and the relative buying power of consumers. Amenity effects relate to the negative physical effects which licensed premises bring to the neighbourhoods they service whereby licensed premises are viewed as magnets for violence, disorder, and 'trouble'. The amenity effect of a new licence is not necessarily additive or 'linear' such that one new licence brings the same number of problems as the one which preceded it. By virtue of their collective appeal, premises which are 'bunched' together may apply a multiplicative pressure on violence and disorder as they draw large numbers of potential perpetrators and victims into close contact with one another. As Livingston et al (2007: 562) describe it: 'At a certain point, a growing bunch of outlets, particularly on-premise outlets such as hotels and bars, becomes fixed in people's mental maps as an entertainment district . . . attracting crowds above and beyond what would be attracted by the same number of outlets on their own . . .'

In the context of a night-time-entertainment district therefore, the clustering or 'bunching' of licensed establishments enhances the likelihood that crowds of people—many young and intoxicated, some unhappily ejected at closing time, others moving on to a change of scene—will spill out, mill around, and traverse the streets, vying for limited food, transport services, personal space, and entertainment.

CONTROLLING THE LATE-NIGHT ENVIRONMENT

Past Australian efforts toward controlling the late-night-entertainment environment can best be described as reactive, enervated, and having a low regard for evidence-based approaches. Police have faced, and continue to face, substantial obstacles to proactively policing licensed premises.

LIQUOR LICENSING: FROM LAW INTO ACTION?

As noted, regulatory control of the liquor industry is vested in state and territory governments which specify jurisdiction-wide controls. The scope and purpose of the various Liquor Acts differ but they typically regulate trading hours; number, type and location of licensed premises; minimum age for drinking on licensed premises and offences regarding provision of alcohol to minors; and stipulations on the illegality of supplying alcohol such that it leads to, or increases, intoxication (Loxley et al, 2007; NDRI, 2007). Most Liquor Acts refer to the minimization of harm as a primary or secondary objective. Despite the strength of local evidence pointing to extended trading hours and high-outlet densities as major contributors to violent crime and disorder, liquor-licensing decision-makers have, by and large, been reluctant to directly employ the legislative power available to them to control or reduce problems which occur in the night-time environment.[22] On top of the already considerable inertia among liquor-licensing decision-makers in this regard, the rise of National Competition Policy brings an additional disincentive to change.

It is widely apparent that deference to harm-minimization principles in most Acts has been of limited practical use to local communities beset with high levels of crime and disorder and which are seeking to reverse the disintegration of public safety and amenity after dark. In 2007, two separate liquor-licence applications in the region of Preston in Darebin, Victoria, highlighted the inequity, inconsistency, and ineffectiveness of current liquor-licensing processes for reducing alcohol-related problems.

In 2006, Preston, Darebin had one licensed premise for very 290 adult residents—a rate which exceeded that of surrounding districts by more than 20 per cent (Chikritzhs 2007). Local police had documented increased levels of assaults and criminal damage following in the wake of a 'burgeoning licensed premises industry' (Zammit, 2006: 3). Convinced of the relationship between growing numbers of licensed premises and the decline in public safety and amenity in their community, the police and local city council were keen to stem any further increase. In 2007, they opposed an application by Cheapa Wines[23] to establish an off-premise liquor outlet in Preston. Heralded at the time as a landmark case, the Cheapa Wines application was rejected by the Liquor Licensing Panel (LLP) of Victoria which concluded that it would be

---

[22] There have been some successful high-profile Indigenous community applications for restrictions on the sale of alcohol in Western Australian in recent years: <http://202.6.74.101/news/stories/2007/09/11/2029870.htm>.

[23] Cheapa Wines proposed specializing in low-cost wine.

'conducive to the further misuses and abuse of alcohol in the Preston area' (Liquor Licensing Panel 2007a: 7).[24]

Several months later, another application for an off-premise licence was presented to the LLP. The applicant was a large supermarket-chain operator, with the trading name of 'Dan Murphy's'. Given their landmark success only a few months earlier, the objectors anticipated victory—especially as the Dan Murphy chain specialized in bulk discount sales and had the capacity to sell many times more alcohol than Cheapa Wines. The LLP, however, 'was not persuaded that the grant of the licence at these premises to this applicant would be conductive to misuse or abuse of liquor' (Liquor Licensing Panel 2007b: 9). One of the reasons given was that since Dan Murphy's would operate in place of a former packaged liquor outlet known as 'Bell Liquor' (surrendered and located next door) it did not constitute an 'additional' licence in the area. The LLP conceded, however, that based on what was known of the usual operation of the Dan Murphy's liquor chain, this particular licence was likely to operate on a 'vastly different scale to the operation of Bell Liquor'. After the unprecedented victory of the Preston community in the *Cheapa Wines* case, the Dan Murphy decision was the subject of community protest and national media coverage:

Liquor giant Dan Murphy's has controversially been granted a licence for a massive new discount store . . . The decision has outraged health groups, who called for a major overhaul of Victoria's liquor licensing laws . . . 'It's hard to understand the logic of granting a licence to a mega-discount liquor store when a smaller discount liquor store was rejected on the grounds that it might exacerbate existing alcohol harms. It's just extraordinary. It's time we had a balanced liquor licensing law that took account of people's health and not just the economic interests of liquor merchants . . .' said Geoff Munro, of the Community Alcohol Action Network.[25]

ENFORCEMENT OF LEGISLATION

Enforcement activities surrounding the operation of licensed venues within the late-night economy are largely the preserve of the police, although private security agencies operate within most venues and some states have introduced Liquor Licensing Officers.[26] There is abundant evidence that effective enforcement is a crucial element in the successful implementation of policy initiatives to reduce alcohol-related crime and disorder. It is not enough, however, to simply enforce—the threat of enforcement must be also be perceived by the target group as real and imminent. Enforcement needs to be frequent, unpredictable, strongly publicized (eg, media promotion), and the punishment must be substantial enough to outweigh the financial or social gains

---

[24] Enthused by the outcome, the Chair of the City of Darebin's Drug and Alcohol Committee was quoted in the media describing the decision as a 'seminal' one which 'proves that the Liquor Control Reform Act actually has some teeth': <http://www.theage.com.au/news/national/suburb-blows-whistle-on-high-alcohol-content/2007/06/28/1182624080039.html> (Jill Stark, 29 June 2007).

[25] <http://www.theage.com.au/news/national/fury-as-dan-murphys-gets-the-nod/2007/08/22/1187462354513.html>.

[26] Queensland has a squad of non-police Liquor Licensing Inspectors.

from non-compliance. The threat of considerable financial loss, when well publicized, is in itself a significant deterrent to those who might otherwise act irresponsibly (Babor et al, 2003; Loxley et al, 2004; NDRI, 2007; Stockwell, 2006).

It is currently illegal in all eight Australian jurisdictions for licensees, managers, and bar staff to supply alcohol to an individual to the point where they reach intoxication or to serve an already intoxicated person (NDRI, 2007).[27] If effectively enforced, liquor-law intoxication provisions could be a powerful and cost-effective mechanism for reducing drunkenness and alcohol-related crime in the licensed drinking environment. This is because for every one vendor deterred from serving irresponsibly, there are potentially hundreds of patrons who will be affected. Despite the prospective gains to be made by a proactive focus on vendors, evidence from a number of sources suggests that police have preferred to focus their efforts on 'reacting' to drinking-related crimes perpetrated by individuals.[28] In New South Wales for instance, some 40 per cent of all actions initiated in relation to liquor-law breaches concerned patrons, and only about 3 per cent involved licensees/managers found to be in breach of their legal requirement not to serve intoxicated patrons (Briscoe and Donnelley, 2003b). The low level of vendors prosecuted for breaching New South Wales intoxication laws is at odds with evidence pointing to a high level of irresponsible beverage service in that state. A survey of 19–39-year-olds found that only 10 per cent of drinkers who self-reported at least one physical sign of intoxication[29] the last time they drank at a licensed venue had experienced some form of 'responsible service' (eg, server asked them to stop drinking, to leave the premises, or suggested they purchase food/non-alcoholic drink) (Donnelly and Briscoe, 2002).

Inattention to enforcement of intoxication provisions is widespread. Loxley et al (2007) estimated that in 2006, 97 per cent of Western Australian and 82 per cent of Victorian Liquor Act infringement notices were issued to patrons. Among infringements which were given to licensees those relating to serving intoxicated patrons contributed between 15 and 20 per cent. A Queensland survey of 750 Police Licensing Officers indicated that over a twelve-month period, more than two-thirds of their activity related to drunk and disorderly conduct or disturbances committed by individuals at licensed premises and only 14 per cent involved breaches by licensees (Findlay et al, 2002).

Personal experience and observation play a major role in determining the degree to which individuals perceive the probability of detection and severity of punishment for illegal acts (Cook, 1980; Homel, 1988). Given what is known from police reports, it is reasonable to assume that most licensees, managers, and staff would deduce—quite accurately—that responsible beverage service is a low priority for police.

---

[27] Since the early 1990s, most states/territories have formally required or recommended that licensees, managers, and bar staff complete Responsible Beverage Service training. The structure and quality of these programmes varies widely but, at a minimum, they include information about the jurisdiction's liquor laws, especially those pertaining to patron intoxication (NDRI, 2007).

[28] Individuals are typically charged with offences such as 'failing to leave a licensed venue' or for being under the legal age for drinking on licensed premises (18 years) (Briscoe and Donnelley, 2001).

[29] Signs of intoxication that servers are trained to look for include: loud, boisterous, and disorderly behaviour; spilling drinks; slurred speech; swaying; bumping into furniture; vomiting; difficulty with balance, coordination, or walking.

There are a range of reasons why police find enforcement of liquor-licensing laws pertaining to the operation of licensed premises a difficult task, rarely pursued with vigour. Central among these are the considerable barriers police face in establishing guilt, prosecuting breaches, and the trivial nature of maximum fines imposed—especially in relation to serving intoxicated patrons. In a highly publicized case, Western Australian police charged staff of a five-star hotel for serving a female guest to intoxication who, the same night, fell to her death from the 15th floor with a blood alcohol level of 0.342 mg/ml. Under the Act it is illegal to sell or supply alcohol to a person who is already intoxicated and penalties range from $2,000 for employees to $5,000 for management. Police submitted that when the woman was served four Martinis she showed obvious signs of intoxication (she had been drinking at other bars in the hotel throughout the day), including an inability to walk unaided and requiring assistance to go to the toilet. At the time, all licensees and managers were required to complete training in responsible beverage service. Nonetheless, the magistrate dismissed the charges on the grounds that bar staff could not be expected to have the capacity to accurately determine whether or not a patron was intoxicated.[30] As commentators have noted, outcomes such as this strengthen the widely held belief among police that 'lack of support by the court system, in every jurisdiction in the country' means that to attempt to enforce illegal behaviour by licensees is 'a waste of time' (Vaughan, 2001: 205).

Other obstacles to enforcement include limited police resources for preventative policing, which is typically viewed as less important than 'serious crime'; the development of overly close relationships between police and licensees which may result in corrupt practices; poor knowledge and understanding of liquor laws due to inadequate training and the high volume of information required to be digested; ambivalence about interfering with people's enjoyment, especially within tight-knit communities where officers may be required to monitor licensee practices within their own social network; and, concern regarding the commercial viability of licensed premises and victimization of licensees (NDRI, 2007; Stockwell, 1995). It has also been observed that heavy social drinking is strongly embedded in the dominant police culture and that intoxication is viewed as an acceptable excuse for aberrant behaviour (Doherty and Roche, 2003). Many police are therefore unwilling to impose restrictions on the actions of others which they may themselves engage in or privately condone.

VOLUNTARY COMMUNITY LIQUOR ACCORDS: LICENSED PREMISES REGULATING THEMSELVES?

Described by some as 'gentlemen's agreements', Voluntary Community Liquor Accords (Accords) are usually police-driven (sometimes initiated by local councils) community-based initiatives which involve licensees/managers of licensed premises, other businesses, local councils, and community representatives, drawing up an (unbinding) agreement or code of practice to reduce alcohol-related harms. Accords

---

[30] <http://www.caan.adf.org.au/newsletter.asp?ContentId=t06062005> and <http://www.caan.adf.org.au/newsletter.asp?ContentId=t20060619>.

were initially developed to proactively address a range of problems concerning the decline of public safety and amenity stemming from licensed premises but which were being borne by local businesses and residents alone.

Accords typically involve the unanimous agreement of participating licensees (usually all or most premises within a defined region) to undertake responsible beverage service practices (eg, not to serve customers to intoxication); discourage 'happy hours', drinking games, and price discounting; remove or re-train aggressive security staff; provide adequate seating; address any access problems to bars and toilets (eg, bottlenecks); and routinely conduct age-identification checks. Police also commit to monitoring licensee reports of incidents on the premises; being available for regular formal communication with licensees; supporting initiatives to improve the late-night environment such as liaising with public-transport providers to ensure adequate services, improving lighting, or installing closed-circuit television cameras; and maintaining a high visible presence in and around licensed premises.[31]

The first Accords emerged in Victoria in the early 1990s and, from there, uptake by police jurisdictions across the country has grown rapidly.[32] The wholehearted embrace of the Accord philosophy reflects the difficulties police face in effectively applying the legal powers vested in them by Liquor Acts and a consequent preference for working 'with' rather than 'against' licensees. As Homel and colleagues (2001: 242) point out, it is a reasonable response to the 'vacuum created by an inadequate regime of legal regulation'.

Reviews of Accord evaluations point to limited positive outcomes with no evidence to suggest any long-term impact on levels of alcohol-related problems. Where improvements have occurred, they have been short term (Loxley et al, 2004; NDRI, 2007; Stockwell, 2006). It is apparent that although Accord coordinators may be able to facilitate initial agreement from licensees, compliance typically degrades over time as competitive pressures come to bear. Some have concluded that in the absence of effective enforcement practices, Accords are a 'look good only measure' (Stockwell, 2006: 272); others have noted that the 'appeal of Accords probably rests more on the development of local communication networks, the facilitation of local input, a sense of local "control", and improving public relations through open negotiations, than in the actual reduction of harm' (NDRI, ibid: 198).

It is unsurprising therefore that despite the proliferation of Accords, violent crime appears unabated (Matthews et al, 2002). Accords are, by definition, cooperative agreements, the forces of which are only as strong as the commitment of their respective signatories (Hawks et al, 1999). In the context of a highly competitive environment, 'there are many responsible members of the alcohol industry who do obey the

---

[31] Since Accord membership is voluntary (although strongly encouraged) and licensees may refuse to participate, police are keen to allay their concerns regarding potential threats to profitability. As Vaughan (2001: 215) has noted, reluctance to participate is a common occurrence and 'needs to be addressed at the outset. Licensees need to be shown that an Accord is a "win–win" proposition for them which presents no threat to their viability.'

[32] Victoria has about 80 Accords; 11 Accords are active in South Australia; New South Wales has over 140 active Accords: <http://www.olgr.nsw.gov.au/liquor_liqaccrds_maps_new.asp>; the Northern Territory has established one in Alice Springs; and they are active throughout most of Western Australia and Queensland (Loxley et al, 2007; NDRI, 2007).

licensing laws; however, self-regulation may never succeed as too many in the industry, at all levels, are motivated by profit alone' (Vaughan, 2001: 205).

LOCKOUTS

In popular late-night locations, maintaining control of street problems associated with large volumes of intoxicated revellers requires resource-intensive policing at substantial cost (Donnelley et al, 2007). In very recent years police have increasingly recognized a need for more prescriptive strategies, the most notable and controversial of these, the 'lockout', is currently being trialled in several jurisdictions.[33] Relatively new to Australia, the lockout strategy is concerned with discouraging the common practice of 'pub-hopping'[34] by revellers and requires licensees to refuse admission to patrons seeking entry after a certain time (usually a few hours after midnight, but before the end of permitted trading hours).

Lockout policies are not well received by licensees and their representatives. The Association of Liquor Licensees Melbourne appealed to the Victorian Civil Administrative Tribunal after the Victorian government announced a three-month trial of lockout restrictions.[35] In late 2007, New South Wales liquor-licensing authorities supported a police proposal[36] to introduce 1.00 am lockouts for licensed premises in Newcastle's high-crime central business district. The affected licensees strongly appealed the decision to the licensing court and after many months, police and licensees struck an out-of-court deal allowing an additional half hour of 'pre-lockout' time.[37] Senior Western Australian police have argued strongly for introducing lockout conditions to an existing Accord agreement covering the entertainment district of Northbridge but have received strong opposition from Accord members:

The Accord meeting was opened by police, who argued that a range of measures such as bike patrols, foot patrols and dog squad patrols had failed to curb the violence in Northbridge. 'The situation is not getting any better . . . my officers just go from fight to fight', Insp Roger Beer said. He said alcohol-related assaults accounted for 62 per cent of violence in Northbridge . . . 58 Accord members raised their hands during an unofficial tally to show they were opposed to a lockout in any form, with only two, including the Superintendent, voting in favour of the lockout.[38]

---

[33] Lockouts are currently in place or being trialled in some areas of Victoria (<http://www.news.com.au/dailytelegraph/story/0,22049,23784550–5001028,00.html>; <http://www.theage.com.au/national/arrests-down-on-first-lockout-weekend-20080609–2nzm.html>), Western Australia (<http://www.news.com.au/perthnow/story/0,21598,23809545–2761,00.html>), South Australia (<http://www.news.com.au/adelaidenow/story/0,22606,23748885–5006301,00.html>) and New South Wales (<http://www.news.com.au/dailytelegraph/story/0,22049,23748707–5006009,00.html>).

[34] Pub-hopping refers to the movement of large numbers of patrons between different late-night venues often in a drunken and disorderly fashion, thus undermining the public safety and amenity of the surroundings.

[35] Subsequently, Liquor Licensing Victoria conceded that some nightclubs which met certain conditions (eg, additional security guards) would be exempt from the lockouts (<http://www.news.com.au/dailytelegraph/story/0,22049,23784550-5001028,00.html>).

[36] Police were backed by highly motivated and coordinated community support.

[37] <http://www.abc.net.au/news/stories/2008/07/30/2318973.htm>.

[38] <http://www.thewest.com.au/default.aspx?MenuID=77andContentID=8876>.

Where enforced, lockouts may be a pragmatic solution for reducing front-line policing costs. Although promising, as a relatively new strategy to Australian policing, there is only limited evidence for the impact of lockouts across a range of problems and little is known about potential negative effects (NDRI, 2007).[39] Nonetheless, available evidence supports the view that levels of alcohol-related disorder may decline where lockouts are implemented—the codicil being that lockouts do not necessarily reduce overall levels of alcohol consumption.

CONCLUSIONS

The current condition of alcohol policy in Australia can best be described as inconsistent. State and territory Liquor Acts include foremost statements about minimizing harm due to the sale and supply of alcohol, but the processes involved rarely allow for the enforcement of such sentiments in practice. At the Federal level of governance, alcohol is now considered an unexceptional commodity—like orange juice or milk—and state laws or practices which unjustifiably reduce industry competitiveness are being weeded out. For policymakers, regulators, and enforcers, deregulation and self-regulation have become the common catchphrases of recent decades.

It is not possible to know with certainty how trends in nightlife-related violence and crime may have changed across the nation as a whole. Emerging crime and health statistics point toward increasing problems in the most deregulated areas, although it may be many more years before the full national impact is known. Media attention on the negative effects of alcohol appears to have grown substantially, somewhat displacing past appetites for news of illicit drugs. National surveys hint at increasing public concern over how licensed premises are regulated and prominent agencies are united in urging the prime minister and premiers to take decisive action against alcohol-related violence.[40] Alcohol-related issues appear to hold more interest for the current Commonwealth government than they have for past administrations.[41]

Perhaps the clearest sign that public order and safety in nightlife environments may be in decline is the degree of concern expressed by those to whom the responsibility for maintaining order in the late-night environment falls. Police—who now regularly find themselves acting as front-line advocates for local communities besieged with alcohol-related problems—increasingly express their dismay at the inequities of the nation's various licensing systems. In 2008, Australian Police Commissioners met to discuss a range of policing issues.[42] A discussion paper prepared at the request of the

---

[39] Police have reported increased levels of problems associated with refusal of entry and higher levels of intoxication (Molloy et al, 2004).

[40] <http://www.news.com.au/heraldsun/story/0,21985,23540518-2862,00.html>.

[41] In its first 12 months of office the Rudd Federal government has introduced higher excise tax on pre-mixed spirit-based beverages, a National 'Binge Drinking Strategy' grant-funding scheme, and has conducted two Senate inquiries into alcohol (<http://www.brisbanetimes.com.au/articles/2008/04/27/1209234617917.html>).

[42] Conference of Commissioners of Police of Australasia and the South West Pacific Region, Tasmania, March 2008.

Commissioners highlighted areas where police have a major role to play in reducing alcohol-related harms. Key among these was a need to ensure that appropriate liquor licensing regulation was in place and that it be supported with enhanced enforcement (Nicholas, 2008). Police are cognizant of the central role they must play in addressing alcohol-related crime in the night-time environment and there is a growing awareness that strategies favoured in the past have not had their desired effects. Progress will be slow and many of the past frameworks will no doubt continue to remain for some time. In the words of one senior Australian police officer, 'it takes many years of co-ordinated effort to turn these virtual juggernauts even a few degrees'.

REFERENCES

All internet sources were accessible 20 August 2008

ABS (Australian Bureau of Statistics) (2002) *Crime and Safety Australia 2002*, Cat No 4509.0, Canberra: ABS.

AERF (Alcohol Education and Rehabilitation Foundation) (2008) *National Alliance Against Alcohol-Related Violence*: Media Release, ACT: AERF, <http://www.aerf.com.au/community/NAAARV/Editorials/Daryl%20Article.pdf>.

—— (2005) *Crime and Safety Australia 2005*, Cat No 4509.0, Canberra: ABS.

AIHW (Australian Institute of Health and Welfare) (2008) *2007 National Drug Strategy Household Survey: First results*, Canberra: AIHW.

BABOR, T, CAETANO, R, CASSWELL, S, EDWARDS, G, GIESBRECHT, N, GRAHAM, K, et al (2003) *Alcohol: No Ordinary Commodity: Research and Public Policy*, Oxford: Oxford University Press.

BRISCOE, S and DONNELLY, N (2001) *Temporal and Regional Aspects of Alcohol-Related Violence and Disorder*, Alcohol Studies Bulletin, No 1, Sydney: NSW Bureau of Crime Statistics and Research.

—— —— (2003a) 'Problematic licensed premises for assaults in inner Sydney, Newcastle and Wollongong', *Australian and New Zealand Journal of Criminology*, 36/1, 18–33.

—— —— (2003b) *Liquor Licensing Enforcement Activity in New South Wales*, Alcohol Studies Bulletin, No 4, Sydney: NSW Bureau of Crime Statistics and Research.

CATALANO, P and STOCKWELL, T (2002) *Drinking after Driving in Western Australia*, Technical report, Perth: National Drug Research Institute, Curtin University of Technology.

CHAPPELL, D, GRBOSKY, P and STRANG, H (eds), (1991) *Australian Violence: Contemporary perspectives*, Canberra: Australian Institute of Criminology.

CHIKRITZHS, T (2004) *The Impact of Extended Trading Hours in Licensed Premises on Indicators of Alcohol-Related Harm*, PhD Thesis, Perth: Curtin University of Technology.

—— (2007) *Submission to the Liquor Licensing Panel of Victoria: Woolworth's Limited packaged liquor application, Bell St Preston*, Perth: National Drug Research Institute, Curtin University of Technology.

—— CATALANO, P, HENRICKSON, N and PASCAL, R (2007) *Predicting Alcohol-Related Harms from Licensed Outlet Density: A feasibility study*, Hobart: National Drug Law Enforcement Research Fund.

—— and STOCKWELL, T (2002) 'The impact of later trading hours for hotels on levels of violence', *Journal of Studies on Alcohol*, 63/5, 591–9.

CHIKRITZHS, T and STOCKWELL, T (2006) 'The impact of later trading hours for hotels on levels of impaired driver road crashes and driver breath alcohol levels', *Addiction,* 101, 1254–64.

—— —— (2007) 'The impact of later trading hours for hotels (public houses) on breath alcohol levels of apprehended impaired drivers', *Addiction,* 102, 1609–17.

—— —— and MASTERS, L (1997) *Evaluation of the Public Health and Safety Impact of Extended Trading Permits for Perth Hotels and Nightclubs,* Technical Report, Perth: National Centre for Research into the Prevention of Drug Abuse, Curtin University of Technology.

COOK, P (1980) 'Research in criminal deterrence: Laying the groundwork for the second decade', *Crime and Justice: An annual review of research,* 2, 211–68.

DEVERY, C (1992) *Mapping Crime in Local Government Areas: Assault and break and enter in Waverley,* Sydney: NSW Bureau of Crime Statistics and Research.

DOHERTY, S and ROCHE, A (2003) *Alcohol and Licensed Premises: Best practice in policing,* South Australia: Australasian Centre for Policing Research.

DONNELLY, N and BRISCOE, S (2002) *Young Adults' Experience of Responsible Service Practice in NSW,* Alcohol Studies Bulletin No 3, Sydney: NSW Bureau of Crime Statistics and Research.

DONNELLEY, N, POYNTON, S, WEATHERBURN, D, BAMFORD, E and NOTTAGE, J (2006) *Liquor Outlet Concentrations and Alcohol-Related Neighbourhood Problems,* Sydney: NSW Bureau of Crime Statistics and Research.

—— SCOTT, L, POYNTON, S, WEATHERBURN, D, SHANAHAN, M and HANSEN, F (2007) *Estimating the Short-Term Cost of Police Time Spent Dealing with Alcohol-Related Crime in NSW,* Monograph series No 25, Tasmania: National Drug Law Enforcement Research Fund.

FINDLAY, RA, SHEEHAN, MC, DAVEY, J, BRODIE, H and RYNNE F (2002) 'Liquor law enforcement: Policy and practice in Australia', *Drugs: Education, prevention and policy,* 9/1, 85–94.

GRAHAM, K and HOMEL, R (1997) 'Creating safer bars', in M Plant, E Single, and T Stockwell (eds), *Alcohol: Minimising the harm,* London: Free Association Press, 171–92.

GRUENEWALD, P, PONICKI, W and HOLDER, H (1993) 'The relationship of outlet densities to alcohol consumption: A time series cross–sectional analysis', *Alcoholism: Clinical and Experimental Research,* 17/1, 38–47.

HAWKS, D, RYDON, P, STOCKWELL, T, WHITE, M, CHIKRITZHS, T and HEALE, P (1999) *The Evaluation of the Fremantle Police–Licensee Accord: Impact of serving practices, harm and the wider community,* Perth: National Drug Research Institute, Curtin University of Technology.

HOMEL, R (1988) *Policing and Punishing the Drinking Driver: A study of general and specific deterrence,* London: Springer-Verlag.

—— and CLARK, J (1994) 'The prediction and prevention of violence in pubs and clubs', *Crime Prevention Studies,* 3, 1–46.

—— MCILWAIN, G and CARVOTH, R (2001) 'Creating safer drinking environments', in N Heather, T Peters and T Stockwell (eds), *International Handbook of Alcohol Dependence and Problems,* London: John Wiley and Sons, 721–40.

—— and TOMSEN, S (1993) *Hot Spots for Violence: the environments of pubs and clubs,* Homicide: Patterns, Prevention and Control, Conference Proceedings No 17, Canberra: Australian Institute of Criminology.

—— —— and THOMMENY, J (1992) 'Public drinking and violence: Not just an alcohol problem', *The Journal of Drug Issues,* 22/3, 679–97.

HORNE, D (1971) *The Lucky Country,* Ringwood, Victoria: Penguin Books.

INDERMAUR, D (1999) 'Situational prevention of violent crime: Theory and practice in Australia', *Studies on Crime and Crime Prevention,* 8/1, 71–87.

IRELAND, C and THOMMENY, J (1993) 'The crime cocktail: Licensed premises, alcohol and street offences', *Drug and Alcohol Review*, 12/2, 143–50.

JOCHELSON, R. (1997) *Crime and Place: An Analysis of Assaults and Robberies in Inner Sydney, NSW*, Sydney: Bureau of Crime Statistics and Research.

LANG, E, STOCKWELL, T, RYDON, P and GAMBLE, C (1992) *Drinking Settings, Alcohol-Related Harm and Support for Prevention Policies*, Perth: National Centre for Research into the Prevention of Drug Abuse, Curtin University of Technology.

LIQUOR LICENSING PANEL (2007a) *Report and Recommendation(s) to the Director of Liquor Licensing, Cheapa Wines, Preston, File No: 44556A01B*, Melbourne, Victoria: Office of the Director of Liquor Licensing, Department of Justice.

—— (2007b) *Report and Recommendation(s) to the Director of Liquor Licensing, Dan Murphy's, Preston, File No: 44523A01G*, Melbourne, Victoria: Office of the Director of Liquor Licensing, Department of Justice.

LIVINGSTON, M (2008a) 'Alcohol outlet density and assault: A spatial analysis', *Addiction*, 103, 619–28.

—— (2008b) 'A Longitudinal analysis of alcohol outlet density and assault', *Alcoholism: Clinical and Experimental Research*, 32/6, 1–6.

—— CHIKRITZHS, T and ROOM, R (2007) 'Changing the density of alcohol outlets to reduce alcohol-related problems', *Drug and Alcohol Review*, 26/5, 557–66.

LOXLEY, W, PASCAL, R, LYONS, Z, CHIKRITZHS, T and ALLSOP, S (2007) *Alcohol Consumption and Harm: A comparison of liquor licensing and other relevant issues in Western Australia and other Australian jurisdictions*, Perth: National Drug Research Institute, Curtin University of Technology.

—— TOUMBOUROU, J, STOCKWELL, T, HAINES, B, SCOTT, K, GODFREY, C et al (2004) *The Prevention of Substance Use, Risk and Harm in Australia: A review of the evidence*, Perth and Melbourne: National Drug Research Institute and Centre for Adolescent Health.

MACINTYRE, S and HOMEL, R (1997) 'Danger on the dance floor: A study of interior design, crowding and aggression in nightclubs', in R Homel (ed), *Policing for Prevention: Reducing crime, public intoxication and injury*, Crime Prevention Studies (7), Monsey, NY: Willow Tree Press, 92–113.

MATTHEWS, S, CHIKRITZHS, T, CATALANO, P, STOCKWELL, T and DONATH, S (2002) *Trends in Alcohol-Related Violence in Australia, 1991/92–1999/2000*, National Alcohol Indicators Technical Report No 5, Perth: National Drug Research Institute, Curtin University of Technology.

MIDFORD, R. (2005) 'Australia and Alcohol: Living Down the Legend', *Addiction*, 100, 891–6.

MOLLOY, M, McDONALD, J, McLAREN, S and HARVEY, J (2004) *Program Evaluation Operation Link: Be safe late program*, Ballarat: Centre for Health Research and Practice, University of Ballarat.

NATIONAL COMPETITION COUNCIL (2005) *Assessment of the Governments' Progress in Implementing the National Competition Policy and Related Reforms*, Melbourne: National Competition Council.

NDRI (National Drug Research Institute) (2007) *Restrictions on the Sale and Supply of Alcohol: Evidence and outcomes*, NDRI Monograph, Perth: National Drug Research Institute, Curtin University of Technology.

NICHOLAS, R (2008) *Understanding and Responding to Alcohol-Related Social Harms in Australia: Options for policing*, Tasmania: National Drug Law Enforcement Fund.

NIEUWENHUYSEN, J (1986) *Review of the Victorian Liquor Control Act 1968*, Melbourne: Government Printer.

Roche, A, Bywood, P, Borlagdan, J, Lunnay, B, Freeman, T, Lawton, L, Tovell, A and Nicholas, R (2007) *Young People and Alcohol: The role of cultural influences*, Adelaide: National Centre for Education and Training on Addiction.

Room, R (1988) 'The dialectic of drinking in Australian life: From the Rum Corps to the wine column', *Australian Drug and Alcohol Review*, 7/4, 413–37.

Scribner, RA, MacKinnin, DP and Dwyer, HH (1995) 'The risk of assaultive violence and alcohol availability in Los Angeles County', *American Journal of Public Health*, 85/3, 335–40.

Single, E (1988) 'The availability theory of alcohol-related problems', in C Chaudron and D Wilkinson (eds), *Theories on Alcoholism*, Canada: Addiction Research Foundation, Toronto.

Stevenson, R, Lind, B and Weatherburn, D (1999a) 'The relationship between alcohol sales and assaults in New South Wales, Australia', *Addiction*, 94/3, 397– 410.

—— —— —— (1999b) 'property damage and public disorder: Their relationship with sales of alcohol in New South Wales, Australia', *Drug and Alcohol Dependence*, 54/3, 163–70.

Stockwell, T (1995) 'Do controls on the availability of alcohol reduce alcohol problems?', in T Stockwell (ed), *Alcohol Misuse and Violence: An examination of the appropriateness and efficacy of liquor laws across Australia*, Report 5: National Symposium on Alcohol Misuse and Violence, Canberra: Australian Government Publishing Service.

—— (1997) 'Regulation of the licensed drinking environment: A major opportunity for crime prevention', in R Homel (ed), *Policing for Prevention: Reducing crime, public intoxication and injury*, Monsey NY: Criminal Justice Press.

—— (2006) Alcohol supply, demand, and harm reduction: What is the strongest cocktail? *International Journal of Drug Policy*, 17, 269–77.

—— Masters, L, Phillips, M, Daly, A, Gahegan, M, Midford, R and Philp, A (1998) 'Consumption of different alcoholic beverages as predictors of local rates of night-time assault and acute alcohol-related morbidity', *Australian and New Zealand Journal of Public Health*, 22/2, 237–42.

—— Somerford, P and Lang E (1992a) 'Levels of drunkenness of customers leaving licensed premises in Perth, Western Australia: A Comparison of High and Low "Risk" Premises', *British Journal of Addiction*, 87, 873–81.

—— —— —— (1992b) 'The relationship between licence type and alcohol-related problems attributed to licensed premises in Perth, Western Australia', *Journal of Studies on Alcohol*, 53/5, 495–8.

Vaughan, S (2001) 'Reducing alcohol-related harm in and around licensed premises: industry accords—a successful intervention', in P Williams (ed), *Alcohol, Young Persons and Violence*, Canberra: Australian Institute of Criminology.

Zammit, G (2006) *Witness Statement Submitted to the Liquor Licensing Panel, Victoria*, Preston Police Complex, Darebin Police Service, Victoria Police.

PART III

CONCLUSIONS

19

NIGHTLIFE HORIZONS

SOME FURTHER THOUGHTS AND CONCLUSIONS

Phil Hadfield

INTRODUCTION

A book of this nature could never hope to provide comprehensive and authoritative analyses of the vast range of social, economic, political, and cultural factors which shape nightlife and its relationships to crime. As previous comparative volumes focusing on the anthropology of drinking have shown, these would necessarily include factors such as religion and other normative frameworks, the influence of the family, youth transitions, and gender relations, to name but a few key variables (Douglas, 1987; Heath, 2000; MacAndrew and Edgerton, 1969; Wilson, 2005). Moreover, national political cultures differ in how they rank social problems, regulate civil behaviour, intervene in the market, and fund related research. Yet, the kind of research a country engages in is also often idiosyncratic and driven by chance. For example, in the early 1990s, Canada and the Nordic countries (Finland and to a lesser extent Norway and Sweden) dominated some types of alcohol research as a result of the research organizations that flourished in those countries. On the other hand, there were few alcohol researchers in the UK, France, Italy, or Spain. Whilst a substantial amount of funding was available in the United States through the National Institute on Alcohol Abuse and Alcoholism (NIAAA), very little of this money was directed toward social problems such as violence in the NTE.[1] In England and Wales, current levels of research activity concerning these social contextual, rather than strictly epidemiological problems, have emerged only within the last decade, chiefly as a result of Home Office prioritization. In no other nations, apart from Scotland and Australia, has the NTE received such sustained attention and the literature on governmental responses to nightlife has so far been limited to analyses of the conditions pertaining within specific nation states, with most work published in scholarly journals. This work has primarily focused on the UK, Scandinavia, and Australasia. One of the key objectives of this book has been to help

---

[1] I am grateful to Kathryn Graham for sharing her thoughts on these matters.

facilitate a more outward-looking internationalist perspective, thus contributing to the development of new theoretical advances and shared knowledge to inform policy and interventions. This book makes the case for a timely and concerted response—a call to action, in this respect.

Rather than attempt a bald thematic summary of 17 chapters and the work of 36 authors, this chapter will seek to extend the analysis of a small selection of salient or innovative themes, including regulation of the alcohol industry and social divisions and exclusions. Tentative conclusions will be drawn as to promising topics for future comparative research, including the impact of new communications and surveillance technologies, and the unexplored realm of contemporary philanthropic governance.

THE REGULATION OF NIGHT-TIME-ECONOMY BUSINESSES AND THE ALCOHOL INDUSTRY

As we have seen in the cases of England and Wales ('Memoranda of Agreements'), Australia (Voluntary Community Liquor Accords), Norway (Bergen Earlier Warning System), Canada and Finland (Responsible Beverage Service Training) and San Francisco, USA (Entertainment Commission), amongst others, one widespread approach adopted by central and local governments is to require those who run bars and serve alcoholic drinks—thus making 'their living selling "risky" substances and pleasures'—to 'take responsibility for managing the risks associated with their business' (Valverde, 2003: 238; also Levi and Valverde, 2001). These initiatives often take the form of putative or formally institutionalized public–private partnerships and may be located within a broader field of neo-liberal governance wherein everyday governmental tasks are contracted out as part of a process of 'responsibilization' (O'Malley, 1996). In the NTE, *self-regulation* forms a core component of responsibilization through privatized security governance, in which leisure businesses are persuaded, coerced, or, more often, voluntarily commit themselves to, non-legally binding agreements with public authorities, principally police and licensing bodies, concerning minimum standards of operational practice. In this volume, self-regulation is described as occurring, to a lesser or greater degree, in England and Wales, Scotland, Ireland, Greece, the United States, Canada, Australia, and New Zealand.

International literature on the evaluation of industry compliance with self-regulatory codes, statutory requirements, and partnership agreements stresses the necessity for such approaches to be combined with adequate enforcement (see the discussion and literature review by Tanya Chikritzhs in Chapter 18); something which is often lacking, as recently identified in the English and Welsh context (DCMS, 2008, and see Chapter 2). Two interesting developments in the UK have further highlighted the need to question the surface appearances and rhetorical appeal of such approaches (Stockwell, 2006). Firstly, one sees the withdrawal of the British Beer and Pub Association's code of practice on discounted drinks promotions (BBPA, 2005) referred to in the licensing conditions of thousands of pubs and bars (Bowers and Pidd, 2008). In justification for this move, the BBPA point to the emergence of new legal opinion which suggests that such guidance may be in breach of European competition law (similar concerns are raised in Chapter 18, concerning the dictates of Australian law). Secondly, *Social Responsibility Standards for the Production and Sale of Alcoholic Drinks in the UK* (Wine and Spirit Trade Association et al, 2005) a document whose signatories comprise 16 trade associations and alcohol industry organizations, was recently the subject of an independent review by consultants KPMG, on behalf of the Home Office (Home Office/KPMG LLP, 2008). This study combined observational and interview-based fieldwork across eight locations in England. It found many pub and club operators to be in breach of both the licensing laws and their own voluntary codes, including those of the BBPA, with:

- people who appear to be under 18 frequently being admitted to age-restricted venues in which they cannot purchase alcohol legally
- the promotion of alcohol through low-price offers, inducements by DJs to consume greater quantities, and glamorization through links with sexual imagery
- encouragement to drink more and faster through shots and shooters being 'downed in one'
- sales to blatantly intoxicated people
- several health and safety issues inside bars and clubs, eg overcrowding, broken glass, and spilled alcohol
- poor dispersal practices (although there is some very good practice). (ibid: 9–10)

These developments, combined with the announcement by *Luminar Leisure*, Britain's biggest nightclub operator, that it would be offering mid-week deals on alcohol at many of its clubs—with prices as low as £0.80 on all drinks—has led to the charge by senior police officers and alcohol campaigners that voluntary self-regulation agreements have 'no teeth' (Alcohol Concern, 2008) and that the time has come for less 'government at a distance' and more direct state intervention in the form of new statutory requirements and the enforcement of operating standards (Harris, 2008a). In a move unprecedented in the recent history of alcohol policy in England and Wales, July 2008 saw the announcement of a Department of Health consultation exercise on proposals for a new mandatory alcohol retailing code 'to end poor retailing practice' (DoH, 2008: 4). The results of this exercise are to be considered by ministers toward the end of 2008 and it will be interesting to follow developments, particularly to the extent that they involve any inter-departmental wrangling with the Home Office, and counter-lobbying by the alcohol industry.

Developments on the other side of the Atlantic have illustrated both the potential for broader crime control measures to impact upon governance of the NTE and the capacity of influential commercial operators to resist such measures. When evidence of alleged 'mob ties', major tax evasion, and 'more than four dozen violations of state law at nine venues' by the operators of the *Cipriani* restaurant chain were brought before the New York State Liquor Authority (SLA) (Bagli, 2008)[2] it looked for a while as though the company's liquor licences would be revoked leading to the downfall of the business—state law prohibiting convicted felons from holding liquor licences (Harris, 1998b). The Ciprianis offered to settle the matter by not contesting the charges and paying a $500,000 civil penalty in return for the retention of their licences. In the light of concerns regarding the effects of closing down several Manhattan nightlife institutions, including the *Rainbow Room* at the *Rockefeller Center* and *Harry Cipriani* on Fifth Avenue, thus knocking 'the fizz out of the city's culture of excess' as one *New York Post* critic put it (Cuozzo, 2008, unpaginated), the SLA voted to accept the offer. In reaching its decision, the Board expressed concern about the potential loss of jobs if the restaurants and catering halls were forced to close. Its vote overruled the Authority's Chair, former police chief, Daniel B Boyle, who had been seeking revocation of the Ciprianis' licences. Mr Boyle had previously commented that the Ciprianis should not be allowed to 'buy their way through the system' and had even threatened them with further fines for what he saw as attempted bribery when making the settlement offer (Harris, 1998b). The eventual outcome of the case was, in his words, 'unfortunate' (Shott, 2008).

As Martin Elvins notes of the Scottish context (Chapter 3), in some jurisdictions the concept of 'social responsibility' has been extended to encompass a 'polluter pays' approach. In this respect, venue operators are enjoined and increasingly obligated to extend their duties of care—that is, in this context, 'duties to know and to manage risks' (Valverde, 2003: 238)—to encompass the behaviour of nightlife patrons in surrounding public spaces. However, as Campbell (2005) has pointed out with regard to Alcohol Disorder Zones (ADZs) (see Chapter 2) significant challenges remain in garnering sufficient empirical evidence of localized disorder such that it can be presented in a legally compelling manner as justification for the imposition of mandatory financial contributions. As Commander Chris Allison, former Association of Chief Police Officers (ACPO) Lead on licensing issues told a British national newspaper, 'they're (the drinks industry) going to fight us, they're going to appeal it, it's going to cost lots of public money' (Doward, 2005: unpaginated). Given the reluctance of licensing authorities and police forces across England and Wales to use the new powers at their disposal, it would appear that Allison's concerns are widely shared, whilst giving rise to the suspicion that this is another part of the regulatory arsenal which 'looks good' to electorates within a context of populist punitiveness, but which is effectively inoperable and thus of little practical value.

In practice, the expansion of privatized forms of security governance over night-time public spaces is emerging most clearly through the placing of enforceable conditions on licences requiring the employment of bouncers and street wardens. Increasingly, these uniformed patrols are tasked not only with the prevention of crime and disorder, but also with the more general preservation of neighbourhood 'quality of life', through actions to deter noise pollution and the fouling of pavements (see Ocejo and Brotherton, Chapter 13.2; Hutton, Chapter 17), or to load patrons safely

---

[2] <http://gothamist.com/2008/08/07/felonious_ciprianis_keep_liquor_lic.php>.

into taxis etc.[3] Much criminological debate surrounding private security governance has focused on 'enclosed' mass private property, such as shopping malls and leisure venues, policed largely in accordance with commercial objectives (Crawford, 2006; Shearing and Stenning, 1985; Wakefield, 2003). Yet, the patrolling tasks adopted by the operators of licensed premises now differ from these earlier forms of responsibilization to the extent that private interests are being co-opted to undertake duties for which the police were formerly regarded as solely responsible, ie the policing of public spaces. These efforts 'to persuade or coerce organizations or non-offending persons . . . to take some responsibility for preventing crime or reducing crime problems' in particular locations is future-oriented and preventative and may therefore be understood as constituting a form of what Mazerolle and Ransley (2006: 2–3) define as 'third party policing'. In performing these duties, the security priorities of licensed operators may well cross-cut those of the public police; however, they are unlikely to match them entirely (McCahill, 2002) and may indeed prove more stringent and exclusionary (Hadfield, 2008), whilst being less democratically accountable (White, 2008).

CHARITY BEGINS AT DUSK

Following the work of Castells (2000) and others, the concept of de-centred 'networks' of governance have become ubiquitous across the social sciences, and an especially interesting development in relation to the governance of public nightlife spaces concerns the increasing involvement of religious and other charitable and voluntary groups in providing patrolling functions and other in-situ services. This new urban philanthropy has prominently involved the introduction of 'Street Pastor' projects in 60 locations around the UK, and one in the West Indies. The project's website, headlined 'The Church in Action on the Streets', describes its aims and origins as:

an inter-denominational response to urban problems, engaging with people on the streets to care, listen and dialogue. It was pioneered in London in January 2003 by Rev Les Isaac, Director of the Ascension Trust . . . Each city project is . . . run by a local coordinator with support from Ascension Trust and local churches and community groups, in partnership with Police, Council and other statutory agencies . . . A Street Pastor is a Church leader/minister or member with a concern for society—in particular young people who feel themselves to be excluded and marginalised—and who is willing to engage people where they are, in terms of their thinking (i.e. their perspective of life) and location (i.e. where they hang out—be it on the streets, in the pubs and clubs or at parties etc.) . . . so that people know that the Church is there for them in a practical way. The role is not about preaching heaven and hell, but one of listening, caring and helping—working in an unconditional way. To be a Street Pastor you need to be over 18 (no upper age limit), a church member and able to commit to our training

---

[3] Taxi marshalling schemes have been introduced in a number of UK cities, including Cardiff, Glasgow, Leeds, and Manchester, wherein security guards monitor key city-centre taxi ranks late at night to reduce tension and ensure orderly queuing behaviour amongst revellers. The schemes are typically funded by the local Crime and Disorder Reduction Partnerships (see Chapter 2).

programme. Each Street Pastor team consists of at least three groups of four, each of which will work a minimum of one night a month, usually from 10pm to around 4am. [4]

Similar voluntary sector patrols known as 'Night Ravens' are described by Arvid Skutle and colleagues as operating in Norwegian towns and cities (Chapter 7).

Further voluntary sector developments in recent years include the establishment of 'safe havens' in central urban-nightlife locations, the most prominent of which have been the so-called 'SOS Bus' schemes. The first SOS Bus Project was established in Norwich in 2001, with similar schemes later emerging in Southend-on-Sea, Leicester, and Belfast, and proposals for further schemes in various stages of development, most progressively in Colchester.[5] The website for the Norwich SOS Bus Project describes how the initial impetus for the scheme was generated by tragic events:

> In late-2000 two teenagers were found dead in the river after a night out in the city clubland area. A short while later a third young person was found dead in the toilets of a city night-club due to alcohol-related problems. The age of these youths was from 17–21 years of age . . . A local church—Proclaimers in Norwich—offered the use of their ex-Berlin city bus as a mobile safe haven. It is a 57 foot-long bendi-bus with running water, power and heating. The community and local businesses provided all the items that were required to make the project work. Within six weeks the SOS Bus was on the streets. (ibid, note 3)

The Norwich SOS Bus is staffed by volunteers from various charities and religious organizations who provide counselling and immediate assistance to persons present-ing themselves at the facility between the hours of 9.00 pm and 3.00 am. The bus operates in conjunction with a nearby First Aid Centre staffed by volunteers from the St John Ambulance Service. A 12-seat support vehicle is used to collect clients and help them get home safely, or to obtain assistance from the emergency services. The facility has access to the city-wide police operated digital radio system, which links bus volunteers to the police, door staff at local pubs and clubs, and the city's public area CCTV operating room. The Southend bus scheme operates along very similar lines, save that the bus is a double-decker and incorporates its own beds and first aid facili-ties. The Norwich scheme's website describes the Project's mission as 'a multi-agency initiative to meet the needs of any person in Norwich's clubland at night. It is a first point of contact for those whose well-being is threatened by: inability to get home, illness or injury, emotional distress or other vulnerability' (ibid, note 3).

Despite their welfare and needs-based objectives, there seems little doubt that such initiatives remain constituents of the broader security governance agenda, their successes being measured partly in relation to reductions in crime and disorder. As the Street Pastor project's website prominently notes, local projects have 'seen some remarkable results, including drops in crime in areas where teams have been work-ing' (ibid); similarly, the cover of a recent Home Office police training DVD, entitled *Effective Practice in the Night-Time Economy*, describes SOS buses as 'A voluntary-sector model to relieve pressure on the police and ambulance' services. Whilst these

---

[4] <http://www.streetpastors.co.uk/Home/tabid/255/Default.aspx>.
[5] See websites for bus schemes in Norwich: <http://www.sosbus.co.uk/>, Southend: <http://www.sosbussouthend.co.uk/>, Belfast: <http://www.sosbusni.com/home_sosbus.htm>, and Colchester: <http://www.colchester.gov.uk/news_det.asp?art_id=7183&sec_id=27>.

developments represent the 'soft side' of urban control—contemporary research into which is sorely lacking—there are many more examples of increased surveillance, criminalization, and selective exclusion.

SURVEILLANCE AND EXCLUSION

A number of chapters in this book, including the entries from Spain, Italy, Greece, New Zealand, Northern Ireland, and Canada, have noted the extent to which nightlife patrons and other young people who populate night-time urban space are subject to various forms of surveillance, social sorting, and exclusion. In England and Wales, following implementation of the Licensing Act 2003 in November 2005 (see Chapter 2), one sees that target hardening and situational crime-prevention measures, such as high-resolution CCTV, metal detectors, identity- and age-verification scanning systems, and other security hardware are being built into the regulated operating procedures of venues through the placing of conditions on trading licences. The popular *Clubscan*[6] system, for example, which 'can read all US, Canadian and Mexican IDs, as well as each EU member ID' and those of South Africa, Australia, and New Zealand, has so far been sold and installed in 32 countries around the world.[7] Its manufacturers point to the system's ability to read 223 different IDs and 162 different passports, including photographs, by means of touchscreen technology which can record an image of the document in seconds. As well as verifying identity and age, the system is used to build a database of patrons which can be used for promotional mail shots and other forms of direct marketing. In answer to the question 'why will a venue *Clubscan* my ID?', the company's website provides a template statement for venues in explaining the system and its uses to customers:

It checks your age and whether you are listed on the venue's database of people who have been barred . . . To maintain a log of customers on our premises . . . to assist the police and other local authorities . . . You are not obliged to permit a venue to scan your identification through Clubscan . . . The venue will do its best to keep your information secure, and will be aware of the main principles of the Data Protection Act. Your information is not normally accessed by any other staff member other than the DPS (Designated Premises Supervisor).[8]

The website further claims that the installation of *Clubscan* can effectively protect a venue's licence by removing the risk of customers failing a police-initiated underage alcohol test-purchase operation. The system also provides the venue with demographic information as to the typical profile of its customers, including their average age and male to female ratio.

Other conditions placed on licences in England and Wales may include the requirement to conduct mandatory body searches, to employ designated numbers and proportions of male and female bouncers, and to limit last-entry times to the premises.

---

[6] <http://www.idscan.co.uk/uk_products_clubscan.php>.
[7] <http://www.idscan.co.uk/uk_faq.php?faq_id=5&category_id=11>.
[8] <http://www.idscan.co.uk/uk_faq.php?faq_id=25&category_id=11>.

Whilst such levels of intrusive surveillance appear, for the most part, to be passively accepted by the British populace, as Graham and Bernards note in Chapter 14, this has not been the case in Canada, where (even!) proposals to install public place CCTV cameras remain controversial on privacy grounds (Hier et al, 2007), requiring the police in Toronto to submit their plans for public consultation.[9]

Combined with a venue's own, largely unaccountable practices concerning whom, amongst those arriving at its door, it will select for admission (Hadfield, 2008), these various security technologies can, in some areas, add up to significant numbers of persons who, though present in nightlife, find themselves excluded from the party; that is to swollen ranks of the dispossessed. One of the more controversial and little recognized forms of social sorting occurs in relation to assumed connections between the type of musical entertainment offered and the type of crowd that a venue may wish to attract, or more pertinently, deter.

SONIC GOVERNANCE

In their case study of San Francisco (Chapter 13.3) Moloney et al discuss two inter-related and under-researched issues of nightlife security governance: first, the role and impact of independent promoters,[10] and secondly, the risk profiling of particu-lar musical genres or music-based subcultures/scenes. Such regulation is not only a facet of police and licensing authority activity (Talbot, 2007); it also forms part of the repertoire of inculcated and largely unspoken occupational codes which constitute industry notions of 'good management'. Here it appears that forms of class-biased and sometimes racist prejudicial attitudes infuse both the public and private governance of nightlife. A police officer cited by Moloney et al recites his advice to venue managers to: 'know who your promoter is' and goes on to narrate a cautionary tale of managers who get 'in way over their head' when dealing with certain promoters, allowing them-selves to get 'pushed around', with problems spiralling out of control.

Similar regulatory forms are apparent in areas of London, the anonymity of which must be retained for legal and ethical reasons. Here licensing authorities and the police are advising 'naïve' bar owners to avoid entering into partnerships with particular DJs and promoters, who are identified as 'trouble'—as in Chapter 13.3: 'bringing in too large a crowd, filled with the "wrong sort" of people' (p 231, n 14). These 'trouble-some' persons and their entourages are said to originate from South London and to

---

[9] <http://www.torontopolice.on.ca/media/text/20061214-tps_cctv_project.pdf>.

[10] Independent promoters with specialist knowledge, skills, or community links are often contracted by nightclub owners to drum up business, especially during quieter weeknight trading periods. The promot-ers typically receive the admission fees, with the venues taking the money from bar sales. A more detailed examination of their role is provided in Chapter 13.3, p 231 and at n 14 of that chapter. Promoted events often take the form of 'niche nights' with different styles of entertainment used to attract different types of customer (for example 'party nights', 'club nights', 'student nights' etc). Each of these operational themes may generate a divergent set of security risks and require an accordingly specialized managerial response (Hadfield, 2004a). In the City of London it is proposed that venues may, as a condition of their licence, have to seek approval from the police concerning their plans to hold events hosted by external promoters in order for the police to conduct a risk assessment. If the police deem the event to be too 'risky' it will not be allowed to proceed.

not 'mix well' with rivals from other parts of the metropolis, when meeting in 'neutral' locations such as Central London bars and clubs. The promoted events 'problem' appears to involve geographical displacement (Felson and Clarke, 1998), with a 'crackdown' by the authorities in one area being followed by a mushrooming of issues in neighbouring boroughs, thus demonstrating that nightlife-related crime flows across jurisdictional borders not only internationally, but also intra-nationally. As in San Francisco, the groups in question are subtly, sometimes explicitly, referred to as 'Black', the music being described as 'RNB', 'Hip Hop', or 'Grime'. These assumptions, then, appear to constitute 'trade' knowledge, learned on the job, 'which can range from racial stereotypes to generalizations made about very specific groups of individuals' of the form that Levi and Valverde (2001: 833) observe in the discourse of Canadian liquor-licensing inspectors and which have been a long-established and salient theme in the sociology of policing (Herbert, 1997; Skolnick, 1994; Sudnow).

In addition, 'music profiling' appears to be an extension of lay assumptions concerning people's emotional responses to music, and other sounds. Sounds are commonly regarded as having the ability to both trigger aggression and soothe or displace it. To the extent that sounds can be deliberately manipulated in order to influence the behaviour of individuals or groups, this might be described as the realm of 'sonic governance'. In the daytime economy, for example, one sees the emergence of the 'Mosquito Alarm', described by its manufacturers as an 'ultrasonic teenage deterrent'.[11] The purpose of this device is to protect properties and businesses from juvenile crime by emitting 'high frequency screeching sounds that carry over a distance of roughly 20 metres, which are audible only to those under about 20–25 years of age' (Crawford, 2008: 18). Here sound is used as a blunt instrument of generalized dispersal, a low-level sonic weapon. Crawford (ibid: 19) links the Mosquito's development to more subtle technologies of control:

Often referred to as the 'Manilow method', many shopping centres have traditionally deliberately played music that is unpopular with young people thereby encouraging them to move away . . . It has been reported that the Local Government Association (LGA) has complied a list of such songs for councils to play in trouble spots in order to move youths on, including Lionel Ritchie's 'Hello' and the St Winifred's School Choir's 'There's No One Quite Like Grandma'!

Returning to the NTE, one finds chip and kebab shop owners in Stockport, northwest England, attempting to reduce disorder in and around their premises by playing mellow down-tempo music between 1.30 am and 3.00 am to influence the mood of those customers who remain 'wound-up' from a heavy night of clubbing (Hadfield, 2004b).

Studies in social psychology indicate that the presentation of music in terms of its tempo and volume can influence the rate at which people drink; these studies include research from the United States (Bach and Schaefer, 1979; Drews, et al, 1992; McElrea and Standing, 1992) and France (Guéguen et al, 2008). In an early Australian study, Homel and Tomsen (1993) found the risk of disorder to reduce in crowds entertained by quality

---

[11] <http://www.compoundsecurity.co.uk/teenage_control_products.html>.

musicians, whilst increasing where patrons were subjected to 'bad bands'—this being the case even when the crowds listening to the 'good music' were significantly larger. More recently, Graham and Homel (2008) note how the style and lyrical content of the songs a band selects may influence the risk of bar-room violence. Qualitative studies focusing on recorded music as played by disc jockeys, have found triggers for disorder linked to the genre, programming style, tempo, and volume of the music presented, in both English (Hadfield, 2006: 94–104; 2007) and Scottish (Forsyth, 2008; Forsyth and Cloonan, 2008) contexts. It appears that the 'wrong' music can soon lead patrons to behave in a boisterous and aggressive manner, bringing them into conflict with other customers. There may also be local sensitivities in relation to different musical styles, or songs which are associated with particular sports teams which give rise to a heightened risk of conflict (Hadfield, 2004a). One of the more interesting themes for future research concerns the way in which venue operators, bands, and disc jockeys use music *strategically* within the context of a 'set' or 'playlist', to not only 'wind the crowd up' into a state of euphoria, but also to 'take them on a journey' containing emotional peaks and troughs, finally 'winding them down' in preparation for closure and orderly clearance of the venue (Hadfield, 2007). In a recent conference paper, Alasdair Forsyth (2008: 25), who is at the forefront of the sonic research agenda, drew together five main findings or hypotheses from the existing literature:

Music is an integral part of the nightlife experience; music can both attract /retain and remove / deter a (particular) clientele or patrons; music can influence levels of alcohol and other drug use (as well as other patterns of consumption); music can both trigger or provide distraction from violence (and worsen or alleviate existing levels of disorder); music is not just entertainment – it's mind control!

The playing out of pre-existing community tensions and rivalries in a nightlife context is a topic touched upon by several contributors to this volume, but with regard to which a great deal of further research is required, especially concerning the thorny issue of nightlife security governance in contexts of social division and multiculturalism.

SOCIAL COHESIONS AND DIVISIONS

Nightlife spaces, particularly NTEs, are often spaces of division (Hollands, 2002). This is perhaps most visible in relation to the construction of stylistic, cultural, and economic hierarchies (Measham and Hadfield, 2009) and in the rise of particular forms of admission policy and consumer stratification processes, as imposed by venues applying 'guest list' or 'membership' criteria (Hadfield, 2008; Spicer, 2007). There also appears to be mounting evidence from British (Böse, 2003: 175; Hobbs et al, 2003: 123; Talbot, 2007: 40), and French (Marlière, 2007:53), cities of racist door policies, giving rise to extensive spatial exclusion, particularly from city centre venues. It should come as no surprise that the social divisions of nightlife reflect those of wider society (Kalra, 2000; Parker, 2000; Song, 1999), and that whilst some minority groups may be disproportionably excluded from 'mainstream' nightlife, others may be less likely to seek participation in the first place. Certainly, the position of intra-national ethnic minorities and cultural diversity appears to be something of a blind spot within the academic literature on nightlife (Huq, 2006).

As Room (2005: 321) notes, 'alcohol or drug use or non-use often becomes an eth- nic marker . . . and use patterns in immigrant communities are thus not simply a mat- ter of acculturation to some "mainstream"'. The 'mainstream' cultures in question, particularly those relating to drinking, may well be understood as a coded reference to 'whiteness', which, as the majority identity in the West, has long been 'the ethnic identity that dare not speak its name' (Huq, 2006: 135). However, people may express identification with their ethnic group to varying degrees and it is, of course, not possi- ble to predict individual behaviour simply on the basis of generalized assumptions of collective identity. Third-generation immigrants may differ from their first-genera- tion grandparents, men from women, those living in ethnically and spatially distinct communities in comparison with those living in 'mixed' environments.[12] Behaviours are therefore relational and context specific and may change over the life course. Abstention, for example, only becomes a marker of ethnic identity if the society in which one lives is one in which participation is widely accepted. Similarly, in specific environments where intoxication is the norm, such as those to be found in many nightlife areas, even the 'light drinker' may mark themselves as distinct. When study- ing these more polarized contexts it may perhaps be easier to draw certain conclu- sions as to collective identities, although, again, this is an area in which research is severely lacking. Based upon what knowledge is available, Room (2007: 21), in his review of cultural differences in drinking habits, comments that 'If one searches today for a cultural political boundary in Europe between abstinence and intoxication, it is Muslim minorities who have taken on the role of a group defining itself in part in terms of abstinence.'

In England, the ethnic-minority presence in nightlife is most visible in specific enclaves that depart from the norm by being predominately food-led rather than alcohol-based. Such areas include the so-called 'Curry Mile' in Rusholme, Manchester, Birmingham's Sparkbrook, Balsall Heath, and Moseley (the 'Balti Triangle'), and Lon- don's Edgware Road and Brick Lane. Similarly, as Parker (2000: 81) notes, '"Going for a Chinese" has become as integral a part of British daily life as "going down the pub", and indeed the two activities are often closely related. This is evident in the spatial distri- bution of Chinese takeaways . . .'. Do such agglomerations of ethnic businesses repre- sent multiculturalism, separatism, or what Parker (ibid) describes as 'zones of contact' between different cultures? Certainly these ethnic enclaves appear to both welcome and have considerable popularity amongst majority white and immigrant communi- ties alike, as their prominence in place-marketing and 'city break' tourism campaigns attests.[13] Many of the restaurants in these areas are not licensed to sell alcohol, thus

---

[12] See Chapter 2, note 10.

[13] See, for example, the official visitor websites for Birmingham: <http://www.visitbirmingham.com/ eating_out/balti_triangle/>, Manchester, <http://www.restaurantsofmanchester.com/rusholme.htm>, and Leicester: <http://www.visitleicester.co.uk/england/leicester-restaurants-indian.php>.

'cultural diffusion flows in both directions' (Room, 2005: 321), notwithstanding the fact that a 'bring your own bottle' policy typically operates. Would a more Western-style NTE be imaginable without significant use of alcohol and drugs? Perhaps not, but a non-Western-style one certainly would, and to some extent already exists within Western countries, as the following case notes from my own observational research describes:

The Edgware Road area of West London has a distinctive character, drawn largely from the preponderance of Middle Eastern restaurants concentrated in the area. A number, though by no means a majority, of these establishments cater overtly for Muslims (that is, they empha-size their provision of halal food, mint tea, and sweet desserts). Previous studies have sug-gested that this factor ensures that the area is popular with Muslims from all parts of London, especially during Ramadan (Town Centres Limited, 2001: 20). The same study suggests that a total of 650,000 Middle Eastern tourists visited the Edgware Road in 2000 (ibid), and it can reasonably be assumed that a significant proportion did so in the night-time dining period. The recognized cultural preference for late-night dining amongst Middle Eastern people inevitably contributes to the late-night use of the area.

The area acts as a community site for Bangladeshi, Nigerian, Egyptian and other North Afri-can and South East Asian communities, Hindu and Muslim, with some venues used for prayer meetings. Late at night the area is youth-centred and principally male-dominated, with activ-ity continuing into the early hours. Early hours activities focus on the Middle Eastern tradi-tional of smoking from Shisha Pipes. This has been described in the following terms:

'Shisha is a Middle-Eastern smoking tradition ... Tobacco is soaked in fruit shavings such as strawberry, apples or grapes. This mixture is then smoked through a large water pipe (called a hookah). The hookah uses a small charcoal tablet to gently heat a special, flavour-infused tobacco blend. The tobacco never burns, but is filtered as it is drawn through the water-filled, hand-blown glass base and inhaled through ornate, embroidered hoses.'[14]

Nightlife, then, offers opportunities for cultural diffusion and exchange in which people living together in the same society can partake in, and gain a greater under-standing of, other cultures—in much the same way as through travel. The following paragraphs, however, consider an equally unexamined area, that of the security risks and criminogenic impacts of civil conflict and external threat.

CIVIL CONFLICT AND EXTERNAL THREAT

Issues of conflict and insecurity as experienced by nightlife participants are raised by a number of authors in this volume, principally those reporting from Italy, Spain, and Northern Ireland. In Chapter 9, Selmini and Nobili describe how the central squares of Bologna in northern Italy become sites of danger, especially for young people visiting from outside the city, for students, and generally for young women. These risks relate to the contestation of these spaces by different and often opposi-tional groups, including urban travellers (the so-called *punka bestia*), drug addicts, and North African drug dealers. Similarly in Chapter 10, Anabel Rodríguez Basanta, reporting from Spain, notes how some clubs and music scenes are dominated by

---

[14] <http://www.shishapipe.net/>.

violent skinheads. She also points to tensions between indigenous Spaniards and in-coming Latin American communities over the establishment of noisy new venues and Latino youths' occupation of parks and other public spaces. Both chapters mention inter-generational conflicts between young people occupying outdoor city spaces and older residents in central urban areas. In Chapter 4, McElrath considers Belfast, a city emerging into a more peaceful era, but still containing divided communities, fear and distrust of the 'other', and sporadic instances of sectarian violence. She describes how, during the years of conflict, nightlife was repressed by the courts through the imposition of 'wartime measures' such as curfews in relation to pub opening hours. In addition, the basic levels of personal security required for development of a vibrant NTE in the city centre proved elusive. These security risks differed from the 'ordinary risks of assault' often associated with public-drinking settings due to the heightened possibilities of being targeted and lynched by opposing and hostile groups. Thus one sees how wider political contexts of civil strife can act to limit and repress nightlife, whilst creating and enforcing particular forms of temporal and spatial exclusion (Body-Gendrot, 2000; Sibley, 1995).

The lethal realities of the conflict in Northern Ireland were transposed to England on 21 November 1974 in one of the nation's most deadly terrorist attacks. Bombs were planted in two central Birmingham pubs, the *Mulberry Bush*, at the foot of the Rotunda, and the *Tavern in the Town*, a basement pub on New Street. The explosions, at 8.25 pm and 8.27 pm resulted in the deaths of 21 people (10 at the *Mulberry Bush* and 11 at the *Tavern in the Town*), with 182 people injured. The attacks were said to be the work of the Provisional IRA, although the organization later issued a denial. The six men arrested shortly after the bombing served 16 years in jail only to be freed on appeal in 1991 when fresh evidence emerged to show that their convictions could 'no longer be considered safe and satisfactory'.[15]

Pubs and nightlife areas have also been the target for domestic 'hate crimes'. On 30 April 1999, a nail bomb was placed in the *Admiral Duncan* in Old Compton Street, Soho, a Central London pub at the heart of the capital's gay community. The bar was packed with drinkers at the start of the bank holiday weekend and the bomb, which detonated just after 6.30 pm, killed three people, one of them a pregnant woman. The incident was the third in a series of three, with previous attacks targeting the black community in Brixton, South London and Bangladeshis in Brick Lane, East London. David Copeland, a 22-year-old right-wing extremist, was captured shortly after the pub bombing, found guilty of murder, and jailed for life in June 2000.

On 12 October 2002, Islamist terrorists attacked a popular night spot in the tourist district of Kuta Beach on the Indonesian island of Bali. The attacks occurred at 11.30 pm when the bars were packed. Three bombs exploded that night: a backpack-mounted device carried by a suicide bomber and a large car bomb, both of which were detonated in or near nightclubs; and a third, much smaller device, detonated outside the United States consulate in Denpasar, causing only minor damage. The blast destroyed the *Sari Club* and the resulting fire then engulfed a neighbouring bar, *Paddy's Irish Club*. The attack killed 202 people, mainly Australians. A further 209

---

[15] <http://news.bbc.co.uk/onthisday/hi/dates/stories/february/25/newsid_2516000/2516525.stm>.

people were injured. No injuries occurred in the American consulate explosion. Three individuals from a regional Islamist group, Jemaah Islamiyah, were convicted in relation to the bombings and sentenced to death.

At the 2006 Old Bailey trial of an Islamist terrorist group, tape recordings made in 2004 by the British Security Service MI5 were played to the jury in which the accused, 22-year-old Jawad Akbar, was heard to discuss his choice of target, London's *Ministry of Sound* nightclub: 'What about easy stuff where you don't need no experience and nothing and you could get a job, yeah, like for example the biggest nightclub in Central London where no one can even turn round and say, "Oh they were innocent", those slags dancing around?' (Bennetto, 2006: unpaginated). Akbar is now serving a life sentence for conspiracy to cause explosions. His plans, however, were almost brought to fruition by others.

At 1.30 am on Friday, 29 June 2007, a car bomb containing 60 litres of petrol, gas cylinders and nails was left outside the *Tiger Tiger* bar on Haymarket, near Piccadilly Circus in Central London. The bomb was defused after police were alerted by an ambulance crew called to *Tiger Tiger* at 1.25 am to deal with someone taken ill. The paramedics spotted what appeared to be vapour inside the Mercedes, which was parked illegally directly outside the glass-fronted venue (*The Times*, 2007). Around 800 revellers were in the bar and by 2.00 am would have been spilling out of the venue at closing time. The plot was revealed to be the work of two Islamist extremists based in Scotland, one of whom subsequently died as a result of the injuries he received in a further attack on Glasgow airport.

The above chronology presents a partial history of the selection of 'soft' nightlife targets by terrorists. The incidents show how domestic social divisions can merge with wider global conflicts to bring terror 'home' to otherwise relatively peaceful and stable leisure environments. Such attacks can also be global in their impact, the Bali bombing, for example, resulted in the death or injury of people from 24 different countries. A recent document produced by the Association of Chief Police Officers (ACPO) National Counter Terrorism Security Office demonstrates the extent to which the British police see the NTE as a high-profile ongoing target:

Terrorist attacks in the UK are a real and serious danger. Crowded places, including bars, pubs and nightclubs, may feature in the attack plans of terrorist organizations in the future; as they are usually locations with limited protective security measures and therefore afford the potential for mass fatalities and casualties. Although terrorist attacks on bars, pubs and nightclubs in the UK have been infrequent recently, there is a long history of such attacks and there have been recent attacks on bars and nightclubs in other countries around the world. (NaCTSO, 2007: 5)

Such warnings remind us that despite the preponderance of 'routine violence', our capacity to enjoy nightlife depends at a more fundamental level on the freedoms we take for granted in politically stable societies, but which have, on occasions, been directly challenged. Van Calster et al (Chapter 6) elucidate how, in the wake of heightened public fears and insecurities, the Netherlands appears to be dismantling its previously liberal criminal justice and social policy paradigms, with the policing of nightlife becoming more repressive, enforcement-focused, and pervasive. Such concerns give rise to a further theme of debate: are nightlife participants under-protected, or over-controlled?

LET'S GO OUTSIDE: ORGANIC NIGHTLIFE FORMS

As the Italian and Spanish contributors (Chapters 9 and 10) to this volume demonstrate, public space offers a more informal context for leisure in which young people are adept at finding their own amusement (Corrigan, 1976). At the same time, commercial entertainment markets are becoming increasingly segmented, presenting various opportunities (and forms of exclusion) to different groups of young people, the greatest gap being in the dichotomy between leisure activity in public space and that which occurs in nightclubs. The former is largely informal, uncontrolled, and partly founded on the attractions of deviance inherent in the infringement of civic rules; the latter is increasingly standardized, regimented, accountable to regulators, and embedded in broader official control mechanisms—some would say sanitized. Given the increasing degrees of surveillance and control exerted by leisure venues over their patrons in these countries and elsewhere (Hadfield, 2008) it is perhaps unsurprising that some young people should enjoy the opportunity to meet in spaces that may be considered 'free'—both in financial terms, and to the extent that their actions remain comparatively ungoverned. In Britain and other more northerly climes, young people traverse public space, but are less likely to linger in it. This is partially due to differences in weather and seasonality, notable exceptions being warm summer nights when young people often choose to remain in public spaces after leisure venues have shut. The familiar quest for further amusement, and sometimes shelter, in the early hours of the morning is demonstrated by the popular ritual of visiting takeaway restaurants after leaving bars and clubs.

It seems that some young people in some countries (including Britain) are choosing these spontaneous gatherings in *preference* to more formally organized indoor entertainments, whether as a response to the necessities of their economic position, or as a proto-political rejection of the highly regulated consumerist NTE (Calafat et al, 2005). These 'organic' nightlife forms may emerge in a number of guises, some of which demonstrate significant enterprise, organizational ability, and the power of communication networks amongst youth. The rave or free-party scene, whilst severely restricted in Britain following the Criminal Justice and Public Order Act 1994, which gave police the power to seize sound equipment (see Hadfield, 2006: 58–60), remains strong in many other countries. Locations typically include residual urban spaces (warehouses, factories, squats, blocks) and rural locations (beaches, caves, and forests), sometimes with, but often without, permission from private-property owners. However, in many countries, the shift to alternative, predominantly open-air environments is most visible during summer months and festive periods, and in the public streets and squares of towns and cities. Such gatherings are sometimes organized at very short notice, through the use of email, texts, and social networking websites, and in England have included what are known as 'flash-mobs'[16] and 'splash-mobs'.[17]

Police, municipal governments and local residents often view these unstructured leisure activities as a threat to public order, particularly when they involve mass drinking or drug-taking. Inspired by Goffman and other symbolic interactionist writers, Martin Innes (2004) has coined the term 'signal disorder' to describe how certain activities, such as the public consumption of alcohol, are widely understood as threatening, being construed as a signifier of the potential for more serious problems to occur. Thus the integration of all nightlife into the commercial NTE is seen as a protective factor which reduces the risk of violence, antisocial behaviour, and public nuisance;[18] similarly, consumption of alcohol on the London Underground has recently been banned, presumably as a measure to assuage public fears, as much as to prevent crime. Yet, official clampdowns on organic nightlife often reveal as much about political economy and the incestuous relations and convergent governmental interests of private- and public-sector elites as they do about moral entrepreneurship and public outcry. In his Opening Ceremony address to the June 2008 Clubhealth conference in Ibiza, Pedro Vidal, president of the Federación de la Salas de Fiesta y Discotecas de España, voiced his support for a clampdown on the island's free beach-party scene. It seems that even on an island renowned for its 'hippy' heritage and enticing climate,

---

[16] *London Victoria, April 2007*
At 6.53 pm on 4 April 2007 more than 4,000 clubbers danced through the rush-hour crowds at London's Victoria station in Britain's largest 'flash-mob' (a group of people brought together via the internet who arrange to perform bizarre acts in a public place, only to disperse as quickly as they have gathered). The event was staged by clubbing website *mobileclubbing.com*. Invitation emails and texts were sent out a week in advance. Revellers responded to e-bulletins urging them to 'dance like you've never danced before'. As the *London Evening Standard* reported:

There were knowing looks and giggles among the casually dressed crowd that gathered from 6.30 pm, wearing earphones. A 10-second countdown startled station staff and commuters before the concourse erupted in whoops and cheers. MP3 players and iPods emerged and the crowd danced wildly to their soundtracks in silence—for two hours . . . University of London student Lucy Dent, 20, was among the flash mobbers. She said: 'It was my first flash mob and I'm hooked. I've been dancing non-stop since we began. I didn't even notice the commuters. When you get into the dancing you're oblivious to them and forget you're at a railway station'. Chris Gale, 39, brought his daughter Sophia, three, and son Jacob, six. Mr Gale, a property entrepreneur from Bromley, said: 'The children were a bit bewildered at first but then had fantastic fun. Some of the commuters are only interested in their trains and had to weave round us to the platforms. But most of them stood and stared, finding it hugely entertaining—and some even joined in. I saw the straightest looking guy in a suit with his briefcase doing the freakiest dance moves.' Last night's flash-mob ended when four vanloads of police dispersed the dancers. One commuter failed to see the funny side: 'I was trying to get my train home but the whole concourse was filled with students dancing and I couldn't get through. The last thing I wanted after a hard day at work was to miss my train because of these idiots.' (Stewart, 2007: unpaginated)

[17] Splash-mobs are a form of flash-mob involving water fighting. These events achieved nationwide notoriety in Britain in the summer of 2008 when 250 people gathered for a *Facebook*-organized splash mob at Kensington Gardens in London. The event got out of hand when one man knocked a woman who had dowsed him in coloured liquid to the ground, passers-by were 'accidentally' splashed and horse-riding children were injured after being thrown from their mounts. Police intervened and made nine arrests (Barkham, 2008).

[18] See Matthew Collin's (1997) account of the close connections between the officially instigated dismantling of the original rave scene and the rise of branded indoor 'superclubs' in mid-1990s England.

opportunities for enjoying the outdoors and escaping the jaws of the official nightlife machine are running low.

There is some evidence, in Britain at least, of a growing resistance to the restriction of free assembly inherent in the increasing use of Designated Public Place Orders (DPPOs) (see Chapter 2) and other measures which govern the consumption of alcohol in public places. As noted above, one of Boris Johnson's first acts when becoming Mayor of London in May 2008 was to introduce a ban on the consumption of alcohol on London's public-transport network, including the London Underground, the Docklands Light Railway, and Transport for London's buses and trams. In response, a number of online groups were set up to organize an evening of protest on Saturday, 31 May 2008, the last night before the ban came into force.[19] This development was followed in July 2008 by police action in Devon to prevent the occurrence of a huge beach party, also organized on *Facebook*.[20]

Such 'booze bans' have drawn criticism from libertarian campaign group The Manifesto Club[21] who identify them as an emergent worldwide phenomenon, stretching, they claim, from 'San Diego beaches, areas of Prague and other cities in the Czech Republic, to streets and street fairs in New York, and Bondi beach in Australia. New

---

[19] *London, Circle Line, May 2008*

The stated aim of the *Facebook* group 'Circle Line Party-Last Day of Drinking on the Tube' was to celebrate 'our freedom to drink', adding, 'We need to make this really big, so spread the word and we'll flash-mob the Tube.' Another group, calling itself 'One Final Tube Booze Party' planned to set off from Liverpool Street in order to 'take over a Circle Line train and go around getting drunk all day just to say "Up yours Boris, you party animal!"' But, according to the *Daily Telegraph* newspaper:

the scenes turned ugly when police and Underground staff attempted to restore order, with drunken mobs fighting workers and wrecking trains leading to the closures of six stations . . . A dossier of the violent assaults and incidents was released by the *Rail Maritime and Transport (RMT)* union which said the violence was 'far uglier' than first reported . . . The RMT said there were at least five 'Mayday' calls from staff, a worker was punched in the face and had beer poured over his head, a driver had his glasses broken by an assailant, a passenger climbed on the roof of a Tube train, several other people got onto the tracks and trains were vandalised.

Police made 17 arrests for offences including assault, drunk and disorderly behaviour, assault on police, public order related offences and drug offences. A British Transport Police spokesman said seven people have been bailed pending further inquiries. (Tibbetts, 2008: unpaginated)

These reports show how ill-planned pranks can go wrong, providing fuel for negative media coverage, especially when direct action and social protest are linked to substance misuse and harm to innocent bystanders. As 26-year-old banker, Alexandre Graham, organizer of 'Circle Line Party', appeared to acknowledge, things can easily get 'out of hand':

You are going to expect a bit of trouble, but I was surprised and disappointed because I don't want to be associated [with it] . . . The point of it [the party] was just to make fun of how ridiculous the ban is. (ibid)

[20] *Torbay, Devon, July 2008*

In the first weekend of July 2008, up to 10,000 young people were expected to gather at one of five beaches near Torbay, Devon for a mass party, the exact location and time of which was not to be posted until a few hours beforehand on the social networking site *Facebook*. The story caught the national media's attention when it emerged that the police and council were threatening to ban alcohol sales in pubs, bars, and off-licences over a wide geographical area as part of a contingency plan to stall the event. The blanket ban would have been the first of its kind under the provisions of s 160 of the Licensing Act 2003. The event was susequently cancelled by the organizers who warned would-be party-goers not to travel to Torbay as there would still be a high police presence around the coast.

[21] <http://www.manifestoclub.com/>.

Zealand's no-drinking zones even ban people from driving through the area with cans in the boot of their car' (Manifesto Club, 2008: 8). In the case of DPPOs, cases are presented where police are said to have exceeded their powers in preventing *all* public drinking, when the intention of statute was to target only 'alcohol-related disorder or nuisance'. Their report is lucid in arguing that:

Genuine civility results from people sharing a space together, and negotiating its rules, not from behavioural codes imposed from above. What is at stake is not just the right to drink alcohol in public, which is a pleasant, but not necessarily crucial part of life. What is also at stake is the principle that public space is for free use and enjoyment, and that we set the terms of acceptable and unacceptable behaviour. The more things that we can only do at police officers' and local councillors' discretion, the less public is public space, and the less we are citizens. (ibid: 21)

What the Manifesto Club identifies here, then, is an insidiously accumulating body of crime-control powers and regulations that gradually infuse the governance of many aspects of our lives, thus eroding the range of freedoms we enjoy. This is the process Simon (1997) refers to as 'governing through crime', wherein domains of social practice which were once considered innocuous become increasingly drawn into the realm of governmental concern as a result of some relationship to crime that was formerly considered tangential. This diffusion is further accentuated by the contracting out of security tasks discussed earlier in this chapter and eluded to in one form or another by many of the authors in this book, including those from the United States, Canada, The Netherlands, Italy, New Zealand, and Australia. The danger is that whenever things 'go wrong' at youth-initiated events, as described in notes 17 and 19 above, public acceptance of the value of spontaneous assembly diminishes, whilst the call for repressive action re-ignites. Perhaps the most unfortunate and telling aspect of this is not that challenging behaviours occur, but that bystanders to such incidents perceive social order to be so fundamentally fragile as to expect, if not demand, that response be made by uniformed agents whose working lives are dedicated to the task.

CONCLUSIONS

Contemporary criminology has witnessed a growth in interest in the comparison of crime control systems 'in order to assess the extent of similarity and difference and to question what this might tell us about processes of globalisation and diffusion' (Jones and Newburn, 2007: 159; Newburn and Sparks, 2004). The entries in his book have illustrated the sociological complexities of this task, particularly when one considers that 'crime control systems' cannot be studied in the abstract; in other words, we need to know a considerable amount about the political cultures and legal frameworks of each of the countries we study before we can hope to generate meaningful results. In comparative research on nightlife and crime, there is also a need to encompass insight into the following three spheres: (1) the economic—labour market, socio-economic, and commercial trends, flows of symbols, commodities and consumers; (2) the constitutional—the extent and distribution of powers and jurisdictions; and (3) the cultural—'complex networks of communicative exchange' (Melossi, 2004) including normative codes, traditions, family and gender relations and roles, cultural divisions and cohesions.

Furthermore, mainstream criminological discourse, in its increasing focus on criminal-justice processes, tends to overlook administrative and private forms of governance, despite their centrality to everyday practices of crime control (Hadfield, 2006 and 2008). On the evidence of this book, many countries are witnessing a withdrawal, or at least a significant reshaping, of the role of the state in its governance of nightlife's social order. Core functions such as licensing and enforcement have long been ceded to municipal or regional governments; however, the discretionary power and reach of local regulatory actors is growing. At the same time, front-line security and patrolling tasks are increasingly contracted out to the private, or even voluntary, sector.

This book began with an observation of street life in my own town. This device was inspired by the belief that empirically grounded comparative research on nightlife and crime can only flourish if researchers think locally and work from the bottom up, as well as thinking globally and from the top down in a process of hypothesis-testing. The challenge is clearly to develop transferable methods to explore the same topic in different contexts. Yet, the question of 'topic' can itself present challenges as 'Any term, even the simplest, is embedded within a cultural context, or milieu, that gives it its meaning' (Melossi, 2004: 80). The initial task when choosing a topic, then, is to interpret local understandings of the problem or research question, rather than simply attempting to transplant one's own.

Many aspects of nightlife, including those deemed marginal or 'anti-authority', can offer young people a sense of belonging and identity, whilst broadening their social horizons and experiences. Yet, there is evidence from across the world of an increasing criminalization of nightlife patrons juxtaposed with a 'light touch' approach to enforcement of the laws which govern nightlife operators; indeed (unequal) partnership approaches and self-regulation appear to be in ascendancy. One cannot escape the conclusion that material economic factors are at play here, in addition to the symbols and rhetoric of populist punitiveness. Levi and Valverde (2001: 823) cite the 1899 PhD thesis of Canadian public-administration lawyer Clement Sites, in which he summarizes the 'crux of the liquor problem' as the 'reconciling of police regulation with sumptuary and social desires'. Over a century on, this statement retains its power to describe not only the governance of alcohol, but the governance of nightlife as a whole and across the world. As long as some people want to party, then others will want to object and police and regulators will be kept busy. This appears to be one of the perennial challenges of living together on an increasingly crowded and urbanized planet. In an age of nightclub identity scanners, databases, and metal detectors, those enjoying a night out might well feel themselves to be well and truly 'bar-coded'. In all of this scrutinizing, ranking, and responsibilizing, nightlife becomes just another part of the daily disciplinary grind to which adult citizens must submit; thus, some of nightlife's innocence and magic is lost. Debate of such matters evokes clashes of values, with interlocutors speaking different normative 'languages' and it often seems as though one is expected to choose 'sides'. Such expectations raise the stakes for all involved: businesses, revellers, policymakers, practitioners, and researchers. As an academic who has tilled this particular research furrow for some time, I have sometimes felt this entrenchment of positions to exert pressure on my sanity. In the words of Big Chris in *Lock, Stock and Two Smoking Barrels*, 'That's all I've come to say. There is one more thing … It's been emotional.'[22]

REFERENCES

All internet sources were accessible as of 8 October 2008

ALCOHOL CONCERN (2008) *Unequal Partners: A report into the limitations of the alcohol regulatory regime*, London: Alcohol Concern.

BACH, PJ and SCHAEFER, JM (1979) 'The tempo of country music and the rate of drinking in bars', *Journal of Studies on Alcohol*, 40, 1058–9.

BAGLI, CV (2008) 'State Board lets Ciprianis keep their liquor licences', *The New York Times*, 6 August, <http://www.nytimes.com/2008/08/07/nyregion/07cipriani.html?_r=2&ref=nyregion&oref=slogin&oref=slogin>.

BARKHAM, P (2008) 'The danger of the summer's "splash mob" craze', *The Guardian*, 4 August, 2.

BBPA (British Beer and Pub Association) (2005) *Point of Sale Promotions: A good practice guide for pub owners and licensees*, London: BBPA.

BENNETTO, J (2006) 'Terror cell plotted to bomb Ministry of Sound, court is told', *The Independent*, 26 May, <http://www.independent.co.uk/news/uk/crime/terror-cell-plotted-to-bomb-ministry-of-sound-court-is-told-479756.html>.

BODY-GENDROT, S (2000) *The Social Control of Cities? A Comparative Perspective*, Oxford: Blackwell.

BÖSE, M (2003) '"Race" and class in the "post-subcultural" economy', in D Muggleton and R Weinzierl (eds), *The Post-Subcultures Reader*, Oxford: Berg, 167–180.

BOWERS, S and PIDD, H (2008) 'Police demand action after pubs ditch drinking code', *The Guardian*, 28 July, 1.

CALAFAT, A, JUAN, M, BECOÑA, E, CASTILLO, A, FERNÁNDEZ, C, FRANCO, M, PEREIRO, C and ROS, M (2005) 'El Consumo de Alcohol en la Lógica del Botellón', *Adicciones*, 17/3, 193–202, <http://www.irefrea.org/archivos/sa/logica_botellon.pdf>.

CAMPBELL, D (2005) 'Alcohol-related disorder and the nature of the problem of social cost', *Public Law*, 4, 749–63.

CASTELLS, M (2000) *The Rise of the Network Society: The information age—economy, society and culture*, vol 1, 2nd edn, Oxford: Blackwell.

COLLIN, M with contributions by GODFREY, J (1997) *Altered State: The story of ecstasy culture and acid house*, London: Serpent's Tail.

CORRIGAN, P (1976) 'Doing nothing', in S Hall and T Jefferson (eds), *Resistance Through Rituals*, Hutchinson: London.

---

[22] *Lock, Stock and Two Smoking Barrels* (1998) scripted and directed by Guy Ritchie, Universal Pictures UK, <http://www.script-o-rama.com/movie_scripts/l/lock-stock-and-two-smoking-barrels-script.html>.

CRAWFORD, A (2006) 'Policing and security as 'club goods': The new enclosures?', in J Wood and B DuPont (eds), *Democracy, Society and the Governance of Security*, Cambridge: Cambridge University Press, 111–38.

—— (2008) *From the Shopping Mall to the Street Corner: Dynamics of exclusion in the governance of public space*, paper presented to the Worldwide Universities Network Colloquium 'International Comparative Criminal Justice and Urban Governance', University of Leeds, 26–28 June.

CUOZZO, S (2008) 'No booze, we lose: Hurting Ciprianis won't help NYC', *New York Post*, 6 August, <http://www.nypost.com/seven/08062008/entertainment/food/no_booze_we_lose_123177.htm>.

DCMS (Department for Culture, Media and Sport) (2008) *Evaluation of the Impact of the Licensing Act 2003*, London: DCMS.

DoH (Department of Health) (2008) *Safe, Sensible, Social: Consultation on further action*, London:DoH,<http://www.dh.gov.uk/en/Consultations/Liveconsultations/DH_086412>.

DOUGLAS, M (1987) *Constructive Drinking: Perspectives on drink from anthropology*, Cambridge: Cambridge University Press.

DOWARD, J (2005) 'Police fear chaos over pub hours', *The Observer*, 20 March, <http://www.guardian.co.uk/society/2005/mar/20/drugsandalcohol.politics>.

DREWS, DR, VAUGHN, DB and ANFITEATRO, A (1992) 'Beer consumption as a function of music and the presence of others', *Journal of Pennsylvania Academy of Science*, 65, 134–6.

FELSON, M and CLARKE, RV (1998) *Opportunity Makes the Thief: Practical theory for crime prevention*, Police Research Series 98, London: HMSO.

FORSYTH, A (2008) 'Lager, lager, shouting! The role of music in nightlife disorder', paper represented at Club Health 2008, Santa Eulària des Riu Eivissa (Ibiza), Parallel Session 1c, 24 June.

—— and CLOONAN, M (2008) 'Alco-pop? The use of popular music in Glasgow pubs', *Popular Music and Society*, 31/1, 57–78.

GRAHAM, K and HOMEL, R (2008) *Raising the Bar: Preventing violence in and around bars, pubs and clubs*, Cullompton: Willan.

GUÉGUEN, N, JACOB, C, Le GUELLEC, H, MORINEAU, T and LOUREL, M (2008) 'Sound level of environmental music and drinking behavior: A field experiment with beer drinkers', *Alcoholism: Clinical and Experimental Research*. 32/10, 1–4.

HADFIELD, P (2004a) 'The operation of licensed premises', in P Kolvin (ed), *Licensed Premises: Law and practice*, London: Tottel.

—— (2004b) 'The prevention of public disorder', in P Kolvin (ed), *Licensed Premises: Law and practice*, London: Tottel.

—— (2006) *Bar Wars: Contesting the Night in Contemporary British Cities*, Oxford: Oxford University Press.

—— (2007) 'Phat controllers: Disc jockeys, security, and the construction of joyful constraint', paper presented at the Gender, Work and Organization Conference *2007*, Alternative Modes of Work Stream, Keele University, 28 June.

—— (2008) 'From threat to promise: Nightclub "security", governance and consumer elites', *British Journal of Criminology*, 48, 429–47.

HARRIS, J (2008a) 'Brown must call time on the booze trade's lack of restraint', *The Guardian*, 2 September, 30.

HARRIS, P (2008b) 'How ex-cop could take down New York's elite food dynasty', *The Observer*, 3 August, World News, 42.

HEATH, D (2000) *Drinking Occasions: Comparative perspectives on alcohol and culture*, Hove: Brunner/Mazel.

HERBERT, S (1997) *Policing Space: Territoriality and the Los Angeles Police Department*, Minneapolis: University of Minnesota Press.

HIER, SP, GREENBERG, J, WALBY, K and LETT, D (2007) 'Media, communication and the establishment of public camera surveillance programmes in Canada', *Media, Culture and Society*, 29, 727–51.

HOBBS, D, HADFIELD, P, LISTER, S, and WINLOW, S (2003) *Bouncers: Violence and Governance in the Night-time Economy*, Oxford: Oxford University Press.

HOLLANDS, R (2002) 'Divisions in the dark: Youth cultures, transitions and segmented consumption spaces in the night-time economy', *Journal of Youth Studies*, 5/2, 153–71.

HOME OFFICE/KPMG LLP (2008) *Review of the Social Responsibility Standards for the Production and Sale of Alcoholic Drinks*, Birmingham: KPMG LLP.

HOMEL, R and TOMSEN, S (1993) 'Hot spots for violence: the environment of pubs and clubs', *Homicide: Patterns, prevention and control*, Canberra: Australian Institute of Criminology, 53–66.

HUQ, R (2006) *Beyond Subculture: Pop, youth and identity in a postcolonial world*, London: Routledge.

INNES, M (2004) 'Signal crimes and signal disorders: Notes on deviance as communicative action', *British Journal of Sociology*, 55/3, 335–55.

JONES, T and NEWBURN, T (2007) *Policy Transfer and Criminal Justice: Exploring US influence over British crime control policy*, Maidenhead: Open University Press.

KALRA, V (2000) *From Textiles Mills to Taxi Ranks: Experiences of migration, labour and social change*, Aldershot: Ashgate.

LEVI, R and VALVERDE, M (2001) 'Knowledge on tap: Police science and common knowledge in the legal regulation of drunkenness', *Law and Social Inquiry*, 26/4, 819–46.

McCAHILL, M (2002) *The Surveillance Web: The rise of visual surveillance in an English city*, Cullompton: Willan.

McELREA, H and STANDING, L (1992) 'Fast music causes fast drinking', *Perceptual and Motor Skills*, 75, 362.

MACANDREW, C and EDGERTON, R (1969) *Drunken Comportment: A social explanation*, London: Thomas Nelson and Sons Ltd.

MANIFESTO CLUB (2008) *Manifesto Club Report: Against the booze bans and the hyper-regulation of public space*, 19 August, London: Manifesto Club, <http://www.manifestoclub.com/files/BoozeBanReport.pdf>.

MARLIÈRE, E (2007) 'Violence between young people going out at night in Paris and the surrounding region', in A Recasens (ed), *Violence between Young People in Night-Time Leisure Zones: A European comparative study*, Brussels: Vubpress, 31–57.

MAZEROLLE, L and RANSLEY, J (2006) *Third Party Policing*, Cambridge: Cambridge University Press.

MEASHAM, F and HADFIELD, P (2009) '"Your name's not down": Fragmentation, gentrification and criminalisation in English clubland', *Addiciones, Special Issue: Selected Papers from the Club Health Conference 2008* (forthcoming).

MELOSSI, D (2004) 'The cultural embeddedness of social control: Reflections on a comparison of Italian and North American cultures of punishment', in T Newburn and R Sparks (eds), *Criminal Justice and Political Cultures: National and international dimensions of crime control*, Cullompton: Willan.

NaCTSO (National Counter Terrorism Security Office) (2007) *Counter Terrorism Protective Security Advice for Bars, Pubs and Nightclubs*, London: NaCTSO.

NEWBURN, T and SPARKS, R (eds), (2004) *Criminal Justice and Political Cultures: National and international dimensions of crime control*, Cullompton: Willan.

O'MALLEY, P (1996) 'Risk and responsibility', in A Barry, T Osborne and N Rose (eds), *Foucault and Political Reason: Liberalism, neo-liberalism, and rationalities of government*. London: UCL Press, 189–207.

PARKER, D (2000) 'The Chinese takeaway and the diasporic habitus: Space, time and power geometries', in B Hesse (ed), *Un/settled Multiculturalisms: Diasporas, entanglements, transruptions*, London: Zed Books.

ROOM, R (2005) 'Multicultural contexts and alcohol and drug use as symbolic behaviour', *Addiction Research and Theory*, 13/4, 321–31.

—— (2007) 'Understanding cultural differences in young people's drinking', in M Jarvinen and R Room (eds), *Youth Drinking Cultures: European experiences*, Aldershot: Ashgate, 17–40.

SHEARING, C and STENNING, P (1985) 'From the panopticon to Disney World: The development of discipline', in A Doob and E Greeenspan (eds), *Perspectives in Criminal Law: Essays in honour of John Ll J Edwards*, Ontario: Canada Law Book Inc, 335–49.

SHOTT, C (2008) 'Cipriani escapes liquor license fiasco', 6 August, *The New York Observer*, <http://www.observer.com/2008/real-estate/cipriani-escapes-liquor-license-fiasco>.

SIBLEY, D (1995) *Geographies of Exclusion: Society and difference in the West*, London: Routledge.

SIMON, J (2007) *Governing Through Crime: How the War on Crime Transformed American Democracy and Created a Culture of Fear*, Oxford: Oxford University Press.

SKOLNICK, JH (1994) *Justice Without Trial: Law enforcement in democratic society*, 3rd edn, New York: Wiley.

SONG, M (1999) *Helping Out: Children's labor in ethnic businesses*, Temple, Phil: Temple University Press.

SPICER, K (2007) 'Very important party people', *Sunday Times Style Supplement*, 29 July, 12–15.

STEWART, T (2007) '4,000 flash mob dancers startle commuters at Victoria', *London Evening Standard*, 5 April, <http://www.thisislondon.co.uk/news/article-23391632-details/4,000+flash+mob+dancers+startle+commuters+at+Victoria/article.do>.

STOCKWELL, T (2006) 'Alcohol supply, demand, and harm reduction: What is the strongest cocktail?', *International Journal of Drug Policy*, 17, 269–77.

SUDNOW, D (1965) 'Normal crimes: Sociological features of the penal code in a public defender office', *Sociological Problems*, XII/3, 255–76.

TALBOT, D (2007) *Regulating the Night: Race, culture and exclusion in the making of the night-time economy*, Aldershot: Ashgate.

The Times (2007) 'Nightclub bomb alert issued two weeks ago: Anti-Terror Office warned of car-bomb threat to Britain's bars, clubs and pubs', 30 June, 1, 4–7.

TIBBETTS, G (2008) 'Tube party organizer was City banker', *Daily Telegraph*, 2 June, <http://www.telegraph.co.uk/news/uknews/2065899/Tube-party-organizer-was-City-banker.html>.

TOWN CENTRES LIMITED (2001) *West End Entertainment Impact Study: Final Report, 2001*, London: City of Westminster.

VALVERDE, M (2003) 'Police science, British style: Pub licensing and knowledges of urban disorder', *Economy and Society*, 32/2, 234–52.

WAKEFIELD, A (2003) *Selling Security: The private policing of public space*, Cullompton: Willan.

WHITE, R (2008) 'Public spaces, consumption, and the social regulation of young people', in SA Venkatesh and R Kassimir (eds), *Youth, Globalisation and the Law*, Stanford: Stanford University Press, 223–48.

WILSON, TM (ed) (2005) *Drinking Cultures: Alcohol and identity*, Oxford: Berg.

WINE AND SPIRIT TRADE ASSOCIATION, BRITISH BEER AND PUB ASSOCIATION, SCOTCH WHISKY ASSOCIATION and others (2005) *Social Responsibility Standards for the Production and Sale of Alcoholic Drinks in the UK*, London: WSTA, <http://www.wsta.co.uk/images/stories/social_responsibility.pdf>.

INDEX